Advances in Japanese Business and Economics

Volume 11

Advances in Japanese Business and Economics (AJBE) showcases the work of Japanese and non-Japanese scholars researching the Japanese economy and Japanese businesses. Published in English, the series highlights for a global readership the unique perspectives of Japan's most distinguished and emerging scholars of business and economics. It covers research of either theoretical or empirical nature, in both authored and edited volumes, regardless of the sub-discipline or geographical coverage, including, but not limited to, such topics as macroeconomics, microeconomics, industrial relations, innovation, regional development, entrepreneurship, international trade, globalization, financial markets, technology management, and business strategy. At the same time, as a series of volumes written by Japanese and non-Japanese scholars studying Japan, it includes research on the issues of the Japanese economy, industry, management practice, and policy, such as the economic policies and business innovations before and after the Japanese "bubble" burst in the 1990s.

AJBE endeavors to overcome a historical deficit in the dissemination of Japanese economic theory, research methodology, and analysis. The volumes in the series contribute not only to a deeper understanding of Japanese business and economics but to revealing underlying universal principles.

Overseen by a panel of renowned scholars led by Editor-in-Chief Professor Ryuzo Sato, AJBE employs a single-blind review process in which the Editor-in-Chief, together with the Managing Editors and specialized scholars designated by the Editor-in-Chief or Managing Editors, rigorously reviews each proposal and manuscript to ensure that every submission is a valuable contribution to the global scholarly readership.

More information about this series at http://www.springer.com/series/11682

W. Erwin Diewert · Kiyohiko G. Nishimura ·
Chihiro Shimizu · Tsutomu Watanabe

Property Price Index

Theory and Practice

Springer

W. Erwin Diewert
University of British Columbia
Vancouver, BC, Canada

Kiyohiko G. Nishimura
National Graduate Institute for Policy Studies (GRIPS)
Tokyo, Japan

Chihiro Shimizu
Nihon University & The University of Tokyo
Tokyo, Japan

Tsutomu Watanabe
The University of Tokyo
Tokyo, Japan

ISSN 2197-8859 ISSN 2197-8867 (electronic)
Advances in Japanese Business and Economics
ISBN 978-4-431-55940-5 ISBN 978-4-431-55942-9 (eBook)
https://doi.org/10.1007/978-4-431-55942-9

This Springer imprint is published by the registered company Springer Japan KK part of Springer Nature.
The registered company address is: Shiroyama Trust Tower, 4-3-1 Toranomon, Minato-ku, Tokyo 105-6005, Japan

Preface

Fluctuations in property prices have substantial impacts on economic activities. In Japan, a sharp rise in property prices during the latter half of the 1980s and its subsequent decline in the early 1990s led to a decade-long stagnation of the Japanese economy dubbed as the "lost decade." Many countries had similar experiences with this kind of problem- for example, Sweden's economic crisis in the 1990s and more recently, a rapid rise in housing prices and its reversal in the United States triggered a global fiscal crisis.

More generally, throughout their histories, most advanced nations have experienced abrupt increases and subsequent decreases in asset prices, especially housing prices. These fluctuations have had substantial impact on the financial system, often leading to a stagnation of economic activity. Reinhart and Rogoff (2008) conducted an exhaustive, long-term, comparative time series analysis of economic data from numerous countries which made it clear that the incidence of various economic phenomena is a common factor underlying banking crises.

In light of this, it was pointed out that the "information gap", which existed between policy-making authorities and the property and financial markets, was a problem.

In such circumstances, the development of appropriate indexes that allow one to capture changes in property prices with precision is extremely important, not only for policy makers but also for market participants who are looking for the time when housing prices hit bottom.

Recent research has focused on methods for compiling appropriate property price indexes. The location, maintenance and the characteristics of each house are different from each other in varying degrees, so there are no two houses that are identical in terms of quality. Even if the location and basic structure are the same at two periods of time, the building ages over time and renovations and extensions mean that the houses are not identical across time. In other words, it is very difficult to apply the usual matching methodology (where the prices of exactly the same item are compared over time) to the construction of constant quality property price indexes. Thus most countries do not have official property price indexes.

In 2009, the IMF proposed that the G20 countries construct official quality adjusted property price indexes in order to fill in this "information gap" and the proposal was adopted. However, as indicated above, the construction of constant quality property price indexes is one of the most difficult tasks for national statistical agencies. In order to address these measurement problems, Eurostat published the *Handbook of Residential Property Price Indices* in 2012 and the *Commercial Property Price Indicators* in 2017. The authors of the present volume played a significant role in the writing of both of these volumes.

This book consists of 3 parts with 8 chapters.

The first part of this volume addresses the following topics: (i) a discussion of the policy uses of Property Price Indices (Chap. 1); (ii) a presentation of the basic theory of property price indexes (Chap. 2) and (iii) an illustration of the characteristics of each estimation method using numerical examples (Chap. 3).

The second part summarizes the academic research results presented in a series of papers written during the time when the Japanese Official Property Price Index was constructed. Chapter 4 discusses the construction of a residential property price index and Chap. 5 discusses the construction of a commercial property price index in the System of National Accounts.

The third part of this volume presents conceptual frameworks for the measurement of housing services in a Consumer Price Index (CPI) (Chap. 6). Chapters 7 and 8 discuss specific measurement issues related to the estimation of housing services in a CPI (Chap. 7) and in the System of National Accounts (Chap. 8). We proposed a new method of calculation of a CPI in the case of Japan.

Each paper has had some influence on international discussions surrounding the construction of Official Property Price Indexes. Each of the Chapters was originally presented at an international conference. Professor Shimizu used these presented papers as the basis for a revised paper which appears in this volume.

We thank the following authors for helpful comments and discussions over the years: Naohito Abe, Bert Balk, Carsten Boldsen, Yongheng Deng, David Fenwick, Kevin Fox, Marc Francke, David Geltner, Xiangyu Guo, Jan de Haan, Robert Hill, Tjeerd Jellema, Daniel McMillen, Jens Mehrhoff, Alice Nakamura, Koji Nomura, Niall O'Hanlon, Alicia Rambaldi, Marshall Reinsdorf, Guebin Sahinbeyoglu, Paul Schreyer, Iqbal Shed, Mick Silver, Miriam Steurer, Bruno Tissot, Iichiro Uesugi and Peter Van de Ven.

Vancouver, Canada — W. Erwin Diewert
Tokyo, Japan — Kiyohiko G. Nishimura
Tokyo, Japan — Chihiro Shimizu
Tokyo, Japan — Tsutomu Watanabe
October 2019

Contents

About the Authors

W. Erwin Diewert is a Professor of Economics at the University of British Columbia and at the University of New South Wales. He has published over 120 papers in Journals and 140 chapters in books. His main areas of research include duality theory, flexible functional forms, index number theory (including the concept of a superlative index number formula), the measurement of productivity, the pure theory of international trade and the calculation of excess burdens of taxation. He has acted as a consultant on measurement and regulatory issues for the International Monetary Fund, the World Bank, the Bureau of Labor Statistics, the Bureau of Economic Analysis, the OECD, the New Zealand Treasury, the Business Roundtable in New Zealand, Bell Canada, B. C. Telephone, the American Association of Railways, the Victorian Treasury and Industry Canada. Diewert is a founding member of two international groups that study measurement issues: the Ottawa Group on Prices and the Canberra Group on Capital Measurement. He is also Chair of the Statistics Canada advisory committee on Prices. His research on flexible functional forms can be described as follows. Thirty years ago, most quantitative macroeconomic models that were based on economic theory used very restrictive functional forms to model consumer and producer theory. Diewert's Ph.D. thesis at the University of California at Berkeley in 1969 introduced more flexible functional forms that could better describe producer and consumer responses and these flexible functional forms are widely used in applied economics today. Diewert's second main area of research is in the area of index number theory and measurement economics. Diewert is a Fellow of the Econometric Society and the Royal Society of Canada and is a Distinguished Fellow of the American Economic Society. In 2003, he also won a Killam Prize for career achievements in the social sciences and humanities in Canada.

Kiyohiko G. Nishimura is emeritus professor of economics at The University of Tokyo and professor in the National Graduate Institute for Policy Studies (GRIPS). He received his Ph.D. (1982) from Yale University. He was associate professor (1983–1994) and professor (1994–2005) at The University of Tokyo. He joined the Bank of Japan as a Member of its Policy Board (2005–2008), and then became deputy governor (2008–2013) in the most turbulent periods in the history of the world economy and central banking. He has been particularly influential in the debates over macroprudential policies, especially in pointing out the critical importance of demographic factors on property bubbles and financial crisis. After returning to academia, he was dean of the Graduate School of Economics at The University of Tokyo (2013–2015). He was chairman of the Statistics Commission of Japan (2014–2019), leading a sweeping reform of economic statistics. Since October 2019, he is Advisor of the Ministry of Internal Affairs and Communications. Dr. Nishimura's academic research focuses on a wide span from economic theory such as mathematical economics to economic policy and management studies. He received numerous awards and prizes, including the Nikkei Prize in 1993 for his work about microeconomic foundations of macroeconomics, the Japan Economist Prize in 1997 for his seminal work about deflationary pressure in Japan, and the TELECOM Social Science Award in 2006 for his work about the impact of ICT on the Japanese economy. He was also the winner of the Japanese Economic Association Nakahara Prize in 1998 for his contribution to economic theory. He was awarded Emperor's Medal of Honor with Purple Ribbon in 2015 for his outstanding contribution to theoretical economics. His current research interests include theory and applications of Knightian uncertainty with Ozaki. Their book Economics of Pessimism and Optimism is widely read and cited, and won the second Nikkei Prize in 2018 for him.

Chihiro Shimizu is Professor of Nihon University, project Professor of Center for Spatial Information Science, The University of Tokyo and Head of Center of AI & Business Studies of Reitaku University in Japan. He is also Research Affiliate of Center of Real Estate in Massachusetts Institute of Technology (MIT). He has held visiting positions at various universities, including University of British Columbia, National University of Singapore and University of Hong Kong. Shimizu's main research area are Index Theory, Real Estate Economics, Applied Econometrics and Machine Learning. He has served as an advisor for various research councils at the Ministry of Finance, Financial Service Agency (FSA), Cabinet Office, Ministry of Economy, Trade and Industry and the Ministry of Land, Infrastructure, Transport and Tourism in Japan. From 2013 to 2015 he participated as a specialist in a project promoted mainly by the IMF, OECD, and others related to preparing international commercial real estate price indices. He has contributed a number of theses to international academic journals as well as published numerous theses and books in Japan. His research has received many awards from a number of academic bodies. He was born in 1967 and received his doctorate from the University of Tokyo.

Tsutomu Watanabe has been a professor of economics at the Graduate School of Economics, The University of Tokyo, since October 2011. He was a professor at Hitotsubashi University (1999–2011) and a senior economist at the Bank of Japan (1982–1999). He has held visiting positions at various universities, including Kyoto University, Bocconi University, and Columbia University. He received his Ph.D. in economics from Harvard University in 1992 and did his undergraduate work at The

University of Tokyo. Watanabe's main research area is monetary policy and inflation dynamics. He is known for his series of papers on monetary policy when nominal interest rates are bounded at zero; in particular, his paper on the optimal monetary policy at the zero lower bound has been widely recognized as the first paper to provide a simple description of the liquidity trap and characterize the optimal policy response to it in a dynamic stochastic general equilibrium model. He is an author of many books and more than 40 academic journal articles on monetary policy, inflation dynamics, and international finance. He is Project Leader of JSPS Grant-in-Aid for Scientific Research projects on "Understand Inflation Dynamics of the Japanese Economy: An Approach Integrating Microeconomic Behaviors and Aggregate Fluctuations" (2006–2011) and "Understanding Persistent Deflation in Japan" (2012–2017). He has developed *Nikkei-UTokyo Daily Price Index* with Kota Watanabe.

Part I
Index Theory for Property Price Indexes

Chapter 1
International Policy Discussion in Property Price Indices

1.1 Introduction

This paper highlights some of the themes that emerged from the OECD-IMF Workshop on Real Estate Price Indexes which was held in Paris, November 6–7, 2006.

Section 1.2 discusses the question: what are appropriate target indexes for Real Estate Prices? This section argues that the present System of National Accounts is a good starting point for a systematic framework for Real Estate Price indexes but the present SNA has to be augmented somewhat to meet the needs of economists who are interested in measuring consumption on a more comprehensive service flow basis and who are interested in measuring the productivity of the economy.

Section 1.3 notes the fundamental problem that makes the construction of constant quality real estate price indexes very difficult: namely depreciation and renovations to structures make the usual matched model methodology for constructing price indexes inapplicable.

Section 1.4 discusses four classes of methods that were suggested at the workshop to deal with the above problem and Sect. 1.5 discusses some additional technical difficulties.

Section 1.6 discusses the problems raised by Verbrugge's (2006) contribution to the Workshop; i.e., why do user costs diverge so much from rents?

Finally, Sect. 1.7 summarizes suggestions for moving the agenda forward.

The base of this chapter is Diewert, W. E. 2007. The Paris OECD-IMF Workshop on Real Estate Price Indexes: conclusions and future directions. Discussion Paper 07–01, University of British Columbia. Presented at OECD-IMF Workshop on Real Estate Price Indexes, Paris, November 6–7, 2006.

W. E. Diewert et al., *Property Price Index*, Advances in Japanese Business and Economics 11, https://doi.org/10.1007/978-4-431-55942-9_1

1.2 What Are Appropriate Target Indexes?

There are many possible target real estate price indexes that could be constructed. Thus it is useful to consider alternative *uses* for real estate price indexes that were suggested at the workshop since these uses will largely determine what type of indexes should be constructed.

Fenwick (2006; 6) suggested the following list of possible uses for house price indexes:

- As a general macroeconomic indicator (of inflation);
- As an input into the measurement of consumer price inflation;
- As an element in the calculation of household (real) wealth and
- As a direct input into an analysis of mortgage lender's exposure to risk of default.

Arthur (2006) also suggested some (related) uses for real estate price indexes:

- Real estate price bubbles (and the subsequent collapses) have repeatedly been related to financial crises and thus it is important to measure these price bubbles accurately and in a way that is comparable across countries and
- Real estate price indexes are required for the proper conduct of monetary policy.

Fenwick also argued that various real estate price indexes are required for deflation purposes in the System of National Accounts:

> The primary focus of a national accountant seeking an appropriate deflator for national accounts will be different. Real estate appears in the National Accounts in several ways;
>
> - the imputed rental value received by owner occupiers for buildings, as opposed to land, is part of household final consumption,
> - the capital formation in buildings, again as opposed to land, is part of gross fixed capital formation, depreciation, and the measurement of the stock of fixed capital,
> - and land values are an important part of the National stock of wealth.
>
> Fenwick (2006; 7–8)

Fenwick (2006; 6) also argued that it would be useful to develop a coherent conceptual framework for an appropriate *family* of real estate price indexes[1] and he provided such a framework towards the end of his paper.[2]

---

[1]

> It can be seen that user needs will vary and that in some instances, more than one measure of house price or real estate inflation may be required. It can also be seen that coherence between different measures and with other economic statistics is important and that achieving this will be especially difficult as statisticians are unlikely to have an ideal set of price indicators available to them. Fenwick (2006; 8).

[2]See Fenwick (2006; 8–11).

Diewert, in his oral presentation to the Workshop, followed Fenwick and argued that in the first instance, real estate price statistics should serve the needs of the System of National Accounts. Why this conclusion?

The answer to this question is that (with one exception to be discussed later) the SNA provides a quantitative framework where value flows and stocks are systematically decomposed in an economically meaningful way into price and quantity (or volume) components. The resulting p's and q's are the basic building blocks which are used in virtually all macroeconomic models. Hence it seems important that price statisticians do their best to meet the deflation needs of the System of National Accounts.

Before the one major problem area with the present SNA is discussed, it will be useful to review a bit of basic economics. There are two basic paradigms or models in economics:

- Consumers or households maximizing utility subject to their budget constraints and
- Producers maximizing profits subject to their production function (or more generally, their technology) constraints.

There are one period "static" and many period "intertemporal" versions of the two models. However, for our purposes, it suffices to say that the SNA provides the necessary data to implement both models *except* that the SNA does not deal adequately with the consumption of consumer durables for applications to consumer models or the use of durable inputs in the producer context. The problem is the following one. When a consumer or producer purchases a good that provides services over a number of years, it is not appropriate to charge the entire purchase cost to the quarter or month when the durable is purchased: the purchase cost needs to be spread out over the useful life of the durable. However, with one exception, the SNA simply charges the entire cost of the durable to the period of purchase.[3] This is not an appropriate treatment of durables for many economic purposes. Thus with respect to the household accounts, in addition to the usual *acquisitions approach* to consumer durables (which simply charges the entire purchase cost to the period of purchase), it is useful to have alternative measures of the service flows generated by household holdings of consumer durables. There are two alternative approaches to constructing such flow measures:

- An *imputed rent approach* which simply imputes market rental prices for the same type of service (if such prices are available) and
- A *user cost approach* which forms an estimate of what the cost would be of buying the durable at the beginning of the period, using the services of the good during the period and then selling it at the end of the period. This estimated cost also includes the interest cost that is associated with value of the capital that is tied up in the purchase of the durable.[4]

---

[3]The one exception is residential housing, where estimates of the period by period flow of housing services are made in the SNA.

[4]The user cost idea can be traced back to Walras in 1874; see Walras (1954).

We will discuss the relative merits of the above two service flow methods for valuing housing services in Sect. 1.6 below. For additional material on the various economic approaches to the treatment of durables and housing in particular, see Diewert (2002; 611–622, 2003a, b, c), Verbrugge (2006) or Chap. 23, "Durables and User Costs", in the International Labour Organization (ILO) Consumer Price Index Manual (2004).

On the producer side of the System of National Accounts, the service flows generated by durable inputs that are used to produce goods and services are buried in Gross Operating Surplus. Jorgenson and Griliches (1967, 1972) showed how gross operating surplus could be decomposed into price and quantity components using the user cost idea and their work led directly to the first national statistical agency productivity program; see the Bureau of Labor Statistics (1983).[5] Schreyer, Diewert and Harrison (2005) argued that this *productivity oriented approach to the System of National Accounts* could be regarded as a natural extension of the present SNA where the extended version provides a decomposition of a value flow (Gross Operating Surplus) into price and quantity (or volume) components.

We will argue below that if the SNA is expanded to exhibit the service flows that are associated with the household and production sectors' purchases of durable goods, then the resulting *Durables Augmented System of National Accounts* (DASNA)[6] provides a natural framework for a family of real estate price indexes.

In this augmented system of national accounts, household wealth and consumption will be measured in real and nominal terms. This will entail measures of the household sector's stock of residential wealth and it will be of interest to decompose this value measure into price and volume (or quantity) components. It will also be useful to decompose the residential housing stock aggregate into various subcomponents such as:

- by type of housing,
- by location or region,
- by the proportion of land and structures in the aggregate value,
- by age (in particular, new housing should be distinguished) and
- whether the residence is rented or owned.

Each of these subaggregates should be decomposed into price and volume components if possible. The DASNA will also require a measure of the flow of services from households' consumption of services from their long lived consumer durables, such as motor vehicles and owner occupied housing.[7] Thus it will be necessary to

---

[5]The list of countries who now have official productivity programs includes the U.S., Canada, the UK, Australia, New Zealand and Switzerland. The EU KLEMS project is developing productivity accounts for many European countries using the Jorgenson and Griliches methodology, which is described in more detail in Schreyer (2001). For recent extensions and modifications, see Schreyer (2006).

[6]Such an accounting system is laid out in great detail and implemented for the U.S. by Jorgenson and Landefeld (2006).

[7]For short lived household durables, it is not worth the bother of capitalizing these stocks and so the usual acquisitions approach will suffice for these assets.

either implement the rental equivalence approach (as is currently recommended in the SNA) or the user cost approach (or both) to valuing the services of Owner Occupied Housing in this extended system of accounts.[8]

Turning now to the producer side of the DASNA, for productivity measurement purposes, we will want user costs for owned commercial, industrial and agricultural properties. In order to form wealth estimates, we will require estimates for the value of commercial, industrial and agricultural properties and decompositions of the values into price and volume components. The price components can be used as basic building blocks to form user costs for these various types of property. It will also be useful to decompose these business property stock aggregates into various subcomponents such as:

- by type of structure,
- by location or region,
- by the proportion of land and structures in the aggregate value,
- by age (in particular, new structures should be distinguished) and
- whether the structure is rented or owned.

If we turn back to the list of uses for real estate price indexes suggested by Fenwick and Arthur earlier in this section, it can be seen that if we had all of the price indexes for implementing the DASNA as suggested above, then virtually all of the user needs could be met by this family of national accounts type real estate price indexes. Thus it seems to me that the Durables Augmented SNA is a natural framework for the development of real estate price indexes that would meet user needs.

We turn now to a discussion of the many technical issues that arise when trying to construct a property price index.

1.3 The Failure of the Traditional Matched Model Methodology in the Real Estate Context

Consider the problems involved in constructing a constant quality price index for say a class of residential dwelling units or for a class of business structures. The starting point for constructing any price index between two time periods is to collect prices on exactly the same product or item for the two time periods under consideration; this is the standard *matched model* methodology.[9]

The *fundamental problem* that price statisticians face when attempting to construct a real estate price index is that *exact matching of properties over time is not possible* for two reasons:

---

[8]We will return to this topic in Sect. 1.6 below.

[9]For a detailed description of how this methodology works, see Chap. 20, "Elementary Indices", in the ILO (2004).

- The property depreciates over time (*the depreciation problem*) and
- The property may have had major repairs, additions or remodeling done to it between the two time periods under consideration (*the renovations problem*).

Because of the above two problems, constructing constant quality real estate price indexes cannot be a straightforward matter; some form of imputation or indirect estimation will be required.

A third problem that faces many European countries is the *problem of low turnover of properties*; i.e., if the sales of properties are very infrequent, then even if the depreciation and renovations problems could be solved, there would still be a problem in constructing a satisfactory property price index because of the low incidence of resales.[10]

A fourth problem should be mentioned at this point. For some purposes, it is desirable to decompose the real estate price index into two separate constant quality components:

- A component that measures the change in the price of the structure and
- A component that measures the change in the price of the underlying land.

In the following section, we will look at some of the methods that were suggested by conference participants to construct constant quality real estate price indexes for the land and structures taken together. The problem of decomposing a real estate price index into its structure and land components will be deferred until Sect. 1.5 below.

1.4 Suggested Methods for Constructing Constant Quality Real Estate Price Indexes

1.4.1 The Repeat Sales Method

The *repeat sales approach* is due to Bailey et al. (1963), who saw their procedure as a generalization of the *chained matched model methodology* that was used by the early pioneers in the construction of real estate price indexes like Wyngarden (1927) and Wenzlick (1952). We will not describe the technical details of the method but just note that the method uses information on properties which trade on the market more than once over the sample period.[11] By utilizing information on "identical"

[10] Related problems are that the mix of transactions can change over time and in fact entirely new types of housing can enter the market.

[11] See Case and Shiller (1989) and Diewert (2013a, b, c; 31–39) for detailed technical descriptions of the method. Diewert showed how the repeat sales method is related to Summers' (1973) country product dummy model used in international price comparisons and the product dummy variable hedonic regression model proposed by Aizcorbe et al. (2001).

properties that trade more than one period, the repeat sales method attempts to hold the quality of the properties constant over time.

We now discuss some of the advantages and disadvantages of the repeat sales method.[12]

The *main advantages* of the repeat sales model are:

- The availability of source data from administrative records on the resale of the same property so that no imputations are involved and
- Reproducibility of the results; i.e., different statisticians given the same data on the sales of housing units will come up with the same estimate of quality adjusted price change.[13]

The *main disadvantages* of the repeat sales model are:

- It does not use all of the available information on property sales; it uses only information on units that have sold more than once during the sample period.[14]
- It cannot deal adequately with depreciation of the dwelling unit or structure.
- It cannot deal adequately with units that have undergone major repairs or renovations.[15] Conversely, a general hedonic regression model for housing or structures

[12]Throughout this section, we will discuss the relative merits of the different methods that have been suggested for constructing property price indexes. For a similar (and perhaps more comprehensive) discussion, see Hoffmann and Lorenz (2006; 2–6).

[13]Hedonic regression models suffer from a reproducibility problem; i.e., different statisticians will use different characteristics variables, use different functional forms and make different stochastic specifications, possibly leading to quite different results. However, the repeat sales model is not as reproducible in practice as indicated in the main text because in some variants of the method, houses that are "flipped" (sold very rapidly) and houses that have not sold for long periods are excluded from the regressions. The exact method for excluding these observations may vary from time to time leading to a lack of reproducibility.

[14]Some of the papers presented at the workshop suggested that the repeat sales method might lead to estimates of price change that were biased upwards, since often sellers of properties undertake major renovations and repairs just before putting their properties on the market, leading to a lack of comparability of the unit from its previous sale. "The repeat sales method does not entirely adjust for changes in quality of the dwellings. If a dwelling undergoes a major renovation or even an extension between two transaction moments, the repeat sales method will not account for this. The last transaction price may in that case be too high, which results in an overestimation of the index." van der Wal et al. (2006; 3). "Research has suggested that appreciation rates for houses that sell may not be the same as appreciation rates for the rest of the housing stock." Leventis (2006; 9). Leventis cites Stephens et al. (1995) on this point. Finally, Gudnason and Jonsdottir made the following observations on the method: "The problem with this method is the risk for bias; e.g., when major renovation and other changes have been made on the house which increases the quality or if the wear of the house has been high, causing a decrease in the quality. Such changes are not captured by this method. In Iceland, this method cannot be used because the number of housing transactions are too few and thus there are not enough repeated sales to be able to calculate the repeated sales index." Gudnason and Jonsdottir (2006; 2).

[15]Case and Shiller (1989) used a variant of the repeat sales method using US data on house sales in four major cities over the years 1970–1986. They attempted to deal with the depreciation and renovation problems as follows: "The tapes contain actual sales prices and other information about the homes. We extracted from the tapes for each city a file of data on houses sold twice for which there

can adjust for the effects of renovations and extensions if (real) expenditures on renovations and extensions are known at the time of sale (or rental).[16]

- The method cannot be used if indexes are required for very fine classifications of the type of property due to a lack of observations. In particular, if monthly property price indexes are required, the method may fail due to a lack of market sales for smaller categories of property.
- In principle, estimates for past price change obtained by the repeat sales method should be updated as new transaction information becomes available.[17] Thus the Repeat Sales property price index is subject to never ending revision.

We turn now to another class of methods suggested by workshop participants in order to form constant quality property price indexes.

1.4.2 The Use of Assessment Information

Most countries tax real estate property. Hence, most countries have some sort of official valuation office that provides periodic appraisals of all taxable real estate property. The paper by van der Wal et al. (2006) presented at the Workshop describes how Statistics Netherlands uses appraisal information in order to construct a property price index. In particular, the *SPAR (Sales Price Appraisal Ratio) Method* is described as follows[18]:

> This method has been used in New Zealand since the early 1960s. It also uses *matched pairs*, but unlike the Repeat Sales method, the SPAR method relies on nearly all transactions that

---

was no apparent quality change and for which conventional mortgages applied." Case and Shiller (1989; 125–126). It is sometimes argued that renovations are approximately equal to depreciation. While this may be true in the aggregate, it certainly is not true for individual dwelling units because over time, many units are demolished.

[16]However, usually information on maintenance and renovation expenditures is not available in the context of estimating a hedonic regression model for housing. Malpezzi et al. (1987; 375–6) comment on this problem as follows: "If all units are identically constructed, inflation is absent, and the rate of maintenance and repair expenditures is the same for all units, then precise measurement of the rate of depreciation is possible by observing the value or rent of two or more units of different ages. … To accurately estimate the effects of aging on values and rents, it is necessary to control for inflation, quality differences in housing units, and location. The hedonic technique controls for differences in dwelling quality and inflation rates but cannot control for most differences in maintenance (except to the extent that they are correlated with location)."

[17]

> Another drawback on the RS method is the fact that previously published index numbers will be revised when new data are added to the sample. van der Wal et al. (2006; 3).

[18]van der Wal et al. (2006; 3) noted that this method is described in more detail in Bourassa et al. (2006). The conference presentation by Statistics Denmark indicated that a variant of this method is also used in Denmark. Jan de Haan brought to my attention that a much more comprehensive analysis of the SPAR method (similar in some respects to the analysis in this section) may be found in de Haan, van der Wal et al. (2006).

have occurred in a given housing market, and hence should be less prone to sample selection bias. The first measure in each pair is the official government appraisal of the property, while the second measure is the matching transaction price. The ratio of the sale price and the appraisal of all sold dwellings in the base period, $t = 0$, serves as the denominator. The numerator is the ratio of the selling price of the reference period, $t = t$, and the appraisal of the base period of all dwellings that have been sold in the reference period. van der Wal et al. (2006; 3).

We will follow the example of van der Wal, ter Steege and Kroese and describe the SPAR method algebraically. Denote the number of sales of a certain type of real estate in the base period by $N(0)$, let the sales prices be denoted as $[S_1^0, S_2^0, ..., S_{N(0)}^0] \equiv \mathbf{S}^0$ and denote the corresponding official appraisal prices as $[A_1^{00}, A_2^{00}, ..., A_{N(0)}^{00}] \equiv \mathbf{A}^{00}$. Similarly, denote the number of sales of the same type of property in the current period by $N(t)$, let the sales prices be denoted as $[S_1^t, S_2^t, ..., S_{N(t)}^t] \equiv \mathbf{S}^t$ and denote the corresponding official appraisal prices in the base period as $[A_1^{0t}, A_2^{0t}, ..., A_{N(t)}^{0t}] \equiv \mathbf{A}^{0t}$. The *value weighted SPAR index* defined by van der Wal et al. (2006; 4) in our notation is defined as follows:

$$P_{\text{DSPAR}}(\mathbf{S}^0, \mathbf{S}^t, \mathbf{A}^{00}, \mathbf{A}^{0t}) \equiv \frac{\sum_{i=1}^{N(t)} S_i^t / \sum_{i=1}^{N(t)} A_i^{0t}}{\sum_{n=1}^{N(0)} S_n^0 / \sum_{n=1}^{N(0)} A_n^{00}}. \tag{1.1}$$

We have labeled the index defined by (1.1) by using the notation P_{DSPAR} where the D stands for Dutot, since the index formula on the right hand side of (1.1) is closely related to the Dutot formula that occurs in elementary index number theory.[19]

What is the intuitive justification for formula (1.1)? One way to justify (1.1) is to suppose that the value S_n^0 for each property transaction in period 0 is equal to a period 0 common price level for the type of property under consideration, P^0 say, times a quality adjustment factor, Q_n^0 say, so that:

$$S_n^0 = P^0 Q_n^0; \quad n = 1, 2, ..., N(0). \tag{1.2}$$

Next, we assume that the period 0 assessed value for transacted property n, A_n^{00}, is equal to the common price level P^0 times the quality adjustment factor Q_n^0 times an independently distributed error term, which we write as $1 + \varepsilon_n^{00}$, where it is likely that the expected value for each of the error terms is 0.[20] Thus we have

$$A_n^{00} = P^0 Q_n^0 (1 + \varepsilon_n^{00}); \quad n = 1, 2, ..., N(0) \tag{1.3}$$

with the error terms having zero expectations; i.e.:

[19]If the term $\sum_{n=1}^{N(0)} S_n^0 / \sum_{n=1}^{N(0)} A_n^{00}$ on the right hand side of (1.1) is equal to 1, then the index reduces to a Dutot index. For the properties of Dutot indexes, see Chap. 20, " Elementary Indices", in ILO (2004) or IMF (2004).

[20]This stochastic specification reflects the fact that the errors are more likely to be multiplicative rather than additive.

$$E\,\varepsilon_n^{00} = 0; \quad n = 1, 2, ..., N(0). \tag{1.4}$$

Turning now to a model for the period t property price transactions, we suppose that the value S_n^t for each property transaction in period t is equal to a period t common price level for the type of property under consideration, P^t say, times a quality adjustment factor, Q_n^t say, so that:

$$S_i^t = P^t Q_i^t; \quad i = 1, 2, ..., N(t). \tag{1.5}$$

Next, we assume that the period 0 assessed value for transacted property i in period t, A_i^{0t}, is equal to the period 0 price level P^0 times the quality adjustment factor Q_i^t times an independently distributed error term, which we write as $1 + \varepsilon_i^{0t}$.[21] Thus we have:

$$A_i^{0t} = P^0 Q_i^t (1 + \varepsilon_i^{0t}); \quad i = 1, 2, ..., N(t). \tag{1.6}$$

Our goal is to obtain an estimator for the level of property prices in period t relative to period 0, which is P^t/P^0. Define the share of transacted property n in period 0 to the total value of properties transacted in period 0, s_n^0, as follows:

$$s_n^0 \equiv \frac{S_n^0}{\sum_{k=1}^{N(0)} S_k^0}; \quad n = 1, 2, ..., N(0). \tag{1.7}$$

Similarly, define the share of transacted property i in period t to the total value of properties transacted in period t, s_i^t, as follows:

$$s_i^t \equiv \frac{S_i^t}{\sum_{k=1}^{N(t)} S_k^t}; \quad i = 1, 2, ..., N(t). \tag{1.8}$$

Now substitute (1.2)–(1.6) into definition (1.1), use definitions (1.7) and (1.8), and we obtain the following expression for the Dutot type SPAR price index:

$$\begin{aligned} P_{\text{DSPAR}}(S^0, S^t, A^{00}, A^{0t}) &= \frac{\sum_{i=1}^{N(t)} P^t Q_i^t / \sum_{i=1}^{N(t)} P^0 Q_i^t (1 + \varepsilon_i^{0t})}{\sum_{n=1}^{N(0)} P^0 Q_n^0 / \sum_{n=1}^{N(0)} P^0 Q_n^0 (1 + \varepsilon_n^{00})} \\ &= \frac{P^t}{P^0} \cdot \frac{1 + \sum_{n=1}^{N(0)} s_n^0 \varepsilon_n^{00}}{1 + \sum_{n=1}^{N(t)} s_n^t \varepsilon_n^{0t}}. \end{aligned} \tag{1.9}$$

Thus the Dutot type SPAR index will be unbiased for the "true" property price index, P^t/P^0, provided that the share weighted average of the period 0 and t quality adjustment errors are equal to zero; i.e., there will be no bias if

[21] It is no longer likely that the expected value of the error term ε_i^{0t} is equal to 0 since the base period assessments cannot pick up any depreciation and renovation biases that might have occurred between periods 0 and t.

$$\sum_{n=1}^{N(0)} s_n^0 \varepsilon_n^{00} = 0 \text{ and} \tag{1.10}$$

$$\sum_{n=1}^{N(t)} s_n^t \varepsilon_n^{0t} = 0. \tag{1.11}$$

It is likely that the weighted sum of errors in period 0 is equal to zero (at least approximately) because it is likely that the official assessed values for period 0 are approximately equal to the market transaction values in the same period; i.e., it is likely that (1.10) is at least approximately satisfied. However, it is not so likely that (1.11) would be satisfied since the period 0 assessed values will not reflect depreciation and renovations done between periods 0 and t. If the economy is growing strongly, then it is likely that the value of renovations will exceed the value of depreciation between periods 0 and t and hence the error terms ε_i^{0t} will tend to be less than 0 and $P_{\text{DSPAR}}(\boldsymbol{S}^0, \boldsymbol{S}^t, \boldsymbol{A}^{00}, \boldsymbol{A}^{0t})$ will be biased upwards. On the other hand, if there is little growth (or a declining population), then it is likely that the value of renovations will be less than the value of depreciation between periods 0 and t and hence the error terms ε_i^{0t} will tend to be greater than 0 and $P_{\text{DSPAR}}(\boldsymbol{S}^0, \boldsymbol{S}^t, \boldsymbol{A}^{00}, \boldsymbol{A}^{0t})$ will be biased downwards.

Variants of the Dutot type SPAR index can be defined; i.e., *the equal weighted SPAR index* defined by van der Wal et al. (2006; 4) in our notation is defined as follows:

$$\begin{aligned} P_{\text{CSPAR}}(\boldsymbol{S}^0, \boldsymbol{S}^t, \boldsymbol{A}^{00}, \boldsymbol{A}^{0t}) &\equiv \frac{\sum_{i=1}^{N(t)} (S_i^t / A_i^{0t}) / N(t)}{\sum_{n=1}^{N(0)} (S_n^0 / A_n^{00}) / N(0)} \\ &= \frac{\sum_{i=1}^{N(t)} \{P^t Q_i^t / P^0 Q_i^t (1 + \varepsilon_i^{0t})\} / N(t)}{\sum_{n=1}^{N(0)} \{P^0 Q_n^0 / P^0 Q_n^0 (1 + \varepsilon_n^{00})\} / N(0)} \quad \text{using (1.2)–(1.6)} \\ &= \frac{P^t}{P^0} \cdot \frac{\sum_{i=1}^{N(t)} (1 + \varepsilon_i^{0t})^{-1} / N(t)}{\sum_{n=1}^{N(0)} (1 + \varepsilon_n^{00})^{-1} / N(0)}. \end{aligned} \tag{1.12}$$

We have labeled the index as P_{CSPAR} since looking at the first line of (1.12), it can be seen that the index is a ratio of two equally weighted indexes of price relatives; i.e., they are a ratio of of two Carli indexes.[22] By looking at (1.12), it can be seen that if all of the error terms ε_i^{0t} and ε_i^{00} are equal to zero, then $P_{\text{CSPAR}}(\boldsymbol{S}^0, \boldsymbol{S}^t, \boldsymbol{A}^{00}, \boldsymbol{A}^{0t})$ will be equal to the target index, P^t/P^0. Of course, it is much more likely that the period 0 error terms, ε_i^{00}, are close to zero than the period t terms, ε_i^{0t}. If in fact all of the period 0 error terms are equal to 0, then it can be seen that $S_n^0 = A_n^{00}$ for all n and P_{C} reduces to the ordinary Carli index, $\sum_{i=1}^{N(t)} (S_i^t / A_i^{0t}) / N(t)$, which is known to be biased upwards.[23]

[22] For the properties of Carli indexes, see Chap. 20, "Elementary Indices", in ILO (2004).

[23] See Chap. 20, "Elementary Indices", in ILO (2004).

The last equation in (1.12) gives us an expression that could be helpful in determining the bias in this Carli type SPAR index in the general case of errors in both periods. However, it proves to be useful to approximate the reciprocal function, $f(\varepsilon) \equiv (1+\varepsilon)^{-1}$, by the following second order Taylor series approximation around $\varepsilon = 0$:

$$\begin{aligned} f(\varepsilon) &\equiv (1+\varepsilon)^{-1} \\ &\approx 1 - \varepsilon + \varepsilon^2. \end{aligned} \tag{1.13}$$

Substituting (1.13) into the last line of (1.12), we find that the Carli type SPAR index is approximately equal to:

$$\begin{aligned} P_{\mathrm{CSPAR}}(\boldsymbol{S}^0, \boldsymbol{S}^t, \boldsymbol{A}^{00}, \boldsymbol{A}^{0t}) &\approx \frac{P^t}{P^0} \cdot \frac{\sum_{i=1}^{N(t)} (1 - \varepsilon_i^{0t} + [\varepsilon_i^{0t}]^2)/N(t)}{\sum_{n=1}^{N(0)} (1 - \varepsilon_n^{00} + [\varepsilon_n^{00}]^2)/N(0)} \\ &= \frac{P^t}{P^0} \cdot \frac{1 + \{\sum_{i=1}^{N(t)} (-\varepsilon_i^{0t} + [\varepsilon_i^{0t}]^2)\}/N(t)}{1 + \{\sum_{n=1}^{N(0)} (-\varepsilon_n^{00} + [\varepsilon_n^{00}]^2)\}/N(0)} \\ &\approx \frac{P^t}{P^0} \cdot \frac{1 + \{\sum_{i=1}^{N(t)} (-\varepsilon_i^{0t} + [\varepsilon_i^{0t}]^2)\}/N(t)}{1 + \sum_{n=1}^{N(0)} [\varepsilon_n^{00}]^2/N(0)} \end{aligned} \tag{1.14}$$

where the last approximation follows from the (likely) assumption that

$$\sum_{n=1}^{N(0)} \varepsilon_n^{00} = 0; \tag{1.15}$$

i.e., that the sum of the assessment measurement errors in period 0 is zero. Now we can use the last line in (1.14) in order to assess the likely size of the bias in P_{CSPAR}. If the economy is growing strongly, then it is likely that the value of renovations will exceed the value of depreciation between periods 0 and t and hence the error terms ε_i^{0t} will tend to be less than 0 so that $\sum_{i=1}^{N(t)} -\varepsilon_i^{0t}$ will be positive. The terms $\sum_{i=1}^{N(t)} [\varepsilon_i^{0t}]^2/N(t)$ and $\sum_{n=1}^{N(0)} [\varepsilon_n^{00}]^2/N(0)$ will both be positive but the period t squared errors will be much larger than the period 0 squared errors so overall, $P_{\mathrm{CSPAR}}(\boldsymbol{S}^0, \boldsymbol{S}^t, \boldsymbol{A}^{00}, \boldsymbol{A}^{0t})$ is likely to have a strong upward bias. On the other hand, if there is little growth (or a declining population), then the upward bias is likely to be smaller but an upward bias is still likely because the terms $\sum_{i=1}^{N(t)} [\varepsilon_i^{0t}]^2/N(t)$ are likely to be very much larger than the terms $-\sum_{i=1}^{N(t)} \varepsilon_i^{0t}/N(t)$ and $\sum_{n=1}^{N(0)} [\varepsilon_n^{00}]^2/N(0)$.

What about the relative sizes of the bias in the Dutot SPAR formula defined by the last line in (1.9) versus the Carli SPAR formula defined by the last line in (1.14)? Assuming that (1.10) holds and using a second order approximation analogous to (1.13) for $[1 + \sum_{n=1}^{N(t)} s_n^t \varepsilon_n^{0t}]^{-1}$, we obtain the following approximation for the Dutot type SPAR formula:

$$P_{\text{DSPAR}}(S^0, S^t, A^{00}, A^{0t}) \approx \frac{P^t}{P^0} \cdot \frac{1}{1 + \sum_{n=1}^{N(t)} s_n^t \varepsilon_n^{0t}}$$
$$\approx \frac{P^t}{P^0} \cdot \left\{ 1 - \sum_{n=1}^{N(t)} s_n^t \varepsilon_n^{0t} + \left[\sum_{n=1}^{N(t)} s_n^t \varepsilon_n^{0t} \right]^2 \right\}. \tag{1.16}$$

Comparing (1.14) with (1.16), it can be seen that the upward bias in the Carli type index will generally be *much greater* than the corresponding bias in the Dutot type index, since the sum of the individual period t errors divided by the number of observations, $\sum_{i=1}^{N(t)} [\varepsilon_i^{0t}]^2 / N(t)$, will usually be very much greater than the square of the period t weighted sum of errors, $[\sum_{n=1}^{N(t)} s_n^t \varepsilon_n^{0t}]^2$.

It is evident that instead of using arithmetic averages of price relatives as in the Carli type formula (1.12), geometric averages could be used, leading to the following *Jevons*[24] *type SPAR index*:

$$P_{\text{JSPAR}}(S^0, S^t, A^{00}, A^{0t}) \equiv \frac{\left[\prod_{i=1}^{N(t)} (S_i^t / A_i^{0t})\right]^{1/N(t)}}{\left[\prod_{n=1}^{N(0)} (S_n^0 / A_n^{00})\right]^{1/N(0)}}$$
$$= \frac{\left[\prod_{i=1}^{N(t)} \{P^t Q_i^t / P^0 Q_i^t (1 + \varepsilon_i^{0t})\}\right]^{1/N(t)}}{\left[\prod_{n=1}^{N(0)} \{P^0 Q_n^0 / P^0 Q_n^0 (1 + \varepsilon_n^{00})\}\right]^{1/N(0)}} \quad \text{using (1.2)–(1.6)}$$
$$= \frac{P^t}{P^0} \cdot \frac{\left[\prod_{n=1}^{N(0)} (1 + \varepsilon_n^{00})\right]^{1/N(0)}}{\left[\prod_{i=1}^{N(t)} (1 + \varepsilon_i^{0t})\right]^{1/N(t)}}. \tag{1.17}$$

Under the assumption that there are no systematic appraisal errors in period 0 so that (1.4) is satisfied, we can assume that $\prod_{n=1}^{N(0)} (1 + \varepsilon_n^{00})$ is close to one but if the value of renovations between periods 0 and t exceeds the value of depreciation, it is likely that $\prod_{i=1}^{N(t)} (1 + \varepsilon_i^{0t})$ is less than one and hence $P_{\text{JSPAR}}(S^0, S^t, A^{00}, A^{0t})$ will have an upward bias.[25]

It is evident that it is not really necessary to have the denominator terms in the right hand sides of definitions (1.1), (1.12) and (1.17) above, provided that the assessments are reasonably close to market values in the base period. Thus define the (regular) *Dutot, Carli and Jevons Market Value to Appraisal indexes* as follows:

$$P_{\text{D}}(S^t, A^{0t}) = \sum_{i=1}^{N(t)} S_i^t / \sum_{i=1}^{N(t)} A_i^{0t}; \tag{1.18}$$

[24]For the properties of Jevons indexes, see Chap. 20, "Elementary Indices", in the ILO (2004) Manual.

[25]Using second order Taylor series approximation techniques, it can be shown that the upward bias in the Jevons type SPAR index will be less than in the corresponding Carli type SPAR index.

$$P_C(S^t, A^{0t}) \equiv \sum_{i=1}^{N(t)} (S_i^t/A_i^{0t})/N(t); \quad (1.19)$$

$$P_J(S^t, A^{0t}) \equiv \left[\prod_{i=1}^{N(t)} (S_i^t/A_i^{0t})\right]^{1/N(t)} \quad (1.20)$$

Using the material in Chap. 20 of the ILO *CPI Manual* (2004), it can be shown that the Jevons index $P_J(S^t, A^{0t})$ is always strictly less than the corresponding Carli index $P_C(S^t, A^{0t})$, unless all of the ratios S_i^t/A_i^{0t} are equal to the same number, in which case the indexes are equal to each other. It is also shown in the ILO Manual that the Dutot index will normally be fairly close to the corresponding Jevons index.[26]

None of the six index number formula discussed above are completely satisfactory because none of these methods can deal with the depreciation and renovations problem. However, if exogenous adjustments can be made to the indexes that make some sort of "average" adjustment to the index for renovations and depreciation, then appraisal methods become quite attractive. If appraisals in the base period are known to be reasonably accurate, then I would vote for the ordinary Jevons index, $P_J(S^t, A^{0t})$, defined by (1.20). If the appraisals in the base period are known to have a systematic bias, then the Jevons type SPAR index defined by (1.17), $P_{JSPAR}(S^0, S^t, A^{00}, A^{0t})$, seems to be the most attractive index.[27]

It is useful to discuss the merits of the above appraisal methods compared to other methods for constructing real estate price indexes.

The *main advantages* of methods that rely on assessment information in the base period and sales information in the current period are:

- The source data on assessment and sales are usually available from administrative records.
- These methods are reproducible conditional on the assessment information; i.e., different statisticians given the same data on the sales of housing units and the same base period assessment information will come up with the same estimate of quality adjusted price change.
- The assessment methods use much more information than the repeat sales method and hence there are fewer problems due to sparse data.
- Information on housing or structure characteristics is not required in order to implement this method.

The *main disadvantages* of the assessment methods discussed above are:

- They cannot deal adequately with depreciation of the dwelling units or structures.
- They cannot deal adequately with units that have undergone major repairs or renovations.

---

[26] The Manual does not recommend the use of the Carli formula since it fails the time reversal test with an upward bias.

[27] These indexes should be further adjusted to take into account depreciation and renovations bias.

- These methods are entirely dependent on the quality of the base period assessment information. How exactly were the base period assessments determined? Were hedonic regression methods used? Were comparable property methods used?[28] How can we be certain that the quality of these base period assessments is satisfactory?[29]
- The methods discussed above do not deal with weighting problems.[30]
- If information on housing characteristics is not available, then the method can be used to form only a single index. However, in most countries, the rate of change in real estate prices is not constant across locations[31] and type of housing and so it is useful to be able to calculate more than one real estate price index.
- These assessment based methods cannot decompose a property price index into structure and land components.[32]

My overall evaluation of these assessment based methods is that they are quite satisfactory (and superior to repeat sales methods) if:

- The assessed values are used for taxation purposes[33];
- The index is adjusted using other information for depreciation and renovations bias and

[28]Leventis (2006) discussed some of the problems with U.S. private sector assessment techniques when he discussed the work of Chinloy et al. (1997) as follows: "Using a sample of 1993 purchase price data for which they also had the appraisal information, they compared purchase prices against appraisals to determine whether there were systematic differences. They estimated an upward bias of two percent and found that appraisals exceeded purchase price in approximately 60% of the cases. ... That appraisers 'extrapolate' valuations from recent results and have a vested interest in ensuring that their valuations appear reasonable (and perhaps consistent) to the originators suggest that the volatility of appraised values may be lower. At the same time, the authors believe that the appraisals' reliance on a small number of comparables 'almost surely' leads to 'more volatility than marketwide prices'. Leventis (2006; 5–6).

[29]If the assessments are used for taxation purposes and they are supposed to be based on market valuations, then the assessed values cannot be too far off the mark since the government has an incentive to make the assessments as large as possible (to maximize tax revenue) and taxpayers have the opposite incentive to have the assessments as small as possible.

[30]This is not really a major problem since the base period assessment information can be used to obtain satisfactory weights. When a new official assessment takes place, superlative indexes can be formed between any two consecutive assessment periods and interpolation techniques can be used to form approximate weights for all intervening periods. For descriptions of superlative indexes and their properties, see Diewert (1976, 1978) or Chaps. 15–20 of ILO (2004).

[31]The paper presented by Girouard et al. (2006; 26) showed that there are regional differences in the rate of housing price change. This paper also showed that real estate bubbles were quite common in many OECD countries. In many countries, bubbles lead to differential rates of housing price increase; i.e., in the upward phase of the bubble, expensive properties tend to increase in price more rapidly than cheaper ones and then in the downward phase, the prices of more expensive properties tend to fall more rapidly. A single index will not be able to capture these differential rates of price change.

[32]We show later in Sect. 1.5.1 that the hedonic method can deal with this problem.

[33]A bit of caution is called for here: sometimes official assessments are not very accurate for various reasons.

- Only a single index is required and a decomposition of the index into structure and land components is not required.

We turn now to another class of methods for constructing property price indexes.

1.4.3 Stratification Methods

Possibly the simplest approach to the construction of a real estate price index is to *stratify* or decompose the market into separate types of property, calculate the mean (or more commonly, the median) price for all properties transacted in that cell for the current period and the base period and then use the ratio of the means as a real estate price index.

The problem with this method can be explained as follows: if there are too many cells in the stratification, then there may not be a sufficient number of transactions in any given period in order to form an accurate cell average price but if there are too few cells in the stratification, then the resulting cell averages will suffer from *unit value bias*; i.e., the mix of properties sold in each period within each cell may change dramatically from period to period, and thus the resulting stratified indexes do not hold quality constant.

The stratification method can work well; for example, see Gudnason and Jonsdottir (2006; 3–5) where they note that they work with some 8,000–10,000 real estate transactions per year in Iceland, which is a sufficient number of observations to be able to produce 30 monthly subindexes.[34] Within each cell, geometric rather than arithmetic averaging of prices is used:

> The geometric mean replaces the arithmetic mean when averaging house prices within each stratum at the elementary level. This is in line with the calculation method used at the elementary level in the Icelandic CPI. The geometric mean is also used in hedonic calculations and the geometric mean is a typical matched model estimator (Diewert 2003b, c; de Haan 2003). Gudnason and Jonsdottir (2006; 5).

Even though geometric averaging is difficult to explain to some users, it has much to recommend it since it is more likely that random "errors" in a particular stratum of real estate are multiplicative in nature rather than being additive; see also Chaps. 16 and 20 of ILO (2004).

The Australian Bureau of Statistics (ABS) is also experimenting with stratification techniques in order to produce constant quality housing price indexes:

> The approach uses location (suburb) to define strata that group together (or 'cluster') houses that are 'similar' in terms of their price determining characteristics. Ideally, each suburb would form its own cluster as this would maximise the homogeneity of the cluster. However, there are insufficient numbers of observations from quarter to quarter to support this

[34] However, the monthly index is produced as a moving average: "The calculation of price changes for real estate is a three month moving average, with a one month delay." Gudnason and Jonsdottir (2006; 4). Gudnason and Jonsdottir (2006; 3) also note that each year about 8–10% of all the housing in the country is bought and sold.

methodology. The ABS has grouped similar suburbs to form clusters with sufficient ongoing observations to determine a reliable median price. ABS research showed HPI (Housing Price Index) strata (or clusters of suburbs) were most effectively determined using an indicator of socio-economic characteristics: the median price, the percentage of three bedroom houses and the geographical location of the suburbs. Branson (2006; 5).

The ABS clustering procedures are very interesting and novel but one must be a bit cautious in interpreting the resulting price changes since any individual suburb might contain a mixture of properties and thus the resulting indexes may be subject to a certain amount of unit value bias.[35]

As usual, we close this section with a discussion of the advantages and disadvantages of the stratification approach to the construction of real estate price indexes.

It is useful to discuss the merits of the above appraisal methods compared to other methods for constructing real estate price indexes.

The *main advantages* of the stratification method are:

- The method is conceptually acceptable but it depends crucially on the choice of stratification variables.
- The method is reproducible, conditional on an agreed list of stratification variables.
- Housing price indexes can be constructed for different types and locations of housing.
- The method is relatively easy to explain to users.

The *main disadvantages* of the stratification method are:

- The method cannot deal adequately with depreciation of the dwelling units or structures.
- The method cannot deal adequately with units that have undergone major repairs or renovations.
- The method requires some information on housing characteristics so that sales transactions can be allocated to the correct cell in the classification scheme.[36]
- If the classification scheme is very coarse, then there may be some unit value bias in the indexes.
- If the classification scheme is very fine, the detailed cell indexes may be subject to a considerable amount of sampling variability due to small sample sizes.
- The method cannot decompose a property price index into structure and land components.

My overall evaluation of the stratification method is that it can be quite satisfactory (and superior to the repeat sales and assessment methods[37]) if:

---

[35]However, Prasad and Richards (2006) show that the stratification method applied to Australian house price data gave virtually the same results as a hedonic model that had locational explanatory variables.

[36]If no information on housing characteristics is used, then the method is subject to tremendous unit value bias.

[37]The standard assessment method leads to only a single price index whereas the stratification method leads to a family of subindexes. However, if stratification variables are available, the assessment method can also produce a family of indexes.

- An appropriate level of detail is chosen for the number of cells;
- The index is adjusted using other information for depreciation and renovations bias and
- A decomposition of the index into structure and land components is not required.

It is well known that stratification methods can be regarded as special cases of general hedonic regressions[38] and so we now turn to this more general technique.

1.4.4 Hedonic Methods

Very detailed expositions of hedonic regression techniques applied to the property market can be found in some of the papers presented at this workshop; see in particular, Gouriéroux and Laferrère (2006) and Li et al. (2006). Although there are several variants of the technique, the basic model regresses the logarithm of the sale price of the property on the price determining characteristics of the property and a time dummy variable is added for each period in the regression (except the base period). Once the estimation has been completed, these time dummy coefficients can be exponentiated and turned into an index.[39]

Since the method assumes that information on the characteristics of the properties sold is available, the data can be stratified and a separate regression can be run for each important class of property. Thus the hedonic regression method can be used to produce a family of indexes.[40]

The issues associated with running weighted hedonic regressions are rather subtle and the recent literature on this topic will not be reviewed here.[41]

---

[38] See Diewert (2003b) who showed that stratification techniques or the use of dummy variables can be viewed as a nonparametric regression technique. In the statistics literature, these partitioning or stratification techniques are known as analysis of variance models; see Scheffé (1959).

[39] An alternative approach to the hedonic method is to estimate separate hedonic regressions for both of the periods compared; i.e., for the base and current period. Predicted prices can then be generated in each period using the estimated hedonic regressions based on a constant characteristics set, say the characteristics of the base period. A ratio of the geometric means of the estimated prices in each period would yield a pure price comparison based on a constant base period set of characteristics. A hedonic index based on a constant current period characteristic could also be compiled, as could such indexes based on a symmetric use of base and current period information. Heravi and Silver (2007) outline alternative formulations and Silver and Heravi (2007) provide a formal analysis of the difference between this approach and that of the time dummy method. The French method also does not use the time dummy method but is too complex to explain here.

[40] This property of the hedonic regression method also applies to the stratification method. The main difference between the two methods is that continuous variables can appear in hedonic regressions (like the area of the structure and the area of the lot size) whereas the stratification method can only work with discrete ranges for the independent variables in the regression.

[41] Basically, this recent literature makes connections between weighted hedonic regressions and traditional index number formula that use weights; see Diewert (2003c, 2004, 2005a, b), de Haan (2003, 2004), Silver (2003) and Silver and Heravi (2005). It is worth noting that a perceived advantage of the stratification method is that *median* price changes can be measured as opposed to

The usual hedonic regression model is not able to separate out the land and structures components of the property class under consideration but in Sect. 1.5.1 below, we will explain how the usual method can be modified to give us this decomposition.

As usual, it is useful to discuss the merits of the hedonic regression method compared to other methods for constructing real estate price indexes.

The *main advantages* of the hedonic regression method are:

- Property price indexes can be constructed for different types and locations of the property class under consideration.
- The method is probably the most efficient method for making use of the available data.
- The method can be modified to give a decomposition of property prices into land and structures components (see Sect. 1.5.1 below); none of the other methods described so far can do this.
- If the list of property characteristics is sufficiently detailed, so that, for example, it can be determined whether major maintenance projects have been undertaken and when they were done (such as a new roof), then it may be possible to deal adequately with the depreciation and renovations problems.

The *main disadvantages* of the hedonic method are:

- The method is data intensive (i.e., it requires information on property characteristics) and thus it is relatively expensive to implement.
- The method is not entirely reproducible; i.e., different statisticians will enter different property characteristics into the regression,[42] assume different functional forms for the regression equation, make different stochastic specifications and perhaps choose different transformations of the dependent variable[43] all of which leads to perhaps different estimates of the amount of overall price change.
- The method is not easy to explain to users.

My overall evaluation of the hedonic regression method is that it is probably the best method that could be used in order to construct constant quality price indexes for various types of property.[44] Note that the paper by Gouriéroux and Laferrère (2006) demonstrates that it is possible to construct an official nationwide credible hedonic regression model for real estate properties.

---

arithmetic mean ones, that are implicit in a say ordinary least squares estimator. However, regression estimates can also be derived from robust estimators from which the parameter estimates for the price change will be similar to a median.

[42]Note that the same criticism can be applied to stratification methods; i.e., different analysts will come up with different stratifications.

[43]For example, the dependent variable could be the sales price of the property or its logarithm or the sales price divided by the area of the structure and so on.

[44]This evaluation agrees with that of Hoffmann and Lorenz: "As far as quality adjustment is concerned, the future will certainly belong to hedonic methods." Hoffman and Lorenz (2006; 15).

In the following 2 sections, we will discuss some additional technical issues that emerged from the workshop. In particular, in Sect. 1.5.1 below, we will show how the hedonic regression technique can be modified to provide a structures and land price decomposition of property price movements.

1.5 Other Technical Issues

1.5.1 The Decomposition of Real Estate Values into Land and Structure Components

If we momentarily think like a property developer who is planning to build a structure on a particular property, the total cost of the property after the structure is completed will be equal to the floor space area of the structure, say A square meters, times the building cost per square meter, α say, plus the cost of the land, which will be equal to the cost per square meter, β say, times the area of the land site, B. Now think of a sample of properties of the same general type, which have prices p_n^0 in period 0 and structure areas A_n^0 and land areas B_n^0 for $n = 1, \ldots, N(0)$, and these prices are equal to costs of the above type times error terms η_n^0 which we assume have mean 1. This leads to the following hedonic regression model for period 0 where α and β are the parameters to be estimated in the regression[45]:

$$p_n^0 = [\alpha A_n^0 + \beta B_n^0]\eta_n^0; \quad n = 1, \ldots, N(0). \tag{1.21}$$

Taking logarithms of both sides of (1.21) leads to the following traditional additive errors regression model[46]:

$$\ln p_n^0 = \ln[\alpha A_n^0 + \beta B_n^0] + \varepsilon_n^0; \quad n = 1, \ldots, N(0) \tag{1.22}$$

where the new error terms are defined as $\varepsilon_n^0 \equiv \ln \eta_n^0$ for $n = 1, \ldots, N(0)$ and are assumed to have 0 means and constant variances.

Now consider the situation in a subsequent period t. The price per square meter of this type of structure will have changed from α to $\alpha\gamma^t$ and the land cost per square meter will have changed from β to $\beta\delta^t$ where we interpret γ^t as the *period 0 to t price index for the type of structure* and δ^t as the *period 0 to t price index for the land that is associated with this type of structure*. The period t counterparts to (1.21) and (1.22) are:

[45]Multiplicative errors with constant variances are more plausible than additive errors with constant variances; i.e., it is more likely that expensive properties have relatively large absolute errors compared to very inexpensive properties. The multiplicative specification for the errors will be consistent with this phenomenon.

[46]However, note that this model is not linear in the unknown parameters to be estimated.

$$p_n^t = [\alpha\gamma^t A_n^t + \beta\delta^t B_n^t]\eta_n^t; \quad n = 1, ..., N(t); \tag{1.23}$$
$$\ln p_n^t = \ln[\alpha\gamma^t A_n^t + \beta\delta^t B_n^t] + \varepsilon_n^t; \quad n = 1, ..., N(t) \tag{1.24}$$

where $\varepsilon_n^t \equiv \ln \eta_n^t$ for $n = 1, ..., N(t)$, the period t property prices are p_n^t and the corresponding structure and land areas are A_n^t and B_n^t for $n = 1, ..., N(t)$.

Equations (1.22) and (1.24) can be run as a system of nonlinear hedonic regressions and estimates can be obtained for the 4 parameters, α, β, γ^t and δ^t. The main parameters of interest are of course, γ^t and δ^t, which can be interpreted as price indexes for the price of a square meter of this type of structure and for the price per meter squared of the underlying land respectively.

The above very basic nonlinear hedonic regression framework can be generalized to encompass the traditional array of characteristics that are used in real estate hedonic regressions. Thus suppose that we can associate with each property n that is transacted in each period t a list of K characteristics $X_{n1}^t, X_{n2}^t, \ldots, X_{nK}^t$ that are price determining characteristics for the structure and a similar list of M characteristics $Y_{n1}^t, Y_{n2}^t, \ldots, Y_{nM}^t$ that are price determining characteristics for the type of land that sits underneath the structure. The equations which generalize (1.22) and (1.24) to the present setup are the following ones:

$$\ln p_n^0 = \ln\left\{\left[\alpha_0 + \sum_{k=1}^{K} X_{nk}^0\alpha_k\right]A_n^0 + \left[\beta_0 + \sum_{m=1}^{M} Y_{nm}^0\beta_m\right]B_n^0\right\} + \varepsilon_n^0; \; n = 1, ..., N(0); \tag{1.25}$$

$$\ln p_n^t = \ln\left\{\gamma^t\left[\alpha_0 + \sum_{k=1}^{K} X_{nk}^t\alpha_k\right]A_n^t + \delta^t\left[\beta_0 + \sum_{m=1}^{M} Y_{nm}^t\beta_m\right]B_n^t\right\} + \varepsilon_n^t; \; n = 1, ..., N(t); \tag{1.26}$$

where the parameters to be estimated are now the $K + 1$ quality of structure parameters, $\alpha_0, \alpha_1, \ldots, \alpha_K$, the $M + 1$ quality of land parameters, $\beta_0, \beta_1, \ldots, \beta_M$, the period t price index for structures parameter γ^t and the period t price index for the land underlying the structures parameter δ^t. Note that $[\alpha_0 + \sum_{k=1}^{K} X_{nk}^0\alpha_k]$ in (1.25) and (1.26) replaces the single structures quality parameter α in (1.22) and (1.24) and $[\beta_0 + \sum_{m=1}^{M} Y_{nm}^0\beta_m]$ in (1.25) and (1.26) replaces the single land quality parameter β in (1.22) and (1.24).

In order to illustrate how X and Y variables can be formed, we consider the list of exogenous variables in the hedonic housing regression model reported by Li et al. (2006; 23). The following variables in their list of exogenous variables can be regarded as variables that affect structure quality; i.e., they are X type variables: number of reported bedrooms, number of reported bathrooms, number of garages, number of fireplaces, age of the unit, age squared of the unit, exterior finish is brick or not, dummy variable for new units, unit has hardwood floors or not, heating fuel is natural gas or not, unit has a patio or not, unit has a central built in vacuum cleaning system or not, unit has an indoor or outdoor swimming pool or not, unit has a hot tub unit or not, unit has a sauna or not, and unit has air conditioning or not. The following variables can be regarded as variables that affect the quality of the land;

i.e., they are Y type location variables: unit is at the intersection of two streets or not (corner lot or not), unit is at a cul-de-sac or not, shopping center is nearby or not, and various suburb location dummy variables.[47]

The nonlinear hedonic regression model defined by (1.25) and (1.26) is very flexible and can accomplish what none of the other real estate price index construction methods were able to accomplish: namely a decomposition of a property price index into structures and land components. However, this model has a cost compared to the usual hedonic regression model discussed in Sect. 1.4.4: the previous class of models was linear in the unknown parameters to be estimated whereas the model defined by (1.25) and (1.26) is highly nonlinear. It remains to be seen whether such a highly nonlinear model can be estimated successfully for a large data set.[48]

1.5.2 Weighting and Formula Issues

Most of the papers presented at the workshop did not delve too deeply into weighting and formula issues, with some exceptions, such as the paper by Gudnason and Jonsdottir (2006). However, for all of the methods except the hedonic regression methods, the advice on formulae and weighting given in the ILO *CPI Manual* (2004) seems relevant and the reader is advised to consult the appropriate chapters. For hedonic methods, we noted the recent literature on weighting and the reader is advised to consult this literature.

Perhaps it is worth repeating some of Diewert's observations on weighting problems that can arise if we use the acquisitions approach to housing:

> Some differences between the acquisitions approach and the other approaches are:
>
> - If rental or leasing markets for the durable exist and the durable has a long useful life, then the expenditure weights implied by the rental equivalence or user cost approaches will typically be much larger than the corresponding expenditure weights implied by the acquisitions approach.
> - the capital formation in buildings, again as opposed to land, is part of gross fixed capital formation, depreciation, and the measurement of the stock of fixed capital,

---

[47]Of course, in practice, some of the land or location variables could act as proxies for unobserved structure quality variables. There are also some interesting conceptual problems associated with the treatment of rental apartments and owner occupied apartments or condominiums. Obviously, separate hedonic regressions would be appropriate for apartments since their structural characteristics are quite different from detached housing. For rental apartments, the sale price of the apartment can be the dependent variable and there will be associated amounts of structure area and land area. For a condo sale, the price of the single unit is the dependent variable while the dependent variables in the bare bones model would be structure area of the apartment plus the apartment's share of commonly owned facilities plus the apartment's share of the lot area. In the end, we want to be able to impute the value of the property into land and structure components and so the hedonic regression should be set up so as to accomplish this task.

[48]Of course, large data sets can be transformed into smaller data sets if we run separate hedonic regressions for various property strata!

- In making comparisons of consumption across countries where the proportion of owning versus renting or leasing the durable varies greatly,[49] the use of the acquisitions approach may lead to misleading cross country comparisons. The reason for this is that opportunity costs of capital are excluded in the net acquisitions approach whereas they are explicitly or implicitly included in the other two approaches. Diewert (2003a, 7–8).

1.5.3 The Frequency Issue and the Consistency of Quarterly with Annual Estimates

For inflation monitoring purposes, central banks would like to have property price indexes produced on a monthly or quarterly basis. Given the fact that the number of observations for a monthly index will only be approximately one third the number for a quarterly index, statistical agencies will have to carefully evaluate the timeliness-quality tradeoff.

Another question arises in this context: how can monthly or quarterly estimates of real estate inflation be made consistent with annual estimates?

The answer to this question is not simple because of two problems:

- The existence of seasonal factors; i.e., during some seasons (e.g., winter) real estate sales tend to be more sparse and there may be seasonal fluctuations in prices.[50]
- For high inflation countries, the price levels in the last month or quarter can be very much higher than those prevailing in the first quarter, leading to various conceptual difficulties.

If there is high inflation within the year, then when annual unit value prices are computed (to correspond to total annual production of the commodities under consideration), "too much" weight will be given to the prices of the fourth quarter compared to the prices in the first quarter.[51] There are possible solutions to this problem but they are rather complex and there is no consensus on what the appropriate solution should be.

For possible solutions to the above problems, the reader is referred to Hill (1996), Diewert (1998, 1999), Bloem et al. (2001) and Armknecht and Diewert (2004).

1.5.4 Revision Policies

Many of the papers presented at this conference noted the difficulties in assembling timely data on property sales. Since many of these difficulties seem rather intractable,

[49] From Hoffmann and Kurz (2002; 3–4), about 60% of German households live in rented dwellings whereas only about 11% of Spaniards rent their dwellings in 1999 (private communication).

[50] Hoffmann and Kurz-Kim (2006) provide some recent evidence of seasonality in German prices.

[51] See Hill (1996) and Diewert (1998) for a discussion of these problems.

it seems sensible to *not* apply the usual Consumer Price Index methodology to Real Estate Price indexes[52]; i.e., revisions should be allowed for Real Estate price indexes. This will create some problems for CPI indexes that apply a user cost approach to Owner Occupied Housing, since the user cost will depend on accurate property price indexes, which will generally only be available with a lag. The same problem will occur if the Harmonized Index of Consumer Prices decides to implement an acquisitions approach to Owner Occupied Housing.[53] One solution might be that users will be given a flagship CPI or HICP that makes use of preliminary or forecasted data and finally adjusted indexes will only be made available as "analytic" series. This issue requires more discussion.

1.5.5 The Renovations Versus Depreciation Problem

Renovations increase the quality of a property and depreciation decreases the quality of a property and typically, both phenomena are not directly observed, making the construction of constant quality real estate price indexes extremely difficult if not impossible. How can we deal with this issue?

Perhaps the best way to deal with this problem is for statistical agencies to have a fairly extensive *renovations and repair survey* for both households and businesses. If renovations expenditures can be tracked over time back to a base period for individual properties that have sold in the current period and a base period estimate for the value of the property is available, then this information can be used in a hedonic regression model along the lines indicated in Sect. 1.5.1 and scientific estimates of depreciation can be obtained. On the business side of property markets, the situation is not as bad, since businesses normally keep track of major renovations in their asset registers and this information could be accessed in investment surveys that also ask questions about asset sales and retirements. Canada,[54] the Netherlands[55] and New Zealand ask such questions on retirements in their investment surveys and Japan is about to follow suit.[56] Diewert and Wykoff (2006) indicate how this type of survey can be used to obtain estimates for depreciation rates.

There are a number of technical details that remain to be explored in this area. It is an important area of research that needs further development.

---

[52]The usual CPI methodology is to never revise the index.

[53]For an update on how thinking is progressing on the treatment of Owner Occupied Housing in the HICP, see Makaronidis and Hayes (2006).

[54]For a description and further references to the Canadian program on estimating depreciation rates, see Baldwin et al. (2005).

[55]Actually, since 1991, the Dutch have a separate (mail) survey for enterprises with more than 100 employees to collect information on discards and retirements: The Survey on Discards; see Bergen et al. (2005; 8) for a description of the Dutch methods.

[56]The Economic and Social Research Institute (ESRI), Cabinet Office of Japan, with the help of Koji Nomura is preparing a new survey to be implemented as of the end of 2006.

The final technical problem that arose out of the workshop is sufficiently important that it deserves a separate section. The question which the paper by Verbrugge (2006) raised is this: are user costs so volatile and unpredictable that they are pretty much useless in a statistical agency real estate price index?

1.6 User Costs Versus Rental Equivalence

Perhaps the most interesting and provocative paper presented at the Workshop was the paper by Verbrugge. He summarized his paper as follows:

> I construct several estimates of *ex ante* user costs for US homeowners, and compare these to rents. There are three novel findings. First, a significant volatility divergence remains even for *ex ante* user cost measures which have been smoothed to mimic the implicit smoothing in the rent data. Indeed, the volatility of smoothed quarterly aggregate *ex ante* user cost growth is about 10 times greater than that of aggregate rent growth. This large volatility probably rules out the use of *ex ante* user costs as a measure of the costs of homeownership.
>
> The second novel finding is perhaps more surprising: not only do rents and user costs diverge in the short run, but the gaps persist over extended periods of time. ...
>
> The divergence between rents and user costs highlights a puzzle, explored in greater depth below: rents do not appear to respond very strongly to their theoretical determinants. ...
>
> Despite this divergence, the third novel finding is that there were evidently no unexploited profit opportunities. While the detached unit rental market is surprisingly thick, and detached housing is readily moved between owner and renter markets ..., the large costs associated with real estate transactions would have prevented risk neutral investors from earning expected profits by using the transaction sequence *buy, earn rent on property, sell*, and would have prevented risk neutral homeowners form earning expected profits by using the transaction sequence *sell, rent for one year, repurchase*. Verbrugge (2006; 3).

How did Verbrugge arrive at the above conclusions? He started off with the following expression for the user cost u_i^t of home i[57]:

$$u_i^t = P_i^t(i^t + \delta - E\pi_i^t) \tag{1.27}$$

where

- P_i^t is the price of home i in period t;
- i^t is a nominal interest rate[58];
- δ is the sum of annual depreciation, maintenance and repair, insurance, property taxes and potentially a risk premium[59]; and

---

[57] See formula (1) in Verbrugge (2006; 11). We have not followed his notation exactly.

[58] Verbrugge (2006; 11) used either the current 30 year mortgage rate or the average one year Treasury bill rate and noted that the choice of interest rate turned out to be inconsequential for his analysis.

[59] Verbrugge (2006; 13) assumed that δ was approximately equal to 7%. Note that the higher the volatility in house prices is, the higher the risk premium would be for a risk averse consumer.

- $E\pi_i^t$ represents the expected annual constant quality home appreciation rate for home i at period t.[60]

Thus the resulting user cost can be viewed as an opportunity cost measure for the annual cost of owning a home starting at the beginning of the quarter indexed by time t. Presumably, landlords, when they set an annual rent for a dwelling unit, would use a formula similar to (1.27) in order to determine the rent for a tenant.[61] So far, there is nothing particularly controversial about Verbrugge's analysis. What is controversial was Verbrugge's determination of the expected house price appreciation term, $E\pi_i^t$:

> Rather than using a crude proxy, I will construct a *forecast* for $E\pi_i^t$, as described below. This choice is crucial, for four reasons. First, expected home price appreciation is extremely volatile; setting this term to a constant is strongly at odds with the data, and its level of volatility will be central to this study. Second, this term varies considerably across cities, and its temporal dynamics might well vary across cities as well. Third, the properties of $(i^t - E\pi_i^t)$ are central to user cost dynamics, yet these properties are unknown (or at least, not documented); again, setting $E\pi_i^t$ to a constant (or even to a long moving average) would be inappropriate for this study, since this choice obviously suppresses the correlation between i^t and $E\pi_i^t$. Finally, the recent surge in $E\pi_i^t$ is well above its 15 year average, and implies that the user cost/rent ratio has fallen dramatically. A *single* year appreciation rate is used since we are considering the *one year* user cost, in order to remain comparable to the typical rental contract. Verbrugge (2006; 12).

Verbrugge (2006; 13) went on to use various econometric forecasting techniques to forecast expected price appreciation for his one year horizon, he inserted these forecasts into the user cost formula (1.27) above and obtained tremendously volatile ex ante user costs and the rest of his conclusions followed.

However, it is unlikely that landlords use econometric forecasts of housing price appreciation one year away and adjust rents for their tenants every year based on these forecasts. Tenants do not like tremendous volatility in their rents and any landlord that attempted to set such volatile rents would soon have very high vacancy rates on his or her properties.[62] It is however possible that landlords may have some idea of the long run average rate of property inflation for the type of property that they manage and this long run average annual rate of price appreciation could be inserted into the user cost formula (1.27).[63]

---

[60] π_i^t is the actual 4 quarter (constant quality) home price appreciation between the beginning of period t and one year from this period.

[61] Diewert (2003a) noted that there would be a few differences between a user cost formula for an owner occupier as compared to a landlord but these differences are not important for Verbrugge's analysis.

[62] Hoffmann and Kurz-Kim find that German rents are changed only once every 4 years on average: "In Germany, as in other euro area countries, prices of most products change infrequently, but not incrementally. Pricing seems to be neither continuous nor marginal. In our sample, prices last on average more than two years—if price changes within a month are not considered—but then change by nearly 10%. The longest price durations are found for housing rents, which, on average, are for more than four years." Hoffmann and Kurz-Kim (2006; 5).

[63] The paper by Girouard, Kennedy, van den Noord and André nicely documents the length of housing booms and busts: "To qualify as a major cycle, the appreciation had to feature a cumulative real price increase equalling or exceeding 15%. This criterion identified 37 such episodes, correspond-

Looking at the opportunity costs of owning a house from the viewpoint of an owner occupier, the relevant time horizon to consider for working out an annualized average rate of expected price appreciation is the expected time that the owner expects to use the dwelling before reselling it. This time horizon is typically some number between 6 and 12 years so again, it does not seem appropriate to stick annual forecasts of expected price inflation into the user cost formula. Once we use annualized forecasts of expected price inflation over longer time horizons, the volatility in the ex ante user cost formula will vanish or at least be much diminished.

Another method for reducing the volatility in the user cost formula is to replace the nominal interest rate less expected price appreciation term $(i^t - E\pi_i^t)$ by a constant or a slowly changing long run average *real interest rate*, r^t say. This is what is done in Iceland[64] and the resulting user cost seems to be acceptable to the population (and it is not overly volatile).

Verbrugge had an interesting section in his paper that helps to explain why user costs and market rentals can diverge so much over the short run. The answer is high transactions costs involved in selling or purchasing real estate properties prevent arbitrage opportunities[65]:

> The first question is thus answered: there is no evidence of unexploited profits for prospective landlords. How about the second: was there ever a period of time in any city during which a 'median' homeowner should have sold his house, rented for a year, and repurchased his house a year later? ... In this case, it appears that for Los Angeles, there was a single year, 1994, during which a homeowner should have sold her house, rented for a year, and repurchased her house. For every other time period, and for the entire period for the other four cities, a homeowner was always better off remaining in his house. Verbrugge (2006; 36).

Since high real estate transactions costs prevent the exploitation of arbitrage opportunities between owning and renting a property, user costs can differ considerably over the corresponding rental equivalence measures over the lifetime of a property cycle.

We conclude this section with the following (controversial) observation: perhaps the "correct" opportunity cost of housing for an owner occupier is not his or her internal user cost but the *maximum* of the internal user cost and what the property could rent for on the rental market. After all, the concept of opportunity cost is supposed to represent the *maximum sacrifice* that one makes in order to consume or use some object and so the above point would seem to follow. If this point of view

---

ing to about two large upswings on average per 35 years for English speaking and Nordic countries and to $1\frac{1}{2}$ for the continental European countries." Girouard et al. (2006; 6). Thus one could justify taking 10 to 20 year (annualized) average rates of property price inflation in the user cost formula rather than one year rates.

[64] See Gudnason (2004) and Gudnason and Jonsdottir (2006; 11).

[65] Verbrugge (2006; 35) assumed that the transactions costs in the U.S. were approximately 8–10% of the sales price.

is accepted, then at certain points in the property cycle, user costs would replace market rents as the "correct" pricing concept for owner occupied housing, which would dramatically affect Consumer Price Indexes and the conduct of monetary policy.[66]

1.7 Summary and Conclusion

The following points emerged as a result of the Workshop:

- The needs of users cannot be met by a single housing (or more generally, by a single real estate) price index.
- There is a demand for official real estate price indexes that are at least roughly comparable across countries.
- Statistical agencies should not produce multiple indexes that measure the same thing.
- The System of National Accounts should be the starting point for providing a systematic framework for a family of real estate price indexes.[67]
- It may well be that cooperation between the private sector and statistical agencies is the way forward in this area; the papers by Gouriéroux and Laferrère (2006) and Li et al. (2006) show that this type of cooperation is possible.
- It would be very useful for the various international agencies to cooperate in producing an international Manual or Handbook of Methods on Real Estate Price Indexes so that national real estate price indexes can be harmonized across countries (or at least be more harmonized).
- It would be useful to produce a country inventory of practices in the real estate price index area.
- The OECD should take the lead in producing the Manual and the inventory of practices.
- There is a need for the Manual writers to talk to users about their needs in this area.
- The listing of properties on the internet may well facilitate the development of high quality property price indexes and may do the same for residential property price indexes as scanner data did for ordinary consumer price indexes.[68]

[66]Woolford (2006) shows that different treatments of Owner Occupied Housing in the Australian context generate very different aggregate consumer price indexes.

[67]As was noted above in Sect. 1.2, it is necessary to look beyond the present SNA to the next version which will probably have a more detailed treatment of durable goods in it so that consumer service flows can be better measured and so that productivity accounts can be constructed for the business sector. A natural family of real estate price indexes emerges from this expanded SNA.

[68]Johannes Hoffmann made this point.

References

Armknecht, P.A., and W.E. Diewert. 2004. Treatment of Seasonal Products. In *Producer Price Index Manual: Theory and Practice*, 553–593. Washington: International Monetary Fund. http://www.imf.org/external/np/sta/tegppi/ch22.pdf.

Arthur, S.V. 2006. Residential Property Prices—What has been Achieved since 2003? Paper presented at the OECD-IMF Workshop on Real Estate Price Indexes held in Paris, November 6–7, 2006. http://www.oecd.org/dataoecd/3/9/37583158.pdf.

Aizcorbe, A., C. Corrado, and M. Doms. 2001. Constructing Price and Quantity Indexes for High Technology Goods. Industrial Output Section, Division of Research and Statistics, Board of Governors of the Federal Reserve System, July.

Bailey, M.J., R.F. Muth, and H.O. Nourse. 1963. A regression method for real estate price construction. *Journal of the American Statistical Association* 58: 933–942.

Baldwin, J., G. Gellatly, M. Tanguay, and A. Patry. 2005. Estimating Depreciation Rates for the Productivity Accounts. Paper presented at the OECD Workshop on Productivity Measurement, Madrid Spain, October 17–19. http://www.oecd.org/document/27/0,2340,en_2649_34409_35100379_1_1_1_1,00.html.

Bergen, Dirk van den, M. de Haan, R. de Heij, and M. Horsten. 2005. Measuring Capital in the Netherlands. Paper presented at the Meeting of the OECD Working Party on National Accounts, Paris, October 11–14. www.unece.org/stats/documents/ece/ces/ge.20/2005/8.e.pdf.

Bloem, A.M., R.J. Dippelsman, and N.Ø. Maehle. 2001. *Quarterly National Accounts Manual: Concepts Data Sources and Compilation*. Washington: International Monetary Fund.

Bourassa, S.C., M. Hoesli, and J. Sun. 2006. A simple alternative house price index. *Journal of Housing Economics* 15: 80–97.

Branson, M. 2006. The Australian Experience in Developing an Established House Price Index. Paper presented at the OECD-IMF Workshop on Real Estate Price Indexes, Paris, November 6–7. http://www.oecd.org/dataoecd/2/26/37583386.pdf.

Bureau of Labor Statistics. 1983. *Trends in Multifactor Productivity, 1948–81, Bulletin 2178*, U.S. Government Printing Office, Washington, D.C.

Case, K.E., and R.J. Shiller. 1989. The efficiency of the market for single family homes. *The American Economic Review* 79: 125–137.

Chinloy, P., M. Cho, and I.F. Megbolugbe. 1997. Appraisals, transactions incentives and smoothing. *Journal of Real Estate Finance and Economics* 14 (1): 45–55.

de Haan, J. 2003. Direct and Indirect Time Dummy Approaches to Hedonic Price Measurement. Paper presented at the 7th Ottawa Group Meeting, Paris, May 27–29. http://www.ottawagroup.org/pdf/07/Time%20dummy%20hedonics%20-%20de%20Haan%20-(2003).pdf Also published in 2004 in the *Journal of Economic and Social Measurement* 29, 427–443.

de Haan, J. 2004. Hedonic Regression: The Time Dummy Index As a Special Case of the Imputation Törnqvist Index. Paper presented at the 8th Ottawa Group Meeting, Helsinki, August 23–25. http://www.stat.fi/og2004/dehaanp_ver2.pdf.

de Haan, J., E. van der Wal, D. ter Steege, and P. de Vries. 2006. The Measurement of House Prices: A Review of the SPAR Method", paper presented at the Economic Measurement Group Workshop 2006, Coogee Australia, December 13–15. http://www.sam.sdu.dk/parn/EMG%20Workshop%20'06%20program.pdf.

Diewert, W.E. 1976. Exact and superlative index numbers. *Journal of Econometrics* 4: 114–145.

Diewert, W.E. 1978. Superlative index numbers and consistency in aggregation. *Econometrica* 46: 883–900.

Diewert, W.E. 1998. High Inflation, Seasonal Commodities and Annual Index Numbers. *Macroeconomic Dynamics* 2: 456–471. http://www.econ.ubc.ca/diewert/highinfl.pdf.

Diewert, W.E. 1999. Index Number Approaches to Seasonal Adjustment. *Macroeconomic Dynamics* 3: 1–21. http://www.econ.ubc.ca/diewert/seasonal.pdf.

Diewert, W.E. 2002. Harmonized Indexes of Consumer Prices: Their Conceptual Foundations. *Swiss Journal of Economics and Statistics* 138: 547–637. http://www.econ.ubc.ca/diewert/harindex.pdf.

Diewert, W.E. 2003a. The Treatment of Owner Occupied Housing and Other Durables in a Consumer Price Index. Discussion Paper 03–08, Department of Economics, University of British Columbia, Vancouver, Canada. http://www.econ.ubc.ca/discpapers/dp0308.pdf.

Diewert, W.E. 2003b. Hedonic Regressions: A Consumer Theory Approach. In *Scanner Data and Price Indexes*, Studies in Income and Wealth, vol. 64, R.C. Feenstra and M.D. Shapiro, 317–348, NBER and University of Chicago Press. http://www.econ.ubc.ca/diewert/scan.pdf.

Diewert, W.E. 2003c. Hedonic Regressions: A Review of Some Unresolved Issues. Paper presented at the 7th Meeting of the Ottawa Group, Paris, May 27–29. http://www.ottawagroup.org/pdf/07/Hedonics%20unresolved%20issues%20-%20Diewert%20-(2003).pdf.

Diewert, W.E. 2004. On the Stochastic Approach to Linking the Regions in the ICP. Discussion Paper 04–16, Department of Economics, University of British Columbia, November. http://www.econ.ubc.ca/diewert/icp.pdf.

Diewert, W.E. 2005a. Weighted Country Product Dummy Variable Regressions and Index Number Formulae. *The Review of Income and Wealth* 51 (4): 561–571. http://www.econ.ubc.ca/diewert/country.pdf.

Diewert, W.E. 2005b. Adjacent Period Dummy Variable Hedonic Regressions and Bilateral Index Number Theory. Discussion Paper 05–11, Department of Economics, University of British Columbia, Vancouver, Canada, V6T 1Z1. http://www.econ.ubc.ca/discpapers/dp0511.pdf.

Diewert, W.E., and F.C. Wykoff. 2006. Depreciation, Deterioration and Obsolescence when there is Embodied or Disembodied Technical Change. Forthcoming in *Price and Productivity Measurement*, ed. W.E. Diewert, B.M. Balk, D. Fixler, K.J. Fox, and A.O. Nakamura. Canada: Trafford Press. http://www.econ.ubc.ca/diewert/dp0602.pdf.

Fenwick, D. 2006. Real Estate Prices: the Need for a Strategic Approach to the Development of Statistics to Meet User Needs. Paper presented at the OECD-IMF Workshop on Real Estate Price Indexes held in Paris, November 6–7, 2006. http://www.oecd.org/dataoecd/22/49/37619259.pdf.

Girouard, N., M. Kennedy, P. van den Noord, and C. André. 2006. Recent House Price Developments: The Role of Fundamentals. Paper presented at the OECD-IMF Workshop on Real Estate Price Indexes, Paris, November 6–7. http://www.oecd.org/dataoecd/3/6/37583208.pdf.

Gouriéroux, C., and A. Laferrère. 2006. Managing Hedonic Housing Price Indexes: the French Experience. Paper presented at the OECD-IMF Workshop on Real Estate Price Indexes, Paris, November 6–7. http://www.oecd.org/dataoecd/2/24/37583497.pdf.

Gudnason, R. 2004. Simple User Costs and Rentals. Paper presented at the 8th Ottawa Group Meeting, Helsinki, August 23–25. http://www.stat.fi/og2004/gudnasonpaper.pdf.

Gudnason, R., and G. Jonsdottir. 2006. House Price Index, Market Prices and Flow of Services Methods. Paper presented at the OECD-IMF Workshop on Real Estate Price Indexes held in Paris, November 6–7, 2006. http://www.oecd.org/dataoecd/2/42/37583740.pdf.

Heravi, S., and M. Silver. 2007. Hedonic Indexes: A Study of Alternative Methods. Forthcoming in *Hard-to-Measure Goods and Services: Essays in Honour of Zvi Griliches*, ed. E.R. Berndt, and C. Hulten. Chicago: University of Chicago Press.

Hill, T.P. 1996. *Inflation Accounting: A Manual on National Accounting Under Conditions of High Inflation*. Paris: OECD.

Hoffmann, J., and C. Kurz. 2002. *Rent Indices for Housing in West Germany: 1985 to 1998*. Discussion Paper 01/02. Frankfurt: Economic Research Centre of the Deutsche Bundesbank.

Hoffmann, J., and J.-R. Kurz-Kim. 2006. *Consumer Price Adjustment Under the Microscope: Germany in a Period of Low Inflation*. Discussion Paper Series 1, Economic Studies, No 16/2006, Deutsche Bundesbank, Wilhelm-Epstein-Strasse 14, 60431, Postfach 10 06 02, 60006, Frankfurt a.M.

Hoffmann, J., and A. Lorenz. 2006. Real Estate Price Indices for Germany: Past, Present and Future. Paper presented at the OECD-IMF Workshop on Real Estate Price Indexes, Paris, November 6–7. http://www.oecd.org/dataoecd/31/20/37625451.pdf.

International Labour Organization (ILO), and Others. 2004. *Consumer Price Index Manual: Theory and Practice*, International Labour Organization, Geneva. http://www.ilo.org/public/english/bureau/stat/guides/cpi/index.htm.

International Monetary Fund (IMF), and Others. 2004. *Producer Price Index Manual: Theory and Practice*. Washington, D.C.: International Monetary Fund. http://www.imf.org/np/sta/tegppi/index.htm.

Jorgenson, D.W., and Z. Griliches. 1967. The explanation of productivity change. *The Review of Economic Studies* 34: 249–283.

Jorgenson, D.W., and Z. Griliches. 1972. Issues in growth accounting: A reply to Edward F. Denison. *Survey of Current Business* 52 (4), Part II (May): 65–94.

Jorgenson, D.W., and J.S. Landefeld. 2006. Blueprint for Expanded and Integrated U.S. National Accounts: Review, Assessment, and Next Steps. In *A New Architecture for the U.S. National Accounts*, ed. D.W. Jorgenson, J.S. Landefeld, and W.D. Nordhaus, 13–112. Chicago: University of Chicago Press.

Leventis, A. 2006. Removing Appraisal Bias from a Repeat Transactions House Price Index: A Basic Approach. Paper presented at the OECD-IMF Workshop on Real Estate Price Indexes held in Paris, November 6–7, 2006. http://www.oecd.org/dataoecd/2/45/37583706.pdf.

Li, W., M. Prud'homme, and K. Yu. 2006. Studies in Hedonic Resale Housing Price Indexes. Paper presented at the OECD-IMF Workshop on Real Estate Price Indexes held in Paris, November 6–7, 2006. http://www.oecd.org/dataoecd/2/25/37583404.pdf.

Makaronidis, A., and K. Hayes. 2006. Owner Occupied Housing for the HICP. Paper presented at the OECD-IMF Workshop on Real Estate Price Indexes held in Paris, November 6–7, 2006. http://www.oecd.org/dataoecd/42/60/37612322.pdf.

Malpezzi, S., L. Ozanne, and T. Thibodeau. 1987. Microeconomic estimates of housing depreciation. *Land Economics* 63: 372–385.

Prasad, N., and A. Richards. 2006. Measuring Aggregate House Prices in Australian Capital Cities: A Review of RBA Research. Paper presented at the Economic Measurement Group Workshop 2006, Coogee Australia, December 13–15. http://www.sam.sdu.dk/parn/EMG%20Workshop%20'06%20program.pdf.

Schreyer, P. 2001. *OECD Productivity Manual: A Guide to the Measurement of Industry-Level and Aggregate Productivity Growth*. Paris: OECD.

Schreyer, P. 2006. Measuring Multi-Factor Productivity when Rates of Return are Exogenous. Forthcoming in *Price and Productivity Measurement*, ed. W.E. Diewert, B.M. Balk, D. Fixler, K.J. Fox, and A.O. Nakamura. Canada: Trafford Press.

Schreyer, P., W.E. Diewert, and A. Harrison. 2005. Cost of Capital Services in the National Accounts. Paper presented to the Meeting of the Canberra II Group on Non-financial Assets in Canberra, April.

Scheffé, H. 1959. *The Analysis of Variance*. New York: Wiley.

Silver, M. 2003. The Use of Weights in Hedonic Regressions: The Measurement of Quality Adjusted Price Changes. Room document for the 7th Meeting of the Ottawa Group, Paris, May. http://www.ottawagroup.org/pdf/07/Weights%20in%20hedonics%20-%20Silver%20(2003).pdf.

Silver, M., and S. Heravi. 2005. A failure in the measurement of inflation: Results from a hedonic and matched experiment using scanner data. *Journal of Business and Economic Statistics* 23 (3): 269–281.

Silver, M., and S. Heravi. 2007. The Difference Between Hedonic Imputation Indexes and Time Dummy Hedonic Indexes. Forthcoming in the *Journal of Business and Economic Statistics*, also published as *IMF Working Paper Series*, No. 181, 2006. http://www.imf.org/external/pubs/cat/longres.cfm?sk=19363.

Stephens, W., Y. Li, V. Lekkas, J. Abraham, C. Calhoun, and T. Kimner. 1995. Conventional home mortgage price index. *Journal of Housing Research* 6 (3): 389–418.

Summers, R. 1973. International comparisons with incomplete data. *Review of Income and Wealth* 29 (1): 1–16.

van der Wal, E., D. ter Steege, and B. Kroese. 2006. Two Ways to Construct a House Price Index for the Netherlands: The Repeat Sale and the Sale Price Appraisal Ratio. Paper presented at the OECD-IMF Workshop on Real Estate Price Indexes held in Paris, November 6–7, 2006.

Verbrugge, R. 2006. The Puzzling Divergence of Rents and User Costs, 1980–2004. Paper presented at the OECD-IMF Workshop on Real Estate Price Indexes held in Paris, November 6–7, 2006. http://www.oecd.org/dataoecd/42/57/37612870.pdf.

Walras, L. 1954. *Elements of Pure Economics*, a translation by W. Jaffé of the Edition Définitive (1926) of the *Eléments d'économie pure*, first edition published in 1874, Homewood. Illinois: Richard D. Irwin.

Wenzlick, R. 1952. As I See the Fluctuations in the Selling Prices of Single Family Residences. *The Real Estate Analyst* 21 (December 24): 541–548.

Woolford, K. 2006. An Exploration of Alternative Treatments of Owner Occupied Housing in a CPI. Paper presented at the Economic Measurement Group Workshop 2006, Coogee Australia, December 13–15. http://www.sam.sdu.dk/parn/EMG%20Workshop%20'06%20program.pdf.

Wyngarden, H. 1927. *An Index of Local Real Estate Prices*. Michigan Business Studies, vol. 1, no. 2. Ann Arbor: University of Michigan.

Chapter 2
Theoretical Background of Hedonic Measure and Repeat Sales Measure-Survey-

2.1 Introduction

When it comes to methods of quality adjustment for property price indexes, if one looks at the *Residential Property Price Indices Handbook*[1] published by EuroStat in 2013, it present a variety of methods along with their advantages and disadvantages: (a) Stratification or Mix Adjustment Methods , (b) Hedonic Regression Methods, (c) Repeat Sales Methods, and (d) Appraisal-Based Methods. This is because, in reality, multiple methods have been applied in the estimation of property price indexes.

Why have approaches other than the hedonic method been applied in practice?

The first reason is the difficulty of quality adjustment. As explained previously, the reason for performing quality adjustment of property is that it is a good for which no homogeneity exists, so it is strongly heterogeneous. In such a case, in addition to the problems relating to quality changes faced in consumer price statistics and the like, one must also address said heterogeneity. In other words, quality adjustment involves a high degree of difficulty.

The second reason is the lack of usable price information at the micro level when estimating property price indexes. If attempting to apply the hedonic method, not only transaction price, transaction time, and land/building size but also location-related information such as the time to the city center and detailed information related to the building age and features are required. When there is no such information, the price index must be estimated with limited data. With the repeat sales method, quality adjustment is possible with just the transaction price and transaction time, so it has the advantage of minimizing the information needed with respect to

[1] The RPPI Handbook may be viewed via the following link: http://epp.eurostat.ec.europa.eu/portal/page/portal/hicp/methodology/hps/rppi_handbook.

The base of this chapter is Shimizu, C. and K. Karato. 2018. Property Price Index Theory and Estimation: A survey. CSIS Discussion Paper 156, The University of Tokyo. Presented at International Conference on Commercial Property Price Indicators (Eurostat, ECB, IMF and BIS, OECD). European Central Bank, Frankfurt, Germany, September 29, 2014.

W. E. Diewert et al., *Property Price Index*, Advances in Japanese Business and Economics 11, https://doi.org/10.1007/978-4-431-55942-9_2

property-related variables. That being the case, when attempting to measure price changes when information is limited, creating an index using only data for properties that are transacted repeatedly is consistent with the general thinking behind price index estimation methods.

However, unlike other goods and service markets, the property transaction market is extremely thin. Thus, when attempting, for example, to create a monthly price index, one may easily anticipate that many problems will occur, since—unlike markets where goods and services of identical quality are transacted frequently—this is a market in which property with identical characteristics is transacted only once every few years.

Third, in actual property transaction practice, it is not uncommon for property appraisal prices to be used. Not only is property strongly heterogeneous but there are few transactions—depending on the region and usage, there are even markets where almost no transactions exist. In light of this, when trying to determine prices, using prices based on property appraisals is a valid approach.

Thus, attempting to estimate property price indexes involves many difficulties. Compared to the housing market, where there is a relatively large number of transactions and the quality gap is small (i.e., it is more homogeneous), these difficulties mean that for commercial property (offices, retail facilities, hotels, logistics facilities, hospitals, farmland, etc.): (1) there will be more heterogeneity and a greater lack of information, (2) there will be a reduction in repeat sales samples, and (3) there is a greater probability of property appraisal prices being used.

For markets for which property price information is relatively easy to obtain, the aim of this paper is to outline the characteristics of the hedonic method and repeat sales method that may be used in creating property price indexes, as well as estimation methods using property appraisal prices. Specifically, focusing on the hedonic method and repeat sales method, it will provide a comprehensive survey relating to quality adjustment methods when estimating property price indexes and clarify the characteristics of the various estimation methods. What's more, drawing on this outline, it will present a view of how property price indexes should be created, from the perspective of estimation method theory.

2.2 The Hedonic Price Method

2.2.1 The Hedonic Approach

The hedonic approach is a technique established theoretically by Rosen (1974). Specifically, it treats a given product's price as an aggregate (bundle of attributes) of the values of the product's various attributes (characteristics) and estimates the various attribute prices using regression analysis. For many products circulating on the market, even when their intended use is the same, considerable differentiation exists based on their performance, functions, etc. Differences in attributes are reflected in the product's production costs. One could also say that consumer evaluations of the product's specific performance and functions are also reflected in the price determined by the market. However, the attributes themselves are not necessarily bought and sold on the market. With the hedonic approach, by regressing product price on variables representing attribute quality and quantity, it is possible to measure the shadow price of non-market goods based on the estimated coefficient value.

Lancaster (1966) has conducted theoretical analysis of consumer behavior based on the assumption that consumer utility depends not on the product itself but on the various features, functions, etc., that comprise the product. The product's market price is thought to be determined based on supply and demand in relation to its various characteristics. However, the market with respect to these characteristics is not necessarily explicit but may be hidden in the background of product price determination. Lancaster's aim was to explicitly treat such underlying mechanisms and analyze consumer behavior in differentiated goods markets.

Rigorously examining the relationship between differentiated product prices and consumer behavior is essential in preparing price indexes. For example, in the case of digital consumer electronics, passenger vehicles, housing, etc., even if the price is the same, quality will improve and functions increase as time passes. With the Laspeyres method, since a market basket is fixed at a baseline point in time, price indexes based on this method ignore changes in quality and functionality. Using the hedonic approach helps estimate the performance ratio between new and old products.

Rosen (1974)'s price analysis of differentiated goods is a study that theoretically clarifies the manner in which product prices comprised by bundles of attributes are generated on the market. The study rigorously examines the relationship between the product supplier offer function, product demander bid function, and hedonic market price function, and characterizes the market price of products based on consumer and producer behavior. When this hedonic market price function is used, it is possible to obtain the acceptable payment amount for product attributes.

Section 2.2.2 below outlines Rosen (1974)'s hedonic approach theory, while Sect. 2.2.3 addresses issues relating to the estimation of hedonic market price functions. Following Diewert (2007), Sect. 2.2.4 summarizes differences based on a hedonic dummy index and hedonic imputed index. Section 2.2.5 explains the characteristics of a producer price-related quality-adjusted hedonic index. Section 2.2.6 summarizes the characteristics of the hedonic price method.

2.2.2 *Hedonic Approach Theory*

2.2.2.1 The Bid Function

Following Rosen (1974)'s method, we will demonstrate the theoretical basis of the hedonic approach, using real estate as an example. The value of characteristic k comprising real estate shall be expressed as z_k $(k = 1, 2, \ldots, K)$. Real estate characteristics represent size, building structure, kitchen, bathroom, accessibility of transportation, natural environment, social environment, and so forth. According to Rosen, the relationship between real estate market price p and characteristic value $z_1, \ldots, z_k, \ldots, z_K$ may be expressed with the following hedonic price function h:

$$p = h(z_1, \ldots, z_k, \ldots, z_K) \tag{2.1}$$

The main objective of Rosen's analysis is to clarify how (2.1) is determined by the market.

Given market price function (2.1), consumers select the optimal combination of real estate characteristics. The issue of utility maximization may be formulated as follows:

$$\max_{x,z} U(x, z) \tag{2.2}$$

$$s.t. \quad I = x + h(z) \tag{2.3}$$

Here, $U(\cdot)$ is a well-behaved, strictly concave function, x is composite goods including goods and services other than real estate, $z = (z_1, \ldots, z_k, \ldots, z_K)$ is the real estate characteristic vector, and I is income. The composite goods price is standardized as 1. Based on the parameters of this optimization issue step, $U_k/U_x = h_k(z)$ is established. Note that $U_k = \frac{\partial U(x,z)}{\partial z_k}$, $U_x = \frac{\partial U(x,z)}{\partial x}$ and $h_k(z) = \frac{\partial h(z)}{\partial z_k}$. In other words, this shows that the marginal utility of the real estate characteristic measured using the marginal utility of income is equal to the marginal contribution value of the attribute in market prices.

It is possible to determine the market price function using the bid function. Based on a given utility level u and income I, if the bid offered by a housing demander for real estate possessing characteristic z is taken as θ, then based on (2.2), this may be written as $U(I - \theta, z) = u$.

If one solves this for θ, the amount that a consumer is able to spend on housing with respect to various combinations of characteristic z may be expressed as the bid function $\theta(z; I, u)$, given the utility level and income. In order to raise (lower) the utility level u, the bid for housing with characteristic z must decrease (increase) $\left(\frac{\partial \theta(z; I, u)}{\partial u} = -U_x^{-1} < 0\right)$. Therefore, this shows that θ, when it reaches utility level u, is the maximum price that may be paid for housing with characteristic z.

Based on (2.2), (2.3), and the bid function $\theta(z; I, u)$, one may write that $U(I - \theta(z; I, u), z) = u$. If this formula is partially differentiated for z_k and 0 is included, the following is obtained:

$$-U_x \frac{\partial \theta(z; I, u)}{\partial z_k} + U_k = 0$$

When the utility is maximized at the level of u^*, since $U_k/U_x = h_k(z^*)$ for the optimal combination of characteristics z^*, the following two equations are definitely established:

$$\frac{\partial \theta(z^*; I, u^*)}{\partial z_k} = h_k(z^*) \quad (2.4)$$

$$\theta(z^*; I, u^*) = h(z^*) \quad (2.5)$$

Equations (2.4) and (2.5) show that when the optimal characteristics are selected, the slope of the bid function and the slope of the market price function are consistent and the bid and market price are also equal. In other words, based on the optimal characteristic value, the bid function and market price function are contiguous.

When consumer incomes and preferences vary, the bid function also varies. However, since the bid function and market price function must be contiguous in market equilibrium, the market price function is an envelope of the bid function for all consumers, with their various incomes and preferences.

2.2.2.2 The Offer Function

It is also possible to define the price offer function for real estate suppliers and theorize the relationship with the market price function from the issue of profit maximization. For a given level of technology, the offer function is the minimum price offered when a given profit is reached. When a company selects the optimal characteristics and produces real estate, the slope of the offer function and the slope of the market price (per unit of real estate) function will be consistent based on profit maximization behavior, and the offer price and market price will also be consistent. Therefore, based on the optimal characteristic value, the offer function and market price function are contiguous. Since heterogeneity exists in real estate producers' technology, offer prices also vary in accordance with this. Since the offer price and market price need to be consistent in equilibrium, the market price function is an envelope of the offer function for various companies.

Based on the above, the hedonic market price function is an envelope of both the bid function for an infinite number of real estate demanders and the offer function for an infinite number of real estate suppliers. As well, in the case of there being one supplier company, the bid function is equal to the marginal cost if one additional unit of real estate is produced (or the average cost per unit of real estate). As a result, the market price function is equal to the supplier's marginal cost.

2.2.2.3 Willingness to Pay

If the bid function is used, it is possible to obtain consumers' willingness to pay with respect to changes in attributes. For z^*, let us now assume that $p^* = \theta(z^*; I, u^*) = h(z^*)$. When real estate K's characteristic z_K^* is increased to (z_K^{**}), the demander's willingness to pay (WTP) may be defined with the following formula:

$$WTP \equiv \theta(z_1^*, \ldots, z_{K-1}^*, z_K^{**}; I, u^*) - p^* \tag{2.6}$$

In other words, when the characteristic value changes incrementally, the willingness to pay is the additional value that may be paid for real estate without changing the utility level. Since the utility function U is

$$\frac{\partial^2}{\partial z_k^2}\theta(z^*; I, u^*) = \frac{U_x^2 U_{kk} - 2U_x U_k U_{xk} + U_k^2 U_{xx}}{U_x^3} < 0$$

when it is a strict concave function (the Hessian matrix is a negative definite matrix), the bid function is a concave function. Equations (2.4) and (2.5) are established based on the optimal characteristic value combination z^*, and given that the bid function is a concave function, one can derive from

$$\theta(z_1^*, \ldots, z_{K-1}^*, z_K^{**}; I, u^*) < h(z_1^*, \ldots, z_{K-1}^*, z_K^{**}) = p'$$

That

$$p' - p^* > WTP \tag{2.7}$$

In other words, caution is required with regard to the limit value of market price function characteristics, since as long as demanders are not homogeneous, it is possible that the willingness to pay is overestimated. However, if it is assumed that changes in characteristic values will be sufficiently small, the market price function limit value may be used as an approximation of the willingness to pay.

2.2.3 *Hedonic Market Price Function Estimation*

2.2.3.1 Function Types

In order to accurately measure willingness to pay, estimation of the bid function is required, but in general an approximation is used by estimating the hedonic market price function (2.1). When estimating the hedonic market price function, the function type is an issue. Given that simple estimation is possible, models such as double logarithms, semi-logs, and line shapes are often used.

When real estate price at multiple points in time is observed as data, the hedonic market price at time t for property n may be described with the following formula:

$$y_n^t = \alpha_t + z_n^{t\prime}\gamma + \varepsilon_n^t \quad (n = 1, 2, \ldots, N(t); t = 0, 1, \ldots, T) \tag{2.8}$$

Here, y_n^t is the housing price logarithm ($\ln p_n^t$) or exact numeric value (p_n^t), α_t is the unknown time effect, $z_n^t = (1, z_{n1}^t, \ldots, z_{nk}^t, \ldots, z_{nK}^t)$ is the explanatory variable (characteristic) vector including a constant term, $\gamma = (\gamma_0, \gamma_1, \ldots, \gamma_k, \ldots, \gamma_K)$ is the coefficient vector, and ε_n^t is the error term. As an example, a semi-log model including the time effect may be written as:

$$y_n^t = \ln p_n^t = \alpha_t + \gamma_0 + \sum_{k=1}^{K} \gamma_k z_{nk}^t + \varepsilon_n^t \tag{2.9}$$

In this model, the estimation value of coefficient γ shows the effect of the characteristic value with respect to real estate price, and if a dummy variable is used for each point in time, estimation may be made estimated based on the method of least squares. To avoid multicollinearity and distinguish all parameters, it is necessary to perform some kind of standardization for α_t and γ_0. Typically, at the observation starting point $t = 0$, it is considered that $\alpha_0 = 0$, and a dummy variable for each point in time is used with respect to $t = 1, 2, \ldots, T$.

Since the function type of the hedonic market price function h cannot be specified in theoretical terms, it must be selected with a statistical technique. Even if specified in a double logarithmic model or semi-log model, the form is not necessarily the ideal one. Studies from the 1980s onward, such as Linneman (1980), have performed non-linear estimation using Box-Cox transformation. In this case, the left side of (2.9) can be rewritten as follows:

$$y = \begin{cases} \frac{p^\lambda - 1}{\lambda} & \lambda \neq 0 \\ \ln p & \lambda = 0 \end{cases} \tag{2.10}$$

Here, λ is an unknown parameter. Halvorsen and Pollakowski (1981) tested various function forms by applying Box-Cox transformation to a flexible function form using a two-step approximation formula including a cross-term between explanatory variables. In response to their paper, Cassel and Mendelsohn (1985) increased the explanatory power by including multiple cross-terms between variables, but pointed out that there is a reduction in the reliability of the coefficient estimation value due to multicollinearity and that interpretation of the marginal effect of hedonic characteristic values becomes more difficult. Cropper et al. (1988) performed statistical tests based on a translog form and Diewert type utility function (Barten 1964; Diewert 1971, 1973), showing that if observational errors are included in the variables, a linear model or linear Box-Cox transformation model is superior to quadratic form Box-Cox transformation when it comes to formulation.

There is also research that has proposed using a non-parametric method or semi-parametric method instead of a parametric function form to formulate the hedonic price function. With these approaches, attribute prices are inferred directly from the data without specifying a function form in advance (Knight et al. 1993; Anglin and Gencay 1996; Pace 1995). However, it has also been pointed out that, as with parametric analysis techniques, these do not free one from data-related problems (multicollinearity). In tests relating to the selection of parametric versus non-parametric models, Anglin and Gencay (1996) have shown that it is relatively easy to dismiss parametric models. It is not that the parametric model variable structure is weak; rather, this result was demonstrated even for parametric models that passed a number of standard tests for model selection. Using a more flexible Generalized Additive Model (GAM), Pace (1998) estimated a semi-parametric-type hedonic price function and demonstrated that it was superior to all types of parametric model. Since GAM itself is an established statistical technique, this finding shows that the incorporation of a non-parametric method in the hedonic approach is extremely effective.

2.2.3.2 The Problem of Distinguishing the Marginal Bid Value Function

If characteristic values have a significant effect on market prices, the willingness to pay will cause divergence between the hedonic market price function and bid value function, so it is necessary to estimate the bid value function or bid value marginal effect. As a method of estimating the bid value function, Rosen (1974) has proposed a method that regresses the market price function marginal effect on characteristic values and other exogenous variables.

$$\widehat{h_k} = D_k(z, \boldsymbol{A}) \tag{2.11}$$

$$\widehat{h_k} = S_k(z, \boldsymbol{B}) \tag{2.12}$$

Here, $\widehat{h_k}$ is the marginal effect for hedonic market price function characteristic k, $D(\cdot)$ and $S(\cdot)$ are the characteristic's demand and supply functions, and $\boldsymbol{A}$ and $\boldsymbol{B}$ are vectors showing the real estate demander and supplier type, respectively (based on income, manufacturing technology, etc.). Since the marginal effect is the shadow price of the characteristic value, (2.11) and (2.12) are supply and demand simultaneous equations using inverse demand (bid value) and inverse supply (offer price), and supply and demand are distinguished using $\boldsymbol{A}$ and $\boldsymbol{B}$ as instrumental variables.

Following Rosen's model, Witte et al. (1979) estimated simultaneous equations for three characteristics covering multiple housing markets. However, as Brown and Rosen (1982) have pointed out, it is not possible to properly distinguish between characteristic value supply and demand with estimation based on this method. Since the market price function marginal effect $\widehat{h_k}$ estimated in the first step is derived from $h(z)$, one may consider that the characteristic price shown with the marginal effect is also a function of z. Demand for z depends on the various characteristic prices, and there is a correlation between characteristic prices and characteristic demand equation errors. In other words, it is possible that the effect of characteristic prices on characteristic demand is estimated with a bias.

This problem of distinguishing the bid value function and offer function has been considered by Diamond and Smith (1985) and Mendelsohn (1985). First, with regard to estimation of the first step hedonic market price function, it is pointed out that, apart from characteristic vectors, there is a need for exogenous variables not included in either the bid value function or offer function as well as for a characteristic value exponential term. Then, in the second step, a marginal bid value function simultaneous equation system is estimated simultaneously using exogenous variables solely to meet the distinction conditions. Sheppard (1999) has discussed the distinction problem in greater detail. Ekeland (2004) and Heckman et al. (2010) proposed a distinction method for hedonic price estimation using a non-parametric approach.

2.2.4 Price Index Estimation Based on the Hedonic Approach

The hedonic approach is a useful technique when creating quality-adjusted price indexes. There are two representative types of hedonic price index: (i) time dummy hedonic indexes and (ii) imputed hedonic indexes . Following Diewert (2007), we discuss differences between the two types of price index below.

2.2.4.1 Time Dummy Hedonic Regression

In (2.8), taking the observation period as two points in time, $(t = 0, 1)$, one may assume the following estimation model that regresses logarithmic price on an explanatory variable vector with the time dummy and constant term excluded:

$$y_n^t \equiv \ln p_n^t = \alpha_t + \sum_{k=1}^{K} \gamma_k z_{nk}^t + \varepsilon_n^t \quad (n = 1, 2, \ldots, N(t); t = 0, 1) \tag{2.13}$$

Here, α_t shows the average level of the product's quality-constant price for each period, and the overall scale of logarithmic price changes from time 0 to time 1 is $\alpha_1 - \alpha_0$.

Let us take $\mathbf{1}_t$ as an $N(t)$ dimension vector comprising everything from 1 and $\mathbf{0}_t$ as an $N(t)$ dimension vector comprising everything from 0. As well, let us take $\boldsymbol{y}^0$ and $\boldsymbol{y}^1$ as the $N(0)$ and $N(1)$ dimension vectors for the time 0 and time 1 logarithmic prices respectively, $\mathbf{Z}^0$ and $\mathbf{Z}^1$ as the $N(t) \times K$ explanatory variable matrices for time 0 and time 1 respectively, and ε^0 and ε^1 as the $N(0)$, $N(1)$ dimension error vectors for time 0 and time 1 respectively. If we represent (2.13) as matrices for time 0 and time 1, they may be written as follows:

$$\boldsymbol{y}^0 = \mathbf{1}_0\alpha_0 + \mathbf{0}_0\alpha_1 + \mathbf{Z}^0\gamma + \varepsilon^0 \tag{2.14}$$

$$\boldsymbol{y}^1 = \mathbf{0}_1\alpha_0 + \mathbf{1}_0\alpha_1 + \mathbf{Z}^1\gamma + \varepsilon^1 \tag{2.15}$$

Here, if we take α_t^*, γ^* as estimators based on the method of least squares, one can formulate the following using the estimators and the realized value $\boldsymbol{e}^t$ of the least squares residual error:

$$\boldsymbol{y}^0 = \mathbf{1}_0\alpha_0^* + \mathbf{0}_0\alpha_1^* + \mathbf{Z}^0\gamma^* + \boldsymbol{e}^0 \tag{2.16}$$

$$\boldsymbol{y}^1 = \mathbf{0}_1\alpha_0^* + \mathbf{1}_0\alpha_1^* + \mathbf{Z}^1\gamma^* + \boldsymbol{e}^1 \tag{2.17}$$

For (2.16) and (2.17), if we define $\boldsymbol{y} = [\boldsymbol{y}^{0\prime}\ \boldsymbol{y}^{1\prime}]'((N(0)+N(1))\times 1$ vector), $\boldsymbol{e} = [\boldsymbol{e}^{0\prime}\ \boldsymbol{e}^{1\prime}]'$ $((N(0)+N(1))\times 1$ vector), $\varphi^* = [\alpha_0^*\ \alpha_1^*\ \boldsymbol{\gamma}^{*\prime}]'$ ($(2+K)\times 1$ vector), and $\mathbf{X} = \begin{bmatrix} \mathbf{1}_0 & \mathbf{0}_0 & \mathbf{Z}^0 \\ \mathbf{0}_1 & \mathbf{1}_1 & \mathbf{Z}^1 \end{bmatrix}$ $((N(0)+N(1))\times(2+K)$ matrix), then (2.16) and (2.17) may be rewritten as follows:

$$\boldsymbol{y} = \mathbf{X}\varphi^* + \boldsymbol{e} \tag{2.18}$$

Here, since $\mathbf{X}$ and the residual error $\boldsymbol{e}$ are orthogonal, we can obtain:

$$\mathbf{X}'\boldsymbol{e} = \mathbf{X}'(\boldsymbol{y} - \mathbf{X}\varphi^*) = \mathbf{0}_{2+K} \tag{2.19}$$

In other words, we can obtain $\mathbf{1}_0'\boldsymbol{e}^0 = 0$, $\mathbf{1}_1'\boldsymbol{e}^1 = 0$, and $\mathbf{Z}^{0\prime}\boldsymbol{e}^0 + \mathbf{Z}^{1\prime}\boldsymbol{e}^1 = \mathbf{0}_K$. Therefore, using the residual errors for (2.16) and (2.17):

$$\mathbf{1}_0'\boldsymbol{y}^0 = N(0)\alpha_0^* + \mathbf{1}_0'\mathbf{Z}^0\boldsymbol{\gamma}^* \tag{2.20}$$

$$\mathbf{1}_1'\boldsymbol{y}^1 = N(1)\alpha_1^* + \mathbf{1}_1'\mathbf{Z}^1\boldsymbol{\gamma}^* \tag{2.21}$$

If we work out α_0^* and α_1^* from this, we can obtain:

$$\alpha_0^* = \frac{\mathbf{1}_0'\boldsymbol{y}^0}{N(0)} - \frac{\mathbf{1}_0'\mathbf{Z}^0\boldsymbol{\gamma}^*}{N(0)} = \frac{\mathbf{1}_0'(\boldsymbol{y}^0 - \mathbf{Z}^0\boldsymbol{\gamma}^*)}{N(0)} \tag{2.22}$$

$$\alpha_1^* = \frac{\mathbf{1}_1'\boldsymbol{y}^1}{N(1)} - \frac{\mathbf{1}_1'\mathbf{Z}^1\boldsymbol{\gamma}^*}{N(1)} = \frac{\mathbf{1}_1'(\boldsymbol{y}^1 - \mathbf{Z}^1\boldsymbol{\gamma}^*)}{N(1)} \tag{2.23}$$

Equations (2.22) and (2.23) show the quality-constant logarithmic price level. $\mathbf{1}_t'\boldsymbol{y}^t/N(t)$ shows the arithmetic mean of the logarithmic price for time $t = 0, 1$ and $\mathbf{1}_t'\mathbf{Z}^t/N(t)$ shows the arithmetic mean of the characteristic value for time $t = 0, 1$. In other words, α_0^* is equal to the result obtained by subtracting the average value of all characteristic values from the average value of the logarithmic price (arithmetic average of the quality-adjusted logarithmic price). Based on the above, the hedonic time dummy estimation value based on the logarithmic price change from time 0 to time 1 is the following differential:

$$LP_{HD} = \alpha_1^* - \alpha_0^* \tag{2.24}$$

The explanatory variable matrices for (2.18) are expressed as follows:

$$\mathbf{V} = \begin{bmatrix} \mathbf{1}_0 & \mathbf{0}_0 \\ \mathbf{0}_1 & \mathbf{1}_1 \end{bmatrix}, \quad \mathbf{Z} = \begin{bmatrix} \mathbf{Z}^0 \\ \mathbf{Z}^1 \end{bmatrix}$$

Here, $\mathbf{V}$ is a $(N(0)+N(1))\times 2$ matrix and $\mathbf{Z}$ is a $(N(0)+N(1))\times K$ matrix. If the explanatory variable is rewritten as $\mathbf{X} = [\mathbf{V}\ \mathbf{Z}]$, since the residual error vector is $\boldsymbol{e} = \boldsymbol{y} - \mathbf{V}\boldsymbol{\alpha}^* - \mathbf{Z}\boldsymbol{\gamma}^*$, the least squares estimator

$$\boldsymbol{\alpha}^* = \begin{bmatrix} \alpha_0^* \\ \alpha_1^* \end{bmatrix} = (\mathbf{V}'\mathbf{V})^{-1}\mathbf{V}'(\boldsymbol{y} - \mathbf{Z}\boldsymbol{\gamma}^*) \tag{2.25}$$

can be obtained from $\partial \boldsymbol{e}'\boldsymbol{e}/\partial\boldsymbol{\alpha}^* = \mathbf{0}$. Based on (2.25), the residual error may be rewritten as $\boldsymbol{e} = \mathbf{M}(\boldsymbol{y} - \mathbf{Z}\boldsymbol{\gamma}^*)$. Here,

$$\mathbf{M} = \begin{bmatrix} \mathbf{M}^0 \\ \mathbf{M}^1 \end{bmatrix} = \mathbf{I} - \mathbf{V}(\mathbf{V}'\mathbf{V})^{-1}\mathbf{V}' = \begin{bmatrix} \mathbf{I}_0 - \mathbf{1}_0\mathbf{1}_0'/N(0) & \mathbf{0} \\ \mathbf{0} & \mathbf{I}_1 - \mathbf{1}_1\mathbf{1}_1'/N(1) \end{bmatrix},$$

$\mathbf{I}$ is a $(N(0)+N(1)) \times (N(0)+N(1))$ identity matrix, and $\mathbf{I}_t$ is a $N(t) \times N(t)$ identity matrix. If we define $\boldsymbol{y}^* = \mathbf{M}\boldsymbol{y}$ and $\mathbf{Z}^* = \mathbf{MZ}$, the error sum of squares is $\boldsymbol{e}'\boldsymbol{e} = (\boldsymbol{y}^* - \mathbf{Z}^*\boldsymbol{\gamma}^*)'(\boldsymbol{y}^* - \mathbf{Z}^*\boldsymbol{\gamma}^*)$, so the least squares estimator for $\boldsymbol{\gamma}$ can be obtained as follows:

$$\boldsymbol{\gamma}^* = \left(\mathbf{Z}^{*\prime}\mathbf{Z}^*\right)^{-1}\mathbf{Z}^{*\prime}\boldsymbol{y}^* = \left(\mathbf{Z}^{0*\prime}\mathbf{Z}^{0*} + \mathbf{Z}^{1*\prime}\mathbf{Z}^{1*}\right)^{-1}\left(\mathbf{Z}^{0*\prime}\boldsymbol{y}^{0*} + \mathbf{Z}^{1*\prime}\boldsymbol{y}^{1*}\right) \tag{2.26}$$

If we first calculate $\boldsymbol{\gamma}^*$ from (2.26) and then plug it into (2.25) (or (2.22) or (2.23)), the time effect estimator $\boldsymbol{\alpha}^*$ can be obtained.

2.2.4.2 Imputed Hedonic Indexes

Instead of performing estimation one time for two periods by pooling data, it is also possible to estimate the characteristic price parameter for each period. Taking $\boldsymbol{\eta}^t$ as the $N(t) \times 1$ error term vector, the regression model for time $t = 0$ and time $t = 1$ may be written as follows:

$$\boldsymbol{y}^t = \mathbf{1}_t\beta_t + \mathbf{Z}^t\boldsymbol{\gamma}^t + \boldsymbol{\eta}^t \tag{2.27}$$

Here, it is assumed that the characteristic price parameters $\boldsymbol{\gamma}^0, \boldsymbol{\gamma}^1$ vary depending on the observation period. If one includes β_t^* and $\boldsymbol{\gamma}^{t^*}$ as least squares estimators, the following formula may be established using the least squares residual error vector $\boldsymbol{u}^t$:

$$\boldsymbol{y}^t = \mathbf{1}_t\beta_t^* + \mathbf{Z}^t\boldsymbol{\gamma}^{t^*} + \boldsymbol{u}^t \tag{2.28}$$

Based on the nature of the residual error, $[\mathbf{1}_t\ \mathbf{Z}^t]'\boldsymbol{u}^t = [0\ \mathbf{0}_K']'$, so the following can be obtained:

$$\mathbf{1}_0'\boldsymbol{y}^0 = N(0)\beta_0^* + \mathbf{1}_0'\mathbf{Z}^0\boldsymbol{\gamma}^{0^*} \tag{2.29}$$

$$\mathbf{1}_1'\boldsymbol{y}^1 = N(1)\beta_1^* + \mathbf{1}_1'\mathbf{Z}^1\boldsymbol{\gamma}^{1^*} \tag{2.30}$$

Therefore, the estimator for (2.29) and the time effect based on (2.29) can be obtained by solving these for β_0^*, β_1^*.

$$\beta_0^* = \frac{\mathbf{1}_0' \mathbf{y}^0}{N(0)} - \frac{\mathbf{1}_0' \mathbf{Z}^0 \gamma^{0^*}}{N(0)} = \frac{\mathbf{1}_0' (\mathbf{y}^0 - \mathbf{Z}^0 \gamma^{0^*})}{N(0)} \tag{2.31}$$

$$\beta_1^* = \frac{\mathbf{1}_1' \mathbf{y}^1}{N(1)} - \frac{\mathbf{1}_1' \mathbf{Z}^1 \gamma^{1^*}}{N(1)} = \frac{\mathbf{1}_1' (\mathbf{y}^1 - \mathbf{Z}^1 \gamma^{1^*})}{N(1)} \tag{2.32}$$

The estimation value of the hedonic time dummy based on the logarithmic price change from time 0 to time 1 may be obtained using the differential $LP_{HD} = \alpha_1^* - \alpha_0^*$. However, since it is assumed that the parameters γ^0, γ^1 for quality adjustment based on the formulation of (2.27) periods for the two times, it is not possible to simply define the logarithmic price change from the differential of β_0^*, β_1^*. Therefore, in order to perform the same quality adjustment for the two periods, we will define the quality-adjusted logarithmic price arithmetic average as follows, using the parameter γ^{0^*} for time 0 instead of γ^{1^*} for quality adjustment of time 1.

$$\delta_1^* = \frac{\mathbf{1}_1' \mathbf{y}^1}{N(1)} - \frac{\mathbf{1}_1' \mathbf{Z}^1 \gamma^{0^*}}{N(1)} = \frac{\mathbf{1}_1' (\mathbf{y}^1 - \mathbf{Z}^1 \gamma^{0^*})}{N(1)} \tag{2.33}$$

Since the quality adjustment performed for (2.33) is the same as for β_0^* in (2.31), a quality-constant logarithmic price is formed for each period. Therefore, the change from time 0 to time 1 may be shown as the following differential of δ_1^* and β_0^*:

$$\phi_L^* = \delta_1^* - \beta_0^*$$

We shall refer to this hedonic imputed scale based on logarithmic price change as a price change-based "Laspeyres-type scale." This logarithmic price change scale depends on the characteristic price vector γ^{0^*} obtained from the regression equation for time 0. Therefore, in contrast, it is also possible to define a logarithmic price change scale using the characteristic price vector γ^{1^*} obtained from the regression equation for time 1. The quality-adjusted logarithmic price arithmetic average using γ^{1^*} in quality adjustment of time 0 may be written as follows:

$$\delta_0^* = \frac{\mathbf{1}_0' \mathbf{y}^0}{N(0)} - \frac{\mathbf{1}_0' \mathbf{Z}^0 \gamma^{1^*}}{N(0)} = \frac{\mathbf{1}_0' (\mathbf{y}^0 - \mathbf{Z}^0 \gamma^{1^*})}{N(0)} \tag{2.34}$$

The quality-adjusted logarithmic price arithmetic average β_1^* in (2.32) and δ_0^* in (2.34) are adjusted with the same characteristic price γ^{1^*}, and the quality-constant price change may be defined with the differential

$$\phi_P^* = \beta_1^* - \delta_0^*$$

We shall refer to this hedonic imputed scale based on logarithmic price change as a price change-based Paasche-type scale. For both the differential ϕ_L^* and ϕ_P^*, adjustment with characteristic price is asymmetrical. Therefore, using the median value of the two differentials, the hedonic imputed estimation value based on the logarithmic price change from time 0 to time 1 is written as follows:

$$
\begin{aligned}
LP_{HI} &= \frac{1}{2}\phi_L^* + \frac{1}{2}\phi_P^* \\
&= \frac{\mathbf{1}_1'\left\{y^1 - \mathbf{Z}^1\left(\frac{1}{2}\gamma^{0^*} + \frac{1}{2}\gamma^{1^*}\right)\right\}}{N(1)} - \frac{\mathbf{1}_0'\left\{y^0 - \mathbf{Z}^0\left(\frac{1}{2}\gamma^{0^*} + \frac{1}{2}\gamma^{1^*}\right)\right\}}{N(0)}
\end{aligned} \tag{2.35}
$$

Here, one can see that quality adjustment of price is performed not with $\mathbf{Z}^t\gamma^{t^*}$ but with $\mathbf{Z}^t\left(\frac{1}{2}\gamma^{0^*} + \frac{1}{2}\gamma^{1^*}\right)$. If the sample sizes for the two times are identical and the characteristics and characteristic prices are constant over time, there is no difference between the two techniques.

2.2.4.3 Differences Between Time Dummy Indexes and Imputed Indexes

In order to look at the differences between LP_{HD} (2.24) and LP_{HI} (2.35), the differential of the two may be expressed as follows:

$$
LP_{HD} - LP_{HI} = \left(\frac{\mathbf{1}_1'\mathbf{Z}^1}{N(1)} - \frac{\mathbf{1}_0'\mathbf{Z}^0}{N(0)}\right)\left(\tfrac{1}{2}\gamma^{0^*} + \tfrac{1}{2}\gamma^{1^*} - \gamma^*\right) \tag{2.36}
$$

In other words, if the average of the characteristic prices is equivalent for each time and if the pooled hedonic regression model characteristic price is equivalent to the hedonic characteristic price median value estimated for each time, (2.24) and (2.35) are fully equivalent.

Based on (2.31) and (2.32), the β_0, β_1 least squares estimator regressed on each observation period is:

$$
\beta_t^* = \mathbf{1}_t'(y - \mathbf{Z}^t\gamma^{t^*})/N(t)
$$

Using this, the least squares residual error may be written as follows:

$$
u^t = \mathbf{M}^t y^t - \mathbf{M}^t\mathbf{Z}^t\gamma^{t^*} \tag{2.37}
$$

Here, $\mathbf{M}^t = \mathbf{I} - \mathbf{1}_t\mathbf{1}_t'/N(t)$. If we define $y^{t^*} = \mathbf{M}^t y^t$ and $\mathbf{Z}^{t^*} = \mathbf{M}^t\mathbf{Z}^t$, the estimated characteristic price vector is as follows:

$$
\gamma^{t^*} = \left(\mathbf{Z}^{t^*\prime}\mathbf{Z}^{t^*}\right)^{-1}\mathbf{Z}^{t^*\prime}y^{t^*} \tag{2.38}
$$

Here, if we multiply $\left(\mathbf{Z}^{0^*\prime}\mathbf{Z}^{0^*} + \mathbf{Z}^{1^*\prime}\mathbf{Z}^{1^*}\right)$ by both sides of (2.26), the characteristic price using pooled data in (2.26) becomes:

$$
\left(\mathbf{Z}^{0^*\prime}\mathbf{Z}^{0^*} + \mathbf{Z}^{1^*\prime}\mathbf{Z}^{1^*}\right)\gamma^* = \left(\mathbf{Z}^{0^*\prime}y^{0^*} + \mathbf{Z}^{1^*\prime}y^{1^*}\right) = \mathbf{Z}^{0^*\prime}\mathbf{Z}^{0^*}\gamma^{0^*} + \mathbf{Z}^{1^*\prime}\mathbf{Z}^{1^*}\gamma^{1^*} \tag{2.39}
$$

Note that, based on (2.38), $\left(\mathbf{Z}^{0^*\prime}\mathbf{Z}^{0^*}\right)\gamma^{0^*} = \mathbf{Z}^{0^*\prime}\mathbf{y}^{0^*}$ and $\left(\mathbf{Z}^{1^*\prime}\mathbf{Z}^{1^*}\right)\gamma^{1^*} = \mathbf{Z}^{1^*\prime}\mathbf{y}^{1^*}$. If γ^{0^*} and γ^{1^*} are equivalent, (2.39) shows that γ^* is necessarily the shared characteristic vector of these. If we multiply the right side of (2.36) $\left(\frac{1}{2}\gamma^{0^*} + \frac{1}{2}\gamma^{1^*} - \gamma^*\right)$ by $2\left(\mathbf{Z}^{0^*\prime}\mathbf{Z}^{0^*} + \mathbf{Z}^{1^*\prime}\mathbf{Z}^{1^*}\right)$ from the right side, we obtain the following:

$$
\begin{aligned}
&2\left(\mathbf{Z}^{0^*\prime}\mathbf{Z}^{0^*} + \mathbf{Z}^{1^*\prime}\mathbf{Z}^{1^*}\right)\left(\tfrac{1}{2}\gamma^{0^*} + \tfrac{1}{2}\gamma^{1^*} - \gamma^*\right)\\
&= \mathbf{Z}^{0^*\prime}\mathbf{Z}^{0^*}\gamma^{0^*} + \mathbf{Z}^{0^*\prime}\mathbf{Z}^{0^*}\gamma^{1^*} + \mathbf{Z}^{1^*\prime}\mathbf{Z}^{1^*}\gamma^{0^*} + \mathbf{Z}^{1^*\prime}\mathbf{Z}^{1^*}\gamma^{1^*} - 2\left(\mathbf{Z}^{0^*\prime}\mathbf{Z}^{0^*} + \mathbf{Z}^{1^*\prime}\mathbf{Z}^{1^*}\right)\gamma^*\\
&= \mathbf{Z}^{0^*\prime}\mathbf{Z}^{0^*}\gamma^{0^*} + \mathbf{Z}^{0^*\prime}\mathbf{Z}^{0^*}\gamma^{1^*} + \mathbf{Z}^{1^*\prime}\mathbf{Z}^{1^*}\gamma^{0^*} + \mathbf{Z}^{1^*\prime}\mathbf{Z}^{1^*}\gamma^{1^*} - 2\mathbf{Z}^{0^*\prime}\mathbf{Z}^{0^*}\gamma^{0^*} - 2\mathbf{Z}^{1^*\prime}\mathbf{Z}^{1^*}\gamma^{1^*}\\
&= -\mathbf{Z}^{0^*\prime}\mathbf{Z}^{0^*}\gamma^{0^*} + \mathbf{Z}^{0^*\prime}\mathbf{Z}^{0^*}\gamma^{1^*} + \mathbf{Z}^{1^*\prime}\mathbf{Z}^{1^*}\gamma^{0^*} - \mathbf{Z}^{1^*\prime}\mathbf{Z}^{1^*}\gamma^{1^*}\\
&= -\left(\mathbf{Z}^{1^*\prime}\mathbf{Z}^{1^*} - \mathbf{Z}^{0^*\prime}\mathbf{Z}^{0^*}\right)\left(\gamma^{1^*} - \gamma^{0^*}\right)
\end{aligned}
$$

In other words,

$$
\left(\tfrac{1}{2}\gamma^{0^*} + \tfrac{1}{2}\gamma^{1^*} - \gamma^*\right) = -\tfrac{1}{2}\left(\mathbf{Z}^{0^*\prime}\mathbf{Z}^{0^*} + \mathbf{Z}^{1^*\prime}\mathbf{Z}^{1^*}\right)\left(\mathbf{Z}^{1^*\prime}\mathbf{Z}^{1^*} - \mathbf{Z}^{0^*\prime}\mathbf{Z}^{0^*}\right)\left(\gamma^{1^*} - \gamma^{0^*}\right) \tag{2.40}
$$

If we plug (2.40) into (2.36), the differential of the time dummy index and imputed index shown with the logarithmic price difference may be rewritten using the following formula:

$$
LP_{HD} - LP_{HI} = -\frac{1}{2}\left(\frac{\mathbf{1}_1'\mathbf{Z}^1}{N(1)} - \frac{\mathbf{1}_0'\mathbf{Z}^0}{N(0)}\right)\left(\mathbf{Z}^{0^*\prime}\mathbf{Z}^{0^*} + \mathbf{Z}^{1^*\prime}\mathbf{Z}^{1^*}\right)\left(\mathbf{Z}^{1^*\prime}\mathbf{Z}^{1^*} - \mathbf{Z}^{0^*\prime}\mathbf{Z}^{0^*}\right)\left(\gamma^{1^*} - \gamma^{0^*}\right) \tag{2.41}
$$

Based on the above, when any of the following conditions are met, the two logarithmic price differentials based on the hedonic time dummy and hedonic imputation method are identical:

- The average value of each characteristic is equivalent for the two times: $\frac{\mathbf{1}_1'\mathbf{Z}^1}{N(1)} = \frac{\mathbf{1}_0'\mathbf{Z}^0}{N(0)}$
- The characteristic value variance/covariance matrices are equivalent for the two times:
  $\mathbf{Z}^{1^*\prime}\mathbf{Z}^{1^*} = \mathbf{Z}^{0^*\prime}\mathbf{Z}^{0^*}$
- The quality-adjusted prices obtained with the hedonic price estimation method for each time are identical: $\gamma^{1^*} = \gamma^{0^*}$

2.2.4.4 Summary of Hedonic Dummy Indexes and Hedonic Imputed Indexes

As shown above, we have identified factors that show the differences between a hedonic dummy index and hedonic imputed index. In the regression equations, if it is possible to use information for two times and formulate the indexes with identical function forms, taking the (geometric) average of the two is perhaps a viable method when the two approaches show different results. However, rather than doing this, using either one index or the other is preferable for various reasons.

A major issue of concern when using the hedonic time dummy (HD) method is that it has the following restriction: the characteristic price is fixed over time. However, the null hypothesis that the characteristic variable parameter is fixed throughout the observation period has in fact been dismissed by a number of papers. In contrast to this, the hedonic imputed index (HI) method is inherently more flexible than the time dummy model, which is a significant advantage.

In Sect. 2.2.4.3, we showed that the difference between the two approaches depends on the following three variable factors:

- The characteristic average value
- The variance/covariance matrix of the characteristic value
- The estimated hedonic characteristic price

What's more, multiplication of the difference between the two periods produces the ultimate difference. Therefore, the stability of the characteristic price parameter alone is not necessarily a problem. For example, even if the parameter is unstable, its instability will be alleviated by slight changes in other characteristics, and the same may be true for the price index.

Due to the nature of the HD method, it uses independent variables observed for the two times, and it is restricted such that the characteristic price parameters are the same for the two times, and regression analysis ends up being executed one time only. In this sense, it may be said that the HD method is not flexible due to the presence of these restrictions. Why, then, are these restrictions imposed? Presumably, the reasons include the following:

- To not lose a degree of freedom.
- To provide an unambiguous estimation value for the overall price change from time 0 to time 1.
- To minimize the effect of abnormal values in conditions where there is a small degree of freedom.

In contrast to this, the HI method allows for diachronic changes in characteristic prices and formulation is more flexible. However:

- A degree of freedom is lost.
- The estimation value for the overall price change in the two times is difficult to reproduce.

Due to these and other issues, analysis costs increase. The latter of the two issues pointed out above may in fact not be all that serious, because Laspeyres- and Paasche-type estimation values for price changes are well established in index theory. Bearing these points in mind, the HI method may be considered the preferred method as long as the degree of freedom is not extremely restricted.

In light of the above, a rolling window hedonic method that merges the hedonic dummy method and hedonic imputed method has been proposed. Market structural changes occur as a result of various exogenous shocks, but it is thought that a certain adjustment period exists until shocks are absorbed by the market and changes are realized. Therefore, the regression coefficient likewise does not change instantaneously but should instead be viewed as changing sequentially.

However, if estimating a model where the data is divided into various periods and observation data for each period is used (as with the HI method), the links to prior and subsequent data are severed. As a result, under the assumption that structural changes occur sequentially, this method ends up making it more difficult to capture price changes within the sequential change process. Instead, as a more natural approach, a method of estimating price indexes within the sequential change process by taking an estimation period of a certain duration and estimating the model while moving this period—as if obtaining a moving average—may be preferable. A method that has been proposed based on this idea is the rolling window hedonic method. This approach is employed in the estimation of housing price indexes in Ireland and Japan.

2.2.5 *Hedonic Production Price Index Measurement and Quality Adjustment*

In this section, we will explain the characteristics of quality-adjusted hedonic indexes for producer prices, based on Diewert (2002). The Konus-type price index proposed in that paper is defined using a revenue function that is a value function of the revenue maximization problem based on company technology and resource constraints. The revenue function is derived from characteristic values constituting the product price, production technology, production factors, and product.

2.2.5.1 The Producer Revenue Maximization Problem

We shall define the hedonic price (producer's willingness to pay) based on the characteristic vector z as:

$$\Pi^t(z) = \rho^t f^t(z) \tag{2.42}$$

Here, ρ^t is the price showing the value of all characteristic values used for the product at time t and $f^t(z)$ shows the cardinal utility separable from the utility function. In (2.42), it is assumed that the utility function is equivalent for the two times.

$$f^0 = f^1 \tag{2.43}$$

Given the hedonic price (2.42), the producer performs revenue maximization. First, we shall define the production function F as follows:

$$q = F^t(z, \boldsymbol{v}) \tag{2.44}$$

Here, q is the production volume and $\boldsymbol{v}$ is the production factor vector. For a given level of production technology, the following revenue-maximizing value function may be obtained:

$$\begin{aligned} R(\rho^s f^s, F^t, \boldsymbol{Z}^t, \boldsymbol{v}) &\equiv \max_{q,z}\{\rho^s f^s(z)q : q = F^t(z, \boldsymbol{v}); z \in \boldsymbol{Z}^t\} \\ &= \max_{z}\{\rho^s f^s(z)F^t(z, \boldsymbol{v}); z \in \boldsymbol{Z}^t\} \end{aligned} \tag{2.45}$$

Here, $\boldsymbol{Z}^t$ shows the feasible set of characteristic values.

When the characteristics and input factors for time t are taken as z^t, v^t, the corresponding production volume is:

$$q^t = F^t(z^t, \boldsymbol{v}^t) \tag{2.46}$$

Therefore, the maximized revenue function for time t may be written as follows:

$$\begin{aligned} R(\rho^t f^t, F^t, \boldsymbol{Z}^t, \boldsymbol{v}) &\equiv \max_{q,z}\{\rho^t f^t(z)q : q = F^t(z, \boldsymbol{v}^t); z \in \boldsymbol{Z}^t\} \\ &= \rho^t f^t(z^t)q^t; \quad t = 0, 1 \end{aligned} \tag{2.47}$$

2.2.5.2 Konus-Type Hedonic Production Price Indexes

Using the maximized revenue function (2.47), the Konus-type hedonic product price index between time 0 and time 1 is defined as follows:

$$P(\rho^0 f^0, \rho^1 f^1, F^t, \boldsymbol{Z}^t, \boldsymbol{v}) = \frac{R(\rho^1 f^1, F^t, \boldsymbol{Z}^t, \boldsymbol{v})}{R(\rho^0 f^0, F^t, \boldsymbol{Z}^t, \boldsymbol{v})} \tag{2.48}$$

The differences between the two revenue functions are caused by the hedonic prices $\rho^1 f^1$ and $\rho^0 f^0$. Since $\max_z\{\rho^1 f^1(z)F^t(z, \boldsymbol{v}^t); z \in \boldsymbol{Z}^t\} = \max_z\{\rho^1 f^0(z)F^t(z, \boldsymbol{v}^t); z \in \boldsymbol{Z}^t\}$ based on hypothesis (2.43), (2.48) may be rewritten as follows:

$$P(\rho^0 f^0, \rho^1 f^1, F^t, \boldsymbol{Z}^t, \boldsymbol{v}) = \frac{\rho^1 R(\rho^0 f^0, F^t, \boldsymbol{Z}^t, \boldsymbol{v})}{\rho^0 R(\rho^0 f^0, F^t, \boldsymbol{Z}^t, \boldsymbol{v})} = \frac{\rho^1}{\rho^0} \tag{2.49}$$

In estimation of the hedonic price, if we assume that the utility of the characteristic portion is diachronically constant, the Konus-type product price index may be estimated very easily.

Let us consider general cases that do not meet hypothesis (2.43). Taking the price index in (2.49) as our base, we can define an observable hedonic Laspeyres production price index and Paasche production price index with the following inequalities, using:

$$P(\rho^0 f^0, \rho^1 f^1, F^0, \mathbf{Z}^0, \boldsymbol{v}^0) = \frac{R(\rho^1 f^1, F^0, \mathbf{Z}^0, \boldsymbol{v}^0)}{R(\rho^0 f^0, F^0, \mathbf{Z}^0, \boldsymbol{v}^0)} \geq \frac{\rho^1 f^1(z^0)}{\rho^0 f^0(z^0)} = P_{HL} \quad (2.50)$$

$$P(\rho^0 f^0, \rho^1 f^1, F^1, \mathbf{Z}^1, \boldsymbol{v}^1) = \frac{R(\rho^1 f^1, F^1, \mathbf{Z}^1, \boldsymbol{v}^1)}{R(\rho^0 f^0, F^1, \mathbf{Z}^1, \boldsymbol{v}^1)} \leq \frac{\rho^1 f^1(z^1)}{\rho^0 f^0(z^1)} = P_{HP} \quad (2.51)$$

Here, $P(\rho^0 f^0, \rho^1 f^1, F^0, \mathbf{Z}^0, \boldsymbol{v}^0)$ and $P(\rho^0 f^0, \rho^1 f^1, F^1, \mathbf{Z}^1, \boldsymbol{v}^1)$ are theoretical production price indexes that cannot be observed. Equation (2.50) shows that the theoretical production price index $P(\rho^0 f^0, \rho^1 f^1, F^0, \mathbf{Z}^0, \boldsymbol{v}^0)$ has the observable Laspeyres production price index P_{HL} as its lower limit, and (2.51) shows that the theoretical production price index $P(\rho^0 f^0, \rho^1 f^1, F^1, \mathbf{Z}^1, \boldsymbol{v}^1)$ has the observable Paasche production price index P_{HP} as its upper limit.

By using these convex combination equations (weighted averages) instead of $F^0, \mathbf{Z}^0, \boldsymbol{v}^0$ or $F^1, \mathbf{Z}^1, \boldsymbol{v}^1$ constituting the production price index, it is possible to define the range that can be covered by the theoretical Laspeyres production price index and Paasche production price index. If the scalar $\lambda \in [0, 1]$ is used, the convex combinations for $F^t, \mathbf{Z}^t, \boldsymbol{v}^t$ for period $t = 0, 1$ may be written as follows.

$$\mathbf{Z}(\lambda) = (1-\lambda)\mathbf{Z}^0 + \lambda \mathbf{Z}^1$$
$$\boldsymbol{v}(\lambda) = (1-\lambda)\boldsymbol{v}^0 + \lambda \boldsymbol{v}^1$$
$$F(\lambda) = (1-\lambda)F^0(z, \boldsymbol{v}(\lambda)) + \lambda F^1(z, \boldsymbol{v}(\lambda))$$

Therefore, the hedonic production price function may be written as:

$$P(\lambda) = \frac{R(\rho^1 f^1, F(\lambda), \mathbf{Z}(\lambda), \boldsymbol{v}(\lambda))}{R(\rho^0 f^0, F(\lambda), \mathbf{Z}(\lambda), \boldsymbol{v}(\lambda))} = \frac{\max_z\{\rho^1 f^1(z)F(\lambda); z \in \mathbf{Z}(\lambda)\}}{\max_z\{\rho^0 f^0(z)F(\lambda); z \in \mathbf{Z}(\lambda)\}} \quad (2.52)$$

When $\lambda = 0$, since $P(\lambda)$ signifies that $P(\rho^0 f^0, \rho^1 f^1, F^0, \mathbf{Z}^0, \boldsymbol{v}^0)$, the following may be derived from inequality (2.50):

$$P(0) \geq P_{HL} = \frac{\rho^1 f^1(z^0)}{\rho^0 f^0(z^0)} \quad (2.53)$$

As well, when $\lambda = 1$, since $P(\lambda)$ signifies that $P(\rho^0 f^0, \rho^1 f^1, F^1, \mathbf{Z}^1, \boldsymbol{v}^1)$, the following may be derived from inequality (2.51):

$$P(1) \leq P_{HP} = \frac{\rho^1 f^1(z^1)}{\rho^0 f^0(z^1)} \quad (2.54)$$

By using Diewert's proof (1983; 1060–1061), if $P(\lambda)$ is a continuous function for [0, 1], it is possible to show that λ^* exists, whereby

$$0 \leq \lambda^* \leq 1 \text{ and } P_{HL} \leq P(\lambda^*) \leq P_{HP} \qquad P_{HP} \leq P(\lambda^*) \leq P_{HL}.$$

In other words, one can see that the theoretical hedonic production price index for the period $t = 0, 1$, when considered via $P(\lambda^*)$ described above, exists between the observable Laspeyres production price index and Paasche production price index. Note that to obtain this result, one must assume the continuity of λ in the hedonic model price functions $\rho^1 f^1(z^0)$, $\rho^0 f^0(z^0)$ in the numerator and denominator of Formula (2.52), the production functions $F^0(z, \boldsymbol{v})$, $F^1(z, \boldsymbol{v})$, and the feasible characteristic value sets $\mathbf{Z}^0$, $\mathbf{Z}^1$. The sufficient conditions for continuity are:

- The production functions $F^0(z, \boldsymbol{v})$, $F^1(z, \boldsymbol{v})$ are positive and continuous for z and $\boldsymbol{v}$.
- The hedonic model price functions $f^0(z)$, $f^1(z)$ are positive and continuous for z.
- ρ^0, ρ^1 are positive.
- Sets $\mathbf{Z}^0$, $\mathbf{Z}^1$ are convex sets, bounded, and closed.

Based on the above, one can see that the boundary range for the theoretical price index is determined by the observable price index. In order to obtain the best value for approximating the theoretical index, it is natural to take the adjusted average of the two boundary values. If the adjusted average function for the Laspeyres and Paasche production price indexes is written as $m(P_{HL}, P_{HP})$, we can confirm, based on Diewert's argument (1997; 138), that $m()$ must be the geometric average. In other words, the best candidate in terms of approximating the theoretical production price index is the following observable Fisher hedonic production price index, using (2.50) and (2.51):

$$P_{HF} = (P_{HL}P_{HP})^{\frac{1}{2}} = \frac{\rho^1}{\rho^0}\left(\frac{f^1(z^0)}{f^0(z^0)}\right)^{\frac{1}{2}}\left(\frac{f^1(z^1)}{f^0(z^1)}\right)^{\frac{1}{2}}$$

If the hypothesis $f^0 = f^1$ is fulfilled by the hedonic model price function being the same for the two times, then this can be transformed into $P_{HF} = \rho^1/\rho^0$. As well, if the respective observable prices are defined as

$$P^0 = \rho^0 f^0(z^0) \text{ and } P^1 = \rho^1 f^1(z^1) \tag{2.55}$$

the Laspeyres and Paasche production price indexes can be shown as quality-adjusted price comparisons:

$$P_{HL} = \frac{\rho^1 f^1(z^0)}{\rho^0 f^0(z^0)} = \frac{P^1/f^1(z^1)}{P^0/f^1(z^0)} \tag{2.56}$$

$$P_{HP} = \frac{\rho^1 f^1(z^1)}{\rho^0 f^0(z^1)} = \frac{P^1/f^0(z^1)}{P^0/f^0(z^0)} \tag{2.57}$$

Therefore, the Fisher hedonic production price index may be written as follows:

$$P_{HF} = (P_{HL}P_{HP})^{\frac{1}{2}} = \left(\frac{P^1/f^1(z^1)}{P^0/f^1(z^0)}\right)^{\frac{1}{2}} \left(\frac{P^1/f^0(z^1)}{P^0/f^0(z^0)}\right)^{\frac{1}{2}} \tag{2.58}$$

In other words, the Fisher hedonic production price index may be obtained from the geometric average of the two quality-adjusted price indexes obtained by estimating the hedonic regression model. The hedonic approach is useful not just for quality adjustment of the product user price but also for quality adjustment of the product supplier price. In this chapter, in order to define a product price index assuming competitive company production activities, we used a revenue function (total willingness to pay) maximized based on Konus. If the cardinal utility function for the characteristic portion is the same at the two points in time, the theoretical production price index may be shown by comparison with the observable product price.

In addition, in general cases, based on certain restrictions, we showed that the theoretical production price index is present in the range that forms the boundary values of the observable Laspeyres and Paasche production price indexes.

2.2.6 Characteristics, Advantages, and Disadvantages of the Hedonic Method

Rosen (1974) developed a market equilibrium theory for differentiated products. This study rigorously examined the relationship between the structures of the product supplier offer function, product demander bid value function, and hedonic market price function, and characterized product market price based on consumer and producer behavior.

If the bid value function is used, it is possible to obtain the consumer's willingness to pay with respect to changes in characteristics. In market equilibrium, not only are the market price and bid value consistent, but the slope of the hedonic function and bid value function are also consistent. Since the bid value function is a concave function, the willingness to pay with respect to incremental changes in characteristics is smaller than the change in the market price. In other words, caution is required with respect to the market price function characteristic limit value, since it is possible that the willingness to pay will be overestimated as long as demanders are not homogeneous. However, if one assumes that changes in characteristic values will be sufficiently small, the market price function limit value may be used as an approximation of the willingness to pay. Therefore, the market price function is generally estimated in existing research.

If the hedonic approach is used, it is possible to measure changes in quality-adjusted price using samples at another point in time. The simplest and most widely used method is to estimate the time effect for the hedonic function based on the characteristic price being constant and using a time dummy with pooled data. Hedonic imputed indexes estimate a hedonic function for each observation time, allowing for changes in characteristic prices, and measure price changes using a Laspeyres-type scale or Paasche-type scale. Hedonic dummy indexes and hedonic imputed indexes produce different results, but this is not caused solely by differences based on whether or not characteristic prices are constant for the two times. Differences between the two indexes occur if the average value for each characteristic varies for the two times or if the characteristic variance /covariance matrices vary for the two periods.

The hedonic approach is useful not just for quality adjustment of the product user price but also for quality adjustment of the product supplier price. It is possible to define a producer price index using a revenue function (total willingness to pay) maximized based on Konus. In this case, if the cardinal utility function for the characteristic portion is the same at the two points in time, the theoretical production price index may be shown by comparison with the observable product price. In general cases, based on certain restrictions, it has been shown that the theoretical production price index is present in the range that forms the boundary values of the observable Laspeyres and Paasche production price indexes.

Thus, one can see that price indexes with what is broadly called the "hedonic method" vary considerably depending on the approach employed in estimation.

The advantages and disadvantages of the hedonic method in the estimation of property price indexes are outlined below. The following may be considered as advantages:

- As well as having a basis in economic theory and index theory, the theoretical biases of the hedonic method are clear.
- Compared to other approaches, it is possible to use all transaction price data, so it may be considered the most efficient approach.
- Since it makes it possible to control for the many characteristics of property, it enables the sorting of data into specialized indexes by purpose/region.
- Since it is already used in the estimation of consumer price statistics and the like, it is possible to be consistent with other economic statistics.

Disadvantages include:

- Since it is necessary to collect many property-related characteristics, information-gathering costs are high.
- In cases where it is not possible to collect important characteristics for determining property prices, one faces the problem of omitted variable bias.
- Calculated indexes vary depending on the function form used. In other words, there is a low level of reproducibility.
- In cases of strong heterogeneity, it may not be possible to control for quality.
- Since the underlying economic theory and statistical procedures are complicated, the organizations creating the indexes require specialized skills, and explaining the indexes to users is difficult.

2.3 Repeat Sales Method

Apart from the hedonic method, the most used approach is the repeat sales method elaborated by Bailey et al. (1963) and Case and Shiller (1987, 1989). With the repeat sales method, since use of the data generation process in the hedonic price regression model is assumed, some of the problems occurring with the hedonic method are inherited. However, since the same product is compared, underestimation bias is eliminated if there is no change in the characteristics or characteristic prices. Given that the estimation method is straightforward, it has the benefits of being a technique with high reproducibility and estimation efficiency.

With either method, there is a bias that exists due to the estimation technique. Since the purpose of a price index is to observe price data over an extended time, as the observation period becomes longer, "aggregation bias" is to be expected, due to changes in the characteristics and characteristic prices of identical properties.

In particular, the fact that it is not possible to separate effects common to the market as a whole (time effects) that are factors in the housing market supply-demand balance from effects related to changes in individual housing, especially deterioration (age effects), is an extremely important issue when using the repeat sales method. If the effects of housing deterioration are ignored, it is to be expected that repeat sales price indexes will have a strong downward bias.

As well, since only properties transacted multiple times are selected for use, the sample size shrinks and there is also concern that selection bias occurs in the samples. Moreover, while it is strongly assumed that there will be no changes in property quality during the period when repeat transactions are conducted, it is easy to predict that property deterioration, investment in renovations, or changes to the surrounding environment will occur, so the assumption is not consistent with the reality.

Below, we provide an overview of the repeat sales method and describe what kinds of problems occur with it. Section 2.3.2 explains the analysis structure and price index characteristics of the standard repeat sales method. Sections 2.3.3 and 2.3.4 present the problems of aggregation bias and sample selection bias with the standard repeat sales method, along with methods of resolving them.

2.3.1 *Standard Repeat Sales Price Index*

When housing prices at multiple points in time are observed as data, the hedonic market price of property n at time t may be described in the form of the following regression model:

$$y_n^t \equiv \ln p_n^t = \alpha_t + z_n^{t\prime}\gamma^t + \varepsilon_n^t \quad (n = 1, 2, \ldots, N(t); t = 0, 1, \ldots, T) \qquad (2.59)$$

Here, y_n^t is the housing price logarithm ($\ln p_n^t$), α_t is the unknown time effect at time t, $z_n^t = (1, z_{n2}^t, \ldots, z_{nk}^t, \ldots, z_{nK}^t)'$ is the explanatory variable (characteristic) vector including a constant term, $\gamma^t = (\gamma_1, \gamma_2^t, \ldots, \gamma_k^t, \ldots, \gamma_K^t)'$ is the unknown coefficient vector, and ε_n^t is the error term. γ_1 is the constant term coefficient for the overall model and $\gamma_2^t, \ldots, \gamma_K^t$ is the characteristic marginal effect (characteristic quality-adjusted parameter).

Let us take it that property n is transacted on the market twice, at time s and time t ($t > s$). In this case, for example, the logarithmic price differential for the two times in (2.59) may be written as follows:

$$Y_n \equiv \ln p_n^t - \ln p_n^s = (\alpha_t - \alpha_s) + (z_n^{t\prime}\gamma^t - z_n^{s\prime}\gamma^s) + v_n \tag{2.60}$$

Here, v_n is the differential of the error terms for the respective times ($\varepsilon_n^t - \varepsilon_n^s$). In other words, the price rate of change (logarithmic differential) may be treated as data occurring based on differences in the time effect, changes in characteristic values (characteristic qualities and quantities), and errors.

The repeat sales method of Bailey et al. (1963) and Case and Shiller (1987, 1989) reformulated (2.60) above by implicitly establishing the following hypotheses:

Hypothesis 1. All characteristics are constant over time.

Hypothesis 2. All characteristic parameters are constant over time.

In other words, hypothesis 1 signifies that $z_n = z_n^t = z_n^s$ and hypothesis 2 that $\gamma = \gamma^t = \gamma^s$. If one takes property n as being transacted for the first time at time s and for the second time at time t, the hedonic regression formula (2.59) may be rewritten as follows for time s and time t, respectively, using time dummy variables based on hypothesis 1 and 2:

$$y_n^s = \overline{\boldsymbol{d}}_n'\boldsymbol{\alpha} + z_n'\gamma + \varepsilon_n^s \tag{2.61}$$

$$y_n^t = \overline{\overline{\boldsymbol{d}}}_n'\boldsymbol{\alpha} + z_n'\gamma + \varepsilon_n^t \tag{2.62}$$

Note that $\overline{\boldsymbol{d}}_n' = (\overline{d}_n^1, \ldots, \overline{d}_n^T)$ is the time dummy variable for the first transaction and $\overline{\overline{\boldsymbol{d}}}_n' = (\overline{\overline{d}}_n^1, \ldots, \overline{\overline{d}}_n^T)$ is the time dummy variable for the second transaction, and they are defined as follows:

$$\overline{d}_n^u = \begin{cases} 1 & u = s \\ 0 & u \neq s \end{cases}, \quad \overline{\overline{d}}_n^u = \begin{cases} 1 & u = t \\ 0 & u \neq t \end{cases}$$

As well, $\boldsymbol{\alpha} = (\alpha_1, \ldots, \alpha_s, \ldots, \alpha_t, \ldots, \alpha_T)$ is the time effect vector. Since there is a linear relationship between the constant term z^1 for the overall model and the dummy variable, the time effect for time 0 is standardized here as $\alpha_0 = 0$. Therefore, the time dummy variables $\overline{d}_n^0$ and $\overline{\overline{d}}_n^0$ for time 0 are omitted.

The differential of the time dummy variables for the first and second hedonic regression equations is defined with the following $T \times 1$ vector.

$$\boldsymbol{D}_n = \overline{\overline{\boldsymbol{d}}}_n - \overline{\boldsymbol{d}}_n \tag{2.63}$$

Note that:

$$D_n^u = \begin{cases} 1 & u = t \text{ (2nd transaction)} \\ -1 & u = s \text{ (1st transaction)} \\ 0 & \text{Other cases} \end{cases} \quad (n = 1, 2, \ldots, N(t);\ u = 1, \ldots, s, \ldots, t, \ldots, T)$$

$\boldsymbol{Y} = (Y_1, \ldots, Y_n, \ldots, Y_N)'$ and $\mathbf{D} = (\boldsymbol{D}_1, \ldots, \boldsymbol{D}_n, \ldots, \boldsymbol{D}_N)'$ are included, the matrix representation repeat sales regression model may be defined as follows:

$$\boldsymbol{Y} = \mathbf{D}\boldsymbol{\alpha} + \boldsymbol{v} \tag{2.64}$$

The least squares estimator for (2.64) is $\widehat{\boldsymbol{\alpha}} = (\mathbf{D}'\mathbf{D})^{-1}\mathbf{D}'\boldsymbol{Y}$. The theoretical value (logarithmic price differential) of a random property transacted for the first time at time s and the second time at time t is:

$$\widehat{\boldsymbol{Y}} = \ln\left(\frac{p_n^t}{p_n^s}\right) = \widehat{\alpha}_t - \widehat{\alpha}_s$$

Therefore, taking time s as the baseline, the price index at time t (price comparison) is $\exp(\widehat{\alpha}_t - \widehat{\alpha}_s)$. Since the time dummy variable for time 0 was omitted and $\alpha_0 = 0$ included in order to avoid multicollinearity, $\exp(\widehat{\alpha}_t)$ is the price index taking time 0 as the baseline. The "BMN" price index presented in Bailey et al. (1963) is:

$$\boldsymbol{I}^{\mathrm{BMN}} = \{\exp(\widehat{\alpha}_t), \exp(\widehat{\alpha}_1), \ldots, \exp(\widehat{\alpha}_T)\} \tag{2.65}$$

2.3.2 *Random Walk Error Term*

The following is assumed with respect to the error terms in (2.61) and (2.62).

$$\begin{aligned} &E(\varepsilon_n^t) = 0,\ E[(\varepsilon_n^t)^2] = \sigma^2 \ n = 1, \ldots, N. \\ &E(\varepsilon_m^s \varepsilon_n^t) = 0 \qquad m, n = 1, \ldots, N;\ s, t = 1, \ldots, T;\ n \neq m, t \neq s \end{aligned} \tag{2.66}$$

Equation (2.66) shows that for the respective hedonic regression equations, the error terms are homogeneously variant and there is no serial correlation. In this case, since the error term for (2.64), which is the differential of (2.61) and (2.62), is

$$\begin{aligned} &E(v_n) = 0,\ E[(v_n)^2] = 2\sigma^2 \ n = 1, \ldots, N. \\ &E(v_n v_m) = 0 \qquad m, n = 1, \ldots, N;\ n \neq m \end{aligned} \tag{2.67}$$

Equation (2.67) fulfills the conditions of being homogeneously variant and having no serial correlation. Bailey et al. (1963)'s price index is also estimated based on this type of assumption.

With regard to this, Case and Shiller (1987, 1989) presented a repeat sales regression model which assumes that as the interval between transactions becomes larger, the variance in noise associated with housing-specific structural factors becomes greater, and logarithmic price changes are not homogeneously variant. In this paper, the error term with respect to logarithmic price fluctuation is hypothesized with the following formulas including a random walk:

$$\varepsilon_n^t = h_n^t + \nu_n^t, \quad \nu_n^t \sim \text{i.i.d. } N(0, \sigma_\nu^2) \quad n = 1, \ldots, N;\ t = 1, \ldots, T \tag{2.68}$$

$$h_n^t = h_n^{t-1} + \eta_n^t \quad \eta_n^t \sim \text{i.i.d. } N(0, \sigma_\eta^2) \quad n = 1, \ldots, N;\ t = 1, \ldots, T \tag{2.69}$$

Here, the left-side first term in (2.68) is the random walk shown in (2.69), and the second item in (2.68) is assumes wide noise ν_n^t, η_n^t:

$$\begin{aligned} E(\nu_n^t \nu_m^s) &= 0,\ n \neq m = 1, \ldots, N;\ t \neq s = 1, \ldots, T \\ E(\nu_n^t \eta_m^s) &= 0,\ n, m = 1, \ldots, N;\ t, s = 0, \ldots, T \\ E(\eta_n^t \eta_m^s) &= 0,\ n \neq m = 1, \ldots, N;\ t \neq s = 0, \ldots, T \end{aligned} \tag{2.70}$$

Equation (2.64) is the repeat sales regression model error term. Here, based on

$$v_n = \varepsilon_n^t - \varepsilon_n^s = (h_n^t - h_n^s) + (\nu_n^t - \nu_n^s),$$

the following can be obtained:

$$E(v_n) = 0 \tag{2.71}$$

$$E(v_n^2) = 2\sigma_\nu^2 + (t - s)\sigma_\eta^2 \tag{2.72}$$

In this case, one can see that if the transaction interval $t - s$ becomes greater, the repeat sales regression model error variance also increases (heterogeneous variance).

With regard to this heterogeneous variance, Case and Shiller (1987, 1989) proposed a three-step estimation method, the Weighted Repeat Sales (WRS) method.

1. Equation (2.64) is estimated in the same way as when a BMN price index is obtained, the logarithmic price differential is regressed on the time dummy differential, and the least squares residual error $\widehat{v}_n$ is obtained.
2. In order to estimate $\sigma_\nu^2, \sigma_\eta^2$ in (2.72), the error value of squares $\widehat{v}_n^2$ is regressed on the constant term and transaction interval $A_n - t - s$. ($\widehat{v}_n^2 = a + bA_n +$ error$_n$)
3. Taking the theoretical value in Step 2 as $\widehat{\widehat{v}_n^2} = \widehat{a} + \widehat{b}A_n$ and its reciprocal square root $1/\widehat{\widehat{v}_n^2}$ as the weight, the weighted method of least squares is implemented for (2.64).

If the weight in Step 3 ($N \times N$ diagonal matrix) is defined as

$$\widehat{\omega} = \begin{pmatrix} 1/\widehat{\widehat{v}}_1 & & 0 \\ & \ddots & \\ 0 & & 1/\widehat{\widehat{v}}_N \end{pmatrix},$$

the weighted repeat sales regression model may be written as follows:

$$\boldsymbol{Y}^* = \mathbf{D}^*\boldsymbol{\alpha} + \boldsymbol{v}^* \tag{2.73}$$

Note that $\boldsymbol{Y}^* = \widehat{\omega}\boldsymbol{Y}$, $\mathbf{D}^* = \widehat{\omega}\mathbf{D}$, and $\boldsymbol{v}^* = \widehat{\omega}\boldsymbol{v}$. Therefore, a workable generalized least squares estimator is:

$$\widehat{\boldsymbol{\alpha}}^{\mathrm{WLS}} = (\mathbf{D}'\widehat{\omega}'\widehat{\omega}\mathbf{D})^{-1}\mathbf{D}'\widehat{\omega}'\widehat{\omega}\boldsymbol{Y} \tag{2.74}$$

Based on (2.74), Case and Shiller's WRS price index is:

$$\boldsymbol{I}^{\mathrm{WRS}} = \{\exp(0), \exp(\widetilde{\alpha}_1), \ldots, \exp(\widetilde{\alpha}_T)\} \tag{2.75}$$

Knight et al. (1997, 1999) define the hedonic price index error term in cases where the serial correlation autoregressive parameter is 1 as:

$$\varepsilon_n^t = \varepsilon_n^{t-1} + \nu_n^t, \quad \nu_n^t \sim \text{i.i.d. } N(0, \sigma_{\nu,n}^2) \quad n = 1, \ldots, N;\ t = 0, \ldots, T$$

Here, ν_n^t assumes unknown heterogeneous variance. Therefore, the repeat sales regression model error variance is:

$$E\left[(\varepsilon_n^t - \varepsilon_n^s)^2\right] = (t - s)\sigma_{\nu,n}^2$$

When the transaction interval is taken as $A_n = t - s$, then

$$v_n \equiv \varepsilon_n^t - \varepsilon_n^s \sim N(0, A_n\sigma_{\nu,n}^2),$$

and the weighted repeat sales regression model may be written as follows:

$$\boldsymbol{Y}^{**} = \mathbf{D}^{**}\boldsymbol{\alpha} + \boldsymbol{v}^{**} \tag{2.76}$$

Note that $\boldsymbol{Y}^{**} = \omega\boldsymbol{Y}$, $\mathbf{D}^{**} = \omega\boldsymbol{D}$, and $\boldsymbol{v}^{**} = \omega\boldsymbol{v}$, and

$$\omega = \begin{pmatrix} 1/\sqrt{A_1} & & & & 0 \\ & \ddots & & & \\ & & 1/\sqrt{A_n} & & \\ & & & \ddots & \\ 0 & & & & 1/\sqrt{A_N} \end{pmatrix}$$

2.3.3 *Aggregation Bias*

With the repeat sales method, aggregation bias is an important issue that has been pointed out in much research. Aggregation bias is a problem relating to the two hypotheses in repeat sales regression model (2.60) (hypothesis 1: all characteristics are constant over time; hypothesis 2: all characteristic parameters are constant over time). For example, if there are changes in characteristic values due to deterioration/obsolescence of real estate capital, renovations and maintenance, changes in the surrounding geographic environment, etc., such hypotheses are not valid. As well, Knight et al. (1997) tested whether or not characteristic parameters change with the observation period (hypothesis 2). In order to estimate a stable price index, an observation period of sufficient length is necessary, but the longer the observation period, the more liable these kinds of structural changes are to occur. The biggest problem is the downward effect on real estate prices due to deterioration pointed out by Bailey et al. (1963), Palmquist (1979), and others. Below, we will show that it is not possible to separate the time effect and age effect in standard repeat sales price indexes and discuss methods for simultaneously estimating the time effect and age effect.

2.3.3.1 Bias Due to Omission of the Age Effect

As the transaction interval becomes greater, real estate depreciates and the market value declines. This is explained by McMillen (2003)'s succinct model. The real estate at time t is defined as $p^t = Q^t H^t$. Here, $p^t = \exp(\alpha_t + \gamma_x x)$ is the price per unit of floor space, which varies based on the location (distance from city center) x, α_t is the time effect, and $\gamma_x < 0$. H^t is the real estate floor space, which is produced using land L and capital K^t (a linear homogeneous Cobb-Douglas production function is hypothesized: $H^t = L^{1-\xi} K^{\xi}$). Since real estate materials deteriorate over time, this is defined as $K^t = K[0]\exp(c\tau)$. Here, $K[0]$ is the real estate capital when the building age is 0, $c < 0$ is the capital decrease rate per period, and τ is the building age. Based on the above, the logarithm of the real estate price at time t may be written as follows:

$$\ln p^t = \ln Q^t + \ln H^t = \alpha_t + \gamma_x x + (1-\xi)\ln L + \xi \ln K[0] + \theta\tau$$

Note that $\theta = \xi c < 0$. Therefore, the logarithmic price differential for property n transacted twice at time s and time t is as follows:

$$\begin{aligned} Y_n &= \ln p^t - \ln p^s \\ &= \alpha_t - \alpha_s + \theta A_n + v_n \end{aligned} \tag{2.77}$$

Here, $A_n = t - s > 0$, and v_n is the error term differential. If taking housing capital deterioration into account, it is necessary to consider not only the time effect difference for the logarithmic price differential but also the age effect difference.

The time effect estimator with the BMN-type repeat sales method is $\widehat{\alpha} = (\mathbf{D}'\mathbf{D})^{-1}\mathbf{D}'\boldsymbol{Y}$, but if the real data generation process is (2.77), then based on

$$\widehat{\alpha} = \alpha + (\mathbf{D}'\mathbf{D})^{-1}\mathbf{D}'(\mathbf{A}\boldsymbol{\theta} + \boldsymbol{v}),$$

one obtains

$$E(\widehat{\alpha}) - \alpha = (\mathbf{D}'\mathbf{D})^{-1}\mathbf{D}'\mathbf{A}\boldsymbol{\theta} \tag{2.78}$$

and as long as it is $\theta < 0$, the BMN-type repeat sales method time effect has a bias. In other words, an age effect is included in the BMN-type time effect.

However, it is not possible to simultaneously estimate the time effect and age effect in (2.77) in order to distinguish them. If (2.63) is used, the linear relationship shown below is formed between the age difference for property n and the time dummy difference (Cannaday et al. 2005):

$$A_n = t - s = \boldsymbol{D}_n'\boldsymbol{u} = \sum_{u=1}^{T} D_n^u u = \underbrace{D_n^1}_{=0} \cdot 1 + \cdots + \underbrace{D_n^s}_{=-1} \cdot s + \cdots + \underbrace{D_n^t}_{=1} \cdot t + \cdots + \underbrace{D_n^T}_{=0} \cdot T$$

Therefore, the repeat sales regression model with the age effect is

$$\boldsymbol{Y} = \mathbf{D}\boldsymbol{\alpha} + \mathbf{A}\boldsymbol{\theta} + \boldsymbol{v} = \mathbf{D}(\boldsymbol{\alpha} + \boldsymbol{u}\boldsymbol{\theta}) + \boldsymbol{v} \tag{2.79}$$

and it is not possible to distinguish between $\boldsymbol{\alpha}$ and $\boldsymbol{\theta}$. Based on the above, there is a difficult problem with the BMN-type repeat sales method: if the effect of deterioration is ignored, a bias occurs in the price index, and if the effect of deterioration is considered, it cannot be estimated due to multicollinearity.

2.3.3.2 Age Effect Estimation

The problem of not being able to distinguish the time effect and age effect with the standard repeat sales method has been pointed out by Bailey et al. (1963), Palmquist (1979), Knight et al. (1997, 1999), Chau et al. (2005), Cannaday et al. (2005), and others. It is common for the age effect to be ignored in the estimation of repeat sales price indexes.

However, estimating the age effect with the repeat sales method is a very significant issue. First, in economic accounting, as typified by the SNA, estimation of housing stocks is performed, but no consistent method has been established for measuring the depreciation rate. In general, the hedonic method is used for this kind of quality adjustment, but a lot of housing characteristic information is needed to estimate the hedonic function. When collecting this information is difficult, it becomes necessary to perform estimation using another approach. If measurement of the depreciation rate is possible within the framework of repeat sales method estimation, it could be applied in many countries. An additional issue is the elimination of the biases inherent in housing price indexes. There is a strong possibility that biases due to being unable to eliminate the age effect with the repeat sales method will be a serious problem, especially in Asian countries like Hong Kong and Japan where high depreciation rates may be expected.

In an attempt to estimate (2.79), Palmquist (1979) estimated θ independently of the repeat sales regression equation, then adjusted the time effect to satisfy (2.79). In order to estimate the age effect, Cannaday et al. (2005) proposed a multivariate repeat sales model that incorporates a dummy variable for building age instead of a continuous term as in (2.77). In addition to this, a method has been proposed that performs estimation by disrupting the linear relationship between the time dummy variable and age. Chau et al. (2005) distinguished the time effect and age effect by hypothesizing non-linearity in the age effect (Box-Cox transformation), and Knight et al. (1997) did so by refining Case and Quigley (1991)'s hybrid method (joint hedonic and repeat sales model estimation).

Cannaday et al. (2005) proposed the following model using an age dummy variable:

$$Y_n = \boldsymbol{D}'_n\boldsymbol{\beta} + \boldsymbol{B}'_n\boldsymbol{\theta} + v_n, \quad n = 1, \ldots, N \tag{2.80}$$

Here, $\boldsymbol{\beta} = (\beta_1, \ldots, \beta_t, \ldots, \beta_T)'$ is the unknown time effect parameter, and $\boldsymbol{B}_n = (B_n^1, \ldots, B_n^j, \ldots, B_n^{J-1})'$ is the dummy variable corresponding to building age, defined as follows:

$$B_n^j = \begin{cases} 1 & j = \tau \quad \text{Building age at second transaction time} \\ -1 & j = \tau - (t - s) \quad \text{Building age at first transaction time} \\ 0 & \text{Other} \end{cases}$$

As well, $\boldsymbol{\theta} = (\theta_1, \ldots, \theta_j, \ldots, \theta_{J-1})'$ is the age dummy coefficient vector. For the building age dummy, in the case of new construction ($j = 0$), B_n^0 is removed, and in the case of the maximum building age value in the sample ($j = J$), B_n^J is removed. By dropping the time dummy for time 0 and removing B_n^0 and B_n^J, it is possible to avoid multicollinearity. According to Cannaday et al. (2005), the reason for this is that since, in general, building age $[0, J]$ has a broader range than the observation period $[0, T]$ in the data used, it may be considered that the degree of freedom lowering effect is less if the two building age dummies are dropped. Dropping the first and last building age dummies is equivalent to assuming that the price change rate is 0 in this sample range. Now, let us take the average value of the price change rate per year of building age as $\overline{\theta}$. However, since in general it may be considered that $\overline{\theta} < 0$, assuming that the price change rate is 0 for the interval between the first and second transactions $t - s$ means overestimating the price change rate average value $\overline{\theta}$, which leads as a result to underestimating the time effect. Therefore, for the time effect, it is necessary to perform upward correction for $-\overline{\theta}(t-s) > 0$ only, and for the age effect, it is necessary to perform downward correction for $\overline{\theta}(t-s) < 0$ only.

Taking the above into account, if we estimate $\widehat{\boldsymbol{\beta}}, \widehat{\boldsymbol{\theta}}$ from (2.80) with the method of least squares, using time s as the baseline year and time t as the comparison year, we can define an age-adjusted multivariate repeat sales price index (AAMRS price index) as follows when the building age for the baseline year is j:

$$I_{s,t,j}^{\mathrm{AAMRS}} = \frac{\exp[\widehat{\beta}_t - \overline{\theta}(t-s) + \theta_{j+(t-s)} + \overline{\theta}(t-s)]}{\exp(\widehat{\beta}_s + \theta_j)} = \exp(\widehat{\beta}_t - \widehat{\beta}_s + \theta_{j+(t-s)} - \theta_j) \quad (2.81)$$

Here, for the period $t-s$, the price change rate based on the time effect is $\widehat{\beta}_t - \widehat{\beta}_s$, and the price change rate based on the age effect is $\theta_{j+(t-s)} - \theta_j$. $\overline{\theta}$ is estimated as

$$\ln p^t = \text{const.} + \theta^t \tau_n^t + \text{error}_n, \quad n = 1, 2, \ldots, N(t)$$

for the sample in each period, and the average value of the change rate in relation to building age is obtained from $\overline{\theta} = \sum_t \theta^t / T$. Here, τ_n^t is the building age of property n at time t (2.81) adjusts the price change based on deterioration in addition to the time effect price change.

A price index in which building age is controlled as a constant (age-constant multivariate repeat sales price index, or ACMRS price index) can be obtained from the following:

$$I_{s,t,j}^{\mathrm{ACMRS}} = \exp(\widehat{\beta}_t - \widehat{\beta}_s - \overline{\theta} t) \quad (2.82)$$

In this paper, this will be referred to as a "pure time index."

When the two price indexes were estimated using four cities (Cleveland, Ohio; Miami, Florida; San Francisco, California; and Champaign, Illinois), the results varied for the AAMRS price index when the initial building age value was set as $j = 1$ and $j = 45$. Compared to the orthodox Case-Shiller price index, the price increase rate was smaller for the recently constructed building ($j = 1$) and the price increase rate was higher for the older building ($j = 45$). In other words, one can see that the price index is important even in terms of what should be the baseline building age level. As well, the ACMRS price index, which separates the age effect included in the orthodox Case-Shiller price index from the time effect and holds the age effect constant, showed that, as predicted with (2.78), three of the cities advanced at a higher level than with the Case-Shiller price index, and the further one gets from the baseline year, the greater the divergence becomes.

Knight et al. (1997) distinguished the time effect and age effect by refining Case and Quigley (1991)'s hybrid method (hedonic and repeat sales method joint model estimation). The hedonic regression model is recognized to be defined as follows:

$$y_n^t \equiv \ln p_n^t = \boldsymbol{z}_n'\gamma + \tau_n^t\theta + \boldsymbol{d}_n'\boldsymbol{\beta} + \varepsilon_n^t \quad (n = 1, 2, \ldots, N(t); t = 0, 1, \ldots, T) \quad (2.83)$$

Here, y_n^t is the logarithm of price p_n^t of property n at time t, z_n is the characteristic vector, τ_n^t is the building age of property n at time t, $\boldsymbol{d}_n$ is the time dummy variable, $(\gamma, \theta, \boldsymbol{\beta})$ is the unknown parameter that should be estimated, and ε_n^t is the error term. θ shows the age effect and $\boldsymbol{\beta}$ the time effect.

From sample $n = 1, \ldots, N(t)$, let us take N_R as a property that is transacted twice. When the building age of property n at the first transaction point s is $\tau - (t - s)$ and the building age at the second transaction point t is τ, the repeat sales regression model may be written as follows:

$$Y_n = A_n\theta + \boldsymbol{D}_n'\boldsymbol{\beta} + v_n \quad (n = 1, 2, \ldots, N_R) \tag{2.84}$$

Here, $A_n = \tau_n - \{\tau_n - (t - s)\}$ is the differential of the building age at time s and time t. If all samples $N + N_R$ for (2.83) and (2.84) are pooled, the following regression model is obtained:

$$\begin{pmatrix} \boldsymbol{y} \\ \boldsymbol{Y} \end{pmatrix} = \begin{pmatrix} z & \tau & \boldsymbol{d} \\ 0 & \boldsymbol{A} & \boldsymbol{D} \end{pmatrix} \begin{pmatrix} \gamma \\ \theta \\ \boldsymbol{\beta} \end{pmatrix} + \begin{pmatrix} \varepsilon \\ \boldsymbol{v} \end{pmatrix} \tag{2.85}$$

Case and Quigley (1991) estimated this with the generalized least squares (GLS) method, assuming the error terms for (2.66) and (2.67). However, Knight et al. (1997) perform the estimation using the maximum-likelihood method, assuming the AR1 process $\varepsilon_n^t = \rho\varepsilon_n^{t-1} + \nu_n^t$ for the hedonic regression model error term. Here, ρ is the autoregressive coefficient, and a time-homogeneous error term is assumed. If $\rho = 1$, the model is the random walk error term in Case and Shiller, but the parameters must be tested. A distinctive feature of this approach is that, by pooling a hedonic regression model and repeat sales regression model, it disrupts the linear relationship between $\boldsymbol{A}$ and $\boldsymbol{D}$ and makes it possible to estimate the age effect θ.

Knight et al. (1997) report that the age effect when hedonic regression model (2.83) is estimated using OLS or GLS and the age effect of the pooled joint model (2.85) are roughly the same value, the error term's autocorrelation coefficient is significant, and $\hat{\rho} = 0.54$. In the case of the repeat sales price index when (2.84) is estimated alone, since a negative age effect is included, it is estimated at a lower value than the hedonic price index when (2.83) is estimated alone. The price index based on the joint model (2.85) maximum-likelihood method progresses with a somewhat higher value than the hedonic price index. As well, it is shown that the estimator based on the serial correlation obtained with the maximum-likelihood method is also efficient in Monte Carlo testing.

For the repeat sales method, estimation is not workable unless some kind of hypothesis is included for the error term's heterogeneous variance based on factors other than age, but Knight et al. (1999) also performed Monte Carlo testing for the repeat sales regression model, assuming various heterogeneous variances and serial correlations, and showed that a model with an error term that assumes time-homogeneous serial correlation provides results that are preferable to a random walk.

2.3.4 *Sample Selection Bias*

2.3.4.1 Selection Bias Elimination

With a repeat sales index, since the price index is estimated using samples that are transacted repeatedly, it has been pointed out that sample selection bias likely exists. For example, Shimizu et al. (2010) used a hedonic index and repeat sales index to analyze the difference between the two indexes. The findings they obtained showed that when a hedonic index was estimated using only repeat sales samples, the extent to which price fluctuations lagged behind market turning points became greater as the number of repeat sales increased. They concluded that this suggests the existence of a structural sampling bias in repeat sales samples.

As a hypothesis for explaining whether or not housing will appear on the market as a good to be exchanged, the following condition may be considered: the seller's offer price must exceed his or her reservation price. Gatzlaff and Haurin (1997, 1998) verified that, if changes in the housing market's economic conditions influence the determination of offer prices and reservation prices, there is a possibility that housing samples that are actually sold are not random samples. In other words, actual observed transaction prices depend on the stochastic process that generates offer prices and reservation prices. With that in mind, selection bias is eliminated by applying a two-stage estimation method (Heckit method) based on Heckman (1979).

Since the transaction prices at the first and second sale times are observed as a paired data-set only if the seller's offer price exceeds his or her reservation price, the use of selected samples in analysis cannot be avoided. In Gatzlaff and Haurin (1997), correction of selection bias is performed by applying the Heckit method, using the simplest repeat sales regression model proposed by Bailey et al. (1963) as a base. In order for a property to be sold on the market, the seller's offer price has to exceed his or her reservation price, and a transaction price is observed only when that happens. Therefore, based on the fact that the conditional expected value for the closed hedonic price error distribution is not 0, selection bias occurs in the hedonic price.

In the hedonic regression model presented by Gatzlaff and Haurin (1998), selection bias elimination is performed using the method below. Taking the seller's reservation (logarithmic) price as y_n^{tR} and offer (logarithmic) price as y_n^{tO}, the following hedonic regression model may be written:

$$y_n^{tR} = z'_n\gamma^R + \boldsymbol{d}'_n\boldsymbol{\alpha} + \varepsilon_n^{tR}, \quad n = 1, \ldots, N; t = 0, 1, \ldots, T \tag{2.86}$$

$$y_n^{tO} = z'_n\gamma^O + \boldsymbol{d}'_n\boldsymbol{\alpha} + \varepsilon_n^{tO} \quad n = 1, \ldots, N; t = 0, 1, \ldots, T \tag{2.87}$$

Here, the average of the error terms $\varepsilon_n^{tR}, \varepsilon_n^{tO}$ is 0, and the variance/covariance matrix is:

$$\Sigma = \begin{pmatrix} \sigma_{RR} & \sigma_{RO} \\ \sigma_{RO} & \sigma_{OO} \end{pmatrix} \tag{2.88}$$

The actual transacted price y_n^t is observed only when the offer price exceeds the reservation price. In other words:

$$y_n^t = \begin{cases} y_n^{tO} & \text{if } y_n^{tO} - y_n^{tR} \geq 0 \\ \text{unobserved} & \text{if } y_n^{tO} - y_n^{tR} < 0 \end{cases} \tag{2.89}$$

Therefore, the transaction price expected value is:

$$E(y_n^t) = z_n'\gamma + \boldsymbol{d}_n'\boldsymbol{\alpha} + E(\varepsilon_n^{tO} \mid y_n^{tO} - y_n^{tR} \geq 0) \tag{2.90}$$

Since the error term expected value is not 0 and selection bias occurs, Heckman (1979)'s approach is used to correct this. That is, probit estimation is performed for the selection function that determines whether or not housing is put up for sale in the first step, and OLS estimation using an inverse Mills ratio is performed in the second step.

Gatzlaff and Haurin (1997) expanded the above model to the repeat sales regression method. Here, for time s, let us take $S_n^{s^*}$ as a latent variable that represents the choice of whether or not to put housing on sale, where the selection mechanism may be written with the following regression equation:

$$S_n^{s^*} = \boldsymbol{W}_n^{s\prime}\boldsymbol{\pi} + \varphi_n^s \tag{2.91}$$

Here, $\boldsymbol{W}_n^s$ is the characteristic vector including the seller's individual characteristics, housing characteristics, geographic environment, etc., $\boldsymbol{\pi}$ is the unknown parameter, and φ_n^s is the error term. The latent variable $S_n^{s^*}$ cannot actually be observed. For the first transaction, since the price is observed only when the offer price surpasses the reservation price—i.e., when $y_n^{1O} - y_n^{1R} \geq 0$ – this is taken as $S_n^1 = 1$. For the second transaction to be observed, the first transaction must actually occur. Therefore, the binary variable expressing this may be defined as follows:

$$S_n^2 - \begin{cases} 1 & \text{if } y_n^{1O} - y_n^{1R} \geq 0 \text{ and if } y_n^{2O} - y_n^{2R} \geq 0 \\ 0 & \text{if } y_n^{1O} - y_n^{1R} \geq 0 \text{ and if } y_n^{2O} - y_n^{2R} < 0 \\ \text{unobserved} & \text{if } y_n^{1O} - y_n^{1R} < 0 \end{cases} \tag{2.92}$$

Therefore, the first and second prices y_n^1, y_n^2 are observed if $S_n^2 = 1$ ($y_n^{1O} - y_n^{1R} \geq 0$ and $y_n^{2O} - y_n^{2R} \geq 0$) and cannot be observed in other cases. Taking the error terms of the selection function that determines the first and second sales as φ_n^1, φ_n^2 and the error terms of the hedonic regression models as ε_n^1, ε_n^2, the variance/covariance matrix may be defined as follows:

$$\Sigma = \begin{pmatrix} 1 & \sigma_{12} & \sigma_{13} & \sigma_{14} \\ \sigma_{12} & 1 & \sigma_{23} & \sigma_{24} \\ \sigma_{13} & \sigma_{23} & \sigma_{33} & \sigma_{34} \\ \sigma_{14} & \sigma_{24} & \sigma_{34} & \sigma_{44} \end{pmatrix} \tag{2.93}$$

Since both the first and second transaction prices y_n^1, y_n^2 are only observed when $S_n^1 = 1$ and $S_n^2 = 1$ are established simultaneously, the hedonic regression model error term expected values, based on the conditional expected values $E(y_n^1 \mid S_n^1 = 1$ and $S_n^2)$ and $E(y_n^2 \mid S_n^1 = 1$ and $S_n^2)$, are:

$$E(\varepsilon_n^1 \mid S_n^1 = 1 \text{ and } S_n^2) = \sigma_{13}\lambda_n^1 + \sigma_{23}\lambda_n^2$$
$$E(\varepsilon_n^2 \mid S_n^1 = 1 \text{ and } S_n^2) = \sigma_{14}\lambda_n^1 + \sigma_{24}\lambda_n^2$$

Here, λ_n^1, λ_n^2 are inverse Mills ratios. Therefore, the repeat sales regression model corrected for sample selection bias may be written as follows:

$$Y_n = \boldsymbol{D}_n'\boldsymbol{\alpha} + (\sigma_{14} - \sigma_{13})\lambda_n^1 + (\sigma_{24} - \sigma_{23})\lambda_n^2 + \eta_n, \quad n = 1, \ldots, N \tag{2.94}$$

Analysis by Gatzlaff and Haurin (1997) using Miami housing market data showed that a standard repeat sales price index has an upward bias compared to a price index estimated with (2.94).

2.3.4.2 Matching Estimation

Properties transacted multiple times are limited even for the housing market as a whole, and with the standard repeat sales method, data transacted only once is not used at all. Therefore, the problem of selection bias discussed in the previous section occurs, and the reduction in sample size also leads to a decrease in estimation efficiency.

McMillen (2012) proposes a price index estimation method using a matching approach to handle this problem. The time effect $\boldsymbol{\alpha}$ in the hedonic regression model corresponds to treatment effects in policy evaluation. As a simple example, the hedonic regression model in the case of the two times $t = 0, 1$ is written as follows:

$$\begin{aligned} y_n^t &= \alpha_0 + \alpha_1 d_n^1 + z_n'\gamma + \varepsilon_n^t \\ &= \alpha_0 + (\alpha_1 - \alpha_0)d_n^1 + z_n'\gamma + \varepsilon_n^t \quad n = 1, \ldots, N(t); t = 0, 1 \end{aligned} \tag{2.95}$$

Here, d_n^1 is a time dummy, where if $t = 1$, then $d_n^1 = 1$; otherwise, $d_n^1 = 0$. Taking the baseline point as $t = 0$, it is possible to measure the price change rate from d_n^1's coefficient estimation value. In the case of the repeat sales method, the price change rate can be obtained by regressing $y_n^2 - y_n^1$ on d_n^1. One can see that the repeat sales method price change rate observes the difference between a representative "post-treatment" value and representative "pre-treatment" value.

Apart from these methods, it is possible to measure the extent to which price changes occur with the average for the whole sample, using the project evaluation method. In other words, it is necessary to obtain the average treatment effect (ATE):

$$ATE = \frac{1}{N(1)} \sum_{n=1}^{N(1)} d_n^1 E(y_n^1 - y_n^0)$$

This shows that the average price change expected value for property transacted at the baseline time $t = 0$ and re-sold at time $t = 1$ is equivalent to ATE. Or, it shows the average difference in the pre-treatment and post-treatment values. To measure the price index with respect to $t = 1, 2, \ldots, T$, it is necessary to obtain the following:

$$ATE = \frac{1}{N(t)} \sum_{n=1}^{N(t)} d_n^t E(y_n^t - y_n^0), \quad t = 1, 2, \ldots, T \tag{2.96}$$

To approximate the ATE as the "treatment group average treatment effect," the data for all observation times must be randomly sampled data. In the case of data used with the repeat sales method, treatment group data may only be observed at the points when properties are actually sold. Therefore, it is necessary to match data corresponding to the baseline year $t = 0$ control group to $t = 1, 2, \ldots, T$ at each point in time. To perform matching, we first obtain a propensity score after performing logit regression of the time dummy on the characteristic variable used in the hedonic regression model. Next, we create the treatment group matching data for each time based on kernel matching (Heckman et al. 1998), and finally measure the price index by calculating (2.96).

McMillen (2012) estimated a price index using quarterly data from 1993 to 2008 (approximately 60 quarters) for single-family housing in Chicago. The data size is approximately 169,000 samples, of which 52,000 are repeat sales data transacted at least twice. The baseline point is Q1 1993, and the control group data consists of 1,651 samples. Due to the nature of repeat sales data, there are few samples at the initial observation time and even fewer samples at the final observation time. The number of matched samples, however, is roughly the same at each point. The total number of matched samples for the period from Q1 1993 to Q4 2008 is 102,000, which exceeds the repeat sales data. When price indexes were estimated based on the hedonic approach using the initial 169,000 samples and 102,000 matched samples, there was almost no difference between the two. In other words, when it comes to the matching estimator, this shows that a hedonic approach-based estimator is extremely robust.

The matching estimator clearly differs from the simple price change average. The price index based on the average value for each period using all 169,000 samples is easily influenced by values that are outliers from the distribution. In the case of Chicago, since the variation in the 2005 data is greater (in particular, the left side is flat) than that of the 1995 data, it is shown that the price index based on the average value for each time is pulled downward.

The repeat sales method of estimating price indexes could be called an extreme version of matching method-based estimation. Matching housing transaction data that is not necessarily identical but is similar has a number of advantages compared to price index estimation with either the repeat sales method or hedonic method. Compared to the standard repeat sales method, the general matching method dramatically increases the sample size and the likelihood of obtaining more efficient estimation values. For example, even in cases where there are few samples (small region, short observation period, etc.), it may make it possible to create a price index. This means that matching-based estimation could be a useful price index estimation method.

2.3.5 Characteristics, Advantages, and Disadvantages of Repeat Sales Indexes

This chapter has presented an overview of the repeat sales method and discussed it, with a focus on what kind of problems occur. Since the repeat sales method involves price comparison of the same property, if there is no change in characteristics or characteristic prices, the problem of underestimation bias that occurs with the hedonic method is eliminated. As well, since the estimation method is simple, it has the benefits of being an approach with high reproducibility and estimation efficiency.

In order to create a more stable price index, it is necessary to observe price data over an extended period. However, when the observation period becomes longer, aggregation bias occurs due to changes in characteristics and characteristic values for the same property.

Since the price of housing changes due to deterioration and investment in renovations (housing age effect), an age effect is included in the time effect in the standard repeat sales method. However, since a perfectly linear relationship exists between the time dummy and the variable indicating the transaction interval, it is not possible to distinguish the time effect and age effect in the standard method. What have been proposed to date are methods that intentionally disrupt the linear relationship between the time dummy and transaction interval variable and methods that extrapolate the price index using exogenous data.

As well, since only property transacted multiple times is selected for use with the repeat sales method, the sample size is reduced and the occurrence of selection bias in the sample is a concern. If changes in housing market economic conditions influence the determination of the offer price and reservation price, since the transactions at the times of the first and second sales are observed as a paired data-set only when the seller's offer price exceeds the reservation price, the use of selected samples in analysis cannot be avoided. In this case, the traditional method of correcting bias by estimating a selection function has been proposed.

Properties transacted multiple times are limited even for the housing market as a whole, and with the standard repeat sales method, data transacted only once is not used at all. It has been shown that the matching method is useful in improving this point. Using data transacted only once as re-sold data based on the matching method increases the sample size dramatically and the likelihood of obtained more efficient estimation values. This may, for example, make it possible to create a price index even in cases where there are few samples (small region, short observation period, etc.).

To summarize the above points, the advantages include:

- Since the index is created by comparing prices of repeatedly transacted properties at different points in time, there is no need for information relating to the property characteristics.
- The problem of omitted variable bias that occurs with the hedonic method is avoided.
- The estimation method is simple and there is a high level of reproducibility.
- Even in the case of strong heterogeneous property, the probability of estimating index is high.
- Due to simple concept, it is easy to explain to users.

The disadvantages include:

- Since the price index is estimated using only information for properties transacted at least twice (information for properties transacted only once is discarded), this method is inefficient. As a result, its use is difficult in countries or regions where liquidity is low, and it often becomes difficult to estimate indexes restricted to certain regions or property uses.
- Since the depreciation that accompanies the aging of the building between the two transaction times is ignored, there is a downward bias if this is not controlled for.
- If investment in renovations is made between the two transaction times, there is an upward bias if this is not controlled for.
- Depending on the database composition, it may be cost-intensive to identify transactions involving the same property (there are quite a few countries where it is difficult to identify transactions involving the same property).
- It is impossible to create separate indexes for land and buildings.
- When new transaction price information is generated, the data—including even past series—changes, so it is not possible to produce definite values.

2.4 Price Indexes Based on Property Appraisal Prices

2.4.1 Property Appraisal Price Indexes

If the property market has few transactions (i.e., it is thin) and property is strongly heterogeneous, price surveys are conducted by property appraisal experts. In addition, in the many countries with property taxes, there are quite a few that use property assessment values for the purpose of tax assessment.

Moreover, in recent years, with the dramatic growth in the property investment market, it has become possible to obtain property appraisal prices that are periodically surveyed for the purpose of measuring the performance of investment properties. In light of this, efforts have been made to create property prices indexes using property appraisal prices.

In particular, when attempting to capture the movements of markets that are strongly heterogeneous with few transactions, using property appraisal prices may be a valuable method of capturing changes.

However, it has been pointed out that there are valuation error, lagging, and smoothing problems surrounding property appraisal prices. The first problem occurs because property appraisal prices are determined based on the judgment of property appraisal experts, so there is a certain degree of error in the price determination absolute value. The second problem occurs because the information property appraisers are able to use in price determination is past information, so there is a certain lag in price determination. The final problem, which is related to the first and second problems, occurs because not only is there a strong possibility of misjudging market turning points, but changes also undergo smoothing, so price changes occur only gradually.

Furthermore, property appraisal systems differ by country, so there are cases where the definition of the price obtained by property appraisers also varies. Furthermore, assessed values for the purpose of tax assessment differ from normal property appraisal values, and since they are assessed values, there is an even stronger possibility that they do not properly capture market changes.

While property appraisal price information is a valuable information source for markets with few transactions, and the possibility of creating an index using this information exists, sufficient care must be taken with regard to its biases.

2.4.2 Hedonic Method Based on Pooling of Property Appraisal Prices And Transaction Prices

When attempting to estimate hedonic price indexes using transaction price information, one faces cases where index estimation is difficult due to a lack of such information. In addition, as mentioned previously, since valuation error and smoothing problems exist with property price information, it is known to have certain biases. In order to control for these biases and compensate for insufficient transaction price information, the following has been proposed: attempting to estimate price indexes by pooling property appraisal price information and transaction price information, then using the hedonic method.

Since assessed values obtained for tax purposes incorporate various factors that are likely included in transaction price information, they are helpful in explaining transaction prices. The regression equation using assessed values is written as follows:

$$\ln p_n^t = \alpha_t + \varsigma \ln a_n^t + \varepsilon_n^t \tag{2.97}$$

Here, p_n^t is the transaction price and a_n^t is the assessed value. Note that there is no guarantee that the true property market value can be assessed correctly, so there is always an error in the assessed value. For example, taking the true property market value as V_n^t, the assessed value a_n^t may be an observation value accompanied by a probability error, as follows:

$$\ln a_n^t = \ln V_n^t + \eta_n^t \tag{2.98}$$

In other words, the assessed value is the true property market value with the probability error η_n^t added to it. If the assessed value in (2.97) is taken as a proxy for the true property market value, since $\ln V_n^t = \ln a_n^t - \eta_n^t$ based on (2.98), (2.97) may be rewritten as follows:

$$\ln p_n^t = \alpha_t + \varsigma(\ln a_n^t - \eta_n^t) + \varepsilon_n^t = \alpha_t + \varsigma \ln a_n^t + (\varepsilon_n^t - \varsigma\eta_n^t) \tag{2.99}$$

Since the explanatory variable $\ln a_n^t$ is clearly correlated to the error term, the coefficient's least-squares estimator has a bias.

This estimation method is currently being researched and developed by the European Central Bank with the aim of applying it in practice.

2.4.3 *The SPAR Method*

Since there is also a lack of price information for properties transacted multiple times when estimating repeat sales indexes, one may be faced with the problem of being unable to estimate the price index. In light of this, along with the method of artificially increasing the number of repeat sales using the previously mentioned matching method, an estimation method known as the SPAR (sale price appraisal ratio) method, which obtains the first transaction price with the property appraisal price, has been proposed and applied in practice.

The sale price of property n at comparison point t is taken as p_n^t $(n = 1, 2, \ldots, N(t))$. In addition, the appraisal price of said property at the baseline point 0 is taken as $(n = 1, 2, \ldots, N(0))$. In this case, the sale-appraisal price ratio is p_n^t/a_n^0. If all quantities are standardized as 1, the appraisal price-based arithmetic average price index may be defined as follows:

$$P_{AP}^{0t} = \frac{\sum_{n=1}^{N(t)} p_n^t}{\sum_{n=1}^{N(t)} a_n^0} = \sum_{n=1}^{N(t)} w_n^0(t) \left(\frac{p_n^t}{a_n^0}\right) \tag{2.100}$$

Here, $w_n^0(t)$ in the second formula on the right side of (2.100) is the weight based on the appraisal price, and $w_n^0(t) = a_n^0/\sum_{n=1}^{N(t)} a_n^0$.. Since this weight is defined by the quantity (standardized as 1) of sample $N(t)$ at the comparison point, $w_n^0(t)$ is the expenditure weight calculated with the baseline point price and comparison point quantity. Therefore, since (2.100) is the weighted average based on $w_n^0(t)$ in the sale-appraisal price ratio p_n^t/a_n^0, one can see that it is a Paasche-type index. Note that in general, the baseline point sample size $N(0)$ and comparison point sample size $N(t)$ are not equivalent.

The problem with (2.100) is that it takes the appraisal value as the baseline point price. Since the sale price is not used, the price index is not 1 at the baseline point. The arithmetic average sales price appraisal ratio method (arithmetic method) index overcomes this problem by dividing by the baseline point sale-appraisal price ratio, as follows:

$$P_{SPAR}^{0t} = \frac{\sum_{n=1}^{N(t)} p_n^t}{\sum_{n=1}^{N(t)} a_n^0} \left(\frac{\sum_{n=1}^{N(0)} p_n^0}{\sum_{n=1}^{N(0)} a_n^0} \right)^{-1} = \frac{\sum_{n=1}^{N(t)} p_n^t / N(t)}{\sum_{n=1}^{N(0)} p_n^0 / N(0)} \left(\frac{\sum_{n=1}^{N(0)} a_n^0 / N(0)}{\sum_{n=1}^{N(t)} a_n^0 / N(t)} \right) \tag{2.101}$$

Equation (2.101) is a reciprocal multiplication of the sale price arithmetic average ratio and appraisal price arithmetic average ratio. The reciprocal of the appraisal price arithmetic average plays a role in adjusting structural changes that occur from the baseline point to the comparison point.

2.4.4 Characteristics, Advantages, and Disadvantages of Property Appraisal Price Indexes

Property appraisal price information is, needless to say, an extremely important source of information in the estimation of property price indexes. In particular, in regions where there are few transactions and markets which are strongly heterogeneous, such as the logistics facility, hotel, or hospital markets, there are quite a few cases where one has to rely on property appraisal price information.

In light of this, not only are there price indexes that make direct use of property appraisal prices, but many inventive approaches have also been developed, such as methods like the SPAR method that correct the repeat sales method by using property appraisal prices and methods that perform estimation by combining property appraisal prices and transaction prices in hedonic method estimation. Their respective advantages and disadvantages are outlined below. First, the SPAR method's advantages include:

- It preserves the advantages of the repeat sales method.
- Since it enables the use of more information than the repeat sales method, it is highly efficient.
- Since it is a method based on traditional index theory, it is easy to understand, and the estimation method is simple, it has a high level of reproducibility.

Its disadvantages include:

- It inherits the disadvantages of the repeat sales method.
- Since the initial transaction is obtained with the property appraisal price, it is affected by the valuation error and smoothing problems with property appraisal prices.
- The quality adjustment issues surrounding property price indexes.

In the case of estimation using property appraisal price information and transaction price information with the hedonic method, while it artificially increases the number of samples and increases the efficiency when estimating the hedonic function, numerous problems remain in terms of estimation theory, such as how to set the probability that transactions will occur.

2.5 Summary and Conclusion

How should property price indexes be estimated? When estimating a property price index, the estimation method varies considerably based on the limitations of available information. If no such limitations exist, the hedonic method has an advantage when one considers the underlying economic theory, the consistency with other types of economic statistics, its application in the System of National Accounts, and so forth. However, in reality, while it may be viable for the housing market, where the transaction quantity is relatively large and quality is relatively high, or even for the office market when it comes to commercial property, in markets that are strongly heterogeneous, there are quite a few cases where it is difficult to apply the hedonic method.

The repeat sales method is effective when there is a sufficient quantity of transactions, even if the market is strongly heterogeneous. However, in markets where the number of transactions is limited, application of the repeat sales method is also difficult.

In such cases, it may be possible to create indexes using property appraisal price information. There are various possibilities, such as the SPAR method, estimation based on the hedonic method using property appraisal prices and transaction prices, and appraisal price indexes that use property appraisal prices as is.

However, when there are few transactions, one faces the problem of how property appraisers determine property appraisal prices and, in light of that, how reliable the determined property appraisal prices are.

Furthermore, in cases where there is a lack of property transaction price information, there is further scope to consider creating indexes using property revenue information and so on.

Going forward, in an attempt to properly capture property market trends, it is likely that multiple indexes will be created by combining various sources of information with appropriate estimation methods for those sources.

References

Anglin, P.M., and R. Gencay. 1996. Semiparametric estimation of hedonic price function. *Journal of Applied Econometrics* 11 (6): 633–648.

Bailey, M.J., R.F. Muth, and H.O. Nourse. 1963. A regression model for real estate price index construction. *Journal of American Statistical Association* 58: 933–942.

Barten, A.P. 1964. Consumer demand functions under conditions of almost additive preferences. *Econometrica* 32 (1/2): 1–38.

Berndt, E.R., Z. Griliches, and N.J. Rappaport. 1995. Econometric estimates of price indexes for personal computers in the 1990s? *Journal of Econometrics* 68: 243–268.

Box, G.E.P., and D.R. Cox. 1964. Ananalysis of transformations. *Journal of the Royal Statistical Society SeriesB (Methodological)* 26 (2): 211–252.

Brown, J.N., and H.S. Rosen. 1982. On the estimation of structural hedonic price models. *Econometrica* 50 (3): 765–768.

Cannaday, R.E., H.J. Munneke, and T.T. Yang. 2005. A multivariate repeat-sales model for estimating house price indices. *Journal of Urban Economics* 57 (2): 320–342.

Case, B., and J.M. Quigley. 1991. The dynamics of real estate prices. *Review of Economics and Statistics* 73 (1): 50–58.

Case, K.E., and R.J. Shiller. 1987. Prices of Single Family Homes Since 1970: New Indexes for Four cities. In *New England Economic Review*, vol. (Sept./Oct.), 45–56.

Case, K.E., and R.J. Shiller. 1989. The effciency of the market for single-family homes. *The American Economic review* 79 (1): 125–137.

Case, B., H.O. Pollakowski, and S.M. Wachter. 1991. On choosing among house price index methodologies. *Real Estate Economics* 19 (3): 286–307.

Cassel, E., and R. Mendelsohn. 1985. The choice of functional forms for hedonic price equations: comment. *Journal of Urban Economics* 18 (2): 135–142.

Chau, K.W., S.K. Wong, and C.U. Yiu. 2005. Adjusting for non-linear age effects in the repeat sales index. *Journal of Real Estate Finance and Economics* 31 (2): 137–153.

Clayton, J., D. Geltner, and S.W. Hamilton. 2001. Smoothing in commercial property valuations: evidence from individual appraisals. *Real Estate Economics* 29 (3): 337–360.

Court, A.T. 1939. Hedonic Price Indexes with Automotive Examples. In *The Dynamics of Automobile Demand*. New York: General Motors.

Cropper, M.L., L.B. Deck, and K.E. McConnell. 1988. On the choice of functional form for hedonic price functions. *The Review of Economics and Statistics* 70 (4): 668–675.

de Haan, J. 2004. Direct and indirect time dummy approaches to hedonic price measurement. *Journal of Economic and Social Measurement* 29 (4): 427–443.

de Haan, J. 2010. Hedonic price indexes: a comparison of imputation, time dummy and re-pricing methods. *Jahrbücher für Nationalökonomie und Statistik* 230 (6): 772–791.

Devaney, S., and R.M. Diaz. 2010. *Transaction Based Indices for the UK Commercial Property Market: Exploration and Evaluation Using IPD Data*, Discussion Paper 2010-02. 1–19. University of Aberdeen Buisiness school.

Diamond Jr., D., and B.A. Smith. 1985. Simultaneity in the market for housing characteristics. *Journal of Urban Economics* 17 (3): 280–292.

Diewert, W.E., S. Heravi, and M. Silver. 2007. *Hedonic Imputation Versus Time Dummy Hedonic Indexes*, 1–29. Discussion Paper 007–07, Department of Economics, University of British Columbia

Diewert, W.E. 1971. An application of the Shepherd duality theorem: a generalized leontief production function. *Journal of Political Economy* 79 (3): 481–507.

Diewert, W.E. 1973. Functional forms for profit and transformation functions. *Journal of Economic Theory* 6 (3): 284–316.

Diewert, W.E. 1976. Exact and superlative index numbers. *Journal of Econometrics* 4 (2): 114–145.

Diewert, W.E. 1983. The Theory of the Output Price Index and the Measurement of Real Output Change. In *Price Level Measurement*, ed. W.E. Diewert, and C. Montmarquette, 1049–1113. Ottawa: Statistics Canada.

Diewert, W.E. 1997. Commentary on Mathew D. Shapiro and David W. Wilcox: Alternative Strategies for Aggregating Price in the CPI. The Federal Reserve Bank of St. Louis Review, Vol. 79, no. 3, pp. 127–137.

Diewert, W.E. 2002. *Hedonic Producer Price Indexes and Quality Adjustment*, Discussion Paper 02–14, 1–11. Department of Economics: University of British Columbia.

Diewert, W.E. 2003. *Hedonic Regressions: A Review of Some Unresolved Issues*. Mimeo: Department of Economics, University of British Colombia.

Diewert, W.E. 2007. *The Paris OECD-IMF Workshop on Real Estate Price Indexes: Conclusions and Future Directions*, Discussion Paper 07-01. University of British Columbia.

Dulberger, E.R. 1989. The Application of a Hedonic Model to a Quality-Adjusted Price Index for Computer Processors. In *Technology and Capital Formation*, ed. D.W. Jorgenson, and R. Landau, 37–75. Cambridge, MA: MIT Press.

Ekeland, I., J.J. Heckman, and L. Nesheim. 2004. Identification and estimation of hedonic models. *Journal of Political Economy* 112 (S1): S60–S109.

Eurostat. 2013. Handbook on Residential Property Price Indices (RPPIs). Methodologies and Working papers, 2013 edn.

Gatzlaff, D.H., and D.R. Haurin. 1997. Sample selection bias and repeat-sales index estimates. *Journal of Real Estate Finance and Economics* 14 (1/2): 33–50.

Gatzlaff, D.H., and D.R. Haurin. 1998. Sample selection and biases in local house value indices. *Journal of Urban Economics* 43 (2): 199–222.

Griliches, Z. 1961. Hedonic Price Indexes for Automobiles: An Econometric Analysis of Quality Change. In *The Price Statistics of the Federal Government*, ed. G. Stigler (chairman). Washington D.C.: Government Printing Office.

Griliches, Z. 1967. Hedonic price indexes revisited: a note on the state of the art. *Proceedings of the Business and Economics Section of the American Statistical Association* 332–334.

Griliches, Z. 1971. Introduction: Hedonic Price Indexes Revisited. In *Price Indexes and Quality Change*, ed. Z. Griliches, 3–15. Cambridge MA: Harvard University Press.

Halvorsen, R., and H.O. Pollakowski. 1981. Choice of functional form for hedonic price equations. *Journal of Urban Economics* 10 (1): 37–49.

Heckman, J.J., H. Ichimura, and P. Todd. 1998. Matching as an econometric evaluation estimator. *Review of Economic Studies* 65 (2): 261–294.

Heckman, J.J., R.L. Matzkin, and L. Nesheim. 2010. Nonparametric identification and estimation of nonadditive hedonic models. *Econometrica* 78 (5): 1569–1591.

Heckman, J.J. 1979. Sample selection bias as a specification error. *Econometrica* 47 (1): 153–161.

Hill, R.C., J.R. Knight, and C.F. Sirmans. 1993. Estimation of hedonic housing price models using non sample information: a montecarlo study. *Journal of Urban Economics* 34 (3): 319–346.

Knight, J.R., J. Dombrow, and C.F. Sirmans. 1997. Aggregation bias in repeat-sales indices. *Journal of Real Estate Finance and Economics* 14 (1/2): 75–88.

Knight, J.R., R.C. Hill, and C.F. Sirmans. 1999. A random walk down main street? *Regional Science and Urban Economics* 29 (1): 89–103.

Lancaster, K.J. 1966. A new approach to consumer theory. *Journal of Political Economy* 74 (2): 132–157.

Linneman, P. 1980. Some empirical results on the nature of the hedonic price function for the urban housing market. *Journal of Urban Economics* 8 (1): 47–68.

Malpezzi, S. 2003. Hedonic Pricing Models: A Selective and Applied Review. In *Housing Economics: Essays in Honor of Duncan Maclennan*, ed. A. O'Sullivan, and K. Gibb, 67–89. Malder, MA: Blackwell.

McMillen, D.P. 2003. The return of centralization to chicago: using repeat sales to identify changes in house price distance gradients. *Regional Science and Urban Economics* 33 (3): 287–304.

McMillen, D.P. 2012. Repeat sales as a matching estimator. *Real Estate Economics* 40 (4): 745–773.

Mendelsohn, R. 1985. Identifying structural equations with single market data. *The Review of Economics and Statistics* 67 (3): 525–529.
Pace, R.K. 1995. Parametric, semiparametric, and nonparametric estimation of characteristic values with in mass assessment and hedonic pricing models. *Journal of Real Estate Finance and Economics* 11 (3): 195–217.
Pace, R.K. 1998. Appraisal using generalized additive models. *Journal of Real Estate Research* 15 (1): 77–99.
Palmquist, R.B. 1979. Hedonic price depreciation indexes for residential housing: a comment. *Journal of Urban Economics* 6 (2): 267–271.
Rosen, S. 1974. Hedonic prices and implicit markets: product differentiation in pure competition. *Journal of Political Economy* 82 (1): 34–55.
Sheppard, S. 1999. Hedonic Analysis of Housing Markets. In *In Handbook of Regional and Urban Economics*, vol. 3, ed. P.C. Cheshire, and E.S. Mills, 1595–1635. Chap. 41.
Shimizu, Chihiro., and Karato, Koji. 2007. *Econometric Analysis of the Property Market (Fudosan Shijo no Keiryokeizai Bunseki)*. Asakura Publishing.
Shimizu, C., K.G. Nishimura, and T. Watanabe. 2010. House prices in Tokyo -a comparison of repeat-sales and hedonic measures-. *Journal of Economics and Statistics* 230 (6): 792–813.
Silver, M., and S. Heravi. 2007. The difference hedonic imputation indexes and time dummy hedonic indexes. *Journal of Business and Economic Statistics* 25 (2): 239–246.
Sirmans, C.F., R.C. Hill, and J.R. Knight. 1997. Estimating capital asset price indexes. *The Review of Economics and Statistics* 79 (2): 226–233.
Witte, A.D., H. Sumka, and J. Erekson. 1979. An estimate of a structural hedonic price model of the housing market: an application of rosen's theory of implicit markets. *Econometrica* 47: 1151–72.

Part II
Empirical Studies for Property Price Indexes

Chapter 3
A Comparison of Alternative Approaches to Measuring House Price Inflation

3.1 Introduction

This paper has two main purposes:

- Some real estate data for sales of detached houses in the Dutch town of "A" is used in order to construct house price indexes using a variety of methods. A main purpose of the paper is to determine whether the different methods generate different empirical results. The data cover 14 quarters of sales, beginning in 2005 and ending in the middle of 2008.
- The second main purpose is to determine whether it is possible to decompose an overall house price index into reliable Land and Structures components. This decomposition is required for some national income accounting purposes, as well as being of general interest.

With respect to the second main purpose, the present paper is a follow up on Diewert et al. (2010). Those authors used a hedonic regression approach to decompose an overall house price index into land and structures components. Their decomposition method relied on the imposition of monotonicity restrictions on the prices of the two components and their approach worked satisfactorily because during the time period they studied, house prices in the Dutch town of "A" only rise. However, during the time period used in the present paper, house prices in the town of "A" both rise and fall and thus the methodology used by Diewert, Haan and Hendriks needs to be modified in order to deal with this problem.

With respect to the comparison of methods purpose, *four main classes of methods* for constructing house price indexes for *sales* of properties will be considered:

The base of this chapter is Diewert, W.E. 2010. Alternative approaches to measuring house price inflation. Discussion Paper 10-10, Department of Economics, University of British Columbia, Vancouver, Canada.

W. E. Diewert et al., *Property Price Index*, Advances in Japanese Business and Economics 11, https://doi.org/10.1007/978-4-431-55942-9_3

- *Stratification methods*; i.e., sales of houses during a period are segmented into relatively homogeneous classes and normal index number theory is applied to the cell data;
- *Time dummy hedonic regression methods*;
- *Hedonic regression imputation methods*;
- *Additive hedonic regression methods* with the imposition of period to period monotonicity restrictions to smooth the estimates for the land and structure components of the overall index.

The last three classes of methods are all variants of hedonic regressions.[1] The additive method is a variant of the method that was used by Diewert et al. (2010). All four classes of methods can be given theoretical justifications so it is of some interest to see how different or similar they are when implemented on the same data set.

A brief outline of the contents of each section follows.

In Sect. 3.2, *stratification methods* are explained along with our data on real estate transactions for the small Dutch town of "A" over a 14 quarter period. This same data set will be used to illustrate how all of the various methods for constructing house price indexes work in practice.

The results from Sect. 3.2 indicate that prices may follow a *seasonal* pattern of decline in the fourth quarter of each year. Solutions to this seasonality problem are explained in Sect. 3.3.

In Sects. 3.4 and 3.5, standard hedonic regressions are implemented on the data set. There are three main characteristics of a detached house that sold in a quarter that are used in the hedonic regression: the age A of the house, its structure floor space area S and the land area of the plot L. The use of just these three characteristics leads to a hedonic regression that explain 84 to 89% of the variation in selling prices. In Sect. 3.4, the dependent variable is the logarithm of the selling price while in Sect. 3.5, we study hedonic regressions that use just the selling price as the dependent variable. The regressions in these two sections use the *time dummy methodology*.

In Sect. 3.6, the time dummy methodology is not used. Instead, a separate hedonic regression for the data of each quarter is estimated and then these regressions are used to create imputed prices for the various "models" of houses that transacted so that a matched model methodology can be applied. This class of methods for constructing a house price index is based on what is called the *hedonic imputation methodology*. This method turns out to be our preferred method for constructing an overall house price index.

In Sect. 3.7, we turn our attention to the problem of constructing *separate price indexes for land and for structures*. There is a multicollinearity problem between structure size and land plot size: large structures tend to be associated with large plots. This multicollinearity problem shows up in this section, where none of the straightforward methods suggested work. Thus in the next two sections, restrictions are imposed upon the hedonic regressions. In Sect. 3.8, the price of constant quality

[1]The difference between time dummy and imputation hedonic regressions has been theoretically analysed by Diewert et al. (2009), de Hann (2009, 2010).

structures is forced to be nondecreasing while in Sect. 3.9, the price movements in constant quality structure prices are forced to follow the movements in an exogenous index of new dwelling construction costs. Both methods seem to work reasonably well but the results they generate are somewhat inconsistent.

A problem with many hedonic regression models is that historical results will generally change as new data become available. This problem is addressed by applying a *rolling window hedonic regression methodology* that is a generalization of the usual adjacent period time dummy hedonic regression methodology. This methodology is explained and illustrated in Sect. 3.10.

Finally, in Sect. 3.11, we show how the hedonic regression models for the *sales* of properties developed in Sects. 3.6 and 3.9 can be adapted to generate indexes for the *stock* of housing properties.

Section 3.12 offers some tentative conclusions.

3.2 Stratification Methods

A dwelling unit has a number of important *price determining characteristics*:

- The *land area* L of the property;
- The *floor space area* S of the structure; i.e., the size of the structure that sits on the land underneath and surrounding the structure;
- The *age* A of the structure, since this determines (on average) how much physical deterioration or depreciation the structure has experienced;
- The amount of *renovations* that have been undertaken for the structure;
- The *location* of the structure; i.e., its distance from amenities such as shopping centers, schools, restaurants and work place locations;
- The *type of structure*; i.e., single detached dwelling unit, row housing, low rise apartment or high rise apartment or condominium;
- The *type of construction* used to build the structure;
- Any *other special price determining characteristics* that are different from "average" dwelling units in the same general location such as swimming pools, air conditioning, elaborate landscaping, the height of the structure or views of oceans or rivers.

The data used in this study consist of observations on quarterly sales of detached houses for a small town (the population is around 60,000) in the Netherlands, town "A", for 14 quarters, starting in the first quarter of 2005 and ending in the second quarter of 2008. The variables used in this study can be described as follows[2]:

[2]Houses which were older than 50 years at the time of sale were deleted from the data set. Two observations which had unusually low selling prices (36,000 and 40,000 Euros) were deleted as were 28 observations which had land areas greater than 1200m^2. No other outliers were deleted from the sample.

- p_n^t is the selling price of property n in quarter t in Euros where $t = 1, ..., 14$;
- L_n^t is the area of the plot for the sale of property n in quarter t in meters squared;
- S_n^t is the living space area of the structure for the sale of property n in quarter t in meters squared;
- A_n^t is the (approximate) age (in decades) of the structure on property n in quarter t.

The values of the fourth variable listed above are determined as follows. The original data were coded as follows: if the structure was built in 1960–1970, the observation was assigned the decade indicator variable $BP = 5$; 1971–1980, $BP = 6$; 1981–1990, $BP = 7$; 1991–2000, $BP = 8$; 2001–2008, $BP = 9$. The age variable A in this study was set equal to $9 - BP$. For a recently built structure n in quarter t, $A_n^t = 0$. Thus the age variable gives the (approximate) age of the structure in decades.

It can be seen that not all of the price determining characteristics of the dwelling unit were used in the present study. In particular, the last five sets of price determining characteristics of the property listed above were neglected. Thus there is an implicit assumption that quarter to quarter changes in the amount of renovations that have been undertaken for the structures sold, the location of the structures, the type of structure, the type of construction used to build the structures and any other special price determining characteristics of the properties sold in the quarter did not change enough to be a significant determinant of the average price for the properties sold once changes in land size, structure size and the age of the structures were taken into account. To support this assumption, it should be noted that the hedonic regression models to be discussed later in the paper consistently explained 80–90% of the variation in the price data using just the three main explanatory variables: L, S and A.[3]

As mentioned above, there were 2289 observations on detached house sales for city "A" over the 14 quarters in the sample. Thus there was an average of 163.5 sales of detached dwelling units in each quarter. The overall sample mean selling price was 190,130 Euros, while the corresponding median price was 167,500 Euros. The average lot or plot size was $257.6\,\text{m}^2$ and the average size of structure was $127.2\,\text{m}^2$. The average age of the properties sold was approximately 18.5 years old.

The *stratification approach* to the construction of a house price index is conceptually very simple: for each important price explaining characteristic, divide up the sales into relatively homogeneous groups. Thus in the present case, sales were classified into 45 groups or cells consisting of 3 groupings for the land area L, 3 groupings for the structure area S and 5 groups for the age A (in decades) of the structure that was sold ($3 \times 3 \times 5 = 45$ separate cells). Once quarterly sales were classified into the 45 groupings of sales, the sales within each cell in each quarter were summed and then divided by the number of units sold in that cell in order to obtain unit value

[3]The R^2 between the actual and predicted selling prices ranged from 0.83 to 0.89. The fact that it was not necessary to introduce more price determining characteristics for this particular data set can perhaps be explained by the nature of the location of the town of "A" on a flat, featureless plain and the relatively small size of the town; i.e., location was not a big price determining factor since all locations have basically the same access to amenities.

prices. These unit value prices were then combined with the number of units sold in each cell to form the usual p's and q's that can be inserted into a bilateral index number formula, like the Laspeyres (1871), Paasche (1874) and Fisher (1922) ideal formulae,[4] yielding a stratified index of house prices of each of these types.[5]

How should the size limits for the L and S groupings be chosen? One approach would be to divide the range of L and S by three and then create three equal size cells. However, this approach leads to a very large number of observations in the middle cells. Thus in the present study, size limits were chosen so that roughly 50% of the observations would fall into the middle sized categories and roughly 25% would fall into the small and large categories. For the land size variable L, the cutoff points chosen were $160\,\mathrm{m}^2$ and $300\,\mathrm{m}^2$, while for the structure size variable S, the cutoff points chosen were $110\,\mathrm{m}^2$ and $140\,\mathrm{m}^2$. Thus if $L < 160\,\mathrm{m}^2$, then the observation fell into the small land size cell; if $160\,\mathrm{m}^2 \leq L < 300\,\mathrm{m}^2$, then the observation fell into the medium land size cell and if $300\,\mathrm{m}^2 \leq L$, then the observation fell into the large land size cell. The resulting sample probabilities for falling into these three L cells over the 14 quarters were 0.24, 0.51 and 0.25 respectively. Similarly, if $S < 110\,\mathrm{m}^2$, then the observation fell into the small structure size cell; if $110\,\mathrm{m}^2 \leq S < 140\,\mathrm{m}^2$, then the observation fell into the medium structure size cell and if $140\,\mathrm{m}^2 \leq S$, then the observation fell into the large structure size cell. The resulting sample probabilities for falling into these three S cells over the 14 quarters were 0.21, 0.52 and 0.27 respectively.

The data that were used did not have an exact age for the structure; only the decade when the structure was built was recorded. Thus there was no possibility of choosing exact cutoff points for the age of the structure. For the first age group, $A = 0$ corresponds to a house that was built during the years 2001–2008; $A = 1$ for houses built during the years 1991–2000; $A = 2$ for houses build in 1981–1990, $A = 3$ for houses built in 1971–1980; and $A = 4$ for houses built in 1961–1970. The resulting sample probabilities for falling into these five cells over the 14 quarters were 0.15, 0.32, 0.21, 0.20 and 0.13 respectively. See Table 3.1 for the sample joint probabilities of a house sale belonging to each of the 45 cells.

There are several points of interest to note about the above table:

- There were no observations for houses built during the 1960s (the $A = 4$ class) which had a small lot ($L =$ small) and a large structure ($S =$ large), so this cell is entirely empty;

[4]The various international manuals on price measurement recommend this unit value approach to the construction of price indexes at the first stage of aggregation; see ILO et al. (2004), IMF et al. (2004, 2009). However, the unit value aggregation is supposed to take place over homogeneous items and this assumption may not be fulfilled in the present context, since there is a fair amount of variability in L, S and A within each cell. But since there are only a small number of observations in each cell for the data set under consideration, it would be difficult to introduce more cells to improve homogeneity since this would lead to an increased number of empty cells and a lack of matching for the cells.

[5]However, since there are only 163 or so observations for each quarter and 45 cells to fill, it can be seen that each cell will have only an average of 3 or so observations in each quarter, and some cells were empty for some quarters. This problem will be addressed subsequently.

Table 3.1 Sample probability of a sale in each stratified cell

		$A = 0$	$A = 1$	$A = 2$	$A = 3$	$A = 4$
$L =$ small	$S =$ small	0.00437	0.02665	0.01660	0.02053	0.02097
$L =$ medium	$S =$ small	0.00349	0.02840	0.01966	0.01092	0.03888
$L =$ large	$S =$ small	0.00087	0.00175	0.00044	0.00218	0.00612
$L =$ small	$S =$ medium	0.01223	0.05242	0.04281	0.02053	0.00699
$L =$ medium	$S =$ medium	0.03277	0.09262	0.08869	0.07907	0.02141
$L =$ large	$S =$ medium	0.00786	0.02315	0.01005	0.01442	0.01398
$L =$ small	$S =$ large	0.00306	0.00218	0.00175	0.00568	0.00000
$L =$ medium	$S =$ large	0.03145	0.03495	0.00786	0.02097	0.00306
$L =$ large	$S =$ large	0.04893	0.05461	0.02315	0.02490	0.01660

- There are many cells which are almost empty; in particular the probability of a sale of a large plot with a small house is very low as is the probability of a sale of a small plot with a large house[6];
- The most *representative model* that is sold over the sample period corresponds to a medium sized lot, a medium sized structure and a house that was built in the 1990s (the $A = 1$ category). The sample probability of a house sale falling into this cell is 0.09262, which is the highest probability cell.

The average selling price of a house that falls into the medium L, medium S and $A = 1$ category is graphed in Fig. 3.1 along with the mean and median price of a sale in each quarter. These average prices have been converted into indexes which start at 1 for quarter 1, which is the first quarter of 2005. It should be noted that these three house price indexes are rather variable!

Two additional indexes are plotted in Fig. 3.1: a fixed base matched model Fisher ideal index and a chained matched model Fisher ideal price index. It is necessary to explain what a matched model index in this context means. If at least one house sold in each quarter for each of the 45 classes of transaction, then the ordinary *Laspeyres*, *Paasche* and *Fisher* price indexes, $P_L(s,t)$, $P_P(s,t)$ and $P_F(s,t)$, that compared the data in quarter s (in the denominator) to the data in quarter t (in the numerator) would be defined as follows:

$$P_L(s,t) \equiv \frac{\sum_{n=1}^{45} p_n^t q_n^s}{\sum_{n=1}^{45} p_n^s q_n^s}; \tag{3.1}$$

$$P_P(s,t) \equiv \frac{\sum_{n=1}^{45} p_n^t q_n^t}{\sum_{n=1}^{45} p_n^s q_n^t}; \tag{3.2}$$

$$P_F(s,t) \equiv [P_L(s,t)P_P(s,t)]^{1/2} \tag{3.3}$$

[6]Thus lot size and structure size are positively correlated with a correlation coefficient of 0.6459. Both L and S are fairly highly correlated with the selling price variable P: the correlation between P and L is 0.8234 and between P and S is 0.8100. These high correlations lead to some multicollinearity problems in the hedonic regression models to be considered later.

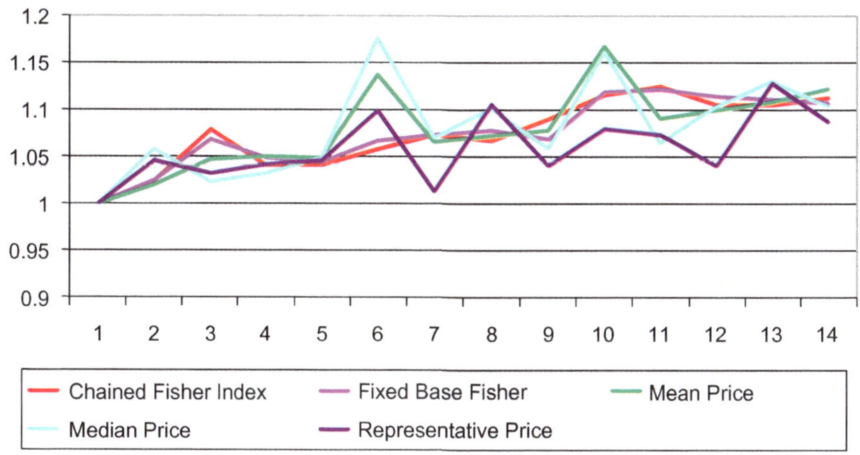

Fig. 3.1 Fisher matched model stratification and various summary statistic indexes

where q_n^t is the *number of properties transacted* in quarter t in cell n and p_n^t is defined as the sum of the *values* for all properties transacted in quarter t in cell n divided by q_n^t and thus p_n^t is the *unit value price* for all properties transacted in cell n during quarter t for $t = 1, \ldots, 14$ and $n = 1, \ldots, 45$.

The above algebra is applicable to the case where there are transactions in all cells for the two quarters being compared. But for the present data set, on average only about 30 out of the 45 cell categories can be matched across any two quarters, s and t. The above formulae (3.1)–(3.3) need to be modified to deal with this lack of matching problem. Thus when considering how to form an index number comparison between quarters s and t, define *the set of cells n that have at least one transaction in each of quarters s and t* as the set $S(s,t)$. Then the *matched model counterparts*, $P_{\text{ML}}(s,t)$, $P_{\text{MP}}(s,t)$ and $P_{\text{MF}}(s,t)$, to the indexes defined by (3.1), (3.2) and (3.3) are defined as follows[7]:

$$P_{\text{ML}}(s,t) \equiv \frac{\sum_{n\in S(s,t)} p_n^t q_n^s}{\sum_{n\in S(s,t)} p_n^s q_n^s}; \tag{3.4}$$

$$P_{\text{MP}}(s,t) \equiv \frac{\sum_{n\in S(s,t)} p_n^t q_n^t}{\sum_{n\in S(s,t)} p_n^s q_n^t}; \tag{3.5}$$

$$P_{\text{MF}}(s,t) \equiv [P_{\text{ML}}(s,t)P_{\text{MP}}(s,t)]^{1/2}. \tag{3.6}$$

[7]A justification for this approach to dealing with a lack of matching in the context of bilateral index number theory can be found in the discussion by Diewert (1980; 498–501) on the related problem of dealing with new and disappearing goods. Other approaches are also possible. For approaches based on imputation methods, see Alterman et al. (1999) and for approaches that are based on maximum matching over all pairs of periods, see Ivancic et al. (2011) and de Haan and van der Grient (2011).

Table 3.2 Matched model Fisher chained and fixed base indexes, mean, median and representative model house price indexes

Quarter	P_{FCH}	P_{FFB}	P_{Mean}	P_{Median}	$P_{\text{Represent}}$
1	1.00000	1.00000	1.00000	1.00000	1.00000
2	1.02396	1.02396	1.02003	1.05806	1.04556
3	1.07840	1.06815	1.04693	1.02258	1.03119
4	1.04081	1.04899	1.05067	1.03242	1.04083
5	1.04083	1.04444	1.04878	1.04839	1.04564
6	1.05754	1.06676	1.13679	1.17581	1.09792
7	1.07340	1.07310	1.06490	1.06935	1.01259
8	1.06706	1.07684	1.07056	1.10000	1.10481
9	1.08950	1.06828	1.07685	1.05806	1.03887
10	1.11476	1.11891	1.16612	1.16048	1.07922
11	1.12471	1.12196	1.08952	1.06290	1.07217
12	1.10483	1.11321	1.09792	1.10323	1.03870
13	1.10450	1.11074	1.10824	1.12903	1.12684
14	1.11189	1.10577	1.12160	1.10323	1.08587

In Fig. 3.1, the Fixed Base Fisher index is the matched model Fisher index defined by (3.6), where the base quarter s is kept fixed at quarter 1; i.e., the indexes $P_{\text{MF}}(1,1)$, $P_{\text{MF}}(1,2)$, ..., $P_{\text{MF}}(1,14)$ are calculated and labelled as the Fixed Base Fisher Index, P_{FFB}. The index that is labelled the Chained Fisher Index, P_{FCH}, is the index $P_{\text{MF}}(1,1)$, $P_{\text{MF}}(1,1)P_{\text{MF}}(1,2)$, $P_{\text{MF}}(1,1)P_{\text{MF}}(1,2)P_{\text{MF}}(2,3)$, ..., $P_{\text{MF}}(1,1)P_{\text{MF}}(1,2)P_{\text{MF}}(2,3)P_{\text{MF}}(3,4)...P_{\text{MF}}(13,14)$. Note that the Fixed Base and Chained Fisher (matched model) indexes are quite close to each other and are *much smoother* than the corresponding Mean, Median and Representative Model indexes.[8] The data for the 5 series plotted in Fig. 3.1 are listed in Table 3.2 in appendix.

The two matched model Fisher indexes must be regarded as being more accurate than the other indexes, which use only a limited amount of the available price and quantity information. Either Fisher index could be used as a headline index of house price inflation. Since both Fisher indexes trend fairly smoothly, the chained Fisher should be preferred over the fixed base Fisher index, following the advice in Hill (1988, 1993) and in the CPI Manual; see the ILO et al. (2004). Note also that there is no need to use Laspeyres or Paasche indexes in this situation since real estate

[8]The means (and standard deviations) of the 5 series are as follows: $P_{\text{FCH}} = 1.0737$ (0.0375), $P_{\text{FFB}} = 1.0737$ (0.0370), $P_{\text{Mean}} = 1.0785$ (0.0454), $P_{\text{Median}} = 1.0785$ (0.0510), and $P_{\text{Representative}} = 1.0586$ (0.0366). Thus the representative model price index is smoother than the two matched model Fisher indexes but it has a substantial bias relative to the two Fisher indexes: the representative model price index is well below the Fisher indexes for most of the sample period.

data on sales of houses contains both value and quantity information. Under these conditions, Fisher indexes are preferred by the above sources over the Laspeyres and Paasche indexes (which do not use all of the available price and quantity information for the two periods being compared).

Since there is a considerable amount of heterogeneity in each cell of the stratification scheme, there is the possibility of some *unit value bias*[9] in the matched model Fisher indexes. However, if a finer cell classification were used, the amount of matching would drop dramatically. Already, with the present classification, only about 2/3 of the cells could be matched across any two quarters. Thus there is a tradeoff between having too few cells with the possibility of unit value bias and having a finer cell classification scheme but with a much smaller degree of matching of the data within cells across the two time periods being compared.[10]

Looking at Table 3.2 and Fig. 3.1, it can be seen that the chained Fisher index considered above shows drops in house prices in the fourth quarter of 2005, 2006 and 2007. Thus there is the possibility that house prices drop for seasonal reasons in the fourth quarter of each year. In order to deal with this possibility, a rolling year matched model Fisher index is constructed in the following section.

3.3 Rolling Year Indexes and Seasonality

Assuming that each commodity in each season of the year is a separate "annual" commodity is the simplest and theoretically most satisfactory method for dealing with seasonal commodities when the goal is to construct *annual* price and quantity indexes. This idea can be traced back to Mudgett in the consumer price context and to Stone in the producer price context:

> The basic index is a yearly index and as a price or quantity index is of the same sort as those about which books and pamphlets have been written in quantity over the years. Mudgett (1955; 97).

> The existence of a regular seasonal pattern in prices which more or less repeats itself year after year suggests very strongly that the varieties of a commodity available at different seasons cannot be transformed into one another without cost and that, accordingly, in all cases where seasonal variations in price are significant, the varieties available at different times of the year should be treated, in principle, as separate commodities. Stone (1956; 74–75).

Diewert (1983) generalized the Mudgett-Stone annual framework to allow for *rolling year comparisons* for 12 consecutive months of data with a base year of

---

[9]See Balk (1998, 2008; 72–74), Silver (2009a, b, 2010) and Diewert and von der Lippe (2010) for discussions of unit value bias.

[10]Diewert and von der Lippe (2010) show that with finer and finer stratification schemes, eventually there is a complete lack of matching and index numbers based on highly stratified unit values become meaningless.

12 months of data or for comparisons of 4 consecutive quarters of data with a base year of 4 consecutive quarters of data; i.e., the basic idea is to compare the current rolling year of price and quantity data to the corresponding data of a base year where the data pertaining to each season is compared.[11] Thus in the present context, we have in principle,[12] price and quantity data for 45 classes of housing commodities in each quarter. If the sale of a house in each season is treated as a separate good, then there are 180 annual commodities.

For the first index number value, the four quarters of price and quantity data on sales of detached dwellings in the town of "A" (180 series) are compared with the same data using the Fisher ideal formula. Naturally, the resulting index is equal to 1. For the next index number value, the data for the first quarter of 2005 are dropped and the data pertaining to the first quarter of 2006 are appended to the data for quarters 2–4 of 2005. The resulting Fisher index is the second entry in the RY Matched Model series that is illustrated in Fig. 3.2. However, as was the case with the chained and fixed base Fisher indexes that appeared in Fig. 3.1 above, not all cells could be matched using the rolling year methodology; i.e., some cells were empty in the first quarter of 2006 which corresponded to cells in the first quarter of 2005 which were not empty and vice versa. Thus when constructing the rolling year index P_{RY} plotted in Fig. 3.2, the comparison between the rolling year and the data pertaining to 2005 was restricted to the set of cells which were non empty in both years; i.e., the Fisher rolling year indexes plotted in Fig. 3.2 are matched model indexes. Unmatched models are omitted from the index number comparison.[13] The results can be observed in Fig. 3.2. Note that there is a definite downturn at the end of the sample period but that the downturns which showed up in Fig. 3.1 for quarters 4 and 8 can be interpreted as seasonal downturns; i.e., the rolling year indexes in Fig. 3.2 did not turn down until the end of the sample period. Note also that the index value for observation 5 compares the data for calendar year 2006 to the corresponding data for calendar year 2005 and the index value for observation 9 compares the data for calendar year 2007 to the corresponding data for calendar year 2005; i.e., these index values correspond to Mudgett-Stone annual indexes.

It is a fairly labour intensive job to construct the rolling year matched model Fisher indexes since the cells that are matched over any two periods vary with the periods. A short cut method for seasonally adjusting a series such as the matched model

---

[11] For additional examples of this rolling year approach, see the chapters on seasonality in ILO et al. (2004), the IMF et al. (2004) and Diewert (1998). In order to theoretically justify the rolling year indexes from the viewpoint of the economic approach to index number theory, some restrictions on preferences are required. The details of these assumptions can be found in Diewert (1999; 56–61). It should be noted that weather and the lack of fixity of Easter can cause "seasons" to vary and a breakdown in the approach; see Diewert et al. (2009). However, with quarterly data, these limitations of the rolling year index are less important.

[12] In practice, as we have seen in the previous section, many of the cells are empty in each period.

[13] There are 11 rolling year comparisons that can be made with the data for 14 quarters that are available. The number of unmatched or empty cells for rolling years 2, 3, ..., 11 are as follows: 50, 52, 55, 59, 60, 61, 65, 65, 66, 67. The relatively low number of unmatched or empty cells for rolling years 2, 3 and 4 is due to the fact that for rolling year 2, 3/4 of the data are matched, for rolling year 3, 1/2 of the data are matched and for rolling year 4, 1/4 of the data are matched.

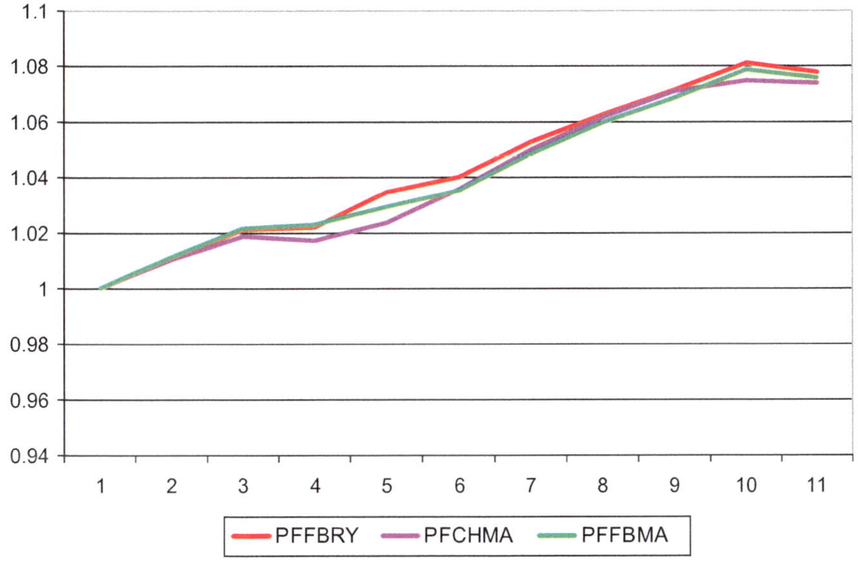

Fig. 3.2 Rolling year fixed base Fisher P_{FFBRY}, Fisher chained moving average P_{FCHMA} and Fisher fixed base moving average P_{FFBMA} house price indexes

Table 3.3 Rolling year fixed base Fisher P_{FFBRY}, Fisher chained moving average P_{FCHMA} and Fisher fixed base moving average P_{FFBMA} house price indexes

Rolling Year	P_{FFBRY}	P_{FCHMA}	P_{FFBMA}
1	1.00000	1.00000	1.00000
2	1.01078	1.01021	1.01111
3	1.02111	1.01841	1.02156
4	1.02185	1.01725	1.02272
5	1.03453	1.02355	1.02936
6	1.04008	1.03572	1.03532
7	1.05287	1.04969	1.04805
8	1.06245	1.06159	1.05948
9	1.07135	1.07066	1.06815
10	1.08092	1.07441	1.07877
11	1.07774	1.07371	1.07556

chained Fisher index P_{FCH} and the fixed base Fisher index P_{FFB} listed in Table 3.2 in the previous section is to simply take a 4 quarter *moving average* of these series. The resulting rolling year series, P_{FCHMA} and P_{FFBMA}, can be compared with the rolling year Mudgett-Stone-Diewert series P_{RY}; see Fig. 3.2. The data that corresponds to Fig. 3.2 are listed in Table 3.3.

It can be seen that a simple moving average of the chained Fisher and fixed base quarter to quarter indexes, P_{FCH} and P_{FFB}, listed in Table 3.2 approximates the theoretically preferred rolling year fixed base Fisher index P_{FFBRY} fairly well. However, there are differences of up to 1% between the preferred rolling year index and the moving average index. Recall that the fixed base Fisher index constructed in the previous section compared the data of quarters 1 to 14 with the corresponding data of quarter 1. Thus the observations for, say, quarters 2 and 1, 3 and 1, and 4 and 1 are not as likely to be as comparable as the rolling year indexes where data in any one quarter is always lined up with the data in the corresponding quarter of the base year. A similar argument applies to the moving average index P_{FCHMA}; the comparisons that go into the links in this index are from quarter to quarter and they are unlikely to be as accurate as comparisons across the years for the same quarter.[14]

We turn now to methods for constructing house price indexes that are based on hedonic regression techniques.

3.4 Time Dummy Hedonic Regression Models Using the Logarithm of Price as the Dependent Variable

The most popular hedonic regression models regress the log of the price of the good on either a linear function of the characteristics or on the logs of the characteristics along with time dummy variables.[15] We will consider each of these models in turn.

The Log Linear Time Dummy Hedonic Regression Model

In quarter t, there were $N(t)$ sales of detached houses in the town of "A" where p_n^t is the selling price of house n sold during quarter t. We have information on three characteristics of house n sold in period t: L_n^t is the area of the plot in square meters (m^2); S_n^t is the floor space area of the structure in m^2 and A_n^t is age in decades of house n in period t. The *Log Linear time dummy hedonic regression model* is defined by the following system of regression equations[16]:

[14]The stronger is the seasonality, the stronger will be this argument in favour of the accuracy of the rolling year index. The strength of this argument can be seen if all house price sales in a given cell turn out to be strongly seasonal; i.e., the sales for that cell occur in say only one quarter in each year. Quarter to quarter comparisons are obviously impossible in this situation but rolling year indexes will be perfectly well defined.

[15]This methodology was developed by Court (1939; 109–111) as his hedonic suggestion number two but there were earlier contributions which were not noticed by the profession until recently.

[16]For all the models estimated in this paper, it is assumed that the error terms ε_n^t are independently distributed normal variables with mean 0 and constant variance and maximum likelihood estimation is used in order to estimate the unknown parameters in each regression model. The nonlinear option in Shazam was used for the actual estimation.

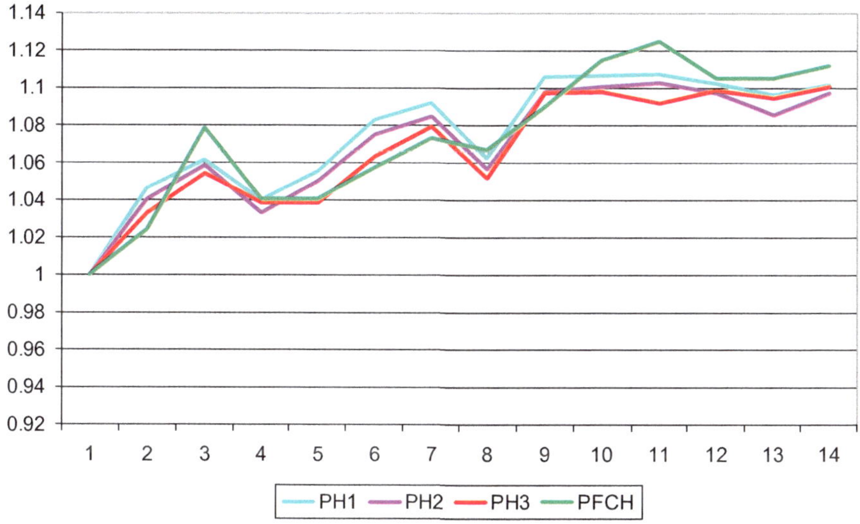

Fig. 3.3 Three time dummy hedonic regression based house price indexes P_{H1}, P_{H2} and P_{H3} and the stratified sample matched model chained Fisher house price index P_{FCH}

$$\ln p_n^t = \alpha + \beta L_n^t + \gamma S_n^t + \delta A_n^t + \tau^t + \varepsilon_n^t; \quad t = 1, \ldots, 14; \; n = 1, \ldots, N(t); \; \tau^1 \equiv 0 \tag{3.7}$$

where τ^t is a quarter t shift parameter which shifts the hedonic surface upwards or downwards as compared to the quarter 1 surface.[17]

Note that if we exponentiated both sides of (3.7) and neglected the error term, then the house price p_n^t would equal $e^\alpha[\exp L_n^t]^\beta[\exp S_n^t]^\gamma[\exp A_n^t]^\delta[\exp \tau^t]$. Thus if we could observe a house with the *same characteristics* in two consecutive periods t and $t+1$, the corresponding price relative (neglecting error terms) would equal $[\exp \tau^{t+1}]/[\exp \tau^t]$ and this can serve as the chain link in a price index. Thus it is particularly easy to construct a house price index using this model; see Fig. 3.3 and Table 3.4 for the resulting index which is labelled as P_{H1} (hedonic house price index 1). The R^2 for this model is 0.8420 which is quite satisfactory for a hedonic regression model with only three characteristics. For later comparison purposes, we note that the log likelihood is 1407.6.

A problem with this model is that the underlying price formation model seems implausible: S and L interact multiplicatively in order to determine the overall house price whereas it seems likely that lot size L and house size S interact in an approximately additive fashion to determine the overall house price.

Another problem with the regression model (3.7) is that age is entered in an additive fashion. The problem with this is that we would expect age to interact directly

[17]The 15 parameters $\alpha, \tau^1, \ldots, \tau^{14}$ correspond to variables that are exactly collinear in the regression (3.7) and thus the restriction $\tau^1 = 0$ is imposed in order to identify the remaining parameters.

Table 3.4 Time dummy house price indexes using hedonic regressions with the logarithm of price as the dependent variable P_{H1}, P_{H2} and P_{H3} and the stratified sample matched model chained Fisher index P_{FCH}

Quarter	P_{H1}	P_{H2}	P_{H3}	P_{FCH}
1	1.00000	1.00000	1.00000	1.00000
2	1.04609	1.04059	1.03314	1.02396
3	1.06168	1.05888	1.05482	1.07840
4	1.04007	1.03287	1.03876	1.04081
5	1.05484	1.05032	1.03848	1.04083
6	1.08290	1.07532	1.06369	1.05754
7	1.09142	1.08502	1.07957	1.07340
8	1.06237	1.05655	1.05181	1.06706
9	1.10572	1.09799	1.09736	1.08950
10	1.10590	1.10071	1.09786	1.11476
11	1.10722	1.10244	1.09167	1.12471
12	1.10177	1.09747	1.09859	1.10483
13	1.09605	1.08568	1.09482	1.10450
14	1.10166	1.09694	1.10057	1.11189

with the structures variable S as a (net) depreciation variable (and not interact directly with the land variable, which does not depreciate). In the following model, we make this direct interaction adjustment to (3.7).

The Log Linear Time Dummy Hedonic Regression Model with Quality Adjustment of Structures for Age

In this model, we argue that age A interacts with the quantity of structures S in a multiplicative manner; i.e., an appropriate explanatory variable for the selling price of a house is $\gamma(1-\delta)^A S$ (geometric depreciation where δ is the decade geometric depreciation rate) or $\gamma(1-\delta A)S$ (straight line depreciation where δ is the decade straight line depreciation rate) instead of the additive specification $\gamma S + \delta A$. In what follows, the straight line variant of this class of models is estimated[18]; i.e., the *Log Linear time dummy hedonic regression model with quality adjusted structures* is the following regression model:

$$\ln p_n^t = \alpha + \beta L_n^t + \gamma(1 - \delta A_n^t)S_n^t + \tau^t + \varepsilon_n^t; \quad t = 1, \ldots, 14;\ n = 1, \ldots, N(t);\ \tau^1 \equiv 0. \tag{3.8}$$

The above regression model was run using the 14 quarters of sales data for the town of "A". Note that only one common straight line depreciation rate δ is estimated.

[18] This regression is essentially linear in the unknown parameters and hence it is very easy to estimate.

The estimated decade (net) depreciation rate[19] was $\delta^* = 11.94\%$ (or around 1.2% per year), which is very reasonable. As was the case with the previous model, if we could observe a house with the *same characteristics* in two consecutive periods t and $t+1$, the corresponding price relative (neglecting error terms) would equal $[\exp \tau^{t+1}]/[\exp \tau^t]$ and this can serve as the chain link in a price index; see Fig. 3.3 and Table 3.4 (see $P_{\rm H2}$) for the resulting index. The R^2 for this model is 0.8345, a bit lower than the previous model and the log likelihood is 1354.9, which is quite a drop from the previous log likelihood of 1407.6. Thus it appears that the imposition of more theory (with respect to the treatment of the age of the house) has led to a drop in the empirical fit of the model. However, it is likely that this model and the previous one is misspecified[20]: they both multiply together land area times structure area in order to determine the price of the house and it is likely that an additive interaction between L and S is more appropriate than a multiplicative one.

Note that once the depreciation rate has been estimated (denote the estimated rate by δ^*), then *quality adjusted structures* (adjusted for the aging of the structure) for each house n in each quarter t can be defined as follows:

$$S_n^{t^*} \equiv (1 - \delta^* A_n^t) S_n^t; \quad t = 1, \dots, 14; \; n = 1, \dots, N(t). \tag{3.9}$$

The Log Log Time Dummy Hedonic Regression Model with Quality Adjustment of Structures for Age

From now on, we will work with quality adjusted (for age) structures, $(1 - \delta A)S$, rather than the unadjusted structures area, S. The Log Log model is similar to the previous Log Linear model, except that now, instead of using L and $(1 - \delta A)S$ as explanatory variables in the regression model, we use the logarithms of the land and quality adjusted structures areas as independent variables. Thus the *Log Log time dummy hedonic regression model with quality adjusted structures* is the following regression model:

$$\ln p_n^t = \alpha + \beta \ln L_n^t + \gamma \ln[(1 - \delta A_n^t) S_n^t] + \tau^t + \varepsilon_n^t; \quad t = 1, \dots, 14; \; n = 1, \dots, N(t); \; \tau^1 \equiv 0. \tag{3.10}$$

[19]It is a net depreciation rate because we have no information on renovation expenditures so δ serves as a net depreciation rate; i.e., it is equal to gross wear and tear depreciation of the house less average expenditures on renovations and repairs.

[20]If the variation in the independent variables is relatively small, the difference in indexes generated by the various hedonic regression models considered in this section and the following sections is likely to be small since virtually all of the models considered can offer roughly a linear approximation to the "truth". But when the variation in the independent variables is large (as it is in the present housing context), then the choice of functional form can have a very substantial effect. Thus a priori reasoning should be applied to both the choice of independent variables in the regression as well as to the choice of functional form. For additional discussion on functional form issues, see Diewert (2003a).

Using the data for "A", the estimated decade (net) depreciation rate[21] is $\delta^* = 0.1050$ (standard error 0.00374), which is a reasonable decade net depreciation rate. Note that if we exponentiated both sides of (3.10) and neglected the error term, the house price p_n^t would equal $e^{\alpha}[L_n^t]^{\beta}[S_n^{t*}]^{\gamma}[\exp \tau^t]$ where S_n^{t*} is defined as quality adjusted structures, $(1 - \delta A_n^t)S_n^t$. Thus if we could observe a house with the *same characteristics* in two consecutive periods t and $t+1$, the corresponding price relative (neglecting error terms) would equal $[\exp \tau^{t+1}]/[\exp \tau^t]$ and this again can serve as the chain link in a price index; see Fig. 3.3 and Table 3.4 (see P_{H3}) for the resulting index. The R^2 for this model is 0.8599, which is a big increase over the previous two models and the log likelihood is 1545.4, a huge increase over the log likelihoods for the previous two models (1407.6 and 1354.9).

It turns out that this hedonic regression model is a variant of McMillen's (2003) *consumer oriented approach to hedonic housing models*. It is worthwhile outlining his theoretical framework.[22]

A very simple way to justify a hedonic regression model from a consumer perspective is to postulate that households have the same (cardinal) utility function, $f(z_1, z_2)$, that aggregates the amounts of two relevant characteristics, $z_1 > 0$ and $z_2 > 0$, into the overall utility of the "model" with characteristics z_1, z_2 yielding the scalar welfare measure, $f(z_1, z_2)$. Thus households will prefer model 1 with characteristics z_1^1, z_2^1 to model 2 with characteristics z_1^2, z_2^2 if and only if $f(z_1^1, z_2^1) > f(z_1^2, z_2^2)$.[23] Thus having more of every characteristic is always preferred by households. The next assumption that we make is that in period t, there is a positive *generic price for all models*, ρ^t, such that the household's *willingness to pay*, $W^t(z_1, z_2)$, for a model with characteristics z_1 and z_2 is equal to the generic model price ρ^t times the utility generated by the model, $f(z_1, z_2)$; i.e., we have for each model n with characteristics z_{1n}^t, z_{2n}^t that is purchased in period t, the following *willingness to pay* for model n[24]:

$$W^t(z_{1n}^t, z_{2n}^t) = \rho^t f(z_{1n}^t, z_{2n}^t) = p_n^t. \tag{3.11}$$

The above willingness to pay for a house is set equal to the selling price of the house, p_n^t. Now all that is necessary is to specify the z characteristics and pick a functional form for the (cardinal) utility function f. In order to relate (3.11) to (3.10), let $z_{1n}^t \equiv L_n^t$ and $z_{2n}^t \equiv [(1 - \delta A_n^t)S_n^t]$ and let $f(z_1, z_2)$ be the following *Cobb-Douglas utility function*:

$$f(z_1, z_2) \equiv e^{\alpha} z_1^{\beta} z_2^{\gamma}; \quad \beta > 0; \; \gamma > 0. \tag{3.12}$$

---

[21] It is a net depreciation rate because we have no information on renovation expenditures so δ serves is equal to average gross wear and tear depreciation of the house less average real expenditures on renovations and repairs.

[22] This exposition follows that of Diewert et al. (2010).

[23] It is natural to impose some regularity conditions on the characteristics aggregator function f like continuity, monotonicity (if each component of the vector z^1 is strictly greater than the corresponding component of z^2, then $f(z^1) > f(z^2)$ and $f(0, 0) = 0$.

[24] For more elaborate justifications for household based hedonic regression models, see Muellbauer (1974) and Diewert (2003a).

Now define $\rho^t \equiv \exp \tau^t$ for $t = 1, ..., 14$ and it can be seen that with these definitions, the hedonic regression model defined by (3.11) is equivalent to the model defined by (3.10), neglecting the error terms.

If β and γ sum to one, then the consumer's characteristics utility function exhibits *constant returns to scale*. Thus if z_1 and z_2 are multiplied by the positive scalar λ, then the consumer's initial utility $f(z_1, z_2)$ is also multiplied by λ; i.e., we have $f(\lambda z_1, \lambda z_2) = \lambda f(z_1, z_2)$ for all $\lambda > 0$. For the data pertaining to the town of "A", we obtained the following estimates for β and γ (standard errors in brackets): $\beta^* = 0.4196$ (0.00748) and $\gamma^* = 0.5321$ (0.0157). Thus the sum of β^* and γ^* is 0.9517, which is reasonably close to one.

Although this model performs the best of the simple hedonic regression models considered thus far, it has the unsatisfactory feature that the quantity of land and quality adjusted structures determine the price of a house in a *multiplicative manner* when it is more likely that house prices are determined by a weighted *sum* of their land and quality adjusted structures amounts. Thus in the following section, an additive time dummy hedonic regression model will be estimated and the expectation is that this model will fit the data better.

The three house price series generated by the three time dummy hedonic regressions described in this section where the logarithm of the selling price is used as the dependent variable, P_{H1}, P_{H2} and P_{H3}, are plotted in Fig. 3.3 along with the stratified sample matched model chained Fisher house price index described in Sect. 3.2 above, P_{FCH}. These four house price series are listed in Table 3.4.

It can be seen that all four indexes capture the same trend but there can be differences of over 2% between the various indexes for some quarters. Note that all of the indexes move in the same direction from quarter to quarter with decreases in quarters 4, 8, 12 and 13 except that P_{H3} (the index that corresponds to the Log Log model) increases in quarter 12.

3.5 Time Dummy Hedonic Regression Models Using Price as the Dependent Variable

The Linear Time Dummy Hedonic Regression Model

There are reasons to believe that the selling price of a property is linearly related to the plot area of the property plus the area of the structure due to the competitive nature of the house building industry.[25] If the age of the structure is treated as another characteristic that has an importance in determining the price of the property, then the following *linear time dummy hedonic regression model* might be an appropriate one:

$$p_n^t = \alpha + \beta L_n^t + \gamma S_n^t + \delta A_n^t + \tau^t + \varepsilon_n^t; \quad t = 1, ..., 14; \; n = 1, ..., N(t); \; \tau^1 \equiv 0. \tag{3.13}$$

[25] Diewert (2007) and Diewert et al. (2010) develop this line of thought in more detail.

Table 3.5 Two time dummy house price indexes using hedonic regressions with price as the dependent variable, P_{H4} and P_{H2}, the log log time dummy index P_{H3} and the stratified sample matched model chained Fisher index P_{FCH}

Quarter	P_{H4}	P_{H5}	P_{H3}	P_{FCH}
1	1.00000	1.00000	1.00000	1.00000
2	1.04864	1.04313	1.03314	1.02396
3	1.06929	1.06667	1.05482	1.07840
4	1.04664	1.03855	1.03876	1.04081
5	1.05077	1.04706	1.03848	1.04083
6	1.08360	1.07661	1.06369	1.05754
7	1.09593	1.09068	1.07957	1.07340
8	1.06379	1.05864	1.05181	1.06706
9	1.10496	1.09861	1.09736	1.08950
10	1.10450	1.10107	1.09786	1.11476
11	1.10788	1.10588	1.09167	1.12471
12	1.10403	1.10044	1.09859	1.10483
13	1.09805	1.08864	1.09482	1.10450
14	1.11150	1.10572	1.10057	1.11189

The above linear regression model was run using the data for the town of "A". The R^2 for this model is 0.8687, much higher than those obtained in our previous regressions and the log likelihood is -10790.4 (which cannot be compared to the previous log likelihoods since the dependent variable has changed from the logarithm of price to just price. Using model (3.13) to form an overall house price index is a bit more difficult than using the time dummy regression models in the previous section. In the previous section, holding characteristics constant and neglecting error terms, the *relative price* for the same model over any two time periods turned out to be constant, leading to an unambiguous overall index. In the present section, holding characteristics constant and neglecting error terms, the *difference in price* for the same model turns out to be constant, but the relative prices for different models will not in general be constant. Thus an overall index will be constructed which uses the prices generated by the estimated parameters in (3.13) and evaluated at the sample average amounts of L, S and the average age of a house A.[26] The resulting quarterly house prices for this "average" model were converted into an index, P_{H4}, which is listed in Table 3.5 and charted in Fig. 3.4.

The hedonic regression model defined by (3.13) is perhaps the simplest possible one but it is a bit too simple since it neglects the fact that the interaction of age with the selling price of the property takes place via a multiplicative interaction with the structures variable and not via a general additive factor. Thus in the following

[26]The sample average amounts of L and S were 257.6 m^2 and 127.2 m^2 respectively and the average age of the detached dwellings sold over the sample period was 1.85 decades.

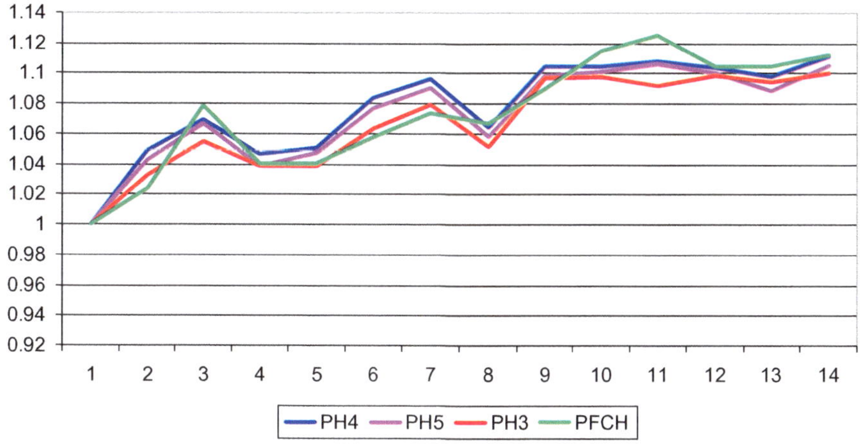

Fig. 3.4 Two time dummy house price indexes using hedonic regressions with price as the dependent variable, P_{H4} and P_{H5}, the log log time dummy index P_{H3} and the stratified sample matched model chained Fisher index P_{FCH}

section, we will rerun the present model but using quality adjusted structures as an explanatory variable rather than just entering age A as a separate stand alone characteristic.

The Linear Time Dummy Hedonic Regression Model with Quality Adjusted Structures
The *linear time dummy hedonic regression model with quality adjusted structures* is the following regression model:

$$p_n^t = \alpha + \beta L_n^t + \gamma(1 - \delta A_n^t)S_n^t + \tau^t + \varepsilon_n^t; \quad t = 1, \ldots, 14; \; n = 1, \ldots, N(t); \; \tau^1 \equiv 0. \tag{3.14}$$

This is the most plausible hedonic regression model so far. It works with quality adjusted (for age) structures S^* equal to $(1 - \delta A)S$ instead of having A and S as completely independent variables that enter into the regression in a linear fashion.

The results for this hedonic regression model were a clear improvement over the results of the previous model, (3.13). The log likelihood increased by 92 to -10697.8 and the R^2 increased to 0.8789 from the previous 0.8687. The estimated decade depreciation rate is $\delta^* = 0.1119$ (0.00418), which is reasonable as usual. This linear regression model has the same property as the previous model: house price *differences* are constant over time for all constant characteristic models but house price *ratios* are not constant. Thus as in the previous model, an overall index will be constructed which uses the prices generated by the estimated parameters in (3.14) and evaluated at the sample average amounts of L, S and the average age of a house A. The resulting quarterly house prices for this "average" model were converted into an index, P_{H5}, which is listed in Table 3.5 and charted in Fig. 3.4. For comparison purposes, P_{H3} (the time dummy Log Log model index) and P_{FCH} (the stratified sample chained matched model Fisher index) will be charted along with P_{H4} and P_{H5}. Our preferred indexes are P_{FCH} and P_{H5}.

It can be seen that again, all four indexes capture the same trend but there can be differences of over 2 percent between the various indexes for some quarters. Note that all of the indexes move in the same direction from quarter to quarter with decreases in quarters 4, 8, 12 and 13, except that P_{H3} increases in quarter 12.

A major problem with the hedonic time dummy regression models considered thus far is that the prices of land and quality adjusted structures are not allowed to change in an unrestricted manner from period to period. The class of hedonic regression models to be studied in the following section does not suffer from this problem.

3.6 Hedonic Imputation Regression Models

The theory of *hedonic imputation indexes* works as follows[27]: for each period, run a linear regression of the following form:

$$p_n^t = \alpha^t + \beta^t L_n^t + \gamma^t (1 - \delta^t A_n^t) S_n^t + \varepsilon_n^t; \quad t = 1, ..., 14; \; n = 1, ..., N(t). \quad (3.15)$$

Note that there are only 4 parameters to be estimated for each quarter: α^t, β^t, γ^t and δ^t for $t = 1, ..., 14$.[28] Note also that (3.15) is similar in form to the model defined by Eq. (3.14), but with some significant differences:

- Only one depreciation parameter is estimated in the model defined by (3.14) whereas in the present model, there are 14 depreciation parameters; one for each quarter.
- In model (3.14), there was only one α, β, γ and δ parameter whereas in (3.15), there are 14 α^t, 14 β^t, 14 γ^t and 14 δ^t parameters to be estimated. On the other hand, model (3.14) had an additional 13 time shifting parameters (the τ^t) that required estimation.

Thus the hedonic imputation model involves the estimation of 56 parameters whereas the time dummy model required the estimation of only 17 parameters. Hence it is likely that the hedonic imputation model will fit the data much better.

---

[27]This theory dates back to Court (1939; 108) as his hedonic suggestion number one. His suggestion was followed up by Griliches (1971a; 59–60, 1971b; 6) and Triplett and McDonald (1977; 144). More recent contributions to the literature include Diewert (2003b), de Haan (2003, 2009, 2010), Triplett (2004) and Diewert et al. (2009).

[28]Due to the fact that the regressions defined by (3.15) have a constant term and are essentially linear in the explanatory variables, the sample residuals in each of the regressions will sum to zero. Hence the sum of the predicted prices will equal the sum of the actual prices for each period. Thus the sum of the actual prices in the denominator of (3.17) will equal the sum of the corresponding predicted prices and similarly, the sum of the actual prices in the numerator of (3.19) will equal the corresponding sum of the predicted prices.

As usual, in the housing context, we almost never have matched models across periods (there are always depreciation and renovation activities that make a house in the exact same location not quite comparable over time). This lack of matching, say between quarters t and $t+1$, is overcome in the following way: take the parameters estimated using the quarter $t+1$ hedonic regression and price out all of the housing models (i.e., sales) that appeared in quarter t. This generates *predicted quarter t+1 prices for the quarter t models*, $p_n^{t+1}(t)$, as follows:

$$p_n^{t+1}(t) \equiv \alpha^{t+1^*} + \beta^{t+1^*} L_n^t + \gamma^{t+1^*}(1 - \delta^{t+1^*} A_n^t) S_n^t; \quad t = 1, \ldots, 13;\ n = 1, \ldots, N(t) \tag{3.16}$$

where α^{t^*}, β^{t^*}, γ^{t^*} and δ^{t^*} are the parameter estimates for the period t regression (3.15) for $t = 1, \ldots, 14$. Now we have a set of "matched" quarter $t+1$ prices for the models that appeared in period t and we can form the following *Laspeyres type matched model index*, going from quarter t to $t+1$:

$$P_{\mathrm{HIL}}(t, t+1) \equiv \frac{\sum_{n=1}^{N(t)} 1 p_n^{t+1}(t)}{\sum_{n=1}^{N(t)} 1 p_n^t}; \quad t = 1, \ldots, 13. \tag{3.17}$$

Note that the quantity that is associated with each price is 1; basically, each housing unit is unique and cannot be matched except through the use of a model.

The same method can be used going backwards from the housing sales that took place in quarter $t+1$; take the parameters for the quarter t hedonic regression and price out all of the housing models that appeared in quarter $t+1$ and generate predicted prices, $p_n^t(t+1)$ for these $t+1$ models:

$$p_n^t(t+1) \equiv \alpha^{t^*} + \beta^{t^*} L_n^{t+1} + \gamma^{t^*}(1 - \delta^{t^*} A_n^{t+1}) S_n^{t+1}; \quad t = 1, \ldots, 13;\ n = 1, \ldots, N(t+1). \tag{3.18}$$

Now we have a set of "matched" quarter t prices for the models that appeared in period $t+1$ and we can form the following *Paasche type matched model index*, going from quarter t to $t+1$:

$$P_{\mathrm{HIP}}(t, t+1) \equiv \frac{\sum_{n=1}^{N(t+1)} 1 p_n^{t+1}}{\sum_{n=1}^{N(t+1)} 1 p_n^t(t+1)}; \quad t = 1, \ldots, 13. \tag{3.19}$$

Once the above Laspeyres and Paasche imputation indexes have been calculated, we can readily form the corresponding *Fisher type matched model index* going from period t to $t+1$ by taking the geometric average of the two indexes defined by (3.17) and (3.19):

$$P_{\mathrm{HIF}}(t, t+1) \equiv [P_{\mathrm{HIL}}(t, t+1) P_{\mathrm{HIP}}(t, t+1)]^{1/2}; \quad t = 1, \ldots, 13. \tag{3.20}$$

The resulting chained Laspeyres, Paasche and Fisher imputation indexes, P_{HIL}, P_{HIP} and P_{HIF}, are plotted in Fig. 3.5 and are listed in Table 3.6.

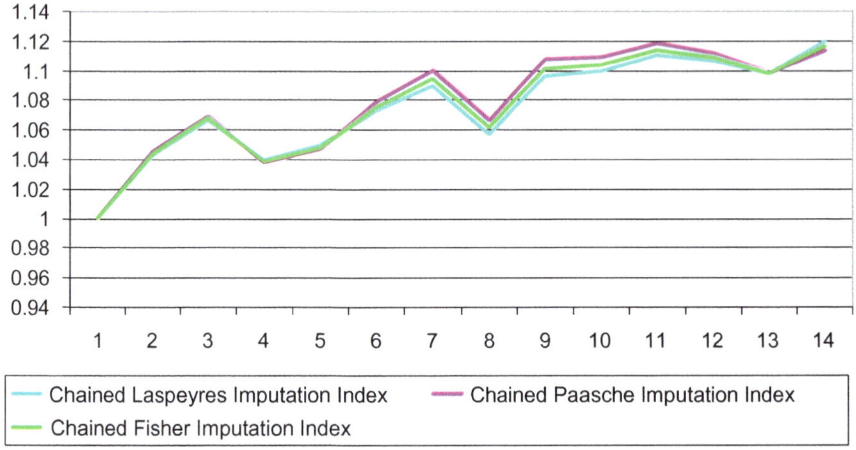

Fig. 3.5 Chained Laspeyres, Paasche and Fisher imputation indexes

Table 3.6 Chained Laspeyres, Paasche and Fisher imputation indexes

Quarter	P_{HIL}	P_{HIP}	P_{HIF}
1	1.00000	1.00000	1.00000
2	1.04234	1.04479	1.04356
3	1.06639	1.06853	1.06746
4	1.03912	1.03755	1.03834
5	1.04942	1.04647	1.04794
6	1.07267	1.07840	1.07553
7	1.08923	1.10001	1.09460
8	1.05689	1.06628	1.06158
9	1.09635	1.10716	1.10174
10	1.09945	1.10879	1.10411
11	1.11062	1.11801	1.11430
12	1.10665	1.11112	1.10888
13	1.09830	1.09819	1.09824
14	1.11981	1.11280	1.11630

The 3 imputation indexes are amazingly close.

The Fisher imputation index is our preferred hedonic index thus far; it is better than the time dummy indexes in the previous two sections because the imputation indexes allow the price of land and quality adjusted structures to change independently over time, whereas the time dummy indexes shift the hedonic surface in a parallel fashion. However, the above empirical results show that the Laspeyres type hedonic imputation index P_{HIL} can provide a very close approximation to the theoretically preferred Fisher type hedonic imputation index P_{HIF}. This is important in

Fig. 3.6 The Fisher hedonic imputation price index P_{HIF}, the chained matched model stratified Fisher index P_{FCH}, the linear time dummy hedonic regression index P_{H5} and the log log time dummy hedonic regression index P_{H3}

the context of producing real time indexes since a reasonably accurate index that covers period $t+1$ can be constructed using only the period t hedonic regression.

Our two "best" indexes thus far are the Fisher imputation index and the Stratified Chained Fisher index. These two "best" indexes are plotted in Fig. 3.6 along with the Log Log time dummy indexes P_{H3} and the Linear time dummy index with quality adjusted structures P_{H5}. Note that all of the indexes except P_{H3} indicate downward movements in quarters, 4, 8, 12 and 13 and upward movements in the other quarters (P_{H3} moves up in quarter 12 instead of falling like the other indexes).

This completes our discussion of basic hedonic regression methods that could be used in order to construct an overall index of house prices. In the following sections, we will study various hedonic regression methods that could be used in order to construct *separate* indexes for the price of housing land and for housing structures.

3.7 The Construction of Land and Structures Price Indexes: Preliminary Approaches

It is reasonable to develop a cost of production approach to the pricing of a newly built house.[29] Thus for a newly built house during quarter t, the total cost of the

[29]This approach was suggested by Diewert (2007) and implemented by Diewert et al. (2010). Thus the model in this section is a supply side model as opposed to the demand side Cobb Douglas model

property after the structure is completed will be approximately equal to the floor space area of the structure, say S square meters, times the building cost per square meter, γ^t say, plus the cost of the land, which will be equal to the cost per square meter, β^t say, times the area of the land site, L. Now think of a sample of newly built properties of the same general type, which have prices p_n^t in quarter t and structure areas S_n^t and land areas L_n^t. The prices of these newly built properties, p_n^t, should be approximately equal to costs of the above type, $\beta^t L_n^t + \gamma^t S_n^t$ plus error terms, which we assume have zero means. This model for pricing the sales of new structures is generalized to include the pricing of used structures by introducing quality adjusted structures in the usual way. This leads to the following hedonic regression model for the entire data set where β^t (the price of land), γ^t (the price of constant quality structures) and δ (the decade depreciation rate) are the parameters to be estimated in the following regression model[30, 31]:

$$p_n^t = \beta^t L_n^t + \gamma^t (1 - \delta A_n^t) S_n^t + \varepsilon_n^t; \quad t = 1, ..., 14; \; n = 1, ..., N(t). \qquad (3.21)$$

Note that a common depreciation rate for all quarters was estimated. Thus the model defined by (3.21) has 14 unknown β^t parameters, 14 unknown γ^t parameters and one unknown δ or 29 unknown parameters in all. The R^2 for this model is equal to 0.8847, which is the highest yet for regressions using the entire data set.[32] The log likelihood is −10642.0, which is considerably higher than the log likelihoods obtained for the two time dummy hedonic regressions that use prices as the dependent variable (recall the regressions associated with the construction of P_{H4} and P_{H5}, where the log likelihoods are −10790.4 and −10697.8). The decade straight line estimated depreciation rate is 0.1068 (0.00284).

---

of McMillen (2003) studied earlier. See Rosen (1974) for a discussion of identification issues in hedonic regression models.

[30] In order to obtain homoskedastic errors, it would be preferable to assume multiplicative errors in Eq. (3.1) since it is more likely that expensive properties have relatively large absolute errors compared to very inexpensive properties. However, following Koev and Santos Silva (2008), we think that it is preferable to work with the additive specification (3.1) since we are attempting to decompose the aggregate value of housing (in the sample of properties that sold during the period) into additive structures and land components and the additive error specification will facilitate this decomposition.

[31] Thorsnes (1997; 101) has a related cost of production model. He assumed that instead of Eq. (3.21), the value of the property under consideration in period t, p^t, is equal to the price of housing output in period t, ρ^t, times the quantity of housing output $H(L, K)$ where the production function H is a CES function. Thus Thorsnes assumed that $p^t = \rho^t H(L, K) = \rho^t[\alpha L^\sigma + \beta K^\sigma]^{1/\sigma}$ where ρ^t, σ, α and β are parameters , L is the lot size of the property and K is the amount of structures capital in constant quality units (the counterpart to our S^*). Our problem with this model is that there is only one independent time parameter ρ^t whereas our model has two, β^t and γ^t for each t, which allow the price of land and structures to vary freely between periods.

[32] The present model is similar in structure to the hedonic imputation model described in the previous section except that this model is more parsimonious; i.e., there is only one depreciation rate in the present model (as opposed to 14 depreciation rates in the imputation model) and there are no constant terms in the present model. The important factor in both models is that the prices of land and quality adjusted structures are allowed to vary independently across time periods.

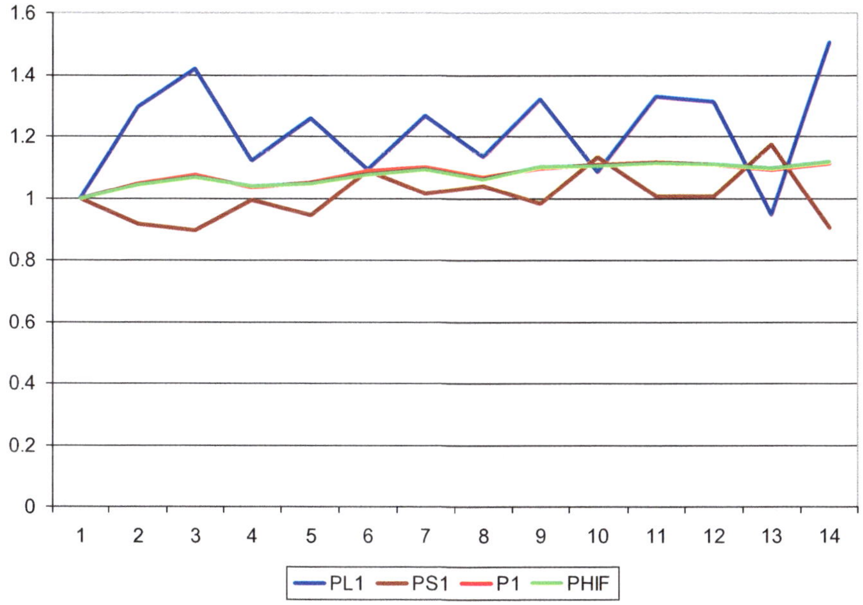

Fig. 3.7 The price of land P_{L1}, the price of quality adjusted structures P_{S1}, the overall cost of production house price index P_1 and the Fisher hedonic imputation house price index P_{HIF}

The model yields an estimated land price for quarter t equal to β^{t^*} and the corresponding quantity of land transacted is equal to $L^t \equiv \sum_{n=1}^{N(t)} L_n^t$. The estimated period t price for a square meter of quality adjusted structures is γ^{t^*} and the corresponding quantity of constant quality structures is $S^{t^*} \equiv \sum_{n=1}^{N(t)}(1 - \delta^* A_n^t)S_n^t$. The land price series $\beta^{1^*}, \ldots, \beta^{14^*}$ (rescaled to equal 1 in quarter 1) is the price series P_{L1} which is plotted in Fig. 3.7 and listed in Table 3.7. The constant quality price series for structures $\gamma^{1^*}, \ldots, \gamma^{14^*}$ (rescaled to equal 1 in quarter 1) is the price series P_{S1} which is plotted in Fig. 3.7 and listed in Table 3.7. Finally, using the price and quantity data on land and constant quality structures for each quarter t, $(\beta^{t^*}, L^t, \gamma^{t^*}, S^{t^*})$ for $t = 1, \ldots, 14$, an overall house price index can be constructed using the Fisher formula. The resulting price series is P_1 which is also plotted in Fig. 3.7 and listed in Table 3.7. For comparison purposes with P_1, the Fisher hedonic imputation index P_{HIF} is also plotted in Fig. 3.7 and listed in Table 3.7.

It can be seen that the new overall hedonic price index based on a cost of production approach to the hedonic functional form, P_1, is very close to the Fisher hedonic imputation index P_{HIF} constructed in the previous section. However, it can also be seen that the price series for land, P_{L1}, and the price series for quality adjusted structures, P_{S1}, are not at all credible: there are large random fluctuation in both series. Note that when the price of land spikes upwards, there is a corresponding dip in the price of structures. This is a sign of multicollinearity between the land and quality adjusted structures variables, which leads to unstable estimates for the prices of land and structures.

Table 3.7 The price of land P_{L1}, the price of quality adjusted structures P_{S1}, the overall cost of production house price index P_1 and the Fisher hedonic imputation house price index P_{HIF}

Quarter	P_{L1}	P_{S1}	P_1	P_{HIF}
1	1.00000	1.00000	1.00000	1.00000
2	1.29547	0.91603	1.04571	1.04356
3	1.42030	0.89444	1.07482	1.06746
4	1.12290	0.99342	1.03483	1.03834
5	1.25820	0.94461	1.05147	1.04794
6	1.09346	1.08879	1.08670	1.07553
7	1.26514	1.01597	1.09941	1.09460
8	1.13276	1.03966	1.06787	1.06158
9	1.31816	0.98347	1.09713	1.10174
10	1.08366	1.13591	1.11006	1.10411
11	1.32624	1.00699	1.11782	1.11430
12	1.30994	1.00502	1.11077	1.10888
13	0.94311	1.17530	1.09373	1.09824
14	1.50445	0.9032	1.11147	1.11630

There is a tendency for the price of land per meter squared to decrease for large lots. Thus in an attempt to improve upon the results of the hedonic regression model defined by (3.21), a *linear spline model for the price of land* is implemented.[33] Thus for lots that are less that 160 m^2, we assume that the price of land per meter squared is β_S^t during quarter t. For sales of properties that have lot sizes between 160 m^2 and 300 m^2, we assume that the cost per m^2 of units of land above 160 m^2 changes to a price of β_M^t per additional square meter during quarter t. Finally, for large plots of land that are above 300m^2, we allow the marginal price of an additional unit of land above 300m^2 to change to the price of β_L^t per additional square meter during quarter t. For quarter t, let the set of sales n of small, medium and large plots be denoted by $N_S(t)$, $N_M(t)$ and $N_L(t)$ respectively for $t = 1, \ldots, 14$. For sales n of properties that fall into the small land size group during period t, the hedonic regression model is described by (3.22); for the medium group, by (3.23) and for the large land size group, by (3.24):

$$p_n^t = \beta_S^t L_n^t + \gamma^t(1 - \delta A_n^t)S_n^t + \varepsilon_n^t; \quad t = 1, \ldots, 14; \ n \in N_S(t); \tag{3.22}$$

$$p_n^t = \beta_S^t[160] + \beta_M^t[L_n^t - 160] + \gamma^t(1 - \delta A_n^t)S_n^t + \varepsilon_n^t; \quad t = 1, \ldots, 14; \ n \in N_M(t); \tag{3.23}$$

$$p_n^t = \beta_S^t[160] + \beta_M^t[140] + \beta_L^t[L_n^t - 300] + \gamma^t(1 - \delta A_n^t)S_n^t + \varepsilon_n^t; \quad t = 1, \ldots, 14; \ n \in N_L(t). \tag{3.24}$$

Using the data for the town of "A", the estimated decade depreciation rate is $\delta^* = 0.1041$ (0.00419). The R^2 for this model is 0.8875, an increase over the previous

[33]This approach follows that of Diewert et al. (2010).

no splines model where the R^2 is 0.8847. The log likelihood is -10614.2 (an increase of 28 from the previous model defined by (3.21) log likelihood.) The first period parameter values for the 3 marginal prices for land are $\beta_S^{1*} = 281.4$ (55.9), $\beta_M^{1*} = 380.4$ (48.5) and $\beta_L^{1*} = 188.9$ (27.5). Thus in quarter 1, the marginal cost per m^2 of small lots is estimated to be 281.4 Euros per m^2. For medium sized lots, the estimated marginal cost is 380.4 Euros/m^2. And, for large lots, the estimated marginal cost is 188.9 Euros/m^2. The first period parameter value for quality adjusted structures is $\gamma^{1*} = 978.1$ Euros/m^2 with a standard error of 82.3. The lowest t statistic for all of the 57 parameters is 3.3, so all of the coefficients in this model are significantly different from zero.

Once the parameters for the model have been estimated, then in each quarter t, we can calculate the *predicted value of land for small, medium and large lot sales*, V_{LS}^t, V_{LM}^t and V_{LL}^t respectively along with the associated *quantities of land*, L_{LS}^t, L_{LM}^t and L_{LL}^t as follows:

$$V_{LS}^t \equiv \sum_{n \in N_S(t)} \beta_S^{t*} L_n^t; \quad t = 1, ..., 14; \tag{3.25}$$

$$V_{LM}^t \equiv \sum_{n \in N_M(t)} \beta_S^{t*}[160] + \beta_M^{t*}[L_n^t - 160]; \quad t = 1, ..., 14; \tag{3.26}$$

$$V_{LL}^t \equiv \sum_{n \in N_L(t)} \beta_S^{t*}[160] + \beta_M^{t*}[140] + \beta_L^{t*}[L_n^t - 300]; \quad t = 1, ..., 14; \tag{3.27}$$

$$L_{LS}^t \equiv \sum_{n \in N_S(t)} L_n^t; \quad t = 1, ..., 14; \tag{3.28}$$

$$L_{LM}^t \equiv \sum_{n \in N_M(t)} L_n^t; \quad t = 1, ..., 14; \tag{3.29}$$

$$L_{LL}^t \equiv \sum_{n \in N_L(t)} L_n^t; \quad t = 1, ..., 14. \tag{3.30}$$

The *corresponding average quarterly prices*, P_{LS}^t, P_{LM}^t and P_{LL}^t, for the three types of lot are defined as the above values divided by the above quantities:

$$P_{LS}^t \equiv \frac{V_{LS}^t}{L_{LS}^t}; \; P_{LM}^t \equiv \frac{V_{LM}^t}{L_{LM}^t}; \; P_{LL}^t \equiv \frac{V_{LL}^t}{L_{LL}^t}; \quad t = 1, ..., 14. \tag{3.31}$$

The average land prices for small, medium and large lots defined by (3.31) and the corresponding quantities of land defined by (3.28)–(3.30) can be used to form a chained *Fisher land price index*, which we denote by P_{L2}. This index is plotted in Fig. 3.8 and listed in Table 3.8. As in the previous model, the estimated period t price for a square meter of quality adjusted structures is γ^{t*} and the corresponding quantity of constant quality structures is $S^{t*} \equiv \sum_{n=1}^{N(t)} (1 - \delta^* A_n^t) S_n^t$. The structures price and quantity series γ^{t*} and S^{t*} were combined with the three land price and quantity series to form a chained *overall Fisher house price index* P_2 which is graphed in Fig. 3.8 and listed in Table 3.8. The *constant quality structures price index* P_{S2} (a normalization of the series $\gamma^{1*}, \ldots, \gamma^{14*}$) is also found in Fig. 3.8 and Table 3.8.

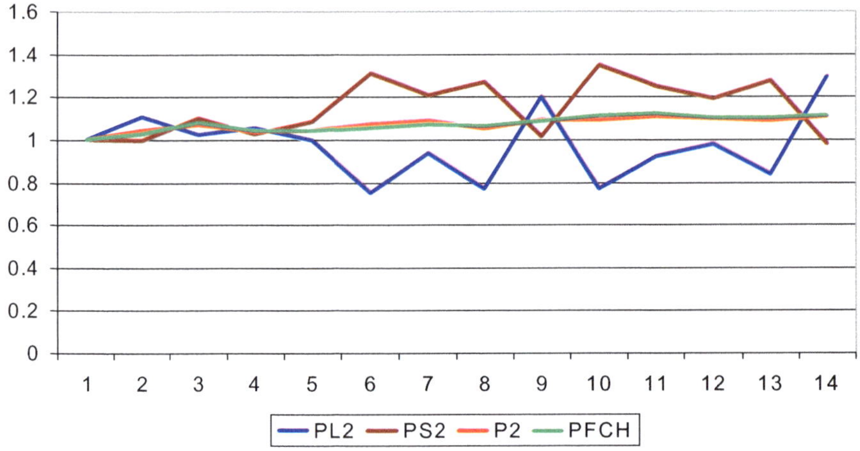

Fig. 3.8 The price of land P_{L2}, the price of quality adjusted structures P_{S2}, the overall house price index P_2 using splines on land and the chained stratified sample Fisher house price index P_{FCH}

Table 3.8 The price of land P_{L2}, the price of quality adjusted structures P_{S2}, the overall house price index P_2 using splines on land and the chained stratified sample Fisher house price index P_{FCH}

Quarter	P_{L2}	P_{S2}	P_2	P_{FCH}
1	1.00000	1.00000	1.00000	1.00000
2	1.10534	0.99589	1.04137	1.02396
3	1.02008	1.09803	1.06465	1.07840
4	1.05082	1.02542	1.03608	1.04081
5	0.99379	1.08078	1.04294	1.04083
6	0.74826	1.31122	1.06982	1.05754
7	0.93484	1.20719	1.08912	1.07340
8	0.77202	1.26718	1.05345	1.06706
9	1.19966	1.01724	1.09425	1.08950
10	0.77139	1.34813	1.09472	1.11476
11	0.92119	1.24884	1.10596	1.12471
12	0.97695	1.19188	1.09731	1.10483
13	0.84055	1.27531	1.08811	1.10450
14	1.29261	0.97875	1.10613	1.11189

It can be seen that the overall house price index that results from the spline model, P_2, is very close to the chained Fisher index P_{FCH} that was calculated using the stratification approach. However, the spline model does not generate sensible estimates for the price of land, $P_{\text{L}2}$ and the price of structures, $P_{\text{S}2}$: both price indexes are volatile but in opposite directions. As was the case with the previous cost of production model, the present model is subject to a multicollinearity problem.[34]

In the following section, an attempt to cure this volatility problem will be made by imposing monotonicity restrictions on the price movements for land and quality adjusted structures.

3.8 The Construction of Land and Structures Price Indexes: Approaches Based on Monotonicity Restrictions

It is likely that Dutch construction costs did not fall significantly during the sample period.[35] If this is the case, then these monotonicity restrictions on the quarterly prices of quality adjusted structures, $\gamma^1, \gamma^2, \gamma^3, \ldots, \gamma^{14}$, can be imposed on the hedonic regression model (3.22)–(3.24) in the previous section by replacing the constant quality quarter t structures price parameters γ^t by the following sequence of parameters for the 14 quarters: $\gamma^1, \gamma^1 + (\phi^2)^2, \gamma^1 + (\phi^2)^2 + (\phi^3)^2, \ldots, \gamma^1 + (\phi^2)^2 + (\phi^3)^2 + \cdots + (\phi^{14})^2$ where $\phi^2, \phi^3, \ldots, \phi^{14}$ are scalar parameters.[36] Thus for each quarter t starting at quarter 2, the price of a square meter of constant quality structures γ^t is equal to the previous period's price γ^{t-1} plus the square of a parameter ϕ^{t-1}, $[\phi^{t-1}]^2$, for $t = 2, 3, \ldots, 14$. Now replace this reparameterization of the structures price parameters γ^t in Eqs. (3.22)–(3.24) in order to obtain a *linear spline model for the price of land with monotonicity restrictions on the price of constant quality structures*.

Using the data for the town of "A", the estimated decade depreciation rate is $\delta^* = 0.1031$ (0.00386). The R^2 for this model is 0.8859, a drop from the previous unrestricted spline model where the R^2 is 0.8875. The log likelihood is -10630.5, a decrease of 16.3 over the previous unrestricted model. Eight of the 13 new parameters ϕ^t are zero in this monotonicity restricted hedonic regression. The first period parameter values for the 3 marginal prices for land are $\beta_S^{1^*} = 278.6$ (37.2), $\beta_M^{1^*} = 380.3$ (41.0) and $\beta_L^{1^*} = 188.0$ (21.4) and these estimated parameters are virtually identical

[34] Comparing Figs. 3.7 and 3.8, it can be seen that in Fig. 3.7, the price index for land is *above* the overall price index for the most part while the price index for structures is below the overall index but in Fig. 3.8, this pattern *reverses*. This instability is again an indication of a multicollinearity problem.

[35] Some direct evidence on this assertion will be presented in the following section.

[36] This method for imposing monotonicity restrictions was used by Diewert et al. (2010) with the difference that they imposed monotonicity on both structures and land prices, whereas here, we impose monotonicity restrictions on structures prices only.

to the corresponding parameters in the previous unrestricted model. The first period parameter value for quality adjusted structures is $\gamma^{1^*} = 980.5$ (49.9) Euros/m^2 which is little changed from the corresponding unrestricted estimate of 978.1 Euros/m^2.

Once the parameters for the model have been estimated, then convert the estimated ϕ^t parameters into γ^t parameters using the following recursive equations:

$$\gamma^{t+1^*} \equiv \gamma^{t^*} + [\phi^{t^*}]^2; \quad t = 2, \ldots, 14. \tag{3.32}$$

Now use Eqs. (3.25)–(3.31) in the previous section in order to construct a chained Fisher index of land prices, which we denote by P_{L3}. This index is plotted in Fig. 3.9 and listed in Table 3.9. As in the previous two models, the estimated period t price for a square meter of quality adjusted structures is γ^{t^*} and the corresponding quantity of constant quality structures is $S^{t^*} \equiv \sum_{n=1}^{N(t)} (1 - \delta^* A_n^t) S_n^t$. The structures price and quantity series γ^{t^*} and S^{t^*} were combined with the three land price and quantity series to form a chained *overall Fisher house price index* P_3 which is graphed in Fig. 3.9 and listed in Table 3.9. The constant quality structures price index P_{S3} (a normalization of the series $\gamma^{1^*}, \ldots, \gamma^{14^*}$) is also found in Fig. 3.9 and Table 3.9.

From Fig. 3.9, it can be seen that the new overall house price index P_3 that imposed monotonicity on the quality adjusted price of structures cannot be distinguished from the previous overall house price index P_2, which was based on a similar hedonic regression model except that the movements in the price of structures were not restricted. It can also be seen that the new land and structures price indexes look "reasonable"; the fluctuations in the price of land and quality adjusted structures are no longer violent. Finally, we note that the overall index P_3 is quite close to our

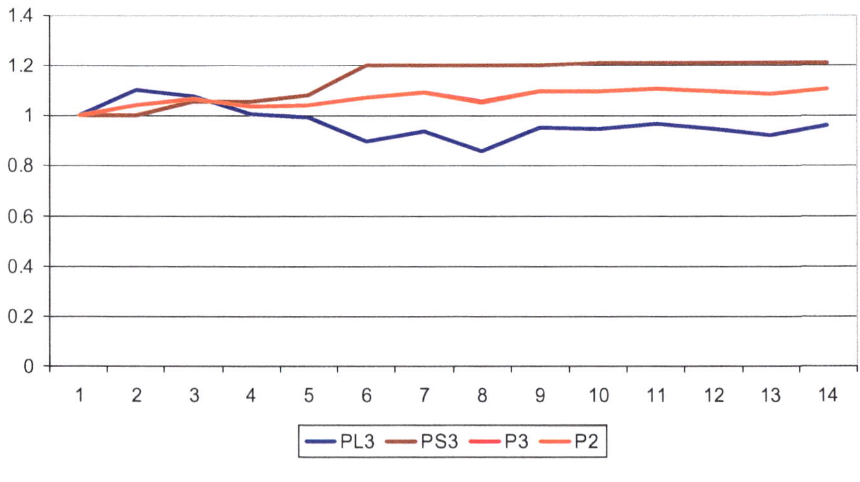

Fig. 3.9 The price of land P_{L3}, the price of quality adjusted structures P_{S3}, the overall house price index with monotonicity restrictions on structures P_3 and the unrestricted overall house price index using splines on land P_2

Table 3.9 The price of land P_{L3}, the price of quality adjusted structures P_{S3}, the overall house price index with monotonicity restrictions on structures P_3 and the unrestricted overall house price index using splines on land P_2

Quarter	P_{L3}	P_{S3}	P_3	P_2
1	1.00000	1.00000	1.00000	1.00000
2	1.10047	1.00000	1.04148	1.04137
3	1.07431	1.05849	1.06457	1.06465
4	1.00752	1.05849	1.03627	1.03608
5	0.99388	1.08078	1.04316	1.04294
6	0.89560	1.20300	1.07168	1.06982
7	0.93814	1.20300	1.08961	1.08912
8	0.85490	1.20300	1.05408	1.05345
9	0.95097	1.20300	1.09503	1.09425
10	0.94424	1.21031	1.09625	1.09472
11	0.96514	1.21031	1.10552	1.10596
12	0.94596	1.21031	1.09734	1.09731
13	0.92252	1.21031	1.08752	1.08811
14	0.96262	1.21031	1.10427	1.10613

previously recommended indexes, the matched model stratified chained Fisher index P_{FCH}, and the Fisher hedonic imputation index, P_{HIF}.

Although the above results look "reasonable", the early rapid increase in the price of structures and the slow growth in the index from quarter 6 to 14 looks a bit odd. Thus in the following section, we will try one more method for extracting separate structures and land components out of real estate sales data.

3.9 The Construction of Land and Structures Price Indexes: An Approach Based on the Use of Exogenous Information on the Price of Structures

Many countries have new construction price indexes available on a quarterly basis. This is the case for the Netherlands.[37] Thus if we are willing to make the assumption that new construction costs for houses have the same rate of growth over the sample period across all cities in the Netherlands, the statistical agency information on

[37] From the Central Bureau of Statistics (2010) online source, Statline, the following series was downloaded for the New Dwelling Output Price Index for the 14 quarters in our sample of house sales in "A" : 98.8, 98.1, 100.3, 102.7, 99.5, 100.5, 100.0, 100.3, 102.2, 103.2, 105.6, 107.9, 110.0, 110.0. This series was normalized to 1 in the first quarter by dividing each entry by 98.8. The resulting series is denoted by $\mu^1(= 1), \mu^2, \ldots, \mu^{14}$.

construction costs can be used to eliminate the multicollinearity problems that we encountered in Sect. 3.6 above.

Recall Eqs. (3.22)–(3.24) in Sect. 3.7 above. These equations are the estimating equations for the unrestricted hedonic regression model based on costs of production. In the present section, the constant quality house price parameters, the γ^t for $t = 2, ..., 14$ in (3.22)–(3.24), are replaced by the following numbers, which involve only the single unknown parameter γ^1:

$$\gamma^t = \gamma^1 \mu^t; \quad t = 2, 3, ..., 14 \tag{3.33}$$

where μ^t is the statistical agency estimated *construction cost price index* for the location under consideration and for the type of dwelling, where this series has been normalized to equal unity in quarter 1. The new hedonic regression model is again defined by Eqs. (3.22)–(3.24) except that the 14 unknown γ^t parameters are now assumed to be defined by (3.33), so that only γ^1 needs to be estimated for this new model. Thus the number of parameters to be estimated in this new restricted model is 44 as compared to the old number, which was 57.

Using the data for the town of "A", the estimated decade depreciation rate is $\delta^* = 0.1028$ (0.00433). The R^2 for this model is 0.8849, a small drop from the previous restricted spline model where the R^2 is 0.8859 and a larger drop from the unrestricted spline model R^2 in Sect. 3.7, which is 0.8875. The log likelihood is -10640.1, a decrease of 10 over the previous monotonicity restricted model. The first period parameter values for the 3 marginal prices for land ae $\beta_S^{1^*} = 215.4$ (30.0), $\beta_M^{1^*} = 362.6$ (46.7) and $\beta_L^{1^*} = 176.4$ (28.4). These new estimates differ somewhat from our previous estimates for these parameters. The first period parameter value for quality adjusted structures is $\gamma^{1^*} = 1085.9$ (22.9) Euros/m^2 which is substantially changed from the corresponding unrestricted estimate which is 980.5 Euros/m^2. Thus the imposition of a nationwide growth rate on the change in the price of quality adjusted structures has had some effect on our previous estimates for the levels of land and structures prices.

As usual, we used Eqs. (3.25)–(3.31) in order to construct a chained Fisher index of land prices, which we denote by P_{L4}. This index is plotted in Fig. 3.10 and listed in Table 3.10. As for the previous three models, the estimated period t price for a square meter of quality adjusted structures is γ^{t^*} (which in turn is now equal to $\gamma^{1^*}\mu^t$) and the corresponding quantity of constant quality structures is $S^{t^*} \equiv \sum_{n=1}^{N(t)} (1 - \delta^* A_n^t) S_n^t$. The structures price and quantity series γ^{t^*} and S^{t^*} were combined with the three land price and quantity series to form a chained *overall Fisher house price index* P_4 which is graphed in Fig. 3.10 and listed in Table 3.10. The *constant quality structures price index* P_{S4} (a normalization of the series $\gamma^{1^*}, \ldots, \gamma^{14^*}$) is also found in Fig. 3.10 and Table 3.10.

Comparing Figs. 3.9 and 3.10, it can be seen that the imposition of the national growth rates for new dwelling construction costs has totally changed the nature of our land and structures price indexes: in Fig. 3.9, the price series for land lies below the overall house price series for most of the sample period while in Fig. 3.10, the pattern is reversed: the price series for land lies above the overall house price series

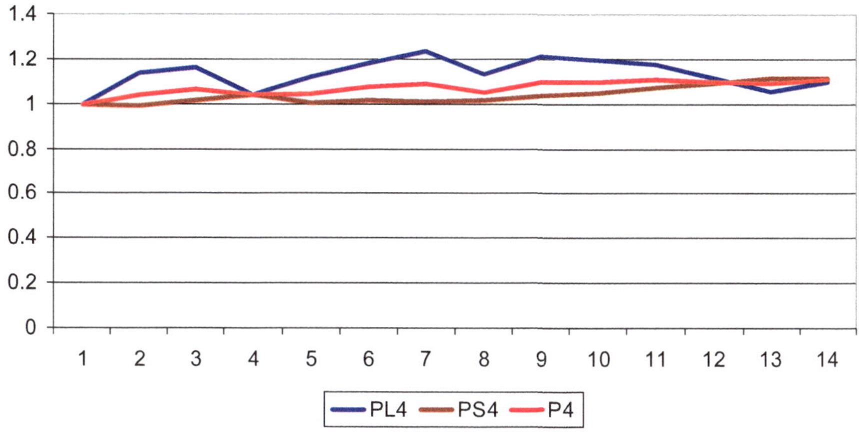

Fig. 3.10 The price of land P_{L4}, the price of quality adjusted structures P_{S4}, and the overall house price index using exogenous information on the price of structures P_4

Table 3.10 The price of land P_{L4}, the price of quality adjusted structures P_{S4}, and the overall house price index using exogenous information on the price of structures P_4

Quarter	P_{L4}	P_{S4}	P_4
1	1.00000	1.00000	1.00000
2	1.13864	0.99291	1.04373
3	1.16526	1.01518	1.06752
4	1.04214	1.03947	1.03889
5	1.11893	1.00709	1.04628
6	1.18183	1.01721	1.07541
7	1.23501	1.01215	1.09121
8	1.13257	1.01518	1.05601
9	1.21204	1.03441	1.09701
10	1.19545	1.04453	1.09727
11	1.17747	1.06883	1.10564
12	1.11588	1.09211	1.09815
13	1.05070	1.11336	1.08863
14	1.09648	1.11336	1.10486

for most of the sample period (and vice versa for the price of structures). Again, this is a reflection of the large amount of variability in the data and the multicollinearity between selling price, the quantity of land and the quantity of structures.

Which model is best? It is difficult to be definitive at this stage: on statistical grounds, the log likelihood is somewhat higher for the previous model that generated the P_3 overall index (and thus it should be preferred from this point of view) but the pattern of price changes for land and structures seems more believable for the present

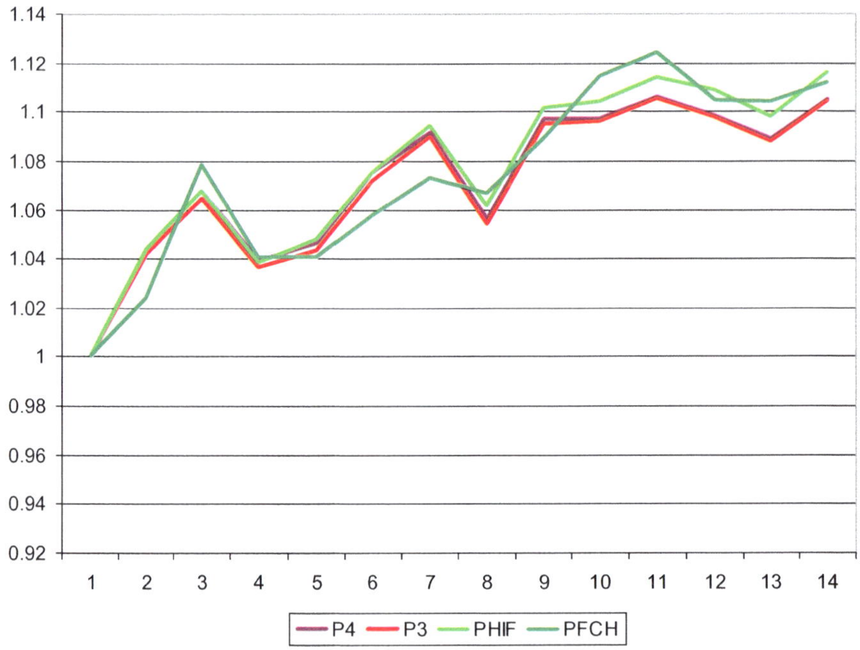

Fig. 3.11 House price indexes using exogenous information P_4 and using monotonicity restrictions P_3, the Fisher chained imputation index P_{HIF} and the chained Fisher stratified sample index P_{FCH}

model using exogenous information on structures prices (and thus the exogenous information model should be preferred).

We conclude this section by listing and charting our four preferred overall indexes. These four indexes are the matched model chained Fisher stratified sample index P_{FCH} studied in Sect. 3.2, the chained Fisher hedonic imputation index P_{HIF} studied in Sect. 3.6, the index P_3 that resulted from the cost based hedonic regression model with monotonicity restrictions studied in Sect. 3.8 and the index P_4 that was generated by the cost based hedonic regression model which used exogenous information on the price of structures studied in the present section. As can be seen from Fig. 3.11, all four of these indexes paint much the same picture. Note that P_3 and P_4 are virtually identical.

All things considered, the hedonic imputation index P_{HIF} is our preferred index (since it has fewer restrictions than the other indexes and seems closest to a matched model index in spirit) followed by the two cost of production hedonic indexes P_4 and P_3 followed by the stratified sample index P_{FCH} (which is likely to have some unit value bias).[38] If separate land and structures indexes are required, then the cost based

[38]However, the hedonic regression based indexes can be biased as well if important explanatory variables are omitted and if an "incorrect" functional form for the hedonic regression is chosen. But in general, hedonic regression methods are probably preferred over stratification methods.

hedonic regression model that used exogenous information on the price of structures is our preferred model.

A problem with the hedonic regression models discussed in Sects. 3.4, 3.5 and in 3.7–3.9 is that as the data for a new quarter are added, the old index values presumably will change as well when a new hedonic regression is run with the additional data. This problem is addressed in the next section.

3.10 Rolling Window Hedonic Regressions

Recall the last hedonic regression model that was discussed in the previous section. This model was defined by Eqs. (3.22)–(3.24) and (3.33), where Eq. (3.33) imposed exogenous information on the price of structures over the sample period. A problem with this hedonic regression model (and all the other hedonic regression models discussed in this paper with the exception of the hedonic imputation models) is that when more data are added, the indexes generated by the model change. This feature of these regression based methods makes these models unsatisfactory for statistical agency use, where users expect the official numbers to remain unchanged as time passes.[39] A simple solution to this difficulty is available. First, one chooses a "suitable" number of periods (equal to or greater than two) where it is thought that the hedonic regression model will yield "reasonable" results; this will be the *window length* (say M periods) for the sequence of regression models which will be estimated. Secondly, an initial regression model is estimated and the appropriate indexes are calculated using data pertaining to the first M periods in the data set. Next, a second regression model is estimated where the data consist of the initial data less the data for period 1 but adding the data for period $M + 1$ (Table 3.11).

Appropriate price indexes are calculated for this new regression model but only the rate of increase of the index going from period M to $M + 1$ is used to update the previous sequence of M index values. This procedure is continued with each successive regression dropping the data of the previous earliest period and adding the data for the next period, with one new update factor being added with each regression. If the window length is a year, then this procedure is called a *rolling year hedonic regression model* and for a general window length, it is called a *rolling window hedonic regression model*. This is exactly the procedure used recently by Shimizu et al. (2011) in their hedonic regression model for Tokyo house prices.[40]

We implement the rolling window procedure for the last model in the previous section with a window length of 9 quarters. Thus the initial hedonic regression model defined by (3.22)–(3.24) and (3.33) is implemented for the first 9 quarters.

---

[39] Users may tolerate a few revisions to recent data but typically, users would not like all the numbers to be revised back into the indefinite past as new data become available.

[40] An analogous procedure has also been recently used by Ivancic et al. (2011) and de Haan and van der Grient (2011) in their adaptation of the GEKS method for making international comparisons to the scanner data context.

Table 3.11 House price indexes using exogenous information P_4 and using monotonicity restrictions P_3, the Fisher chained imputation index P_{HIF} and the chained Fisher stratified sample index P_{FCH}

Quarter	P_4	P_3	P_{HIF}	P_{FCH}
1	1.00000	1.00000	1.00000	1.00000
2	1.04373	1.04148	1.04356	1.02396
3	1.06752	1.06457	1.06746	1.07840
4	1.03889	1.03627	1.03834	1.04081
5	1.04628	1.04316	1.04794	1.04083
6	1.07541	1.07168	1.07553	1.05754
7	1.09121	1.08961	1.09460	1.07340
8	1.05601	1.05408	1.06158	1.06706
9	1.09701	1.09503	1.10174	1.08950
10	1.09727	1.09625	1.10411	1.11476
11	1.10564	1.10552	1.11400	1.12471
12	1.09815	1.09734	1.10888	1.10483
13	1.08863	1.08752	1.09824	1.10450
14	1.10486	1.10427	1.11630	1.11189

The resulting indexes for the price of land, constant quality structures and the overall index are denoted by P_{RWL4}, P_{RWS4} and P_{RW4} respectively and are listed in the first 9 rows of Table 3.12.[41] Next a regression covering the data for quarters 2–10 was run and the land, structures and overall price indexes generated by this model were used to update the initial indexes in the first 9 rows of Table 3.12; i.e., the price of land in quarter 10 of Table 3.12 is equal to the price of land in quarter 9 times the price relative for land (quarter 10 land index divided by the quarter 9 land index) that was obtained from the second regression covering quarters 2–10, etc. Similar updating was done for the next 4 quarters using regressions covering quarters 3–11, 4–12, 5–13 and 6–14. The rolling window indexes can be compared to their one big regression counterparts (the model in the previous section) by looking at Table 3.12 and Fig. 3.12. Recall that the estimated depreciation rate and the estimated Quarter 1 price of quality adjusted structures for the last model in the previous section are $\delta^* = 0.1028$ and $\gamma^{1^*} = 1085.9$ respectively. If by chance, the 6 rolling window hedonic regressions each generate the same estimates for δ and γ, then the indexes generated by the rolling window regressions would coincide with the indexes P_{L4}. P_{S4} and P_4 that were described in the previous section. The 6 estimates for δ generated by the 6 rolling window regressions are 0.10124, 0.10805, 0.11601, 0.11103, 0.10857 and 0.10592. The 6 estimates for γ^1 generated by the 6 rolling window regressions are 1089.6, 1103.9, 1088.1, 1101.0, 1123.5 and 1100.9. While these estimates are not identical to the

[41] We imposed the restrictions (3.33) on the rolling window regressions and so the rolling window constant quality price index for structures, P_{RWS}, is equal to the constant quality price index for structures listed in Table 3.10, P_{S4}.

Table 3.12 The price of land P_{L4}, the price of quality adjusted structures P_{S4}, the overall house price index using exogenous information on the price of structures P_4 and their rolling window counterparts P_{RWL} and P_{RW}

Quarter	P_{RWL}	P_{L4}	P_{RW}	P_4	P_{S4}
1	1.00000	1.00000	1.00000	1.00000	1.00000
2	1.14073	1.13864	1.04381	1.04373	0.99291
3	1.16756	1.16526	1.06766	1.06752	1.01518
4	1.04280	1.04214	1.03909	1.03889	1.03947
5	1.12055	1.11893	1.04635	1.04628	1.00709
6	1.18392	1.18183	1.07542	1.07541	1.01721
7	1.23783	1.23501	1.09123	1.09121	1.01215
8	1.13408	1.13257	1.05602	1.05601	1.01518
9	1.21417	1.21204	1.09698	1.09701	1.03441
10	1.19772	1.19545	1.09738	1.09727	1.04453
11	1.18523	1.17747	1.10718	1.10564	1.06882
12	1.11889	1.11588	1.09779	1.09815	1.09201
13	1.05191	1.05070	1.08893	1.08863	1.11335
14	1.09605	1.09648	1.10436	1.10486	1.11335

corresponding P_4 estimates of 0.1028 and 1085.9, they are fairly close and so we can expect the rolling window indexes to be fairly close to their counterparts for the last model in the previous section. The R^2 values for the 6 rolling window regressions are 0.8803, 0.8813, 0.8825, 0.8852, 0.8811 and 0.8892.

The rolling window series for the price of quality adjusted structures, P_{RWS}, is not listed in Table 3.12 because it is identical to the series P_{S4}, which was described in the previous section.[42] It can be seen that the new rolling window price series for land, P_{RWL}, is extremely close to its counterpart in the previous section, P_{L4}, and the overall rolling window price series for detached dwellings in "A", P_{RW}, is also close to its counterpart in the previous section, P_4. These series are so close to each other that a chart shows practically no differences, which explains why we have not provided a chart for the series in Table 3.12.

Our conclusion here is that rolling window hedonic regressions can give pretty much the same results as a longer hedonic regression that covers the sample period. Thus the use of rolling window hedonic regressions can be recommended for statistical agency use.

A final topic of interest is: how can the results of hedonic regression models for sales of houses be adapted to give estimates for a price index for the stock of houses? This topic is briefly addressed in the following section.

[42]By construction, P_{S4} and P_{RWS} are both equal to the official CBS construction price index for new dwellings, μ^t/μ^1 for $t = 1, \ldots, 14$.

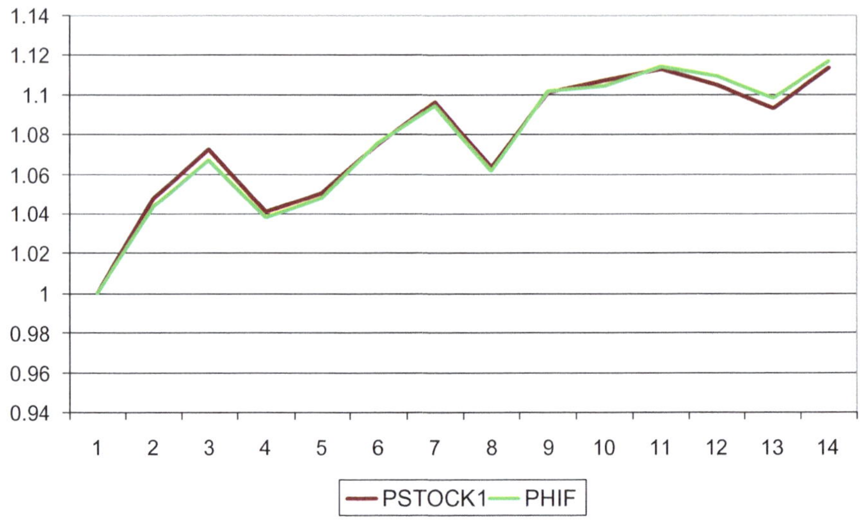

Fig. 3.12 An approximate stock price index P_{Stock1} and the corresponding Fisher hedonic imputation sales price index P_{HIF}

3.11 The Construction of Price Indexes for the Stock of Dwelling Units Using the Results of Hedonic Regressions on the Sales of Houses

In this section, we will show how the hedonic regression models estimated in Sects. 3.6 and 3.9 can be used in order to form approximate price indexes for the stock of dwelling units.

Recall that the system of hedonic regression equations for the hedonic imputation model discussed in Sect. 3.6 was Eq. (3.15), where L_n^t, S_n^t and A_n^t denote, respectively, the land area, structure area, and age (in decades) of the detached house n which was sold in period t. In order to form a price index for the stock of dwelling units in the town of "A", it would be necessary to know L, S and A for the entire stock of detached houses in "A" for some base period. This information is not available to us but we treat the total number of houses sold over the 14 quarters as an approximation to the stock of dwellings of this type.[43] Thus there are $N \equiv N(1) + N(2) + \cdots + N(14)$ houses that were transacted during the 14 periods in our sample.[44]

[43]This approximation would probably be an adequate one if the sample period were a decade or so. Obviously, our sample period of 14 quarters is too short to be a good approximation but the method we are suggesting can be illustrated using this rough approximation. There are also sample selectivity problems with this approximation; i.e., new houses will be over represented using this method.

[44]We did not delete the observations for houses that were transacted multiple times over the 14 quarters since the same house transacted during two or more of the quarters is not actually the same house due to depreciation and renovations.

Recall the hedonic regression Eq. (3.15) in Sect. 3.6 and let α^{t^*}, β^{t^*}, γ^{t^*} and δ^{t^*} denote the estimates for the unknown parameters in (3.15) for quarter t for $t = 1, ..., 14$. Our approximation to *the total value of the housing stock for quarter t*, V^t, is defined as follows:

$$V^t \equiv \sum_{s=1}^{14} \sum_{n=1}^{N(s)} \left[\alpha^{t^*} + \beta^{t^*} L_n^s + \gamma^{t^*}(1 - \delta^t A_n^s) S_n^s\right]; \quad t = 1, ..., 14. \tag{3.34}$$

Thus V^t is simply the imputed value of all of the houses that traded during the 14 quarters in our sample using the estimated regression coefficients for the quarter t hedonic imputation regression as weights for the characteristics of each house. Dividing the V^t series by the value for Quarter 1, V^1, is our estimated stock price index, P_{Stock1}, for the town of "A". This is a form of a Lowe index; see the CPI Manual (ILO et al. 2004) for additional material on the properties of Lowe indexes. This price index for the stock of housing units is compared with the corresponding Fisher hedonic imputation price index, P_{HIF}, from Sect. 3.6 in Table 3.13 and Fig. 3.12.

It can be seen that the differences between the two series are generally quite small, less than one half of a percentage point for each quarter.

The same kind of construction of a stock index can be done for the other hedonic regression models that were implemented for sales of houses in previous sections. We will conclude this section by constructing an approximate stock price index using the results of the cost based hedonic regression model that used exogenous information on the price of structures that was explained in Sect. 3.9 above. Recall that this model

Table 3.13 An approximate stock price index P_{Stock1} and the corresponding Fisher hedonic imputation sales price index P_{HIF}

Quarter	P_{Stock1}	P_{HIF}
1	1.00000	1.00000
2	1.04791	1.04356
3	1.07255	1.06746
4	1.04131	1.03834
5	1.05040	1.04794
6	1.07549	1.07553
7	1.09594	1.09460
8	1.06316	1.06158
9	1.10137	1.10174
10	1.10708	1.10411
11	1.11289	1.11430
12	1.10462	1.10888
13	1.09278	1.09824
14	1.11370	1.11630

was defined by Eqs. (3.22)–(3.24) and (3.33). Recall also that the sets of period t sales of small, medium and large lot houses were defined as $N_S(t)$, $N_M(t)$ and $N_L(t)$ respectively and the total number of sales in period t was defined as $N(t)$ for $t = 1, \ldots, 14$. Denote the estimated parameter values for the model (3.22)–(3.24) and (3.33) by δ^*, γ^{1^*}, and $\beta_S^{t^*}$, $\beta_M^{t^*}$, $\beta_L^{t^*}$ for $t = 1, \ldots, 14$. The *estimated period t values of all small, medium and large lot houses* traded over the 14 quarters, V_{LS}^t, V_{LM}^t, V_{LL}^t for $t = 1, \ldots, 14$, are defined by (3.35)–(3.37) respectively:

$$V_{LS}^t \equiv \sum_{r=1}^{14} \sum_{n \in N_S(r)} \beta_S^{t^*} L_n^r; \quad t = 1, \ldots, 14; \tag{3.35}$$

$$V_{LM}^t \equiv \sum_{r=1}^{14} \sum_{n \in N_M(r)} \{\beta_S^{t^*}[160] + \beta_M^{t^*}[L_n^r - 160]\}; \quad t = 1, \ldots, 14; \tag{3.36}$$

$$V_{LL}^t \equiv \sum_{r=1}^{14} \sum_{n \in N_L(r)} \{\beta_S^{t^*}[160] + \beta_M^{t^*}[140] + \beta_L^{t^*}[L_n^r - 300]\}; \quad t = 1, \ldots, 14; \tag{3.37}$$

$$V_S^t \equiv \sum_{r=1}^{14} \sum_{n=1}^{N(r)} \gamma^{1^*} \mu^t (1 - \delta^* A_n^r) S_n^r; \quad t = 1, \ldots, 14. \tag{3.38}$$

The estimated period t value of quality adjusted structures, V_S^t, is defined by (3.38) above, where all structures traded during the 14 quarters are included in this imputed total value. The *quantities* that correspond to the above period t valuations of the stock of structures and the 3 land stocks are defined as follows[45]:

$$Q_{LS}^t \equiv \sum_{r=1}^{14} \sum_{n \in N_S(r)} L_n^r; \quad t = 1, \ldots, 14; \tag{3.39}$$

$$Q_{LM}^t \equiv \sum_{r=1}^{14} \sum_{n \in N_M(r)} L_n^r; \quad t = 1, \ldots, 14; \tag{3.40}$$

$$Q_{LL}^t \equiv \sum_{r=1}^{14} \sum_{n \in N_L(r)} L_n^r; \quad t = 1, \ldots, 14; \tag{3.41}$$

$$Q_S^t \equiv \sum_{r=1}^{14} \sum_{n=1}^{N(r)} (1 - \delta^* A_n^r) S_n^r; \quad t = 1, \ldots, 14. \tag{3.42}$$

The *approximate stock prices*, P_{LS}^t, P_{LM}^t, P_{LL}^t and P_S^t, that correspond to the values and quantities defined by (3.35)–(3.42) are defined in the usual way:

[45] The quantities defined by (3.39)–(3.42) are constant over the 14 quarters: $Q_{LS}^t = 77455$, $Q_{LM}^t = 258550$, $Q_{LL}^t = 253590$ and $Q_S^t = 238476.3$ for $t = 1, \ldots, 14$.

Table 3.14 Approximate price indexes for the stock of houses P_{Stock}, the stock of land P_{LStock}, the stock of structures P_{SStock} and the corresponding sales indexes P_{L4}, P_{S4} and P_4

Quarter	P_{Stock}	P_4	P_{LStock}	P_{L4}	P_{SStock}	P_{S4}
1	1.00000	1.00000	1.00000	1.00000	1.00000	1.00000
2	1.04331	1.04373	1.13279	1.13864	0.99291	0.99291
3	1.06798	1.06752	1.16171	1.16526	1.01518	1.01518
4	1.04042	1.03889	1.04209	1.04214	1.03947	1.03947
5	1.04767	1.04628	1.11973	1.11893	1.00709	1.00709
6	1.07540	1.07541	1.17873	1.18183	1.01721	1.01721
7	1.09192	1.09121	1.23357	1.23501	1.01215	1.01215
8	1.05763	1.05601	1.13299	1.13257	1.01518	1.01518
9	1.09829	1.09701	1.21171	1.21204	1.03441	1.03441
10	1.10065	1.09727	1.20029	1.19545	1.04453	1.04453
11	1.10592	1.10564	1.17178	1.17747	1.06883	1.06883
12	1.10038	1.09815	1.11507	1.11588	1.09211	1.09211
13	1.08934	1.08863	1.04668	1.05070	1.11336	1.11336
14	1.10777	1.10486	1.09784	1.09648	1.11336	1.11336

$$P_{LS}^t \equiv \frac{V_{LS}^t}{Q_{LS}^t};\ P_{LM}^t \equiv \frac{V_{LM}^t}{Q_{LM}^t};\ P_{LL}^t \equiv \frac{V_{LL}^t}{Q_{LL}^t};\ P_S^t \equiv \frac{V_S^t}{Q_S^t};\quad t = 1, \ldots, 14. \quad (3.43)$$

With prices defined by (3.43) and quantities defined by (3.39)–(3.42), an approximate stock index of land prices, P_{LStock}, is formed by aggregating the three types of land and an overall approximate stock index of house prices, P_{Stock}, is formed by aggregating the three types of land with the constant quality structures. Since quantities are constant over all 14 quarters, the Laspeyres, Paasche and Fisher indexes are all equal.[46] An approximate constant quality stock price for structures, P_{SStock}, is formed by normalizing the series P_S^t. The approximate stock price series, P_{LStock}, P_{SStock} and P_{Stock} are listed in Table 3.14 and are charted in Fig. 3.13. For comparison purposes, the corresponding price indexes based on sales of properties for the model presented in Sect. 3.9, P_{L4}, P_{S4} and P_4, are also listed in Table 3.14.

From Table 3.14, it can be seen that the new stock price index for structures, P_{SStock}, coincides with the sales type price index for constant quality structures, P_{S4}, that was described in Sect. 3.9 above. Thus P_{S4} is not charted in Fig. 3.13. From Fig. 3.13, it can be seen that the overall approximate price index for the stock of houses in "A", P_{Stock}, cannot be distinguished from the corresponding overall sales price index P_4 which was discussed in Sect. 3.9 and similarly, the overall approximate price index for the stock of land in "A", P_{LStock}, cannot be distinguished from the corresponding overall sales price index for land in "A", P_{L4}. However, Table 3.14 shows that there are small differences between the stock and sales indexes.

[46]Fixed base and chained Laspeyres, Paasche and Fisher indexes are also equal under these circumstances.

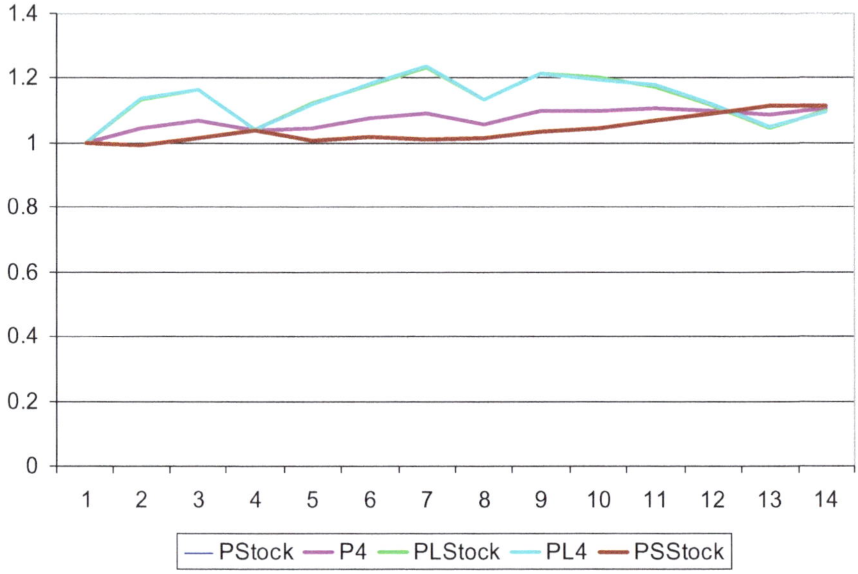

Fig. 3.13 Approximate price indexes for the stock of houses P_{Stock}, the stock of land P_{LStock}, the stock of structures P_{SStock} and the corresponding sales indexes P_{L4} and P_4

Our conclusion here is that the hedonic regression models for the sales of houses can readily be adapted to yield Lowe type price indexes for the stocks of houses and generally, there do not appear to be major differences between the two index types.

3.12 Summary and Conclusion

Several tentative conclusions can be drawn from this study:

- If information on the sales of houses during a quarter or month is available by location and if information on the age of the houses, the type of housing and their living space and lot size areas is also available, then stratification methods and hedonic regression methods for constructing house price indexes of sales will give approximately the same answers, provided the information on age, lot size and house size is used for both types of method.
- Our preferred method for constructing a sales price index is the hedonic imputation method explained in Sect. 3.6 but virtually all forms of hedonic regression model using the three main characteristics used in this study give much the same answer, at least when the target index is an overall house price index.
- However, when a linear specification based on a cost of production approach to hedonic regressions is used, the fit to the data is usually considerably better than the fits that result when alternative hedonic regression models are used.
- Rolling year indexes can be used to eliminate seasonality or traditional econometric methods can be applied to the unadjusted house price series; see Sect. 3.3 above.

- A problem with many hedonic regression models for house prices is that as new data become available, the historical series must constantly be revised. However, if the rolling window technique pioneered by Shimizu et al. (2011) is used, this problem is solved and the results do not differ materially from the one big regression approach that leads to constant revisions; see Sect. 3.10.
- If separate land and structures house price indexes are required, then the methods based on the cost of production approach with restrictions seem promising; see the method based on imposing monotonicity restrictions on the price of structures explained in Sect. 3.8 and the method based on the use of exogenous information on the price of structures explained in Sect. 3.9.
- Hedonic regression methods based on the sales of dwelling units can readily be adapted to yield price indexes for the stock of dwellings; see Sect. 3.11.

Of course, this is only one study and the results here need to be confirmed using other data sets. However, it seems likely that at least some of the above conclusions will not be overturned by future research.

Some problems that require future research are:

- There is a need to introduce sensible imputation procedures for the prices that correspond to empty cells when using stratification methods. This is particularly important if it is desired to use stratification methods to construct price indexes for the stock of houses.
- The techniques here need to be extended to encompass the use of additional characteristics.
- It would be useful to extend the spline treatment of plot size to the size of the structure; i.e., it is likely that the price per meter squared of structure increases as the structure size increases and a spline model could capture this variation.
- The basic method used here that concentrated on holding location constant and using information on three main characteristics needs to be adapted to deal with sales of apartments and row houses, where other characteristics are likely to be important.

3.13 Appendix: Tables of Values for the Figures in the Text

See Tables 3.2, 3.3, 3.4, 3.5, 3.6, 3.7, 3.8, 3.9, 3.10, 3.11, 3.12, 3.13 and 3.14.

References

Alterman, W., W.E. Diewert, and R.C. Feenstra. 1999. *International Trade Price Indexes and Seasonal Commodities*. Washington, DC: Department of Labor, Bureau of Labor Statistics, U.S. Government Printing Office.

Balk, B.M. 1998. On the use of unit value indices as consumer price subindices. In *Proceedings of the Fourth Meeting of the International Working Group on Price Indices*, ed. W. Lane. Washington, DC: Bureau of Labour Statistics.
Balk, B.M. 2008. *Price and Quantity Index Numbers*. New York: Cambridge University Press.
Central Bureau of Statistics. 2010. *New Dwelling Output Price Indices, Building Costs, 2005 = 100, Price Index: Building Costs including VAT, October 15*. Den Haag: Statline, CBS.
Court, A.T. 1939. Hedonic price indexes with automotive examples. In *The Dynamics of Automobile Demand*, 98–117. New York: General Motors Corporation.
de Haan, J. 2003. Time Dummy Approaches to Hedonic Price Measurement. Paper presented at the Seventh Meeting of the International Working Group on Price Indices, (Ottawa Group), May 27–29, 2003. Paris: INSEE. http://www.insee.fr/en/nom_def_met/colloques/ottawa/ottawa_papers.htm.
de Haan, J. 2009. Comment on hedonic imputation versus time dummy hedonic indexes. In *Studies in Income and Wealth 70*, ed. Price Index Concepts, W.E. Measurement, J.S.Greenlees Diewert, and C.R. Hulten, 196–200. Chicago: University of Chicago Press.
de Haan, J. 2010. Hedonic price indexes: A comparison of imputation, time dummy and re-pricing methods. *Jahrbücher für Nationalökonomie und Statistik* 230 (6): 772–791.
de Haan, J., and H. van der Grient. 2011. Eliminating chain drift in price indexes based on scanner data. *Journal of Econometrics*. (forthcoming).
Diewert, W.E. 1980. Aggregation problems in the measurement of capital. In *The Measurement of Capital*, ed. D. Usher, 433–528. Chicago: The University of Chicago Press.
Diewert, W.E. 1983. The treatment of seasonality in a cost of living index. In *Price Level Measurement*, ed. W.E. Diewert, and C. Montmarquette, 1019–1045. Ottawa: Statistics Canada.
Diewert, W.E. 1998. High inflation, seasonal commodities and annual index numbers. *Macroeconomic Dynamics* 2: 456–471.
Diewert, W.E. 1999. Index number approaches to seasonal adjustment. *Macroeconomic Dynamics* 3: 1–21.
Diewert, W.E. 2003a. Hedonic regressions: A consumer theory approach. In *Scanner Data and Price Indexes*, Studies in Income and Wealth, vol. 64, ed. R.C. Feenstra and M.D. Shapiro, 317–348. NBER and University of Chicago Press.
Diewert, W.E. 2003b. Hedonic Regressions: A Review of Some Unresolved Issues. Paper presented at the 7th Meeting of the Ottawa Group, Paris, May 27–29. http://www.ottawagroup.org/pdf/07/Hedonics%20unresolved%20issues%20-%20Diewert%20(2003).pdf.
Diewert, W.E. 2007. The Paris OECD-IMF Workshop on Real Estate Price Indexes: Conclusions and Future Directions. Discussion Paper 07-01, Department of Economics, University of British Columbia, Vancouver, British Columbia, Canada, V6T 1Z1.
Diewert, W.E., Y. Finkel, and Y. Artsev. 2009. Empirical evidence on the treatment of seasonal products: The israeli experience. In *Price and Productivity Measurement: Volume 2; Seasonality*, ed. W.E. Diewert, B.M. Balk, D. Fixler, K.J. Fox, and A.O. Nakamura, 53–78. Trafford Press.
Diewert, W.E., J. de Haan, and R. Hendriks. 2010. The Decomposition of a House Price Index into Land and Structures Components: A Hedonic Regression Approach. Discussion Paper 10-01, Department of Economics, University of British Columbia, Vancouver, Canada, V6T 1Z1.
Diewert, W.E., S. Heravi, and M. Silver. 2009. Hedonic imputation versus time dummy hedonic indexes. In *Studies in Income and Wealth 70*, ed. Price Index Concepts, W.E. Measurement, J.S.Greenlees Diewert, and C.R. Hulten, 161–196. Chicago: University of Chicago Press.
Diewert, W.E., and P. von der Lippe. 2010. Notes on unit value bias. *Journal of Economics and Statistics*. (forthcoming).
Fisher, I. 1922. *The Making of Index Numbers*. Boston: Houghton-Mifflin.
Griliches, Z. 1971a. Hedonic price indexes for automobiles: An econometric analysis of quality change. In *Price Indexes and Quality Change*, ed. Z. Griliches, 55–87. Cambridge, MA: Harvard University Press.
Griliches, Z. 1971b. Introduction: Hedonic price indexes revisited. In *Price Indexes and Quality Change*, ed. Z. Griliches, 3–15. Cambridge, MA: Harvard University Press.

Hill, T.P. 1988. Recent developments in index number theory and practice. *OECD Economic Studies* 10: 123–148.

Hill, T.P. 1993. Price and volume measures. In *System of National Accounts 1993*, 379–406. Eurostat, IMF, OECD, UN and World Bank, Luxembourg, Washington, DC, Paris, New York, and Washington, DC.

ILO, IMF, OECD, UNECE, Eurostat, and World Bank. 2004. *Consumer Price Index Manual: Theory and Practice*, ed. P. Hill. ILO: Geneva.

IMF, ILO, OECD, Eurostat, UNECE, and the World Bank. 2004. *Producer Price Index Manual: Theory and Practice*, ed. Paul Armknecht. Washington, DC: International Monetary Fund.

IMF, ILO, OECD, UNECE, and World Bank. 2009. *Export and Import Price Index Manual*, ed. M. Silver. IMF: Washington, DC.

Ivancic, L., W.E. Diewert, and K.J. Fox. 2011. Scanner data, time aggregation and the construction of price indexes. *Journal of Econometrics*. (forthcoming).

Koev, E., and J.M.C. Santos Silva. 2008. *Hedonic Methods for Decomposing House Price Indices into Land and Structure Components, October, Unpublished Paper*. England: Department of Economics, University of Essex.

Laspeyres, E. 1871. Die Berechnung einer mittleren Waarenpreissteigerung. *Jahrbücher für Nationalökonomie und Statistik* 16: 296–314.

McMillen, D.P. 2003. The return of centralization to chicago: Using repeat sales to identify changes in house price distance gradients. *Regional Science and Urban Economics* 33: 287–304.

Mudgett, B.D. 1955. The measurement of seasonal movements in price and quantity indexes. *Journal of the American Statistical Association* 50: 93–98.

Muellbauer, J. 1974. Household production theory, quality and the 'Hedonic technique'. *American Economic Review* 64: 977–994.

Paasche, H. 1874. Über die Preisentwicklung der letzten Jahre nach den Hamburger Borsennotirungen. *Jahrbücher für Nationalökonomie und Statistik* 12: 168–178.

Rosen, S. 1974. Hedonic prices and implicit markets: Product differentiation in pure competition. *Journal of Political Economy* 82: 34–55.

Shimizu, C., K.G. Nishimura, and T. Watanabe. 2011. Housing prices in Tokyo: A comparison of hedonic and repeat sales measures. *Journal of Economics and Statistics*. (forthcoming).

Silver, M. 2009a. *Do Unit Value Export, Import, and Terms of Trade Indices Represent or Misrepresent Price Indices? IMF Staff Papers 56, 297–322*. Washington, DC: IMF.

Silver, M. 2009b. Unit value indices. In IMF, ILO, OECD, UNECE and World Bank (2008), *Export and Import Price Index Manual*, ed. M. Silver. IMF: Washington, DC.

Silver, M. 2010. The Wrongs and Rights of Unit Value Indices. Review of Income and Wealth, Series 56. *Special Issue* 1: S206–S223.

Statistics Portugal (Instituto Nacional de Estatistica). 2009. Owner-Occupied Housing: Econometric Study and Model to Estimate Land Prices, Final Report. In Paper presented to the Eurostat Working Group on the Harmonization of Consumer Price Indices, March 26–27. Luxembourg: Eurostat.

Stone, R. 1956. *Quantity and Price Indexes in National Accounts*. Paris: OECD.

Thorsnes, P. 1997. Consistent estimates of the elasticity of substitution between land and non-land inputs in the production of housing. *Journal of Urban Economics* 42: 98–108.

Triplett, J.E. 2004. *Handbook on Hedonic Indexes and Quality Adjustments in Price Indexes: Special Application to Information Technology Products*. STI Working Paper 2004/9, OECD Directorate for Science, Technology and Industry, DSTI/DOC(2004)9, Paris: OECD.

Triplett, J.E., and R.J. McDonald. 1977. Assessing the quality error in output measures: The case of refrigerators. *The Review of Income and Wealth* 23 (2): 137–156.

Chapter 4
Estimation of Residential Property Price Index: Methodology and Data Sources

4.1 Introduction

Fluctuations in real estate prices have substantial impacts on economic activities. In Japan, a sharp rise in real estate prices during the latter half of the 1980s and its decline in the early 1990s led to a decade-long stagnation of the Japanese economy. More recently, a rapid rise in housing prices and its reversal in the United States triggered a global financial crisis. In such circumstances, the development of appropriate indexes that allow one to capture changes in real estate prices with precision is extremely important, not only for policy makers but also for market participants who are looking for the time when housing prices hit bottom. Recent research has focussed on methods of compiling appropriate residential property price indexes. The location, maintenance and the facilities of each house are different from each other in varying degrees, so there are no two houses that are identical in terms of quality. Even if the location and basic structure are the same at two periods of time, the building ages over time and the houses are not identical across time. In other words, it is very difficult to apply the usual *matching methodology* (where the prices of exactly the same item are compared over time) to housing.

As a result, one may say that the construction of constant quality real estate price indexes is one of the most difficult tasks for national statistical agencies. In order to address these measurement problems, Eurostat published the *Residential Property Price Indices Handbook* in 2012. This chapter through Chap. 7 of this Handbook are devoted to methods for constructing constant quality price indexes.[1] Chapter 8 deals with the problems associated with decomposing an overall property price index

[1] This chapter–Chap. 7 deal with the following methods: stratification or mix adjustment methods, hedonic regression methods, repeat sales methods, and appraisal based methods.

The base of this chapter is Shimizu, C., W.E. Diewert, K.G. Nishimura and T. Watanabe. 2014. Residential property price indexes for Japan: an outline of the Japanese official RPPI. Discussion Paper 14-05, Vancouver School of Economics, University of British Columbia. Presented at OECD Workshop on House Price Statistics 2014, OECD, Paris, France, March 24 –25, 2014.

W. E. Diewert et al., *Property Price Index*, Advances in Japanese Business and Economics 11, https://doi.org/10.1007/978-4-431-55942-9_4

into land and structure components,[2] Section 4.3 reviews methods currently used by private and government index providers and Section 4.4 discusses data sources for PPI.

In the wake of the release of this *Handbook*, how should different countries construct residential property price indexes? With the start of the Residential Property Price Indices Handbook project, the government of Japan set up an Advisory Board through the Ministry of Land, Infrastructure, Transport, and Tourism (MLIT) and is proceeding with the development of a new Japanese official residential property price index. This paper outlines the results of the advisory board's ongoing review with regard to the development of a residential property price index for Japan.[3]

Sections 4.2 and 4.3 below summarize the results of deliberations by the Advisory Board regarding residential property price indexes estimation methods. The material in these sections is based on the paper by Shimizu et al. (2010a). Section 4.4 summarizes the results of deliberations regarding selection of data sources. Section 4.5 then outlines the results of analysis of an outstanding issue: methods for separating housing prices into land and building component prices. Finally, Sect. 4.6 summarizes what kind of index the government of Japan intends to publish as an official Residential Property Price Index.[4]

4.2 Alternative Methods for Constructing Residential Property Price Indexes

4.2.1 Introduction: The Two Main Methods for Making Quality Adjustments

A key starting point in estimating a housing price index is to recognize that each property at each point in time is a unique item. Even if the location and basic structure of the housing unit are the same at two points in time, depreciation, alternative maintenance policies and renovations alter the quality of the structure so that like cannot be precisely compared with like. Given this special feature of houses and hence housing services, an important task for researchers is to make adjustments for differences in quality. There are two methods widely used by practitioners and researchers: the *hedonic method* and the *repeat sales method*. A primary purpose

[2]This decomposition is required in order to construct the national accounts for a country.

[3]The Advisory Board was set up by the Ministry of Land, Infrastructure, Transport and Tourism, with the participation of the Bank of Japan, Financial Services Agency, Ministry of Justice (which is the department responsible for the land registry), Statistics Japan (the department responsible for the consumer price index), the Cabinet Office (the department responsible for SNA), the Japan Association of Real Estate Appraisers and various realtor associations. As of 2013, the Advisory Board also began developing a official Commercial Property Price Index in addition to developing the Residential Property Price Index.

[4]Sections 4.2 and 4.3 draw heavily on the paper by Shimizu et al. (2010a).

of the paper by Shimizu et al. (2010a) was to compare these two methods using a unique dataset that we they compiled from individual listings in a widely circulated real estate advertisement magazine.

Previous studies on house price indexes have identified several problems for each of the two main methods for quality adjustment. The real estate literature has identified the following problems with the repeat sales method:

- The repeat sales method may suffer from *sample selection bias* because houses that are traded multiple times have different characteristics than a typical house.[5]
- The repeat sales method basically assumes that *property characteristics remain unchanged over time*. In particular, the repeat sales method neglects depreciation and possible renovations to the structure.[6]

On the other hand, the hedonic method suffers from the following problems:

- The *failure to include relevant variables* in hedonic regression may result in estimation bias.[7]
- An *incorrect functional form* may be assumed for the hedonic regression model.[8]
- The assumption of *no structural change* (i.e., no changes in parameters over time) over the entire sample period may be too restrictive.[9]

Given that true quality adjusted price changes are not observable, it is difficult to say which of the two measures performs better. However, at least from a practical perspective, it is often said that the repeat sales method represents a better choice because it is less costly to implement.[10] However, as far as the Japanese housing market is concerned, there are some additional concerns about the repeat sales method:

- The Japanese housing market is less liquid than those in the United States and European countries, so that a house is less likely to be traded multiple times.[11]

---

[5]See Clapp and Giaccotto (1992). Repeat sales that occur in very short time periods are often not regarded as " typical" sales. In particular, the initial sale may take place at a below market price and the subsequent rapid resale takes place at the market price, and this phenomenon may lead to an upward bias in the resulting repeat sales price index. Of course, this source of upward bias is partially offset by the downward bias in the repeat sales method due to its neglect to make a quality adjustment for the depreciation of the structure.

[6]See Case and Shiller (1987, 1989), Clapp and Giaccotto (1992, 1998), Goodman and Thibodeau (1998), Case et al. (1991) and Diewert (2010).

[7]See Case and Quigley (1991) and Ekeland et al. (2004).

[8]See Diewert (2003a, b).

[9]See Case et al. (1991), Clapp and Giaccotto (1992, 1998), Shimizu and Nishimura (2006, 2007) and Shimizu et al. (2010a).

[10]See Bourassa et al. (2006). The hedonic method requires information on property characteristics whereas the repeat sales method does not require any characteristics information. However, this informational advantage of the repeat sales method is offset by its *informational sparseness disadvantage*; i.e., repeat sales information may be so infrequent so as to make the construction of accurate price indexes impossible. Moreover, unless the sample selection bias exactly offsets the depreciation bias, we can say that the repeat sales method is definitely biased whereas we cannot definitely assert that the hedonic method is biased.

[11]This may be partly due to the presence of legal restrictions in Japan on reselling a house within a short period of time.

- The quality of a house declines more rapidly over time in Japan because of the short lifespan of houses and the fact that—for various reasons—renovations to restore the quality of a house play a relatively unimportant role. This implies that depreciation plays a more important role in the determination of house prices, which is not taken into account in the repeat sales method.

Given these features of the Japanese housing market, Shimizu et al. (2010a) argued that, at least in Japan, the hedonic method is a better choice. Another important advantage of the hedonic method over the repeat sales method is that the former method can lead to a decomposition of the sales price of a property into land and structure components. This decomposition cannot be obtained using the repeat sales method.

In the remainder of this section, we will discuss the various variants of the hedonic regression and repeat sales models that are used in practice.

4.2.2 *The Standard Hedonic Regression Model*

We begin with a description of the standard hedonic regression model. Suppose that we have data for house prices and property characteristics for periods $t = 1, 2, \ldots, T$. It is assumed that the price of house i in period t, P_{it}, is given by a *Cobb-Douglas function* of the lot size of the house, L_i, and the amount of structures capital in constant quality units, K_{it}:

$$P_{it} = P_t L_i^{\alpha} K_{it}^{\beta} \tag{4.1}$$

where P_t is the logarithm of the *quality adjusted house price index for period t* and α and β are positive parameters.[12] It is assumed that housing capital, K_{it}, is subject to *generalized exponential depreciation* so that the housing capital in period t is given by

$$K_{it} = B_i \exp[-\delta A_{it}^{\lambda}] \tag{4.2}$$

where B_i is the floor space of the structure, A_{it} is the age of the structure in period t, δ is a parameter between 0 and 1, and λ is a positive parameter. Note that if $\lambda = 1$, Eq. (4.2) reduces to the usual exponential model of depreciation with a constant rate of

[12]McMillen (2003) adopted the same Cobb-Douglas production function for housing services. Thorsnes (1997) described housing output as a constant elasticity substitution production function of the lot size and housing capital, and provided some empirical evidence that the elasticity of substitution is close to unity, which implies that the Cobb-Douglas production function is a good approximation of the technology used in the production of housing services. In contrast, Diewert (2010, 2011) suggested some possible hedonic regression models that might lead to additive decompositions of an overall property price into land and structures components. Additive decomposition models have been estimated by Diewert et al. (2011a, b) and Eurostat (2011) using Dutch data and by Diewert and Shimizu (2013) using data for Tokyo. We will discuss these additive models in Sect. 4.5 below.

depreciation over time; if $\lambda > 1$, the depreciation rate increases with time; if $\lambda < 1$, the depreciation rate decreases with time.

By substituting (4.2) into (4.1), and taking the logarithm of both sides of the resulting equation, we obtain the following equation:

$$\ln P_{it} = \ln P_t + \alpha \ln L_i + \beta \ln B_i - \beta \delta A_{it}^{\lambda}. \tag{4.3}$$

Adding a vector of attributes of house i in period t other than A_{it}, L_i and K_{it}, denoted by $\boldsymbol{x}_i$[13] and an error term υ_{it} leads to an estimating equation of the form:

$$\ln P_{it} = d_t + \alpha \ln L_i + \beta \ln B_i - \beta \delta A_{it}^{\lambda} + \boldsymbol{\gamma} \cdot \boldsymbol{x}_i + \upsilon_{it} \tag{4.4}$$

where $d_t \equiv \ln P_t$ is the logarithm of the constant quality population price index for period t, P_t, $\boldsymbol{\gamma}$ is a vector of parameters associated with the vector of house i characteristics $\boldsymbol{x}_i$, $\boldsymbol{\gamma} \cdot \boldsymbol{x}_i$ is the inner product of the vectors $\boldsymbol{\gamma}$ and $\boldsymbol{x}_i$ and υ_{it} is an iid normal disturbance.[14]

Running an OLS regression of Eq. (4.4) yields estimates for the coefficients on the time dummy variables, d_t for $t = 1, \ldots, T$ as well as for the parameters α, β, $\boldsymbol{\gamma}$, and δ. After making the normalization $d_1 = 0$, the series of estimated coefficients for the time dummy variables, d_t^* for $t = 1, \ldots, T$, can be exponentiated to yield the time series of constant quality price indexes, $P_t \equiv \exp[d_t^*]$ for $t = 1, \ldots, T$. Note that the coefficients α, β, $\boldsymbol{\gamma}$, and δ are all identified in this regression model.

4.2.3 *The Standard Repeat Sales Model*

The standard repeat sales method[15] starts with the assumption that property characteristics do not change over time and that the parameters associated with these characteristics do not change either. The underlying price determination model is basically the same as in Eq. (4.4). However, the repeat sales method focuses on houses that appear multiple times in the dataset. Suppose that house i is transacted twice, and that the transactions occur in periods s and t with $s < t$. Using Eq. (4.4), the change in the logarithms of the house prices between the two time periods is given by

$$\ln(P_{it}/P_{is}) = d_t - d_s - \beta\delta(A_{it}^{\lambda} - A_{is}^{\lambda}) + \upsilon_{it} - \upsilon_{is}. \tag{4.5}$$

Note that the terms that do not include time subscripts in Eq. (4.4), namely $\alpha \ln L_i$, $\beta \ln B_i$ and $\boldsymbol{\gamma} \cdot \boldsymbol{x}_i$, all disappear by taking differences with respect to time, so

---

[13]Note that we are assuming that the vector of house i attributes $\boldsymbol{x}_i$ does not depend on the time of sale, t.

[14]Time dummy hedonic regression models date back to Court (1939).

[15]The repeat sales method is due to Bailey et al. (1963).

that the resulting equation is simpler than the original one.[16] Furthermore, assuming no renovation expenditures between the two time periods and no depreciation of housing capital so that $\delta = 0$, Eq. (4.5) reduces to:

$$\ln(P_{it}/P_{is}) = d_t - d_s + \upsilon_{it} - \upsilon_{is}. \tag{4.6}$$

The above equation can be rewritten as the following linear regression model:

$$\ln(P_{it}/P_{is}) = \sum_{j=1}^{T} D_j^{its} d_j + \upsilon_{its} \tag{4.7}$$

where $\upsilon_{its} \equiv \upsilon_{it} - \upsilon_{is}$ is a consolidated error term and D_j^{its} is a dummy variable that takes on the value 1 when $j = t$ (where t is the period when house i is resold), the value -1 when $j = s$ (where s is the period when house i is first sold) and D_j^{its} takes on the value 0 for j not equal to s or t. In order to identify all of the parameters d_j, a normalization is required such as $d_1 \equiv 0$. This normalization will make the house price index equal to unity in the first period. The *standard repeat sales house price indexes* are then defined by $P_t \equiv \exp[d_t^*]$ for $t = 1, 2, \ldots, T$, where the d_t^* are the least squares estimators for the d_t.

4.2.4 *Heteroskedasticity and Age Adjustments to the Repeat Sales Index*

Aspointed out by previous studies, the standard repeat sales index defined above may be biased for two reasons:

- The disturbance term in Eq. (4.7) may be heteroskedastic in the sense that the variance of the disturbance term may be larger when the two transaction dates are further apart.[17]
- The assumption of no depreciation is too restrictive.

Case and Shiller (1987, 1989) address the heteroskedasticity problem in the disturbance term by assuming that the variance of the residual υ_{its} in (4.7) increases as t and s are further apart; i.e., they assume that $E(\upsilon_{its}) = 0$ and $E(\upsilon_{its})^2 = \xi_0 + \xi_1(t - s)$ where ξ_0 and ξ_1 are positive parameters. The Case-Shiller repeat sales index is estimated as follows. First, Eq. (4.7) is estimated, and the resulting squared disturbance term is regressed on $\xi_0 + \xi_1(t - s)$ in order to obtain estimates for ξ_0 and ξ_1.

---

[16] Thus the regression model defined by (4.5) does not require characteristics information on the house(except that information on the age of the house at the time of each transaction is required).

[17] However, if s and t are very close, the variance could also increase due to the "flipping phenomenon"; i.e., a house that is sold twice in a short time period may have a rate of price change between the two time periods that is unusually large on an annualized basis, causing the error variance to increase.

Denote these estimates by ξ_0^* and ξ_1^*. Then Eq. (4.7) is reestimated by Generalized Least Squares (GLS) where observation i, $\ln(P_{it}/P_{is})$, is adjusted by the weight $[\xi_0^* + \xi_1^*(t - s)]^{1/2}$. Denote the resulting GLS estimates for the coefficients d_t on the time dummy variables by d_t^*. The Case-Shiller *heteroskedasticity adjusted repeat sales indexes* are then defined by $P_t \equiv \exp[d_t^*]$ for $t = 1, 2, \ldots, T$.[18]

We turn now to the lack of an age adjustment problem with the repeat sales method. Previous studies on the repeat sales method, including Bailey et al. (1963) and Case and Shiller (1987, 1989), do not pay much attention to the possibility that property characteristics change over time. However, there are no houses that do not depreciate, implying that the quality of a house at the time of selling depends on its age. Also, the quality of a house may change over time because of maintenance and renovation. Finally, its quality may change over time due to changes in the environment surrounding the house, such as the availability of public transportation, the quality of neighbourhood schools and so on.[19] As far as the Japanese housing market is concerned, the structure of a house typically depreciates more quickly than in the United States and Europe, which is likely to cause a larger bias in price indexes if house price depreciation is ignored.

To take account of the depreciation effect, we go back to Eq. (4.5) and rewrite it as follows:[20]

$$\ln(P_{it}/P_{is}) = d_t - d_s - \beta\delta[(A_{is} + t - s)^{\lambda} - A_{is}^{\lambda}] + v_{its}. \tag{4.8}$$

Note that repeat sales indexes that do not include an age term (such as the term involving A_{is} on the right hand side of the above equation) will suffer from a downward bias.[21]

McMillen (2003) considered a simpler version of this model with $\lambda = 1$, so that the depreciation rate is constant over time. When $\lambda = 1$, (4.8) reduces to (4.9):

$$\ln(P_{it}/P_{is}) = d_t - d_s - \beta\delta(t - s) + v_{its}. \tag{4.9}$$

Note that there is exact collinearity between $d_t - d_s$ and $t - s$, so that it is impossible to obtain estimates for the coefficients on the time dummies. McMillen (2003) measured the age difference between two consecutive sales in days while using quar-

[18]As usual, set $d_1^* \equiv d_1 \equiv 1$ so that $P_1 \equiv 1$.

[19]Note that the depreciation model defined by (4.2) can be regarded as a *net depreciation model*; i.e., it is depreciation less "normal" renovation and maintenance expenditures. See Diewert (2011) for more on the topic of constructing a house price index taking depreciation and renovation into consideration.

[20]The analysis which follows is due to Shimizu et al. (2010a).

[21]It should be noted that the official S&P/Case-Shiller home price index is adjusted in the following way to take the age effect into account. Standard and Poor's (2008: 7) states that "sales pairs are also weighted based on the time interval between the first and second sales. If a sales pair interval is longer, then it is more likely that a house may have experienced physical changes. Sales pairs with longer intervals are, therefore, given less weight than sales pairs with shorter intervals."

terly time dummy variables, thereby eliminating the exact collinearity between the time dummies and the age difference.[22]

Shimizu et al. (2010a) eliminated exact multicollinearity by estimating the nonlinear model defined by (4.8).[23] Once the d_t parameters have been estimated by maximum likelihood or nonlinear least squares (denote the estimates by d_t^* with d_1^* set equal to 0), then the *Shimizu, Nishimura and Watanabe repeat sales indexes* P_t are defined as $P_t \equiv \exp[d_t^*]$ for $t = 1, 2, \ldots, T$.

Note that the parameters β and δ are not identified in the nonlinear regression (4.8) because they appear only in the form of $\beta\delta$. This is in sharp contrast with the hedonic regression model defined by (4.4), in which β appears not only as a coefficient of the age term but also as a coefficient on $\ln B_i$, so that β and δ are identified.[24]

4.2.5 Rolling Window Hedonic Regressions: Structural Change Adjustments to the Hedonic Index

Shimizu et al. (2010b, a) modified the standard hedonic model given by Eq. (4.4) so that the parameters associated with the attributes of a house are allowed to change over time. Structural changes in the Japanese housing market have two important features. First, they usually occur only gradually, triggered, with a few exceptions, by changes in regulations by the central and local governments. Such gradual changes are quite different from "regime changes" discussed by econometricians such as Bai and Perron (1998) in which structural parameters exhibit a discontinuous shift at multiple times. Second, changes in parameters reflect structural changes at various time frequencies. Specifically, as found by Shimizu et al. (2010a), some changes in parameters are associated with seasonal changes in housing market activity. For example, the number of transactions is high at the end of a fiscal year, namely, between January and March, when people move from one place to another due to seasonal reasons such as job transfers, while the number is low during the summer. One way to allow for gradual shifts in parameters is to employ an *adjacent period regression*,[25] in which Eq. (4.4) is estimated using only two periods that are adjacent to each other so that the parameter vector $\boldsymbol{\gamma}$ in (4.4) is only held constant for two consecutive periods (as are the other parameters, α, β, δ and λ). The estimated second period price level, $P_2 \equiv \exp[d_2^*]$, is regarded as a chain type index which is used to update

---

[22] However, one would expect approximate multicollinearity to hold in McMillen's model so that the estimated dummy variable parameters may not be too reliable.

[23] See Chau et al. (2005) for another example where a nonlinear specification of the age effect was introduced into the hedonic regression in order to eliminate multicollinearity between the age variable and the time dummy variables.

[24] If the estimated λ parameter for the model defined by (4.8) turns out to be close to one, then as is the case for McMillen's model, there may be an approximate multicollinearity problem with the Shimizu, Nishimura and Watanabe repeat sales model.

[25] The two period time dummy variable hedonic regression was considered explicitly by Court (1939: 109–111) as his hedonic suggestion number two. Griliches (1971: 7) coined the term "adjacent year regression" to describe the two period dummy variable hedonic regression model.

the previously determined index level for the first period, P_1. This method of index construction allows for gradual taste changes thereby minimizing the rigidity disadvantage of the pooled regression model defined by (4.4). Triplett (2004), based on the presumption that coefficients usually change less between two adjacent periods than over more extended intervals, argued that the adjacent-period estimator is "a more benign constraint on the hedonic coefficients." However, as far as seasonal changes in parameters are concerned, this presumption may not necessarily be satisfied, so that an adjacent period regression may not work very well. To cope with this problem, Shimizu et al. (2010a, b) proposed a regression method using multiple "neighborhood periods," typically 12 or 24 months, rather than two adjacent periods. Specifically, they estimated parameters by taking a certain length as the estimation window and shifting this period as in rolling regressions. This method should be able to handle seasonal changes in parameters better than adjacent period regressions, although it may suffer more from the rigidity disadvantage associated with pooling.

To apply this method, estimate the model defined by Eq. (4.4) for periods $t = 1, \ldots, \tau$, where $\tau < T$ represents the *window width.* As usual, set $d_1 = d_1^* \equiv 1$ and denote the remaining estimated time parameters for this first regression by $d_2^*, \ldots, d_\tau^*$. These parameters are exponentiated to define the sequence of house price indexes P_t for the first τ periods; i.e., $P_t \equiv \exp[d_t^*]$ for $t = 1, 2, \ldots, \tau$. Then this τ period regression model using the data for the periods $2, 3, \ldots, \tau + 1$ can be repeated and a new set of estimated time parameters, $d_2^{2*} \equiv 1, d_3^{2*}, \ldots, d_{\tau+1}^{2*}$ can be obtained. The new *price levels* P_t^2 for periods 2 to $\tau + 1$ can be defined as $P_t^2 \equiv \exp[d_t^{2*}]$ for $t = 2, 3, \ldots, \tau + 1$. Obviously, this process of adding the data of the next period to the rolling window regression while dropping the data pertaining to the oldest period in the previous regression can be continued. The focus in the Shimizu et al. (2010b) paper was on determining how the structural parameters in (4.8) changed as the window of observations changed.[26] They did not address the problem of obtaining a coherent time series of price levels from the multiple estimates of price levels that result from these overlapping hedonic regressions.

A coherent strategy for forming a single set of price level estimates from the sequence of Rolling Window regressions works as follows. As indicated in the previous paragraph, the sequence of final price levels P_t for the first τ periods is obtained by exponentiating the estimated time dummy parameters taken from the first Rolling Window regression; i.e., $P_t \equiv \exp[d_t^*]$ for $t = 1, 2, \ldots, \tau$. The next Rolling window regression the data for periods $2, 3, \ldots, \tau + 1$ generates the new set of estimated time parameters, $d_2^{2*} \equiv 1, d_3^{2*}, \ldots, d_{\tau+1}^{2*}$ and the new set of price levels P_t^2 for periods 2 to $\tau + 1$, defined as $P_t^2 \equiv \exp[d_t^{2*}]$ for $t = 2, 3, \ldots, \tau + 1$. Now use only the last two price levels generated by the new regression to define the *final price level* for period $\tau + 1$, $P_{\tau+1}$, as the period τ price level generated by the first regression, P_τ, times (one plus) the rate of change in the price level over the last two periods using the results of the second regression model; i.e., define $P_{\tau+1} \equiv P_\tau(P_{\tau+1}^2/P_\tau^2)$. The next step is to repeat the τ period regression model using the data for the periods $3, 4, \ldots, \tau + 2$ and obtain a new set of estimated time parameters, $d_3^{3*} \equiv 1, d_4^{3*}, \ldots, d_{\tau+2}^{3*}$. Define new

[26]They called their method the *Overlapping Period Hedonic Housing Model* (OPHM).

preliminary price levels $P_t^3 \equiv \exp[d_t^{3*}]$ for $t = 3, 4, \ldots, \tau + 2$ and update $P_{\tau+1}$ by multiplying it by $(P_{\tau+2}^3/P_{\tau+1}^3)$ so that the final price level for period $\tau + 2$ is defined as $P_{\tau+2} \equiv P_{\tau+1}(P_{\tau+2}^3/P_{\tau+1}^3)$. Carry on with the same process until P_T has been defined. This model can be called the *Rolling Window Hedonic Regression model.*[27] *A major advantage of this method over the repeat sales model is that as new data become available each period, previous period index levels are not revised.* Note that the Rolling Window Hedonic Regression method reduces to an adjacent period hedonic regression model if τ equals 2.

In the following section, the various models defined in this section will be illustrated and compared using data for Tokyo on both houses and condominiums.

4.3 A Comparison of Alternative Housing Models for Tokyo

4.3.1 Data Description

Section 4.3 of this paper summarizes the results in Shimizu et al. (2010a), (henceforth referred to as SNW). The data for the SNW paper were collected from a weekly magazine, Shukan Jutaku Joho (Residential Information Weekly), published by Recruit Co., Ltd., one of the largest vendors of residential property listings information in Japan. The Recruit dataset covered the 23 special wards of Tokyo for the period 1986 to 2008, which included the bubble period in the late 1980s and its collapse in the early 1990s. It contained 157,627 listings for condominiums and 315,791 listings for single family houses, for 473,418 listings in total.[28] Shukan Jutaku Joho provided time series for the price of an advertised for sale unit from the week it is first posted

[27] This is the approach used by Shimizu et al. (2010a) to form an overall price index. Ivancic et al. (2009) recommended a variant of the rolling window model where their basic hedonic regression model was the Time Product Dummy model which is the application of Summer's (1973) Country Product Dummy model to the time series context (from the original application to multilateral comparisons of prices across countries). IDF recommended a (weighted) Rolling Year Time Product Dummy method where the window length was chosen to be 13 months. For extensions of the IDF model to more general hedonic regression models, see de Haan and Krsinich (2014). Diewert and Shimizu (2013) implemented a Rolling Window hedonic regression model for Tokyo houses which will be described later in Sect. 4.5. The Rolling Window Hedonic Regression approach to the construction of house price indexes has also been applied by Eurostat (2011; Chap. 8) and by Diewert et al. (2011b).

[28] Shimizu et al. (2004) reported that the Recruit data cover more than 95% of all transactions in the 23 special wards of Tokyo but the coverage for suburban areas is very limited. Therefore the study by Shimizu, Nishimura and Watanabe used only information for the units located in the special wards of Tokyo.

until the week it is removed.[29] SNW used only the price in the final week of listing because that price was close to the final contract price.[30]

Table 4.1 shows a list of the attributes of a house. Key attributes include the *ground area* of the land plot (GA), the *floor space area* of the structure (FS), and the front *road width* of the land plot (RW). The land plot area was available in the original dataset for single family houses but not for condominiums, so SNW estimated the land area that could be attributed to a condominium unit by dividing the land area of the property by the number of units in the structure.[31] The age of a detached house was defined as the number of quarters between the date of the construction of the house and the transaction. SNW constructed a dummy (south-facing dummy, SD) to indicate whether the windows of a house are south-facing or not.[32] The private road dummy, PD, indicated whether a house had an adjacent private road or not. The land only dummy, LD, indicated whether a transaction was only for land without a building or not. The convenience of public transportation from a house was represented by the travel time to the central business district (CBD),[33] which was denoted by TT, and the time to the nearest station,[34] which was denoted by TS. SNW used a ward dummy, WD, to indicate differences in the quality of public services available in each district, and a railway line dummy, RD, to indicate along which railway or subway line a house is located.

SNW used their Tokyo data sets on detached houses and condominiums to construct housing price indexes that used the hedonic regression and repeat sales models that were described in Sect. 4.2 above. Table 4.2 compares the sample SNW used in their hedonic regressions and the sample used in their repeat sales regressions. Since repeat sales regressions use only observations from houses that are traded multiple

---

[29]There are two reasons for removal of the listing of a unit from the magazine: a successful deal or a withdrawal; i.e., in the second case, the seller gives up looking for a buyer and thus withdraws the listing. SNW were allowed to access information regarding which of the two reasons applied for individual cases and they discarded prices where the seller withdrew the listing.

[30]Recruit Co. Ltd. provided SNW with information on contract prices for about 24% of the population of listings. Using this information, SNW were able to confirm that prices in the final week were almost always identical to the contract prices; i.e., they differed at less than a 0.1% probability.

[31]More specifically, the imputed land area attributed to a condo unit was calculated by dividing the sum of the floor space for each unit in the structure by $FAR \times BLR$, where FAR and BLR stand for the floor area ratio and the building to land ratio, respectively. The sum of the floor space of each unit in a structure was available in the original dataset. The maximum values for FAR and BLR are subject to regulation under city planning law. It was assumed that this regulation was binding.

[32]Japanese people are particularly fond of sunshine!

[33]Travel time to the CBD was measured as follows. The metropolitan area of Tokyo is composed of wards and contains a dense railway network. Within this area, SNW chose seven railway or subway stations as central business district stations: Tokyo, Shinagawa, Shibuya, Shinjuku, Ikebukuro, Ueno, and Otemachi. SNW then defined travel time to the CBD as the minutes needed to commute to the nearest of the seven stations in the daytime.

[34]The time to the nearest station, TS, was defined as the walking time to the nearest station if a house was located within walking distance from a station, and the sum of the walking time to a bus stop and the bus travel time from the bus stop to the nearest station if a house is located in a bus transportation area. SNW used a bus dummy, BD, to indicate whether a house was located in walking distance from a railway station or in a bus transportation area.

Table 4.1 List of variables

Abbreviation	Variable	Description	Unit
GA	Ground area	Ground area	m^2
FS	Floor space	Floor space of building	m^2
RW	Front road width	Front road width	10 cm
AGE	Age of a building at the time of transaction	Age of a building at the time of transaction	Quarters
TS	Time to the nearest station	Time distance to the nearest station (walking time or time by bus or car)	Min
TT	Travel time to central business district	Minimum railway riding time in daytime to one of the seven major business district stations	Min
UV	Unit volume	Unit volume/The total number of units of the condominium	Unit
RT	Market reservation time	Period between the date when the data appear in the magazine for the first time and the date of being deleted	Weeks
BD	Bus dummy	Time distance to the nearest station includes taking the bus = 1; Does not include taking the bus = 0	(0, 1)
CD	Car dummy	Time distance to the nearest station includes taking the car = 1; Does not include taking the car = 0	(0, 1)
FD	First floor dummy	The property is on the ground floor = 1 The property is not on the ground floor = 0	(0, 1)
BBD	Before new building standard law dummy	Construction year is before 1980(when New Building Standard Law enacted)[a] = 1; Construction year is after 1981 = 0	(0, 1)
SRC	Steel reinforced concrete dummy	"Steel" reinforced concrete frame structure = 1; Other structure (Reinforced concrete frame structure) = 0	(0, 1)
SD	South-facing dummy	Main windows facing south = 1 Main windows facing no facing south = 0	(0, 1)
PD	Private road dummy	Site includes a part of private road[b] = 1 Site does not include any part of private road = 0.	(0, 1)
LD	Land only dummy	The transaction includes "land" only (no building is on the site) = 1; The transaction includes land and building = 0	(0, 1)
OD	Old house dummy[c]	The transaction includes existing buliding which can not be used = 1; The transaction doesn't include exsitng building which can be used = 0	(0, 1)

(continued)

Table 4.1 (continued)

Abbreviation	Variable	Description	Unit
BA	Balcony area	Balcony area	m^2
BLR	Building-to-land ratio	Building-to-land ratio regulated by City Planning Law	%
FAR	Floor area ratio	Floor area ratio regulated by City Planning Law	%
WD_k	Ward dummies	Located in ward $k = 1$; Located in other ward $= 0$ $(k = 0, \ldots, K)$	(0, 1)
RD_l	Railway line dummies	Located on railway line $l = 1$; Located on other railway line $= 0$ $(l = 0, \ldots, L)$	(0, 1)
TD_m	Time dummies (monthly)	Month $m = 1$; Other month $= 0$ $(m = 0, \ldots, M)$	(0, 1)

[a]The new building standard law established earthquake-resistance standards.

[b] The building standard law prohibits the construction of a building if the site faces a road which is narrower than 2 m. If the site does not face a road which is wider than 2 m, the site must provide a part of its own site as a part of the road.

[c] If there is an existing building which cannot be used, the buyer has to pay the demolition costs.

Table 4.2 Hedonic versus repeat sales samples

Variable	Condominiums		Single family houses	
	Hedonic sample	Repeat sales sample	Hedonic sample	Repeat sales sample
Average price (10,000 yen)	3, 862.26 (3, 190.83)	4, 463.43 (4284.10)	7, 950.65 (8275.04)	7, 635.24 (7055.96)
FS: Floor space (m^2)	58.31 (21.47)	59.54 (24.09)	102.53 (43.47)	105.82 (45.60)
GA: Ground area (m^2)	23.39 (12.79)	20.53 (11.97)	108.20 (71.19)	101.41 (63.17)
Age: Age of building (quarters)	55.61 (33.96)	60.07 (34.05)	54.06 (32.28)	21.26 (30.88)
TS: Time to the nearest station (minutes)	7.96 (4.43)	7.77 (4.28)	9.85 (4.54)	9.60 (4.37)
TT: Travel time to central business district (minutes)	12.58 (7.09)	10.73 (6.88)	13.23 (6.34)	11.89 (6.18)
	$n = 157,627$	$n = 67,436$	$n = 315,791$	$n = 19,428\%$

times, the repeat sales sample is a subset of the hedonic sample. The ratio of the repeat sales sample to the hedonic sample is 42.7% for condominiums and 6.1% for single family houses, indicating that single family houses are less likely to appear multiple times on the market.

The average price for condominiums was 38 million yen in the hedonic sample, while it was 44 million yen in the repeat sales sample. On the other hand, the average price for single family houses was 79 million yen in the hedonic sample and 76 million yen in the repeat sales sample. Turning to the attributes or characteristics of houses and condos, houses in the repeat sales sample tended to be larger in terms of the floor space, and more conveniently located in terms of time to the nearest station and travel time to a central business district, although these differences are not statistically significant. An important and statistically significant difference between the two samples was the average age of units in the case of single family houses: namely, the repeat sales sample consisted of houses that were constructed relatively recently. Somewhat interestingly, single family houses in the repeat sales sample were larger in terms of floor space, more conveniently located, more recently constructed, but were less expensive.

4.3.2 Estimation Results

Table 4.3 presents the regression results obtained by Shimizu et al. (2010a) for the standard hedonic model given by Eq. (4.4). This model worked well, both for condominiums and single family houses: the adjusted R^2 was 0.882 for condominiums and 0.822 for single family houses. The coefficients of interest are the ones associated with the age effect. The estimates of δ and λ are 0.033 and 0.691 for condominiums, implying that the initial capital stock of structures declines to 0.457 after 100 quarters, and that the average annual geometric depreciation rate for 100 quarters is 0.031. On the other hand, the estimates of δ and λ for single family houses are 0.020 and 0.688, implying that the initial capital stock of structures declines to 0.619 after 100 quarters, and that the average annual depreciation rate for 100 quarters is 0.019. These estimated depreciation rates seem to be quite reasonable.

Table 4.4 presents the SNW regression results for the age adjusted repeat sales model given by Eq. (4.8). The estimates for $\beta\delta$ and λ were 0.0098 and 0.894 for condominiums, and 0.002 and 1.104 for single family houses. Note that the repeat sales regressions do not allow us to estimate β and δ separately. If estimates of β are borrowed from the hedonic regressions, the repeat sales regression value of δ turned out to be 0.019 for condominiums and 0.004 for single family houses. These estimates imply that the average annual rate of depreciation for 100 quarters is 0.045 for condominiums and 0.025 for single family houses. Figure 4.1 compares the hedonic and repeat sales regressions in terms of the estimated age effect. It can be seen that the estimates from the repeat sales regressions indicate slightly faster depreciation than the ones from the hedonic regressions both for condominiums and for single family houses, although the difference is not very large.

Table 4.3 Hedonic regressions

Variable	Condominiums		Single family houses	
	Coefficient	t-value	Coefficient	t-value
Constant	3.263	372.920	4.508	265.376
GA: Ground area (m^2)	0.593	21.499	0.548	48.189
TS: Time to the nearest station (min)	−0.083	−86.748	−0.118	−129.946
Bus: Bus dummy	−0.313	−11.461	−0.079	−2.862
Car: Car Dummy	–	–	−0.408	−6.497
$Bus \times TS$	0.070	6.453	−0.026	−2.580
$Car \times TS$	–	–	0.068	2.330
TT: Travel time to central business district (min)	−0.041	−30.952	−0.076	−83.494
MC: Management cost	0.045	16.135	–	–
UV: Unit volume	0.024	33.752	–	–
BBD: Before new building standard law dummy	−0.085	−126.640	−0.093	−48.965
SRC: Steel reinforced concrete dummy	0.018	33.620	–	–
BA: Balcony area (m^2)	0.029	69.850	–	–
RW: Road width (10 cm)	–	–	0.190	142.685
PD: Private road dummy	–	–	−0.001	−2.973
LD: Land only dummy	–	–	0.227	45.634
SD: South facing dummy	0.003	2.203	0.004	1.940
OD: Old house dummy	–	–	−0.103	−56.412
BLR: Building-to-land ratio	0.075	56.572	0.065	18.677
FAR: Floor area ratio	0.039	6.807	0.029	16.347
FS: Floor space (m^2)				
β	0.528	20.171	0.487	45.103
Age: Age of building (quarters)				
δ	0.033	4.153	0.020	2.423
λ	0.691	98.590	0.688	45.850
	$n = 714, 506$		$n = 1, 540, 659$	
Log likelihood	391552.980		−5138.987	
Prob $> \chi^2 =$	0.000		0.000	
Adjusted $R^2 =$	0.882		0.822	

Note The dependent variable in each case is the log of the price

Table 4.4 Age-adjusted repeat sales regressions

	$\beta\delta$	λ
Condominiums		
Coef.	0.0098	0.8944
Std. err.	0.0004	0.0113
p-value	[.000]	[.000]
Single family houses		
Coef.	0.0019	1.1041
Std. err.	0.0002	0.0269
p-value	[.000]	[.000]

	Standard error of reg.	Adjusted R^2	S.B.I.C.
Condominiums			
Standard repeat sales	0.175	0.751	−20311.0
Case-Shiller repeat sales	0.191	0.760	−12925.4
Age-adjusted repeat sales	0.190	0.761	−13246.6
Single family houses			
Standard repeat sales	0.211	0.478	−2087.0
Case-Shiller repeat sales	0.218	0.511	−1136.1
Age-adjusted repeat sales	0.218	0.513	−1176.4

S.B.I.C.: Schwarz's Bayesian information criterion

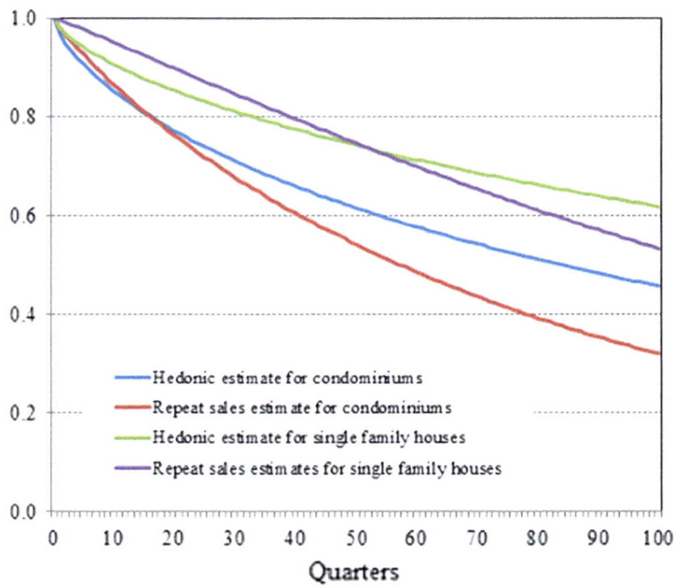

Fig. 4.1 Estimated depreciation curves

Table 4.5 Standard versus rolling window regressions

	Const.	FS	GA	Age		TS	TT
				($\beta\delta$)	(λ)		
Condonimium prices							
Standard hedonic model	3.263	0.528	0.593	0.017	0.691	−0.083	−0.041
12-month rolling regression							
Average	3.200	0.517	0.608	0.016	0.690	−0.082	−0.042
Standard deviation	0.086	0.079	0.040	0.001	0.035	0.015	0.013
Minimum	2.988	0.508	0.562	0.019	0.654	−0.097	−0.069
Maximum	3.429	0.539	0.613	0.011	0.710	−0.051	−0.025
Single family house prices							
Standard hedonic model	4.508	0.487	0.548	0.010	0.688	−0.118	−0.076
12-month rolling regression							
Average	4.691	0.485	0.532	0.006	0.681	−0.101	−0.079
Standard deviation	0.176	0.021	0.098	0.001	0.029	0.003	0.002
Minimum	4.496	0.480	0.512	0.007	0.670	−0.110	−0.079
Maximum	4.742	0.495	0.558	0.006	0.700	−0.041	−0.048
Number of models = 265							

Note FS: Floor space
GA: Ground area
Age: Age of building
TS: Time to the nearest station
TT: Travel time to central business district

Next, turn to the bottom panel of Table 4.4, which looks at the regression performance of the three types of repeat sales measures: the standard repeat sales index defined by Eqs. (4.6) or (4.7), the heteroskedasticity adjusted repeat sales index (i.e., the Case-Shiller index), and the age adjusted repeat sales index defined by (4.8).[35] It can be seen that the age adjusted repeat sales index performed better than the standard one for both condominiums and single family houses. On the other hand, SNW failed to find a significant difference between the age adjusted index and the Case-Shiller index.

Following the Rolling Year methodology introduced by Shimizu et al. (2010b, a) estimated the hedonic model defined by (4.4) using a window length of 12 months. Their results for the structural parameters (averaged over all regressions of window length 12) are presented in Table 4.5, which compares key parameters of the standard hedonic model and the corresponding rolling year hedonic models. For condomini-

[35]Note that the estimated coefficient for λ in the age adjusted repeat sales model was 0.89 for condos and 1.10 for single family houses. Thus the exact multicollinearity problem does not arise for these regressions.

ums, it can be seen that the average value of each parameter estimated by the rolling hedonic regression was close to the estimate obtained by the standard hedonic regression. For example, the parameter associated with the floor space of a house was 0.528 using the standard time dummy hedonic regression model defined by (4.4) where the entire sample was used in the single regression, while the average value of the corresponding parameters estimated by the rolling window regression was 0.517. More importantly, SNW found that the estimated structural parameters fluctuated considerably during the sample period. For example, the parameter associated with the floor space of a house fluctuated between 0.508 and 0.539, indicating that non-negligible structural changes occurred during the sample period. Similar structural changes occurred for single family houses.

4.3.3 Reconciling the Differences between the Five Models

Shimizu et al. (2010a) estimated the 5 models explained in Sect. 4.2 above using their Tokyo data sets for both detached houses and condominiums.[36] Figure 4.2 shows the estimated five indexes for condominiums. The age adjusted repeat sales index starts in the fourth quarter of 1989, while the other four indexes start in the first quarter of 1986. To make the comparison easier, the indexes are normalized so that they are all equal to unity in the fourth quarter of 1989. The first thing that can be seen from this Figure is that there is almost no difference between the standard repeat sales index and the Case-Shiller repeat sales index. This suggests that heteroskedasticity due to heterogeneous transaction intervals may not be very important as far as the Japanese housing market is concerned. Second, the age adjusted repeat sales index behaves differently from the other two repeat sales indexes. Specifically, it exhibits a less rapid decline in the 1990s, i.e., the period when the bubble burst. This difference reflects the relative importance of the age effect, implying that the other two repeat sales indexes, which pay no attention to the age effect, tend to overestimate the magnitude of the burst of the bubble; i.e., the standard repeat sales indexes have the predictable downward bias due to their neglect of depreciation. Third, the two hedonic indexes exhibit a less rapid decline in the 1990s than the standard and the Case-Shiller repeat sales indexes, and the discrepancy between them tends to increase over time in the rest of the sample period.[37]

Figure 4.3 shows the estimated indexes for single family houses. We see that the three repeat sales indexes and the standard hedonic index tend to move together, but the rolling hedonic index behaves differently from them. The spread between

[36]Their Rolling Window results used a window length of 12 months and used the updating procedure explained at the end of Sect. 4.2 above.

[37]Note that the age adjusted repeat sales index is well above the other two repeat sales indexes which do not make an adjustment for depreciation of the structure. This result is to be expected. What is perhaps more surprising is that the age adjusted repeat sales index ends up well below the two hedonic indexes. This result may be due to sample selectivity bias in the repeat sales method or to an incorrect specification of the hedonic models.

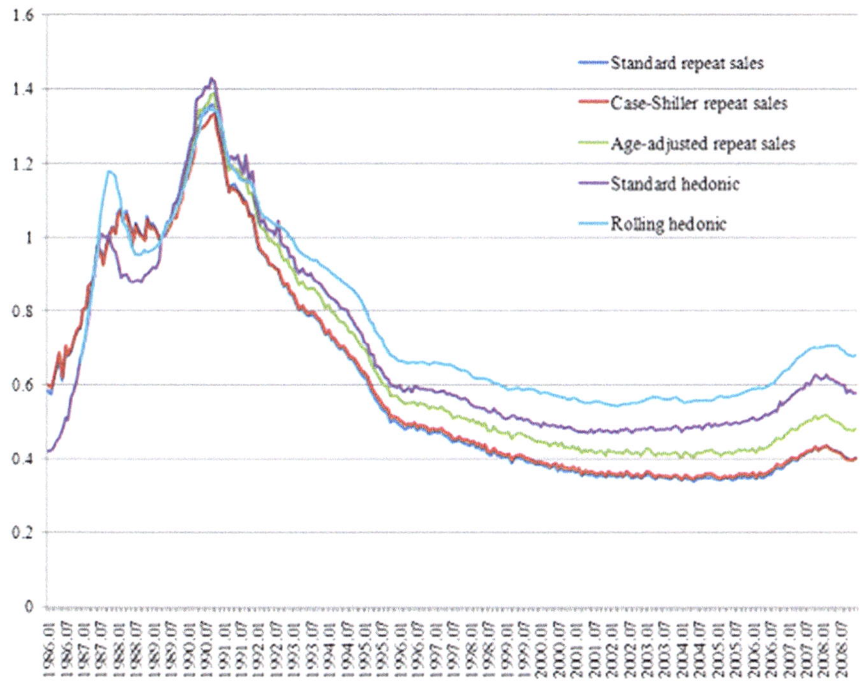

Fig. 4.2 Estimated five indices for condominiums

the rolling hedonic index and the other four indexes tends to expand gradually in the latter half of the 1990s, suggesting the presence of some gradual shifts in the structural parameters during this period.[38]

SNW compared the five indexes for condominiums in terms of their quarterly growth rates. The results are presented in Fig. 4.4. The horizontal axis in the upper left panel represents the growth rate of the standard repeat sales index, while the vertical axis represents the growth rate of the Case-Shiller repeat sales index. One can clearly see that almost all dots in this panel are exactly on the 45 degree line, implying that these two indexes are closely correlated with each other. In fact, the coefficient of correlation is 0.995 at the quarterly frequency, and 0.974 at the monthly frequency. Regressing the quarterly growth rate of the Case-Shiller repeat sales index, denoted by y, on that of the standard repeat sales index, denoted by x, SNW obtained $y = 0.9439x - 0.0002$, indicating that the coefficient on x and the constant term are very close to unity and zero, respectively. Similarly, the lower left panel of Fig. 4.4

[38]The annual depreciation rate for houses appears to be much smaller than the corresponding rate for condos and thus the age bias in the repeat sales models will be much smaller for houses than for condos. The relatively large differences in the two hedonic indexes is a bit of a puzzle. Diewert and Shimizu (2013) also compared Rolling Window house price indexes with a corresponding index based on a single time dummy regression and did not find large differences (but the sample period was much shorter in the Diewert and Shimizu study).

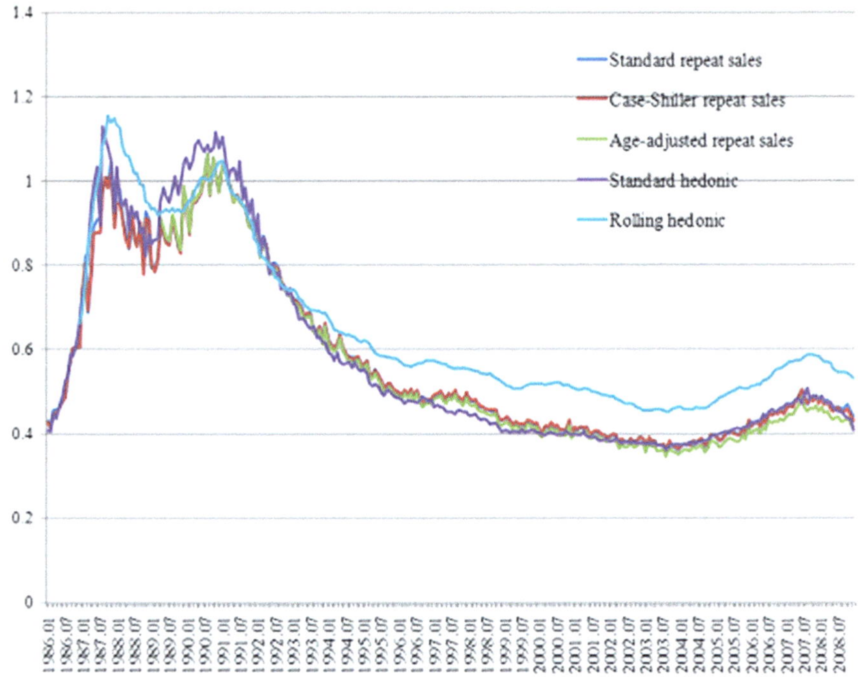

Fig. 4.3 Estimated five indices for single family houses

compares the growth rate of the standard repeat sales index and the age-adjusted repeat sales index. Again, almost all dots are on the 45 degree line, indicating a high correlation between the two indexes (the coefficient of correlation is 0.991 at the quarterly frequency and 0.953 at the monthly frequency). However, the regression results show that the constant term is slightly above zero, indicating that the growth rates for the age adjusted repeat sales index are, on average, slightly higher than those for the standard repeat sales index. Turning to the upper right panel, which compares the standard hedonic index and the standard repeat sales index, the dots are again scattered along the 45 degree line but not exactly on it, indicating a lower correlation than before (0.845 at the quarterly frequency and 0.458 at the monthly frequency). More importantly, SNW obtained $y = 1.0948x + 0.0036$ by regressing the standard hedonic index on the standard repeat sales index, and the constant term turned out to be positive and significantly different from zero. In other words, the standard hedonic index tends to grow faster than the standard repeat sales index, which is consistent with what is seen in Fig. 4.2.[39] Finally, the lower right panel compares the standard

[39]It can be seen from the upper right panel of Fig. 4.4 that several dots in the right upper quadrant are well above the 45 degree line, indicating that the growth rates of the standard hedonic index are substantially higher than those of the standard repeat sales index at least for these quarters. These dots correspond to the quarters between 1986 and 1987, during which the standard hedonic index exhibited much more rapid growth than the standard repeat sales index, as was seen in Fig. 4.2.

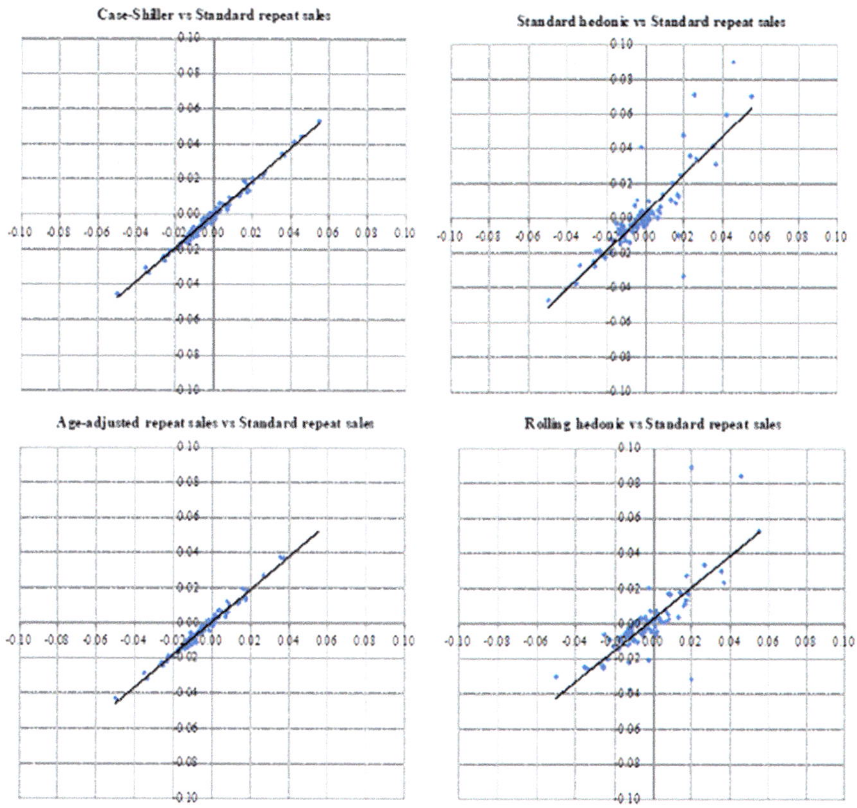

Fig. 4.4 Comparison of the five indexes in terms of the quarterly growth rate

repeat sales index and the rolling hedonic index, showing that the two indexes are more weakly correlated (0.773 at the quarterly frequency and 0.444 at the monthly frequency), and that the rolling hedonic index tends to grow faster than the standard repeat sales index.

SNW also regressed the quarterly growth rate of one of the five indexes, say index A, on the quarterly growth rate of another index, say index B, to obtain a simple linear relationship $y = a + bx$. They then conducted an F-test against the null hypothesis that $a = 0$ and $b = 1$. The results of this exercise are presented in Table 4.6, where the number in each cell represents the p-value associated with the null hypothesis that $a = 0$ and $b = 1$ in a regression in which the index in the corresponding row is the dependent variable while the index in the corresponding column is the independent variable. For example, the number in the lower left corner of the upper panel, 0.0221, represents the p-value associated with the null hypothesis in the regression in which the growth rate of the rolling hedonic index is the dependent variable and the growth rate of the standard repeat sales index is the independent variable. The upper panel, which presents the results for condominiums, shows that in almost all cases the null

Table 4.6 Contemporaneous relationship between the five measures

	Standard repeat sales	Case-Shiller repeat sales	Age-adjusted repeat sales	Standard hedonic	Rolling hedonic
Condominiums					
Standard repeat sales	–	0.0015	0.0001	0.0001	0.0001
Case-Shiller RS	0.0001	–	0.0001	0.0001	0.0001
Age-adjusted RS	0.0001	0.0001	–	0.0216	0.0058
Standard hedonic	0.0121	0.0028	0.2120	–	0.0057
Rolling hedonic	0.0221	0.0408	0.0001	0.1208	–
Single family houses					
Standard repeat sales	–	0.8740	0.0104	0.0001	0.1029
Case-Shiller RS	0.6461	–	0.0001	0.0002	0.1122
Age-adjusted RS	0.0369	0.0001	–	0.0070	0.2819
Standard hedonic	0.7661	0.8889	0.0008	–	0.6547
Rolling hedonic	0.0001	0.0001	0.0001	0.0001	–

Note We regress the quarterly growth rate of index A, y, on the quarterly growth rate of index B, x, to obtain the simple linear relationship $y = a + bx$. The number in each cell represents the p-value associated with the null hypothesis that $a = 0$ and $b = 1$ in the regression in which the index in the row is the dependent variable and the index in the column is the independent variable

hypothesis cannot be rejected. However, there are two cases in which the p-value exceeds 10%: when the standard hedonic index is regressed on the age adjusted repeat sales index (p-value $= 0.2120$), and when the rolling hedonic index is regressed on the standard hedonic index (p-value $= 0.1208$). Looking at the lower panel of Table 4.6, which presents the results for single family houses, we see that there are more cases in which the null hypothesis is rejected. For example, the p-value is very high at 0.7661 when the standard hedonic index is regressed on the standard repeat sales index, so that the null hypothesis that the hedonic and the repeat sales indexes are close to each other can easily be rejected.

The presence of a close contemporaneous correlation in terms of quarterly growth rates between the five indexes does not immediately imply that the five indexes perfectly move together. It is still possible that there exist some lead-lag relationships between the five indexes. For example, one index may tend to precede the other four indexes. To investigate such dynamic relationships between the five indexes, SNW conducted pairwise Granger causality tests. The results for condominiums and single family houses are presented, respectively, in the upper and lower panels of Table 4.7. The number in each cell represents the p-value associated with the null hypothesis that the index in a particular row does not Granger-cause the index in the column. For example, the number in the cell in the third row and second column, 0.2018, represents the p-value associated with the null hypothesis that the Case-Shiller type repeat sales index does not cause the standard repeat sales index. The panel for condominiums shows that one can easily reject the null that the standard hedonic index does not cause the other four indexes. On the other hand, one cannot reject the

Table 4.7 Pairwise Granger-causality tests

	Standard repeat sales	Case-Shiller repeat sales	Age-adjusted repeat sales	Standard hedonic	Rolling hedonic
Condominiums					
Standard repeat sales	–	0.0120	0.0019	0.0039	0.0000
Case-Shiller RS	0.2018	–	n.a.	0.0398	0.0000
Age-adjusted RS	0.0568	n.a.	–	0.1258	0.0000
Standard hedonic	0.0004	0.0001	0.0000	–	0.0000
Rolling hedonic	0.0053	0.0082	0.0022	0.1528	–
Single family houses					
Standard repeat sales	–	0.2726	0.4345	0.1919	0.0048
Case-Shiller RS	0.2397	–	n.a.	0.1810	0.0088
Age-adjusted RS	0.3275	n.a.	–	0.1962	0.0078
Standard hedonic	0.0028	0.0028	0.0027	–	0.0048
Rolling hedonic	0.0812	0.0784	0.0781	0.1089	–

Note The number in each cell represents the p-value associated with the null hypothesis that the variable in the row does not Granger-cause the variable in the column

null that each of the other four indexes does not cause the standard hedonic index. These two results indicate that fluctuations in the standard hedonic index tend to precede those in the other four indexes. The same property was observed for single family houses. To illustrate such lead-lag relationships between the five indexes, SNW compared them in terms of the timing in which each index bottomed out after the bursting of the housing bubble in the early 1990s. The result for condominiums is presented in Fig. 4.5. It can be seen that all of the three repeat sales indexes bottom out simultaneously in the first quarter of 2004. In contrast, the two hedonic indexes bottom out in the first quarter of 2002, indicating that the turn in the hedonic indexes preceded the one in the repeat sales indexes by two years.

An important issue that needs to be addressed is where such lead-lag relationships between the hedonic and repeat sales indexes come from. There are at least two possibilities. First, the presence of the lead-lag relationships may be related to the omitted variable problem in hedonic regressions. It is possible that the variables omitted in hedonic regressions move only with some lags relative to the other variables, leading to an excessively quick response of the estimated hedonic indexes to various shocks. The second possibility is related to sample selection bias in the estimated repeat sales indexes.

As we saw in Table 4.2, the sample employed for producing the repeat sales index makes up only a very limited fraction of the total numbers of observations and, more importantly, might be biased in that it consists of houses whose prices exhibit a delayed response to various shocks.

How can we discriminate between these two possibilities? One way to identify the reason behind the relationships is to apply the hedonic regressions to the repeat sales sample (i.e., the sample consisting of houses that are traded multiple times).

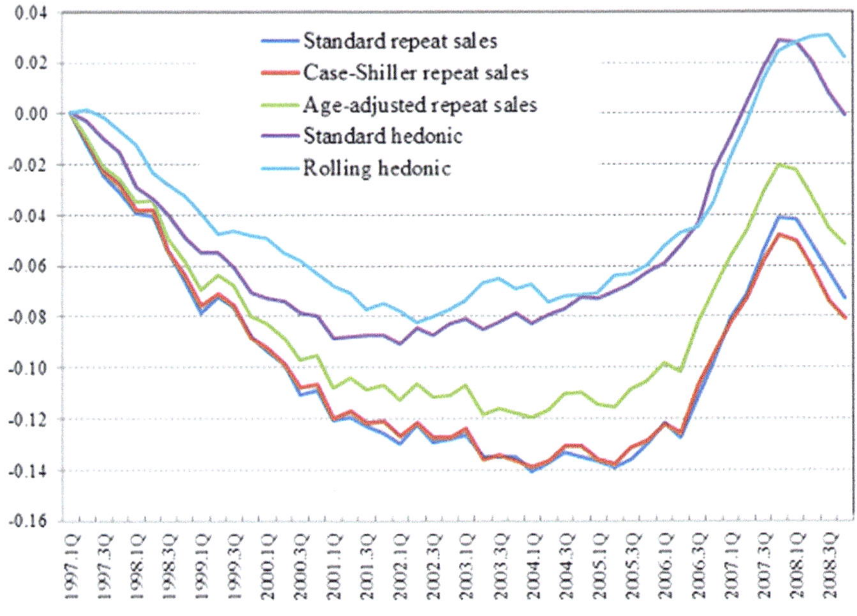

Fig. 4.5 When did condominium prices hit bottom?

The new hedonic index produced in this way and the standard hedonic index differ in terms of the sample employed but otherwise are identical in terms of the explanatory variables used, so that they suffer from the same omitted variables problem. Therefore, any remaining differences between the new and the standard hedonic index can be regarded as stemming from the difference in the sample employed. If a lead-lag relationship between the new and the standard hedonic index is still observed, this would imply that this lead-lag relationship is due to the sample selection bias in the repeat sales indexes.

Figure 4.6 presents the result of this exercise. SNW applied the hedonic regressions to four different samples: a sample of houses that were traded at least once (i.e., the entire sample); a sample of houses that were traded more than once (i.e., the original repeat sales sample); a sample of houses that were traded more than twice; and a sample of houses that were traded more than three times. SNW found that the indexes using the samples of houses that were traded more than once ("traded more than once," "traded more than twice," and "traded more than three times") exhibited a later turn than the index estimated from the larger sample of houses that were " traded at least once," suggesting that the lead-lag relationships between the hedonic and repeat sales indexes in Fig. 4.5 mainly come from sample selection bias in the repeat sales indexes. Moreover, consistent with this interpretation, the delay in the turning point becomes even more pronounced when using the samples of houses " traded more than twice" and " traded more than three times."

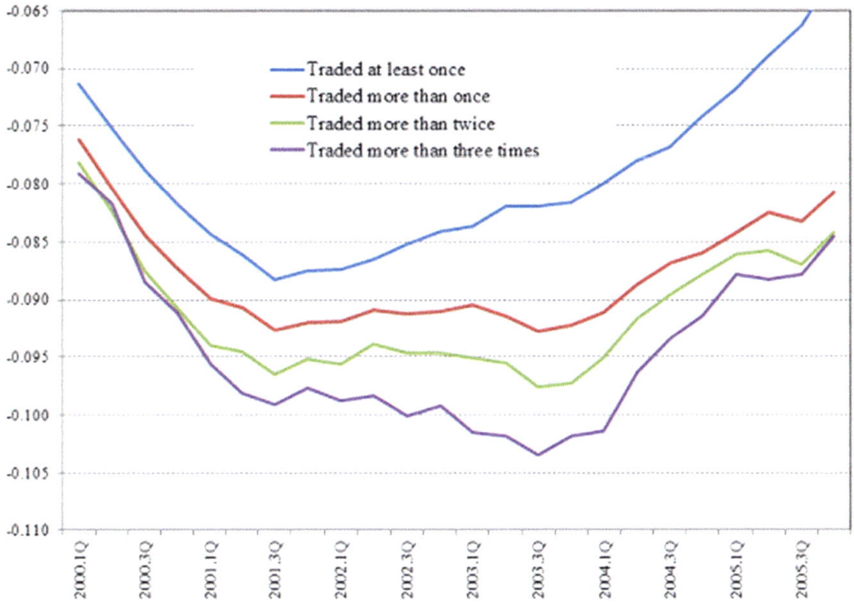

Fig. 4.6 Hedonic indexes estimated using repeat-sales samples

4.4 The Selection of Data Sources for the Construction of Housing Price Indexes

4.4.1 Alternative Types of Real Estate Sales Prices

In[40] constructing a housing price index, one has to make several nontrivial choices. One of them is the choice among alternative estimation methods, such as those discussed in Sect. 4.2 above. There are numerous papers on this issue, both theoretical and empirical.[41] However, there is another important issue which has not been discussed much in the literature, but has been regarded as critically important from a practical viewpoint: the *choice among different data sources for housing prices*. This is the topic to be discussed in this section.

There are several sources of data for housing prices:[42]

---

[40]The material in this section is drawn from Shimizu et al. (2011, 2012). In this section, we will refer to these two papers as SNW.

[41]See for example Case et al. (1991), Diewert (2010), Dorsey et al. (2010), Eurostat (2011) and Sect. 4.2 above. Recently, McMillen and Thorsnes (2006), McMillen (2012) and Deng et al. (2012) proposed a new index estimation method, the matching model method, which focused on the distribution of housing prices.

[42]Eurostat (2011) provides a summary of the sources of price information in various countries. For example, in Bulgaria, Canada, the Czech Republic, Estonia, Ireland, Spain, France, Latvia,

- Data collected by real estate agencies and associations;
- Data collected by mortgage lenders;
- Data provided by government departments or institutions and
- Data gathered and provided by newspapers, magazines, and websites.

Needless to say, different data sets contain different types of prices, including *seller asking prices, transaction prices*, assessor *valuation prices*, and so on.

With multiple data sets available, one may ask several questions. Are these prices different? If so, how do they differ from each other? Given the specific purpose of the housing price index one seeks to construct, which data set is the most suitable? Alternatively, with only one data set available in a particular country, one may ask whether this is suitable for the purpose of the index one seeks to construct. Shimizu et al. (2011), Shimizu et al. (2012) (abbreviated to SNW in this section) addressed these questions.[43] They conducted a statistical comparison of different house prices collected at different stages of the house buying and selling process. SNW collected four different types of prices:

(1) Asking prices at which properties are initially listed in a realtor magazine;
(2) Asking prices when an offer for a property is eventually made and the listing is removed from the magazine;
(3) Contract prices reported by realtors after mortgage approval and
(4) Land Registry prices.

SNW prepared data sets for these four types of price for condominiums traded in the Greater Tokyo Area from September 2005 to December 2009. The four prices are collected by different institutions and therefore recorded in different datasets: (1) and (2) are collected by a real estate advertisement magazine; (3) is collected by an association of real estate agents and (4) is collected jointly by the Land Registry and the Ministry of Land, Infrastructure, Transport and Tourism.

An important advantage of prices at earlier stages of the house buying/selling process, such as initial asking prices in a magazine, is that they are likely to be available earlier, so that house price indexes based on these prices become available in a timely manner. The issue of timeliness is important given that it takes more than 30 weeks before registry prices in Japan become available. On the other hand, it is often said that prices at different stages of the buying/selling process behave quite differently. For example, it is sometimes asserted that when the housing market is, say, in a downturn, prices at earlier stages of the buying/selling process, such as initial asking prices, will tend to be higher than prices at later stages. It is also asserted

---

Luxembourg, Poland and the USA price data collected by statistical institutes or ministries is used. In Denmark, Lithuania, the Netherlands, Norway, Finland, Hong Kong, Slovenia, Sweden and the UK information gathered for registration or taxation purposes is used. In Belgium, Germany, Greece, France, Italy, Portugal and Slovakia data from real estate agents and associations, research institutes or property consultancies is used. Finally, in Malta, Hungary, Austria and Romania data from newspapers or websites is used.

[43]There are several papers that focused on data sources for housing price indexes; see Gatzlaff and Haurin (1998), Genesove and Mayer (2001), Goetzmann and Peng (2006). However, these papers did not compare multiple data sources.

that, for various reasons, prices at earlier stages contain non-negligible amounts of " noise.[44] For instance, prices can be renegotiated extensively before a deal is finalized, and not all of the prices appearing at earlier stages end in transactions because a potential buyer's mortgage application is not always approved.[45]

Do the four types of price for the same dwelling unit differ from each other, and if so, by how much? SNW focussed on the entire cross-sectional distribution for each of the four prices in order to determine whether the four prices are different or not.[46]

Note that the cross sectional distributions for the four types of price may differ from each other simply because the datasets in which they are recorded contain houses with different characteristics. For example, the dataset from a realty magazine may contain more houses with a small floor space than the registry data set, which may give rise to different price distributions. Therefore, SNW tried to make adjustments to the various data sets so that like can be compared to like before comparing price distributions. They called this the *quality adjustment problem.*

SNW conducted quality adjustments in two different ways. The first was to only use the intersection of two different datasets, that is, observations that appeared in two data sets. For example, when testing whether initial asking prices in the magazine had a similar distribution as registry prices, they first identified houses that appear in both the magazine and registry data sets and then they compared the resulting two price distributions for those houses. In this way, they ensured that the two price distributions were not affected by differences in house attributes between the two data sets. This idea is quite similar to the one adopted in the repeat sales method, which is extensively used in constructing quality adjusted house price indexes. As is often pointed out, however, repeat sales samples may not necessarily be representative because houses that are traded multiple times may have certain characteristics that make them different from other houses.[47] A similar type of sample selection bias may arise even in the intersection approach. Houses in the intersection of the magazine dataset and the registry dataset are cases which successfully ended in a transaction. Put differently, houses whose initial asking prices were listed in the magazine but which failed to get an offer from buyers, or where potential buyers failed to get approval for a mortgage, are not included in the intersection.

The second method of quality adjustment used by SNW was based on hedonic regressions. This method is also widely used in constructing quality adjusted house

[44]See Allen and Dare (2004), Haurin et al. (2010), Knight et al. (1998).

[45]See Genesove and Mayer (1997, 2001) and Engelhardt (2003).

[46]An alternative approach would be to compare the four prices in terms of their average prices or in terms of their median prices. However, these summary statistics capture only one aspect of cross-sectional price distributions.

[47]As was noted in the previous section, Shimizu et al. (2010a) constructed five different house price indexes, including hedonic and repeat sales indexes, using Japanese data for 1986 to 2008. They found that there were substantial differences in terms of turning points between hedonic and repeat sales indexes. In particular, the repeat sales measure signaled turning points later than the hedonic measure. For example, the hedonic measure of condominium prices bottomed out at the beginning of 2002, while the corresponding repeat sales measure exhibited a reversal only in the spring of 2004.

price indexes. The hedonic regression that SNW employed differed from those used in previous studies, which are based on the assumption that the hedonic coefficient on, say, the size of a house is identical for high-priced and low-priced houses. This restriction on hedonic coefficients may not be problematic as long as one is interested in the mean or the median of a price distribution, but it is a serious problem when one is interested in the shape of the entire price distribution. In their papers, SNW used quantile hedonic regression techniques in which the hedonic coefficients were allowed to differ for high-priced and low-priced houses.

4.4.2 Condominium Prices in the Greater Tokyo Area from Alternative Sources

SNW collected the prices of condominiums traded in the Greater Tokyo Area from September 2005 to December 2009.[48] According to the register information published by the Japanese Legal Affairs Bureau, the total number of transactions for condominiums carried out in the Greater Tokyo Area during this period was 360,243. Ideally, SNW would have liked to collect price information for this entire "universe," but they were only able to collect three subsets of this universe data set.

The first data set was collected by a weekly magazine, Shukan Jutaku Joho (Residential Information Weekly) published by Recruit Co., Ltd. This data set contains initial asking prices (i.e., the asking prices initially set by sellers), denoted by P_1, and final magazine asking prices (i.e., asking prices immediately before they were removed from the magazine because potential buyers had made an offer), denoted by P_2. The number of observations for P_1 and P_2 is 155,347, meaning that this dataset covers 43% of the universe. There may exist differences between P_1 and P_2 for various reasons. For example, if the housing market is in a downturn, a seller may have to lower the price to attract buyers. Then P_2 will be lower than P_1. If the market is very weak, it is even possible that a seller may give up trying to sell the house and thus withdraws it from the market. If this is the case, P_1 is recorded but P_2 is not.

The second data set is a data set collected by an association of real estate agents. This dataset is compiled and updated through the Real Estate Information Network System, or REINS, a data network that was developed using multiple listing services in the United States and Canada as a model. This dataset contains transaction prices at the time when the actual sales contract are made, after the approval of any mortgages. They are denoted by P_3. Each price in the dataset is reported by the real estate agent who is involved in the transaction as a broker. The number of observations is 122,547, for a coverage of 34%. Note that P_3 may be different from P_2 because a seller and a buyer may renegotiate the price even after the listing is removed from the magazine. It is possible that P_3 for a particular house is not recorded in the realtor data set although P_2 for that house is recorded in the magazine data set. Specifically, there

[48] See Chapter 11 of Eurostat (2011) for detailed information on house price datasets currently available in Japan.

are more than a few cases where the sale was not successfully concluded because a mortgage application was turned down after the listing had been removed from the magazine.

The third data set was compiled by the Ministry of Land, Infrastructure, Transport and Tourism (MLIT). We refer to this data set as P_4. In Japan, each transaction must be *registered* with the Legal Affairs Bureau, but the registered information does not contain transaction prices. To find out transaction prices, the MLIT sends a questionnaire to buyers to collect price information. The number of observations contained in this registry dataset is 58,949, for a coverage ratio of 16%. Since P_3 and P_4 are both transaction prices, there is no clear institutional reason for any discrepancy between the two prices for the sale of the same unit; however, it is still possible that these two prices differ, partly because they are reported by different parties: a real estate agent for P_3 and the buyer for P_4. There may be reporting mistakes, intentional and unintentional, on the side of real estate agents, or on the side of buyers, or on both sides. Summary statistics for the three data sets are presented in Table 4.8.

Some housing units appear only in one of the three data sets, but others appear in two or three data sets. Using address information, SNW identified those housing units which appeared in two or all three of the data sets. For example, the number of dwelling units that appear both in the magazine data set and in the registry data set is 15,015; the number of housing units that are in the magazine data set but not in the registry data set is 140,332; and the number of housing units that are in the registry data set but not in the magazine data set is 43,934.[49] This clearly indicates that these two data sets contain a large number of different housing units, implying that the statistical properties of the two data sets may be substantially different. This suggests that it may be possible that the three data sets produce three different house price indexes, which behave quite differently, even if the identical estimation method is applied to each of the data sets.

Figure 4.7 shows the timing at which each of the four prices, P_1, P_2, P_3 and P_4, was observed in the house buying/selling process in Japan. There was a time lag of 70 days, on average, between the time when P_1 is observed (i.e., the time at which a seller posts an initial asking price in the magazine) and the time when P_2 was observed (i.e., the time when an offer was made by a buyer and the listing was removed from the magazine). Similarly, there was a lag of 38 days between the time at which P_3 was observed (i.e., the time at which a mortgage was approved and a contract was made) and the time at which P_2 was observed. Finally, there was a lag of 108 days between the time at which P_4 was observed (i.e., the time at which the MLIT received price information from a buyer) and the time at which P_3 was observed. In total, the time lag between P_1 and P_4 is, on average, 216 days, implying that a house price index can be available to the public much earlier by using P_1 instead of P_4. At the same time, it may be the case that prices at the earlier stages of the house buying/selling

[49]The number of housing units that appear both in the realtor data set and in the registry data set is 22,613; the number of housing units that are in the realtor data set but not in the registry data set is 99,934; and the number of housing units that are in the registry data set but not in the realtor data set is 36,336.

Table 4.8 Summary of the three datasets

Magazine data (P_1, P_2): completed

	Mean	Std. Dev.	Min.	Max.
	Magazine data: completed (155,347 observations)			
P_1: First asking price (10,000 Yen)	2,958.51	1,875.16	200	33,000
P_2: Final asking price (10,000 Yen)	2,889.27	1,831.34	200	29,800
$\log P_1$: Log of P_1	7.84	0.54	5.77	10.40
$\log P_2$: Log of P_2	7.82	0.54	5.77	10.30
FS: Floor space (m^2)	66.77	18.97	10.39	243.90
P_1/FS (10,000 Yen)	43.59	21.65	10.87	195.68
P_2/FS (10,000 Yen)	42.58	21.16	10.00	189.08
AGE: Age of building (years)	16.59	10.26	1.50	58.93
DS: Distance to the nearest station (m)	850.42	729.86	80	9,900
TT: Travel time to terminal station (min)	20.97	12.61	2	89

Magazine data (P_{1w}): not completed

	Mean	Std. Dev.	Min.	Max.
	Magazine data: not completed (58,300 observations)			
P_{1w}: First asking price (10,000 Yen)	3,156.06	2,385.91	198	34,800
$\log P_{1w}$: Log of P_{1w}	7.86	0.61	5.29	10.46
FS: Floor space (m^2)	66.99	20.91	10.60	250.00
P_{1w}/FS (10,000 Yen)	46.90	26.01	4.44	561.17
AGE: Age of building (years)	17.08	10.63	1.00	51.42
DS: Distance to the nearest station (m)	717.27	408.95	50	9,120
TT: Travel time to terminal station (min)	21.05	13.05	2	89

Realtor data (P_3)

	Mean	Std. Dev.	Min.	Max.
	Realtor data (122,547 observations)			
P_3: Sales price (10,000 Yen)	2,431.81	1,632.88	160	29,074
$\log P_3$: Log of P_3	7.60	0.64	5.08	10.28
FS: Floor space (m^2)	64.87	20.27	10.10	238.81
P_3/FS (10,000 Yen)	37.44	19.65	10.00	187.96
AGE: Age of building (years)	16.79	10.38	1.50	57.14
DS: Distance to the nearest station (m)	881.37	804.67	80	9,900
TT: Travel time to terminal station (min)	23.21	13.65	2	89

Registry data (P_4)

	Mean	Std. Dev.	Min.	Max.
	Registry data (58,949 observations)			
P_4: Sales price (10,000 Yen)	2,316.32	1,633.34	130	28,000
$\log P_4$: Log of P_4	7.53	0.68	4.87	10.24
FS: Floor space (m^2)	57.52	23.58	10.09	196.46
P_4/FS (10,000 Yen)	41.38	21.53	10.00	189.83
AGE: Age of building (years)	16.21	9.83	1.50	59.40
DS: Distance to the nearest station (m)	842.77	719.73	50	9,910
TT: Travel time to terminal station (min)	21.23	13.51	2	89

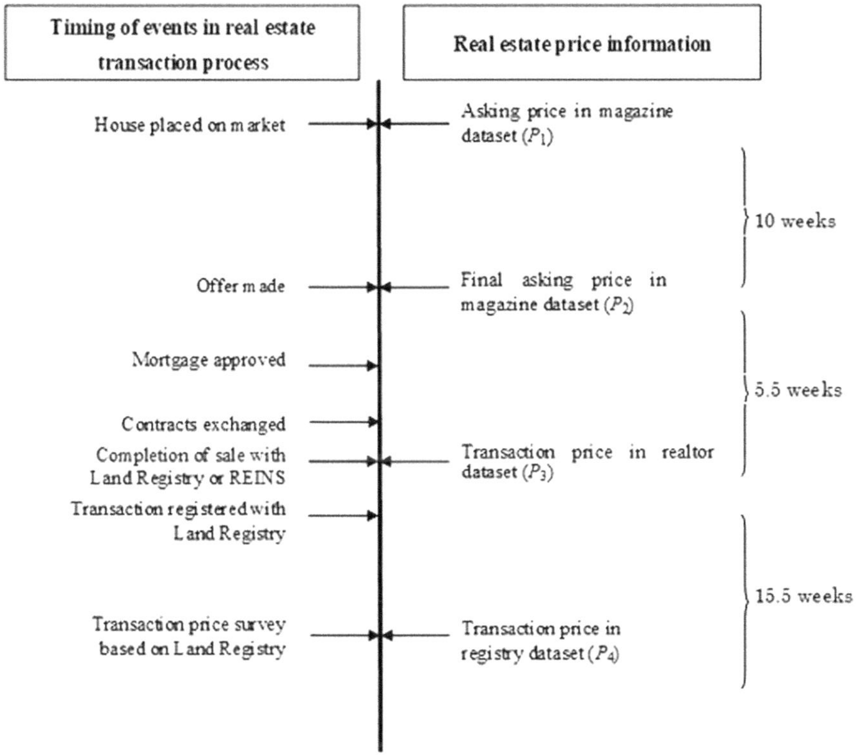

Fig. 4.7 House purchase timeline

process, such as P_1, are not reliable since they are frequently updated up or down until a final contract has been reached. In addition, it is often pointed out that not all of the prices observed at the earlier stage of the house buying/selling process end in transactions.[50]

According to the land registry information, the day on which P_3 was observed and the day on which registration was made at the land registry were identical for 93% of all transactions. This means that the time lag between P_3 and P_4 mainly reflected the number of days it took for the MLIT to collect price information from buyers. Note that this type of time lag does not occur in most other industrialized countries, including the U.S. and the U.K., where the land registry requires sellers and/or buyers to report transaction prices as part of the registration information. However, according

[50]Eurostat (2011: 147) sums up the situation as follows: "Each source of prices information has its advantages and disadvantages. For example a disadvantage of advertised prices and prices on mortgage applications and approvals is that not all of the prices included end in transactions, and the price may differ from the final negotiated transaction price. But these prices are likely to be available sometime before the final transaction price. Indices that measure the price earlier in the purchase process are able to detect price changes first, but will measure final prices with error because prices can be renegotiated extensively before the deal is finalized."

to Eurostat (2011), even in the U.K., there exists a long time lag between completion of the contract and the registration of property ownership transfers; that is, registration is typically completed only 4–6 weeks after the completion of transactions. This lack of timeliness means that price information gathered from the land registry is of limited usefulness in constructing *timely* house price indexes.

Figure 4.8 shows how time lags are distributed for the four prices. For example, the solid line represents the distribution of the time lag between the day P_1 and the day P_2 are observed for a particular property. It can be seen that more than fifty percent of all observations are concentrated at a time lag of 50 days, but there is a non-negligible probability that the time lag exceeds 150 days. Similarly, the time lag between P_1 and P_4 is most likely to be 200 days, but it is possible, although with a low probability, that it may be more than 300 days.

Figure 4.9 shows the cross-sectional distributions for the log of the four prices that SNW obtained in their empirical study of condo prices in Tokyo. The horizontal axis represents the log price while the vertical axis represents the corresponding density.

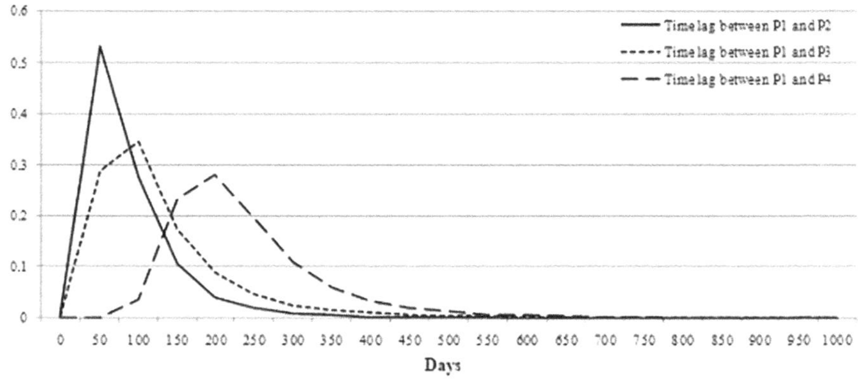

Fig. 4.8 Intervals between events in the house buying/selling process

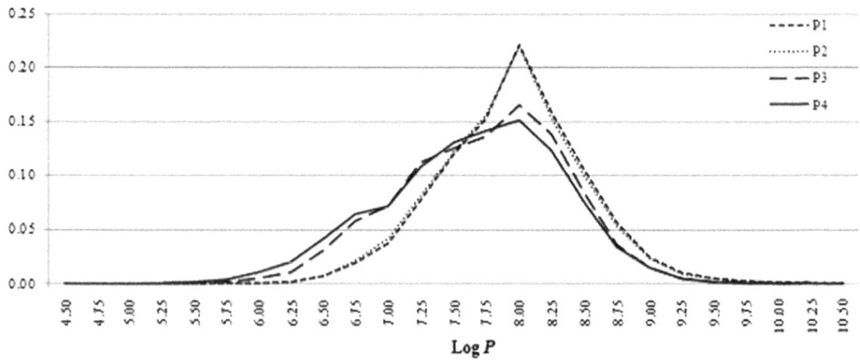

Fig. 4.9 Price densities for P_1, P_2, P_3 and P_4

It can be seen that the distributions of P_1 and P_2 are quite similar to each other. On the other hand, the distribution of P_3 differs substantially from the distribution of P_2; namely, the distribution of P_2 is almost symmetric, while the distribution of P_3 has a thicker lower tail, implying that the sample of P_3 contains more low-priced houses than the sample of P_2. This difference in the two distributions may be a reflection of differences in prices at different stages of the house buying/selling process, but it is also possible that the difference in the price distributions may come from differences in the characteristics of the houses in the two datasets.

To investigate differences in the data sets in more detail, SNW compared the distributions of house attributes for each of the three data sets. The top panel of Fig. 4.10 shows the distributions of floor space, measured in square meters, for the three data sets. The distribution labeled "P_1 and P_2," which was compiled from the magazine data set, is almost symmetric, while the distribution labeled "P_3," which is from the realtor data set, has a thicker lower tail, indicating that the realtor data set contains more small-sized condos whose floor space is 30 square meters or less. This pattern is even more pronounced in the land registry data set, i.e., in the distribution labelled "P_4."

Turning to the middle and bottom panels of Fig. 4.10, it can be seen that there are substantial differences between the three datasets in terms of the age of buildings and the distance to the nearest station. These differences in the distributions of house attributes may be related to the differences in the distributions of house prices. More specifically, the different price distributions exhibited in Fig. 4.9 may be mainly due to differences in the composition of houses in terms of their size, age, location, etc. Put differently, it could be that the price distributions are identical once quality differences are controlled for in an appropriate manner.

4.4.3 The Quality Adjustment Problem

Shimizu et al. (2011, 2012) (SNW) go on to consider two methods for making the distribution of condominium prices in their 3 Tokyo samples of prices more comparable with each other. They considered two methods.

Their first method for achieving greater comparability was to use prices only for condos that are present in two of the data sets. They refer to this approach as the *intersection approach*. They used address information to identify these houses. We will discuss their results for this approach in more detail below.

Their second method was based on running quantile hedonic regressions and SNW called this method the *quantile hedonic approach*. This method is based on the work by Machado and Mata (2005) and McMillen (2008). Since the method is rather complex, the reader is referred to the work of Shimizu et al. (2011, 2012) for the results of this method.

We now describe the intersection method results obtained by SNW. Their magazine data set, which contained P_1 and P_2, and the registry dataset, which contained P_4, had 15,015 observations in common. On the other hand, there were 22,613 obser-

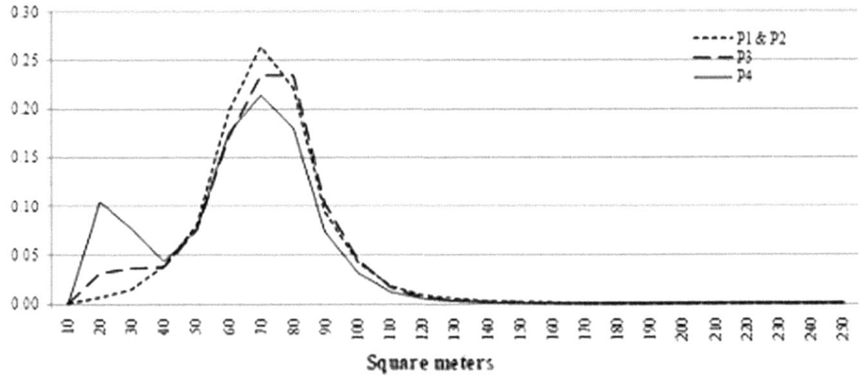

FS: Floor space

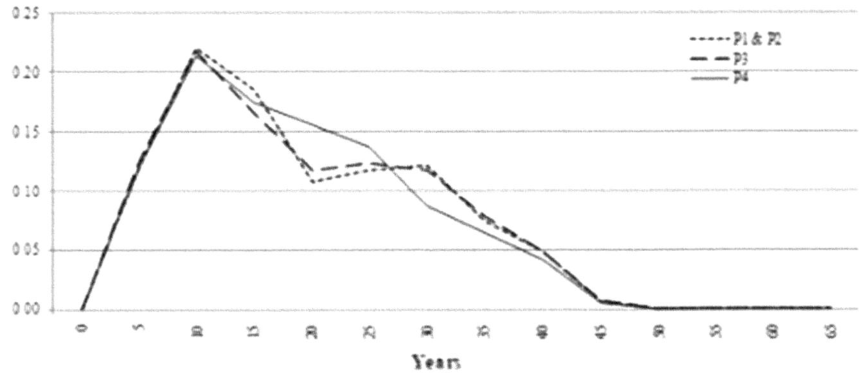

AGE: Age of building

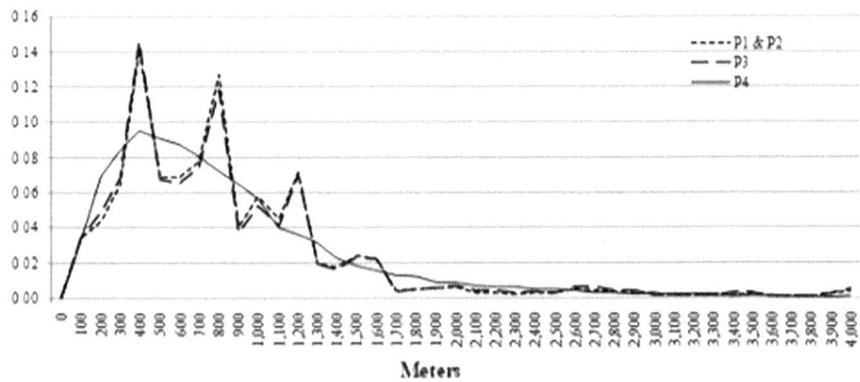

DS: Distance to the nearest station

Fig. 4.10 Density functions for house attributes

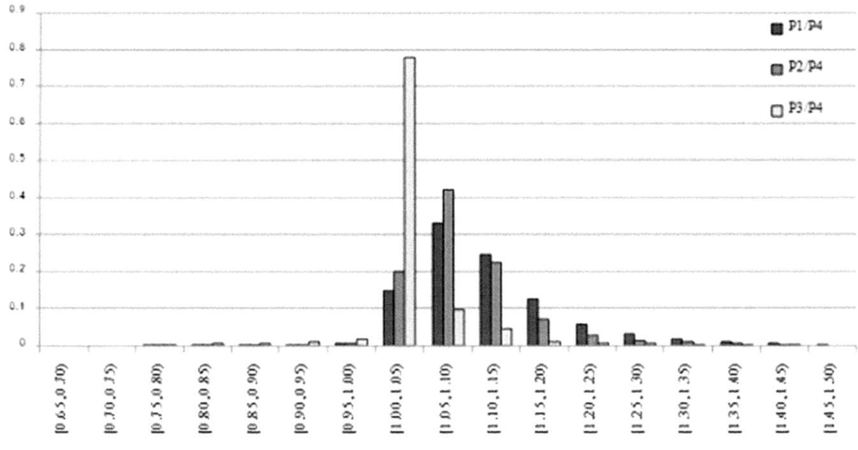

Fig. 4.11 Densities for relative prices

vations in the intersection of the realtor data set, which contained P_3, and the land registry data set, which contained P_4. SNW used these intersection samples to estimate the distance between the distributions of prices at different stages of the house buying/selling process.

SNW started by looking at the distribution of relative prices between P_1 and P_4 in the intersection of the magazine and land registry datasets. Figure 4.11 shows that the distribution of P_1/P_4 has the largest density at the range of 1.05 to 1.10, with more than thirty percent of the total observations being concentrated in this range, and that the densities above 1.10 are not negligible. In contrast, the number of houses for which P_4 exceeds P_1 is very limited, indicating that initial asking prices tend to be higher than registry prices. This may reflect the weak housing demand in the period from 2005 to 2009 when the price data was collected

Turning to the distribution of the relative prices in the intersection of the P_2 and P_4 samples, SNW found that the densities in the range of 1.00 and 1.05, and in the range of 1.05 and 1.10, are slightly higher than those for the relative prices in the P_1/P_4 intersection sample, indicating that final asking prices listed in the magazine tended to be closer to registry prices than initial asking prices. This tendency is more clearly seen for the relative prices in the intersection sample P_3/P_4 between realtor prices and land registry prices: more than 70are concentrated in the range of 1.00 to 1.05 for P_3/P_4. These results are of course in line with our intuition.

Next, Fig. 4.12 shows the distribution of prices using the intersection samples. The top panel compares the distributions of the prices in samples P_1 and P_4 using the intersection sample of the magazine and the land registry data sets. In Fig. 4.9, we saw that the distributions of P_1 and P_4 were quite different. However, now it can be seen that the difference between the two distributions (restricted to their common observations) is much smaller than before, clearly showing the importance of adjusting for quality. However, the two distributions are not exactly identical

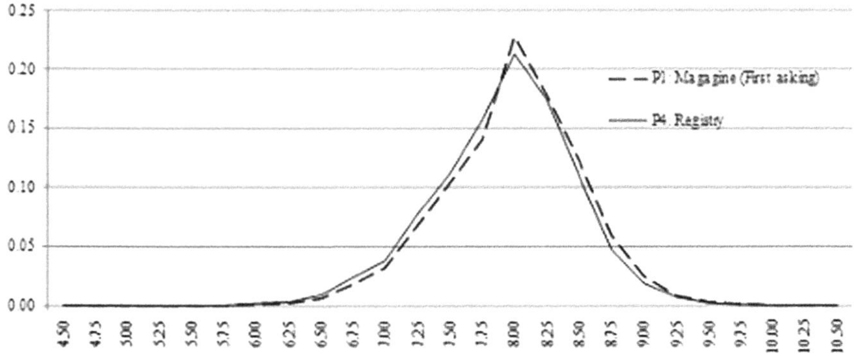

Densities for P_1 and P_4

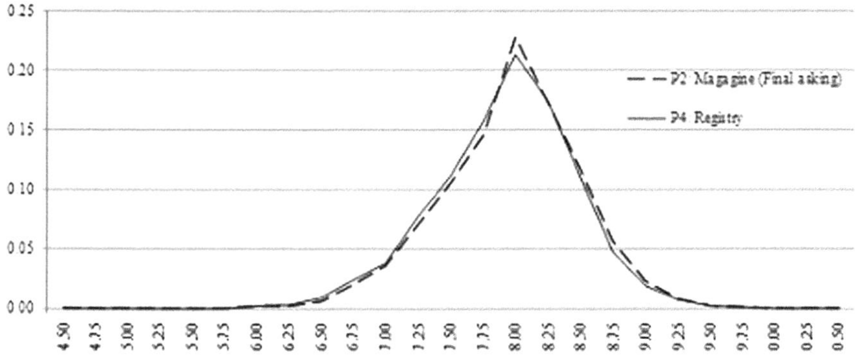

Densities for P_2 and P_4

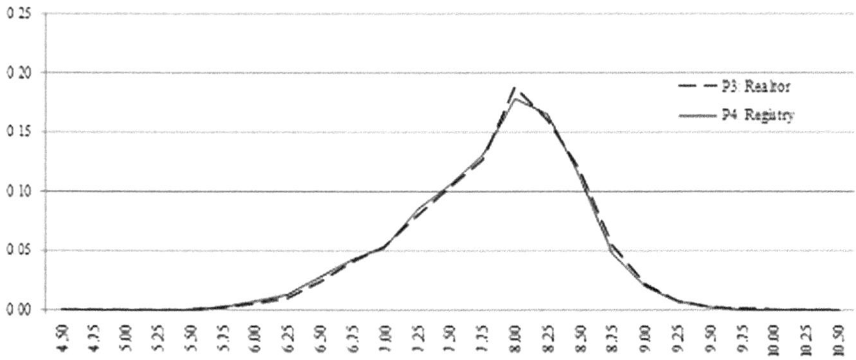

Densities for P_3 and P_4

Fig. 4.12 Price densities for housing units observed in two datasets

even after the quality adjustment. Specifically, the distribution of P_4 has a thicker lower tail than the distribution of P_1. This may be interpreted as reflecting the fact that asking prices initially listed in the magazine were revised downward during the house selling/purchase process.

The middle panel in Fig. 4.12 compares the distributions of the prices in the samples P_2 and P_4 using the intersection sample of the magazine and registry datasets, while the bottom panel compares the distributions of P_3 and P_4 using the intersection sample of the realtor and registry datasets. Both panels show that the differences between the distributions are much smaller than we saw in Fig. 4.9, but there still remain some differences.

One may wonder how the deviations between the standard hedonic indexes generated by (4.4) using the four samples of prices compare over time. In particular, an important question to be asked is whether these indexes differ substantially depending on whether the housing market is in a downturn or in an upturn. To address this, SNW presented in Fig. 4.13 a time series for the hedonic indexes generated by the P_1 and P_2 samples; see the top panel in Fig. 4.13. In the bottom panel of Fig. 4.13, the price ratio between the P_1 and P_2 prices is plotted, as well as a time series for the interval between the time when P_1 is observed (i.e., the time at which a seller posts an initial asking price in the magazine) and the time when P_2 is observed (i.e., the time when an offer is made by a buyer and the listing is removed from the magazine). The price ratio for a particular month is defined and calculated as the average of the ratios between P_2 and P_1 for housing units for which an offer is made in that month and for which an initial asking price P_1 was listed in the magazine some time prior to that month. As shown in the lower panel of Fig. 4.11, the price ratio fluctuates between 0.97 and 0.99, indicating that P_2 tends to be lower than P_1 by one to three percent. More importantly, it can be seen that fluctuations in the price ratio are closely correlated with the overall price movement in the housing market, which is represented by the hedonic indexes for P_1 and P_2 shown in the upper panel of Fig. 4.11. Specifically, the hedonic index for P_1 declined by more than ten percent during the period between March 2008 and April 2009 indicated by the shaded area. During this downturn period, the price ratio exhibited a substantial decline, and more interestingly, changes in the price ratio preceded changes in the hedonic indexes.

Specifically, the price ratio started to decline in December 2007, three months earlier than the hedonic index for P_1, and bottomed out in February 2009, two months earlier than the hedonic index for P_1. As noted above, the interval for a particular month is calculated as the average of the time lags between the time P_2 is observed and the time P_1 is observed for those housing units for which an offer is made in that month. The interval fluctuates between 55 and 78 days, and more importantly, it is closely correlated with the hedonic indexes for P_1 and P_2. Focusing on the downturn period, which is indicated by the shaded area, it can be seen that the interval increased from 65 days to 78 days, suggesting that, due to weak demand, sellers had to wait longer until an offer is made by a buyer. As in the case of the price ratio, changes in the listing interval tended to precede changes in the hedonic indexes; specifically, the interval peaked in December 2008, four months before than the hedonic index for P_1 hit bottom.

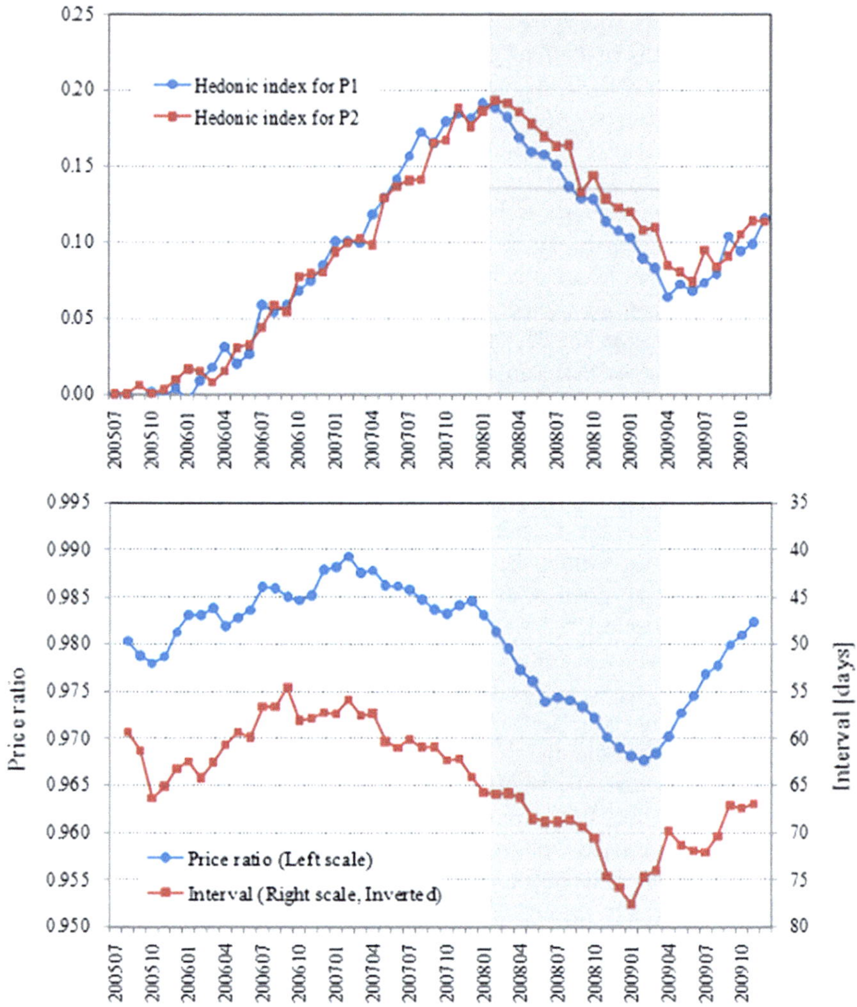

Fig. 4.13 Fluctuations in the price ratio and the interval for P_1 and P_2

In the following section, we will outline a hedonic regression model that will allow one to obtain a decomposition of the sale price of a house into land and structure components.

4.5 The Decomposition of an RPPI into Land and Structure Components

4.5.1 *Introduction*

The usual application of a time dummy hedonic regression model to sales of houses does not lead to a decomposition of the sale price into a structure component and a land component. But such a decomposition is required for many purposes. This section of the paper will describe the results of Diewert and Shimizu (2013) (abbreviated to DS) to address this problem.

Section 4.5.2 below explains the data that DS used in their study. In Sects. 4.5.3 and 4.5.4 below, their hedonic regression model will be explained, which requires information on the selling price of the property V along with the following *basic characteristics* of the property:

- The land area of the property (L);
- The floor space area of the structure (S);
- The age of the structure (A) and
- The location of the property.

Using only information on these 4 characteristics plus the use of an exogenous residential house construction price index for Tokyo, DS were able to explain 81.68% of the variation in the sales data for Tokyo. Their basic nonlinear regression model is a generalization of the *builder's hedonic regression model* introduced by Diewert et al. (2011a, b).

Section 4.5.5 contains a discussion of how DS aggregated up their separate land and structure indexes to form an overall house price index for Tokyo.

4.5.2 *The Tokyo Housing Data*

The basic data set used by DS included information on V, L, S, A, the location of the property and some additional characteristics to be explained below. The data were obtained from a weekly magazine, *Shukan Jutaku Joho* (Residential Information Weekly) published by Recruit Co., Ltd. The Recruit data set covered the 23 special wards of Tokyo for the period 2000 to 2010, including the mini-bubble period in the middle of 2000s and its later collapse caused by the Great Recession. As was explained in Sect. 4.4 above, *Shukan Jutaku Joho* provides time series of housing prices from the week when it is first posted until the week it is removed due to its sale. DS used the price in the final week of listing. There were a total of 5578 observations (after range deletions) in the sample of sales of single family houses in the Tokyo area over the 44 quarters covering 2000–2010.[51] The definitions for the above variables and their units are as follows:

V = The value of the sale of the house in 10,000,000 Yen
S = Structure area (floor space area) in units of 100 m^2
L = Lot area in units of 100 m^2
A = Approximate age of the structure in years
NB = Number of bedrooms
WI = Width of the lot in meters
TW = Walking time in minutes to the nearest subway station
TT = Subway running time in minutes to the Tokyo station from the nearest station during the day (not early morning or night)

Over the sample period, the sample average sale price was approximately 62.3 million Yen, the average structure space was 110 m^2, the average lot size was 103 m^2, the average age of the structure was 14.7 years, the average number of bedrooms in the houses that were sold was 3.95, the average lot width was 4.7 m, the average walking time to the nearest subway station was 9.9 min and the average subway travelling time from the nearest station to the Tokyo Central station was 31.7 min.

There were fairly high correlations between the V, S and L variables. The correlations of the selling price V with structure and lot area S and L were 0.689 and 0.660 respectively and the correlation between S and L was 0.668. Given the large amount of variability in the data and the relatively high correlations between V, S and L, one can expect multicollinearity problems in a simple linear regression of V on S and L.[52]

DS used the address information on each transaction in order to allocate each sale into one of 21 Wards for the Tokyo area. They constructed Ward dummy variables and made use of these variables in most of their regressions as locational explanatory variables.

4.5.3 *The Basic Builder's Model*

A basic model for valuing a residential property postulates that the value of a residential property is the sum of two components: the value of the land which the structure sits on plus the value of the residential structure.

In order to justify the model, consider a property developer who builds a structure on a particular property. The total cost of the property after the structure is completed

[51] DS deleted 9.2% of the observations because they fell outside their range limits for the variables V, L, S, A, NB and W. DS noted that it is risky to estimate hedonic regression models over wide ranges when observations are sparse at the beginning and end of the range of each variable. The a priori range limits for these variables were as follows: $2 \le V \le 20$; $0.5 \le S \le 2.5$; $1 \le A \le 50$; $2 \le NB \le 8$; $2.5 \le W \le 9$.

[52] See Diewert et al. (2011a,b) for evidence on this multicollinearity problem using Dutch data.

will be equal to the floor space area of the structure, say S square meters, times the building cost per square meter, β say, plus the cost of the land, which will be equal to the cost per square meter, α say, times the area of the land site, L. Now think of a sample of properties of the same general type, which have prices or values V_{tn} in period t[53] and structure areas S_{tn} and land areas L_{tn} for $n = 1, \ldots, N(t)$ where $N(t)$ is the number of observations in period t. Assume that these prices are equal to the sum of the land and structure costs plus error terms ε_{tn} which we assume are independently normally distributed with zero means and constant variances. This leads to the following *hedonic regression model* for period t where the α_t and β_t are the parameters to be estimated in the regression:[54]

$$V_{tn} = \alpha_t L_{tn} + \beta_t S_{tn} + \varepsilon_{tn}; \qquad t = 1, \ldots, 44; n = 1, \ldots, N(t). \tag{4.10}$$

Note that the two characteristics in this simple model are the quantities of land L_{tn} and the quantities of structure floor space S_{tn} associated with property n in period t and the two *constant quality prices* in period t are the price of a square meter of land α_t and the price of a square meter of structure floor space β_t. Finally, note that separate linear regressions can be run of the form (4.10) for each period t in the sample.

The hedonic regression model defined by (4.10) applies to new structures. But it is likely that a model that is similar to (4.10) applies to older structures as well. Older structures will be worth less than newer structures due to the depreciation of the structure. Assuming that we have information on the age of the structure n at time t, say A_{tn}, and assuming a straight line depreciation model, a more realistic hedonic regression model than that defined by (4.10) above is the following *basic builder's model*:[55]

$$V_{tn} = \alpha_t L_{tn} + \beta_t (1 - \delta_t A_{tn}) S_{tn} + \varepsilon_{tn}; \qquad t = 1, \ldots, 44; n = 1, \ldots, N(t) \tag{4.11}$$

where the parameter δ_t reflects the *net depreciation rate* as the structure ages one additional period. Thus if the age of the structure is measured in years, we would expect an annual *net* depreciation rate to be between 0.25 and 2.5%.[56] Note that (4.11) is now a nonlinear regression model whereas (4.10) was a simple linear regression

[53]The period index t runs from 1 to 44 where period 1 corresponds to Q1 of 2000 and period 44 corresponds to Q4 of 2010.

[54]Other papers that have suggested hedonic regression models that lead to additive decompositions of property values into land and structure components include Clapp (1980), Francke and Vos (2004), Gyourko and Saiz (2004), Bostic et al. (2007), Davis and Heathcote (2007), Francke (2008), Koev et al. (2008), Statistics Portugal (2009), Diewert (2010, 2011), Rambaldi et al. (2010) and Diewert et al. (2011a, b).

[55]This formulation follows that of Diewert (2010, 2011) and Diewert et al. (2011a, b). It is a special case of Clapp's (1980; 258) hedonic regression model.

[56]This estimate of depreciation is regarded as a *net depreciation rate* because it is equal to a " true" gross structure depreciation rate less an average renovations appreciation rate. Since we do not have information on renovations and additions to a structure, our age variable will only pick up average gross depreciation less average real renovation expenditures. Note that we excluded sales of houses

model. Both models (4.10) and (4.11) can be run period by period; it is not necessary to run one big regression covering all time periods in the data sample. The period t price of land will be the estimated coefficient for the parameter α_t and the price of a unit of a newly built structure for period t will be the estimate for β_t. The period t quantity of land for property n is L_{tn} and the period t quantity of structure for property n, expressed in constant quality units of a new structure, is $(1 - \delta_t A_{tn})S_{tn}$ where S_{tn} is the floor space area of property n in period t.

Note that the above model is a *supply side model* as opposed to the *demand side models* of Muth (1971) and McMillen (2003). Basically, the builder's model assumes that housing is supplied competitively so that we are in Rosen's (1974: 44) Case (a), where the hedonic surface identifies the structure of supply. This assumption is justified for the case of newly built houses but it is less well justified for sales of existing homes.

DS used 5578 observations on sales of houses in Tokyo over the 44 quarters in years 2000–2010. Thus Eq. (4.11) above could be combined into one big regression and a single depreciation rate $\delta = \delta_t$ could be estimated along with 44 land prices α_t and 44 new structure prices β_t so that 89 parameters would have to be estimated. However, experience has shown that it is usually not possible to estimate sensible land and structure prices in a hedonic regression like that defined by (4.11) due to the *multicollinearity* between lot size and structure size.[57] Thus in order to deal with the multicollinearity problem, DS drew on *exogenous information* on new house building costs from the Japanese Ministry of Land, Infrastructure, Transport and Tourism (MLIT) and they assumed that the price of new structures is proportional to this index of residential building costs. Thus the new builder's model that uses exogenous information on structure prices was the following one:

$$V_{tn} = \alpha_t L_{tn} + \beta p_{Ct}(1 - \delta A_{tn})S_{tn} + \varepsilon_{tn}; \qquad t = 1, \ldots, 44; n = 1, \ldots, N(t) \tag{4.12}$$

where all variables have been defined above except that p_{Ct} is the MLIT house construction cost index for Tokyo for quarter t. Thus DS had 5578 degrees of freedom to estimate 44 land price parameters α_t, one structure price parameter β that determines the level of prices over the sample period and one annual straight line depreciation rate parameter δ, a total of 46 parameters.

The R^2 for the resulting nonlinear regression model was only 0.5704,[58] which was not very satisfactory. Thus the simple Builder's Model defined by (4.12) applied to Tokyo house prices was not as satisfactory as was the corresponding Builder's Model for the small town of " A" in the Netherlands where the R^2 was 0.8703 using

---

from our sample if the age of the structure exceeded 50 years when sold. Very old houses tend to have larger than normal renovation expenditures and thus their inclusion can bias the estimates of the net depreciation rate for younger structures.

[57] See Schwann (1998), Diewert et al. (2011a, b) and Eurostat (2011) on the multicollinearity problem.

[58] All of the R^2 reported in this section are equal to the square of the correlation coefficient between the dependent variable in the regression and the corresponding predicted variable. The estimated net annual straight line depreciation rate was $\delta = 1.25\%$, with a T statistic of 17.3.

the same information on characteristics of the house and lot.[59] However, in the case of the town of "A", the structures were all much the same and all houses in the town had access to basically the same amenities. The situation in the huge city of Tokyo is very different: different neighbourhoods have access to very different amenities and Tokyo is not situated on a flat, featureless plain and so we would expect substantial variations in the price of land across the various neighbourhoods.

4.5.4 The Builder's Model with Locational Dummy Variables

In order to take into account possible neighbourhood effects on the price of land, DS introduced *ward dummy variables*, $D_{W,tn,j}$, into the hedonic regression (4.12). These 21 dummy variables are defined as follows: for $t = 1, \ldots, 44$; $n = 1, \ldots, N(t)$; $j = 1, \ldots, 21$:[60]

$$D_{W,tn,j} \equiv \begin{cases} 1 \text{ if observation } n \text{ in period } t \text{ is in Ward } j \text{ of Tokyo;} \\ 0 \text{ if observation } n \text{ in period } t \text{ is } \textit{not} \text{ in Ward } j \text{ of Tokyo.} \end{cases} \tag{4.13}$$

DS modified the model defined by (4.12) to allow the *level* of land prices to differ across the 21 Wards of Tokyo. Their new nonlinear regression model was the following one:

$$V_{tn} = \alpha_t \left(\sum_{j=1}^{21} \omega_j D_{W,tn,j} \right) L_{tn} + \beta p_{Ct}(1 - \delta A_{tn}) S_{tn} + \varepsilon_{tn}; \quad t = 1, \ldots, 44; n = 1, \ldots, N(t). \tag{4.14}$$

Comparing the models defined by Eqs. (4.12) and (4.14), it can be seen that DS added an additional 21 *ward relative land value parameters*, $\omega_1, \ldots, \omega_{21}$, to the model defined by (4.12). However, looking at (4.14), it can be seen that the 44 land time parameters (the α_t) and the 21 ward parameters (the ω_j) cannot all be identified. Thus it is necessary to impose at least one identifying normalization on these parameters. DS chose the following normalization:

$$\omega_{10} \equiv 1. \tag{4.15}$$

---

[59] See Eurostat (2011).

[60] The 21 Wards of Tokyo that had at least one transaction during the DS sample period (with the total number of transactions for that Ward in brackets) are as follows: 1: Minato (69); 2: Shinjuku (136); 3: Bunkyo (82); 4: Taito (15); 5: Sumida (32); 6: Koto (38); 7: Shinagawa (144); 8: Meguro (349); 9: Ota (409); 10: Setagaya (1158); 11: Shibuya (107); 12: Nakano (305); 13: Suginami (773); 14: Toshima (124); 15: Kita (53); 16: Arakawa (34); 17: Itabashi (214); 18: Nerima (925); 19: Adachi (271); 20: Katsushika (143); 21: Edogawa (197). Note that for each observation tn, $\sum_{j=1}^{21} D_{W,tn,j} = 1$; i.e., for each observation tn, the 21 ward dummy variables sum to one.

The tenth ward, Setagaya, had the most transactions in the sample (1158 transactions over the sample period) and thus the level of land prices in this Ward should be fairly accurately determined. Hence the remaining ω_j represent the level of land prices in Ward j *relative* to the level in Ward 10 so if say $\omega_1 > 1$, this means that on average, the price of land in Ward 1 was higher than the average price of land in Ward 10. Taking into account the normalization (4.15), it can be seen that the DS *builder's model with locational dummy variables* had 44 unknown land price parameters α_t, 20 ward relative land price parameters ω_j, one structure price level parameter β and one annual net depreciation parameter δ that needed to be estimated. DS estimated these parameters using the nonlinear regression option in Shazam; see White (2004). The detailed parameter estimates are listed in Table 4.9.[61] The R^2 for this model turned out to be 0.8168 and the log likelihood (LL) was −9233.0, a huge increase of 2270.6 over the LL of the model defined by (4.12). Thus the Ward variables are very significant determinants of Tokyo house prices.

Diewert and Shimizu regarded this model as a minimally satisfactory model. Note that they used only four characteristics for each house sale: the land area L, the structure area S, the age of the structure A and its Ward location.[62]

4.5.5 *The Construction of Land, Structure and Overall House Price Indexes*

DS addressed the problem of how exactly should the land, structure and overall Tokyo house price index be constructed? The DS nonlinear regression model defined by (4.14) decomposes into two terms: one which involves the land area L_{tn} of the house, $\alpha_t(\sum_{j=1}^{21} \omega_j D_{W,tn,j})L_{tn}$, and another which involves the structure area S_{tn} of the house, $\beta p_{Ct}(1 - \delta A_{tn})S_{tn}$. The first term can be regarded as an estimate of the land value of house n that was sold in quarter t while the second term is an estimate of the structure value of the house. The problem now is how exactly should these two value terms be decomposed into constant quality price and quantity components? The view expressed by DS is that a suitable constant quality land price index for all houses sold in period t should be α_t and for house n sold in period t, the corresponding constant quality quantity should be $(\sum_{j=1}^{21} \omega_j D_{W,tn,j})L_{tn}$ which in turn is equal to $\omega_j L_{tn}$ if house n sold in period t is in Ward j.[63] The basic idea here is that DS

[61] The annual net depreciation rate for this model was estimated as $\delta = 1.39\%$ with a T statistic of 26.8.

[62] Diewert and Shimizu (2013) estimated several additional models that were generalizations of the model defined by (4.14). These models made use of the NB, WI, TW and TT variables defined above in Sect. 4.5.2. Their final most general Model 5 had an R^2 equal to 0.8476 and the corresponding log likelihood was −8709.9.

[63] An alternative way of viewing the land model is that land in each Ward can be regarded as a distinct commodity with its own price and quantity. But since all Ward land prices move proportionally over time, virtually all index number formulae will generate an overall land price series that is proportional to the α_t.

Table 4.9 Estimated coefficients for model 1

Name	Est Coef	T Stat	Name	Est Coef	T Stat	Name	Est Coef	T Stat
ω_1	2.1348	41.112	α_3	3.7863	28.383	α_{25}	4.4053	35.093
ω_2	1.0020	30.511	α_4	3.9980	32.103	α_{26}	4.3998	35.979
ω_3	1.1553	30.269	α_5	3.7944	32.603	α_{27}	4.7558	31.124
ω_4	1.0552	11.541	α_6	3.7475	27.506	α_{28}	5.1506	40.423
ω_5	0.38569	5.621	α_7	3.3218	26.688	α_{29}	5.1939	37.356
ω_6	0.62467	9.992	α_8	3.4285	30.338	α_{30}	5.4013	37.140
ω_7	1.0214	27.35	α_9	3.7525	27.488	α_{31}	5.2080	33.905
ω_8	1.2304	58.353	α_{10}	3.3802	28.813	α_{32}	5.6581	39.967
ω_9	0.88449	46.691	α_{11}	3.0205	23.868	α_{33}	5.1146	31.804
ω_{11}	1.6639	41.882	α_{12}	3.3602	31.929	α_{34}	5.0592	31.877
ω_{12}	0.67269	34.870	α_{13}	3.8478	29.689	α_{35}	5.3721	32.813
ω_{13}	0.79505	64.468	α_{14}	3.7603	32.321	α_{36}	4.0782	23.219
ω_{14}	0.89487	26.294	α_{15}	3.5570	28.634	α_{37}	4.0863	22.016
ω_{15}	0.54123	8.8738	α_{16}	3.7025	22.845	α_{38}	3.9651	24.827
ω_{16}	0.44453	6.0919	α_{17}	3.8440	34.010	α_{39}	3.9528	24.771
ω_{17}	0.45904	16.009	α_{18}	3.8632	29.935	α_{40}	3.8021	23.690
ω_{18}	0.49218	39.188	α_{19}	3.4764	28.183	α_{41}	4.2077	27.508
ω_{19}	0.21120	8.9117	α_{20}	4.0631	30.474	α_{42}	4.4752	28.542
ω_{20}	0.28298	7.9508	α_{21}	4.1170	31.375	α_{43}	3.9829	25.538
ω_{21}	0.33419	12.273	α_{22}	4.1321	31.351	α_{44}	4.1515	29.487
α_1	3.7342	32.491	α_{23}	4.1994	28.264	β	3.4071	59.780
α_2	3.9089	33.202	α_{24}	4.2315	35.553	δ	0.01394	26.830

regarded the term $\alpha_t(\sum_{j=1}^{21} \omega_j D_{W,tn,j})L_{tn}$ as a time dummy hedonic model for the land component of the house with α_t acting as the time dummy coefficient. Thus if we priced out house n that sold in period t in period s, our hedonic imputation for the land value component of this " model" would be $\alpha_s(\sum_{j=1}^{21} \omega_j D_{W,tn,j})L_{tn}$. Thus the quarterly time coefficients α_t act as *proportional time shifters of the hedonic surface for the land component* of the value of each house in our sample and the relative period t to period s land price for each constant quality house is α_t/α_s.

Similarly, a suitable *constant quality structure price index* for all houses sold in period t is βp_{Ct} and for house n sold in period t, the corresponding *constant quality quantity* should be approximately equal to the depreciated structure quantity $(1 - \delta A_{tn})S_{tn}$. Thus DS regarded the term $\beta p_{Ct}(1 - \delta A_{tn})S_{tn}$ as a time dummy hedonic model for the structure component of the house with βp_{Ct} acting as the time dummy coefficient. The quarterly time coefficients βp_{Ct} (or just the p_{Ct}) act as proportional time shifters of the hedonic surface for the structure component of each house in our sample and the period t to period s land price for each house in our sample turns out to be p_{Ct}/p_{Cs}.[64]

Thus the *constant quality residential land price index* for Tokyo for quarter t was defined to be $P_{L,t} \equiv \alpha_t/\alpha_1$ and the corresponding *constant quality residential structures price index* for Tokyo for quarter t was defined to be $P_{S,t} \equiv p_{Ct}/p_{C1}$.[65] These price indexes were regarded by DS as quarter t price levels for land and structures respectively and the corresponding Model 1 quarter t *constant quality quantity levels*, $Q_{L,t}$ and $Q_{S,t}$, were defined as the total quarter t values of land and structures divided by the corresponding price levels for $t = 1, \ldots, 44$:

$$Q_{L,t} \equiv \sum_{n=1}^{N(t)} \left(\sum_{j=1}^{21} \omega_j D_{W,tn,j} \right) \alpha_t L_{tn} / P_{L,t} = \alpha_1 \sum_{n=1}^{N(t)} \left(\sum_{j=1}^{21} \omega_j D_{W,tn,j} \right) L_{tn}; \tag{4.16}$$

$$Q_{S,t} \equiv \sum_{n=1}^{N(t)} \beta p_{Ct}(1 - \delta A_{tn}) S_{tn} / P_{S,t} = \beta \sum_{n=1}^{N(t)} (1 - \delta A_{tn}) S_{tn}. \tag{4.17}$$

The price and quantity series for land and structures need to be aggregated into an overall Tokyo house price index. DS used the Fisher (1922) ideal index to perform this aggregation. Thus they defined the *overall house price level for quarter t*, P_t, as the chained Fisher price index applied to the land and structure series $\{P_{L,t}, P_{S,t}, Q_{L,t}, Q_{S,t}\}$.[66]

The overall DS house price index for Tokyo, P_t, as well as the land and structure price indexes, P_{Lt} and P_{St}, for Tokyo over the 44 quarters in the years 2000-2010 are graphed in Fig. 4.14. DS also computed the quarterly mean and median house prices transacted in each quarter and then normalized these averages to start at 1 in Quarter 1 of 2000. These overall average price index series, $P_{\text{Mean},t}$ and $P_{\text{Median},t}$ are also graphed in Fig. 4.14.

The land price series P_{Lt} is the top line in Fig. 4.14, followed by the overall hedonic house price index P_t, followed by the structure price index P_{St} (at the end

[64]Our method for aggregating over different house "models" that have varying amounts of constant quality land and structures can be viewed as a hedonic imputation method but it can also be viewed as an application of Hicks' Aggregation Theorem; i.e., if the prices in a group of commodities vary in strict proportion over time, then the factor of proportionality can be taken as the price of the group and the deflated group expenditures will obey the usual properties of a microeconomic commodity. "Thus we have demonstrated mathematically the very important principle, used extensively in the text, that if the prices of a group of goods change in the same proportion, that group of goods behaves just as if it were a single commodity." Hicks (1946; 312–313).

[65]DS normalized the price indexes P_{Lt} and P_{St} to equal 1 in quarter 1, which is quarter 1 of the year 2000.

[66]The Fisher chained index P_t is defined as follows. For $t = 1$, define $P_t \equiv 1$. For $t > 1$, define P_t in terms of P_{t-1} and $P_{F,t}$ as $P_t \equiv P_{t-1} P_{F,t}$ where $P_{F,t}$ is the quarter t Fisher chain link index. The chain link Fisher index for $t \geq 2$ is defined as $P_{F,t} \equiv [P_{La,t} P_{Pa,t}]^{1/2}$ where the Laspeyres and Paasche chain link indexes are defined as $P_{La,t} \equiv [P_{L,t} Q_{L,t-1} + P_{S,t} Q_{S,t-1}]/[P_{L,t-1} Q_{L,t-1} + P_{S,t-1} Q_{S,t-1}]$ and $P_{Pa,t} \equiv [P_{L,t} Q_{L,t} + P_{S,t} Q_{S,t}]/[P_{L,t-1} Q_{L,t} + P_{S,t-1} Q_{S,t}]$. Diewert (1976, 1992) showed that the Fisher formula had good justifications from both the perspectives of the economic and axiomatic approaches to index number theory.

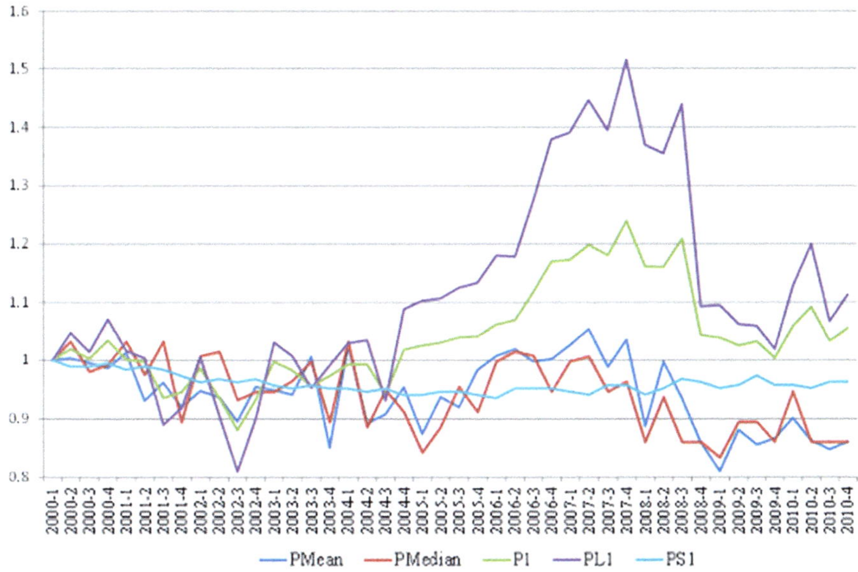

Fig. 4.14 Mean Median and overall prices, land prices and structure price indexes

of the sample period). The mean and median price series track each other and the overall hedonic index price series P_t reasonably well until 2004 but in the following years, the mean and median series fall well below the overall quality adjusted house price series P_t.[67] Thus quality adjusting the sales of residential housing in Tokyo made a big difference to the resulting index.

4.6 Summary and Conclusion

In the wake of the release of the *Residential Property Price Indices Handbook*, the following questions arise:

- Do the different methods suggested in the Eurostat Handbook (and in Sect. 4.2 above) lead to different estimates of housing price changes?
- If the methods do generate different results, which method should be chosen.
- Which data source should be used for housing information?

Section 4.2 of this paper reviewed the 5 methods used by Shimizu et al. (2010a) to construct housing price indexes and Sect. 4.3 presented their empirical results. SNW

[67] The mean and median series cannot adjust properly for changes in the relative prices of land and structures or for changes in the average age of the houses sold. Also our mean and median series are for all sales of houses in Tokyo and thus these series were not adjusted for changes in the number of properties sold in expensive wards and less expensive wards. We cannot expect the mean and median series to be very accurate constant quality indexes of house prices; see Eurostat (2011).

found no significant differences between the five indexes in terms of contemporaneous correlation. They found that the five indexes are almost identical in terms of quarterly growth rates. However, they found significant differences between the five indexes in terms of dynamic relationships. Specifically, they found that there exists a substantial discrepancy in terms of turning points between the hedonic and repeat sales indexes, even though the hedonic index is adjusted for structural change and the repeat sales index is adjusted in the way that Case and Shiller suggested. The repeat sales measure tends to exhibit a delayed turn compared with the hedonic measure; for example, the hedonic measure of condominium prices hit the sample low point at the beginning of 2002, while the corresponding repeat-sales measure exhibits reversal only in the spring of 2004. Such a discrepancy cannot be fully removed even if the repeat sales index is adjusted for depreciation (age effects). SNW presented empirical evidence suggesting that such differences between the hedonic and repeat sales indexes mainly come from non-randomness in the repeat sales samples. Although the 5 types of house index exhibited similar quarterly growth rates (with the exception of the Rolling Year Hedonic index which ended up well above the other 4 house price indexes), looking at Fig. 4.2 that plots these 5 indexes for condominiums, it can be seen that 4 of the methods generate index levels at the end of the sample period that are quite different.[68] Thus it appears that the method of calculation does matter.

Given that the method matters, the question of which method is " best" remains open but the depreciation bias in the standard repeat sales method tends to lead us to prefer hedonic methods.[69]

Given these results, the government of Japan decided to prepare an official residential property price index based on the hedonic method. In particular, it has been determined that it will be estimated with the rolling window hedonic method proposed by Shimizu et al. (2010a, b) and system development is underway.

The next issue is the question of what data sources should be used. The choice of the data set has been regarded as critically important from the practical viewpoint, but has not been discussed much in the literature. Section 4.4 of this paper sought to fill this gap by comparing the distribution of prices collected at different stages of the house buying/selling process, including (1) asking prices at which properties are initially listed in a magazine, (2) asking prices when an offer is eventually made, (3) contract prices reported by realtors, and (4) land registry prices. These four prices, denoted by P_1, P_2, P_3 and P_4 are collected by different parties and recorded in different data sets.

Our findings in Sect. 4.4 have some practical implications for the construction of property price indexes. The first implication is that we may be able to rely on online data to construct a flash or preliminary estimate. Specifically, we may be able to use online asking price data recorded at the time when an offer is eventually made

[68]The end of sample period price levels range from approximately 0.4 to 0.7. These differences were generated over a period of approximately 30 years so that the small differences in quarterly growth rates eventually cumulate into fairly substantial differences between the indexes.

[69]We note that in order to implement the age adjusted repeat sales model, a form of hedonic regression is required.

(i.e., using the P_2 prices) although we still have to cope with various practical issues, including how to identify the timing of a sale and how to find out if the disappearance of the listing price is due to a withdrawal or a sale. Second, the resulting preliminary price indexes could be revised as additional transaction information (i.e., P_3 and P_4 prices) become available. However, it should be noted that P_3 and P_4 information becomes available only gradually. As the P_3 and P_4 information comes in, we could gradually build up actual sales information for the past 4 quarters or so and at the end of each quarter, it would be possible to rerun the preliminary hedonic regressions or repeat sales regressions for the past 4 quarters using the newest relevant data set. Thus the preliminary index would be revised for at least 4 quarters until it becomes " final". Importantly, the quality of the flash estimate as a predictor of the final one depends not only on how prices evolve over time in the buying/selling process, which we empirically examined in Sect. 4.4, but also on the extent of sample selection in the sense that properties listed online do not necessarily proceed to the contract and finally to the registration. Since the government of Japan has a responsibility with regard to data source quality, it was decided to use the transaction price information collected by MLIT as the basis for the construction of the final price index. There was another reason for deciding to use MLIT data. Online information and information collected by realtors is concentrated on urban areas. But since the official housing price index is required to cover the entire country, it is preferable to use land registry data.

However, there are two major problems associated with the use of the land registry data base:

- The only information that can be obtained from the registry are the following variables: (i) the address of the property; (ii) the building floor space; (iii) the land area of the plot; (iv) the time of the transaction and (v) the transaction price. The quality of a hedonic regression model can be improved considerably if additional information on the characteristics of the property can be collected.[70] That being the case, when attempting to perform quality adjustment using the hedonic method, there may be insufficient information on housing-related characteristics in the MLIT data base.
- As was indicated in Sect. 4.4 of this paper, the MLIT information is not particularly timely. The Eurostat Handbook calls for a lag between data collection and publication of less than 3 months, which is problematic.

In order to address the second problem, the Japanese government decided to publish preliminary figures and final figures. Thus alternative data sources that are more timely will be used in order to form preliminary property price indexes.

As part of the above deliberations, MLIT began a trial implementation in August 2012. Full-scale implementation is now planned for the Fall 2014. Even once full-scale implementation of the official residential property price index has begun in

[70] In particular, the MLIT data base does not include the age of the structure, which is a key variable. MLIT has therefore constructed a system that collects location related information using Geographic Information Systems or GIS. In addition, a system was established for real estate appraisers to survey detailed characteristics.

Japan, issues will remain. One of these is the decomposition of property value into land and structure components. Section 4.5 of this paper summarized the results of research on this issue. For purposes of constructing the national accounts, it will be necessary to consider separating the residential property price index into a land index and structure index.

The present paper has indicated that constructing practical residential property price indexes will not be an easy task. Many difficult problems remain but a good start on the required methodology has been made.

References

Allen, M.T., and W.H. Dare. 2004. The effects of Charm listing prices on house transaction prices. *Real Estate Economics* 32: 696–713.

Bai, J., and P. Perron. 1998. Estimating and testing linear models with multiple structural changes. *Econometrica* 66: 47–78.

Bailey, M.J., R.F. Muth, and H.O. Nourse. 1963. A regression model for real estate price index construction. *Journal of the American Statistical Association* 58: 933–942.

Bostic, R.W., S.D. Longhofer, and C.L. Readfearn. 2007. Land leverage: decomposing home price dynamics. *Real Estate Economics* 35 (2): 183–208.

Bourassa, S.T., M. Hoesli, and J. Sun. 2006. A simple alternative house price index method. *Journal of Housing Economics* 15: 80–97.

Case, B., H.O. Pollakowski, and S.M. Wachter. 1991. On choosing among house price index methodologies. *AREUEA Journal* 19: 286–307.

Case, B., and J.M. Quigley. 1991. The dynamics of real estate prices. *Review of Economics and Statistics* 22: 50–58.

Case, K.E., and R.J. Shiller. 1987. Prices of single family homes since 1970: new indexes for four cities. *New England Economic Review*:45–56.

Case, K.E., and R.J. Shiller. 1989. The efficiency of the market for single family homes. *The American Economic Review* 79: 125–137.

Chau, K.W., S.K. Wong, and C.Y. Yiu. 2005. Adjusting for non-linear age effects in the repeat sales index. *Journal of Real Estate Finance and Economics* 31: 137–153.

Clapp, J.M. 1980. The elasticity of substitution for land: the effects of measurement errors. *Journal of Urban Economics* 8: 255–263.

Clapp, J.M., and C. Giaccotto. 1992. Estimating price trends for residential property: a comparison of repeat sales and assessed value methods. *Journal of Real Estate Finance and Economics* 5: 357–374.

Clapp, J.M., and C. Giaccotto. 1998. Price indexes based on the hedonic repeat-sales method: application to the housing market. *Journal of Real Estate Finance and Economics* 16: 5–26.

Court, A. T. 1939. Hedonic Price Indexes with Automotive Examples. In *The Dynamics of Automobile Demand*, pp. 98–117. New York: General Motors Corporation.

Davis, M.A., and J. Heathcote. 2007. The price and quantity of residential land in the United States. *Journal of Monetary Economics* 54: 2595–2620.

de Haan, J., and F. Krsinich. 2014. Scanner Data and the Treatment of Quality Change in Rolling Year GEKS Price Indexes. *Journal of Business and Economic Statistics*. forthcoming.

Deng, Y.D., and McMillen and T.F. Sing, 2012. Private residential price indices in Singapore: a matching approach. *Regional Science and Urban Economics* 42: 485–494.

Diewert, W.E. 1976. Exact and superlative index numbers. *Journal of Econometrics* 4: 114–145.

Diewert, W.E. 1992. Fisher ideal output, input and productivity indexes revisited. *Journal of Productivity Analysis* 3: 211–248.

Diewert, W.E. 2003a. Hedonic Regressions: A Consumer Theory Approach. In *Studies in Income and Wealth 64*, ed. Scanner Data, R.C. Price Indexes, and Feenstra and M.D. Shapiro, 317–348. Chicago: University of Chicago.

Diewert, W.E. 2003b. Hedonic Regressions: A Review of Some Unresolved Issues. In Paper Presented at the 7th Meeting of the Ottawa Group, Paris, May 27–29.

Diewert, W.E. 2010. Alternative Approaches to Measuring House Price Inflation. Discussion Paper 10-10, Department of Economics, The University of British Columbia, Vancouver, Canada, V6T 1Z1.

Diewert, W.E. 2011. The Paris OECD-IMF Workshop on Real Estate Price Indexes: Conclusions and Future Directions. In *Price and Productivity Measurement, Vol. 1: Housing*, W.E. Diewert, B.M. Balk, D. Fixler, K.J. Fox and A.O. Nakamura, eds., pp. 87–116. Trafford Press.

Diewert, W.E. and C. Shimizu 2013. Residential Property Price Indexes for Tokyo. Discussion Paper 13-07, School of Economics, The University of British Columbia, Vancouver, Canada, V6T 1Z1. Forthcoming in *Macroeconomic Dynamics*.

Diewert, W.E., J. de Haan, and R. Hendriks. 2011a. The decomposition of a house price index into land and structures components: a hedonic regression approach. *The Valuation Journal* 6 (2011): 58–106.

Diewert, W.E., J. de Haan and R. Hendriks 2011b. Hedonic Regressions and the Decomposition of a House Price index into Land and Structure Components. Discussion Paper 11-01, Department of Economics, University of British Columbia, Vancouver, Canada, V6T1Z1. Forthcoming in *Econometric Reviews*.

Dorsey, R.E., H. Hua, W.J. Mayera, and H. Wanga. 2010. Hedonic versus repeat-sales housing price indexes for measuring the recent boom-bust cycle. *Journal of Housing Economics* 19: 75–93.

Ekeland, I., J.J. Heckman, and L. Nesheim. 2004. Identification and estimation of hedonic models. *Journal of Political Economy* 112: 60–109.

Engelhardt, G.V. 2003. Nominal loss aversion, housing equity constraints and household mobility: evidence from the United States. *Journal of Urban Economics* 53: 171–195.

Eurostat. 2011. *Handbook on Residential Property Price Indices*. Luxembourg: Eurostat.

Fisher, I. 1922. *The Making of Index Numbers*. Boston: Houghton-Mifflin.

Francke, M.K. 2008. The Hierarchical Trend Model. In *Mass Appraisal Methods: An International Perspective for Property Valuers*, T. Kauko and M. Damato, eds., pp. 164–180. Oxford: Wiley-Blackwell.

Francke, M.K., and G.A. Vos. 2004. The hierarchical trend model for property valuation and local price indices. *Journal of Real Estate Finance and Economics* 28 (2/3): 179–208.

Gatzlaff, D.H., and D.R. Haurin. 1998. Sample selection and biases in local house value indices. *Journal of Urban Economics* 43: 199–222.

Genesove, D., and C. Mayer. 1997. Equity and time to sale in the real estate market. *American Economic Review* 87: 255–269.

Genesove, D., and C. Mayer. 2001. Loss aversion and seller behavior: evidence from the housing market. *Quarterly Journal of Economics* 116: 1233–1260.

Goetzmann, W. and L. Peng 2006. Estimating house price indexes in the preference of seller reservation prices.

Goodman, A.C. and T.G. Thibodeau. 1998. Dwelling age heteroskedasticity in repeat sales house price equations.

Griliches, Z. 1971. Introduction: hedonic price indexes revisited. In *Price Indexes and Quality Change*, Z. Griliches, ed., pp. 3–15. Cambridge MA: Harvard University Press.

Gyourko, J., and A. Saiz. 2004. Reinvestment in the housing stock: the role of construction costs and the supply side. *Journal of Urban Economics* 55: 238–256.

Hicks, J.R. 1946. *Value and Capital*, 2nd ed. Oxford: Clarendon Press.

Haurin, D.R., J.L. Haurin, T. Nadauld, and A. Sanders. 2010. List prices, sale prices and marketing time: an application to U.S. housing markets. *Real Estate Economics* 38: 659–685.

Ivancic, L., W.E. Diewert, and K.J. Fox. 2009. *Scanner Data, Time Aggregation and the Construction of Price Indexes, Discussion Paper 09–09*. Department of Economics: The University of British Columbia, Vancouver, Canada.

Ivancic, L., W.E. Diewert, and K.J. Fox. 2011. Scanner data, time aggregation and the construction of price indexes. *Journal of Econometrics* 161: 24–35.

Knight, J.R., C.F. Sirmans, and G.K. Turnbull. 1998. List price information in residential appraisal and underwriting. *Journal of Real Estate Research* 15: 59–76.

Koev, E., and J.M.C. Santos Silva. 2008. *Hedonic Methods for Decomposing House Price Indices into Land and Structure Components, unpublished paper*. Department of Economics: University of Essex, England, October.

Machado, J.A.F., and J. Mata. 2005. Counterfactual decomposition of changes in wage distributions using quantile regression. *Journal of Applied Econometrics* 20: 445–465.

McMillen, D.P. 2003. The return of centralization to Chicago: using repeat sales to identify changes in house price distance gradients. *Regional Science and Urban Economics* 33: 287–304.

McMillen, D.P. 2008. Changes in the distribution of house prices over time: structural characteristics, neighborhood or coefficients? *Journal of Urban Economics* 64: 573–589.

McMillen, D.P. 2012. Repeat sales as a matching estimator. *Real Estate Economics* 40: 745–773.

McMillen, D.P., and P. Thorsnes. 2006. Housing renovations and the quantile repeat sales price index. *Real Estate Economics* 34: 567–587.

Muth, R.F. 1971. The derived demand for Urban residential land. *Urban Studies* 8: 243–254.

Pollakowski, H.O. 1995. Data sources for measuring house price changes. *Journal of Housing Research* 6 (3): 377–387.

Rambaldi, A.N., R.R.J. McAllister, K. Collins and C.S. Fletcher. 2010. *Separating Land from Structure in Property Prices: A Case Study from Brisbane Australia*. School of Economics, The University of Queensland, St. Lucia, Queensland 4072, Australia.

Rosen, S. 1974. Hedonic prices and implicit markets: product differentiation in pure competition. *Journal of Political Economy* 82: 34–55.

Schwann, G.M. 1998. A real estate price index for thin markets. *Journal of Real Estate Finance and Economics* 16 (3): 269–287.

Shimizu, C., and K.G. Nishimura. 2006. Biases in appraisal land price information: the case of Japan. *Journal of Property Investment and Finance* 26: 150–175.

Shimizu, C., and K.G. Nishimura. 2007. Pricing structure in Tokyo metropolitan land markets and its structural changes: pre-bubble, bubble, and post-bubble periods. *Journal of Real Estate Finance and Economics* 35: 475–496.

Shimizu, C., K.G. Nishimura, and Y. Asami. 2004. Search and vacancy costs in the Tokyo housing market: an attempt to measure social costs of imperfect information. *Review of Urban and Regional Development Studies* 16: 210–230.

Shimizu, C., K.G. Nishimura, and T. Watanabe. 2010. Housing prices in Tokyo: a comparison of hedonic and repeat sales measures. *Journal of Economics and Statistics* 230 (6): 792–813.

Shimizu, C., K.G. Nishimura and T. Watanabe. 2011. House Prices at Different Stages in Buying/Selling Process. Hitotsubashi University Research Center for Price Dynamics Working Paper Working Paper,No. 69.

Shimizu, C., K.G. Nishimura and T. Watanabe. 2012. House Prices from Magazines, Realtors, and the Land Registry. *Property Market and Financial Stability*, BIS Papers No.64, Bank of International Settlements, March 2012, pp. 29-38.

Shimizu, C., H. Takatsuji, H. Ono, and K.G. Nishimura. 2010. Structural and temporal changes in the housing market and hedonic housing price indices. *International Journal of Housing Markets and Analysis* 3 (4): 351–368.

Standard and Poor's. 2008. *S&P/Case-Shiller Home Price indexes: Index Methodology*, March 2008.

Statistics Portugal (Instituto Nacional de Estatistica). 2009. *Owner-Occupied Housing: Econometric Study and Model to Estimate Land Prices, Final Report, paper presented to the Eurostat Working Group on the Harmonization of Consumer Price Indices, March 26–27*. Luxembourg: Eurostat.

Summers, R. 1973. International comparisons with incomplete data. *Review of Income and Wealth* 29 (1): 1–16.
Triplett, Jack. 2004. *Handbook on Hedonic Indexes and Quality Adjustments in Price Indexes*. OECD Science, Technology and Industry Working Papers 2004/9.
Thorsnes, P. 1997. Consistent estimates of the elasticity of substitution between land and non-land inputs in the production of housing. *Journal of Urban Economics* 42: 98–108.
White, K.J. 2004. *Shazam: User's Reference Manual, Version 10*. Vancouver, Canada: Northwest Econometrics Ltd.

Chapter 5
The System of National Accounts and Alternative Approaches to the Construction of Commercial Property Price Indexes

5.1 Introduction

How can a commercial property price index (CPPI) be defined and constructed? And what kind of relationship does the measurement of commercial property's value have to the System of National Accounts and to concerns about national financial sectors? In order to answer such questions, this paper aims to outline the concepts that can be used to define and measure the value of commercial property, and to clarify the relationship of such measurement to the System of National Accounts and to the financial system.

In constructing CPPI's in the National Accounts, we should use transaction prices. However, due to a lack of commercial property sales, it may be necessary to use appraisal based information combined with transaction prices in a mixed approach.

In the case of price indexes, prices transacted on the market are in principle the most fundamental or relevant type of data. However, in the creation of real estate price indexes—especially commercial real estate price indexes—it is not unusual for real estate appraisal values to be used directly in the index construction rather than transaction prices, in part due to the low number of actual transactions.[1] As a prominent example, MSCI-IPD (IPD), a private company based in the U.K. which supplies property return (income return and capital return) indexes for more 30 countries, creates its indexes based on appraisal values.[2] The NCREIF capital returns—a leading

[1]Note however that there are circumstance where transaction price information is more plentiful than appraisal valuation information, notably in countries (such as the U.S.) where IFRS accounting rules are not yet prevalent, such that assets are normally carried on companies' books at historical cost rather than at current "fair value." In the United States, only specialized populations of commercial properties are frequently and professionally appraised.

[2]For details of IPD's real estate investment index, see http://www1.ipd.com/Pages/default.aspx

The base of this chapter is Diewert, W.E. and C. Shimizu. 2019. The system of national accounts and alternative approaches to the construction of commercial property price indexes. Discussion Paper 19–9, Vancouver School of Economics, University of British Columbia. Presented at the 62nd ISI World Statistics Congress, invitation session. Kuala Lumpur, Malaysia, August 19, 2019.

W. E. Diewert et al., *Property Price Index*, Advances in Japanese Business and Economics 11, https://doi.org/10.1007/978-4-431-55942-9_5

U.S. real estate investment index—are also, like IPD's index, based on appraisal valuations.[3]

In recent years, commercial price indexes based on transaction prices have also been published, such as the U.S. Moody's/RCA Commercial Property Price Index (CPPI) and the MIT/CRE Transaction Based Index (TBI).[4] Beyond that, new indexes based on stock market share prices of companies specialized in the ownership of commercial property equity are beginning to be developed, such as the NAREIT Pure Property Index Series which was launched in 2012 in the United States. Thus, an important point that arises with regard to the creation of commercial real estate price indexes is the question of selecting the type of value indication data, along with the issue of the index calculation method. The question is whether to use transaction price data, to use real estate appraisal value, or to use a different method altogether, such as stock market data.

Commercial property investment, like housing, plays an extremely important part in the System of National Accounts. Investment in buildings as part of new property development must be recorded in the System of National Accounts, and while the economy is growing rapidly, new building investment represents a significant share of total national investment in the System of National Accounts. In addition, since buildings are finite-lived durable goods, it is necessary to correctly measure depreciation that occurs with the passage of time. What's more, maintenance is conducted and investments are made in renovations or improvements in order to increase the value. Such investment in maintenance and improvements/renovations also comprises a significant share of investment.

The following issues should be considered in preparing commercial property price indexes:

- We should use transaction prices. However, since transactions may be few in number and only observed sporadically in many markets, we may be forced to consider combining transactions values with appraisal values to construct CPPI's.
- The characteristics that determine the market value of commercial property are extremely heterogeneous and include characteristics both of the property itself and of its site and location. As well, " commercial property" covers a broad range; depending on the source of income, it may refer to offices, retail facilities, investment housing, factories, distribution facilities, hotels, hospitals, care facilities, and land as well as other categories.
- Economic indicators as typified by price indexes of market or transaction prices (such as the CPI) generally track the prices of the same items through time and observe the changes in those prices. But for non-durable goods the "same item" refers to exactly that, a new example of the same good, bought at different points in time. But real estate is not only durable but is unique. No two properties are identical, and when the same property transacts repeatedly at different points in

[3]NCREIF: (http://www.ncreif.org/. (Note that the NCREIF Index is based on a little over 7,000 properties, out of a universe of probably some 3,000,000 commercial properties in the U.S.)).

[4]http://mitcre.mit.edu/research-publications/cred/transaction-based-index. (Note that the TBI is now produced and published by NCREIF as the "NTBI.").

time it is older at the later point in time, and a property's age is one feature determining its value. Indeed, the price of a commercial property can change over time even if depreciation of the structure does not occur, either because some characteristics affecting value can change (e.g., the distance to the nearest subway station may change if a new station is built, or the building's features/structure may change if there are renovations), or because the imputed prices of the property characteristics that determine its value may have changed (e.g., it may be more valuable to be located near an airport or near an internet data center and less valuable to be located near a railway station). Thus, from an SNA (System of National Accounts) perspective, defining what is a change in "price" and what is a change in "quantity" (including "quality") of real estate is non-trivial, and is particularly complicated when dealing with commercial property.
- Current CPPIs compiled largely in the private sector from observing the commercial property market in actual business dealings, may be either transaction based or (more frequently) appraisal based.
- CPPIs produced by the private sector are normally confined to those properties that fall in to the professionally managed investment industry. Smaller non-professionally managed commercial properties, including owner occupied commercial properties, are often not included in these indexes. Even large buildings, if owner-occupied and not in the investment market, are not tracked. As such, the universe of commercial properties is often only partially covered and is biased towards the professionally managed property sector. While CPIs for instance aim to sample the universe of all household transactions, CPPIs produced by the private sector generally refer only to the sub-sector of transactions or properties which fall within the scope of their clients.

With the above general considerations in mind, an outline of the paper is as follows: In Sect. 5.2, we will consider the differences between stock and flow price indexes for commercial real estate and the relationship of these indexes in the System of National Accounts. In subsequent sections, we will concentrate on the construction of stock indexes. In particular, we will look at methods of index construction that enable one to decompose commercial property sales prices into land and structure components with separate price indexes for both components. Sections 5.3–5.6 will work with indexes based on transaction prices for commercial office properties. Section 5.3 introduces the *builder's model* which enables us to construct separate land and structure price indexes for commercial office properties for Tokyo. The model also allows us to estimate a geometric depreciation rate for these properties. Section 5.4 extends the Sect. 5.3 model to allow for geometric depreciation rates that change as the structure ages. Section 5.5 looks at the estimation of straight line structure depreciation rates and also generalizes this simple model with a single rate to a model that allows for a piecewise linear depreciation schedule. The final models in Sects. 5.4 and 5.5 end up producing very similar price indexes for land as well as similar structure aging functions.

Due to the scarcity of transactions in commercial properties in Tokyo, the land price indexes that result from the final models in Sects. 5.4 and 5.5 are fairly volatile. Thus in Sect. 5.6, we look at some simple methods for smoothing these volatile series.

Section 5.7 uses appraisal data and Sect. 5.8 uses tax assessment data in order to construct commercial property land price indexes. It will be seen that the resulting indexes appear to be too smooth and they significantly lag the turning points in the transaction based indexes that are exhibited in Sects. 5.4 and 5.5.

In Sect. 5.9, overall property price indexes based on transactions data and on appraisal data are constructed and these overall indexes are compared to a simple average type of index and to a traditional log price hedonic regression overall commercial property price index. It turns out that the traditional hedonic price index is reasonably close to our overall commercial property transactions based index. However, the traditional log price hedonic index cannot provide separate land and structure subindexes. These separate indexes are required in the country's National Balance Sheet Accounts as well in national multifactor productivity accounts (if the country produces these accounts).

Section 5.10 shows how stock market information on Real Estate Investment Trusts (REITs) can be used to provide additional "transactions" that could be used to increase sample size when running a hedonic regression on sales of commercial properties.

Section 5.11 concludes.

5.2 The System of National Accounts and Stock and Flow Prices for Commercial Properties

Commercial Property Price Indexes (CPPIs) play an important role in economic statistics and especially for the System of National Accounts (SNA). Decomposing the value of a commercial property into price and quantity components is important for financial system oversight and important for guiding macroeconomic policy. The SNA Balance Sheet Accounts require information on the price and quantity (or volume) of commercial properties located in the country. Moreover, the SNA also requires a separate decomposition of property value into *separate* price and quantity components for the *structure* on the commercial property and for the *land* that the structure sits on. This information is essential for measuring the Total Factor Productivity (or Multifactor Productivity) of the commercial property sector and hence, it is also essential to measure the productivity of the national economy. Given the recent increase in the value of land in many advanced economies, determining the value, price and quantity of land used by the commercial property sector is important to guide economic policy.

It is useful to develop a general relationship between the value of an asset and the period by period rents that it can generate as it ages.[5] In general, the value of an asset

[5] See Diewert (2005; 480–485) and Diewert et al. (2016).

at the beginning of an accounting period is equal to the discounted stream of future rental payments that the asset is expected to yield. Thus the *stock value* of the asset is equal to the discounted future *service flows* that the asset is expected to yield in future periods.

The System of National Accounts also requires information on the flow of services generated by the commercial property sector and on the flow of inputs used by the sector over an accounting period.

We introduce some notation for modeling the output and input flows for the commercial property sector for accounting period t. Consider commercial property n in period t which has $I(n)$ separate units in it which are rented out at the rental price p_{tni} for $n = 1, \ldots, N$ and $i = 1, \ldots, I(n)$. The owner of the property provides various intermediate and primary inputs to the renters such as electricity, heating, air conditioning, security services which have prices w_{tnij} for $n = 1, \ldots, N$, $i = 1, \ldots, I(n)$ and $j = 1, \ldots, J$ where there are J separate inputs used by the owners of the commercial properties.[6] Price indexes for rented outputs, (i.e., for the p_{tni}) and price indexes for intermediate inputs used in order to produce the rented outputs (i.e., for the w_{tnij}) are required in the System of National accounts. But note that these prices depend not only on the age of the structure on property n and the time period t but also on the particular characteristics of the property and the particular rented unit . The reason for this dependence is that each unit i in property n will generally offer a different mix of amenities associated with the rented space s_{tni}. Thus the rental price of a unit in a commercial property will generally depend on the following *quality adjusting factors*:

- The floor space area of the unit;
- Is electricity provided?
- Is heating or air conditioning provided?
- Are cleaning services provided and how much maintenance is provided?
- Does the rented space offer a view?
- What is the average vacancy rate?
- Is parking provided?
- How close to rapid transit is the property?
- What is the ratio of structure area to the land area of the building?
- How much landscaping is provided?
- Are other amenity areas provided, such as laundry facilities or recreation areas?

The fact that the quality of rented space will depend heavily on what amenities are associated with the rented space and these amenities can vary greatly across properties means that the output and intermediate input prices p_{tni} and w_{tnij} will generally depend on the *characteristics* associated with unit i in property n. The way to deal with these difficult quality adjustment problems is to use *hedonic regression techniques* to adjust observed unit rental prices for quality differences.[7]

[6] In most cases, the input prices w_{tnij} will not depend on the particular rented unit i in property n.

[7] Hedonic regression analysis dates back to Court (1939) who introduced the term. For more recent expositions of the method and references to the literature, see Triplett (2004) and Diewert (2019).

Similar quality adjustment problems occur when constructing price indexes for *stocks* of commercial properties. Thus for property n in period t, we need the beginning of the period current value of the property, say V_{tn}, and a decomposition of this value into a land value, V_{Ltn}, and a corresponding structure value, V_{Stn}. Furthermore, these two value components need to be further decomposed into price and constant quality quantity components, say $V_{Ltn} = P_{Ltn}Q_{Ltn}$ and $V_{Stn} = P_{Stn}Q_{Stn}$ where P_{Ltn} and P_{Stn} are constant quality prices for land and structures and Q_{Ltn} is the land plot area of property n and Q_{Stn} is floor space area of property n in period t. But the land quality may not remain constant from period to period: new amenities may be built (such as a new subway line that has a station near the property) or new "bads" may occur (such as increased pollution or increased traffic congestion) which will affect the land component of the price of the property. Similarly, the quality of the structure will not remain constant across time periods: depreciation of the structure and renovation expenditures will change the structure component of the price of the property. Thus there are also quality adjustment problems when constructing commercial property price indexes for the values of properties. In the following section, we will show how hedonic regression analysis can be used in order to deal with these quality adjustment problems.

In order to construct a commercial property price index, it is first necessary to obtain information on the *period by period value* of these properties. We conclude this section by noting that there are several methods that could be used to measure the value of a commercial property:

- Use transaction prices for commercial properties.
- Use appraisal values.
- Use property tax assessment values.
- Use estimates of future cash flows generated by the property.
- Use stock market information on Real Estate Investment Trusts (REITs).

The problem with using transactions prices is that commercial properties do not transact very frequently. Moreover, commercial properties are very heterogeneous and hence the selling price of a particular commercial property may not be very relevant for other properties. The problem with using appraisal or assessed values is that they may be somewhat arbitrary. They may be based on market transactions for comparable properties which are in fact, not really comparable. Or appraisals may be based on estimates of future cash flows, which are inherently uncertain and require many somewhat arbitrary assumptions about inflation rates for rents, input prices and interest rates. The use of stock market information is also problematic: REIT investors may rely on published appraisal values to justify their investment decisions and as we have indicated, appraisal values are somewhat subjective. Moreover, there are some technical problems that arise when one attempts to construct property values from stock market values; i.e., information on the outstanding debt of the REIT is required and the current value of the debt may not be easy to construct because it may not be very liquid. Furthermore, a REIT may hold a changing portfolio of buildings which will lead to complications. Finally, the portfolio of REIT properties may not be representative of the entire commercial property market.

To conclude this section, we will look at the pros and cons of using different data sources for commercial property values in more detail.

Research studies on commercial property price indexes have emphasized the problem of data selection when formulating indexes. Traditionally, transaction prices (also called market prices in the literature) have usually been used to estimate price indexes. However, the number of commercial property market transactions is extremely small. Furthermore, even if a sizable number of transaction prices can be obtained, the heterogeneity of the properties is so pronounced that it is difficult to compare like with like and thus the construction of reliable constant quality price indexes becomes very difficult.

Under such circumstances, many commercial property price indexes have been constructed using either appraisal prices from the real estate investment market, or using assessment prices for property tax purposes. The rationale for these price indexes is that, since appraisal prices and assessment prices for property tax purposes are regularly surveyed for the same commercial property, indexes based on these surveys hold most characteristics of the property constant,[8] thus greatly reducing the heterogeneity problem as well as generating a wealth of data.

However, while appraisal prices look attractive for the construction of price indexes, they are somewhat subjective; i.e., exactly how are these appraisal prices constructed? Thus these prices lack the objectivity of market selling prices. Such considerations have led to the development of various arguments concerning the precision and accuracy of appraisal and assessment prices when used in measuring price indexes; see Shimizu and Nishimura (2006) on these issues. In particular, the literature on this issue has pointed out that an appraisal based index will typically lag actual turning points in the real estate market.[9] Geltner et al. (1994) clarified the structure of bias in the NCREIF Property Index, a representative U.S. index based on appraisal prices. In a later study Geltner and Goetzmann (2000), estimated an index using commercial property transaction prices and demonstrated the magnitude of errors and the degree of smoothing in the NCREIF Property Index. These problems plague not only the NCREIF Property Index, but all indexes based on appraisal prices, including the MSCI-IPD Index.

In the case of appraisal prices for investment properties, a systemic factor of appraiser incentives emerges as an additional problem. This problem differs intrinsically from the lagging and smoothing problems that arise in appraisal based methods. Specifically, the incentive problem involves inducing higher valuations from appraisers in order to bolster investment performance; see Crosby et al. (2010) on this point.

In this connection Bokhari and Geltner (2012) and Geltner and Bokhari (2019), estimated quality adjusted price indexes by running a time dummy hedonic regression

[8]Two important characteristics which are not held constant are the age of the structure and the amount of capital expenditures on the property between the survey dates. Changes in these characteristics are an important determinant of the property price.

[9]Another problem with appraisal based indexes is that they tend to be smoother than indexes that are based on market transactions. This can be a problem for real estate investors since the smoothing effect will mask the short term riskiness of real estate investments. However, for statistical agencies, smoothing short term fluctuations will probably not be problematic.

using transaction price data. Geltner (1997) also used real estate prices determined by the stock market in order to examine the smoothing effects of the use of appraisal prices. Finally, Geltner et al. (2010), Shimizu et al. (2015), Shimizu (2016) and Diewert and Shimizu (2017, 2019) proposed various estimation methods for commercial property price indexes using REIT data.

The above paragraphs indicate that it will not be easy to construct a Commercial Property Price Index. However, in the following sections of this paper, we will look at some attempts to construct a Tokyo CCPI using alternative data sources. We will also attempt to construct separate subindexes for the land and structure components of a CCPI.

In the following sections, we will examine three alternative data sources suggested in the literature that enable one to construct land price indexes for commercial properties in Tokyo Special District: (i) sales transactions data (1907 observations) in Sects. 5.3 and 5.4; (ii) appraisal data for Real Estate Investment Trusts (REITs) (1804 observations) in Sect. 5.5 and (iii) assessed values of land for property taxation purposes (6242 observations) in Sect. 5.6. We will utilize these three sources of data for commercial properties in Tokyo over 44 quarters covering the period Q1:2005 to Q4:2015 and compare the resulting land prices.

5.3 The Builder's Model with a Single Geometric Depreciation Rate

The *builder's model* for valuing a commercial property postulates that the value of a commercial property is the sum of two components: the value of the land which the structure sits on plus the value of the commercial structure.

In order to justify the model, consider a property developer who builds a structure on a particular property. The total cost of the property after the structure is completed will be equal to the floor space area of the structure, say S square meters, times the building cost per square meter, β_t during quarter or year t, plus the cost of the land, which will be equal to the cost per square meter, α_t during quarter or year t, times the area of the land site, L. Now think of a sample of properties of the same general type, which have prices or values V_{tn} in period t[10] and structure areas S_{tn} and land areas L_{tn} for $n = 1, \ldots, N(t)$ where $N(t)$ is the number of observations in period t. Assume that these prices are equal to the sum of the land and structure costs plus error terms ε_{tn} which we assume are independently normally distributed with zero means and constant variances. This leads to the following *hedonic regression model* for period t where the α_t and β_t are the parameters to be estimated in the regression[11]:

---

[10]The period index t runs from 1 to 44 where period 1 corresponds to Q1 of 2005 and period 44 corresponds to Q4 of 2015.

[11]Other papers that have suggested hedonic regression models that lead to additive decompositions of property values into land and structure components include Clapp (1980; 257–258), Bostic et al. (2007; 184), Diewert (2008, 2010), Koev and Santos Silva (2008), de Haan and Diewert (2011), Francke (2008; 167), Rambaldi et al. (2010), Diewert et al. (2011, 2015), Diewert and Shimizu

$$V_{tn} = \alpha_t L_{tn} + \beta_t S_{tn} + \varepsilon_{tn}; \qquad t = 1, \ldots, T; n = 1, \ldots, N(t). \qquad (5.1)$$

Note that the two characteristics in our simple model are the quantities of land L_{tn} and the quantities of structure floor space S_{tn} associated with property n in period t and the two *constant quality prices* in period t are the price of a square meter of land α_t and the price of a square meter of structure floor space β_t.

The hedonic regression model defined by (5.1) applies to new structures. But it is likely that a model that is similar to (5.1) applies to older structures as well. Older structures will be worth less than newer structures due to the (net) depreciation of the structure. Assuming that we have information on the age of the structure n at time t, say $A(t, n)$, and assuming a geometric (or declining balance) depreciation model, a more realistic hedonic regression model than that defined by (5.1) above is the following *basic builder's model*[12]:

$$V_{tn} = \alpha_t L_{tn} + \beta_t (1 - \delta)^{A(t,n)} S_{tn} + \varepsilon_{tn}; \qquad t = 1, \ldots, T; n = 1, \ldots, N(t) \quad (5.2)$$

where the parameter δ reflects the *net geometric depreciation rate* as the structure ages one additional period. Thus if the age of the structure is measured in years, we would expect an annual *net* depreciation rate to be between 2 and 3%.[13] Note that (5.2) is now a nonlinear regression model whereas (5.1) was a simple linear regression model.[14] The period t constant quality price of land will be the estimated coefficient for the parameter α_t and the price of a unit of a newly built structure for period t will be the estimate for β_t. The period t quantity of land for commercial property n is L_{tn} and the period t quantity of structure for commercial property n, expressed in equivalent units of a new structure, is $(1 - \delta)^{A(t,n)} S_{tn}$ where S_{tn} is the space area of commercial property n in period t.

Note that the above model can be interpreted as a *supply side model* as opposed to the *demand side model* of Muth (1971) and McMillen (2003) since the value of a property with a new structure is equal to the cost of production. Basically, for

(2015a, b, 2016, 2017, 2019), Burnett-Issacs et al. (2016), Rambaldi et al. (2016) and Diewert et al. (2017).

[12]This formulation follows that of Diewert (2008, 2010), de Haan and Diewert (2011), Diewert et al. (2015) and Diewert and Shimizu (2015b, 2016, 2017) in assuming property value is the sum of land and structure components but movements in the price of structures are proportional to an exogenous structure price index. This formulation is designed to be useful for national income accountants who require a decomposition of property value into structure and land components. They also need the structure index which in the hedonic regression model to be consistent with the structure price index they use to construct structure capital stocks. Thus the builder's model is particularly suited to national accounts purposes; see Schreyer (2001, 2009), Diewert and Shimizu (2015a) and Diewert et al. (2016).

[13]This estimate of depreciation is regarded as a net depreciation rate because it is equal to a "true" gross structure depreciation rate less an average renovations appreciation rate. Since we do not have information on renovations and major repairs to a structure, our age variable will only pick up average gross depreciation less average real renovation expenditures.

[14]We used Shazam to perform the nonlinear estimations; see White (2004). Note that (5.2) is estimated as a single nonlinear regression using the data for all 44 quarters.

newly developed properties, we are assuming competitive suppliers of commercial properties so that we are in Rosen's (1974; 44) Case (a), where the hedonic surface identifies the structure of supply. This assumption is justified for the case of newly built offices but it is less well justified for sales of existing commercial properties.[15]

This study compiled the following three types of micro-data relating to commercial properties in the Tokyo office market: (i) the transaction price data compiled by the Japanese Ministry of Land, Infrastructure, Transport and Tourism; (ii) the appraisal prices periodically determined in the Tokyo office REIT market; and (iii) the "official land prices" surveyed by the Japanese Ministry of Land, Infrastructure, Transport and Tourism since 1970.[16] Official land prices are based on appraisals that are released on January 1st of each year. In Japan, asset taxes relating to land, such as inheritance taxes and fixed assets taxes, are assessed on the basis of these official land prices. Thus official land prices are considered as assessment data for tax purposes. As official land prices are exclusively based on surveys of land prices, they do not include structure prices.

Using the first two data sources, land price indexes were estimated using the Builder's Model. These land price indexes will be compared with those estimated using official land prices in later section of the paper. Our analysis covers the period from 2005 to 2015.

In estimating builder's model using transaction or appraisal prices in Tokyo, there is a major problem with the hedonic regression model defined by (5.2): The multicollinearity problem. Experience has shown that it is usually not possible to estimate sensible land and structure prices in a hedonic regression like that defined by (5.2) due to the multicollinearity between lot size and structure size.[17] Thus in order to deal with the multicollinearity problem, we drew on *exogenous information* on the cost of building new commercial properties from the Japanese Ministry of Land, Infrastructure, Transport and Tourism (MLIT) and we assumed that the price of new structures is equal to an official measure of commercial building costs (per square meter of building structure), p_{St}. Thus we replaced β_t in (5.2) by p_{St} for $t = 1, \ldots, 44$. This reduced the number of free parameters in the model by 44.

Experience has also shown that it is difficult to estimate the depreciation rate before obtaining quality adjusted land prices. Thus in order to get preliminary land price estimates, we temporarily assumed that the annual geometric depreciation rate δ in Eq. (5.2) was equal to 0.025. The resulting regression model became the model defined by (5.3) below:

$$V_{tn} = \alpha_t L_{tn} + p_{St}(1 - 0.025)^{A(t,n)} S_{tn} + \varepsilon_{tn}; \quad t = 1, \ldots, 44; n = 1, \ldots, N(t). \tag{5.3}$$

[15]For sold properties with older structures on them, we are basically following National Accounting conventions which postulates that property value is equal to the current value of the depreciated structure plus the current value of land; see Schreyer (2001, 2009).

[16]For more details on the data and the regressions used in this study, see Diewert and Shimizu (2019).

[17]See Schwann (1998) and Diewert et al. (2011, 2015) on the multicollinearity problem.

The final log likelihood for this **Model 1** was -13328.15 and the R^2 was 0.4003.[18]

In order to take into account possible neighbourhood effects on the price of land, we introduced *ward dummy variables*, $D_{W,tnj}$, into the hedonic regression (5.3). There are 23 wards in Tokyo special district. We made 23 ward or locational dummy variables.[19] These 23 dummy variables were defined as follows: for $t = 1, \ldots, 44; n = 1, \ldots, N(t); j = 1, \ldots, 23$:

$$D_{W,tnj} \equiv \begin{cases} 1 \text{ if observation } n \text{ in period } t \text{ is in ward } j \text{ of Tokyo;} \\ 0 \text{ if observation } n \text{ in period } t \text{ is not in ward } j \text{ of Tokyo.} \end{cases} \tag{5.4}$$

We modified the model defined by (5.3) to allow the *level* of land prices to differ across the Wards. The new nonlinear regression model is the following one[20]:

$$V_{tn} = \alpha_t \left(\sum_{j=1}^{23} \omega_j D_{W,tnj} \right) L_{tn} + p_{St}(1 - 0.025)^{A(t,n)} S_{tn} + \varepsilon_{tn};$$
$$t = 1, \ldots, 44; n = 1, \ldots, N(t). \tag{5.5}$$

Not all of the land time dummy variable coefficients (the α_t) and the ward dummy variable coefficients (the ω_j) can be identified. Thus we imposed the following normalization on our coefficients:

$$\alpha_1 = 1. \tag{5.6}$$

The final log likelihood for the model defined by (5.5) and (5.6) was -12956.60 and the R^2 was 0.5925. Thus there was a large increase in the R^2 and a huge increase in the log likelihood of 371.55 over the previous model. However, many of the wards had only a small number of observations and thus it is unlikely that our estimated ω_j for these wards are very accurate.

In order to deal with the problem of too few observations in many wards, we used the results of the above model to group the 23 wards into 4 Combined Wards based on their estimated ω_j coefficients. The *Group 1 high priced wards* were 1, 2, 3 and 13 (their estimated ω_j coefficients were greater than 1), the *Group 2 medium high priced wards* were 4, 5, 6, 9 and 14 ($0.6 < \omega_j \leq 1$), the *Group 3 medium low priced wards* were 7, 8, 10, 12, 15 and 16 ($0.4 < \omega_j \leq 0.6$), and the *Group 4 low priced*

[18] Our R^2 concept is the square of the correlation coefficient between the dependent variable and the predicted dependent variable.

[19] The 23 wards (with the number of observations in brackets) are as follows: 1: Chiyoda (191), 2: Chuo (231), 3: Minato (205), 4: Shinjuku (203), 5: Bunkyo (97), 6: Taito (122), 7: Sumida (74), 8: Koto (49), 9: Shinagawa (69), 10: Meguro (28), 11: Ota (64), 12: Setagaya (67), 13: Shibuya (140), 14: Nakano (39), 15: Suginami (39), 16: Toshima (80), 17: Kita (30), 18: Arakawa (42), 19: Itabashi (35), 20: Nerima (40), 21: Adachi (19), 22: Katsushika (18), 23:Edogawa (25).

[20] From this point on, our nonlinear regression models are nested; i.e., we use the coefficient estimates from the previous model as starting values for the subsequent model. Using this nesting procedure is essential to obtaining sensible results from our nonlinear regressions. The nonlinear regressions were estimated using Shazam; see White (2004).

wards were 11, 17, 18, 19, 20, 21, 22 and 23 ($\omega_j \leq 0.4$).[21] We reran the nonlinear regression model defined by (5.5) and (5.6) using just the 4 Combined Wards (call this **Model 2**) and the resulting log likelihood was −12974.31 and the R^2 was 0.5850. Thus combining the original wards into grouped wards resulted in a small loss of fit and a decrease in log likelihood of 17.71 when we decreased the number of ward parameters by 19. We regarded this loss of fit as an acceptable tradeoff.

In our next model, we introduced some nonlinearities into the pricing of the land area for each property. The land plot areas in our sample of properties ran from 100 to 790 meters squared. Up to this point, we have assumed that land plots in the same grouped ward sell at a constant price per m^2 of lot area. However, it is likely that there is some nonlinearity in this pricing schedule; for example, it is likely that very large lots sell at an average price that is below the average price of medium sized lots. In order to capture this nonlinearity, we initially divided up our 1907 observations into 7 groups of observations based on their lot size. The Group 1 properties had lots less than 150 m^2, the Group 2 properties had lots greater than or equal to 150 m^2 and less than 200 m^2, the Group 3 properties had lots greater than or equal to 200 m^2 and less than 300 m^2, … and the Group 7 properties had lots greater than or equal to 600 m^2. However, there were very few observations in Groups 4–7 so we added together these groups to form Group 4.[22] For each observation n in period t, we defined the 4 *land dummy variables*, $D_{L,tnk}$, for $k = 1, \ldots, 4$ as follows:

$$D_{L,tnk} \equiv \begin{cases} 1 \text{ if observation } tn \text{ has land area that belongs to group } k \\ 0 \text{ if observation } tn \text{ has land area that does not belong to group } k. \end{cases} \tag{5.7}$$

These dummy variables are used in the definition of the following piecewise linear function of L_{tn}, $f_L(L_{tn})$, defined as follows:

$$\begin{aligned} f_L(L_{tn}, \boldsymbol{\lambda}) \equiv\; & D_{L,tn1}\lambda_1 L_{tn} + D_{L,tn2}[\lambda_1 L_1 + \lambda_2(L_{tn} - L_1)] \\ & + D_{L,tn3}[\lambda_1 L_1 + \lambda_2(L_2 - L_1) + \lambda_3(L_{tn} - L_2)] \\ & + D_{L,tn4}[\lambda_1 L_1 + \lambda_2(L_2 - L_1) + \lambda_3(L_3 - L_2) + \lambda_4(L_{tn} - L_3)] \end{aligned} \tag{5.8}$$

where $\boldsymbol{\lambda} \equiv [\lambda_1, \lambda_2, \lambda_3, \lambda_4]$ and the λ_k are unknown parameters and $L_1 \equiv 150$, $L_2 \equiv 200$ and $L_3 \equiv 300$. The function $f_L(L_{tn})$ defines a *relative valuation function for the land area of a commercial property* as a function of the plot area.

The new nonlinear regression model is the following one:

$$V_{tn} = \alpha_t \left(\sum_{j=1}^{4} \omega_j D_{W,tnj} \right) f_L(L_{tn}, \boldsymbol{\lambda}) + p_{St}(1 - \delta)^{A(t,n)} S_{tn} + \varepsilon_{tn}; \quad t = 1, \ldots, 44;\ n = 1, \ldots, N(t). \tag{5.9}$$

---

[21] The estimated combined ward relative land price parameters turned out to be: $\omega_1 = 1.3003$; $\omega_2 = 0.75089$; $\omega_3 = 0.49573$ and $\omega_4 = 0.25551$. The sample probabilities of an observation falling in the combined wards were 0.402, 0.278, 0.177 and 0.143 respectively.

[22] The sample probabilities of an observation falling in the 7 initial land size groups were: 0.291, 0.234, 0.229, 0.130, 0.050, 0.034 and 0.033.

Comparing the models defined by Eq. (5.5)[23] and (5.9), it can be seen that we have added an additional 4 *land plot size parameters*, $\lambda_1, \ldots, \lambda_4$, to the model defined by (5.5) (with only 4 ward dummy variables). However, looking at (5.9), it can be seen that the 44 land time parameters (the α_t), the 4 ward parameters (the ω_j) and the 4 land plot size parameters (the λ_k) cannot all be identified. Thus we imposed the following identification normalizations on the parameters for **Model 3** defined by (5.9):

$$\alpha_1 \equiv 1; \lambda_1 \equiv 1. \tag{5.10}$$

Note that if we set all of the λ_k equal to unity, Model 3 collapses down to Model 2. The final log likelihood for Model 3 was an improvement of 59.65 over the final LL for Model 2 (for adding 3 new marginal price of land parameters) which is a highly significant increase. The R^2 increased to 0.6116 from the previous model R^2 of 0.5850. The parameter estimates turned out to be $\lambda_2 = 1.4297$, $\lambda_3 = 1.2772$ and $\lambda_4 = 0.2973$. For small land plot areas less than 150 m^2, the (relative) marginal price of land was equal to 1 per m^2. As lot sizes increase from 150 m^2 to 200 m^2, the (relative) marginal price of land increased to $\lambda_2 = 1.4297$ per m^2. For the next 100 m^2 of lot size, the (relative) marginal price of land decreased to $\lambda_3 = 1.2772$ per m^2. For lot sizes greater than 200 m^2, the (relative) marginal price of land decreased to 0.2973 per m^2. Thus the average cost of land per m^2 initially increased and then tends to decrease as lot size becomes large.

For property n in period t, we set the *price* of land for this property equal to $PL_{tn} = \alpha_t^*$, the estimated parameter value for α_t for $t = 2, 3, \ldots, 44$ and we set $\alpha_1^* \equiv 1$. The corresponding constant quality *quantity* for property n in period t is $QL_{tn} \equiv (\sum_{j=1}^{4} \omega_j^* D_{W,tnj}) f_L(L_{tn}, \boldsymbol{\lambda}^*)$ for $t = 1, \ldots, 44$ and $n = 1, 2, \ldots, N(t)$. For property n in period t, the *price* and *quantity* of constant quality structure is set equal to p_{St} and $(1 - \delta^*)^{A(t,n)} S_{tn}$ respectively for $t = 1, \ldots, 44$ and $n = 1, 2, \ldots, N(t)$ where δ^* is the estimated depreciation rate. Since all properties in period t have the same price of land α_t^* and the same price for the structure p_{St}, the *overall period t price indexes for land and structures*, PL^t and PS^t, are set equal to α_t^* and p_{St}/p_{S1} respectively for $t = 1, \ldots, 44$. The same definitions are used to define the aggregate price indexes for land and structures ($PL^t \equiv \alpha_t^*$ and $PS^t \equiv p_{St}/p_{S1}$)[24] for all of the hedonic regression models in this section and the subsequent two sections.

The *footprint* of a building is the area of the land that directly supports the structure. An approximation to the footprint land for property n in period t is the total structure area S_{tn} divided by the total number of stories in the structure H_{tn}. If we

---

[23] We compare (5.9) to the modified Eq. (5.5) where we have only 4 combined ward dummy variables in the modified (5.5) rather than the original 23 ward dummy variables.

[24] Thus PS^t is a normalization of the official construction price series p_{St} so that $PS^t = 1$ when $t = 1$. The series PS^t is plotted in Fig. 5.2.

subtract footprint land from the total land area, TL_{tn}, we get *excess land*, [25] EL_{tn}, defined as follows:

$$EL_{tn} \equiv L_{tn} - (S_{tn}/H_{tn}); \qquad t = 1, \ldots, 44; n = 1, \ldots, N(t). \tag{5.11}$$

In our sample, excess land ranged from 1.083 to 562.58 m^2. We grouped our observations into 5 categories, depending on the amount of excess land that pertained to each observation. Group 1 consists of observations tn where 1: $EL_{tn} < 50$; 2: observations such that $50 \leq EL_{tn} < 100$; 3: $100 \leq EL_{tn} < 150$; 4: $150 \leq EL_{tn} < 300$; 5: $EL_{tn} \geq 300$.[26] Now define the excess land dummy variables, $D_{EL,tnm}$, as follows: for $t = 1, \ldots, 44$; $n = 1, \ldots, N(t)$; $m = 1, \ldots, 5$:

$$D_{EL,tnm} \equiv \begin{cases} 1 \text{ if observation } n \text{ in period } t \text{ is in excess land group } m; \\ 0 \text{ if observation } n \text{ in period } t \text{ is not in excess land group } m. \end{cases} \tag{5.12}$$

We will use the above dummy variables as adjustment factors to the price of land. As will be seen, in general, the more excess land a property possessed, the lower was the average per meter squared value of land for that property.[27]

The new **Model 4** excess land nonlinear regression model is the following one:

$$V_{tn} = \alpha_t \left(\sum_{j=1}^{4} \omega_j D_{W,tnj}\right)\left(\sum_{m=1}^{5} \chi_m D_{EL,tnm}\right) f_L(L_{tn}, \boldsymbol{\lambda}) + p_{St}(1-\delta)^{A(t,n)} S_{tn} + \varepsilon_{tn}; \quad t = 1, \ldots, 44; n = 1, \ldots, N(t). \tag{5.13}$$

However, looking at the model defined by (5.9) and (5.13), it can be seen that the 44 land price parameters (the α_t), the 4 combined ward parameters (the ω_j), the 4 land plot size parameters (the λ_k) and the 5 excess land parameters (the χ_m) cannot all be identified. Thus we imposed the following identifying normalizations on these parameters:

$$\alpha_1 \equiv 1; \lambda_1 \equiv 1; \chi_1 \equiv 1. \tag{5.14}$$

Note that if we set all of the χ_m equal to unity, Model 4 collapses down to Model 3. The final log likelihood for Model 4 was an improvement of 23.99 over the final LL for Model 3 (for adding 4 new excess land parameters) which is a significant increase. The R^2 increased to 0.6207 from the previous model R^2 of 0.6116. The χ_m parameter estimates turned out to be $\chi_2 = 0.9173$, $\chi_3 = 0.7540$, $\chi_4 = 0.7234$ and $\chi_5 = 0.8611$. Thus excess land does reduce the average per meter price of land.

---

[25] This is land that is usable for purposes other than the direct support of the structure on the land plot. Excess land was first introduced as an explanatory variable in a property hedonic regression model for Tokyo condominium sales by Diewert and Shimizu (2016; 305).

[26] The sample probabilities of an observation falling in the 4 excess land size groups were: 0.352, 0.343, 0.149, 0.114 and 0.041.

[27] The excess land characteristic was also used by Diewert and Shimizu (2016) and Burnett-Issacs et al. (2016) in their studies of condominium prices. The same phenomenon was observed in these studies: the more excess land that a high rise property had, the lower was the per meter land price.

The nonlinear estimating equations for **Model 5** are exactly the same as those defined by Eq. (5.13) above except that we estimated the geometric depreciation rate δ instead of assuming that it was equal to 0.025. The final LL increase for Model 5 (for adding one new parameter) was 50.58 which was highly significant. However, the estimated δ turned out to be 0.00165 with a standard error of 0.00152, which seemed low. The R^2 for this model was 0.6399.

It is likely that the height of the building affects the quality of the structure. In our sample of commercial property prices, the height of the building (the H variable) ranged from 3 stories to 14 stories. Thus initially, we had 12 building height categories. Define the building height dummy variables, $D_{H,tnh}$, as follows: for $t = 1, \ldots, 44; n = 1, \ldots, N(t); h = 3, \ldots, 14$:

$$D_{H,tnh} \equiv \begin{cases} 1 \text{ if observation } n \text{ in period } t \text{ is a building which has height } h; \\ 0 \text{ if observation } n \text{ in period } t \text{ is not a building which has height } h. \end{cases} \tag{5.15}$$

Due to the small number of observations in the last 5 height categories, we combined these dummy variables into a single height category that included all buildings of height 10–14 stories; i.e., the new $D_{H,tn10}$ was defined as $\sum_{h=10}^{14} D_{H,tnh}$. The new **Model 6** nonlinear regression model is the following one:

$$\begin{aligned} V_{tn} = {} & \alpha_t \left(\sum_{j=1}^{4} \omega_j D_{W,tnj} \right) \left(\sum_{m=1}^{5} \chi_m D_{EL,tnm} \right) \left(\sum_{h=3}^{10} \mu_h D_{H,tnh} \right) f_L(L_{tn}, \boldsymbol{\lambda}) \\ & + p_{St}(1-\delta)^{A(t,n)} \left(\sum_{h=3}^{10} \phi_h D_{H,tnh} \right) S_{tn} + \varepsilon_{tn}; \quad t = 1, \ldots, 44; n = 1, \ldots, N(t). \end{aligned} \tag{5.16}$$

In addition to the normalizations (5.14), we also imposed the normalization $\phi_3 \equiv 1$. Note that if we set all of the μ_h equal to unity, the new model collapses down to Model 5.

The final log likelihood for the new model was $-12, 649.26$, a big improvement of 190.83 over the final log likelihood for Model 5 (for adding 7 new height parameters). The R^2 increased to 0.7036 from the previous model R^2 of 0.6207. The ϕ_4 to ϕ_{10} parameter estimates turned out to be 1.2071, 1.4599, 1.5720, 1.5114, 2.0950, 2.3062, 2.5437 respectively. Recall that ϕ_3 is set equal to 1. It can be seen that the structure value of a property increased (with one exception) as the height of the building increased. The estimated geometric depreciation rate for this model was $\delta = 0.0212$ (with a standard error of 0.0020). This is a reasonable estimate for a wear and tear (net) depreciation rate.

Recall that we used building height as a quality adjustment factor for the structure portion of the property value. In our next model, we use building height as a possible quality adjustment factor for the land component of the property. Consider two adjacent commercial office properties with the same lot size and building footprint but Property A has a 10 story tower while property B has a 4 story modest office building. In theory, the land plot for each property should be valued at its best potential use. But the local market may not be able to support two high rise buildings in the same area. Hence the land component of Property B may not be valued at the same level as that of Property A, due to an accident of history. Moreover, placing a high rise building on Property B may lead to a decline in the land value of Property A due to an impairment of views (or sunlight) from the higher stories of Property A. In any case, we will introduce one new building height parameter μ that reflects possible changes in land value due to the height H of the building on the property. Thus **Model 7** is defined as the following nonlinear regression model:

$$V_{tn} = \alpha_t\left(\sum_{j=1}^{4}\omega_j D_{W,tnj}\right)\left(\sum_{m=1}^{5}\chi_m D_{EL,tnm}\right)(1+\mu(H_{tn}-3))f_L(L_{tn},\boldsymbol{\lambda}) + p_{St}(1-\delta)^{A(t,n)}\left(\sum_{h=3}^{10}\phi_h D_{H,tnh}\right)S_{tn} + \varepsilon_{tn};\quad t=1,\ldots,44;\ n=1,\ldots,N(t). \tag{5.17}$$

For identification purposes, we imposed the following restrictions on the parameters in (5.17):

$$\alpha_1 \equiv 1;\ \lambda_1 \equiv 1;\ \chi_1 \equiv 1;\ \phi_3 \equiv 1. \tag{5.18}$$

The final log likelihood for Model 7 was −12640.40, an improvement of 8.86 log likelihood points over the final log likelihood for Model 6 (for adding one new parameter μ). The R^2 increased to 0.7063 from the previous model R^2 of 0.7036. The estimated depreciation rate δ was 3.41% with a standard error of 0.0077. The estimated $\phi_4, \ldots, \phi_{10}$ were equal to 1.11, 1.31, 1.32, 1.11, 1.83, 2.01 and 2.12 (recall that ϕ_3 was set equal to 1). The estimate for μ was 0.1135 with a standard error of 0.0339. Thus as the building height increased by one story, the land value appears to increase by approximately 11%. Thus some of the extra cash flow generated by an extra story for the structure appears to leak over into the land value of the property.[28]

This completes our description of our preliminary hedonic regression models for Tokyo office buildings. In the following section, we will extend these preliminary models by estimating more complex depreciation schedules.

5.4 The Builder's Model with Multiple Geometric Depreciation Rates

In the following model, we allowed the geometric depreciation rates to differ after each 10 year interval (except for the last interval).[29] We divided up our 1907 observations into 5 groups of observations based on the age of the structure at the time of

[28]It should be pointed out that our estimate for μ in our final model is 0.0602 instead of 0.1135.

[29]The analysis in this section and the subsequent section follows the approach taken by Diewert et al. (2017). Geltner and Bokhari (2019) estimate a much more flexible model of commercial property depreciation using US transaction data by allowing an age dummy variable for each age of building. This methodological approach generates a combined land and structure depreciation rate whereas our approach will generate depreciation rates that apply only to the structure portion of property value.

the sale. The Group 1 properties had structures with structure age less than 10 years, the Group 2 properties had structure ages greater than or equal to 10 years but less than 20 years, the Group 3 properties had structure ages greater than or equal to 20 years but less than 30 years, the Group 4 properties had structure ages greater than or equal to 30 years but less than 40 years and the Group 5 properties had structure ages greater than or equal to 40 years.[30] For each observation n in period t, we define the 5 *age dummy variables*, $D_{A,tni}$, for $i = 1, \ldots, 5$ as follows:

$$D_{A,tni} \equiv \begin{cases} 1 \text{ if observation } tn \text{ has structure age that belongs to age group } i; \\ 0 \text{ if observation } tn \text{ has structure age that does not belong to age group } i. \end{cases} \tag{5.19}$$

These age dummy variables are used in the definition of the following *aging function*, $g_A(A_{tn}, \boldsymbol{\delta})$, defined as follows where $\boldsymbol{\delta} \equiv [\delta_1, \delta_2, \delta_3, \delta_4]$[31]:

$$\begin{aligned} g_A(A_{tn}, \boldsymbol{\delta}) &\equiv D_{A,tn1}(1-\delta_1)^{A(t,n)} + D_{A,tn2}(1-\delta_1)^{10}(1-\delta_2)^{(A(t,n)-10)} \\ &+ D_{A,tn3}(1-\delta_1)^{10}(1-\delta_2)^{10}(1-\delta_3)^{(A(t,n)-20)} \\ &+ D_{A,tn4}(1-\delta_1)^{10}(1-\delta_2)^{10}(1-\delta_3)^{10}(1-\delta_4)^{(A(t,n)-30)} \\ &+ D_{A,tn5}(1-\delta_1)^{10}(1-\delta_2)^{10}(1-\delta_3)^{10}(1-\delta_4)^{10}(1-\delta_5)^{(A(t,n)-40)}. \end{aligned} \tag{5.20}$$

Thus the annual geometric depreciation rates are allowed to change at the end of each decade that the structure survives.

The new **Model 8** nonlinear regression model is the following one:

$$\begin{aligned} V_{tn} &= \alpha_t \left(\sum_{j=1}^{4} \omega_j D_{W,tnj}\right)\left(\sum_{m=1}^{5} \chi_m D_{EL,tnm}\right)(1+\mu(H_{tn}-3)) f_L(L_{tn}, \boldsymbol{\lambda}) \\ &+ p_{St} g_A(A_{tn}, \boldsymbol{\delta})\left(\sum_{h=3}^{10} \phi_h D_{H,tnh}\right) S_{tn} + \varepsilon_{tn}; \quad t = 1, \ldots, 44; n = 1, \ldots, N(t). \end{aligned} \tag{5.21}$$

We imposed the normalizations $\alpha_1 \equiv 1, \lambda_1 \equiv 1, \chi_1 \equiv 1$ and $\phi_3 \equiv 1$. Note that Model 8 collapses down to Model 7 if $\delta_1 = \delta_2 = \delta_3 = \delta_4 = \delta_5 = \delta$. Thus the number of unknown parameters in Model 8 increased by 4 over the number of parameters in Model 7. The final log likelihood for Model 8 was -12631.21, an improvement of 9.19 over the final log likelihood for Model 7 (for adding 4 additional parameters). The R^2 increased to 0.7091 from the previous model R^2 of 0.7063. The estimated depreciation rates (with standard errors in brackets) were

[30] There were only 28 properties which had age greater than 50 years so these properties were combined with the age 40–50 properties.

[31] A_{tn} is the same as $A(t, n)$. The aging function $g_A(A_{tn})$ quality adjusts a building of age A_{tn} into a comparable number of units of a new building.

as follows: $\delta_1 = 0.0487(0.0111)$, $\delta_2 = 0.0270(0.0097)$, $\delta_3 = 0.0096(0.0106)$, $\delta_4 = 0.0403(0.0154)$, $\delta_5 = -0.0319(0.0185)$.[32] Thus properties with structures which are over 40 years old tended to have a negative depreciation rate; i.e., the value of the structure tends to *increase* by 3.19% per year.

There are two additional explanatory variables in our data set that may affect the price of land. Recall that DS was defined as the distance to the nearest subway station and TT as the subway running time in minutes to the Tokyo station from the nearest station. DS ranges from 0 to 1500 m while TT ranges from 1 to 48 min. Typically, as DS and TT increase, land value decreases.[33] **Model 9** introduces these new variables into the previous nonlinear regression model (5.21) in the following manner:

$$V_{tn} = \alpha_t \left(\sum_{j=1}^{4} \omega_j D_{W,tnj} \right) \left(\sum_{m=1}^{5} \chi_m D_{EL,tnm} \right) (1 + \mu(H_{tn} - 3))(1 + \eta(DS_{tn} - 0)) \times (1 + \theta(TT_{tn} - 1)) f_L(L_{tn}, \boldsymbol{\lambda}) + p_{St} g_A(A_{tn}, \boldsymbol{\delta}) \left(\sum_{h=3}^{10} \phi_h D_{H,tnh} \right) S_{tn} + \varepsilon_{tn}; \quad t = 1, \ldots, 44; n = 1, \ldots, N(t). \tag{5.22}$$

Thus two new parameters, η and θ, are introduced. If these new parameters are both equal to 0, then Model 9 collapses down to Model 8.

The final log likelihood for Model 9 was -12614.70, an improvement of 16.51 over the final log likelihood for Model 8 (for adding 2 additional parameters). The R^2 increased to 0.7142 from the previous model R^2 of 0.7091. The estimated walking distance parameter was $\eta = -0.00023(0.000066)$, which indicates that commercial property land value does tend to decrease as the walking distance to the nearest subway station increases. However, the estimated travel time to Tokyo Central Station parameter was $\theta = 0.0209(0.0053)$ which indicates that land value increases on average as the travel time to the central station increases, a relationship which was not anticipated.

Recall that α_1 was set equal to 1. The sequence of coefficients $\alpha_1, \alpha_2, \ldots, \alpha_{44}$ comprise our estimated quarterly commercial office building price index for the land component of property value. This land price index is quite volatile due to the sparseness of commercial property sales and the heterogeneity of the properties. In the following section, we will show how this volatile land price index can be smoothed in a fairly simple fashion.

Turning to the other estimated coefficients, the ward relative land price parameters, ω_1–ω_4, decline (substantially) in magnitude as we move from the first more expensive composite ward to the less expensive composite wards. The marginal value of land

[32]Recall that these depreciation rates are net depreciation rates. As surviving structures approach their middle age, renovations become important and thus a decline in the net depreciation rate is plausible. The pattern of depreciation rates is similar to the comparable geometric depreciation rates that were observed for Richmond (a suburb of Vancouver, Canada) detached houses by Diewert et al. (2017).

[33]See Diewert and Shimizu (2015b) where these relationships also held for Tokyo detached houses.

parameters, λ_1 (set equal to 1), λ_2, λ_3 and λ_4, exhibit the same inverted U pattern that emerged in Model 3 (and persisted through all of the subsequent models). The excess land parameters, χ_1 (set equal to 1), χ_2, χ_3, χ_4 and χ_5, show that excess land is generally valued less than footprint land but the decline in land value as excess land increases is not monotonic. The building height land parameter $\mu = 0.0602$ is no longer as large as it was in Model 5 but an extra story of building height still adds 6% to the land value of the structure which is a significant premium for extra building stories. The walking distance to the nearest subway station parameter $\eta = -0.00023$ seems small but it tells us if the property is 1000 meters away from the nearest station, then the land value of the property is expected to fall by 23% compared to a nearby property. The travel time to Tokyo station parameter $\theta = 0.0209$ has a counterintuitive sign; it is possible that this variable is correlated with other land price determining characteristics and hence is not reliably determined. The height parameters, $\phi_3 = 1$ and ϕ_4–ϕ_{10}, are very significant determinants of structure value; the value of the structure increases almost monotonically as the number of stories increases. Finally, the decade by decade estimated geometric depreciation rates, δ_1–δ_5, show much the same pattern as was shown by the results for the previous model. Overall, the results of Model 9 seem to be reasonable.

5.5 The Builder's Model with Multiple Straight Line Depreciation Rates

Thus far, we have assumed that geometric depreciation models can best describe our data. In this section, we check the robustness of our approach in the previous section by assuming alternative depreciation models.

Recall that the structure aging (or survival) function for Model 9, $g_A(A_{tn}, \boldsymbol{\delta})$, was defined by (5.20) above. In this section, we switch from a geometric model of depreciation to a *straight line* or *linear depreciation model*. Thus for **Model 10**, we define the aging function as follows:

$$g_A(A_{tn}, \delta) \equiv (1 - \delta A_{tn}) \tag{5.23}$$

where δ is the straight line depreciation rate. Our new nonlinear regression model is the same as the previous model defined by Eq. (5.22) except that the function g_A is defined by (5.23). The starting parameter values were taken to be the final parameter values from Model 7 except that the initial δ was set equal to 0.01 and the initial values for the parameters η and θ were set equal to 0.

The final log likelihood for Model 10 was −12635.83 and the R^2 was 0.7078. The estimated straight line depreciation rate was $\delta = 0.01357(0.00127)$. This model generated reasonable parameter estimates and the imputed value of the structure component of property value was positive for all observation.[34]

[34]This does not always happen for straight line depreciation models; i.e., for properties with very old structures, the imputed value of the structure can become negative if the estimated depreciation

The straight line model of depreciation is not very flexible. Thus following the approach used by Diewert and Shimizu (2015b), we implemented a *piece-wise linear depreciation model*. Recall definitions (5.19) above which defined the 5 age dummy variables, $D_{A,tni}$, for $i = 1, \ldots, 5$. We use these age dummy variables to define the piece-wise linear aging function, $g_A(A_{tn}, \boldsymbol{\delta})$, as follows:

$$\begin{aligned} g_A(A_{tn}, \boldsymbol{\delta}) \equiv\ & D_{A,tn1}(1 - \delta_1 A_{tn}) + D_{A,tn2}(1 - 10\delta_1 - \delta_2(A_{tn} - 10)) \\ & + D_{A,tn3}(1 - 10\delta_1 - 10\delta_2 - \delta_3(A_{tn} - 20)) \\ & + D_{A,tn4}(1 - 10\delta_1 - 10\delta_2 - 10\delta_3 - \delta_4(A_{tn} - 30)) \\ & + D_{A,tn5}(1 - 10\delta_1 - 10\delta_2 - 10\delta_3 - 10\delta_4 - \delta_5(A_{tn} - 40)) \end{aligned} \tag{5.24}$$

where $\boldsymbol{\delta}$ is now defined as $\boldsymbol{\delta} \equiv [\delta_1, \delta_2, \delta_3, \delta_4, \delta_5]$. The **Model 11** nonlinear regression model is the same as the model defined by Eq. (5.22) except that the function g_A is defined by (5.24). The starting parameter values were taken to be the final parameter values from Model 10 except that the new depreciation parameters $\delta_1, \ldots, \delta_5$ were all set equal to the final straight line depreciation rate δ estimated in Model 10. If all $5\delta_i$ are set equal to a common δ, then Model 11 collapses down to Model 10.

The final log likelihood for Model 11 was −12614.35, which was an increase in log likelihood of 21.48 over the Model 10 log likelihood. The R^2 for Model 11 was 0.7143.[35] The estimated piecewise linear depreciation rates (with standard errors in brackets) were as follows: $\delta_1 = 0.0393(0.0057)$, $\delta_2 = 0.0125(0.0049)$, $\delta_3 = 0.0302(0.0041)$,[36] $\delta_4 = 0.0159(0.0054)$, $\delta_5 = -0.0135(0.0074)$. Thus as was the case with the multiple geometric depreciation rate model, properties with structures which are over 40 years old tended to *increase* in value by 1.35% per year.

Comparing the estimated coefficients, the parameter estimates for Models 9 and 11 were very similar except that there were some differences in the estimated depreciation rates δ_1–δ_5. However, it turns out that the ageing functions generated by these alternative depreciation models approximate each other reasonably well. Thus both depreciation models describe the underlying data to the same degree of approximation.

The determination of depreciation schedules for commercial office buildings is important for tax purposes, for investors and for the estimation of commercial office structure stocks, which in turn feed into the computation of the Multifactor Productivity of the Commercial Office Sector. The methodology explained above should

rate is large enough. This phenomenon cannot occur with geometric depreciation models, which is an advantage of assuming this form of depreciation.

[35]Recall that the log likelihood for the comparable geometric model of depreciation, Model 9, was −12614.70 and the R^2 for Model 9 was 0.7142. Thus the descriptive power of both models is virtually identical.

[36]Recall that these depreciation rates are net depreciation rates. As surviving structures approach their middle age, renovations become important and thus a decline in the net depreciation rate is plausible. The pattern of depreciation rates is similar to the comparable geometric depreciation rates that were observed for Richmond (a suburb of Vancouver, Canada) detached houses by Diewert et al. (2017).

be helpful to national income accountants and tax offices who require estimates for depreciation rates.

As was mentioned in Sect. 5.3 above, all of the above models generate land and structure price indexes which are equal to the sequence of estimated α_t^* estimates for Models 1–11 for the land indexes PL_t and are equal to the sequence of official new building cost series p_{St}. Thus the structure price series remain constant across models but the land price series will vary across the various models. In the following section, we will chart the land price series for Model 11.

5.6 Smoothing the Land Price Series

In Fig. 5.1, it can be seen that our Model 11 estimated land price series, $PL_{\text{MLIT}}^t \equiv \alpha_t^*$, is somewhat volatile. This is due to the fact that commercial properties are very heterogeneous and we have relatively few transactions per quarter. Thus the raw series PL_{MLIT}^t does not accurately represent the *trend* in commercial land prices in Tokyo; the raw series requires some smoothing in order to model the trends in land prices.[37] Patrick (2017) found the same problem for Irish house price sales and we will follow his example and smooth the raw series.[38]

We used the LOWESS nonparametric smoother in Shazam[39] in order to construct a preliminary smoothed land price series, PL_{S}^t, using the Model 11 land price series, PL_{MLIT}^t, as the input series.[40] We used the cross-validation criterion to choose the smoothing parameter which turned out to be $f = 0.12$. The Model 11 land prices PL_{MLIT}^t and their smoothed counterparts PL_{S}^t are plotted in Fig. 5.1.

The jagged black line in Fig. 5.1 represents the unsmoothed land price index PL_{MLIT} that we estimated from Model 11 while the lowest line represents the LOWESS nonparametric smoothed series PL_{S} that was generated using Shazam. It can be seen that while PL_{S} is reasonably smooth, it is not quite centered; i.e., it is consistently below the raw series. Thus we considered some alternative methods for smoothing the raw series.

[37]The volatility in the raw series could be real phenomenon in that land prices are inherently volatile. If this is the case, it would be useful for statistical offices to publish the unsmoothed series as well as the smoothed series. As noted by Geltner et al. (2014), property investors would find unsmoothed property price indexes useful in order to evaluate the riskiness of property investments. On the other hand, the volatility may be due to the heterogeneity of commercial properties (and the scarcity of market transactions). Thus there are important price determining characteristics of these properties that we have not taken into account in our regressions and this leads to volatility in our indexes.

[38]Patrick initially smoothed his series by taking a three month rolling average of the raw index prices for Ireland. He found that the resulting index was still too volatile to publish and he ended up using a double exponential smoothing procedure.

[39]The method is due to Cleveland (1979).

[40]The initial smoothed series was divided by the Quarter 1 value so that the resulting normalized series equalled 1 in Quarter 1. Recall that Quarter 1 is the first quarter in 2005 and Quarter 44 is the last quarter in 2015.

Henderson (1916) was the first to realize that various moving average smoothers could be related to rolling window least squares regressions that would exactly reproduce a polynomial curve. Thus we apply his idea to derive the moving average weights that would be equivalent to fitting a linear function to 5 consecutive quarters of a time series, which we represent by the vector $\boldsymbol{Y}^T \equiv [y_1, \ldots, y_5]$ where $\boldsymbol{Y}^T$ denotes the transpose of a vector $\boldsymbol{Y}$. Define the 5 dimensional column vectors $\boldsymbol{X}_1$ and $\boldsymbol{X}_2$ as $\boldsymbol{X}_1 \equiv [1, 1, 1, 1, 1]^T$ and $\boldsymbol{X}_2 \equiv [-2, -1, 0, 1, 2]^T$. Define the 5×2 dimensional $\mathbf{X}$ matrix as $\mathbf{X} \equiv [\boldsymbol{X}_1, \boldsymbol{X}_2]$. Denote the linear smooth of the vector $\boldsymbol{Y}$ by $\boldsymbol{Y}^*$. Then least squares theory tells us that $\boldsymbol{Y}^* = \mathbf{X}(\mathbf{X}^T\mathbf{X})^{-1}\mathbf{X}^T\boldsymbol{Y}$. Thus the 5 rows of the 5×5 projection matrix $\mathbf{X}(\mathbf{X}^T\mathbf{X})^{-1}\mathbf{X}^T$ give us the weights that can be used to convert the raw $\boldsymbol{Y}$ series into the smoothed $\boldsymbol{Y}^*$ series. For our particular example, the 5 rows of the projection matrix are as follows: Row 1 = $(1/10)[6, 4, 2, 0, -2]$; Row 2 = $(1/10)[4, 3, 2, 1, 0]$; Row 3 = $(1/5)[1, 1, 1, 1, 1]$; Row 4 = $(1/10)[0, 1, 2, 3, 4]$; Row 5 = $(1/10)[-2, 0, 2, 4, 6]$. Note that Row 3 tells us that the third component of the smoothed vector $\boldsymbol{Y}^*$ is equal to $y_3^* = (1/5)(y_1 + y_2 + y_3 + y_4 + y_5)$. a simple equally weighted moving average of the raw data for 5 periods. Thus the way this smoothing method could be applied in practice to 44 consecutive quarters of PL_{MLIT} data is as follows. The first 3 components of the smoothed series are set equal to the inner products of the first 3 rows of the projection matrix $\mathbf{X}(\mathbf{X}^T\mathbf{X})^{-1}\mathbf{X}^T$ times the first 5 components of the PL_{MLIT} series. This would generate the first 3 components of the smoothed series, PL_{L}^t for $t = 1, 2, 3$. For $t = 3, 4, \ldots, 42$, define $PL_{\text{L}}^t \equiv (1/5)[PL_{\text{MLIT}}^{t-2} + PL_{\text{MLIT}}^{t-1} + PL_{\text{MLIT}}^{t} + PL_{\text{MLIT}}^{t+1} + PL_{\text{MLIT}}^{t+2}]$. Thus for all observations t except for the first two and last two observations, the smoothed series PL_{L}^t would be defined as the simple centered moving average of 5 consecutive PL_{MLIT} observations with equal weights. The final two observations would be defined as the inner products of Rows 4 and 5 of $\mathbf{X}(\mathbf{X}^T\mathbf{X})^{-1}\mathbf{X}^T$ with the last 5 observations in the PL_{MLIT} series. In practice, as the data of a subsequent period became available, the last two observations in the existing series would be revised but after receiving the data of two subsequent periods, there would be no further revisions; i.e., the final smoothed value of an observation would be set equal to the centered 5 period moving average of the raw data.

We implemented the above procedure but the above algorithm does not ensure that the value of the smoothed series in the first quarter of the sample is equal to 1 and so the generated series had to be divided by a constant to ensure that the first observation in the smoothed series is equal to unity. We found that this division caused the smoothed series to lie below the raw series for the most part.[41] Patrick (2017; 25–26) found that a similar problem occurred with his initial simple moving average smoothing method. He solved the problem by setting the smoothed values equal to the actual values for the first two observations when he applied his second smoothing method. We solved the centering problem in a similar manner: we set the initial value

[41] A similar problem of a lack of centering occurred when we implemented the LOWESS smoothing procedure; i.e., we had to divide by a constant to make the first component of the smoothed series equal to one. As a result, the Lowess smooth tended to lie below the raw series as can be seen in Fig. 5.2.

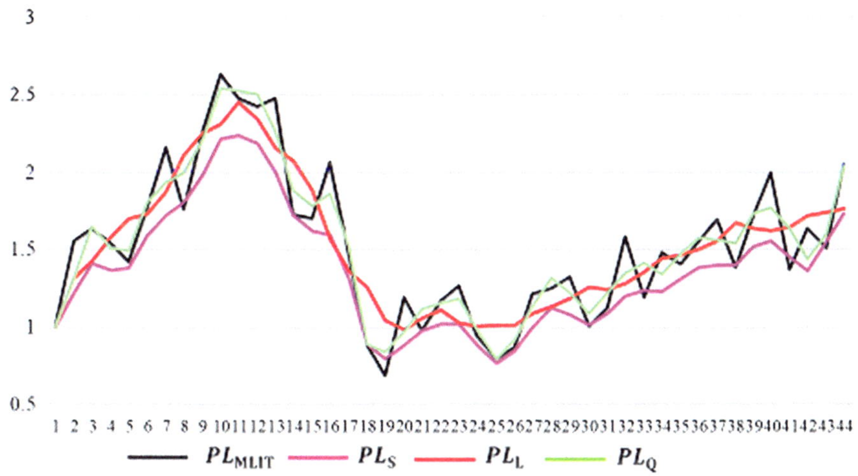

Fig. 5.1 MLIT land prices, lowess smoothed prices and linear and quadratic smoothed prices

of the smooth equal to the corresponding raw number (so that $PL_{\mathrm{L}}^{1} \equiv PL_{\mathrm{MLIT}}^{1}$) and we set the second value of the smooth equal to the average of the first and third observations in the raw series (so that $PL_{\mathrm{L}}^{2} \equiv (1/2)[PL_{\mathrm{MLIT}}^{1} + PL_{\mathrm{MLIT}}^{3}]$). For the Quarter 3 value of the smooth, we used the simple 5 term centered moving average so that $PL_{\mathrm{L}}^{3} \equiv (1/5)[PL_{\mathrm{MLIT}}^{1} + PL_{\mathrm{MLIT}}^{2} + PL_{\mathrm{MLIT}}^{3} + PL_{\mathrm{MLIT}}^{4} + PL_{\mathrm{MLIT}}^{5}]$ and we carried on using this moving average until Quarters 43 and 44 where we used Rows 4 and 5 of the matrix $\mathbf{X}(\mathbf{X}^T\mathbf{X})^{-1}\mathbf{X}^T$ defined above for our moving average weights. The resulting smoothed series PL_{L}^{t} plotted in Fig. 5.1. It can be seen that it does a good job of smoothing the initial PL_{MLIT}^{t} series.

We also applied the same least squares methodology to a rolling window 5 term quadratic regression model. Define the 5 dimensional column vectors X_1 and X_2 as before and define $X_3 \equiv [4, 1, 0, 1, 4]^T$. Define the 5×3 dimensional $\mathbf{X}$ matrix as $\mathbf{X} \equiv [X_1, X_2, X_3]$. Denote the quadratic smooth of the vector Y by Y^{**}. Again least squares theory tells us that $Y^{**} = \mathbf{X}(\mathbf{X}^T\mathbf{X})^{-1}\mathbf{X}^T Y$. The 5 rows of the new 5×5 projection matrix $\mathbf{X}(\mathbf{X}^T\mathbf{X})^{-1}\mathbf{X}^T$ give us the weights that can be used to convert the raw Y series into the smoothed Y^{**} series. The 5 rows of the new projection matrix are as follows: Row 1 = (1/35)[31, 9, −3, −5, 3]; Row 2 = (1/35)[9, 13, 12, 6, −5]; Row 3 = (1/35)[−3, 12, 17, 12, −3]; Row 4 = (1/35)[−5, 6, 12, 13, 9]; Row 5 = (1/35)[3, −5, −3, 9, 31]. Now repeat the steps that were used to construct the linear smooth PL_{L}^{t} to construct a preliminary quadratic smooth PL_{Q}^{t}, except that the new 5×5 projection matrix $\mathbf{X}(\mathbf{X}^T\mathbf{X})^{-1}\mathbf{X}^T$ replaces the previous one. A final PL_{Q}^{t} series was constructed by replacing the first 2 values in the smoothed series by the same initial 2 values that we used to construct the final versions of PL_{L}^{1} and PL_{L}^{2}. The resulting smoothed series PL_{Q}^{t} plotted in Fig. 5.1. It can be seen that PL_{Q}^{t} is not nearly as smooth as the linear smoothed series PL^t_{L} but of course, it is a lot closer to the unadjusted series PL^t_{MLIT}. For our particular data set, we would recommend the linear smoother over the quadratic smoother.[42]

5.7 The Use of Appraisal Prices as the Data Source in the Builder's Model

We turn now to the construction of land prices using commercial property appraisal data.

As was indicated in the introduction, we have quarterly appraisal data for 41 commercial office REIT office buildings located in Tokyo for the 44 quarters starting at Q1:2005 and ending at Q4:2015, which of course, is the same period that was covered by the MLIT selling price data. We will implement the builder's model for this data set in this section.

The builder's model using appraisal data is somewhat different from the builder's model using selling price data. The panel nature of the REIT data means that we can use a single property specific dummy variable as a variable that concentrates all of the location attributes of the property into a single property dummy variable; i.e., we do not have to worry about how close to a subway line the property is or how many stories the building has or how much excess land is associated with the property. The single property specific dummy variable will take all of these characteristics into account.

There are 41 separate properties in our REIT data set. For each of our 44 quarters, we assume that the 41 properties appear in the appraised property value for property n in period t, V_{tn}, in the same order. Our initial regression model is the following one where the variables have the same definitions as in Eq. (5.5) above except that ω_n is now the *property n sample average land price* (per m^2) rather than a Ward n relative price of land:

$$V_{tn} = \sum_{n=1}^{41} \omega_n L_{tn} + p_{St}(1 - 0.025)^{A(t,n)} S_{tn} + \varepsilon_{tn}; \quad t = 1, \ldots, 44; n = 1, \ldots, 41. \tag{5.25}$$

Thus in **Model 1** above, there are no quarter t land price parameters in this very simple model with 41 unknown property average land price ω_n parameters to estimate. Note that the geometric (net) depreciation rate in the model defined by (5.25) was assumed to be 2.5% per year.

[42] A quadratic Henderson type smoother would be much smoother if we lengthened the window. But a longer window would imply a longer revision period before the series would be finalized. Since the linear smoother with window length 5 seems to do a nice job of smoothing, we would not recommend moving to a longer window length for this particular application.

The final log likelihood for this model was -14968.77 and the R^2 was 0.9426. Thus the 41 property average price of land parameters ω_n explain a large part of the variation in the data.

In **Model 2**, we introduce quarterly land prices α_t into the above model. The new nonlinear regression model is the following one:

$$V_{tn} = \sum_{n=1}^{41} \alpha_t \omega_n L_{tn} + p_{St}(1 - 0.025)^{A(t,n)} S_{tn} + \varepsilon_{tn}; \quad t = 1, \ldots, 44; n = 1, \ldots, 41. \tag{5.26}$$

Not all of the quarterly land price parameters (the α_t) and the average property price parameters (the ω_n) can be identified. Thus we impose the following normalization on our coefficients:

$$\alpha_1 = 1. \tag{5.27}$$

We used the final parameter values for the ω_n from Model 1 as starting coefficient values for Model 2 (with all α_t initially set equal to 1).[43] The final log likelihood for Model 2 was -13999.00, a huge improvement of 969.77 for adding 43 new parameters. The R^2 was 0.9804. Thus the 41 property average price parameters ω_n and the 43 quarterly average land price parameters α_t explain most of the variation in the data.

Model 3 is the following nonlinear regression model:

$$V_{tn} = \sum_{n=1}^{41} \alpha_t \omega_n L_{tn} + p_{St}(1 - \delta)^{A(t,n)} S_{tn} + \varepsilon_{tn}; \quad t = 1, \ldots, 44; n = 1, \ldots, 41 \tag{5.28}$$

where δ is the annual geometric (net) depreciation rate. The normalization (5.27) is also imposed. Thus Model 3 is the same as Model 2 except that we now estimate the single geometric depreciation rate δ.

We used the final parameter values for the α_t and ω_n from Model 2 as starting coefficient values for Model 3 (with δ initially set equal to 0.025). The final log likelihood for this model was -13993.47, and increase of 5.53 for one additional parameter, and the R^2 was 0.9806. The estimated geometric (net) depreciation rate was $\delta = 0.01353$.[44] Recall that α_1 was set equal to 1. The sequence of land price

[43] The reader may well wonder why we estimated the ω_n in Model 1 rather than first estimating the α_t in Model 1. When this alternative strategy was implemented, we found that the resulting Model 2 did not converge to the "right" parameter values; i.e., the resulting R^2 was very low. This is the reason for following our nested estimation methodology where each successive model uses the final coefficient values from the previous model. It is not possible to simply estimate our final models in one step and obtain sensible results.

[44] We also estimated the straight line depreciation model counterpart to Model 3. The resulting estimated straight line depreciation rate δ was equal to 0.01317 (t statistic = 45.73). The R^2 for this model was 0.9806 and the final log likelihood was -13989.83. The resulting land price series was very similar to the land price series generated by Model 3 above.

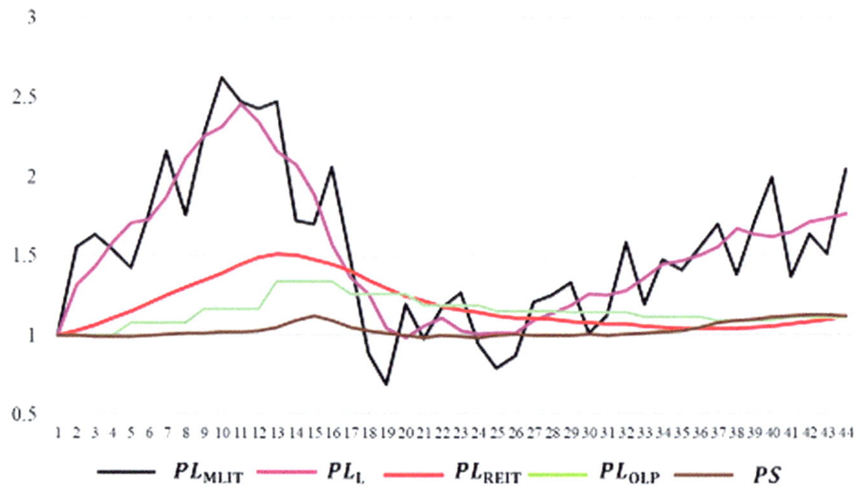

Fig. 5.2 Alternative land price series and the price of structures

(per m^2) α_t, for $t = 1, 2, \ldots, 44$ is our estimated sequence of quarterly Tokyo land prices, PL^t_{REIT}, which appears in Fig. 5.2.

The implied standard errors on the quarterly land price coefficients, the α_t, were fairly large whereas they were fairly small for the property coefficients, the ω_n. This means that our estimated land price indexes, $PL^t_{\text{REIT}} = \alpha_t$, were not reliably determined. Note also that our estimated geometric depreciation rate δ is only 1.35% per year which is much lower than our estimated depreciation rate from Model 7 in Sect. 5.3 above which was 3.41% per year. One factor which may help to explain this divergence in estimates of wear and tear depreciation is that appraisers take into account capital expenditures on the properties. However, our current data base did not have information on capital expenditures and it is likely that not having capital expenditures as an explanatory factor affected our estimates for the depreciation rate. In our earliest study of land prices using REIT data for Tokyo, Diewert and Shimizu (2017), we adjusted our nonlinear regressions for capital expenditures and found that the resulting estimated quarterly wear and tear geometric depreciation rate was 0.005 which implied an annual (single) geometric depreciation rate of about 2%.[45]

[45]In the multiple geometric depreciation rate model estimated by Diewert and Shimizu (2017), the various rates averaged out to an annual rate of 2.6% per year. Our earlier study covered the 22 quarters starting at Q1 of 2007 and ending at Q2 of 2012. The correlation coefficient between the price of land series in this model in Diewert and Shimizu (2017) and the above Model 3 price of land series for the overlapping 22 quarters is 0.9901 so these two studies using REIT appraisal data show much the same trends in Tokyo commercial property land prices even though the estimated wear and tear depreciation rates are different. Note that in addition to wear and tear depreciation, depreciation due to the early demolition of a structure before it reaches "normal" retirement age should be taken into account. Our current study does not estimate this extra component of depreciation. However, Diewert and Shimizu (2017) estimated *demolition depreciation* for Tokyo commercial office buildings at 1.2% per year.

In the following section, we will estimate our final land price series for Tokyo commercial office buildings using official estimates for the land values of commercial properties for taxation purposes.

5.8 The Use of Land Tax Assessment Values as the Data Source

In this section, we will use the Official Land Price (OLP) data described in Sect. 5.2 above. We have 6242 annual assessed values for the land components of commercial properties in Tokyo covering the 11 years 2005–2015. We will label these years as $t = 1, 2, \ldots, 11$. The assessed land value for property n in year t is denoted as V_{tn}.[46] We have information on which Ward each property is located and the ward dummy variables $D_{W,tnj}$ are defined by definitions (5.4) above. The land plot area of property n in year t is denoted by L_{tn} and the subway variables DS_{tn} and TT_{tn} are defined as in previous section above. The number of observations in year t is $N(t)$.

Our initial regression model is the following one where we regress property land value on the ward dummy variables times the land plot area:

$$V_{tn} = \left(\sum_{j=1}^{23} \omega_j D_{W,tnj}\right) L_{tn} + \varepsilon_{tn}; \qquad t = 1, \ldots, 11; n = 1, \ldots, N(t). \quad (5.29)$$

Thus in **Model 1** above, there are no year t land price parameters in this very simple model and ω_j is an estimate of the average land price (per m^2) in Ward j for $j = 1, \ldots, 23$. The final log likelihood for this model was -67073.91 and the R^2 was 0.3647.

In **Model 2**, we introduce annual land prices α_t into the above model. The new nonlinear regression model is the following one:

$$V_{tn} = \alpha_t \left(\sum_{j=1}^{23} \omega_j D_{W,tnj}\right) L_{tn} + \varepsilon_{tn}; \qquad t = 1, \ldots, 11; n = 1, \ldots, N(t). \quad (5.30)$$

Not all of the 11 annual land price parameters (the α_t) and the 23 Ward average property relative price parameters (the ω_n) can be identified. Thus we impose the normalization $\alpha_1 = 1$.

We used the final parameter values for the ω_n from Model 1 as starting coefficient values for Model 2 (with all α_t initially set equal to 1). The final log likelihood for Model 2 was -67022.90, an increase of 51.01 for adding 43 new parameters. The R^2 was 0.3748.

In our next model, we allowed the price of land to vary as the lot size increased. We divided up our 6242 observations into 5 groups of observations based on their lot size. The Group 1 properties had lots less than 100 m^2, the Group 2 properties had lots greater than or equal to 100 m^2 and less than 150 m^2, the Group 3 properties had

[46]The units of measurement used in this section are in 100,000 yen.

lots greater than or equal to 150 m^2 and less than 200 m^2, the Group 4 properties had lots greater than or equal to 200 m^2 and less than 300 m^2 and the Group 5 properties had lots greater than or equal to 300 m^2.[47] For each observation n in period t, we define the 5 *land dummy variables*, $D_{L,tnk}$, for $k = 1, \ldots, 5$ as follows:

$$D_{L,tnk} \equiv \begin{cases} 1 \text{ if observation } tn \text{ has land area that belongs to group } k; \\ 0 \text{ if observation } tn \text{ has land area that does not belong to group } k. \end{cases} \tag{5.31}$$

Define the constants L_1–L_4 as 100, 150, 200 and 300 respectively. These constants and the dummy variables defined by (5.31) are used in the definition of the following piecewise linear function of L_{tn}, $f(L_{tn})$:

$$\begin{aligned} f(L_{tn}) \equiv\ & D_{L,tn1}\lambda_1 L_{tn} + D_{L,tn2}[\lambda_1 L_1 + \lambda_2(L_{tn} - L_1)] \\ & + D_{L,tn3}[\lambda_1 L_1 + \lambda_2(L_2 - L_1) + \lambda_3(L_{tn} - L_2)] \\ & + D_{L,tn4}[\lambda_1 L_1 + \lambda_2(L_2 - L_1) + \lambda_3(L_3 - L_2) + \lambda_4(L_{tn} - L_3)] \\ & + D_{L,tn5}[\lambda_1 L_1 + \lambda_2(L_2 - L_1) + \lambda_3(L_3 - L_2) + \lambda_4(L_4 - L_3) + \lambda_5(L_{tn} - L_4)]. \end{aligned} \tag{5.32}$$

Model 3 was defined as the following nonlinear regression model:

$$V_{tn} = \alpha_t \left(\sum_{j=1}^{23} \omega_j D_{W,tnj} \right) f(L_{tn}) + \varepsilon_{tn}; \qquad t = 1, \ldots, 11; n = 1, \ldots, N(t). \tag{5.33}$$

We imposed the normalizations $\alpha_1 = 1$ and $\lambda_1 = 1$ so that all of the remaining parameters in (5.33) could be identified. These normalizations were also imposed in Model 4 below.

We used the final parameter values for the α_t and ω_j from Model 2 as starting coefficient values for Model 3 (with all λ_k initially set equal to 1). Thus Model 3 adds the 4 new marginal prices of land, λ_2, λ_3, λ_4 and λ_5 to Model 2. The final log likelihood for Model 3 was −66044.02, an increase of 978.88 for adding 4 new parameters. The R^2 was 0.4668.

Our final land price model added the subway variables to Model 3. Thus **Model 4** was defined as the following nonlinear regression model[48]:

$$V_{tn} = \alpha_t \left(\sum_{j=1}^{23} \omega_j D_{W,tnj} \right) (1 + \eta(DS_{tn} - 50))(1 + \theta(TT_{tn} - 4)) f(L_{tn}) + \varepsilon_{tn}; \quad t = 1, \ldots, 11; n = 1, \ldots, N(t). \tag{5.34}$$

[47] The sample probabilities of an observation falling in the 5 land size groups were: 0.171, 0.285, 0.175, 0.178 and 0.191.

[48] The minimum value for the distance to the nearest subway station DS_{tn} is 50 meters and the minimum value for the subway running time from the nearest station to the central Tokyo subway station was 4 min.

Thus Model 4 has added two new subway parameters, η and θ, to Model 3. We used the final parameter values for the α_t, ω_j and λ_k from Model 3 as starting coefficient values for Model 4 (with η and θ initially set equal to 0). The final log likelihood for Model 4 was -65584.56, an increase of 459.46 for adding 2 new parameters. The R^2 was 0.5401. The α_t sequence of estimated parameters (along with $\alpha_1 \equiv 1$) forms an annual (quality adjusted) Official Land Price series. For comparison purposes, we repeat each α_t four times and convert the annual Official Land Price series into the quarterly Official Land Price series, PL^t_{OLP}. It will be listed and compared with our final transactions based MLIT land price series PL^t_{MLIT} and its linear smooth PL^t_{L} along with our final REIT based land price series PL^t_{REIT} in the following section.

The standard errors on the estimated annual land prices α_t were fairly small; they were fairly large for the REIT based quarterly land price series, PL^t_{REIT}. The estimated λ_2, λ_3, λ_4 and λ_5 were 0.7011, -0.3331, 0.3568 and 0.1440 respectively. Except for λ_3, it can be seen that the λ_k monotonically decrease as k increases; this indicates that the marginal price of land decreases (for the most part) as the land plot size increases. The estimates for the subway parameters were $\eta^* = -0.000740$ and $\theta^* = -0.022807$. These estimates have the expected negative sign and are reasonable in magnitude. Since we do not have additional information on the height or size of the buildings, we cannot add more explanatory variables to the Model 4 regression.

The 4 land price series, PL^t_{MLIT} (the transaction price based series), PL^t_{L} (our preferred smoothed version of PL^t_{MLIT}), PL^t_{REIT} (the appraisal based series) and PL^t_{OLP} (the tax assessment based series), along with the official (normalized) construction price series PS^t plotted in Fig. 5.2.

It can be seen that the land price series based on transactions data, PL^t_{MLIT} and its linear smooth, PL^t_{L}, paint a very different picture of land price movements as compared to the series based on appraisal values for commercial land in Tokyo, PL^t_{REIT}, and the series based on property tax assessed values, PL^t_{OLP}. As was noted in previous section above, appraisal prices tend to lag behind the movements in transaction prices and they also smooth the sales data. The same phenomenon evidently applies to assessed value prices. Figure 5.2 shows that the appraisal and assessed value based price indexes for commercial land fluctuate far less than the index based actual transactions prices. However, it can be seen that the appraisal and assessed value series do tend to move in the same direction as the transactions prices but with a lag. The Figure also shows the problem with the transactions based series: its quarter to quarter fluctuations are massive. But it also can be seen that the linear smoothed series PL^t_{L} (which is essentially a centered five quarter moving average of the unsmoothed series PL^t_{MLIT}) captures the trend in transactions prices quite well. This series can be finalized after a two quarter delay. Our preferred land price series is the linear smoothed transaction series PL^t_{L}.

In the following section, we will use the MLIT and REIT data to construct alternative commercial property price indexes; i.e., we will aggregate the land and structure price data into overall property price indexes and compare these indexes with other indexes which are simpler to construct.

5.9 Overall Commercial Property Price Indexes

Recall that in Sect. 5.3, the MLIT value of property n in quarter t was defined as V_{tn} in period t and the corresponding property land and structure areas were defined as S_{tn} and L_{tn} for $n = 1, \ldots, N(t)$ and $t = 1, \ldots, 44$. In the property price literature, a frequently used index of overall property prices is the period average of the individual property values V_{tn} divided by the corresponding structure areas S_{tn}. Thus define the (preliminary) quarter t mean property price P^t_{MEANP} as follows:

$$P^t_{\text{MEANP}} \equiv (1/N(t)) \sum_{n=1}^{N(t)} V_{tn}/S_{tn}; \qquad t = 1, \ldots, 44. \tag{5.35}$$

The final mean property price index for quarter t, P^t_{MEAN}, is defined as the corresponding preliminary index P^t_{MEANP} divided by P^1_{MEANP}; i.e., we normalize the series defined by (5.35) to equal 1 in quarter 1.

As could be expected, the mean property price series P^t_{MEAN} is rather volatile and so in order to capture the trends in Tokyo commercial property prices, it is necessary to smooth this series. We used the same linear smoothing procedure that was explained in previous section above to construct the smoothed land price series PL^t_{L}. Thus we set the initial value of the smoothed mean series, P^1_{MEANS}, equal to the corresponding unsmoothed value P^1_{MEAN}. We set the quarter 2 value of the smooth equal to the average of the first and third observations in the raw series (so that $P^2_{\text{MEANS}} \equiv (1/2)[P^1_{\text{MEAN}} + P^3_{\text{MEAN}}]$). For the Quarter 3 value of the smooth, we used the simple 5 term centered moving average so that $P^3_{\text{MEANS}} \equiv (1/5)[P^1_{\text{MEAN}} + P^2_{\text{MEAN}} + P^3_{\text{MEAN}} + P^4_{\text{MEAN}} + P^5_{\text{MEAN}}]$ and we carried on using this 5 term centered moving average until Quarters 43 and 44 where we used Rows 4 and 5 of the matrix $\mathbf{X}(\mathbf{X}^T\mathbf{X})^{-1}\mathbf{X}^T$ defined in Sect. 5.7 for our Henderson linear regression smoother. The resulting smoothed mean price series, P^t_{MEANS}, plotted in Fig. 5.3. We note that the average value of the unsmoothed series P^t_{MEAN} is 1.1644 while the average value of the corresponding smoothed series P^t_{MEANS} is 1.1614.

We can use the predicted values from the Model 11 regression explained in previous section above in order to construct the imputed value of land sold during quarter t. This quarter t value of land is defined as follows:

$$V^t_L \equiv \alpha_t \sum_{n=1}^{N(t)} \left(\sum_{j=1}^{4} \omega_j D_{W,tnj} \right) \left(\sum_{m=1}^{5} \chi_m D_{EL,tnm} \right) (1 + \mu(H_{tn} - 3))(1 + \eta(DS_{tn} - 0)) \times$$
$$(1 + \theta(TT_{tn} - 1)) f_L(L_{tn}); \qquad t = 1, \ldots, 44. \tag{5.36}$$

In a similar fashion, we can use the predicted values from the Model 11 regression in order to define the imputed value of structures sold during quarter t, V^t_S, as follows:

$$V^t_S \equiv p_{St} \sum_{n=1}^{N(t)} g_A(A_{tn}) \left(\sum_{h=3}^{10} \phi_h D_{H,tnh} \right) S_{tn} \qquad t = 1, \ldots, 44. \tag{5.37}$$

The *quality adjusted quarter t quantities of land and of structures*, Q_L^t and Q_S^t, are defined as follows:

$$Q_L^t \equiv V_L^t / PL_{\text{MLIT}}^t; \; Q_S^t \equiv V_S^t / PS^t; \qquad t = 1, \ldots, 44. \tag{5.38}$$

With the prices and quantities of land and structures defined for each quarter, we calculated Fisher (1922) property price indexes, which are listed as P_{FMLIT}^t plotted on Fig. 5.3.[49]

From viewing Fig. 5.3, it can be seen that the Fisher property price indexes using MLIT data, P_{FMLIT}^t, are quite volatile (due of course to the volatility of the MLIT land price component indexes, PL_{MLIT}^t). The Henderson linear regression smooth of the unsmoothed land price series PL_{MLIT}^t was calculated as PL_{L}^t. We use this smoothed land price series along with the new land quantities defined as $Q_L^t \equiv V_L^t / PL_{\text{L}}^t$ in order to define the smoothed Fisher property price index, P_{FMLITS}^t, which plotted on Fig. 5.3. This series is our preferred measure of overall commercial property prices for Tokyo.

Recall Model 3 in Sect. 5.3 above that used REIT data to implement a version of the builder's model. We can use the predicted values from the Model 3 regression in order to construct the imputed value of land sold during quarter t. This quarter t value of land is defined as follows:

$$V_L^t \equiv \sum_{n=1}^{41} \alpha_t \omega_n L_{tn}; \qquad t = 1, \ldots, 44. \tag{5.39}$$

In a similar fashion, we can use the predicted values from the Model 3 REIT regression in order to define the impute value of structures sold during quarter t, V_S^t, as follows:

$$V_S^t \equiv \sum_{n=1}^{41} p_{St}(1 - \delta)^{A(t,n)} S_{tn}; \qquad t = 1, \ldots, 44. \tag{5.40}$$

The (REIT data based) quality adjusted land price for quarter t is the α_t which appears in (5.39) and is calculated as PL_{REIT}^t. The price of structures is $PS^t = p_{St} S_{tn}$ where p_{St} is the official construction price per m^2 in period t. The corresponding period t quantities of land and structure are defined as follows:

$$Q_L^t \equiv V_L^t / PL_{\text{REIT}}^t; \; Q_S^t \equiv V_S^t / PS^t; \qquad t = 1, \ldots, 44. \tag{5.41}$$

[49] The Laspeyres and Paasche price indexes for quarter t are defined as $P_L^t \equiv [PL_{\text{MLIT}}^t Q_L^1 + PS_t Q_S^1]/[PL_{\text{MLIT}}^1 Q_L^1 + PS_1 Q_S^1]$ and $P_P^t \equiv [PL_{\text{MLIT}}^t Q_L^t + PS_t Q_S^t]/[PL_{\text{MLIT}}^1 Q_L^t + PS_1 Q_S^t]$ respectively. The quarter t Fisher index is defined as $P_{\text{FMLIT}}^t \equiv [P_L^t P_P^t]^{1/2}$ for $t = 1, \ldots, 44$. See Fisher (1922) for additional materials on these indexes. The Fisher index has strong economic and axiomatic justifications; see Diewert (1976, 1992). We also calculated chained Fisher property price indexes using the same data but these indexes were virtually the same as the Fisher fixed base indexes.

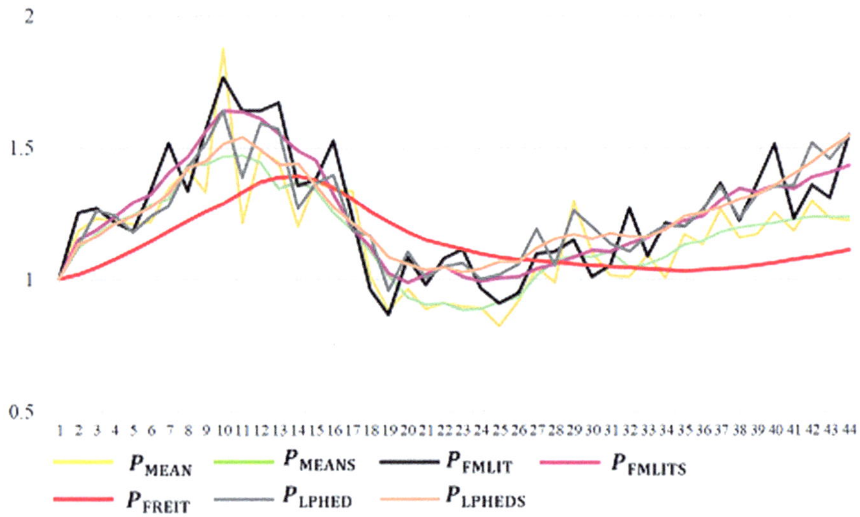

Fig. 5.3 Alternative commercial property price indexes using MLIT and REIT data

The overall REIT based property price index for quarter t is defined as the Fisher index P^t_{FREIT} using the above prices and quantities for land and structures as the basic building blocks. The REIT based overall property price series P^t_{FREIT} plotted in Fig. 5.3. It can be seen that this series is not volatile and does not require any smoothing.

Our final property price index will be generated by a traditional log price time dummy hedonic regression using the MLIT data.[50]

We use the same notation and definitions of variables as was used in previous sections. Define the natural logarithms of V_{tn}, L_{tn} and S_{tn} as LV_{tn}, LL_{tn} and LS_{tn} for $t = 1, \ldots, 44$ and $n = 1, \ldots, N(t)$. The *log price time dummy hedonic regression model* is the following linear regression model:

$$
\begin{aligned}
LV_{tn} = \beta_t + \sum_{j=2}^{4} \omega_j D_{W,tnj} + \gamma A_{tn} + \lambda LL_{tn} + \mu LS_{tn} + \sum_{h=4}^{10} \phi_h D_{H,tnh} + \eta DS_{tn} \\
+ \theta TT_{tn} + \varepsilon_{tn}; \qquad t = 1, \ldots, 44; n = 1, \ldots, N(t). \qquad (5.42)
\end{aligned}
$$

The 4 combined ward dummy variables $D_{W,tnj}$ were defined below definitions (5.4) and the discussion around Model 3 in Sect. 5.3. The building height dummy variables, $D_{H,tnh}$, were defined by (5.22) in Sect. 5.3. However, due to the small number of observations in the heights equal to 10-14 stories, all buildings in this range were aggregated into the height 10 stories category. As usual, A_{tn} is the age of building n sold in quarter t and DS_{tn} and TT_{tn} are the two subway variables pertaining to

[50]Recent developments in estimating traditional log price hedonic regression property models are reviewed by Hill et al. (2018) and Silver (2018).

building n in quarter t. The 44 time dummy variable coefficients are $\beta_1, \ldots, \beta_{44}$. Note that the dummy variable for the first combined ward, $D_{W,tn1}$, is not included in the linear regression defined by (5.42) in order to prevent multicollinearity. Similarly, the dummy variable for building height equal to 3 was also excluded from the regression to prevent multicollinearity. There are 59 unknown parameters in the regression. The R^2 for this regression was 0.7593. This is higher than our Model 9 and Model 11 R^2 using the same data, which were 0.7091 and 0.7143 respectively.

The standard errors for the time coefficients β_t^* were fairly large (in the 0.13–0.15 range). Define the unnormalized land price for quarter t, α_t^*, as the exponential of β_t^*; i.e., $\alpha_t^* \equiv \exp(\beta_t^*)$ for $t = 1, \ldots, 44$. The log price hedonic regression property price for quarter t, P^t_{LPHED} is defined as α_t^*/α_1^* for $t = 1, \ldots, 44$. This traditional hedonic regression model property price index P^t_{LPHED} graphed in Fig. 5.3.

The estimated λ and μ parameters were $\lambda^* = 0.5296$ and $\mu^* = 0.4939$ and hence, they almost sum to unity. Thus a generic commercial property sold in quarter t at price P with land and structure areas L and S respectively has a price that is approximately proportional to the Cobb-Douglas function $\alpha_t L^\lambda S^\mu$ which has returns to scale that are approximately equal to $\lambda^* + \mu^* \approx 1$. The estimated ω_j followed the same pattern that was estimated in Models 9 and 11 in Sect. 5.3; the composite Ward 1 was the most expensive ward, Ward 2 the next most expensive, Ward 3 less expensive again and Ward 4 had the lowest level of property prices. The height dummy variables exhibited the same trends that were observed in our MLIT builder's models: the higher the height of the structure, the higher was the price of the property. Finally, the distance from the nearest subway station parameter η was significantly negative indicating that property value falls as the distance increases. The subway travel time parameter θ had an unexpected positive sign but was not significantly different from 0. Finally, it is possible to convert the estimated age coefficient γ^* into an estimate for a geometric rate of structure depreciation, δ. The formula for this conversion is $\delta \equiv 1 - e^{\gamma/\beta}$.[51] When this conversion formula was utilized, we found that the estimated δ^* was 0.01945; i.e., the traditional hedonic regression model generated an implied annual geometric depreciation rate equal to 1.945% per year, which is a reasonable estimate.

Viewing Fig. 5.3, it can be seen that the time dummy hedonic regression model implied property price index P^t_{LPHED} is just as volatile as the corresponding builder's model property price index P^t_{FMLIT}. Thus we applied our modified Henderson linear smoothing operator to P^t_{LPHED} which produces the smoothed series, P^t_{LPHEDS}, which is also plotted in Fig. 5.3.

The two top jagged lines in Fig. 5.3 are the Fisher property price index using the builder's model, P^t_{FMLIT}, and the log price time dummy hedonic regression property price index, P^t_{LPHED}. Both of these series use the MLIT sales transaction data. Their linear smooths are P^t_{FMLITS} and P^t_{LPHEDS}. It can be seen that these two smoothed series

[51]See McMillen (2003; 289–290), Shimizu et al. (2010; 795) and Diewert et al. (2017; 24) for derivations of this formula.

approximate each other reasonably well.[52] What is somewhat surprising is that the smoothed mean index P^t_{MEANS} (which uses the same transactions data) approximates the two smoothed hedonic indexes to some degree but the series gradually diverge due to the fact that an index based on average prices per m^2 cannot take depreciation into account.[53] The hills and valleys in the P^t_{MEANS} series are less pronounced than the corresponding fluctuations in the P^t_{FMLITS} and P^t_{LPHEDS} series but the turning points are the same. Finally, it can be seen that the Fisher property price series that is based on appraised values of properties, P^t_{FREIT}, does not provide a good approximation to the two smoothed series based on transactions, the P^t_{FMLITS} and P^t_{LPHEDS} series. The fluctuations in P^t_{FREIT} are too small and the turning points in this series lag well behind our preferred series.

5.10 Commercial Property Price Indexes Based on Stock Market Data

As was seen in the previous section, the use of appraisal or tax assessment data in constructing a commercial property price index can result in an index which has been excessively smoothed and has lagged turning points. Thus the use of the resulting indexes can render early warning signals for monetary policy ineffective and distort SNA national land asset value estimates.

Under these circumstances, there are advantages to using the transaction price. However, the problems of property heterogeneity and the scarcity of sales of commercial properties lead to difficulties in constructing transaction based indexes. Furthermore, many countries do not collect data on transaction prices. Hence, estimating price indexes using the *stock price* of real estate investment trusts (REIT) has been proposed as a fourth data source, following the transaction price, appraisal price, and assessment price methods.

The stock market method of property valuation can be applied to REITs that have only a single structure in their real estate portfolio. Suppose there are N such single asset REITs. At any point of time in period t, the value of the property in the REIT n, V_{tn}, will be equal to the stock market value of REIT n, say V_{Stn}, plus the value of outstanding debt at that time, V_{Dtn}. Now simply apply the model that was explained in Sect. 5.7 above using the stock market values $V_{tn} = V_{Stn} + V_{Dtn}$ in place of the corresponding appraised values. However, Model 3 defined by Eq. (5.28) does require information on the land plot area, the floor space area of the structure and an exogenous cost of construction index.

---

[52]Diewert (2010) noticed that the Fisher property price index generated by the builder's model frequently approximated the traditional log price time dummy property price index using the same data. However, the key to close approximation is that the time dummy model must generate a reasonable implied structure depreciation rate, which is the case for our particular data set.

[53]If the age structure of the quarterly sales of properties remains reasonably constant, then this neglect of depreciation will probably not be a factor.

The advantage in using stock market data in place of transactions data is that stock market data may be more plentiful than data on sales of commercial properties. But there are some disadvantages as well:

- Stock market data may be more volatile than sales data;
- Stock market data may not be representative of the entire market.

The first difficulty can be overcome by using the smoothing methods discussed in the paper (or alternative methods). The second difficulty can be overcome if stock market data is used to supplement transactions data.

5.11 Summary and Conclusion

Appraisal based commercial property price indexes have been published for many years, focusing on Japan, the U.S., and the U.K. As noted in the paper, these indexes tend to diverge from actual market conditions due to the smoothing and turning points problems. Thus in recent years, commercial property price indexes based on transactions have been developed and are published in the U.S and Japan.

However, in many countries (including Japan), many difficulties accompany the estimation of indexes based on transaction prices due to the lack of transactions. In addition, compared to housing, commercial properties have a high level of heterogeneity, so quality adjustment must be performed.

In addressing problems such as this lack of data and rigorous quality adjustment, one may refer to past experience and efforts that have been made in the practical property appraisal. Property appraisal prices are determined based on the sales comparison approach, using comparables for similar transactions in the vicinity of the property being appraised. For housing price indexes, this approach leads to these appraisal type price indexes being estimated essentially by performing quality adjustment through the use of transaction prices.

For commercial properties, on the other hand, since there is lack of transaction comparables as well as a high level of heterogeneity, it is difficult to construct appraisal based indexes on the sales comparison approach. As a result, commercial property appraisals are generally determined using present values, based on a method known as the capitalization method. This means that the difficulty level of estimating commercial property price indexes using transaction prices is extremely high compared to housing.

In this paper, based on past experience in the practical property appraisal, in addition to a price index using property appraisal prices and price index using transaction prices, we explored the possibility of estimating a price index based on the Builder's Model proposed by Diewert and Shimizu (2019). Specifically, focusing on the Tokyo area, we estimated a transaction based CPPI, along with an appraisal-based price index, using transaction prices and published J-REIT data with the same characteristics as data possessed by NCREIF in the U.S., MSCI-IPD in the U.K., etc. The following provides an overview of the analysis and results obtained.

Here are our main conclusions in comparison with transaction based CPPI using Builder's model, appraisal based index, assessment price index:

- It is possible to construct a quarterly transactions based commercial property price index that can be decomposed into land and structure components.
- The main characteristics of the properties that are required in order to implement our approach are: (i) the property location (or neighbourhood); (ii) the floor space area of the structure on the property; (iii) the area of the land plot; (iv) the age of the structure and (v) the height of the building. We also require an appropriate exogenous commercial property construction cost index that gives the average cost of construction per square meter for each period in the sample.
- The land price index that our hedonic regression model generates may be too volatile and hence may need to be smoothed. We found that a slightly modified five quarter moving average of the raw land price indexes did an adequate job of smoothing. This means that the final land price index could be produced with a two quarter lag.
- We found that a smoothed version of a traditional log price time dummy hedonic regression model produced an acceptable approximation to our preferred smoothed builder's model overall price index.
- We also found that a very simple overall price index which is proportional to the quarterly arithmetic average of each property price divided by the corresponding structure area provided a rough approximation to our preferred price index. This model cannot take depreciation into account and hence will in general have an downward bias but it has the advantage of requiring information on only a single property characteristic (the structure floor space area) in order to be implemented.
- The price indexes that were based on appraisal and assessed value information were not satisfactory approximations to the transactions based indexes. The turning points in these series lagged our preferred series and the appraisal based series smoothed the data based series to an unacceptable degree.[54]

Numerous problems still remain. In the realm of commercial properties, there are many other structures with diverse uses, e.g. commercial establishments, hotels, and warehousing & distribution facilities. In such markets, it is to be expected that transactions prices are even more scarce, and properties, even more heterogeneous, when compared to the office market. Furthermore, certain quantities of transaction price data and appraisal prices from the real investment market are available for use in large cities such as Tokyo. However, it is highly probable that sufficient data will be hard to come by in regional cities.

---

[54]These points are well known in the real estate literature; see Chap. 25 in Geltner et al. (2014).

References

Bokhari, S., and D. Geltner. 2012. Estimating real estate price movements for high frequency tradable indexes in a scarce data environment. *Journal of Real Estate Finance and Economics* 45 (2): 522–543.

Bostic, R.W., S.D. Longhofer, and C.L. Redfearn. 2007. Land leverage: Decomposing home price dynamics. *Real Estate Economics* 35 (2): 183–2008.

Burnett-Issacs, K., N. Huang, and W.E. Diewert. 2016. *Developing Land and Structure Price Indexes for Ottawa Condominium Apartments*. Discussion Paper 16–09, Vancouver School of Economics: University of British Columbia, Vancouver, B.C., Canada.

Clapp, J.M. 1980. The elasticity of substitution for land: The effects of measurement errors. *Journal of Urban Economics* 8: 255–263.

Cleveland, W.S. 1979. Robust locally weighted regression and smoothing scatterplots. *Journal of the American Statistical Association* 74: 829–836.

Court, A.T. 1939. Hedonic price indexes with automotive examples. In *The Dynamics of Automobile Demand*, pp. 99–117. New York: General Motors Corporation.

Crosby, N., C. Lizieri, and P. McAllister. 2010. Means, motive and opportunity? disentangling client influence on performance measurement appraisals. *Journal of Property Research* 27 (2): 181–201.

de Haan, Jan, and W.E. Diewert (eds.). 2011. *Residential Property Price Handbook*. Luxembourg: Eurostat.

Diewert, W.E. 1976. Exact and superlative index numbers. *Journal of Econometrics* 4: 114–145.

Diewert, W.E. 1992. Fisher ideal output, input and productivity indexes revisited. *Journal of Productivity Analysis* 3: 211–248.

Diewert, W.E. 2005. Issues in the measurement of capital services, depreciation, asset price changes and interest rates. In *Measuring Capital in the New Economy*, ed. C. Corrado, J. Haltiwanger, and D. Sichel, 479–542. Chicago: University of Chicago Press.

Diewert, W.E. 2008. The paris OECD-IMF workshop on real estate price indexes: Conclusions and further directions. In *Proceedings from the OECD Workshop on Productivity Measurement and Analysis*, 11–36. Paris: OECD.

Diewert, W.E. 2010. Alternative approaches to measuring house price inflation. Discussion Paper 10–10, Department of Economics, The University of British Columbia, Vancouver, Canada, V6T 1Z1.

Diewert, W.E. 2019. Quality adjustment and hedonics: A unified approach. Discussion Paper 19–01, Vancouver School of Economics, University of British Columbia, Vancouver, B.C., Canada, V6T 1L4.

Diewert, W.E., and C. Shimizu. 2015a. A conceptual framework for commercial property price indexes. *Journal of Statistical Science and Application* 3 (9–10): 131–152.

Diewert, W.E., and C. Shimizu. 2015b. Residential property price indexes for Tokyo. *Macroeconomic Dynamics* 19: 1659–1714.

Diewert, W.E., and C. Shimizu. 2016. Hedonic regression models for Tokyo condominium sales. *Regional Science and Urban Economics* 60: 300–315.

Diewert, W.E., and C. Shimizu. 2017. Alternative approaches to commercial property price indexes for Tokyo. *Review of Income and Wealth* 63 (3): 492–519.

Diewert, W.E., and C. Shimizu. 2019. Alternative land price indexes for commercial properties in Tokyo. *Review of Income and Wealth*. (Forthcoming).

Diewert, W.E., J. de Haan, and R. Hendriks. 2011. The decomposition of a house price index into land and structures components: A hedonic regression approach. *The Valuation Journal* 6: 58–106.

Diewert, W.E., J. de Haan, and R. Hendriks. 2015. Hedonic regressions and the decomposition of a house price index into land and structure components. *Econometric Reviews* 34: 106–126.

Diewert, W.E., K. Fox, and C. Shimizu. 2016. Commercial property price indexes and the system of national accounts. *Journal of Economic Surveys* 30 (5): 913–943.

Diewert, W.E., N. Huang and K. Burnett-Isaacs. 2017. Alternative approaches for resale housing price indexes. Discussion Paper 17–05, Vancouver School of Economics, The University of British Columbia, Vancouver, Canada, V6T 1L4.

Fisher, I. 1922. *The Making of Index Numbers*. Boston: Houghton-Mifflin.

Francke, M.K. 2008. The hierarchical trend model. In *Mass Appraisal Methods: An International Perspective for Property Valuers*, ed. T. Kauko, and M. Damato, 164–180. Oxford: Wiley-Blackwell.

Geltner, D. 1997. The use of appraisals in portfolio valuation and index. *Journal of Real Estate Finance and Economics* 15: 423–445.

Geltner, D., and W. Goetzmann. 2000. Two decades of commercial property returns: A repeated-measures regression-based version of the NCREIF index. *Journal of Real Estate Finance and Economics* 21: 5–21.

Geltner, D., and S. Bokhari. 2019. Commercial buildings capital consumption and the United States national accounts. *Review of Income and Wealth* 65 (3): 561–591.

Geltner, D., R.A. Graff, and M.S. Young. 1994. Random disaggregate appraisal error in commercial property, evidence from the russell-NCREIF database. *Journal of Real Estate Research* 9 (4): 403–419.

Geltner, D., H. Pollakowski, H. Horrigan, and B. Case. 2010. REIT-based pure property return indexes. United States Patent Application Publication, Publication Number: US 2010/0174663 A1, Publication Date: July 8, 2010.

Geltner, D.M., N.G. Miller, J. Clayton, and P. Eichholtz. 2014. *Commercial Real Estate Analysis and Investments*, 3rd ed. Mason Ohio: On Course Learning.

Henderson, R. 1916. Note on graduation by adjusted average. *Actuarial Society of America Transactions* 17: 43–48.

Hill, R.J., M. Scholz, C. Shimizu, and M. Steurer. 2018. An evaluation of the methods used by European countries to compute their official house price indices. *Economie et Statistique/Economics and Statistics Numbers* 500–502: 221–238.

Koev, E., and J.M.C. Santos Silva. 2008. *Hedonic Methods for Decomposing House Price Indices Into Land and Structure Components*. unpublished paper, Department of Economics: University of Essex, England.

McMillen, D.P. 2003. The return of centralization to Chicago: Using repeat sales to identify changes in house price distance gradients. *Regional Science and Urban Economics* 33: 287–304.

Muth, R.F. 1971. The derived demand for urban residential land. *Urban Studies* 8: 243–254.

Patrick, G. 2017. *Redeveloping Ireland's residential property price index (RPPI)*. Germany: In Paper presented at the Ottawa Group Meeting at Eltville.

Rambaldi, A.N., R.R.J. McAllister, K. Collins and C.S. Fletcher. 2010. Separating land from structure in property prices: A case study from Brisbane Australia. In *School of Economics, The University of Queensland, St. Lucia*, 4072. Queensland, Australia.

Rambaldi, A.N., R.R.J McAllister and C.S. Fletcher. 2016. Decoupling land values in residential property prices: Smoothing methods for hedonic imputed price indices. In *Paper presented at the 34th IARIW General Conference*. Dresden, Germany.

Rosen, S. 1974. Hedonic prices and implicit markets: Product differentiation in pure competition. *Journal of Political Economy* 82: 34–55.

Schreyer, P. 2001. *OECD productivity manual: A guide to the measurement of industry-level and aggregate productivity growth*. Paris: OECD.

Schreyer, P. 2009. *Measuring Capital, Statistics Directorate, National Accounts, STD/NAD(2009) 1*. Paris: OECD.

Schwann, G.M. 1998. A real estate price index for thin markets. *Journal of Real Estate Finance and Economics* 16 (3): 269–287.

Shimizu, C. 2016. Microstructure of asset prices, property income, and discount rates in Tokyo residential market. *International Journal of Housing Markets and Analysis* 10 (4): 552–571.

Shimizu, C., and K.G. Nishimura. 2006. Biases in appraisal land price information: The case of Japan. *Journal of Property Investment & Finance* 24 (2): 150–175.

Shimizu, C., K.G. Nishimura, and T. Watanabe. 2010. Housing prices in Tokyo: A comparison of hedonic and repeat sales measures. *Journal of Economics and Statistics* 230: 792–813.

Shimizu, C., W.E. Diewert, K.G. Nishimura, and T. Watanabe. 2015. Estimating quality adjusted commercial property price indexes using Japanese REIT data. *Journal of Property Research* 32 (3): 217–239.

Silver, M.S. 2018. How to measure hedonic property price indexes better. *EURONA* 1 (2018): 35–66.

Triplett, J. 2004. *Handbook on Hedonic Indexes and Quality Adjustments in Price Indexes, Directorate for Science, Technology and Industry, DSTI/DOC(2004) 9*. Paris: OECD.

White, K.J. 2004. *Shazam: User's Reference Manual, Version 10*. Vancouver, Canada: Northwest Econometrics Ltd.

Part III
Housing Services in CPI and SNA

Chapter 6
Measuring the Services of Durables and Owner Occupied Housing

6.1 Introduction

When a durable good (other than housing) is purchased by a consumer, national Consumer Price Indexes typically attribute *all* of that expenditure to the period of purchase, even though the use of the good extends beyond the period of purchase.[1] This is known as the *acquisitions approach* to the treatment of consumer durables in the context of determining a pricing concept for the CPI. However, if one takes a *cost of living* approach to the Consumer Price Index, then it may be more appropriate to take the cost of using the services of the durable good during the period under consideration as the pricing concept. There are two broad methods for estimating this imputed cost for using the services of a durable good during a period:

- If rental or leasing markets for a comparable consumer durable exist, then this market rental price could be used as an estimate for the cost of using the durable during the period. This method is known as the *rental equivalence approach.*
- If used or second hand markets for the durable exist, then the imputed cost of purchasing a durable good at the beginning of the period and selling it at the end could be computed and this net cost could be used as a estimate for the cost of using the durable during the period. This method is known as the *user cost approach.*

The major *advantages* of the acquisitions approach to the treatment of consumer durables are:

[1]This treatment of the purchases of durable goods dates back to Marshall (1898; 594–595) at least: "We have noticed also that though the benefits which a man derives from living in his own house are commonly reckoned as part of his real income, and estimated at the net rental value of his house; the same plan is not followed with regard to the benefits which he derives from the use of his furniture and clothes. It is best here to follow the common practice, and not count as part of the national income or dividend anything that is not commonly counted as part of the income of the individual.".

The base of this chapter is Diewert, W. E. and C. Shimizu. 2019. Measuring the services of durables and owner occupied housing. Discussion Paper 19-02, Vancouver School of Economics, University of British Columbia, Vancouver, Canada.

W. E. Diewert et al., *Property Price Index*, Advances in Japanese Business and Economics 11, https://doi.org/10.1007/978-4-431-55942-9_6

- It is conceptually simple and entirely similar to the treatment of nondurables and services and
- No complex imputations are required.

The major *disadvantage* of the acquisitions approach compared to the other two approaches is that the acquisitions approach is not likely to reflect accurately the consumption services of consumer durables in any period. Thus suppose that real interest rates in a country are very high due to a macroeconomic crisis. Under these conditions, purchases of automobiles and houses and other long lived consumer durables may drop dramatically, perhaps to zero. However, the actual consumption of automobile and housing services of the country's population will not fall to zero under these circumstances: households will still be consuming the services of their existing stocks of motor vehicles and houses. Thus for at least some purposes, rather than taking the cost of *purchasing* a consumer durable as the pricing concept, it will be more useful to take the cost of *using* the services of the durable good during the period under consideration as the pricing concept.

The above paragraphs provide a brief overview of the three major approaches to the treatment of consumer durables. In the remainder of this introduction, we explore these approaches in a bit more detail and give the reader an outline of the detailed discussion that will follow in subsequent sections.

Since the benefits of using the consumer durable extend over more than one period, it does not seem to be appropriate to charge the entire purchase cost of the durable to the initial period of purchase. If this point of view is taken, then the initial purchase cost must be distributed somehow over the useful life of the asset. This is *the fundamental problem of accounting*.[2] Hulten (1990) explains the accounting problems that arise from the purchase of a durable good as follows:

> Durability means that a capital good is productive for two or more time periods, and this, in turn, implies that a distinction must be made between the value of using or renting capital in any year and the value of owning the capital asset. This distinction would not necessarily lead to a measurement problem if the capital services used in any given year were paid for in that year; that is, if all capital were rented. In this case, transactions in the rental market would fix the price and quantity of capital in each time period, much as data on the price and quantity of labor services are derived from labor market transactions. But, unfortunately, much capital is utilized by its owner and the transfer of capital services between owner and user results in an implicit rent typically not observed by the statistician. Market data are thus inadequate for the task of directly estimating the price and quantity of capital services, and this has led to the development of indirect procedures for inferring the quantity of capital, like the perpetual inventory method, or to the acceptance of flawed measures, like book value. Hulten (1990; 120–121).

[2]"The third convention is that of the annual accounting period. It is this convention which is responsible for most of the difficult accounting problems. Without this convention, accounting would be a simple matter of recording completed and fully realized transactions: an act of primitive simplicity." Gilman (1939; 26). "*All* the problems of income measurement are the result of our desire to attribute income to arbitrarily determined short periods of time. Everything comes right in the end; but by then it is too late to matter." Solomons (1961; 378). Note that these authors do not mention the additional complications that are due to the fact that future revenues and costs must be discounted to yield values that are equivalent to present dollars. For more recent papers on the fundamental problem of accounting, see Cairns (2013), Diewert and Fox (2016).

Thus the treatment of durable goods is more complicated than the treatment of non-durable goods and services due to the simple fact that the period of time that a durable is used by the consumer extends beyond the period of purchase. For nondurables and services, the price statistician's measurement problems are conceptually simpler: prices for the same commodity need only be collected in each period and compared. However, for a durable good, the periods of payment and use do not coincide and so complex imputation problems arise if the goal of the price statistician is to measure and compare the price of *using* the services of the durable in two time periods.

As mentioned above, there are 3 main methods for dealing with the durability problem:

- Ignore the problem of distributing the initial cost of the durable over the useful life of the good and allocate the entire charge to the period of purchase. As noted above, this is known as the *acquisitions approach* and it is the present approach used by Consumer Price Index statisticians for all durables with the exception of housing.
- The *rental equivalence approach*. In this approach, a period price is imputed for the durable which is equal to the rental price or leasing price of an equivalent consumer durable for the same period of time.
- The *user cost approach*. In this approach, the initial purchase cost of the durable is decomposed into two parts: one part which reflects an estimated cost of using the services of the durable for the period and another part, which is regarded as an investment, which must earn some exogenous rate of return.

These three major approaches will be discussed more fully in Sects. 6.2–6.4 below. There is fourth approach that has not been applied but seems conceptually attractive that will be discussed in Sect. 6.5: the *opportunity cost approach*. This approach takes the *maximum* of the rental equivalence and user cost as the price for the use of the services of a consumer durable over a period of time. Finally, there is a fifth approach to the treatment of consumer durables that has only been used in the context of pricing owner occupied housing and that is the *payments approach*.[3] This is a kind of cash flow approach, which is not entirely satisfactory. It will be discussed in Sect. 6.17 after we have discussed the other approaches in more detail.

The main three approaches to the treatment of durable purchases can be applied to the purchase of any durable commodity. However, historically, it turns out that the rental equivalence and user cost approaches have *only* been applied to owner occupied housing. In other words, the acquisitions approach to the purchase of consumer durables has been universally used by statistical agencies, with the exception of owner occupied housing. A possible reason for this is tradition; i.e., Marshall (1898) set the standard and statisticians have followed his example for the past century. However, another possible reason is that unless the durable good has a very long useful life, it usually will not make a great deal of difference in the long run whether the acquisitions approach or one of the two alternative approaches is used. This point is discussed in more detail in Sect. 6.10 below.

---

[3]This is the term used by Goodhart (2001; F350–F351).

A major component of the user cost approach to valuing the services of Owner Occupied Housing (OOH) is the depreciation component. In Sect. 6.6, a general model of depreciation for a consumer durable is presented and then it is specialized in Sects. 6.7–6.9 to the three most common models of depreciation that are widely used.

The general model presented in Sect. 6.6 assumes that homogeneous units of the durable are produced in each period so that information on the prices of the various vintages of the durable at any point in time can be used to determine the pattern of depreciation. However, many durables (like housing) are custom produced and thus the methods for determining the form of depreciation explained in Sect. 6.6 are not immediately applicable. The special problems caused by *uniquely* produced consumer durables are considered in Sect. 6.11.

The remainder of this paper looks at the particular problems associated with measuring the services of housing. Sections 6.12–6.14 show how information on the sales of dwelling units can be used to decompose the sales price into land and structure components. This information is required for the country's national balance sheet accounts. The decomposition into land and structure components is also required for the construction of rental prices and user costs.[4] Section 6.12 looks at land and structure decompositions for the sale of detached housing units while Sect. 6.13 does the same for the sales of condominium units. Hedonic regression models are explained in Sects. 6.12 and 6.13 that are basically supply side models while Sect. 6.14 looks at a demand side hedonic regression model for the sales of detached houses. Section 6.15 considers hedonic regression models for rents. Section 6.16 looks at the factors that influence rents. This section also explains why the amount that an owned dwelling unit could rent for is in general different from the user cost that could be used to price the services of the unit to an owner. This section brings up important issues that pertain to the measurement of the services of OOH. Thus Sect. 6.16 revisits issues surrounding the use of either the rental equivalence or user cost approaches to the valuation of Owner Occupied Housing.

As mentioned early, Sect. 6.17 explains the payments approach while Sect. 6.18 concludes.

6.2 The Acquisitions Approach

The *net acquisitions approach* to the treatment of owner occupied housing is described by Goodhart as follows:

> The first is the net acquisition approach, which is the change in the price of newly purchased owner occupied dwellings, weighted by the net purchases of the reference population. This is an asset based measure, and therefore comes close to my preferred measure of inflation as a change in the value of money, though the change in the price of the stock of existing houses rather than just of net purchases would in some respects be even better. It is, moreover,

[4]Depreciation applies to the structure part of property value but not to the land part.

> consistent with the treatment of other durables. A few countries, e.g., Australia and New Zealand, have used it, and it is, I understand, the main contender for use in the Euro-area Harmonized Index of Consumer Prices (HICP), which currently excludes any measure of the purchase price of (new) housing, though it does include minor repairs and maintenance by home owners, as well as all expenditures by tenants. Goodhart (2001; F350).

Thus the weights for the net acquisitions approach are the net purchases of the household sector of houses from other institutional sectors in the base period. Note that in principle, purchases of second-hand dwellings from other sectors are relevant here; e.g., a local government may sell rental dwellings to owner occupiers. However, typically, newly built houses form a major part of these types of transactions. Thus the long term price relative for this category of expenditure will be primarily the price of (new) houses (quality adjusted) in the current period relative to the price of new houses in the base period.[5] If this approach is applied to other consumer durables, it is extremely easy to implement: the purchase of a durable is treated in the same way as a nondurable or service purchase is treated.

One additional implication of the net acquisition approach is that major renovations and additions to owner occupied dwelling units could also be considered as being in scope for this approach. In practice, major renovations to a house are treated as investment expenditures and not covered as part of a consumer price index. Normal maintenance expenditures on a dwelling unit are usually treated in a separate category in the CPI.

Traditionally, the net acquisitions approach also includes transfer costs relating to the buying and selling of second hand houses as expenditures that are in scope for an acquisitions type consumer price index. These costs are mainly the costs of using a real estate agent's services and asset transfer taxes. These costs can be measured but the question arises as to what is the appropriate deflator for these costs. An overall property price index is probably a satisfactory deflator.[6]

The major advantage of the acquisitions approach is that it treats durable and nondurable purchases in a completely symmetric manner and thus no special procedures have to be developed by a statistical agency to deal with durable goods.[7] As will be seen in Sect. 6.5 below, the major disadvantage of this approach is that the

---

[5]This price index may or may not include the price of the land that the new dwelling unit sits on; e.g., a new house price construction index would typically not include the land cost. The acquisitions approach concentrates on the purchases by households of goods and services that are provided by suppliers from outside the household sector. Thus if the land on which a new house sits was previously owned by the household sector, then presumably, the cost of this land would be excluded from an acquisitions type new house price index. In this case, the price index that corresponds to the acquisitions approach is basically a new house price index (excluding land) or a modification of a construction cost index where the modification takes into account builder's margins.

[6]See the discussion in Sect. 6.16 below on transfer costs.

[7]The acquisitions approach is straightforward and simple for most durable goods but not for housing, if the land component of property value is regarded as out of scope. Properties are sold with a single price that includes both the land and structure components of housing and so if the land part of property value is regarded as out of scope for the index, then there is a problem in decomposing property value into land and structure components. This decomposition problem can be avoided if information on the construction costs for building a new housing unit are available. In this case,

expenditures associated with this approach will tend to *understate* the corresponding expenditures on durables that are implied by the rental equivalence and user cost approaches.

Some differences between the acquisitions approach and the other approaches are:

- If rental or leasing markets for the durable exist and the durable has a long useful life, then as mentioned above, the expenditure weights implied by the rental equivalence or user cost approaches will typically be much larger than the corresponding expenditure weights implied by the acquisitions approach; see Sect. 6.16 below.
- If the base year corresponds to a boom year (or a slump year) for the durable, then the base period expenditure weights may be too large or too small. Put another way, the aggregate expenditures that correspond to the acquisitions approach are likely to be more volatile than the expenditures for the aggregate that are implied by the rental equivalence or user cost approaches.[8]
- In making comparisons of consumption across countries where the proportion of owning versus renting or leasing the durable varies greatly,[9] the use of the acquisitions approach may lead to misleading cross country comparisons. The reason for this is that opportunity costs of capital are excluded in the net acquisitions approach whereas they are explicitly or implicitly included in the other two approaches.

More fundamentally, whether the acquisitions approach is the right one or not depends on the overall purpose of the index number. If the purpose is to measure the price of current period *consumption services*, then the acquisitions approach can only be regarded as an approximation to a more appropriate approach (which would be either the rental equivalence or user cost approach). If the purpose of the index is to measure *monetary* (or nonimputed) *expenditures* by households during the period, then the acquisitions approach might be preferable (provided the land component of property value is in scope), since the rental equivalence and user cost approaches necessarily involve imputations.[10]

---

the construction cost index (including builder's markups) can serve as the price index for newly constructed dwelling units.

[8] Hill et al. (2017; 6) summarize the problem of variable weights as follows: "Hence the expenditure weights on OOH under the acquisitions approach can fluctuate very significantly over the housing cycle. If the weights are updated regularly this may have a destabilizing effect on the CPI. If the weights are not updated regularly, then the treatment of OOH may be highly sensitive to the choice of reference year.".

[9] From Hoffmann and Kurz (2002; 3–4), about 60% of German households lived in rented dwellings whereas only about 11% of Spaniards rented their dwellings in 1999.

[10] Fenwick (2009, 2012) laid out the case for the use of the acquisitions approach as a useful measure of general inflation. He also argued for the construction of multiple consumer price indexes to suit different purposes.

The details of the acquisitions approach (as applied to OOH) are discussed in great detail in Eurostat (2017).[11] Eurostat is considering the use of the acquisitions approach for the treatment of OOH in its Harmonized Index of Consumer Prices (HICP) but at this date, no decision has been finalized. At present, OOH is simply omitted in the HICP. Eurostat is considering the use of the acquisitions approach for OOH because at first sight, it seems that no imputations have to be made in order to implement it. The HICP was created as an index of consumer prices that used *actual transactions prices* without the use of any imputations.[12] As such, it was thought to be particularly useful for monitoring inflation by central banks. However, the sale of a newly constructed dwelling unit typically includes a land component which Eurostat wishes to exclude but existing methods for excluding the land component involve imputations.[13]

6.3 The Rental Equivalence Approach

The *rental equivalence approach* simply values the services yielded by the use of a consumer durable good for a period by the corresponding market rental value for the same durable for the same period of time (if such a rental value exists). This is the approach taken in the *System of National Accounts: 1993* for owner occupied housing:

> As well-organized markets for rented housing exist in most countries, the output of own-account housing services can be valued using the prices of the same kinds of services sold on the market with the general valuation rules adopted for goods and services produced on own account. In other words, the output of housing services produced by owner-occupiers is valued at the estimated rental that a tenant would pay for the same accommodation, taking into account factors such as location, neighbourhood amenities, etc. as well as the size and quality of the dwelling itself. Eurostat, IMF, OECD, UN and World Bank (1993; 134).

However, the *System of National Accounts: 1993* follows Marshall (1898; 595) and does *not* extend the rental equivalence approach to consumer durables other than housing. This seemingly inconsistent treatment of durables is explained in the *SNA 1993* as follows:

> The production of housing services for their own final consumption by owner-occupiers has always been included within the production boundary in national accounts, although it constitutes an exception to the general exclusion of own-account service production. The ratio of owner-occupied to rented dwellings can vary significantly between countries and even

---

[11]This very useful publication also discusses the main methods for the treatment of OOH and it also covers the methods used to construct residential property price indexes. The latter topic is also covered in Eurostat (2013).

[12]However, with the passage of time, it became apparent that some imputations for changes in the quality of consumer goods and services had to be made. Thus the current HICP is not completely free from imputations. See Astin (1999) for the methodological foundations of the HICP.

[13]The use of a construction cost index also involves an imputation (but it is a reasonably straight-forward one).

> over short periods of time within a single country, so that both international and intertemporal comparisons of the production and consumption of housing services could be distorted if no imputation were made for the value of own-account services. Eurostat, IMF, OECD, UN and World Bank (1993; 126).

Eurostat's (2001) *Handbook on Price and Volume Measures in National Accounts* also recommends the rental equivalence approach for the treatment of the dwelling services for owner occupied housing:

> The output of dwelling services of owner occupiers at current prices is in many countries estimated by linking the actual rents paid by those renting similar properties in the rented sector to those of owner occupiers. This allows the imputation of a notional rent for the service owner occupiers receive from their property. Eurostat (2001; 99).

To summarize the above material, it can be seen that the rental equivalence approach to the treatment of durables is conceptually simple: impute a current period rental or leasing price for a comparable dwelling unit as the price for the services of an owned dwelling unit.[14]

But where will the statistical agency find the relevant rental data to price the services of OOH? There are at least three possible methods:

- Ask home owners what they think the market rent for their dwelling unit is[15];
- Undertake a survey of owners of rental properties or managers of rental properties and ask what rents they charge for their rental properties by type of property or
- Use one of the above two methods to get a rent to value ratio for various types of property for a benchmark period and then link these ratios to indexes of purchase prices for the various types of property.[16]

There are some disadvantages associated with the use of the rental equivalence approach to the valuation of OOH services:

- Homeowners may not be able to provide very accurate estimates for the rental value of their dwelling unit.
- On the other hand, if the statistical agency tries to match the characteristics of an owned dwelling unit with a comparable unit that is rented in order to obtain the imputed rent for the owned unit, there may be difficulties in finding such comparable units. Furthermore, even if a comparable unit is found, the rent for the comparable unit may not be an appropriate opportunity cost for valuing the services of the owned unit.[17]

---

[14] As will be seen in Sect. 6.16 below, the situation is not quite as simple as indicated above.

[15] This approach is used by the Bureau of Labor Statistics (1983) in order to determine *expenditure weights* for owner occupied housing; i.e., homeowners are asked to estimate what their house would rent for if it were rented to a third party.

[16] Lebow and Rudd (2003; 169) note that the US Bureau of Economic Analysis applies a benchmark rent to value ratio for rented properties to the value of the owner occupied stock of housing. It can be seen that this approach is essentially a simplified user cost method where all of the key variables in the user cost formula (to be discussed later) are held constant except the asset price of the property.

[17] We will return to this point after we have discussed the opportunity cost approach to the valuation of OOH services.

- The statistical agency should make an adjustment to these estimated rents over time in order to take into account the effects of depreciation, which causes the quality of the unit to slowly decline over time (unless this effect is completely offset by renovation and repair expenditures).[18]
- Care must be taken to determine exactly what extra services are included in the homeowner's estimated rent; i.e., does the rent include insurance, electricity and fuel or the use of various consumer durables in addition to the structure? If so, these extra services should be stripped out of the rent, if they are covered elsewhere in the consumer price index.[19]

In order to overcome the first difficulty listed above, statistical agencies, including the Japanese government, are currently collecting housing rent data from property management companies or owners who rent out their dwelling units; i.e., Japan uses the second method to value the services of OOH. However, the characteristics of the owner occupied population of dwelling units are generally quite different from the characteristics of the rental population.[20] Thus typically, it is difficult to find rental units that are comparable to owned dwelling units. The use of hedonic regression techniques can mitigate this lack of matching problem. Moreover the use of hedonic regressions can deal with the depreciation or quality decline problem mentioned above. We will discuss hedonic regression techniques later in this paper in Sects. 6.12–6.15.

In addition to the above possible biases in using the rental equivalence approach to the valuation of the services of OOH, there are differences between *contract rent* and *market rent*. Contract rent refers to the rent paid by a renter who has a long term rental contract with the owner of the dwelling unit and market rent is the rent paid by the renter in the first period after a rental contract has been negotiated. In a normal economy which is experiencing moderate or low general inflation, typically market rent will be higher than contract rent. However, if there are rent controls or a temporary glut of rental units, then market rent could be lower than contract rent. In any case, it can be seen that if we value the services of an owner occupied dwelling at its current opportunity cost on the rental market, we should be using market rent rather than contract rent.

The rents used to estimate the cost of rented dwellings in the Japanese CPI is the aggregate of rents paid for rental accommodation. These rents include a combination

[18]This issue will be discussed in more detail in Sect. 6.16 below.

[19]However, it could be argued that these extra services that might be included in the rent are mainly a weighting issue; i.e., it could be argued that the *trend* in the homeowner's estimated rent would be a reasonably accurate estimate of the trend in the rents after adjusting for the extra services included in the rent.

[20]For example, according to the 2013 Japanese Housing and Land Survey, the average floor space (size) of owner occupied housing in Tokyo was 110.64 m^2 for single family houses and 82.71 m^2 for rental housing, a difference of over 30 m^2. For condominiums, an even greater discrepancy exists: the average floor space is 65.73 m^2 for owner-occupied housing and 37.64 m^2 for rental housing. Moreover, in addition to the difference in floor space between rented and owned units, the quality of the owned units tends to be higher than the rented units and these quality differences need to be taken into account.

of newly signed rental contracts and rollover contracts for existing tenants. It is appropriate to use both types of contract to measure the actual cost of rental housing (but of course, these rents should be quality adjusted for depreciation and other changes in quality). But it is not appropriate to use both types of contract to impute rents for owner occupied housing: only market rents should be used. It is known that price adjustments are basically not made for rollover contracts (i.e. renewed leases). As a result, it is to be expected that new contract rents determined freely by the market will diverge considerably from rollover contract rents.[21]

Genesove (2003), based on a study using individual data from the American Housing Survey and survey research, analyzed the stickiness of rents by dividing them into new contracts and rollover contracts.

In Japan, Shimizu et al. (2010b), Shimizu and Watanabe (2011) used data from a housing listing magazine and a property management company to measure the extent of housing rent stickiness in the country and analyzed the micro structure of rental adjustments.

In the following section, we provide an introduction to user cost theory for a non-housing durable good. In subsequent sections, we will deal with the problems associated with measuring depreciation and the aggregation of user costs over different ages of the same good. And later yet, we will look at the additional difficulties that are associated with the formation of user costs for housing.

6.4 The User Cost Approach for Pricing the Services of a Non-housing Durable Good

The user cost approach to the treatment of durable goods is in some ways very simple: it calculates the cost of purchasing the durable at the beginning of the period, using the services of the durable during the period and then netting off from these costs the benefit that could be obtained by selling the durable good at the end of the period. However, there are several details of this procedure that are somewhat controversial. These details involve the use of opportunity costs, which are usually imputed costs, the treatment of interest and the treatment of capital gains or holding gains.

Another complication with the user cost approach is that it involves making distinctions between current period (flow) purchases within the period under consideration and the holdings of physical stocks of the durable at the beginning and the end of the accounting period. Typically, when constructing a consumer price index, we think of all quantity purchases as taking place at a single point in time, say the middle of the period under consideration, at the (unit value) average prices for the period. In constructing user costs, prices at the beginning and end of an accounting period play an important role.

To determine the net cost of using a durable good during say period 0, it is assumed that one unit of the durable good is purchased at the beginning of period 0 at the price

[21] On this point, see also Lewis and Restieaux (2015).

P^0. The "used" or "second-hand" durable good can be sold at the end of period 0 at the price P_S^1.[22] It might seem that a reasonable *net cost* for the use of one unit of the consumer durable during period 0 is its initial purchase price P^0 less its end of period 0 "scrap value", P_S^1. However, *money received at the end of the period is not as valuable as money that is received at the beginning of the period.* Thus in order to convert the end of period value into its beginning of the period equivalent value, it is necessary to *discount* the term P_S^1 by the term $1 + r^0$ where r^0 is the beginning of period 0 nominal interest rate that the consumer faces. Hence the *period 0 user cost* u^0 for the consumer durable[23] is defined as

$$u^0 \equiv P^0 - P_S^1/(1 + r^0). \tag{6.1}$$

There is another way to view the user cost formula (6.1): the consumer purchases the durable at the beginning of period 0 at the price P^0 and charges himself or herself the rental price u^0. The remainder of the purchase price, I^0, defined as

$$I^0 \equiv P^0 - u^0 \tag{6.2}$$

can be regarded as an *investment*, which is to yield the appropriate opportunity cost of capital r^0 that the consumer faces. At the end of period 0, this rate of return could be realized provided that I^0, r^0 and the selling price of the durable at the end of the period P_S^1 satisfy the following equation:

$$I^0(1 + r^0) = P_S^1. \tag{6.3}$$

Given P_S^1 and r^0, (6.3) determines I^0, which in turn, given P^0, determines the user cost u^0 via (6.2).[24]

Thus user costs are not like the prices of nondurables or services because the user cost concept involves pricing the durable at *two* points in time rather than at a single point in time. Because the user cost concept involves prices at two points in time, money received or paid out at the first point in time is more valuable than money paid out or received at the second point in time and so *interest rates* creep into the user cost formula. Furthermore, because the user cost concept involves prices at two points in time, *expected prices* can be involved if the user cost is calculated at the beginning of the period under consideration instead of at the end. With all of these complications, it is no wonder that many price statisticians would like to avoid using user costs as a pricing concept. However, even for price statisticians who would prefer to use the rental equivalence approach to the treatment of durables over the

[22]Note that this approach to pricing the services of a durable good assumes the existence of second hand markets for units of the durable that have aged. This assumption may not be satisfied for many consumer durables including unique assets such as dwelling units and works of art, which are not bought and sold every period. We will deal with this situation later in Sect. 6.12.

[23]This approach to the derivation of a user cost formula was used by Diewert (1974) who in turn based it on an approach due to Hicks (1946; 326).

[24]This derivation for the user cost of a consumer durable was also made by Diewert (1974; 504).

user cost approach, there is some justification for considering the user cost approach in some detail, since this approach gives insights into the economic determinants of the *rental* or *leasing price* of a durable.

The user cost formula (6.1) can be put into a more familiar form if the period 0 *economic depreciation rate* δ and the period 0 ex post *asset inflation rate* i^0 are defined. Define δ by:

$$(1-\delta) \equiv P_S^1/P^1 \tag{6.4}$$

where P_S^1 is the price of a one period old used asset at the end of period 0 and P^1 is the price of a new asset at the end of period 0. Typically, if a new asset and a one period older asset are sold at the same time, then the new asset will be worth more than the used asset and hence δ will be a positive number between 0 and 1. The *period 0 inflation rate* for the new asset, i^0, is defined by:

$$1+i^0 \equiv P^1/P^0. \tag{6.5}$$

Eliminating P^1 from Eqs. (6.4) and (6.5) leads to the following formula for the *end of period 0 used asset price*:

$$P_S^1 = (1-\delta)(1+i^0)P^0. \tag{6.6}$$

Substitution of (6.6) into (6.1) yields the following expression for the *period 0 user cost* u^0:

$$u^0 = [(1+r^0) - (1-\delta)(1+i^0)]P^0/(1+r^0). \tag{6.7}$$

Note that $r^0 - i^0$ can be interpreted as a period 0 *real interest rate* and $\delta(1+i^0)$ can be interpreted as an *inflation adjusted depreciation rate*.

The user cost u^0 is expressed in terms of prices that are discounted to the *beginning* of period 0. However, it is also possible to express the user cost in terms of prices that are "anti-discounted" or *appreciated* to the *end* of period 0.[25] Thus define the *end of period 0 user cost* p^0 as[26]:

---

[25]Thus the beginning of the period user cost u^0 discounts all monetary costs and benefits into their dollar equivalent at the beginning of period 0 whereas p^0 discounts (or appreciates) all monetary costs and benefits into their dollar equivalent at the end of period 0. This leaves open how flow transactions that take place within the period should be treated. Following the conventions used in financial accounting suggests that flow transactions taking place within the accounting period be regarded as taking place at the end of the accounting period and hence following this convention, end of period user costs should be used by the price statistician; see Peasnell (1981).

[26]Christensen and Jorgenson (1969) derived a user cost formula similar to (6.7) in a different way using a continuous time optimization model. If the inflation rate i equals 0, then the user cost formula (6.7) reduces to that derived by Walras (1954; 269) (first edition 1874). This zero inflation rate user cost formula was also derived by the industrial engineer A. Church (1901; 907–908), who perhaps drew on the work of Matheson: "In the case of a factory where the occupancy is assured for a term of years, and the rent is a first charge on profits, the rate of interest, to be an appropriate rate, should, so far as it applies to the buildings, be equal (including the depreciation rate) to the

$$p^0 \equiv (1 + r^0)u^0 = [(1 + r^0) - (1 - \delta)(1 + i^0)]P^0 \tag{6.8}$$

where the last equation follows using (6.7). If the real interest rate r^{0*} is defined as the nominal interest rate r^0 less the asset inflation rate i^0 and the small term δi^0 is neglected, then the end of the period user cost defined by (6.8) reduces to:

$$p^0 = (r^{0*} + \delta)P^0. \tag{6.9}$$

Abstracting from transactions costs and inflation, it can be seen that the end of the period user cost defined by (6.9) is an *approximate rental cost*; i.e., the rental cost for the use of a consumer (or producer) durable good should equal the (real) opportunity cost of the capital tied up, $r^{0*}P^0$, plus the decline in value of the asset over the period, δP^0. Formulae (6.8) and (6.9) thus cast some light on what are the economic determinants of rental or leasing prices for consumer durables.

If the simplified user cost formula defined by (6.9) above is used, then at first glance, forming a price index for the user cost of a durable good is not very much more difficult than forming a price index for the purchase price of the durable good, P^0. The price statistician needs only to:

- Make a reasonable assumption as to what an appropriate monthly or quarterly real interest rate r^{0*} should be;
- Make an assumption as to what a reasonable monthly or quarterly depreciation rate δ should be[27];
- Collect purchase prices P^0 for the durable and use formula (6.9) to calculate the simplified user cost.[28]

If it is thought necessary to implement the more complicated user cost formula (6.8) in place of the simpler formula (6.9), then the situation is more complicated. As it stands, the end of the period user cost formula (6.8) is an ex post (or after the fact) *user cost*: the asset inflation rate i^0 cannot be calculated until the end of period

---

rental which a landlord who owned but did not occupy a factory would let it for." Matheson (1910; 169), first published in 1884. Additional derivations of user cost formulae in discrete time have been made by Katz (1983; 408–409), Diewert (2005a). Hall and Jorgenson (1967) introduced tax considerations into user cost formulae.

[27]The geometric model for depreciation to be explained in more detail in Sect. 6.6 below requires only a single monthly or quarterly depreciation rate. Other models of depreciation may require the estimation of a sequence of vintage depreciation rates. If the estimated annual geometric depreciation rate is δ_a, then the corresponding monthly geometric depreciation rate δ can be obtained by solving the equation $(1 - \delta)^{12} = 1 - \delta_a$. Similarly, if the estimated annual real interest rate is r_a^*, then the corresponding monthly real interest rate r^* can be obtained by solving the equation $(1 + r^*)^{12} = 1 + r_a^*$.

[28]Iceland uses a variant of the simplified user cost formula (6.9) to estimate the services of OOH with a real interest rate approximately equal to 4% and depreciation rate of 1.25%. The depreciation rate is relatively low because it is applied to the entire property value and not to just the structure portion of property value; see Gudnason and Jonsdottir (2011). Eurostat (2005) also uses a simplified user cost formula. Additional simplified user cost formulae have been developed by Hill et al. (2017) and many others.

0 has been reached. Formula (6.8) can be converted into an ex ante (or before the fact) *user cost* formula if i^0 is interpreted as an *anticipated asset inflation rate*. The resulting formula should approximate a market rental rate for the durable good.[29]

Note that in the user cost approach to the treatment of consumer durables, the *entire* user cost formula (6.8) or (6.9) is the period 0 price. Thus in the time series context, it is *not* necessary to deflate each component of the formula *separately*; the period 0 price $p^0 \equiv [r^0 - i^0 + \delta(1 + i^0)]P^0$ is compared to the corresponding period 1 price, $p^1 \equiv [r^1 - i^1 + \delta(1 + i^1)]P^1$ and so on.

In principle, depreciation rates can be estimated using information on the selling prices of used units of the durable good.[30] However, for housing, the situation is more complex, as will be explained later.

We conclude this introductory section by noting some practical problems that statistical agencies will face when calculating user costs for durable goods[31]:

- It is difficult to determine what the relevant nominal interest rate r^0 is for each household. If a consumer has to borrow to finance the cost of a durable good purchase, then this interest rate will typically be much higher than the safe rate of return that would be the appropriate opportunity cost rate of return for a consumer who had no need to borrow funds to finance the purchase.[32] It may be necessary to simply use a benchmark interest rate that would be determined by either the government, a national statistical agency or an accounting standards board.[33]

---

[29]Since landlords must set their rent at the beginning of the period (and in fact, they usually set their rent for an extended period of time), if the user cost approach is used to model the economic determinants of market rental rates, then the asset inflation rate i^0 should be interpreted as *an expected inflation rate* rather than an after the fact actual inflation rate. This use of ex ante prices in this price measurement context should be contrasted with the preference of national accountants to use actual or ex post prices in the system of national accounts.

[30]For housing, the situation is more complex because typically, a dwelling unit is a *unique good*; its location is a price determining characteristic and each housing unit has a unique location and thus is a unique good. It also changes its character over time due to renovations and depreciation of the structure. Thus the treatment of housing is much more difficult than the treatment of other durable goods. Note that the definitions (6.4) and (6.5) of the depreciation rate δ and the asset inflation rate i^0 implicitly assumed that prices for a new asset and a one period old asset were available in both periods 0 and 1. This assumption is not satisfied for a unique asset.

[31]For additional material on difficulties with the user cost approach, see Diewert (1980; 475–479), Katz (1983; 415–422).

[32]Katz (1983; 415–416) comments on the difficulties involved in determining the appropriate rate of interest to use: "There are numerous alternatives: a rate on financial borrowings, on savings, and a weighted average of the two; a rate on nonfinancial investments. e.g., residential housing, perhaps adjusted for capital gains; and the consumer's subjective rate of time preference. Furthermore, there is some controversy about whether it should be the maximum observed rate, the average observed rate, or the rate of return earned on investments that have the same degree of risk and liquidity as the durables whose services are being valued.".

[33]One way for choosing the nominal interest rate for period t, r^t, is to set it equal to $(1 + r^*)(1 + \rho^t) - 1$ where ρ^t is a consumer price inflation rate for period t and r^* is a reference real interest rate. The Australian Bureau of Statistics has used this method for determining r^t with $r^* \equiv 0.04$; i.e., a 4% real interest rate was chosen. Other methods for determining the appropriate interest rate that

- It will generally be difficult to determine what the relevant depreciation rate is for the consumer durable.[34]
- Ex post *user costs* based on formula (6.8) may be too volatile to be acceptable to users[35] (due to the volatility of the ex post asset inflation rate i^0) and hence an ex ante *user cost* concept may have to be used. For most durable goods, the asset inflation rates are smaller than the reference nominal interest rate so that subtracting an ex post asset inflation rate from the sum of the nominal interest rate plus the asset depreciation rate will usually lead to reasonably stable positive user costs. However, for durable goods with very low depreciation rates, like a housing structure or like land (which has a zero depreciation rate), the resulting ex post user costs may turn out to be negative for some periods. This means that the resulting negative user costs are not useful approximations to rental prices for these long lived durable goods. This creates difficulties in that different national statistical agencies will generally make different assumptions and use different methods in order to construct forecast inflation rates for structures and land and hence the resulting ex ante user costs of the durable may not be comparable across countries.[36]
- The user cost formula (6.8) should be generalized to accommodate various taxes that may be associated with the purchase of a durable or with the continuing use of the durable.[37]

---

should be inserted into user cost formula are discussed by Harper et al. (1989), Schreyer (2001), Hill et al. (2017).

[34]We will discuss geometric or declining balance depreciation and one hoss shay depreciation below. For references to the depreciation literature and for empirical methods for estimating depreciation rates, see Hulten and Wykoff (1981a, b, 1996), Beidelman (1973, 1976), Jorgenson (1996), Diewert and Lawrence (2000).

[35]Goodhart (2001; F351) commented on the practical difficulties of using ex post user costs for housing as follows: "An even more theoretical user cost approach is to measure the cost foregone by living in an owner occupied property as compared with selling it at the beginning of the period and repurchasing it at the end … But this gives the absurd result that as house prices rise, so the opportunity cost falls; indeed the more virulent the inflation of housing asset prices, the more negative would this measure become. Although it has some academic aficionados, this flies in the face of common sense; I am glad to say that no country has adopted this method." As noted above, Iceland and Eurostat have in fact adopted a simplified user cost framework which seems to work well enough. Moreover, the user cost concept is used widely in production function and productivity studies and by national statisticians who construct multifactor productivity accounts for their countries.

[36]For additional material on the difficulties involved in constructing ex ante user costs, see Diewert (1980; 475–486), Katz (1983; 419–420). For empirical comparisons of different user cost formulae, see Harper et al. (1989), Diewert and Lawrence (2000), Diewert and Fox (2018). In the latter paper, the authors calculated Jorgensonian (ex post) user costs for US land used in residential housing and found that negative user costs occurred. Diewert and Fox then replaced the ex post capital gains term in the user cost for land with the long term inflation rate for land over the previous rolling window of 25 years and this substitution led to positive user costs for land that were relatively smooth. Hill et al. (2017) also recommend the use of long run asset inflation rates to avoid chain drift in housing indexes based on user costs.

[37]For example, property taxes are associated with the use of housing services and hence should be included in the user cost formula; see Sect. 6.16 below. As Katz (1983; 418) noted, taxation issues

Some of the problems associated with estimating depreciation rates will be discussed in Sect. 6.6 below.

6.5 The Opportunity Cost Approach

The opportunity cost approach to the valuation of the services of a consumer durable during a time period is very easy to describe: the opportunity cost valuation is simply the *maximum* of the foregone rental or leasing price for the services of the durable during a period of time and the corresponding user cost for the durable. It is easy to see that when a household has a consumer durable in its possession, the household forgoes the money that one could earn by renting out the services of the durable good for the period of time under consideration. (Such rental markets may not exist, in which case, this opportunity cost is 0). Thus the rental equivalent (at current market rates) is one opportunity cost that the household incurs by continuing to own and use the services of the durable during the period. However, there is another opportunity cost that is applicable to using the services of the durable good during the period under consideration. By using the services of the durable good, the household also forgoes a *financial opportunity cost*. Thus the durable good could be sold on the second hand market at the beginning of the period at the price P^0. This amount of money could be invested in some financial instrument that earns the one period rate of return of r^0. Thus at the end of the period, the household would have accumulated $P^0(1 + r^0)$ dollars as a result of selling the consumer durable at the beginning of the period. Now suppose at the end of the period, the household buys back the consumer durable that it sold at the beginning of the period. The value of the durable good at the end of the period will be $(1 + i^0)(1 - \delta^0)P^0$ where i^0 is the asset appreciation rate over period 0 and δ^0 is the depreciation rate for the durable good. Thus the net opportunity cost of using the services of the durable for period 0 from the financial perspective is $P^0(1 + r^0) - (1 + i^0)(1 - \delta^0)P^0$ which is exactly the *end of period user cost* for the durable good that was derived earlier; see Eq. (6.8) above. A true opportunity cost for using the services of a durable good should equal the maximum of the benefits that are foregone by not using these services. Thus the opportunity cost approach to pricing the services of a consumer durable is equivalent to taking the maximum of the rent and user cost that the durable could generate over the period under consideration.[38]

---

also impact the choice of the interest rate: "Should the rate of return be a before or after tax rate?" From the viewpoint of a household that is not borrowing to finance the purchase of the durable, an after tax rate of return seems appropriate but from the point of a leasing firm, a before tax rate of return seems appropriate. This difference helps to explain why rental equivalence prices for the durable might be higher than user cost prices; see also Sect. 6.16 below.

[38]The opportunity cost approach to pricing the services of Owner Occupied Housing was first proposed by Diewert (2008). It was further developed by Diewert and Nakamura (2011), Diewert et al. (2009). To our knowledge, there have been only two studies that implemented the opportunity cost approach to the valuation of the services of OOH; see Shimizu et al. (2012), Aten (2018).

6.6 A General Model of Depreciation for Consumer Durables

In this section, a "general" model of depreciation for durable goods that appear on the market each period without undergoing quality change will be presented. In the following three sections, this general model will be specialized to the three most common models of depreciation that appear in the literature. In Sect. 6.11 below, the additional problems that occur when the durable is a unique good (or when second hand markets do not exist) will be discussed.

The main tool that can be used to identify depreciation rates for a durable good is the cross sectional sequence of asset prices classified by their age that units of the good sell for on the second hand market at any point of time.[39] Thus in order to apply this method of measurement, it is necessary that such second hand markets exist.

Some notation is required. Let P_0^t be the price of a newly produced unit of the durable good at the *beginning* of period t. Let P_v^t be the second hand market price at the beginning of period t of a unit of the durable good that is v periods old.[40] The *beginning of period t cross sectional depreciation rate* for a brand new unit of the durable good, δ_0^t, is defined as follows:

$$1 - \delta_0^t \equiv P_1^t / P_0^t. \tag{6.10}$$

Once δ_0^t has been defined by (6.10), the *period t cross sectional depreciation rate* for a unit of the durable good that is one period old at the beginning of period t, δ_1^t, can be defined using the following equation:

$$(1 - \delta_1^t)(1 - \delta_0^t) \equiv P_2^t / P_0^t. \tag{6.11}$$

Note that P_2^t is the beginning of period t asset price of a unit of the durable good that is 2 periods old and it is compared to the price of a brand new unit of the durable, P_0^t.

Given that the period t cross sectional depreciation rates for units of the durable that are $0, 1, 2, \ldots, v-1$ periods old at the beginning of period 0 are defined (these are the depreciation rates $\delta_0^t, \delta_1^t, \delta_2^t, \ldots, \delta_{v-1}^t$), then the *period t cross sectional depreciation rate for units of the durable that are v periods old* at the beginning of period t, δ_v^t, can be defined using the following equation:

---

[39] Another information source that could be used to identify depreciation rates for the durable good is the sequence of vintage rental or leasing prices that might exist for some consumer durables. In the closely related capital measurement literature, the general framework for an internally consistent treatment of capital services and capital stocks in a set of vintage accounts was set out by Jorgenson (1989), Hulten (1990; 127–129, 1996; 152–160).

[40] If these second hand vintage prices depend on how intensively the durable good has been used in previous periods, then it will be necessary to further classify the durable good not only by its vintage v but also according to the intensity of its use. In this case, think of the sequence of vintage asset prices P_v^t as corresponding to the prevailing market prices of the various vintages of the good at the beginning of period t for assets that have been used at "average" intensities.

$$(1 - \delta_v^t)(1 - \delta_{v-1}^t) \cdots (1 - \delta_1^t)(1 - \delta_0^t) \equiv P_{v+1}^t / P_0^t. \tag{6.12}$$

Thus it is clear how the sequence of *period 0 vintage asset prices* P_v^t can be converted into a sequence of *period t vintage depreciation rates*, δ_v^t. In the depreciation literature, it is usually assumed that the sequence of vintage depreciation rates, δ_v^t, is independent of the period t so that:

$$\delta_v^t = \delta_v \qquad \text{for all periods } t \text{ and all ages v.} \tag{6.13}$$

The above material shows how the sequence of vintage or used durable goods prices at a point in time can be used in order to estimate depreciation rates. This method for estimating depreciation rates using data on second hand assets, with a few extra modifications to account for differing ages of retirement, was pioneered by Beidelman (1973, 1976), Hulten and Wykoff (1981a, b, 1996).[41]

Recall the user cost formula for a new unit of the durable good under consideration which was defined by (6.1) above. The same approach can be used in order to define a sequence of period 0 user costs for all vintages v of the durable. Thus suppose that P_{v+1}^{1a} is the *anticipated end of period 0 price* of a unit of the durable good that is v periods old at the beginning of period 0 and let r^0 be the consumer's opportunity cost of capital for period 0. Then the discounted to the beginning of period 0 *user cost* of a unit of the durable good that is v periods old at the beginning of period 0, u_v^0, is defined as follows:

$$u_v^0 \equiv P_v^0 - P_{v+1}^{1a}/(1 + r^0); \qquad v = 0, 1, 2, \ldots \tag{6.14}$$

It is now necessary to specify how the *end* of period 0 anticipated vintage asset prices P_v^{1a} are related to their counterpart *beginning* of period 0 vintage asset prices P_v^0. The assumption that is made now is that the entire sequence of vintage asset prices at the end of period 0 is equal to the corresponding sequence of asset prices at the beginning of period 0 times a general anticipated period 0 inflation rate factor, $(1 + i^0)$, where i^0 is the *anticipated period 0 (general) asset inflation rate*. Thus it is assumed that[42]

$$P_v^{1a} = (1 + i^0) P_v^0; \qquad v = 0, 1, 2, \ldots \tag{6.15}$$

---

[41] See also Jorgenson (1996) for a review of the empirical literature on the estimation of depreciation rates.

[42] More generally, we assume that assumptions (6.15) hold for subsequent periods t as well; i.e., it is assumed that $P_v^{t+1a} = (1 + i^t) P_v^t$ for $v = 0, 1, 2, \ldots$ and $t = 0, 1, 2, \ldots$ where P_v^{t+1a} is the anticipated price of a unit of the durable good that is v periods old at the end of period t, i^t is a period t expected asset inflation rate for all ages of the durable and P_v^t is the second hand market price for a unit of the durable good that is v periods old at the beginning of period t.

Substituting (6.15) and (6.10)–(6.13) into (6.14) leads to the following beginning of *period 0 sequence of vintage user costs*[43]:

$$\begin{aligned} u_v^0 &= (1-\delta_{v-1})(1-\delta_{v-2})\cdots(1-\delta_0)[(1+r^0)-(1-\delta_v)(1+i^0)]P_0^0/(1+r^0) \\ &= (1-\delta_{v-1})(1-\delta_{v-2})\cdots(1-\delta_0)[r^0-i^0+\delta_v(1+i^0)]P_0^0/(1+r^0); \quad v=1,2,\ldots \end{aligned} \tag{6.16}$$

If $v=0$, then $u_0^0 \equiv [r^0-i^0+\delta_0(1+i^0)]P_0^0/(1+r^0)$ and this agrees with the user cost formula for a new purchase of the durable u^0 that was derived earlier in (6.7) (with our changes in notation; i.e., P^0 is now called P_0^0).

The sequence of vintage user costs u_v^0 defined by (6.16) are expressed in terms of prices that are discounted to the *beginning* of period 0. However, as was done in Sect. 6.4 above, it is also possible to express the user costs in terms of prices that are "anti-discounted" to the *end* of period 0. Thus define the sequence of vintage *end of period 0 user cost* p_v^0 as follows:

$$p_v^0 \equiv (1+r^0)u_v^0 = (1-\delta_{v-1})(1-\delta_{v-2})\cdots(1-\delta_0)[r^0-i^0+\delta_v(1+i^0)]P_0^0; \quad v=1,2,\ldots \tag{6.17}$$

with p_0^0 defined as follows:

$$p_0^0 \equiv (1+r^0)u_0^0 = [r^0-i^0+\delta_v(1+i^0)]P_0^0. \tag{6.18}$$

Thus if the price statistician has estimates for the vintage depreciation rates δ_v and the real interest rate r^{0*} and is able to collect a sample of prices for new units of the durable good P_0^0, then the sequence of vintage user costs defined by (6.17) can be calculated. To complete the model, the price statistician should gather information on the stocks held by the household sector of each vintage of the durable good and then normal index number theory can be applied to these p's and q's, with the p's being vintage user costs and the q's being the vintage stocks pertaining to each period. For some worked examples of this methodology under various assumptions about depreciation rates and the calculation of expected asset inflation rates, see Diewert and Lawrence (2000), Diewert (2005a).[44]

In the following three sections, the general methodology described above is specialized by making additional assumptions about the form of the vintage depreciation rates δ_v.[45]

[43]When $v=0$, define $\delta_{-1} \equiv 1$; i.e., the terms in front of the square brackets on the right hand side of (6.16) are set equal to 1.

[44]Additional examples and discussion can be found in two recent OECD Manuals on productivity measurement and the measurement of capital; see Schreyer (2001, 2009).

[45]In the case of one hoss shay depreciation, assumptions are made about the sequence of user costs, u_v^t, as the age v varies.

6.7 Geometric or Declining Balance Depreciation

The *declining balance method of depreciation* dates back to Matheson (1910; 55) at least.[46] In terms of the algebra presented in the previous section, the method is very simple: all of the cross sectional vintage depreciation rates δ_v^t defined by (6.10)–(6.12) are assumed to be equal to the same rate δ, where δ is a positive number less than one; i.e., for all time periods t and all vintages v, it is assumed that

$$\delta_v^t = \delta; \qquad v = 0, 1, 2, \ldots . \tag{6.19}$$

Substitution of (6.19) into (6.17) leads to the following formula for the sequence of *end of period 0 vintage user costs*:

$$\begin{aligned} p_v^0 &= (1-\delta)^v[r^0 - i^0 + \delta(1+i^0)]P^0; \qquad v = 0, 1, 2, \ldots \\ &= (1-\delta)^v p_0^0 \end{aligned} \tag{6.20}$$

where the second equation follows using definition (6.18). The second set of equations in (6.20) says *that all of the vintage user costs are proportional to the user cost for a new asset*. This proportionality means that it is not necessary to use an index number formula to aggregate over vintages to form a durable services aggregate. To see this, it is useful to calculate the aggregate value of services yielded by all vintages of the consumer durable at the beginning of period 0. Let q^{-v} be the quantity of the new durable purchased by the household sector v periods ago for $v = 1, 2, \ldots$ and let q^0 be the new purchases of the durable during period 0. The beginning of period 0 user cost for the holdings of the durable of age v will be p_v^0 defined by (6.20) above. Thus the aggregate value of services over all vintages of the good, including those purchased in period 0, will have the value v^0 defined as follows:

$$\begin{aligned} v^0 &= p_0^0 q^0 + p_1^0 q^{-1} + p_2^0 q^{-2} + \cdots \\ &= p_0^0 q^0 + (1-\delta) p_0^0 q^{-1} + (1-\delta)^2 p_0^0 q^{-2} + \cdots \qquad \text{using (6.20)} \\ &= p_0^0[q^0 + (1-\delta)q^{-1} + (1-\delta)^2 q^{-2} + \cdots] \\ &= p_0^0 Q^0 \end{aligned} \tag{6.21}$$

where the period 0 aggregate (quality adjusted) quantity of durable services consumed in period 0, Q^0, is defined as

$$Q^0 \equiv q^0 + (1-\delta)q^{-1} + (1-\delta)^2 q^{-2} + \cdots . \tag{6.22}$$

[46] A case for attributing the method to Walras (1954; 268–269) could be made but he did not lay out all of the details. Matheson (1910; 91) used the term "diminishing value" to describe the method. Hotelling (1925; 350) used the term "the reducing balance method" while Canning (1929; 276) used the term the "declining balance formula". For a modern exposition of the geometric model of depreciation, see Jorgenson (1989).

Thus the *period 0 services quantity aggregate* Q^0 is equal to new purchases of the durable in period 0, q^0, plus one minus the depreciation rate δ times the purchases of the durable in the previous period, q^{-1}, plus the square of one minus the depreciation rate times the purchases of the durable two periods ago, q^{-2}, and so on. The service price that can be applied to this quantity aggregate is p_0^0, the imputed rental price or user cost for a new unit of the durable purchased in period 0.

The above result greatly simplifies the valuation of consumer durables. Normally, the price statistician would have to keep track of all new purchases of the durable good by the reference population by period, calculate the relevant user costs p_v^0 and p_v^t for periods 0 and t, and apply the relevant index number formula (Laspeyres, Paasche, Fisher or whatever formula is being used in the CPI) to these age specific prices and quantities for periods 0 and t. But because under assumptions (6.13), (6.15) and (6.19), *all vintage user costs vary in a proportional manner over time*,[47] so any reasonable index number formula will find that the price index going from period 0 to t is equal to p_0^t/p_0^0, the ratio of user costs for a new unit of the durable good. Moreover the corresponding *aggregate quantity index* will be equal to Q^t/Q^0, where Q^0 is defined by (6.22) and Q^t is defined by

$$\begin{aligned} Q^t &\equiv q^t + (1-\delta)q^{t-1} + (1-\delta)^2 q^{t-2} + \cdots \\ &= q^t + (1-\delta)Q^{t-1}. \end{aligned} \tag{6.23}$$

Note that the second equation simplifies the calculation of the period t aggregate service flow (in real terms) over all vintages of the consumer durable: the period t aggregate flow, Q^t, is equal to period t new purchases of the durable, q^t, plus $(1-\delta)$ times the aggregate flow of services in the previous period, Q^{t-1}.

If the depreciation rate δ and the purchases of the durable in prior periods are known, then the aggregate service quantity Q^0 can readily be calculated using (6.22). Then using (6.21), it can be seen that the period 0 value of the services of the durable (over all vintages), v^0, decomposes into the price term p_0^0 times the quantity term Q^0. Hence, it is not necessary to use an index number formula to aggregate over vintages using this depreciation model.

The stock of consumer durables held by the household sector of a country should appear in the balance sheets of the country. Using the geometric model of depreciation, it is very easy to calculate the nominal and real value of the stock of consumer durables held by households. At time t, the stocks held by the household sector for the particular type of consumer durable under consideration are $q^t, q^{t-1}, q^{t-2}, \ldots$ and the corresponding asset prices by age of asset are $P_0^t, P_1^t, P_2^t, \ldots$. Assumptions

[47] Equation (6.20) for period t are the following ones: $p_v^t = (1-\delta)^v p_0^t$ for $v = 1, 2, \ldots$ and so the entire sequence of user costs by age of asset vary in a proportional manner over time under our assumptions. Thus an aggregate period t price for the entire group of assets of varying ages is p_0^t and the corresponding aggregate quantity will be Q^t defined by (6.23). This is an application of Hicks' (1946; 312–313) Aggregation Theorem: "Thus we have demonstrated mathematically the very important principle, used extensively in the text, that if the prices of a group of goods change in the same proportion, that group of goods behaves just as if it were a single commodity.".

(6.12), (6.13) and (6.19) imply that these period t asset prices satisfy the following equations:

$$P_v^t = (1-\delta)^v P_0^t; \qquad v = 1, 2, \ldots . \tag{6.24}$$

Equation (6.24) can be used to define period t *aggregate asset value* for the stocks held by households for the durable good over all ages of the durable good, V^t:

$$\begin{aligned} V^t &\equiv P_0^t q^t + P_1^t q^{t-1} + P_2^t q^{t-2} + P_3^t q^{t-3} + \cdots \\ &= P_0^t [q^t + (1-\delta)^1 q^{t-1} + (1-\delta)^2 q^{t-2} + \cdots] \quad \text{using (6.24)} \\ &= P_0^t Q^t \end{aligned} \tag{6.25}$$

where Q^t is defined by (6.23). Thus Q^t serves as a measure of the real capital stock of the consumer durable at the end of period t *and* it also serves as a measure of the real consumption services provided by this capital stock during period t.

The above algebra explains why the geometric model of depreciation is used so widely in production function studies and in the measurement of Total Factor Productivity or Multifactor Productivity in the production accounts of countries: it is very simple to work with![48]

6.8 Straight Line Depreciation

Another very common model of depreciation is the *straight line model*.[49] In this model, a most probable length of life for the durable is somehow determined, say L periods, so that after being used for L periods, the durable is scrapped. In the straight line depreciation model, it is assumed that the period 0 cross sectional vintage asset prices P_v^0 decline in a linear fashion relative to the period 0 price of a new asset P_0^0:

$$P_v^0 / P_0^0 = [L - v]/L \qquad \text{for } v = 0, 1, 2, \ldots, L-1. \tag{6.26}$$

For $v = L, L+1, \ldots$, it is assumed that $P_v^0 = 0$. Now use definitions (6.14) and (6.17) along with assumptions (6.15) in order to obtain the following sequence of *end of period 0 vintage user costs* for a unit of the durable good of age v at the beginning of period 0:

$$\begin{aligned} p_v^0 &= P_v^0(1+r^0) - (1+i^0)P_{v+1}^0 \qquad \text{for } v = 0, 1, 2, \ldots, L-1 \\ &= [1/L][(L-v)(1+r^0) - (L-v-1)(1+i^0)]P_0^0 \quad \text{using assumptions (6.26)} \\ &= [(r^0 - i^0)(L-v)L^{-1} + (1+i^0)L^{-1}]P_0^0. \end{aligned} \tag{6.27}$$

48 See Jorgenson (1989) who popularized the use of the geometric model of depreciation in production function and Total Factor Productivity studies.

49 This model of depreciation dates back to the late 1800s; see Matheson (1910; 55), Garcke and Fells (1893; 98) or Canning (1929; 265–266).

The user costs for units of the durable good that are older than L periods are zero; i.e., $p_v^0 \equiv 0$ for $v \geq L$. Looking at the terms in square brackets on the right hand side of (6.27), it can be seen that the first term $(r^0 - i^0)(L - v)P_0^0/L$ is a real interest opportunity cost for holding and using the unit of the durable that is v periods old (and this imputed real interest cost declines as the durable good ages; i.e., as the age v increases) and the second term $(1 + i^0)(1/L)P_0^0$ is an inflation adjusted depreciation term that is equal to the constant straight line depreciation rate $1/L$ times the adjustment factor for asset inflation over the period, $(1 + i^0)$, times the price of a new unit of the durable good P_0^0. Note that in period t, the corresponding end of period user cost for a unit of the durable good that is v periods old is $p_v^t \equiv [(r^t - i^t)(L - v)L^{-1} + (1 + i^t)L^{-1}]P_0^t$ for $v = 0, 1, 2, \ldots, L - 1$. Thus in both periods 0 and t, the sequences of end of period user costs by age, $\{p_v^0\}$ and $\{p_v^t\}$ for $v = 0, 1, 2, \ldots, L - 1$, are proportional to the price of a new unit of the durable for periods 0 and t, P_0^0 and P_0^t respectively[50] but if r^0 and/or i^0 change to a different r^t or i^t, then the factors of proportionality will change as we go from period 0 to t and so we cannot apply Hicks' Aggregation Theorem in this case. Thus in the case of changing nominal interest rates r and/or changing expected or actual asset price inflation rates, i^t, we cannot assume that the overall inflation rate between periods 0 and t for all ages of the durable good is equal to P_0^t/P_0^0 as was the case with the geometric model of depreciation. Thus for the straight line model of depreciation, it is necessary to keep track of household purchases of the durable for L periods and weight up each vintage quantity q^{-v} of these purchases by the corresponding end of period user costs vintage user cost p_v^0 defined by (6.27) for period 0 and a similar calculation of household holdings of the durable good by age for period t along with the period t counterparts to the period 0 user costs defined by (6.27) will be necessary. Once these vectors of prices and quantities have been calculated for both periods, then normal index number theory can be applied to get the overall price index for the household holdings of the durable good and this index can be used to deflate the user cost aggregate values to get an appropriate volume index.[51] Thus the straight line model of depreciation is considerably more complicated to implement than the geometric model of depreciation explained in the previous section.[52]

[50]Thus as the price of a new unit of the durable good changes over time, the value of depreciation will also change in line with the change in the price of the new unit. Thus economic depreciation as we have defined it is different from historical cost accounting depreciation which does not adjust depreciation allowances for changes in the levels of asset prices over time.

[51]Diewert and Lawrence (2000) noted this problem with the straight line model of depreciation; i.e., that in general, *an index number formula* should be used to aggregate over the different ages of the asset in order to obtain an aggregate of the capital services of the different vintages of the asset.

[52]However, if one is willing to assume that the reference interest rate for period t, r^t, and the expected asset inflation rate over all ages of the asset, i^t, both remain constant, then all reasonable index number formula will estimate the overall rate of user cost inflation between periods 0 and t as the new good price ratio, P_0^t/P_0^0. However, the assumption that r^t and i^t remain constant over time is only a rough approximation to reality. Note that in order to calculate real and nominal consumption of the durable (over all ages of the durable), it will be necessary to use the vintage user costs defined by (6.27) for a constant r and i to weight up past purchases of the durable good. Thus define the constants $\alpha_v \equiv [(r - i)(L - v)L^{-1} + (1 + i)L^{-1}]$

6.9 One Hoss Shay or Light Bulb Depreciation

The final model of depreciation that is in common use is the "light bulb" or *one hoss shay model of depreciation*.[53] In this model, the durable delivers the *same* services for each vintage: a chair is a chair, no matter what its age is (until it falls to pieces and is scrapped). Thus this model also requires an estimate of the most probable life L of the consumer durable.[54] In this model, it is assumed that the sequence of vintage beginning of the period user costs u_v^0 defined by (6.14) and (6.15) is *constant* for all vintages younger than the asset lifetime L; i.e., it is assumed that

$$u_v^0 \equiv P_v^0 - (1+i^0)P_{v+1}^0/(1+r^0) = u^0; \qquad v = 0, 1, 2, \ldots, L-1 \tag{6.28}$$

where $u^0 > 0$ is a constant. Equation (6.28) can be rewritten in the following form:

$$u^0 = P_v^0 - \gamma P_{v+1}^0; \qquad v = 0, 1, 2, \ldots, L-1 \tag{6.29}$$

where the *discount factor* γ is defined as

$$\gamma \equiv (1+i^0)/(1+r^0) = 1/(1+r^{0*}). \tag{6.30}$$

The interest rate r^{0*} can be regarded as an *asset specific real interest rate*; i.e., $1 + r^{0*} \equiv (1+r^0)/(1+i^0)$ so that one plus the nominal interest rate r^0 is deflated by one plus the expected asset price inflation rate, i^0. Note that Eq. (6.29) can be rewritten as follows:

$$P_v^0 = u^0 + \gamma P_{v+1}^0; \qquad v = 0, 1, 2, \ldots, L-1. \tag{6.31}$$

---

for $v = 0, 1, 2, \ldots, L-1$ and $\alpha_v \equiv 0$ for $v \geq L$. Then the period t *nominal value of durable services* is defined as $v^t \equiv p_0^t q^t + p_1^t q^{t-1} + p_2^t q^{t-2} + \cdots + p_{L-1}^t q^{t-L+1} = \alpha_0 P_0^t q^t + \alpha_1 P_0^t q^{t-1} + \alpha_2 P_0^t q^{t-2} + \cdots + \alpha_{L-1} P_0^t q^{t-L+1} = P_0^t Q^t$ where Q^t is the real value or volume of durable services defined as $Q^t \equiv \alpha_0 q^t + \alpha_1 q^{t-1} + \alpha_2 q^{t-2} + \cdots + \alpha_{L-1} q^{t-L+1}$. Define $\beta_v \equiv (L-v)/L$ for $v = 0, 1, 2, \ldots, L-1$. The period t *asset value* of consumer holdings of the durable good is defined as $V^t \equiv P_0^t q^t + P_1^t q^{t-1} + P_2^t q^{t-2} + \cdots + P_{L-1}^t q^{t-L+1} = P_0^t[\beta_0 q^t + \beta_1 q^{t-1} + \beta_2 q^{t-2} + \cdots + \beta_{L-1} q^{t-L+1}] = P_0^t Q^{t*}$ where we have used assumptions (6.26) applied to period t and the real value of durable stocks held by households at the end of period t is defined as $Q^{t*} \equiv \beta_0 q^t + \beta_1 q^{t-1} + \beta_2 q^{t-2} + \cdots + \beta_{L-1} q^{t-L+1}$. The decomposition of V^t into $P_0^t Q^{t*}$ does not require the assumption of constant r^t and i^t.

[53]This model can be traced back to Böhm-Bawerk (1891; 342). For a more comprehensive exposition, see Hulten (1990; 124) or Diewert (2005a).

[54]The assumption of a single life L for a durable can be relaxed using a methodology due to Hulten: "We have thus far taken the date of retirement T to be the same for all assets in a given cohort (all assets put in place in a given year). However, there is no reason for this to be true, and the theory is readily extended to allow for different retirement dates. A given cohort can be broken into components, or subcohorts, according to date of retirement and a separate T assigned to each. Each subcohort can then be characterized by its own efficiency sequence, which depends among other things on the subcohort's useful life T_i." Hulten (1990; 125).

Use Eq. (6.31) with $v = 0$ to express P_0^0 in terms of u^0 and P_1^0. Now use (6.31) with $v = 1$ to express P_2^0 in terms of u^0 and P_1^0 and then substitute out P_1^0 using the previous expression that expressed P_1^0 in terms of P_0^0 and u^0. Continue this substitution process until finally it ends after L such substitutions when P_L^0 is reached and of course, P_L^0 equals zero. The following equation is obtained:

$$\begin{aligned} P_0^0 &= u^0 + \gamma u^0 + \gamma^2 u^0 + \cdots + \gamma^{L-1} u^0 \\ &= u^0[1 + \gamma + \gamma^2 + \cdots + \gamma^{L-1}] \\ &= \{u^0/(1-\gamma)\} - \{u^0\gamma^L/(1-\gamma)\} \qquad \text{provided that } \gamma < 1 \\ &= u^0(1-\gamma^L)/(1-\gamma). \end{aligned} \tag{6.32}$$

Now[55] use the last equation in (6.32) in order to solve for the constant over vintages (beginning of the period) *user cost* for this model, u^0, in terms of the period 0 price for a new unit of the durable, P_0^0, and the discount factor γ defined by (6.31):

$$u^0 = (1-\gamma)P_0^0/(1-\gamma^L) = u_v^0; \qquad v = 0, 1, 2, \ldots, L-1. \tag{6.33}$$

The sequence of *end of period 0 user cost*, p_v^0, is as usual, equal to the corresponding beginning of the period 0 user cost, u_v^0, times the period 0 nominal interest rate factor, $1 + r^0$:

$$p_v^0 \equiv (1+r^0)u_v^0 = [1+r^0][1-\gamma^0][1-(\gamma^0)^L]^{-1}P_0^0 = p_0^0; \qquad v = 0, 1, 2, \ldots, L-1 \tag{6.34}$$

and $p_v^0 = 0$ for $v = L, L+1, \ldots$ and $\gamma^0 \equiv (1+i^0)/(1+r^0)$.

The *aggregate services of all vintages* of the good for period 0, including those purchased in period 0, will have the following value, v^0:

$$\begin{aligned} v^0 &= p_0^0 q^0 + p_1^0 q^{-1} + p_2^0 q^{-2} + \cdots + p_{L-1}^0 q^{-(L-1)} \\ &= p_0^0[q^0 + q^{-1} + q^{-2} + \cdots + q^{-(L-1)}] \\ &= p_0^0 Q^0 \end{aligned} \tag{6.35}$$

where the *period 0 aggregate (quality adjusted) quantity of durable services* consumed in period 0, Q^0, is defined as follows for this depreciation model:

$$Q^0 \equiv q^0 + q^{-1} + q^{-2} + \cdots + q^{-(L-1)}. \tag{6.36}$$

Thus in this model of depreciation, the service quantity aggregate is the simple sum of household purchases over the last L periods.[56] As was the case with the geo-

---

[55]If $\gamma \geq 1$, then use the second equation in (6.32) to express u^0 in terms of P_0^0 and the various powers of γ.

[56]In the national income accounting literature, this measure is sometimes called the gross capital stock.

metric depreciation model, the one hoss shay model does not require index number aggregation over vintages when calculating aggregate services from all vintages of the durable: there is a constant service price p_0^0 for all assets that are less than L periods old and the associated period 0 quantity Q^0 is the simple sum defined by (6.36) over the purchases of the last L periods for the one hoss shay model.[57]

The first two models of depreciation considered in Sects. 6.6 and 6.7 made assumptions about the pattern of depreciation rates for durables of different ages. The model in this section made assumptions about the pattern of user costs for durable goods of different ages. For a more general model of depreciation that allows for an arbitrary pattern of user costs by age of asset, see Diewert and Wei (2017).

How can the different models of depreciation be distinguished empirically? For durable goods that do not change in quality over time, there are *three possible methods* for determining the sequence of vintage depreciation rates[58]:

- By making a rough estimate of the average length of life L for the durable good and then by *assuming* a depreciation model that seems most appropriate.[59]
- By using cross sectional information on used durable prices at a single point in time and then using Eqs. (6.10)–(6.12) above to determine the corresponding sequence of vintage depreciation rates.
- By using cross sectional information on the rental or leasing prices of the durable as a function of the age of the durable and then Eqs. (6.17) and (6.18), along with information on the appropriate nominal interest rate r^0 and expected durables inflation rate i^0 along with information on the price of a new unit of the durable good P^0 can be used to determine the corresponding sequence of vintage depreciation rates.

6.10 The Relationship Between User Costs and Acquisition Costs

In this section, the user cost approach to the treatment of consumer durables will be compared to the acquisitions approach. Obviously, in the short run, the value flows associated with each approach could be very different. For example, if real

---

[57]Using Eq. (6.31), it can be shown that $P_v^0 = u^0[1 + (\gamma^0) + (\gamma^0)^2 + \cdots + (\gamma^0)^{L-1-v}]$ for $v = 0, 1, 2, \ldots, L-1$ where $\gamma^0 \equiv (1+i^0)/(1+r^0)$ and $P_v^0 = 0$ for $v \geq L$. Thus the period 0 value of the stock of consumer durables is $\sum_{v=0}^{L-1} P_v^0 q^{-v}$. The corresponding asset prices for period t are equal to $P_v^t = u^t[1 + (\gamma^t) + (\gamma^t)^2 + \cdots + (\gamma^t)^{L-1-v}]$ for $v = 0, 1, 2, \ldots, L-1$ where $u^t \equiv [1 - (\gamma^t)]P_0^t/[1 - (\gamma^t)^L]$, $\gamma^t \equiv (1+i^t)/(1+r^t)$ and $P_v^t = 0$ for $v \geq L$. The period t value of the stock of consumer durables is $\sum_{v=0}^{L-1} P_v^t q^{t-v}$. An index number formula will have to be used to form aggregate price and quantity indexes for the *stocks* of consumer durables using the one hoss shay model of depreciation.

[58]These three classes of methods were noted in Malpezzi et al. (1987; 373–375) in the housing context.

[59]A length of life L is can be converted into an equivalent geometric depreciation rate δ by setting δ equal to a number between $1/L$ and $2/L$.

interest rates, $r^0 - i^0$, are very high and the economy is in a severe recession or depression, then purchases of new consumer durables, q^0 say, could be very low and even approach 0 for very long lived assets, like houses. On the other hand, using the user cost approach, existing stocks of consumer durables would be carried over from previous periods and priced out at the appropriate user costs and the resulting consumption value flow could be quite large. Thus in the short run, the monetary values of consumption under the two approaches could be vastly different. Hence, in what follows, a (hypothetical) longer run comparison is considered where real interest rates are held constant.[60]

Suppose that in period 0, the reference population of households purchased q^0 units of a consumer durable at the purchase price P^0. Then *the period 0 value of consumption from the viewpoint of the acquisitions approach* is:

$$V_A^0 \equiv P^0 q^0. \tag{6.37}$$

Recall that the end of period user cost for one new unit of the asset purchased at the beginning of period 0 was p^0 defined by (6.8) above. In order to simplify the analysis, the *geometric model of depreciation* is assumed; i.e., at the beginning of period 0, a one period old asset is worth $(1 - \delta)P^0$, a two period old asset is worth $(1 - \delta)^2 P^0$, ... , a t period old asset is worth $(1 - \delta)^t P^0$, etc. Under these hypotheses, the corresponding end of period 0 user cost for a new asset purchased at the beginning of period 0 is p^0; the end of period 0 user cost for a one period old asset at the beginning of period 0 is $(1 - \delta)p^0$; the corresponding user cost for a two period old asset at the beginning of period 0 is $(1 - \delta)^2 p^0; \ldots;$ the corresponding user cost for a t period old asset at the beginning of period 0 is $(1 - \delta)^t p^0$; etc. The final simplifying assumption is that household purchases of the consumer durable have been growing at the geometric rate g into the indefinite past. This means that if household purchases of the durable were q^0 in period 0, then in the previous period they purchased $q^0/(1 + g)$ new units, two periods ago, they purchased $q^0/(1 + g)^2$ new units, ..., t periods ago, they purchased $q^0/(1 + g)^t$ new units, etc. Putting all of these assumptions together, it can be seen that *the period 0 value of consumption services from the viewpoint of the user cost approach* is:

$$\begin{aligned} V_U^0 &\equiv p^0q^0 + [(1-\delta)p^0q^0/(1+g)] + [(1-\delta)^2 p^0q^0/(1+g)^2] + \cdots \\ &= (1+g)p^0q^0/(g+\delta) \qquad \text{summing the infinite series} \\ &= (1+g)[(1+r^0) - (1-\delta)(1+i^0)]P^0q^0/(g+\delta) \qquad \text{using (6.8).} \end{aligned} \tag{6.38}$$

Equation (6.38) can be simplified by letting the asset inflation rate i^0 be 0 (or by replacing $r^0 - i^0$ by the real interest rate r^{0*} and by ignoring the small term δi^0) and under these conditions, the ratio of the user cost flow of consumption (6.38) to the acquisitions measure of consumption in period 0, (6.37) is:

[60] The following material is based on Diewert (2002).

$$V_U^0/V_A^0 = (1+g)(r^{0*}+\delta)/(g+\delta). \tag{6.39}$$

Using formula (6.39), it can be seen that if $1+g>0$ and $\delta+g>0$, then V_U^0/V_A^0 will be greater than unity if $r^{0*}>g(1-\delta)/(1+g)$, a condition that will usually be satisfied. Thus under normal conditions and over a longer time horizon, *household expenditures on consumer durables using the user cost approach will tend to exceed the corresponding expenditures on new purchases of the consumer durable*. Since the value of consumption services using the rental equivalence approach will tend to approximate the value of consumption services using the user cost approach, it can be seen that the acquisitions approach to household expenditures will tend to understate the value of consumption services estimated by the user cost and rental equivalence approaches. The difference between the user cost and acquisitions approach will tend to grow as the depreciation rate δ decreases.

To get a rough idea of the possible magnitude of the value ratio for the two approaches, V_U^0/V_A^0, Eq. (6.39) is evaluated for a "housing" example using annual data where the depreciation rate is 2% (i.e., $\delta=0.02$), the real interest rate is 3% (i.e., $r^{0*}=0.03$) and the growth rate for the production of new houses is 1% (i.e., $g=0.01$). In this base case, the ratio of user cost expenditures on housing to the purchases of new housing in the same period, V_U^0/V_A^0, is 1.68. If the depreciation rate is *decreased* to 1%, then V_U^0/V_A^0 *increases* to 2.02. If the real interest rate is *decreased* to 2% (with $\delta=0.02$ and $g=0.01$) then V_U^0/V_A^0 *decreases* to 1.35 while if the real interest rate is *increased* to 4%, then V_U^0/V_A^0 *increases* to 2.02. *Thus an acquisitions approach to housing in the CPI is likely to give a substantially smaller weight to housing services than a user cost approach would give.*

However, or shorter lived consumer durables like clothing, the difference between the acquisitions approach and the user cost approach will not be so large and hence, the acquisitions approach can be justified as being an approximately "correct" as a measure of consumption services for these high depreciation rate durable goods.[61]

[61]Let $r^{0*}=0.03$, $g=0.01$ and $\delta=0.2$. Under these assumptions, using (6.39), we find that $V_U^0/V_A^0=1.11$; i.e., using a geometric depreciation rate of 20%, the user cost approach leads to an estimated value of consumption that is 11% higher than the acquisitions approach under the conditions specified. Thus the acquisitions approach for consumer durables with high depreciation rates is probably satisfactory. However, for longer lived durables such as houses, automobiles and household furnishings, it would be useful for a national statistical agency to produce user costs for these goods and for the national accounts division to produce the corresponding consumption flows as "analytic series". This would extend the present national accounts treatment of housing to other long lived consumer durables. Note also that this revised treatment of consumption in the national accounts would tend to make rich countries richer, since poorer countries hold fewer long lived consumer durables on a per capita basis.

6.11 Calculating User Costs for Unique Durable Goods

Calculating rental prices or user costs for durable goods that are unique so that second hand markets for this type of good are either very thin or nonexistent will in general be impossible. Examples of such goods are paintings and unique jewels.[62] It should be noted that dwelling units are also examples of unique goods in that the location of each dwelling unit is unique and a house at a certain location does not remain the same over time due to renovations and depreciation of the structure. However, as we shall see in subsequent sections, the measurement situation is not so dire with respect to measuring housing service as it is for measuring valuable services.

As was mentioned above, it is impossible to measure the services of a unique good that never trades. If the good trades sporadically, it is possible to make estimates of the service flows generated by the good between sales of the good in an ex post fashion. We will indicate how this can be done below. The resulting estimates will not be very accurate but some kind of estimate is probably better than no estimate at all.

Suppose that a valuable is purchased at the beginning of period 0 at the price P^0 and it is sold at the beginning of period T at the price P^T. It is assumed that both asset prices are observed and there is an average *one period nominal interest rate r* that provides an opportunity cost of borrowing or lending for the owner of the asset over the T periods. An average *geometric asset inflation rate i* for the asset over the T periods is defined as follows:

$$1 + i \equiv [P^T/P^0]^{1/T}. \tag{6.40}$$

We assume that the purchase price of the asset, P^0, is set equal to the discounted imputed flow of services that the asset generates for its owner plus the discounted selling price of the asset at the beginning of period T; i.e., we assume that the following equation holds:

$$P^0 = u^0 + \gamma u^1 + \gamma^2 u^2 + \cdots + \gamma^{T-1} u^{T-1} + (1+r)^{-T} P^T \tag{6.41}$$

where u^t is the constant quality consumption value for the durable's services in period t[63] for $t = 0, 1, \ldots, T-1$ and the *discount factor* γ is defined as follows:

$$\gamma \equiv (1+i)/(1+r). \tag{6.42}$$

Make the further assumption that the quality of the service rendered by the unique durable good is constant over the T periods so that:

$$u^t = u^0; \qquad t = 1, 2, \ldots, T-1. \tag{6.43}$$

---

[62] In the international System of National Accounts, these unique goods are listed as valuables.

[63] The nominal imputed user cost for period t is $(1+i)^t u^t$.

Substitution of assumptions (6.43) into (6.41) enables one to solve for u^0:

$$u^0 = [P^0 - P^T(1+r)^{-T}]/[1+\gamma+\gamma^2+\cdots+\gamma^{T-1}]. \tag{6.44}$$

Once u^0 has been calculated, the sequence of imputed rental prices for the unique asset for periods $0, 1, \ldots, T-1$ is u^0, $(1+i)u^0$, $(1+i)^2u^0, \ldots, (1+i)^{T-1}u^0$. The corresponding quantities are all equal to 1. Note that these computations can only be done once P^T is known; i.e., these user cost valuations cannot be made until period T occurs.

The above analysis assumes that $P^0 > P^T/(1+r)^T$ which ensures that $u^0 > 0$. If $P^0 = P^T/(1+r)^T$, then $u^0 = 0$ and the services of the valuable for the T periods are provided to the owner at no (imputed) charge! If $P^0 < P^T/(1+r)^T$, then $u^0 < 0$ and the services of the valuable for the T periods are provided to the owner for no charge and in addition, the *valuable provides a source of income to the owner*. The total benefit to the owner in terms of dollars at the beginning of period 0 is $P^T/(1+r)^T - P^0$. The income benefit to the owner in terms of dollars at the end of period $T-1$ is $P^T - (1+r)^T P^0$.

For some unique assets, the quality of the service flow from using the services of the durable may decline over time. For example, the service flow from a custom built automobile or custom built horse trailer may decline over time due to the aging of the asset. The above model can be modified to take into account this complication but it is necessary to *assume* an *exogenous service flow quality diminution rate* δ where $0 < \delta < 1$. Thus in place of the constant relative quality assumption (6.43), the following assumption is made:

$$u^t = (1-\delta)^t u^0; \qquad t = 1, 2, \ldots, T-1. \tag{6.45}$$

Assumptions (6.41) and (6.42) still hold. Now substitute assumptions (6.45) into (6.41) in order to obtain the following equation:

$$P^0 = u^0 + \gamma(1-\delta)u^0 + \gamma^2(1-\delta)^2u^0 + \cdots + \gamma^{T-1}(1-\delta)^{T-1}u^0 + (1+r)^{-T}P^T. \tag{6.46}$$

Define the constant ϕ as follows:

$$\phi \equiv \gamma(1-\delta) = (1+i)(1-\delta)/(1+r). \tag{6.47}$$

There is a new definition for i as a *constant quality asset inflation rate* over the T periods between period 0 and period T:

$$1+i = [P^T/P^0]^{1/T}/(1-\delta). \tag{6.48}$$

Thus the quality adjusted asset inflation rate is now adjusted upwards by dividing the old asset inflation rate by $1-\delta$. Using definition (6.47), Eq. (6.46) can be rewritten as follows:

$$P^0 = u^0[1 + \phi + \phi^2 + \cdots + \phi^{T-1}] + (1 + r)^{-T} P^T. \tag{6.49}$$

Thus u^0 can be determined from equation (6.49) as follows[64]:

$$u^0 = [P^0 - P^T(1 + r)^{-T}]/[1 + \phi + \phi^2 + \cdots + \phi^{T-1}]. \tag{6.50}$$

Once u^0 has been calculated, the sequence of imputed rental prices for the unique asset for periods $0, 1, \ldots, T-1$ is u^0, $(1+i)(1-\delta)u^0$, $(1+i)^2(1-\delta)^{-2}u^0, \ldots, (1+i)^{T-1}(1-\delta)^{-T+1}u^0$. The corresponding sequence of constant quality quantities is $1, (1-\delta)^{-1}, (1-\delta)^{-2}, \ldots, (1-\delta)^{-T+1}$. Again, note that these computations can only be done once P^T is known; i.e., these user cost valuations cannot be made in real time.

The above models for measuring the services of a unique durable good are subject to many criticisms but perhaps these models can serve as starting points for more realistic models. In any case, having an imperfect model for measuring the services of a unique durable good is better than having no model at all.

In the remaining sections of this paper, the focus will be on the special problems that are associated with both measuring the value of the housing stock as well as on valuing the services of Owner Occupied Housing (OOH).

6.12 Decomposing Residential Property Prices into Land and Structure Components

In this section, the problems associated with the construction of constant quality residential property price indexes will be studied. In this section, we will look at the construction of constant quality indexes for the *stock of residential housing units*; in subsequent sections, we will look at the problems associated with pricing the services of a residential dwelling unit.

There are two difficult measurement problems associated with the construction of a constant quality house price index:

- A dwelling unit is a *unique consumer durable good*; i.e., the location of a housing unit is a price determining characteristic of the unit and each house or apartment has a unique location.
- There are two main components of a dwelling unit: (i) *the size of the structure* (measured in square meters of floor space) and (ii) *the size of the land plot* that the structure sits on (also measured in square meters). However, the purchase price of a dwelling unit is for the entire property and thus the decomposition of property price into its two main components will involve imputations.

[64] If $P^0 - P^T(1+r)^{-T} < 0$, then as before, u^0 becomes negative (and $u^1, \ldots, u^{T-1}$ become negative as well) and again, the services of the unique durable are free of charge and $-(1+i)^{t-1}(1-\delta)^{t-1}u^t = -(1+i)^{t-1}u^0 > 0$ becomes an addition to household income for period t.

The first problem area listed above might not be a problem if the same dwelling unit sold at market prices at a frequent rate so that the location would be held constant and it would seem that the usual matched model methodology that is used in constructing price indexes could be applied. But houses do not transact all that frequently; typically, a house is held for 10–20 years by the same owner before it is resold. Moreover, the structure is not constant over time; depreciation of the structure occurs over time and owners renovate and replace aging components of the structure. For example, the roofing materials for many dwellings are replaced every 20 or 30 years. Thus depreciation and renovation constantly change the quality of the structure.

The second problem area is associated with the difficulty of decomposing the transaction price for a housing unit into *separate components* representing the structure value and the land value; i.e., the single property price is for both components of the housing unit but for many purposes, we require separate valuations for the two components. The international System of National Accounts, requires separate valuations for the land and structure components of residential housing in the National Balance Sheets of the country. Many countries construct estimates for the Total Factor Productivity or Multifactor Productivity of the various sectors in the economy and the methodology used to construct these estimates requires separate price and quantity information on both structures and the land that the structures sit on. In this section, we will indicate a possible method that can be used to accomplish this decomposition of property value into constant quality land and structure components.

The *builder's model* for valuing a detached dwelling unit postulates that the value of the property is the sum of two components: the value of the land which the structure sits on plus the value of the structure. This model can be justified in two situations:

- A household purchases a residential land plot with no structure on it (or if there are structures on the land plot, they are immediately demolished).[65]
- A household purchases a land plot and immediately builds a new dwelling unit on the property.

In the first case, it is clear that the property value is equal to the land value. In the second case, The total cost of the property after the structure is completed will be equal to the floor space area of the structure, say S square meters, times the building cost per square meter β_t during period t, plus the cost of the land, which will be equal to the cost per square meter α_t times the area of the land site, say L square meters. Now think of a sample of properties of the same general type in the same general location, which have prices or values V_{tn} in period t (where $t = 1, \ldots, T$) and structure floor space areas S_{tn} and land areas L_{tn} for $n = 1, \ldots, N(t)$ where $N(t)$ is the number of observations in period t. Assume that these prices are equal to the sum of the land and structure costs plus error terms ε_{tn} which we assume are independently normally distributed with zero means and constant variances. This

[65]The cost of the demolition should be added to the purchase price for the land to get the overall land price for the land plot.

leads to the following *hedonic regression model* for period t where the α_t and β_t are the parameters to be estimated in the regression[66]:

$$V_{tn} = \alpha_t L_{tn} + \beta_t S_{tn} + \varepsilon_{tn}; \qquad t = 1, \ldots, T; n = 1, \ldots, N(t). \tag{6.51}$$

The hedonic regression model defined by (6.51) applies to new structures and to purchases of vacant residential lots in the neighbourhood under consideration where $S_{tn} = 0$. Note that there are some strong simplifying assumptions built into the model defined by (6.51): (i) the period t land price α_t (per m^2) is assumed to be constant across all properties in the neighbourhood under consideration and (ii) the construction cost (per m^2) is also assumed to be constant across all housing units built in the neighbourhood during period t. The above model applies to raw land purchases and the purchases of new dwelling units during period t in the neighbourhood under consideration. It is likely that a model that is similar to (6.51) applies to sales of older structures as well. Older structures will be worth less than newer structures due to the *depreciation* of the structure. Assuming that we have information on the age of the structure n at time t, say $A(t, n)$, and assuming a geometric (or declining balance) depreciation model, a more realistic hedonic regression model than that defined by (6.51) above is the following *basic builder's model*:

$$V_{tn} = \alpha_t L_{tn} + \beta_t (1 - \delta)^{A(t,n)} S_{tn} + \varepsilon_{tn}; \qquad t = 1, \ldots, T; n = 1, \ldots, N(t) \tag{6.52}$$

where the parameter δ reflects the *net geometric depreciation rate* as the structure ages one additional period. Thus if the age of the structure is measured in years, we would expect an annual *net* depreciation rate to be around 1–3 percent per year.[67] Note that (6.52) is now a nonlinear regression model whereas (6.51) was a simple linear regression model. The period t constant quality price of land will be the estimated coefficient for the parameter α_t and the price of a unit of a newly built structure for period t will be the estimate for β_t. The period t quantity of land for property n is L_{tn} and the period t quantity of structure for property n, expressed in equivalent units of a new structure, is $(1 - \delta)^{A(t,n)} S_{tn}$ where S_{tn} is the floor space area of the structure for property n in period t.

Note that the above model can be viewed as a *supply side model* as opposed to a *demand side model*.[68] Basically, we are assuming a valuation of a housing structures that is equal to the cost per unit floor space area of a new unit times the floor space area times an adjustment for structure depreciation. The corresponding land value

---

[66]Other papers that have suggested hedonic regression models that lead to additive decompositions of property values into land and structure components include Clapp (1980; 257–258), Bostic et al. (2007; 184), Francke and Vos (2004), Diewert (2008; 19–22, 2010), Francke (2008; 167), Koev and Santos Silva (2008), Rambaldi et al. (2010), Diewert et al. (2011, 2015), Eurostat (2013), Diewert and Shimizu (2015, 2016, 2017a), Burnett-Issacs et al. (2016), Diewert et al. (2017).

[67]This estimate of depreciation is regarded as a *net depreciation rate* because it is equal to a "true" gross structure depreciation rate less an average renovations appreciation rate. Since typically information on renovations and major repairs to a structure is not available, the age variable will only pick up average gross depreciation less average real renovation expenditures.

[68]We will pursue a demand side model in Sect. 6.14 below.

of the property is determined residually as total property value minus the imputed value of structures quality adjusted for the age of the structure. This assumption is justified for the case of newly built houses and sales of vacant lots but it is less well justified for sales of properties with older structures where a demand side model may be more relevant.

There is a major practical problem with the hedonic regression model defined by (6.52): The multicollinearity problem. Experience has shown that it is usually not possible to estimate sensible land and structure prices in a hedonic regression like that defined by (6.52) due to the multicollinearity between lot size and structure size.[69] Thus in order to deal with the multicollinearity problem, the parameter β_t in (6.52) is replaced by p_{St}, an *exogenous period t construction cost price* for houses in the area under consideration.[70] The exogenous construction price index may be an official construction price index estimated by the national statistical agency or a relevant commercially available residential construction price index. Thus the new model that replaces (6.52) is the following nonlinear hedonic regression model:

$$V_{tn} = \alpha_t L_{tn} + p_{St}(1-\delta)^{A(t,n)} S_{tn} + \varepsilon_{tn}; \qquad t = 1, \ldots, T; n = 1, \ldots, N(t). \tag{6.53}$$

This model has T land price parameters (the α_t) and one (net) geometric depreciation rate δ. Note that the replacement of the β_t by the exogenous construction price level, p_{St}, means that we have saved T degrees of freedom as well as eliminated the multicollinearity problem.

In order to allow for a finer structure of local land prices, the sales data may be further classified into a finer classification of locations. For example, the initial regression (6.53) may be applied to say city wide sales of residential properties. Suppose that the postal code of each sale is also available and there are J postal codes. Then one can introduce the following *postal code dummy variables*, $D_{PC,tn,j}$, into the hedonic regression (6.53). These J dummy variables are defined as follows: for $t = 1, \ldots, T; n = 1, \ldots, N(t); j = 1, \ldots, J$:

$$\begin{aligned} D_{PC,tn,j} &\equiv 1 \text{ if observation } n \text{ in period } t \text{ is in Postal Code } j; \\ &\equiv 0 \text{ if observation } n \text{ in period } t \text{ is } \textit{not} \text{ in Postal Code } j. \end{aligned} \tag{6.54}$$

We now modify the model defined by (6.53) to allow the *level* of land prices to differ across the J postal codes. The new nonlinear regression model is the following one:

$$V_{tn} = \alpha_t \left(\sum_{j=1}^{J} \omega_j D_{PC,tn,j} \right) L_{tn} + p_{St}(1-\delta)^{A(t,n)} S_{tn} + \varepsilon_{tn}; \; t = 1, \ldots, T; n = 1, \ldots, N(t). \tag{6.55}$$

---

[69] See Schwann (1998), Diewert et al. (2011, 2015) on the multicollinearity problem.

[70] This formulation follows that of Diewert (2010), Diewert et al. (2011, 2015, 2017), Eurostat (2013), Diewert and Shimizu (2015, 2016, 2017a), Burnett-Issacs et al. (2016). These authors assume that property value is the sum of land and structure components but movements in the price of structures are proportional to an exogenous structure price index. Note that the index p_{St} should be a levels price that gives the period t cost of building one square meter of structure.

Comparing the models defined by Eqs. (6.53) and (6.55), it can be seen that we have added an additional J *neighbourhood relative land value parameters*, $\omega_1, \ldots, \omega_J$, to the model defined by (6.53). However, looking at (6.55), it can be seen that the T land time parameters (the α_t) and the J location parameters (the ω_j) cannot all be identified. Thus it is necessary to impose at least one identifying normalization on these parameters. The following normalization is a convenient one[71]:

$$\omega_1 \equiv 1. \tag{6.56}$$

Thus Model 2 is defined by Eqs. (6.55) and (6.56) has $J - 1$ additional parameters compared to Model 1 defined by (6.53). Note that if we initially set *all* of the ω_j equal to unity, Model 2 collapses down to Model 1. It is useful to make use of this fact in running a sequence of nonlinear hedonic regressions. The models that are proposed in this section are *nested* so that the final parameter estimates from a previous model can be used as starting parameter values in the next model's nonlinear regression.[72]

In the next model, some nonlinearities in the pricing of the land area for each property are introduced. The land plot areas in a typical sample of properties can vary 5 or 10 fold.[73] Up to this point, we have assumed that land plots in the same neighbourhood sell at a constant price per square meter of lot area. However, it is likely that there is some nonlinearity in this pricing schedule; for example, it is likely that large lots sell at a per m^2 price that is well below the per m^2 price of medium sized lots. In order to capture this nonlinearity, divide up the total number of observations into K groups of observations based on their lot size. The Group 1 properties have lot size less than L_1 m^2, the Group 2 properties L_{tn} have lot sizes which satisfy the inequalities $L_1 \leq L_{tn} < L_2$; the Group 3 properties L_{tn} have lot sizes which satisfy the inequalities $L_2 \leq L_{tn} < L_3; \ldots$; the Group K properties L_{tn} have lot sizes which satisfy the inequalities $L_{K-1} \leq L_{tn}$. The break points $L_1 < L_2 < \cdots < L_{K-1}$ should be chosen so that the sample probability that any property in the sample will fall into

[71]Equivalently, one could make the normalization $\alpha_1 = 1$ and not normalize the ω_j. The resulting estimated α_t for $t = 2, 3, \ldots, T$ can then be interpreted as a constant quality land price index for the entire region relative to period 1 where $\alpha_1 \equiv 1$. In this section, we are drawing heavily on Diewert et al. (2017) and using the normalization used in that paper.

[72]In order to obtain sensible parameter estimates in our final (quite complex) nonlinear regression model, it is absolutely necessary to follow our procedure of sequentially estimating gradually more complex models, using the final coefficients from the previous model as starting values for the next model. The models that are being described in this section were implemented in Diewert et al. (2017) where the econometric software Shazam was used to perform the nonlinear regressions; see White (2004).

[73]This brings up an important point that has not been mentioned up to now. Panel data on the selling prices of properties and on the characteristics of the properties are subject to tremendous variations in the ratio of the say highest price property to the lowest price property, to the largest lot size to the smallest lot size, to the largest floor space area to the smallest floor space area and so on. The observations that appear in the tales of the distribution of prices and in the distributions of property characteristics are inevitably sparse and subject to measurement error. Thus in order to obtain sensible estimates in running these hedonic regressions, it is typically necessary to delete the observations that are in the tales of these distributions.

any one of the groups is approximately equal. For each observation n in period t, the K *land dummy variables*, $D_{L,tn,k}$, for $k = 1, \ldots, K$ are defined as follows:

$$\begin{aligned} D_{L,tn,k} &\equiv 1 \text{ if observation } tn \text{ has land area that belongs to group } k; \\ &\equiv 0 \text{ if observation } tn \text{ has land area that does not belong to group } k. \end{aligned} \tag{6.57}$$

These dummy variables are used in the definition of the following piecewise linear function of L_{tn}, $f_L(L_{tn})$, defined as follows:

$$\begin{aligned} f_L(L_{tn}) \equiv\; & D_{L,tn,1}\lambda_1 L_{tn} + D_{L,tn,2}[\lambda_1 L_1 + \lambda_2(L_{tn} - L_1)] \\ & + D_{L,tn,3}[\lambda_1 L_1 + \lambda_2(L_2 - L_1) + \lambda_3(L_{tn} - L_2)] \\ & + \cdots + D_{L,tn,K}[\lambda_1 L_1 + \lambda_2(L_2 - L_1) + \cdots + \lambda_K(L_{tn} - L_{K-1})] \end{aligned} \tag{6.58}$$

where the λ_k are unknown parameters. The function $f_L(L_{tn})$ defines a *relative valuation function for the land area of a house* as a function of the plot area, L_{tn}. The new nonlinear regression model is the following one:

$$\begin{aligned} V_{tn} = \alpha_t \left(\sum_{j=1}^{J} \omega_j D_{PC,tn,j} \right) f_L(L_{tn}) + p_{St}(1-\delta)^{A(t,n)} S_{tn} + \varepsilon_{tn};\; t = 1, \ldots, T; \\ n = 1, \ldots, N(t). \end{aligned} \tag{6.59}$$

Comparing the models defined by Eqs. (6.55) and (6.59), it can be seen that we have added an additional K *land plot size parameters*, $\lambda_1, \ldots, \lambda_K$, to the model defined by (6.55). However, looking at (6.59), it can be seen that the T land time parameters (the α_t), the J postal code parameters (the ω_j) and the K land plot size parameters (the λ_k) cannot all be identified. Thus the following identification normalizations on the parameters for Model 3 defined by (6.59) and (6.60) are imposed:

$$\omega_1 \equiv 1;\; \lambda_1 \equiv 1. \tag{6.60}$$

Note that if all of the λ_k are set equal to unity, Model 3 collapses down to Model 2. Typically, the log likelihood for Model 3 will be considerably higher than for Model 2.[74] Land prices as functions of lot size do not always decline monotonically but for very large land plots, the marginal price of an extra square foot of land is typically quite low.

The next model is similar to Model 3 except that now the marginal price of adding an extra amount of structure is allowed to vary as the size of the structure increases. It is likely that the quality of the structure increases as the size of the structure increases. In order to capture this nonlinearity, divide up the sample observations into M groups

[74]For the example in Diewert et al. (2017) where the models described in this section were estimated, the log likelihood increased by 1762 log likelihood points and the R^2 jumped from 0.7662 for Model 2 to 0.8283 for Model 3 for the addition of 6 new λ_k parameters.

of observations based on their structure size. The Group 1 properties have structures with floor space area S_{tn} less than S_1 m^2, the Group 2 properties have structure areas S_{tn} satisfying the inequalities $S_1 \leq S_{tn} < S_2$, ..., the Group $M - 1$ properties have structure areas S_{tn} satisfying the inequalities $S_{M-2} \leq S_{tn} < S_{M-1}$, and the Group M properties have structure areas S_{tn} satisfying the inequalities $S_{M-1} < S_{tn}$ where the $M - 1$ break points satisfy the inequalities $S_1 < S_2 < \cdots < S_{M-1}$. Again, the break points should be chosen so that the sample probability that any property in the sample will fall into any one of the groups is approximately equal. For each observation n in period t, we define the M *structure dummy variables*, $D_{S,tn,m}$, for $m = 1, \ldots, M$ as follows:

$$\begin{aligned} D_{S,tn,m} &\equiv 1 \text{ if observation } tn \text{ has structure area that belongs to structure group } m; \\ &\equiv 0 \text{ if observation } tn \text{ has structure area that does not belong to group } m. \end{aligned} \tag{6.61}$$

These dummy variables are used in the definition of the following piecewise linear function of S_{tn}, $g_S(S_{tn})$, defined as follows:

$$\begin{aligned} g_S(S_{tn}) \equiv{}& D_{S,tn,1}\mu_1 S_{tn} + D_{S,tn,2}[\mu_1 S_1 + \mu_2(S_{tn} - S_1)] \\ &+ D_{S,tn,3}[\mu_1 S_1 + \mu_2(S_2 - S_1) + \mu_3(S_{tn} - S_2)] \\ &+ D_{S,tn,4}[\mu_1 S_1 + \mu_2(S_2 - S_1) + \mu_3(S_3 - S_2) + \mu_4(S_{tn} - S_3)] + \cdots \\ &+ D_{S,tn,M}[\mu_1 S_1 + \mu_2(S_2 - S_1) + \mu_3(S_3 - S_2) + \cdots + \mu_M(S_{tn} - S_{M-1})]. \end{aligned} \tag{6.62}$$

where the μ_m are unknown parameters. The function $g_S(S_{tn})$ defines a *relative valuation function for the structure area of a house* as a function of the structure area.

The new nonlinear regression model is the following Model 4:

$$V_{tn} = \alpha_t \left(\sum_{j=1}^{J} \omega_j D_{PC,tn,j} \right) f_L(L_{tn}) + p_{St}(1 - \delta)^{A(t,n)} g_S(S_{tn}) + \varepsilon_{tn}; \quad t = 1, \ldots, T; n = 1, \ldots, N(t). \tag{6.63}$$

Comparing the models defined by Eqs. (6.59) and (6.63), it can be seen that an additional M *structure floor space parameters*, $\mu_1, \ldots, \mu_M$, have been added to the model defined by (6.59).[75] Again, we add the normalizations (6.60) in order to identify all of the parameters in the model. Note that if all of the μ_m are set equal to

[75] At this stage of the sequential estimation procedure, it is usually not necessary to impose a normalization on the parameters $\mu_1 - \mu_M$. This lack of a normalization means that the scale of the exogenous structure price levels p_{St} is allowed to change; i.e., essentially, allowance is now made to quality adjust the exogenous index to a certain extent. However, if the resulting estimated structure values turn out to be unreasonably large or small, then it will be necessary to set one of the μ_m to equal 1.

unity, Model 4 collapses down to Model 3. Typically, the log likelihood for Model 4 will be considerably higher than for Model 3.[76]

At this stage, it is often the case that an acceptable model has been estimated. How can the estimated parameters from the final model be used in order to form price and quantity indexes?

The sequence of price levels for the land component of residential property sales is defined to be $\alpha_1, \alpha_2, \ldots, \alpha_T$ and the corresponding sequence of price levels for the structure component of residential property sales in the T periods is defined to be the exogenous sequence of indexes, $p_{S1}, p_{S2}, \ldots, p_{ST}$. The land and structure values of properties transacted in period t, V_{Lt} and V_{St}, are defined by using the estimated land and structure additive components of transacted properties in period t, $\alpha_t(\sum_{j=1}^{J}\omega_j D_{PC,tn,j}) f_L(L_{tn})$ and $p_{St}(1-\delta)^{A(t,n)} g_S(S_{tn})$ respectively, and summing over properties that were sold in period t:

$$V_{Lt} \equiv \sum_{n\in N(t)} \alpha_t \left(\sum_{j=1}^{J} \omega_j D_{PC,tn,j}\right) f_L(L_{tn}); \qquad t = 1, \ldots, T; \tag{6.64}$$

$$V_{St} \equiv \sum_{n\in N(t)} p_{St}(1-\delta)^{A(t,n)} g_S(S_{tn}); \qquad t = 1, \ldots, T. \tag{6.65}$$

Using the prices $\alpha_1, \alpha_2, \ldots, \alpha_T$ and the corresponding estimated land values, $V_{L1}, \ldots, V_{LT}$ and the prices $p_{S1}, p_{S2}, \ldots, p_{ST}$ and the corresponding estimated structure values, $V_{S1}, \ldots, V_{ST}$, one can just apply normal index number theory using these data to construct Laspeyres, Paasche, Fisher or whatever index formula is being used by the statistical agency in order to construct constant quality price and quantity overall property indexes for the sales of residential properties in the area under consideration for the T periods.

However, constant quality land and structure price indexes for *sales* of Owner Occupied Residential houses is not what is needed for most purposes; what is required are constant quality price and quantity indexes for the *stock* of residential houses. In order to accomplish this task, it is necessary to have a census of the housing stock in the country which would include information on the characteristics that are used in the hedonic regression model that is defined by (6.63). The information that is required in order to estimate (6.63) is information on the following variables:

- The selling price of the residential properties (P_{tn});
- The age of the structure on the property (A_{tn});
- The area of the land plot (L_{tn});
- The floor space area of the structure (S_{tn});
- The neighbourhood of the property (or the postal code) and
- An exogenous structure price index which provides the construction cost of a new structure per meter squared or per square foot (p_{St}).

[76]For the example in Diewert et al. (2017), the log likelihood increased by 935 log likelihood points and the R^2 jumped from 0.8283 for Model 3 to 0.8520 for Model 4 for the addition of 5 new μ_M parameters.

If a national housing Census has information on the above property characteristics (excluding the information on selling prices P_{tn} and on the exogenous structure price index p_{St})[77] then it will be possible to insert the characteristics of each residential dwelling unit into the right hand side of (6.63) and then using appropriate modifications of definitions (6.64) and (6.65), it will be possible to obtain estimates for the land and structure value for each dwelling unit in the area covered by the regression. If there is no national housing census information or the required characteristics are not included in the census, then it will be very difficult to form estimates for the value of residential land.

Additional information on house and property characteristics will lead to more accurate land and structure decompositions of property value. Examples of useful additional structure price determining characteristics are: (i) the number of bathrooms; (ii) the number of bedrooms; (iii) the type of construction material; (iv) the number of stories; etc. Examples of useful additional land price determining characteristics are: (i) the distance to the nearest subway station; (ii) the distance to the city core; (iii) the quality of neighbourhood schools; (iv) the existence of various neighbourhood amenities; etc. For examples of how these characteristics can be integrated into the builder's model, see Diewert et al. (2011, 2015, 2017), Eurostat (2013, 2017), Diewert and Shimizu (2015).[78]

The estimates for the geometric depreciation rate generated by the application of the builder's model are useful for national income accountants because they facilitate the accurate estimation of structure depreciation, which is required for the national accounts. However, the depreciation estimates that are generated by the builder's model are *wear and tear depreciation* estimates that apply to structures that continue in existence over the sample period. The estimated depreciation rate measures (net) depreciation[79] of a structure that has survived from its birth to the period of its sale. However, there is another form of structure depreciation that the estimated depreciation rate misses; namely the loss of residual structure value that results from the *early demolition* of the structure. This problem was noticed and addressed by Hulten and Wykoff (1981a; 377–379, b, 1996). Wear and tear depreciation is often called *deterioration* depreciation and *demolition* or *early retirement depreciation* is sometimes called *obsolescence* depreciation.[80] Methods for estimating this form of depreciation have been proposed by Hulten and Wykoff as mentioned above and by Diewert and Shimizu (2017a; 512–516). Both methods require information on the distribution of the ages of retirement for the asset class. The Hulten and Wykoff

---

[77] Every country will have a national residential construction deflator because this deflator is required in order to form estimates of real investment in residential structures. However, this national deflator may not be entirely appropriate for the type of buildings in a particular neighbourhood.

[78] It is also possible to estimate more general models of depreciation using the builder's model; see Diewert and Shimizu (2017a), Diewert et al. (2017).

[79] It is a net estimate since renovation and replacement investments in the building tend to extend the life of the building or augment its value. Thus the gross wear and tear depreciation rate for the structure will tend to be larger than the estimated net depreciation rate.

[80] Crosby et al. (2012; 230) distinguish the two types of depreciation and in addition, they provide a comprehensive survey of the depreciation literature as it applies to commercial properties.

method absorbs demolition depreciation into the wear and tear depreciation rate whereas the Diewert and Shimizu method uses the wear and tear depreciation rate that is generated by sales of surviving buildings but adds a separate depreciation rate that is due to early demolishment of the structures in the asset class.

The above paragraph simply warns the reader that wear and tear depreciation[81] for surviving buildings is not the entire depreciation story: there is also a loss of asset value that results from the early retirement of a building that needs to be taken into account when constructing national income accounting estimates of depreciation.

There is one additional complication that needs to be taken into account when running a hedonic regression on the sales of houses; i.e., what happens when the sales information for an additional period becomes available? The simplest way of dealing with this problem dates back to Court (1939). His method works as follows: set $T = 2$ and run a hedonic regression that has a time dummy variable in it. In the context of the hedonic regression model defined by (6.63), estimates for the price of land for periods 1 and 2 would be obtained, say α_1^1 and α_2^1. The price index for land for periods 1 and 2 is defined as $P_L^1 = 1$ and $P_L^2 = \alpha_2^1/\alpha_1^1$. Now run a new hedonic regression using (6.63) for $t = 2, 3$ and obtain new estimates for the price of land in periods 2 and 3, say α_2^2 and α_3^2. The price index for land in period 3 is defined as $P_L^3 = P_L^2(\alpha_3^2/\alpha_2^2)$; i.e., we update the price index value for period 2, P_L^2, by the rate of change in land prices going from period 2 to 3, (α_3^2/α_2^2). Thus the previously estimated index is updated each period as new information becomes available. This *adjacent period time dummy model* has the advantage that it does not revise the previously estimated indexes as the new information becomes available.[82]

The above method does not always work well in the context of estimating property price indexes due to the sparseness of sales in a neighbourhood and the multiplicity of parameters that are required to adequately control for differences in housing characteristics. Thus Shimizu et al. (2010a; 797) suggested extending the number of periods from 2 to a longer window of T consecutive periods, leading to the *rolling window time dummy hedonic regression model*. Thus for the model defined by (6.63),

---

[81]What has been labeled as wear and tear depreciation could be better described as *anticipated amortization of the structure* rather than wear and tear depreciation. Once a structure is built, it becomes a fixed asset which cannot be transferred to alternative uses (like a truck or machine). Thus amortization of the cost of the structure should be proportional to the cash flows or to the service flows of utility that the building generates over its expected lifetime. However, technical progress, obsolescence or unanticipated market developments can cause the building to be demolished before it is fully amortized. See Diewert and Fox (2016) for a more complete discussion of the fixity problem.

[82]The two period time dummy variable hedonic regression (and its extension to many periods) was first considered explicitly by Court (1939; 109–111) as his hedonic suggestion number two. Court used adjacent period time dummy hedonic regressions as links in a longer chain of comparisons extending from 1920 to 1939 for US automobiles: "The net regressions on time shown above are in effect price link relatives for cars of constant specifications. By joining these together, a continuous index is secured." If the two periods being compared are consecutive years, Griliches (1971; 7) coined the term "adjacent year regression" to describe this method for updating the index as new information becomes available. Diewert (2005b) looked at the axiomatic properties of adjacent year time dummy hedonic regressions.

the land price parameters that are estimated by the first regression using the data for periods 1 to T are $\alpha_1^1, \alpha_2^1, \ldots, \alpha_T^1$ and the corresponding land price indexes for periods 1 to t are $P_L^t \equiv \alpha_t^1/\alpha_1^1$ for $t = 1, \ldots, T$. The second hedonic regression uses the data for periods $2, 3, \ldots, T, T+1$ and the estimated land price parameters are $\alpha_2^2, \alpha_3^2, \ldots, \alpha_T^2, \alpha_{T+1}^2$. The price index for land in period $T+1$ is defined as $P_L^{T+1} = P_L^T(\alpha_{T+1}^2/\alpha_T^2)$; i.e., the price index for period T, P_L^t, is updated by the rate of change in land prices going from period T to $T+1$, $\alpha_{T+1}^2/\alpha_T^2$.

There are two additional issues that need to be addressed when using a rolling window time dummy hedonic regression model:

- How long should the window length be? A longer window length will probably lead to more stable estimates for the unknown parameters in the hedonic regression. A shorter window length will allow for taste changes to take place more quickly. A window length of one year plus one period will allow for seasonal effects. At this stage of our knowledge, it is difficult to give definitive advice on the length of the window.
- When a new window is computed, how should the index results from the new window be linked to the previous index values? The same issue applies when a multilateral method is used in the time series context. Ivancic et al. (2011) along with Shimizu et al. (2010a, c) suggested that the movement of the indexes for the last two periods in the new window be linked to the last index value generated by the previous window. However Krsinich (2016) suggested that the movement of the indexes generated by the new window over the entire new window period be linked to the previous window index value for the second period in the previous window. Krsinich called this a *window splice* as opposed to the *movement splice* explained above. De Haan (2015; 27) suggested that perhaps the linking period should be in the middle of the old window which the Australian Bureau of Statistics (2016; 12) termed a *half splice*. Ivancic et al. (2011; 33) suggested that the average of all possible links of the new window to the old window be used and they called this a *mean splice* method for linking the results of the new window to the previous window.[83] Again, there is no consensus at this time on which linking method is "best". However, it is likely that all of these linking methods will generate much the same results.

It can be seen that estimating price indexes for houses (or detached dwelling units) is not a straightforward task, particularly if one wants separate constant quality indexes for the land and structure components of property value.[84] In the following section, it will be seen that it is even more complicated to obtain separate indexes for the land and structure components for condominium sales.

[83] For the details on how the mean splice method works, see Diewert and Fox (2017).

[84] For additional hedonic regression models for detached houses, see Verbrugge (2008), Garner and Verbrugge (2011), Eurostat (2013, 2017), Hill (2013), Hill et al. (2018), Rambaldi and Fletcher (2014), Silver (2018).

6.13 Decomposing Condominium Sales Prices into Land and Structure Components

A starting point for applying the builder's model to condominium sales is the hedonic regression model defined by Eq. (6.53) in the previous section.[85] For convenience, Eq. (6.53) are repeated below as Eq. (6.66):

$$V_{tn} = \alpha_t L_{tn} + p_{St}(1-\delta)^{A(t,n)} S_{tn} + \varepsilon_{tn}; \qquad t = 1, \ldots, T; n = 1, \ldots, N(t) \tag{6.66}$$

where V_{tn} is the selling price of a condominium property in a neighbourhood in period t, α_t is the price of the land that the structure sits on (per m^2), L_{tn} is the land area that can be attributed to the condo unit, p_{St} is an exogenous period t construction cost for the type of condo under consideration (per m^2), δ is the one period wear and tear geometric depreciation rate for the structure, $A_{tn} = A(t, n)$ is the age of the structure in periods, S_{tn} is the floor space of unit n that is sold in period t (in m^2) and ε_{tn} is an error term.

A problem with the above model is that it is not appropriate to allocate the entire land value of the condominium property to any particular unit that is sold in period t. Thus each condo unit in the building should be allocated a *share* of the total land value of the property. The problem is: how exactly should this imputed land share be calculated? There are two simple methods for constructing an appropriate land share: (i) Use the unit's share of floor space to total structure floor space or (ii) simply use $1/N$ as the share where N is the total number of units in the building. Thus define the following two land share imputations for unit n in period t:

$$L_{Stn} \equiv (S_{tn}/TS_{tn})TL_{tn}; \; L_{Ntn} \equiv (1/N_{tn})TL_{tn}; \qquad t = 1, \ldots, T; n = 1, \ldots, N(t) \tag{6.67}$$

where S_{tn} is the floor space area of unit n which is sold in period t, TS_{tn} is the total building floor space area, TL_{tn} is the total land area of the building and N_{tn} is the total number of units in the building for unit n sold in period t. The first method of land share imputation is used by the Japanese land tax authorities. The second method of imputation implicitly assumes that each unit can enjoy the use of the entire land area and so an equal share of land for each unit seems "fair".

There is a problem with the definition of L_{Stn} in (6.67): the floor space "share" of unit n, S_{tn}/TS_{tn} if summed over all units in the building would be less than 1 because the privately held floor space of each unit in the building does not account for shared building floor spaces such as halls, elevators, storage spaces, furnace rooms and other "public" floor spaces, which are included in total building floor space, TS_{tn}. Thus the "share" S_{tn}/TS_{tn} must be adjusted upward by some percentage to account for these shared building facilities.[86] In what follows, it is assumed that this

[85] The analysis in this section follows that of Diewert and Shimizu (2016).

[86] Diewert and Shimizu (2016; 303) constructed estimates of Tokyo total building private floor space to total building floor space for each observation nt as $N_{tn}S_{tn}/TS_{tn}$, where N_{tn} is the number of units in the building which contained condo sale n in period t, S_{tn} is the private floor space of the sold unit

adjustment has been made to S_{tn} (so that S_{tn} is now interpreted as adjusted condo floor space area).

In order to obtain sensible decompositions of the condominium selling price into land and structure components, it may be necessary to assume a structure value and focus on the determinants of land value at the initial stages of the sequential estimation procedure. Thus following Diewert and Shimizu (2016), assume that the *imputed structure value* for unit n in period t, V_{Stn}, is defined as follows:

$$V_{Stn} \equiv p_{St}(1-\delta)^{A(t,n)}S_{tn}; \qquad t=1,\ldots,T; n=1,\ldots,N(t) \tag{6.68}$$

where δ is an assumed geometric depreciation rate.[87] Once the imputed value of the structure has been defined by (6.68), the *imputed land value* for condo n in period t, V_{Ltn}, is defined by subtracting the imputed structure value from the total value of the condo unit, which is V_{tn}:

$$V_{Ltn} \equiv V_{tn} - V_{Stn}; \qquad t=1,\ldots,T; n=1,\ldots,N(t). \tag{6.69}$$

In the hedonic regressions which follow immediately, the imputed value of land for the condominium unit, V_{Ltn}, is used as the dependent variable in a hedonic regression. The following regressions explain variations in these imputed land values in terms of the property characteristics.

Suppose that the postal code of each sale is also available and there are J postal codes. Then one can introduce the following *postal code dummy variables*, $D_{PC,tn,j}$, as explanatory variables into a hedonic regression. Define these J dummy variables using definitions (6.54) in the previous section and estimate the following hedonic regression which is a *land counterpart* to the hedonic regression defined by (6.55) in the previous section: are defined as follows:

$$V_{Ltn} - \alpha_t\left(\sum_{j=1}^{J}\omega_j D_{PC,tn,j}\right)L_{Stn} + \varepsilon_{tn}, \qquad t=1,\ldots,T; n=1,\ldots,N(t). \tag{6.70}$$

Note that the imputed value of land, V_{Ltn} defined by (6.69), replaces total property value V_{tn} which was the dependent variable in (6.55).[88]

---

and TS_{tn} is the total floor space of the building. The sample wide average of these ratios was 0.899. Thus the first imputation method in definitions (6.67) was changed from $L_{Stn} \equiv (S_{tn}/TS_{tn})TL_{tn}$ to $L_{Stn} \equiv (1/0.899)(S_{tn}/TS_{tn})TL_{tn} = (1.1)(S_{tn}/TS_{tn})TL_{tn}$. Burnett-Issacs et al. (2016) estimated a similar condo model and consulted with construction experts and determined that on average, the ratio of total space to private space for Ottawa condominium apartments was approximately 1.33. Thus they changed $L_{Stn} \equiv (S_{tn}/TS_{tn})TL_{tn}$ to $L_{Stn} \equiv (1.33)(S_{tn}/TS_{tn})TL_{tn}$.

[87] Diewert and Shimizu (2016) assumed $\delta = 0.03$ and Burnett-Issacs et al. (2016) assumed $\delta = 0.02$ where the age variable A_{tn} is measured in years. Later, δ will be estimated.

[88] As usual, we need a normalization on the parameters such as $\alpha_1 = 1$ in order to identify all of the remaining parameters, $\alpha_2,\ldots,\alpha_T,\omega_1,\ldots,\omega_J$. Note that this regression uses the first method of land imputation defined by (6.67). Later, the second method will also be considered.

It is likely that the height of the building (number of stories) increases the value of the land plot supporting the building, all else equal. Thus define the number of stories dummy variables, $D_{NS,tn,s}$, as follows: $t = 1, \ldots, T; n = 1, \ldots, N(t); s = 1, \ldots, NS$:

$$\begin{aligned} D_{NS,tn,s} &\equiv 1 \text{ if observation } n \text{ in period } t \text{ is in a building with } s \text{ stories ;} \\ &\equiv 0 \text{ if observation } n \text{ in period } t \text{ is } \textit{not} \text{ in building with } s \text{ stories.} \end{aligned} \quad (6.71)$$

The new nonlinear regression model is the following one:

$$V_{Ltn} = \alpha_t \left(\sum_{j=1}^{J} \omega_j D_{PC,tn,j} \right) \left(\sum_{s=1}^{NS} \chi_s D_{NS,tn,s} \right) L_{Stn} + \varepsilon_{tn}; \; t = 1, \ldots, T; n = 1, \ldots, N(t). \quad (6.72)$$

Comparing the models defined by Eqs. (6.70) and (6.72), it can be seen that an additional NS *building height parameters*, $\chi_1, \ldots, \chi_{NS}$, have been added to the model defined by (6.70).[89] As usual, the models defined by (6.70) and (6.72) are nested so that the finishing parameter values from the nonlinear regression (6.70) can be used as starting values for (6.72) along with the starting values $\chi_1 = \chi_2 = \cdots = \chi_{NS} = 1$.

The higher up a unit is, the better is the view on average and so it could be expected that the price of the unit increases as its height increases. The quality of the structure probably does not increase as the height of the unit increases so it seems reasonable to impute the height premium as an adjustment to the land price component of the unit.

It is possible to introduce the height of the unit (the H variable) as a categorical variable (like the number of stories NS in the last hedonic regression model). However, both Diewert and Shimizu (2016) (hereafter DS) and Burnett-Issacs et al. (2016) (hereafter BHD) found that this dummy variable approach could be replaced by using H as a continuous variable with little change in the fit of the model. Thus the new nonlinear regression model is the following one where $t = 1, \ldots, T; n = 1, \ldots, N(t)$:

$$V_{Ltn} = \alpha_t \left(\sum_{j=1}^{J} \omega_j D_{PC,tn,j} \right) \left(\sum_{s=1}^{NS} \chi_s D_{NS,tn,s} \right) (1 + \gamma(H_{tn} - 3)) L_{Stn} + \varepsilon_{tn}; \quad (6.73)$$

where H_{tn} is the height of the sold unit n in period t (measured in number of stories from ground level) and γ is a height of the unit parameter to be estimated.[90] The above model assumes that the lowest height for the units sold in the sample was $H_{tn} = 3$. Thus for all the observations that correspond to the sold unit being located on the third floor of the building, the new parameter γ in (6.73) will not affect the predicted value in the regression. However, for heights of the sold units that were

[89] Again normalizations like $\alpha_1 \equiv 1; \chi_1 \equiv 1$ are required in order to identify the remaining parameters. If all $\chi_s = 1$, then the model defined by (6.72) collapses down to the model defined by (6.70).

[90] Normalizations like $\alpha_1 \equiv 1; \chi_1 \equiv 1$ need to be imposed in order to identify the remaining parameters.

greater than 3, the regression implies that the land value will increase by γ for each story that is above 3.[91]

As was mentioned earlier, there are two simple methods for imputing the share of the building's total land area to the sold unit. Up until now, we have used the first method of imputation defined by (6.67) which set the share of total land imputed to unit n in period t, L_{Stn}, equal to $(S_{tn}/TS_{tn})TL_{tn}$ whereas the second method set L_{Ntn} equal to $(1/N_{tn})TL_{tn}$. In the next model, the land imputation for unit n in period t is set equal to a *weighted average* of the two imputation methods and the best fitting weight, λ, is estimated. Thus define:

$$L_{tn}(\lambda) = [\lambda(S_{tn}/TS_{tn}) + (1-\lambda)(1/N_{tn})]TL_{tn}; \qquad t = 1, \ldots, T; n = 1, \ldots, N(t). \tag{6.74}$$

The new nonlinear regression model is the following one where $t = 1, \ldots, T; n = 1, \ldots, N(t)$ and $L_{tn}(\lambda)$ is defined by (6.74).[92]

$$V_{Ltn} = \alpha_t \left(\sum_{j=1}^{J} \omega_j D_{PC,tn,j}\right)\left(\sum_{s=1}^{NS} \chi_s D_{NS,tn,s}\right)(1+\gamma(H_{tn}-3))L_{tn}(\lambda) + \varepsilon_{tn}. \tag{6.75}$$

Conditional on the land area of the building, one would expect the sold unit's land imputation value to increase as the number of units in the building increases. Thus one could use the total number of units in the building, N_{tn}, as a quality adjustment variable for the imputed land value of a condo unit. DS introduced this variable as a continuous variable. The smallest number of units in the buildings in their sample was 11. Thus they introduced the term $1 + \kappa(N_{tn} - 11)$ as an explanatory term in the nonlinear regression. The new parameter κ is the percentage increase in the unit's imputed value of land as the number of units in the building grows by one unit. The new nonlinear regression model is the following one where $t = 1, \ldots, T; n = 1, \ldots, N(t)$ and $L_{tn}(\lambda)$ is defined by (6.74):

$$V_{Ltn} = \alpha_t \left(\sum_{j=1}^{J} \omega_j D_{PC,tn,j}\right)\left(\sum_{s=1}^{NS} \chi_s D_{NS,tn,s}\right)(1+\gamma(H_{tn}-3)) \\ (1+\kappa(N_{tn}-11))L_{tn}(\lambda) + \varepsilon_{tn}. \tag{6.76}$$

where $L_{tn}(\lambda)$ is defined by (6.74).

The next explanatory variable to be introduced into the hedonic regression model is one which is not obvious but turned out to be very significant in the regressions run by DS and BHD. The *footprint* of a building is the area of the land that directly

[91]The studies that have implemented this model found that the estimated γ was in the 2–4% range. Thus the imputed land value of a unit increases by 2–4% for each story above the threshold level of 3.

[92]For the DS Tokyo condo data, the estimated λ turned out to be $\lambda^* = 0.3636$ ($t = 9.84$) so that the very simple land imputation method that just divided the total land plot size by the number of units in the building got a higher weight (0.6364) than the weight for the floor space allocation method (0.3636). For the Ottawa condo data, the estimated λ turned out to be $\lambda^* = 0.2525$ ($t = 12.10$).

supports the structure. An approximation to the footprint land for unit n in period t is the total structure area TS_{tn} divided by the total number of stories in the structure TH_{tn}. If footprint land is subtracted from the total land area, TL_{tn}, the resulting variable is *excess land*,[93] EL_{tn}, defined as follows:

$$EL_{tn} \equiv TL_{tn} - (TS_{tn}/TH_{tn}); \qquad t = 1, \ldots, T; n = 1, \ldots, N(t). \tag{6.77}$$

In the Tokyo data used by DS, excess land ranged from 47 to 2912 m^2. Now group the sample observations into M categories, depending on the amount of excess land that pertained to each observation. Group 1 consists of observations tn where EL_{tn} is less than some number EL_1; Group 2: observations such that $EL_1 \leq EL_{tn} < EL_2$; ...; Group M: $EL_{M-1} \leq EL_{tn}$. The break points, $EL_1, EL_2, \ldots, EL_{M-1}$ should be chosen so that the number of observations in each group is approximately equal. Define the *excess land dummy variables*, $D_{EL,tn,m}$, as follows for $t = 1, \ldots, T; n = 1, \ldots, N(t); m = 1, \ldots, M$:

$$\begin{aligned} D_{EL,tn,m} &\equiv 1 \text{ if observation } n \text{ in period } t \text{ is in excess land group } m; \\ &\equiv 0 \text{ if observation } n \text{ in period } t \text{ is } \textit{not} \text{ in excess land group } m. \end{aligned} \tag{6.78}$$

The new regression model is the following one:

$$V_{Ltn} = \alpha_t \left(\sum_{j=1}^{J} \omega_j D_{PC,tn,j} \right) \left(\sum_{s=1}^{NS} \chi_s D_{NS,tn,s} \right) \left(\sum_{m=1}^{M} \mu_m D_{EL,tn,m} \right) \times (1 + \gamma(H_{tn} - 3))(1 + \kappa(N_{tn} - 11))L_{tn}(\lambda) + \varepsilon_{tn}; \; t = 1, \ldots, T; n = 1, \ldots, N(t). \tag{6.79}$$

Not all of the parameters in (6.79) can be identified so the following normalizations on the parameters in (6.79) are imposed:

$$\alpha_1 \equiv 1; \chi_1 \equiv 1; \mu_1 \equiv 1. \tag{6.80}$$

Introducing the excess land dummy variables led to huge jumps in the log likelihoods for the hedonic regressions run by DS and BHS: 1020 for DS and 2652 for BHS.[94] Both studies found that the estimated μ_m were positive but their magnitudes decreased monotonically as the excess land variable increased.

There are three additional explanatory variables that were used by DS that may affect the price of land. Define TW as the walking time in minutes to the nearest subway station; TT as the subway running time in minutes to the Central Tokyo

[93]This is land that is usable for purposes *other* than the direct support of the structure on the land plot.

[94]Recall the hedonic regression model defined by (6.59) in the previous section which introduced linear splines on the valuation of the land area of a stand alone housing unit. This introduction also greatly increased the log likelihood of the regression. In the present context, the excess land dummy variables take the place of the linear spline functions in (6.59).

station from the nearest station and the SOUTH dummy variable is set equal to 1 if the sold condo unit faces south and 0 otherwise. Let $D_{S,tn,2}$ equal the SOUTH dummy variable for sale n in period t. Define $D_{S,tn,2} = 1 - D_{S,tn,1}$. In the Tokyo data set used by DS, TW ranged from 1 to 19 min while TT ranged from 12 to 48 min. These new variables are inserted into the previous nonlinear regression model (6.79) in the following manner for $t = 1, \ldots, T$; $n = 1, \ldots, N(t)$:

$$V_{Ltn} = \alpha_t \left(\sum_{j=1}^{J} \omega_j D_{PC,tn,j} \right) \left(\sum_{s=1}^{NS} \chi_s D_{NS,tn,s} \right) \left(\sum_{m=1}^{M} \mu_m D_{EL,tn,m} \right) \times$$
$$(\phi_1 D_{S,tn,1} + \phi_2 D_{S,tn,2})(1 + \gamma(H_{tn} - 3))(1 + \kappa(N_{tn} - 11)) \times$$
$$(1 + \eta(TW_{tn} - 1))(1 + \theta(TT_{tn} - 12))L_{tn}(\lambda) + \varepsilon_{tn}; \qquad (6.81)$$

where $L_{tn}(\lambda)$ is defined by (6.74). Not all of the parameters in (6.81) can be identified so the following normalizations (6.82) are imposed on the parameters in (6.81):

$$\alpha_1 \equiv 1; \chi_1 \equiv 1; \mu_1 \equiv 1; \phi_1 \equiv 1. \qquad (6.82)$$

Using the DS Tokyo data, the R^2 for this model turned out to be 0.6308 and the log likelihood increased by 406 points over the log likelihood of the previous model defined by (6.79) for the addition of 3 new parameters. The estimated parameters had the expected signs and had reasonable magnitudes.

At this point, DS concluded that the imputed land value for each condominium in their sample was predicted reasonably well by the hedonic regression defined by (6.81) and (6.82). Thus in the following regression, they switched from using the imputed land value V_{Ltn} defined by (6.69) as the dependent variable in the regressions to using the actual selling price of the property, V_{tn}. They used the specification for the land component of the property that that is defined by (6.81) and (6.82) but they also added the structure term $p_{St}(1 - \delta)^{A(t,n)} S_{tn}$ to account for the structure component of the value of the condo unit. Note that the annual depreciation rate δ is now estimated by the new hedonic regression model, rather than assuming that it was equal to 3%. Thus the number of unknown parameters in the new model increased by 1. They used the estimated values for the coefficients in (6.81) as starting values in this new nonlinear regression.[95]

Using their Tokyo data, DS found that the R^2 for this new model was 0.8190 and the estimated depreciation rate was $\delta^* = 0.0367$ ($t = 27.1$). Note that the R^2 is satisfactory; i.e., the new model explains a substantial fraction of the variation in condo prices.

DS and BHD introduced some additional explanatory variables as quality adjusting variables for the imputed value of structures. DS introduced the number of bed-

[95] Attempting to estimate the parameters in (6.83) without good starting values for the nonlinear regression will not lead to sensible parameter estimates. Thus it is necessary to obtain good starting values for (6.83) by estimating the rather long sequence of regressions explained above, starting with a very simple model and gradually introducing additional explanatory variables. Each regression in the sequence contains the previous one as a special case so that the final estimates of one regression can be used as starting values for the subsequent one.

rooms and the type of building as quality adjusters for the value of the structure. BHD introduced the number of bedrooms, the number of bathrooms, the presence of balconies, the use of natural gas as the heating fuel and whether there was commercial space in the building as additional variables that could determine the value of the structure. These variables were significant explanatory variables but the overall R^2 for the final hedonic regression did not increase by a large amount with the addition of these variables to the regression. The details may be found in Diewert and Shimizu (2016), Burnett-Issacs et al. (2016).

Once the final hedonic regression has been run, the sequence of land prices is given by $\alpha_1, \alpha_2, \ldots, \alpha_T$ and the sequence of condo structure prices is given by the exogenous structure price indexes, $p_{S1}, p_{S2}, \ldots, p_{ST}$. To obtain overall property price indexes for sales of condos, form the following counterparts to Eqs. (6.64) and (6.65) in the previous section to obtain an estimate of period t condo land value, V_{Lt}, and estimated period t structure value, V_{St}, for $t = 1, \ldots, T$:

$$\begin{aligned} V_{Lt} \equiv \sum_{n \in N(t)} \alpha_t \left(\sum_{j=1}^{J} \omega_j D_{PC,tn,j} \right) \left(\sum_{s=1}^{NS} \chi_s D_{NS,tn,s} \right) \left(\sum_{m=1}^{M} \mu_m D_{EL,tn,m} \right) \times \\ (\phi_1 D_{S,tn,1} + \phi_2 D_{S,tn,2})(1 + \gamma(H_{tn} - 3))(1 + \kappa(N_{tn} - 11)) \times \\ (1 + \eta(TW_{tn} - 1))(1 + \theta(TT_{tn} - 12))L_{tn}(\lambda); \end{aligned} \quad (6.83)$$

$$V_{St} \equiv \sum_{n \in N(t)} p_{St}(1 - \delta)^{A(t,n)} S_{tn}. \quad (6.84)$$

Using the prices $\alpha_1, \alpha_2, \ldots, \alpha_T$ and the corresponding estimated land values, $V_{L1}, \ldots, V_{LT}$ and the prices $p_{S1}, p_{S2}, \ldots, p_{ST}$ and the corresponding estimated structure values, $V_{S1}, \ldots, V_{ST}$, one can again apply normal index number theory using these data to construct Laspeyres, Paasche, Fisher or whatever index formula is being used by the statistical agency in order to construct constant quality price and quantity overall property indexes for the sales of condominium units in the area under consideration for the T periods.

In summary: the builder's model can be modified to apply to the sales of condominium units and reasonable decompositions of property value into land and structure components can be obtained. However, the nonlinear regressions that are required in order to implement the model end up being rather complex. In addition, information on more characteristics of the condominium properties needs to be collected in order to implement the models. The information that is required in order to estimate the final model and calculate (6.83) and (6.84) is as follows:

- The selling prices of the condominium properties in the sample (P_{tn});
- The age of the structure on the property (A_{tn});
- The total area of the land plot (TL_{tn});
- The floor space area of the condo unit (S_{tn});
- The total floor space area of the entire building (TS_{tn});
- The neighbourhood of the property (or the postal code);
- An exogenous structure price index which provides the construction cost of a new structure per meter squared or per square foot (p_{St});

- The number of stories of the building (NS_{tn});
- The height of the sold unit (the number of stories from ground level) (H_{tn});
- The number of units in the building (N_{tn});
- The walking time in minutes to the nearest subway station (TW_{tn}) and
- The subway running time in minutes to the city center from the nearest station (TT_{tn}).

The last two variables are not essential (and are not relevant in small towns and cities). Other non-essential variables which could be useful are the number of bedrooms, the number of bathrooms, the existence of balconies, the type of construction, the number of parking spaces and so on.

The hedonic regression models that were considered in the last two sections are essentially modified supply side models. In the following section, demand side hedonic regressions are considered.

6.14 Demand Side Property Price Hedonic Regressions

A way of rationalizing the traditional log price time dummy hedonic regression model for properties with varying amounts of land area L and constant quality structure area S^* is that the utility that these properties yield to consumers is proportional to the Cobb-Douglas utility function $L^{\alpha}S^{*\beta}$ where α and β are positive parameters (which do not necessarily sum to one).[96] Initially, assume that the constant quality structure area S^* is equal to the floor space area of the structure, S, times an age adjustment, $(1-\delta)^A$, where A is the age of the structure in years and δ is a positive depreciation rate that is less than 1. Thus S^* is related to S as follows:

$$S^* \equiv S(1-\delta)^A. \tag{6.85}$$

In any given time period t, assume that the sale price of transacted property n, V_{tn}, with the amount of land L_{tn} and the amount of quality adjusted structure S^*_{tn} is equal to the following expression:

$$\begin{aligned} V_{tn} &= p_t L_{tn}^{\alpha} S_{tn}^{*\beta} \\ &= p_t L_{tn}^{\alpha}[S_{tn}(1-\delta)^{A(t,n)}]^{\beta} \qquad \text{using (6.85)} \\ &= p_t L_{tn}^{\alpha} S_{tn}^{\beta}(1-\delta)^{\beta A(t,n)} \\ &= p_t L_{tn}^{\alpha} S_{tn}^{\beta}\phi^{A(t,n)} \end{aligned} \tag{6.86}$$

where $A(t,n) = A_{tn}$ is the age of house n sold in period t, p_t can be interpreted as a *period t property price index* and the constant ϕ is defined as follows:

---

[96]The early analysis in this section follows that of Diewert and Fox (2017), McMillen (2003; 289–290), Shimizu et al. (2010a; 795). McMillen assumed that $\alpha+\beta=1$. We follow Shimizu, Nishimura and Watanabe in allowing α and β to be unrestricted.

$$\phi \equiv (1-\delta)^{\beta}. \tag{6.87}$$

Thus if V_{tn} is deflated by the period t property price index p_t, the real value or utility u_{tn} of the property with characteristics L_{tn} and S^*_{tn} is obtained:

$$V_{tn}/p_t = L^{\alpha}_{tn}S^{*\beta}_{tn} \equiv u_{tn}. \tag{6.88}$$

Thus $u_{tn} \equiv q_t$ is the *aggregate real value of the property* with characteristics L_{tn} and S^*_{tn}.

Define ρ_t as the logarithm of p_t and γ as the logarithm of ϕ; i.e.,

$$\rho_t \equiv \ln p_t; \gamma \equiv \ln \phi. \tag{6.89}$$

After taking logarithms of both sides of the first equation in (6.88), using definitions (6.85) and (6.89) and adding error terms, the following system of estimating equations is obtained[97]:

$$\ln V_{tn} = \rho_t + \alpha \ln L_{tn} + \beta \ln S_{tn} + \gamma A_{tn} + \varepsilon_{tn}; \qquad t = 1, \ldots, T; n = 1, \ldots, N(t) \tag{6.90}$$

where the ε_{tn} are independently distributed error terms with 0 means and constant variances. It can be seen that (6.90) is a traditional log price time dummy hedonic regression model with a minimal number of characteristics. The unknown parameters in (6.90) are the constant quality log property prices, $\rho_1, \ldots, \rho_T$, and the taste parameters α, β and the transformed depreciation rate γ. Once these parameters have been determined, the geometric depreciation rate δ which appears in Eq. (6.86) can be recovered from the regression parameter estimates as follows:

$$\delta \equiv 1 - e^{\gamma/\beta}. \tag{6.91}$$

We now explain how the hedonic pricing model defined by (6.86) can be manipulated to provide a decomposition of property value in period t into land and quality adjusted structure components.

Once estimates for α, β and δ have been obtained, define period t value of a property with characteristics L_{tn} and S^*_{tn} is given by the following *period t property valuation function* by the right hand side of (6.86); i.e., define $V(p_t, L_{tn}, S^*_{tn}) \equiv p_t L^{\alpha}_{tn} S^{*\beta}_{tn}$. In empirical applications of the hedonic regression model defined by (6.90), it will often happen that estimates for α and β are such that $\alpha + \beta$ is less than 1.[98] This means that a property in a given period that has double the land and quality adjusted structure than another property will sell for less than double the price of the smaller property. This follows from the fact that the Cobb-Douglas hedonic utility function, $u(L, S^*) \equiv L^{\alpha} S^{*\beta}$, exhibits diminishing returns to scale when $\alpha + \beta < 1$; i.e., we have:

[97] Log price hedonic regressions for property prices date back to Bailey et al. (1963).

[98] See for example the estimated model in Diewert et al. (2017).

$$u(\lambda L, \lambda S^*) = \lambda^{\alpha+\beta} u(L, S^*) \tag{6.92}$$

for all $\lambda > 0$. This behavior is roughly consistent with our builder's Models 5–7 where there was a tendency for property prices to increase less than proportionally as L and S^* increased.

The *marginal prices of land and constant quality structure* in period t for a property with characteristics L and S^*, $\pi_L(p_t, L, S^*)$ and $\pi_{S^*}(p_t, L, S^*)$, are defined by partially differentiating the property valuation function with respect to L and S^* respectively:

$$\pi_L(p_t, L_{tn}, S^*_{tn}) \equiv \frac{\partial V(p_t, L_{tn}, S^*_{tn})}{\partial L} \equiv p_t \alpha L^{\alpha}_{tn} S^{*\beta}_{tn} / L_{tn} = \alpha V(p_t, L_{tn}, S^*_{tn})/L_{tn}; \tag{6.93}$$

$$\pi_{S^*}(p_t, L_{tn}, S^*_{tn}) \equiv \frac{\partial V(p_t, L_{tn}, S^*_{tn})}{\partial S^*} \equiv p_t \beta L^{\alpha}_{tn} S^{*\beta}_{tn} / S^*_{tn} = \beta V(p_t, L_{tn}, S^*_{tn})/S^*_{tn}. \tag{6.94}$$

Multiply the marginal price of land by the amount of land in the property and add to this value of land the product of the marginal price of constant quality structure by the amount of constant quality structure on the property in order to obtain the following identity:

$$(\alpha + \beta) V(p_t, L_{tn}, S^*_{tn}) = \pi_L(p_t, L_{tn}, S^*_{tn}) L_{tn} + \pi_{S^*}(p_t, L_{tn}, S^*_{tn}) S^*_{tn}. \tag{6.95}$$

If $\alpha + \beta$ is less than one, then using marginal prices to value the land and constant quality structure in a property will lead to a property valuation that is less than its selling price. Thus to make the land and structure components of property value add up to property value, divide the marginal prices defined by (6.93) and (6.94) by $\alpha + \beta$ in order to obtain the following *adjusted prices of land and structures for property n sold in period t*, $p_{tL}(p_t, L_{tn}, S^*_{tn})$ and $p_{tS^*}(p_t, L_{tn}, S^*_{tn})$:

$$p_{tL}(p_t, L_{tn}, S^*_{tn}) \equiv \pi_L(p_t, L_{tn}, S^*_{tn})/(\alpha + \beta) = \alpha(\alpha + \beta)^{-1} V(p_t, L_{tn}, S^*_{tn})/L_{tn}; \tag{6.96}$$

$$p_{tS^*}(p_t, L_{tn}, S^*_{tn}) \equiv \pi_{S^*}(p_t, L_{tn}, S^*_{tn})/(\alpha + \beta) = \beta(\alpha + \beta)^{-1} V(p_t, L_{tn}, S^*_{tn})/S^*_{tn}. \tag{6.97}$$

The above material outlines a theoretical framework that can generate a decomposition of property value into land and structure components using the results of a traditional log price time dummy hedonic regression model. To complete the analysis, it is necessary to fill in the details of how the individual property land and structure prices that are generated by the model can be aggregated into period t overall land and structure price indexes.

Run the hedonic regression model defined by (6.90). Define the *constant quality property price index* p_t for period t as follows:

$$p_t \equiv \exp(\rho_t); \qquad t = 1, \ldots, T. \tag{6.98}$$

Define the geometric depreciation rate δ by (6.91). Once δ has been defined, the amount of quality adjusted structure for property n in period t, S_{tn}^* is defined as follows:

$$\ln(S_{tn}^*) \equiv \ln(S_{tn}) + A_{tn}\ln(1-\delta); \qquad t = 1, \ldots, T; n = 1, \ldots, N(t). \tag{6.99}$$

Now that p_t, L_{tn}, S_{tn}^*, α and β have all been defined, we use these data in order to define the predicted prices for property n sold in period t, V_{tn}^*:

$$V_{tn}^* \equiv p_t(L_{tn})^\alpha(S_{tn}^*)^\beta; \qquad t = 1, \ldots, T; n = 1, \ldots, N(t). \tag{6.100}$$

Use Eqs. (6.96) and (6.97) in order to define *constant quality land and structure prices* for sold property n in period t, p_{tnL} and p_{tnS^*}, as follows:

$$p_{tnL} \equiv \alpha(\alpha+\beta)^{-1}V_{tn}^*/L_{tn}; \qquad t = 1, \ldots, T; n = 1, \ldots, N(t); \tag{6.101}$$

$$p_{tnS^*} \equiv \beta(\alpha+\beta)^{-1}V_{tn}^*/S_{tn}^*; \qquad t = 1, \ldots, T; n = 1, \ldots, N(t). \tag{6.102}$$

Finally, *unit value constant quality land and structure prices* for all properties sold in period t, p_{tL} and p_{tS^*}, are defined as follows:

$$p_{tL} \equiv \sum_{n=1}^{N(t)} p_{tnL}L_{tn} \Big/ \sum_{n=1}^{N(t)} L_{tn} \qquad t = 1, \ldots, T; \tag{6.103}$$

$$p_{tS^*} \equiv \sum_{n=1}^{N(t)} p_{tnS^*}S_{tn}^* \Big/ \sum_{n=1}^{N(t)} S_{tn}^* \qquad t = 1, \ldots, T. \tag{6.104}$$

The period t land and structure prices that are defined by (6.103) and (6.104) are reasonable summary statistic prices for land and structures sold in period t that are generated by the log price time dummy hedonic regression model defined by (6.90).

The time dummy log price hedonic regression model defined by (6.90) will generate very different constant quality land and structure subindexes when compared to the corresponding indexes estimated by the builder's model. To see this, suppose the same house n sold in period t and sold again in the following period $t+1$. The period t data for this house are V_{tn}^*, L_{tn} and S_{tn}^* while the period $t+1$ data are V_{t+1n}^*, $L_{t+1n} = L_{tn}$ and $S_{t+1n}^* = (1-\delta)S_{tn}^*$. Use definitions (6.101) and (6.102) for this house for periods t and $t+1$ and calculate the following land and structure inflation rates for this house going from period t to period $t+1$:

$$p_{t+1nL}/p_{tnL} = [\alpha(\alpha+\beta)^{-1}V_{t+1n}^*/L_{tn}]/[\alpha(\alpha+\beta)^{-1}V_{tn}^*/L_{tn}] = V_{t+1n}^*/V_{tn}^*; \tag{6.105}$$

$$p_{t+1nS^*}/p_{tnS^*} = [\beta(\alpha+\beta)^{-1}V_{t+1n}^*/(1-\delta)S_{tn}^*]/[\beta(\alpha+\beta)^{-1}V_{tn}^*/S_{tn}^*] = (1-\delta)^{-1}(V_{t+1n}^*/V_{tn}^*). \tag{6.106}$$

Thus (one plus) the imputed land inflation rate, p_{t+1nL}/p_{tnL}, will equal (one plus) the growth in property value, V_{t+1n}^*/V_{tn}^*, and (one plus) the imputed constant quality structure inflation rate, p_{t+1nS^*}/p_{tnS^*}, will equal $(1-\delta)^{-1}(V_{t+1n}^*/V_{tn}^*)$. Hence if δ is small, then the land and structure inflation rates will be almost identical and approximately equal to (one plus) the growth rate for overall property value. Thus the constant quality price indexes for land and structures will move in an almost proportional manner. In most countries, the price of land will grow much more rapidly than the price of structures so the hedonic regression model defined by (6.90) is not suitable for finding usable land price indexes for residential housing.

However, the hedonic regression model defined by (6.90) (and its generalizations) can generate very reasonable overall constant quality property price indexes, provided that the model generates a plausible estimate for the structure depreciation rate. To see why this result might occur, a highly simplified comparison of a builder's model and the log price traditional hedonic regression model studied in this section will be undertaken below.

Consider the valuation of a representative property in periods 1 and 2 using both the builders model and the traditional hedonic regression model explained in this section. In period 1, the quantity of land and constant quality structure is L_1 and S_1^* with total property value equal to V_1. In period 2, the quantity of land and constant quality structure is $L_2=(1+g_L)L_1$ and $S_2^*=(1+g_S)S_1^*$ with total property value equal to V_2. The L_t and S_t^* are known and hence the growth rates g_L and g_S are also known. Using the property valuation function defined by (6.100), the two properties have the following value decompositions where p_1 and p_2 are the constant quality property price levels for periods 1 and 2:

$$V_1 = p_1 L_1^{\alpha} S_1^{*\beta}; \tag{6.107}$$

$$\begin{aligned} V_2 &= p_2 L_2^{\alpha} S_2^{*\beta} \\ &= p_1(1+\rho)[L_1(1+g_L)]^{\alpha}[S_1^*(1+g_S)]^{\beta} \qquad \text{where } 1+\rho = p_2/p_1 \\ &= V_1(1+\rho)(1+g_L)^{\alpha}(1+g_S)^{\beta} \\ &\approx V_1(1+\rho)[\alpha(1+g_L)+\beta(1+g_S)] \end{aligned} \tag{6.108}$$

where the last approximate equality follows if $\alpha+\beta=1$ and the geometric mean $(1+g_L)^{\alpha}(1+g_S)^{\beta}$ is approximated by the corresponding arithmetic mean, $\alpha(1+g_L)+\beta(1+g_S)$.

Now use the builder's model to value the same properties. Let p_{L1} and p_{L2} be the price levels for land in periods 1 and 2 and let p_{S1} and p_{S2} be the constant quality price levels for structures in periods 1 and 2. The builder's model imputes the following values for the properties in the two periods:

$$V_1 = p_{L1}L_1 + p_{S1}S_1^*; \tag{6.109}$$

$$\begin{aligned} V_2 &= p_{L2}L_2 + p_{S2}S_2^* \\ &= p_{L1}(1+\rho_L)(1+g_L)L_1 + p_{S1}(1+\rho_S)(1+g_S)S_1^* \end{aligned} \tag{6.110}$$

where the land and structure constant quality price indexes are defined as $1+\rho_L = p_{L2}/p_{L1}$ and $1+\rho_S = p_{S2}/p_{S1}$. Define the land and structure share of property value in period 1 as $s_{L1} \equiv p_{L1}L_1/V_1$ and $s_{S1} \equiv p_{S1}S_1^*/V_1$ respectively. The *Laspeyres quantity* and *Paasche price indexes* for properties, Q_L and P_P, are defined as follows:

$$\begin{aligned} Q_L &\equiv s_{L1}(L_2/L_1) + s_{S1}(S_2^*/S_1^*) \\ &= s_{L1}(1+g_L) + s_{S1}(1+g_S); \qquad (6.111) \\ P_P &\equiv [V_2/V_1]/Q_L \\ &= [V_2/V_1]/[s_{L1}(1+g_L) + s_{S1}(1+g_S)] \qquad (6.112) \end{aligned}$$

where the last equality follows using (6.111). Using (6.108), we have the following approximate expression for $1+\rho$, which is the property price index generated by the traditional hedonic regression model:

$$1+\rho \approx [V_2/V_1]/[\alpha(1+g_L) + \beta(1+g_S)]. \qquad (6.113)$$

Comparing (6.112)–(6.113), it can be seen that the Paasche property price index that is generated by the builder's model, P_P, will be approximately equal to the property price index $1+\rho$ that is generated by a traditional log price time dummy hedonic regression model provided that α is approximately equal to the land share s_{L1} and β is approximately equal to structure share s_{S1}.[99] Since the hedonic utility function for the traditional model is Cobb Douglas, this approximate equality is likely to hold. Thus the traditional model is likely to generate approximately the same overall property price indexes as would be generated by the builder's model.[100]

The approximation result in the previous paragraph opens up another possible method for obtaining aggregate land values for residential housing. There are residential property price indexes for many countries that are based on traditional hedonic regression models. Consider such a country that also conducts periodic censuses of housing where owners of residential dwelling units are asked to value their properties. Let the estimated value of housing in periods 1 and t be V_1 and V_t. Suppose the aggregate housing price index levels for these two periods are p_1 and p_t. Using these data, one can form aggregate volume estimates for residential housing as $q_1 \equiv V_1/p_1$ and $q_t \equiv V_t/p_t$. From the country's system of national accounts, it should be possible to obtain estimates for the aggregate price and quantity or volume of residential structures which we denote by p_{S1} and q_{S1} for period 1 and p_{St} and q_{St} for period t. With these data in hand, aggregate Laspeyres, Paasche and Fisher (1922) price and quantity indexes for residential land can be formed using (p_1, p_{S1}) and (p_t, p_{St}) as period 1 and t price vectors and using $(q_1, -q_{S1})$ and $(q_t, -q_{St})$ as period 1 and t quantity vectors. The resulting land prices (p_{L1}, p_{Lt}) and volumes (q_{L1}, q_{Lt}) would fill a gap in the System of National Accounts for the country.

For data series on residential property prices for either the sales of properties or the stock of properties, see the European Central Bank (2018) (which lists 228

[99] To obtain this approximation result, it is also necessary that the depreciation rate that is estimated by the log price time dummy model be reasonable.

[100] For examples of studies where it was found that this approximate equality held, see Diewert (2010; 21), Diewert and Shimizu (2015; 1692), Diewert et al. (2017; 32).

series for European countries) and the Bank for International Settlements (2018), which lists long series for 18 advanced economies. For additional information on alternative approaches for the measurement of residential property price indexes for sales of properties and for making estimates for the stock of residential properties, see Statistics Portugal (Instituto Nacional de Estatistica) (2009), Eurostat (2013, 2017), Hill (2013), Hill et al. (2018), Silver (2018).

6.15 Price Indexes for Rental Housing

At first sight, it would seem that the construction of price indexes for rental housing would be fairly straightforward since typically, rents are paid to owners every month. Thus all that seems to be necessary is to collect information on rents paid (from either the tenants or from the owners), say R_{tn} and R_{t+1n} for rental unit n in periods t and $t+1$, form the price ratios, R_{t+1n}/R_{tn}, and take a suitable average of these ratios to form a rent index. However, the problem is that the quality of the rental unit does not in general remain constant going from one period to the next due to depreciation of the structure and possible renovations and improvements to the structure. Thus the structure is a unique good in general.

Three procedures for dealing with the above problem will be outlined in this section. The first procedure assumes that the builder's model has been run on sales of dwelling units that could be rented and so asset prices, P_{Ltn} and P_{Stn}[101] can be assigned to the land and structure areas, L_{tn} and S_{tn}, that can be imputed for rental dwelling n in period t. The rental price R_{tn} is approximated by the sum of its (end of period) user cost components for land and structures, p_{Ltn} and p_{Stn} respectively. The geometric model of depreciation for structures is used and the one period depreciation rate is $0 < \delta < 1$. The depreciation rate for land is 0. The age of the structure for rental unit n in period t is $A(t, n)$ periods. Setting the rental price of unit n in period t and $t+1$ to the corresponding user costs leads to the following equations:

$$\begin{aligned} R_{tn} &= p_{Ltn}L_{tn} + p_{Stn}(1-\delta)^{A(t,n)-1}S_{tn}; \qquad n = 1, \ldots, N \\ &= [r_t - i_{Lt}]P_{Ltn}L_{tn} + [r_t - i_{St} + (1+i_{St})\delta]P_{Stn}(1-\delta)^{A(t,n)-1}S_{tn}; \end{aligned} \tag{6.114}$$

$$\begin{aligned} R_{t+1n} &= p_{Lt+1n}L_{tn} + p_{St+1n}(1-\delta)^{A(t,n)}S_{tn}; \qquad n = 1, \ldots, N \\ &= [r_{t+1} - i_{Lt+1}]P_{Lt+1n}L_{tn} + [r_{t+1} - i_{St+1} + (1+i_{St+1})\delta]P_{St+1n}(1-\delta)^{A(t,n)}S_{tn} \end{aligned} \tag{6.115}$$

where r_t is the period t opportunity cost of capital for the owner of the rental unit and i_{Lt} and i_{St} are the land and structure price inflation rates that the owner expects at the beginning of period t. Note that the land and structure areas for unit n, L_{tn} and S_{tn}, do not change over time since by hypothesis, we are collect-

[101] P_{Stn} is the price of a square meter of new structure of the type used by rental unit n at the beginning of period t.

ing rent information for the same units over time. It is well known in the housing literature that user costs for dwelling units are much more volatile than the corresponding rents for the same units.[102] Thus in order for the rents R_{tn} and R_{t+1n} to approximate their corresponding user costs on the right hand sides of (6.114) and (6.115), it is necessary to use a nominal smoothed values for the nominal interest rates r_t and particularly for the expected asset inflation rates, i_{Lt} and i_{St}.[103] Note that the quantity of constant quality structure for property n in periods t and $t+1$ are $S^*_{tn} \equiv (1-\delta)^{A(t,n)-1}S_{tn}$ and $S^*_{t+1n} \equiv (1-\delta)^{A(t,n)}S_{tn}$; i.e., the imputed constant quality amount of structure constant quality quantity declines as time increases. The corresponding constant quality amount of land rent, L_{tn}, remains constant over all periods when the dwelling unit is rented. To form a constant quality overall price index for rents, calculate Laspeyres, Paasche or Fisher indexes where the price data for periods t and $t+1$ are the vectors $[p_{Lt1}, \ldots, p_{LtN}; p_{St1}, \ldots, p_{StN}]$ and $[p_{Lt+11}, \ldots, p_{Lt+1N}; p_{St+11}, \ldots, p_{St+1N}]$ and the quantity data for periods t and $t+1$ are the vectors $[L_{t1}, \ldots, L_{tN}; (1-\delta)^{A(t,1)-1}S_{t1}, \ldots, (1-\delta)^{A(t,N)-1}S_{tN}]$ and $[L_{t1}, \ldots, L_{tN}; (1-\delta)^{A(t,1)}S_{t1}, \ldots, (1-\delta)^{A(t,N)}S_{tN}]$.

If estimates for the price of land for the rented units, P_{Ltn}, are not available, then with some additional simplifying assumptions, it is possible to turn Eq. (6.114) into a system of estimating equations. Thus assume that the price of land and the price of a new structure per m^2 is constant across the N rented properties in each period so that $P_{Ltn} = P_{Lt}$ and $P_{Stn} = P_{St}$ for $t = 1, \ldots, T$. Further assume that the new structure price level for period t is known so that P_{St} is a given exogenous variable. Then Eq. (6.114) simplify into the following nonlinear regression model:

$$R_{tn} = p_{Lt}L_{tn} + \mu_t P_{St}(1-\delta)^{A(t,n)-1}S_{tn}; \qquad n = 1, \ldots, N; t = 1, \ldots, T \tag{6.116}$$

where the user cost of land in period t, $p_{Lt} \equiv [r_t - i_{Lt}]P_{Lt}$, is a parameter which is estimated and $\mu_t \equiv [r_t - i_{St} + (1+i_{St})\delta]$[104] is also a parameter which is estimated for $t = 1, \ldots, T$. The depreciation parameter δ is also estimated.[105] The period t price and quantity vectors generated by this model are $[p_{L1}, \ldots, p_{Lt}; \mu_1 P_{S1}, \ldots, \mu_t P_{St}]$ and $[L_{t1}, \ldots, L_{tN}; (1-\delta)^{A(t,1)-1}S_{t1}, \ldots, (1-\delta)^{A(t,N)-1}S_{tN}]$ and normal index number theory can be applied to these vectors. Of course, this simple model can be generalized along the same lines as was done in Sects. 6.12 and 6.13 above for the basic builder's model. If the geometric model of depreciation for the structure

[102] On this point, see Genesove (2003), Verbrugge (2008), Shimizu et al. (2010b), Diewert and Nakamura (2011), Garner and Verbrugge (2011), Suzuki et al. (2018).

[103] The expected land inflation rate i_{Lt} should be an average of land price inflation over the past 15–25 years to reflect the long holding periods that investors have for rental properties and the high transactions costs of buying and selling properties. Diewert and Fox (2018) used a rolling window annualized 25 year inflation rate for land for the 25 years prior to period t to generate very smooth estimates for the expected land inflation rate in their user costs for land in the US.

[104] μ_t is also known as a *capitalization rate*; i.e., it is the ratio of the rental price of the structure to its capital value.

[105] If multicollinearity becomes a problem, it may be necessary to set $\mu_t = \mu$ or assume that that the μ_t are slowly trending over time.

component of the rental unit is changed to another model of depreciation such as one hoss shay depreciation, then the estimating equations must be modified to suit the alternative depreciation model. Finally, a rolling window approach to this model can be implemented which will allow for gradually changing parameters over time.

The second method for dealing with the quality adjustment problems for rents due to the aging of the structure does not require as much information and can be implemented with guesses on the magnitude of a few key parameters. Recall that the market rents for rented unit n in periods t and $t+1$ were define above by (6.114) and (6.115). Define a *constant quality rent* for unit n in period $t+1$, R^*_{t+1n}, as follows:

$$\begin{aligned} R^*_{t+1n} &\equiv p_{Lt+1n}L_{tn} + p_{St+1n}(1-\delta)^{A(t,n)-1}S_{tn}; \qquad n = 1,\ldots,N \\ &= R_{t+1n}[1+\delta(1-\delta)^{-1}s_{St+1n}] \end{aligned} \tag{6.117}$$

where R_{t+1n} is the period $t+1$ market rent for unit n defined by (6.115) and s_{St+1n} is the following *share of structures* in the market rent for unit n in period $t+1$:

$$s_{St+1n} \equiv p_{St+1n}(1-\delta)^{A(t,n)}S_{tn}/R_{t+1n}; \qquad n = 1,\ldots,N. \tag{6.118}$$

Thus R^*_{t+1n}/Rtn is a *constant quality rent index for unit* n for period $t+1$ for $n = 1,\ldots,N$. This index can be calculated if the market rents for both periods, R_{tn} and R_{t+1n}, are known along with the geometric depreciation rate δ and the imputed share of structures in market rent for unit n in period $t+1$, s_{St+1n} defined by (6.118). Thus if market rents are known and the statistician makes educated guesses on the magnitudes of the geometric depreciation rate δ and on s_{St+1n}, then R^*_{t+1n} defined by (6.117) can be calculated as can $1+\delta(1-\delta)^{-1}s_{St+1n}$. To form a constant quality price index for rents, calculate the Laspeyres, Paasche or Fisher indexes where the price data for periods t and $t+1$ are the vectors $[R_{t1},\ldots,R_{tN}]$ and $[R^*_{t1},\ldots,R^*_{tN}]$ and the quantity data for periods t and $t+1$ are the vectors $[1,\ldots,1]$ and $[\{1+\delta(1-\delta)^{-1}s_{St+11}\}^{-1},\ldots,[\{1+\delta(1-\delta)^{-1}s_{St+1N}\}^{-1}]$. This adjustment to rents for the aging of the units will *increase the rental price index* for period $t+1$ and *decrease the corresponding quantity index* for period $t+1$ as compared to an index which just assumed that there was no aging bias.

The third method for dealing with the quality adjustment problems for rents due to the aging of the structure is to run a hedonic regression with the logarithm of rents as the dependent variable. Thus recall the demand side hedonic regression for property prices that was described by Eqs. (6.86)–(6.91) above. Using these equations, replace the period t selling price for property n, V_{tn}, by the observed rent for unit n in period t, R_{tn}, and reinterpret the constant quality price for property sales in period t, p_t, as the period t *constant quality price level for rents* for the dwelling units in scope. With these changes, the rent counterparts to Eq. (6.86) are the following equations:

$$\begin{aligned} V_{tn} &= p_t L^{\alpha}_{tn}[S_{tn}(1-\delta)^{A(t,n)}]^{\beta} \qquad n = 1,\ldots,N;\ t = 1,\ldots,T \\ &= p_t L^{\alpha}_{tn} S^{\beta}_{tn}\phi^{A(t,n)} \end{aligned} \tag{6.119}$$

where $A(t, n) = A_{tn}$, L_{tn} and S_{tn} are the age, land plot area and floor space area of rental unit n and the constant ϕ is defined as $(1-\delta)^{\beta}$. Define ρ_t as the logarithm of p_t and γ as the logarithm of ϕ. Take logarithms of both sides of (6.119) and add error terms in order to obtain the following system of estimating equations:

$$\ln R_{tn} = \rho_t + \alpha \ln L_{tn} + \beta \ln S_{tn} + \gamma A_{tn} + \varepsilon_{tn}; \qquad t = 1, \ldots, T; n = 1, \ldots, N. \tag{6.120}$$

Once the unknown parameters in the linear regression model (6.120) have been determined, the geometric depreciation rate δ which appears in Eq. (6.119) can be recovered from the regression parameter estimates as $\delta \equiv 1 - e^{\gamma/\beta}$. The sequence of constant quality rent levels can be recovered as $p_t \equiv \exp[\rho_t]$ for $t = 1, \ldots, T$.

The estimated depreciation rate δ could equal 0. In this case, renters do not experience any reduction in the quality of the rented structure as the structure ages. This corresponds to one hoss shay or light bulb depreciation. It this case were to occur, it would imply that the aging bias adjustments made in the above two models are not warranted and the estimating equations for those two models would need to be changed to reflect the one hoss shay depreciation of the structures. However, the empirical evidence is that depreciation rates are positive.[106]

Other explanatory variables could be added to the basic log price time dummy hedonic regression model.[107] The explanatory variables that were used in Sects. 6.12 and 6.13 could also be added to the present model defined by Eq. (6.120).

6.16 Valuing the Services of OOH: User Cost Versus Rental Equivalence

In this section, various factors that cause the user cost of an owned dwelling unit to differ from a rental price for a comparable property will be examined.[108] In addition, other factors that affect user costs in general will be discussed.

---

[106] "The average [annual] depreciation rate for rental property is remarkably constant, ranging from 0.58 to 0.60% over the 25 year period. Depreciation rates for owner occupied units show more variation than the estimated rates for renter occupied units. The average depreciation rate for owner occupied housing ranges from 0.9% in year 1 to 0.28% in year 20." Stephen Malpezzi et al. (1987; 382). Note that these depreciation rates are underestimates for the "true" rates since demolition depreciation is not taken into account using this methodology. Put another way, the geometric model of depreciation may not be the "right" model of depreciation for rental housing.

[107] For example, see Malpezzi et al. (1987), Crone et al. (2000, 2011), Verbrugge (2008), Shimizu et al. (2010a), Garner and Verbrugge (2011).

[108] Our discussion here is similar to that of Hill et al. (2017; 7): "The services a household obtains from renting a dwelling are not the same as the services obtained by owner-occupying." They consider some additional factors that can cause rents to differ from user costs. They also assert that since OOH services are derived from both the structure and land, it follows that there is no need to try and separate land from structure in the rental house price index. However, depreciation affects only the structure part of rents and if one attempts to adjust a market rent for this aging factor, it is necessary to apply the depreciation adjustment to only the structure part of rents.

- Utilities such as electricity, water and natural gas may be included in the rent for a dwelling unit that is similar to an owned unit. The net benefit of renting an owned unit should exclude these costs since these expenditures are covered in other categories of a Consumer Price Index.
- When calculating the benefit to the owner of a dwelling unit of renting the unit, there is a problem of determining what is the correct market rental opportunity cost. It turns out that all rents paid in say period t for comparable units to an owned unit can be classified into 3 categories: (i) the rental agreement is not being renegotiated during this period; (ii) the rental agreement is renegotiated during this period with the same tenants and (iii) the rental agreement is a new one with new tenants. Typically, there are no escalations of rents for continuing tenants during the leasehold period and often, renegotiated rents with continuing tenants are also sticky; i.e., there is not much change in these renegotiated rents.[109] For purposes of measuring the net benefit to an owner of renting an owned unit, category (iii) rents should be used as the appropriate comparable market rent.[110]
- Property taxes will be included in market rents and they should also be included in an owner's user cost. However, if property tax payments are treated as a separate category in the CPI, then property taxes should be deducted from the comparable market rents to avoid double counting of these tax expenditures.
- Normal maintenance expenditures on the structure will be part of market rents. These expenditures should be deducted from the comparable market rents since these expenditures by home owners should already be included in other expenditure categories in the CPI. Again, it is necessary to avoid double counting these expenditures. Landlords may also have considerable overhead expenses that are associated with the management of rental properties. These expenses can perhaps be grouped together with maintenance expenditures.
- The structure depreciation rate for rented dwelling units will probably be higher than the rate for comparable owned dwelling units, since owners are likely to take better care of their property and will avoid property damage. This expected difference in the value of depreciation should be deducted from the market rent that is applied to a comparable owned home.
- The owners of rental properties need to charge a small premium to the rents that they receive from rented units in order to cover the loss of rental income due to vacancies. This vacancy premium does not apply to the user cost of an owned unit and thus the comparable market rent for an owned unit should be adjusted downward to account for this vacancy factor.

---

[109]On the stickiness of rents, see Shimizu et al. (2010b), Lewis and Restieaux (2015; 72–75), Suzuki et al. (2018), Hill et al. (2017; 9). Lewis and Restieaux label their three categories as (i) Occupied Let, (ii) Renewal and (iii) New Let. Their category (i) is a stock measure that includes all occupied rental units while their categories (ii) and (iii) match up with categories (ii) and (iii) in the text above. Rents in categories (ii) and (iii) may be subject to rent controls which means that rents in these categories do not reflect current opportunity costs.

[110]However, when constructing a rental price index for renters, rents for all 3 categories should be used.

- Insurance payments are included in market rents. However, in the CPI, insurance payments are included in another category so the imputed insurance premiums should be deducted from the market rent that is applied to a comparable owned home.
- The opportunity cost of capital for a landlord and for an owner may be different. In particular, the owner of a house may be risk averse and have a very low opportunity cost of capital. A landlord who rents properties to tenants will have to include a risk premium in his or her cost of capital to account for possible downturns in the rental market.

Consider the user cost formula for a dwelling unit that was defined by the right hand side of (6.114) in Sect. 6.15. Using the same notation for property n, define period t property value for property n as:

$$V_{tn} \equiv P_{Ltn}L_{tn} + P_{Stn}(1-\delta)^{A(t,n)-1}S_{tn}; \qquad n = 1, \ldots, N. \tag{6.121}$$

Define the period t, property n share of property land value as $s_{Ltn} \equiv P_{Ltn}L_{tn}/V_{tn}$ and the share for constant quality structure as $s_{Stn} \equiv P_{Stn}(1-\delta)^{A(t,n)-1}S_{tn}/V_{tn}$ for $n = 1, \ldots, N$. The using (6.114) and the above definitions the ratio of user cost to property value (or the implied rent capitalization ratio) can be written as follows:

$$R_{tn}/V_{tn} = [r_t - i_{Lt}]s_{Ltn} + [r_t - i_{St} + (1+i_{St})\delta]s_{Stn}; \qquad n = 1, \ldots, N. \tag{6.122}$$

Recall that r_t is a smoothed longer term opportunity cost of capital for period t, i_{Lt} is the long term expected land price inflation rate, i_{St} is a long term expected structure price inflation rate and δ is the geometric structure depreciation rate. The rent to capital value ratio defined by (6.122) or capitalization rate[111] does not take into account the complications that were discussed above. Thus it is necessary to modify (6.122) to take into account these complications. Define v_t as the period t rate of expected loss of rental income due to vacancies (as a fraction of period t capital value), define m_{tn} as expected period t maintenance and overhead expenditures for property n divided by the corresponding period t structure value,[112] define the land tax rate τ_{Ltn} as the ratio of land taxes paid by the owners of property n in period t to the imputed land value $P_{Ltn}L_{tn}$ and the structure tax rate τ_{Stn} as the ratio of structure property taxes paid in period t for property n to imputed structure value, $P_{Stn}(1-\delta)^{A(t,n)-1}S_{tn}$. Finally define π_{tn} as the ratio of insurance payments made in period t by property n to imputed structure value, $P_{Stn}(1-\delta)^{A(t,n)-1}S_{tn}$. Using the

[111]Crone et al. (2000) used hedonic techniques to estimate both a rent index and a selling price index for housing in the U.S. They also suggested that *capitalization rates* (i.e., the ratio of the market rent of a housing property to its selling price) can be applied to an index of housing selling prices in order to obtain an imputed rent index for OOH. As will be shown below, capitalization rates are functions of many variables, some of which can change considerably over time. Also it will be seen that capitalization rates for rented houses are not exactly appropriate as estimators for capitalization rates for owned houses.

[112]Older structures will probably have higher m_{tn} ratios.

above discussion on complications to the standard user cost model, it can be seen that a more meaningful rent to value ratio decomposition for property n in period t is given by the following modification of (6.122) for $n = 1, \ldots, N$:

$$R_{tn}/V_{tn} = [r_t - i_{Lt} + v_t + \tau_{Ltn}]s_{Ltn} + [r_t - i_{St} + (1 + i_{St})\delta + v_t + \tau_{Stn} + m_{tn} + \pi_{tn}]s_{Stn}. \tag{6.123}$$

If property tax payments are not a separate category in the CPI, then the appropriate user cost for an owner of property n in period t, U_{tn}, as a fraction of property value, V_{tn}, is equal to the following expression:

$$U_{tn}/V_{tn} = [r_t - i_{Lt} + \tau_{Ltn}]s_{Ltn} + [r_t - i_{St} + (1 + i_{St})\delta + \tau_{Stn}]s_{Stn} \tag{6.124}$$

Note that the terms v_t, m_{tn} and π_{tn} have been dropped from (6.124). Thus the differences between (6.123) and (6.124) are equal to the following expressions for $n = 1, \ldots, N$:

$$R_{tn}/V_{tn} - U_{tn}/V_{tn} = v_t + [m_{tn} + \pi_{tn}]s_{Stn}. \tag{6.125}$$

Thus looking at (6.125), it can be seen that simply applying the rent of a comparable rented dwelling unit to an owned unit will overstate the appropriate user cost that should be applied to the owned unit. However, the above computations did not take into account the likelihood that the depreciation rate for a rental property is greater than the corresponding depreciation rate for a similar owned property. Thus let δ_O be the depreciation rate for an owned property and suppose that $0 < \delta_O < \delta$ where δ is the depreciation rate for a comparable rented property. Rewriting (6.123) in absolute form rather than in ratio form leads to the following expression for the user cost value of rented property n in period t:

$$\begin{aligned} R_{tn} = {} & [r_t - i_{Lt} + v_t + \tau_{Ltn}]P_{Ltn}L_{tn} \\ & + [r_t - i_{St} + (1 + i_{St})\delta + v_t + \tau_{Stn} + m_{tn} + \pi_{tn}]P_{Stn}(1 - \delta)^{A(t,n)-1}S_{tn}. \end{aligned} \tag{6.126}$$

Taking into account that the depreciation rate is different, the corresponding user cost of a similar owned property n in period t is the following one:

$$U_{tn} = [r_t - i_{Lt} + \tau_{Ltn}]P_{Ltn}L_{tn} + [r_t - i_{St} + (1 + i_{St})\delta_O + \tau_{Stn}]P_{Stn}(1 - \delta_O)^{A(t,n)-1}S_{tn}. \tag{6.127}$$

If δ_O is considerably smaller than δ, then $P_{Stn}(1 - \delta_O)^{A(t,n)-1}S_{tn}$ will be considerably larger than $P_{Stn}(1 - \delta)^{A(t,n)-1}S_{tn}$ and thus in this case, it is likely that U_{tn} will be *larger* than R_{tn} for older properties. Thus the rental equivalence imputation for the services of a comparable owned unit could be considerably smaller than the corresponding imputed long run user cost for the owned unit.[113]

[113]The algebra will be different for different models of depreciation but the same conclusion will follow.

The user cost formulae defined by (6.124)–(6.127) look rather complicated and they require information that may not be available to the statistician. Thus additional assumptions may have to be made which allow approximate user costs for owned dwelling units to be calculated. In situations where equivalent rental prices are not available, this may be the only feasible method to value the services of OOH. For example, the European Union issued the following regulation in 2005 that gives guidance in forming estimates of the services of OOH when equivalent rental prices are not available:

> Under the user-cost method, the output of dwelling services is the sum of intermediate consumption, consumption of fixed capital (CFC), other taxes less subsidies on production and net operating surplus (NOS). For owner occupied dwellings, no labour input is recorded for work done by the owners (1). Experience suggests that CFC and NOS are the two largest items, each representing 30 to 40% of output.
>
> CFC should be calculated based on a perpetual inventory model (PIM) or other approved methods. A separate estimate for the owner-occupied residential buildings should be available.
>
> The net operating surplus should be measured by applying a constant real annual rate of return of 2.5% to the net value of the stock of owner-occupied dwellings at current prices (replacement costs). The real rate of return of 2.5% is applied to the value of the stock at current prices since the increase in current value of dwellings is already taken account of in the PIM. The same rate of return should be applied to the value of the land at current prices on which the owner-occupied dwellings are located.
>
> The value of land at current prices may be difficult to observe annually. Ratios of land value to the value of buildings in different strata may be derived from an analysis of the composition of the costs of new houses and associated land. Eurostat (2005).

To value the services of OOH in Iceland, the highly simplified user cost formula $U_t = (r_t^* + \delta)P_t$ was used where U_t is the period t property user cost, r_t^* is a real interest rate (varied between 3.6 and 4.3%), δ is a property depreciation rate (set equal to 1.25%) and P_t is a period t constant quality property price index.[114]

The Office for National Statistics in the UK used the user cost formula $U_t = (r + m + \delta - i)P_t$ to value the services of OOH where r is a rate of return which includes a risk premium, δ is a depreciation rate, m is the maintenance rate, i is the expected capital appreciation rate of the unit and P_t is a period t property price index.[115]

Returning back to the user cost formulae defined by (6.126) and (6.127), there is another factor which will tend to make the user cost valuation of the services of an owned dwelling unit much bigger than the corresponding actual rental price: households who rent tend to be poorer than households who own. *Thus renters simply cannot afford to rent high end housing units.* High end dwelling units that do rent

---

[114]See Gudnason and Jonsdottir (2011; 148). Note that as in the case of Iceland, the depreciation rate is applied to total property value and not to just the structure value. This may be an acceptable approximation if the shares of land and structure in total property value remain roughly constant over time.

[115]See Lewis and Restieaux (2015; 156). We have changed their notation to match up with our notation.

will tend to rent for prices that are much less than their long run user costs.[116] Thus in advanced countries, the rent to property value ratio for the more expensive properties tends to be about one half the rent to property value ratio for the least expensive properties.[117] Thus it is likely that the widespread use of the rental equivalence approach to the valuation of the services of owner occupied housing results in a measures of the value of housing services which give much lower valuations than valuations based on long run user costs.

There is one additional troublesome issue that has not been discussed thus far and that is the issue of what to do with transfer costs. Transfer costs are the costs associated with the purchase of a dwelling unit. These costs include transactions taxes, legal fees and real estate agent fees. These costs can be substantial. Thus when a household purchases a dwelling unit, the final cost of the purchase should include all of the associated transfer costs. According to user cost theory, the appropriate valuation of the property at the end of the period should be the value of the sale of the house after transfer costs. This viewpoint suggests that the transactions costs of the purchaser should be immediately expensed in the period of purchase. However, from the viewpoint of a landlord who has just purchased a dwelling unit for rental purposes, it would not be sensible to charge the tenant the full cost of these transaction fees in the first month of rent. The landlord would tend to capitalize these costs and recover them gradually over the time period that the landlord expects to own the property. Thus take the capitalized transfer costs that are charged to property n in period t and divide by total property value V_{tn} to obtain the imputed property transfer cost ratio, λ_{tn}. The new rental cost formula for rented unit n in period t, the counterpart to (6.126), becomes the following formula:

$$\begin{aligned} R_{tn} &= [r_t - i_{Lt} + v_t + \tau_{Ltn} + \lambda_{tn}]P_{Ltn}L_{tn} \\ &\quad + [r_t - i_{St} + (1 + i_{St})\delta + v_t + \tau_{Stn} + m_{tn} + \pi_{tn} + \lambda_{tn}]P_{Stn}(1-\delta)^{A(t,n)-1}S_{tn}. \end{aligned} \tag{6.128}$$

From the viewpoint of an owner of a newly purchased dwelling unit, the owner does not actually sell the unit in the next period; the owner holds on to the dwelling unit for average periods that range from 10 to 20 years. Thus it is probably best to regard the transfer costs as a fixed cost that should be amortized over the expected holding period before the dwelling unit is sold again. If this amortisation is appropriate, then the new user cost formula that is the counterpart to (6.127) is the following formula which should be used to value the services of the owned unit if it is not rented out to tenants:

[116] Often high end houses that are not being used by their owners are rented out at prices that are far below their user costs just so someone will be in the house to maintain it and deter theft and vandalism.

[117] See Heston and Nakamura (2011). Hill et al. (2017; 8) find similar results for Australia and Aten (2018) finds similar results for the US. Shimizu et al. (2012) found that user cost valuations for OOH in Tokyo were about 1.7 times as big as the equivalent rent estimates.

$$\begin{aligned}U_{tn} &= [r_t - i_{Lt} + \tau_{Ltn} + \lambda_{tn}]P_{Ltn}L_{tn} \\ &\quad + [r_t - i_{St} + (1 + i_{St})\delta_O + \tau_{Stn} + \lambda_{tn}]P_{Stn}(1 - \delta_O)^{A(t,n)-1}S_{tn}.\end{aligned} \tag{6.129}$$

The above discussion indicates that it is not a straightforward matter to determine the conceptually correct rental equivalent price to value the services of an owned dwelling unit.[118]

6.17 The Payments Approach

The fifth possible approach to the treatment of owner occupied housing in a CPI, the *payments approach*, is described by Goodhart as follows:

> The second main approach is the payments approach, measuring actual cash outflows, on down payments, mortgage repayments and mortgage interest, or some subset of the above. … Despite its problems, such a cash payment approach was used in the United Kingdom until 1994 and still is in Ireland. Goodhart (2001; F350–F351).

Thus the *payments approach* to owner occupied housing is a kind of a *cash flow approach* to the costs of operating an owner occupied dwelling. It consists mainly of mortgage interest and principle payments along with property taxes. Imputations for capital gains, for the cost of capital tied up in house equity and depreciation are ignored in this approach. This leads to the following objections to this approach; i.e., it ignores the opportunity costs of holding the equity in the owner occupied dwelling, it ignores depreciation and it uses nominal interest rates without any offset for inflation in the price of land and the structure. In general, the payments approach will tend to lead to much smaller monthly expenditures on owner occupied housing than the other 4 main approaches, except during periods of high inflation, when the nominal mortgage rate term may become very large without any offsetting item for inflation. One reason for implementing this approach is that it may be useful for indexing the pensions of homeowners; i.e., as the cash costs of home ownership increase, it may be popular to increase pensions to offset these costs.[119] This line of argument has some validity but in recent years, perhaps it is less compelling in many countries due to the ability of homeowners to draw on their equity with reverse mortgages and to postpone paying property taxes until the property is sold. However, a cash flow or payments approach to the valuation of the costs of home ownership may be useful for some users.[120]

---

[118]For a more comprehensive decomposition of the user cost formula for an owned dwelling unit with a mortgage on the unit, see Diewert et al. (2009), Diewert and Nakamura (2011).

[119]Thus the UK still uses the payments approach to value OOH in its Retail Prices Index.

[120]Fenwick (2009, 2012) has argued strongly that statistical agencies responsible for consumer price indexes should produce a range of indexes that suit different purposes. Thus the payments approach to OOH could be produced by statistical agencies that provide multiple consumer price indexes to suit different purposes. However, the payments approach cannot serve as a reliable guide for pricing the services of OOH.

At this point, it is useful to review the three ways which can be used to measure consumption expenditures. The following quotation from the Office for National Statistics (2010; 6):

> Consumption expenditure can be measured in three ways which it is important to distinguish. These ways are:
>
> *Acquisition* means that the total value of all goods and services delivered during a given period is taken into account, whether or not they were wholly paid for during the period.
>
> *Use* means that the total value of all goods and services consumed during a given period is taken into account.
>
> *Payment* means that the total payments made for goods and services during a given period is taken into account, whether or not they were delivered.
>
> For practical purposes, these three concepts cannot be distinguished in the case of non-durable items bought for cash, and they do not need to be distinguished for many durable items bought for cash. The distinction is, however, important for purchases financed by some form of credit, notably major durable goods, which are acquired at a certain point of time, used over a considerable number of years, and paid for, at least partly, some time after they were acquired, possibly in a series of installments. Housing costs paid by owner-occupiers are an obvious example.

In what follows, we will look at the problems associated with the three methods of valuation in a number of specific cases.

Case 1: The payment period coincides with the acquisition period. Let P_1 be the acquisition price for such a unit of a durable good in period 1. Then the acquisition price in period 1 is obviously P_1, the payments price is also P_1 and the period 1 user cost price is p_1 and its exact form depends on the model of depreciation that is applicable for this particular durable good. In other words, there are no problems in sorting out the three methods of valuation in this case.

Case 2: The initial payment period coincides with the acquisition period but payments for the purchase of the durable continue on for subsequent periods. Suppose that payments must be made for T periods and the sequence of monetary payments is $\pi_1, \pi_2, \ldots, \pi_T$. Suppose also that the sequence of expected one period financial opportunity costs of capital for the purchasing household is $r_1, r_2, \ldots, r_{T-1}$. Then the discounted stream of payments, P_1, is the period 1 (expected) cost of purchasing the good where P_1 is defined as follows:

$$P_1 \equiv \pi_1 + (1+r_1)^{-1}\pi_2 + (1+r_1)^{-1}(1+r_2)^{-1}\pi_3 + \cdots + (1+r_1)^{-1}(1+r_2)^{-1}\cdots(1+r_{T-1})^{-1}\pi_T. \quad (6.130)$$

In this case, the acquisitions price for the durable good in period 1 is defined to be P_1, the payments price is π_1 and the user cost will be determined using the appropriate depreciation model where P_1 is taken to be the beginning of the period price for the durable good. In a subsequent period $t \leq T$, the acquisitions price for the used durable good will be 0, the payments price will be π_t and the period t user cost value v_t will be determined using the appropriate depreciation model for this type of durable good. *If* the useful life of the durable good happens to equal T and *if* the period t payment is equal to the corresponding period t user cost valuation v_t

for $t = 1, 2, \ldots, T$, then obviously, the period t user cost valuation v_t will be equal to the observable period t payment π_t.[121]

There are problems associated with the computation of the P_1 defined by (6.130); i.e., in order to compute P_1 when the durable good is purchased during period 1, the sequence of future payments π_t has to be known and guesses will have to be made on the magnitudes of the sequence of expected nominal interest rates r_t. However, the important point to be made here is that P_1 defined by (6.130) will be *less* than the simple sum of the π_t, $\sum_{t=1}^{T} \pi_t$, provided that the nominal interest rates r_t are positive.

Case 3: *The full payment for the good (or service) is made in period 1 but the services of the commodity are not delivered until period t*. Let the period 1 payment be π_1 as usual. Thus the sequence of payments associated with the purchase of the commodity under consideration is π_1 for period 1 and 0 for all subsequent periods. The acquisition of the commodity does not take place until period t but the appropriate acquisition price P_t is not the period 1 payment, π_1, but the following *escalated period 1 price*:

$$P_t \equiv (1 + r_1)(1 + r_2) \cdots (1 + r_{t-1})\pi_1. \tag{6.131}$$

The logic behind this valuation is the following one. During period 1 when the product was paid for, the payment could have been used to pay down debt (at the interest rate r_1) or the payment could have been used to invest in an asset that earned the rate of return r_1. Thus after one period, the opportunity cost of the investment in the pre-purchased product has grown to $\pi_1(1 + r_1)$, after 2 periods, the opportunity cost has grown to $\pi_1(1 + r_1)(1 + r_2), \ldots$, and by period t when the good or service is acquired, the opportunity cost has grown to $\pi_1(1 + r_1)(1 + r_2) \cdots (1 + r_{t-1})$, which is (6.131). The important point to be made here is that P_t defined by (6.131) will be *greater* than the period 1 prepayment, π_1, provided that the nominal interest rates r_t are positive. Since the product has not been acquired by the household for periods $1, 2, \ldots, t - 1$, the corresponding user cost valuations, $v_1, v_2, \ldots, v_{t-1}$ should be set equal to 0. However, when period t is reached, "normal" user costs can be calculated for durable goods using the P_t defined by (6.131) as the beginning of period t price of the durable, assuming that the form of depreciation is known.

Prepayment for services or durable goods is widespread; e.g., trip and hotel reservations made in advance and paid for in advance are service examples and prepayment for condominium units that are under construction is a durable good example.

Case 4: *The good or service is acquired in period 1 but is not paid for until period 2*. In this case, the sequence of payments is $0, \pi_2, 0, \ldots, 0$. The commodity is acquired in period 1 and the appropriate period 1 acquisition price is P_1 defined as follows:

---

[121] The period t user cost valuation v_t for a unit of the durable good that is t periods old can be converted into an equivalent amount of a new unit of a durable good if the geometric or one hoss shay model of depreciation is applicable for the durable good under consideration. Otherwise, units of the durable good of different ages at the same point in time need to be aggregated using an index number formula.

$$P_1 \equiv (1 + r_1)^{-1}\pi_2. \tag{6.132}$$

The justification for this acquisition price runs as follows: The purchasing household lays aside the amount of money P_1 to buy the product in period 1. This money is invested and earns the one period rate of return r_1. Thus when period 2 comes along, the household has $P_1(1 + r_1) = \pi_2$ which is just enough money to complete the purchase in period 2. Thus P_1 is an appropriate period 1 acquisitions price. If the commodity is a durable good, then assuming that the form of depreciation is known, P_1 defined by (6.132) can be used as the beginning of period 1 price for the period 1 user cost and the entire sequence of user costs can be calculated.

This form of pricing is used as a way of offering lower prices for a wide variety of products. A particular application of this model to a service is the use of credit cards to purchase consumption items. A household that pays its balance owing on time can avoid interest charges and thus can postpone payment for its household purchases for up to one month in many cases.[122]

If interest rates are very low, then statistical agencies may well find it is not worth taking into account the above refinements. However, if nominal interest rates are high, it may be necessary to make some of the above adjustments.

6.18 Summary and Conclusion

It is clear that constructing constant quality price indexes for consumer durables is not as conceptually simple as constructing price indexes for nondurables and services where the matched model approach can guide index construction. The fundamental problem of accounting arises when constructing a price index for the services of a durable good: imputations will have to be made in order to decompose the initial purchase cost into period by period components over the life time of the durable good. The method of imputation will involve assumptions which may not be accepted by all interested parties. In spite of this difficulty, it will be useful for statistical agencies to construct analytical series for the services of long lived consumer durables that can be made available to the public. This will meet the needs of different users.[123]

When constructing property price indexes based on sales of properties, there is another factor that reinforces the argument for multiple price indexes: when transactions are sparse, property indexes based on the sparse data can be very volatile. Thus for some purposes, it may be useful to construct a smoothed index (that is revised for a certain number of months) in addition to a volatile real time index.[124]

[122] However, a household that does not pay off its balance owing in a timely fashion will find itself in Case 3 above.

[123] Hill et al. (2017), using Australian data, found substantial differences using the three main approaches to the valuation of OOH. This emphasizes the need for statistical agencies to produce estimates for all three approaches if possible.

[124] See Rambaldi and Fletcher (2014) on various smoothing methods that could be used. Diewert and Shimizu (2017b) suggested a very simple method which worked well in their empirical application.

For non-housing consumer durables, at present, statistical agencies produce consumer price indexes based on the *acquisitions approach*. This type of index is useful for measuring consumer price inflation based on market transactions, with minimal imputations (except for possible quality change). In addition to this standard index, statistical agencies should produce supplementary indexes based on the *user cost approach* in order to more accurately measure the flow of services generated by stocks of consumer durables.[125]

The valuation of the services of housing is very difficult due to the fact that housing services are unique: the location of each dwelling unit is unique and the location affects the land price component of the property and thus affects rents and user costs. Moreover, the structure component of housing does not remain constant over time due to depreciation of the structure and to renovation expenditures. Various methods that can deal with these difficulties (to some degree at least) were explained in Sects. 6.12–6.16. The details of the methods are too complex to summarize here but the suggested methods based on various hedonic regression models have been applied and offer possible ways forward.

For Owner Occupied Housing, the three main approaches should be implemented. There are two possible versions for the *acquisitions approach*: (i) construct a price index for the purchase of new dwelling units in an inclusive basis, including the price of land and (ii) exclude land cost from the purchase cost. The latter index should be well approximated by a construction cost index (with appropriate margins added for developer margins). The inclusive index will be useful for new house buyers, who have to pay for the land plot as well as the new structure. A *rental equivalence price index* for the services of OOH should also be constructed. For many countries, such an (implicit) index is already available as part of the national accounts valuation for the services of OOH.[126] A *user cost index* for the services of OOH should also be constructed since the user cost valuation for the services of a high end dwelling unit will typically be much greater than the corresponding price that the unit could rent for.[127] If the rental equivalent rent and user cost for an owned unit are constructed and are of the same quality, then applying the *opportunity cost approach* to the valuation of the services of the owned unit is appropriate.

For rented housing, the measurement problems are perhaps not so severe; monthly or weekly rents can be observed for the same rental unit and so it would seem that the usual matched model methodology could be applied in this situation. However, an index based on the matched model methodology and normal index number theory will generally have an upward bias due to the neglect of depreciation or a lowering

---

[125]The rental equivalence approach could be used for durables that are rented or leased but typically, most consumer durables are not rented. Depreciation rates will in most cases be based on educated guesses. Durable stock estimates can be made once depreciation rates have been determined. The current value of household stocks of consumer durables should also be constructed and added to household balance sheets.

[126]However, the equivalent rents should be based on new contract rents if possible in order to provide a current opportunity cost for using the services of an owned dwelling unit; recall the discussion on this point in Sect. 6.16.

[127]Recall the evidence on this point in Heston and Nakamura (2011).

of quality due to the aging of the structure. In order to deal with this bias, it will in general require a hedonic regression approach with age as one of the explanatory variables.

We will conclude by noting some specific recommendations that emerge from the paper:

- There are three main approaches for the treatment of consumer durables in a CPI: the acquisitions approach, the rental equivalence approach and the user cost approach.
- The acquisitions approach is suitable (for most purposes) for durable goods with a relatively short expected useful life.
- The acquisitions approach is particularly useful for central bankers who want consumer inflation indexes that are largely free from imputations.
- The acquisitions approach provides an index for purchases of a durable good and this index is a required input into the construction of a user cost index.
- The remaining two approaches are useful for measuring the flow of services yielded by consumer durables over their useful lives.
- At present, only the flow of services for OOH is estimated by national statistical agencies (using the rental equivalence or user cost approaches) because this information is required for the international System of National Accounts.
- The acquisitions approach will substantially understate the value of the service flow from consumer durables that have relatively long lives. Hence at least one of the rental equivalence or user cost approaches should be implemented by statistical agencies for durables with long lives.[128] Examples of long lived durables are automobiles and household furnishings.
- The rental equivalence approach to the valuation of the services provided by consumer durables is the preferred method of valuation when rental or leasing markets for the class of durables exist, because, in principle, no imputations are required to implement this method.[129]
- However, when rental markets for the durable good under consideration are thin or do not exist, then the user cost approach should be used to value the services of the durable good.
- The user cost approach requires the construction of a price index for new acquisitions of the durable. It also requires a model of depreciation and assumptions about the opportunity cost of capital and about expected asset inflation rates. Thus the user cost approach necessarily involves imputations.
- In order to avoid unnecessary volatility in the user costs, long run expected asset inflation rates should be used in the user cost formula.[130]

[128]If the acquisitions approach is used in the headline CPI, the alternative approaches can be published as experimental or supplementary series.

[129]However, for housing, the "comparable" rental property may not be exactly the same as the owned unit. Moreover, the observed rents may include insurance services and the services of some utilities and possibly furniture. It will be difficult to extract these costs from the observed rent.

[130]The long run asset inflation rate over the past 20 or 25 years or the long run rate of inflation in housing rents could be used to predict future asset inflation rates. Many other prediction methods

- Rental markets for high end dwelling units are generally nonexistent or very thin and hence, it may not be possible to use the rental equivalence approach for high end OOH. Even if some rental information on high end housing units is available, usually these rents are far below the corresponding user costs.
- The "true" opportunity cost for using the services of a consumer durable is the maximum of its rental price (if it exists) and its user cost. Thus the use of the rental equivalence approach to value the services of a high end housing unit will understate the "true" service flow by a substantial amount.[131]
- In order to construct national balance sheets and to measure national multifactor productivity, it is necessary to decompose the selling prices of dwelling units into structure and land components. This can be done for both detached housing and condominium units using hedonic regression techniques; see Sects. 6.12 and 6.13 above. This decomposition is also required in order to construct accurate user costs for housing units since depreciation applies to the structure but not to the land component of the property.
- When constructing price indexes for rental housing, statistical agencies need to make an adjustment to observed rents for the same unit for depreciation of the structure and possible improvements to the structure.
- When using observed rents to measure the service flow for comparable owned properties, statistical agencies should use new contract rents to evaluate the service flow for the owned units since rents for continuing tenants may be sticky and not reflect current opportunity costs.
- When constructing user costs for OOH, statistical agencies need to avoid double counting of some housing related costs that may appear elsewhere in the CPI such as insurance costs. Similar double counting problems may arise with housing rents, which may include the services of some utilities or furniture and of course, the housing rent will include insurance costs. In principle, these associated costs should be deducted from the observed rent and placed in the appropriate classification of the CPI. In practice, this is a difficult imputation problem.
- A variant of the acquisitions approach is sometimes applied to OOH. This variant excludes the land component of the purchase of a new house. Thus this variant reduces to a construction cost index for housing with some allowance made for builders' profit margins. This variant generates valuations for OOH that are far below the comparable rental equivalent and user cost valuations. It is difficult to justify the use of this variant in a CPI.[132]

---

could be used; see for example Verbrugge (2008). However, the focus should be on predicting long run asset inflation rather than period to period inflation.

[131] Long run user costs and rents will tend to be approximately equal to each other for lower end housing units since this type of housing unit will be built by property developers who provide rental housing and they need to set rents that are approximately equal to their long run user costs. However, short run dynamics can cause user costs and rents to diverge even for lower end housing units.

[132] It is not a "true" acquisitions price that is observed in the marketplace since it involves imputations to subtract the land value from the property sale. The resulting acquisitions price obviously does not reflect the total services provided by the purchase.

Which of the three main methods for valuing the purchase of a consumer durable should be used for indexing pensions or indexing salaries for consumer inflation? This is a difficult question to answer. If we start out with the idea that we want a national consumer price index, then if there were no durable goods, a national acquisitions price index would be the target index. But it is not clear that this is the "correct" price index once we recognize the existence of consumer durables: an acquisitions index does not recognize the imputed costs of previously purchased consumer durable goods. Thus in order to deal with this difficulty, we need to move to a rental equivalence index or a user cost index if rental markets are thin. But if a national index based on say the rental equivalence approach were used to determine pension payments for veterans or retired civil servants or for employees in an industry, the resulting payments do not take into account that different households have different holdings of consumer durables (housing in particular) and they do not need to be compensated for their consumption of existing holdings. There are additional complications that need to be addressed:

- If the goal is to maintain the purchasing power of a certain group of households (such as retirees or veterans), then an appropriate index needs to be constructed for the relevant group.
- The relevant group may live in different regions of the country and so in principle, separate indexes need to be constructed for each region by group.
- The index may be a plutocratic one (where well off members of the group get a higher weight in the index) or a democratic one (where each individual gets an equal weight in the index).

The resolution of these difficulties is not available at present.

References

Astin, J. 1999. The European union harmonized indices of consumer prices (HICP). *Statistical Journal of the United Nations ECE* 16 (1999): 123–135.

Aten, B.H. 2018. Valuing owner-occupied housing: An empirical exercise using the American community survey (ACS) housing files. Research Paper, Bureau of Economic Analysis, Washington DC, March.

Australian Bureau of Statistics. 2016. Making greater use of transactions data to compile the consumer price index. Information Paper 6401.0.60.003, Nov 29, Canberra: ABS.

Bailey, M.J., R.F. Muth, and H.O. Nourse. 1963. A regression method for real estate price construction. *Journal of the American Statistical Association* 58: 933–942.

Bank for International Settlements. 2018. BIS property prices. BIS Statistics Warehouse, Basel: BIS.

Beidelman, C. 1973. Valuation of used capital assets. Sarasota Florida: American Accounting Association.

Beidelman, C.R. 1976. Economic depreciation in a capital goods industry. *National Tax Journal* 29: 379–390.

Böhm-Bawerk, E.V. 1891. *The Positive Theory of Capital*. New York: G.E. Stechert. W. Smart (translator of the original German book published in 1888).

Bostic, R.W., S.D. Longhofer, and C.L. Readfearn. 2007. Land leverage: Decomposing home price dynamics. *Real Estate Economics* 35 (2): 183–2008.

Bureau of Labor Statistics. 1983. Changing the home ownership component of the consumer price index to rental equivalence. CPI Detailed Report, Washington DC: BLS.

Burnett-Issacs, K., N. Huang, and W.E. Diewert. 2016. Developing land and structure price indexes for Ottawa condominium apartments. Discussion Paper 16–09, Vancouver School of Economics: University of British Columbia, Vancouver, B.C., Canada.

Cairns, R.D. 2013. The fundamental problem of accounting. *Canadian Journal of Economics* 46 (2): 634–655.

Canning, J.B. 1929. *The Economics of Accountancy*. New York: The Ronald Press Co.

Christensen, L.R., and D.W. Jorgenson. 1969. The measurement of U.S. real capital input, 1929–1967. *Review of Income and Wealth* 15 (4): 293–320.

Church, A.H. 1901. The proper distribution of establishment charges, part III. *The Engineering Magazine* 21: 904–912.

Clapp, J.M. 1980. The elasticity of substitution for land: The effects of measurement errors. *Journal of Urban Economics* 8: 255–263.

Court, A.T. 1939. Hedonic price indexes with automotive examples. In *The Dynamics of Automobile Demand*, 98–117. New York: General Motors Corporation.

Crone, T.M., L.I. Nakamura, and R. Voith. 2000. Measuring housing services inflation. *Journal of Economic and Social Measurement* 26: 153–171.

Crone, T.M., L.I. Nakamura, and R.P. Voith. 2011. Hedonic estimates of the cost of housing services: Rental and owner occupied units. In *Price and Productivity Measurement: Volume 1: Housing*, ed. Diewert, W.E., B.M. Balk, D. Fixler, K.J. Fox, and A.O. Nakamura, 51–68. Victoria: Trafford Press.

Crosby, N.S.Devaney, and V. Law. 2012. Rental depreciation and capital expenditure in the UK commercial real estate market, 1993–2009. *Journal of Property Research* 29 (3): 227–246.

de Haan, J. 2015. Rolling year time dummy indexes and the choice of splicing method. Room Document at the 14th meeting of the Ottawa Group, May 22, Tokyo. http://www.stat.go.jp/english/info/meetings/og2015/pdf/t1s3room.

Diewert, W.E. 1974. Intertemporal consumer theory and the demand for durables. *Econometrica* 42: 497–516.

Diewert, W.E. 1980. Aggregation problems in the measurement of capital. In *The Measurement of Capital*, ed. D. Usher, 433–528. Chicago: University of Chicago Press.

Diewert, W.E. 2002. Harmonized indexes of consumer prices: their conceptual foundations. *Swiss Journal of Economics and Statistics* 138 (4): 547–637.

Diewert, W.E. 2005a. Issues in the measurement of capital services, depreciation, asset price changes and interest rates. In *Measuring Capital in the New Economy*, ed. C. Corrado, J. Haltiwanger, and D. Sichel, 479–542. Chicago: University of Chicago Press.

Diewert, W.E. 2005b. Adjacent period dummy variable hedonic regressions and bilateral index number theory. *Annales d'Économie et de Statistique* 79 (80): 759–786.

Diewert, W.E. 2008. OECD workshop on productivity analysis and measurement: Conclusions and future directions. In *Proceedings From the OECD Workshops on Productivity Measurement and Analysis*, 11–36. Paris: OECD.

Diewert, W.E. 2010. Alternative approaches to measuring house price inflation. Discussion Paper 10-10, Department of Economics, The University of British Columbia, Vancouver, Canada, V6T 1Z1.

Diewert, W.E., and K.J. Fox. 2016a. Sunk costs and the measurement of commercial property depreciation. *Canadian Journal of Economics* 49 (4): 1340–1366.

Diewert, W.E., and K.J. Fox. 2017. Substitution bias in multilateral methods for CPI construction using scanner data. Discussion Paper 17-02, Vancouver School of Economics, The University of British Columbia, Vancouver, Canada, V6T 1L4.

Diewert, W.E., and K.J. Fox. 2018. Alternative user costs, productivity and inequality in US business sectors. In *Productivity and Inequality*, ed. Greene, W.H., L. Khalaf, P. Makdissi, R. Sickles, M. Veall, and M.-C. Voia, 21–69. New York: Springer.

Diewert, W.E., and D.A. Lawrence. 2000. Progress in measuring the price and quantity of capital. In *Econometrics Volume 2: Econometrics and the Cost of Capital: Essays in Honor* Dale W. Jorgenson, L.J. Lau, 273–326. Cambridge, MA: The MIT Press.

Diewert, W.E., and A.O. Nakamura. 2011a. Accounting for housing in a CPI. In Diewert, W.E., B.M. Balk, D. Fixler, K.J. Fox, and A.O. Nakamura, *Price and Productivity Measurement: Volume 1: Housing*, 7–32. Victoria: Trafford Press.

Diewert, W.E., A.O. Nakamura, and L.I. Nakamura. 2009. The housing bubble and a new approach to accounting for housing in a CPI. *Journal of Housing Economics* 18 (3): 156–171.

Diewert, W.E., and C. Shimizu. 2015. Residential property price indexes for Tokyo. *Macroeconomic Dynamics* 19: 1659–1714.

Diewert, W.E., and C. Shimizu. 2016b. Hedonic regression models for Tokyo condominium sales. *Regional Science and Urban Economics* 60: 300–315.

Diewert, W.E., and C. Shimizu. 2017a. Alternative approaches to commercial property price indexes for Tokyo. *Review of Income and Wealth* 63 (3): 492–519.

Diewert, W.E., and C. Shimizu. 2017b. Alternative land prices for commercial properties in Tokyo. Discussion Paper 17-07, Vancouver School of Economics, The University of British Columbia, Vancouver, Canada, V6T 1L4.

Diewert, W.E., J. de Haan, and R. Hendriks. 2011b. The decomposition of a house price index into land and structures components: A hedonic regression approach. *The Valuation Journal* 6: 58–106.

Diewert, W.E., J. de Haan, and R. Hendriks. 2015. Hedonic regressions and the decomposition of a house price index into land and structure components. *Econometric Reviews* 34: 106–126.

Diewert, W.E., N. Huang, and K. Burnett-Issacs. 2017. Alternative approaches for resale housing price indexes. Discussion Paper 17-05,Vancouver School of Economics, The University of British Columbia, Vancouver, Canada, V6T 1L4.

Diewert, W.E., and H. Wei. 2017. Getting rental prices right for computers: Reconciling different perspectives on depreciation. *Review of Income and Wealth*, 63S1:149-168.

European Central Bank. 2018. *Residential Property Price Index Statistics*, Statistical Data Warehouse. Frankfurt: European Central Bank.

Eurostat, IMF, OECD, UN and World Bank. 1993. System of national accounts 1993, United Nations. New York.

Eurostat. 2001. *Handbook on Price and Volume Measures in National Accounts*. Luxembourg: European Commission.

Eurostat. 2005. On the principles for estimating dwelling services for the purpose of Council Regulation (EC, Euratom) No 1287/2003 on the harmonisation of gross national income at market prices. *Official Journal of the European Union*, Commission Regulation (EC) No 1722/2005, October 20.

Eurostat. 2013. *Handbook on Residential Property Prices Indices (RPPIs)*. Luxembourg: Publications Office of the European Union.

Eurostat. 2017. *Technical Manual on Owner-Occupied Housing and House Price Indices*. Brussels: European Commission.

Fenwick, D. 2009. A statistical system for residential property price indices. In *Eurostat-IAOS-IFC Conference on Residential Property Price Indices*, Bank for International Settlements, November.

Fenwick, D. 2012. A family of price indices, the meeting of groups of experts on consumer price indices, UNECE/ILO, United Nations Palais des Nations, Geneva Switzerland, May 30–June 1.

Fisher, I. 1922. *The Making of Index Numbers*. Boston: Houghton-Mifflin.

Francke, M.K. 2008. The Hierarchical Trend Model. In *Mass Appraisal Methods: An International Perspective for Property Valuers*, ed. Kauko, T., and M. Damato, 164–180. Oxford: Wiley-Blackwell.

Francke, M.K., and G.A. Vos. 2004. The hierarchical trend model for property valuation and local price indices. *Journal of Real Estate Finance and Economics* 28: 179–208.

Garcke, E., and J.M. Fells. 1893. *Factory Accounts: Their Principles and Practice, Fourth Edition, (First Edition 1887)*. London: Crosby, Lockwood and Son.

Garner, T.I., and R. Verbrugge. 2011. The puzzling divergence of rents and user costs, 1980–2004: Summary and extensions. In Diewert, W.E., B.M. Balk, D. Fixler, K.J. Fox, and A.O. Nakamura, *Price and Productivity Measurement: Volume 1: Housing*, 125–146. Victoria: Trafford Press.

Genesove, D. 2003. The nominal rigidity of apartment rents. *The Review of Economics and Statistics* 85 (4): 844–853.

Gilman, S. 1939. *Accounting Concepts of Profit*. New York: The Rolland Press Co.

Goodhart, C. 2001. What weights should be given to asset prices in the measurement of inflation? *The Economic Journal* 111: F335–F356.

Griliches, Z. 1971. Introduction: Hedonic price indexes revisited. In *Price Indexes and Quality Change*, ed. Z. Griliches, 3–15. Cambridge, MA: Harvard University Press.

Gudnason, R., and G. Jonsdottir. 2011. Owner occupied housing in the icelandic CPI. In *Price and Productivity Measurement: Volume 1: Housing*, ed. W.E. Diewert, B.M. Balk, D. Fixler, K.J. Fox, and A.O. Nakamura. Victoria: Trafford Press.

Hall, R.E., and D.W. Jorgenson. 1967. Tax policy and investment behavior. *American Economic Review* 57: 391–414.

Harper, M.J., E.R. Berndt, and D.O. Wood. 1989. Rates of return and capital aggregation using alternative rental prices. In *Technology and Capital Formation*, ed. D.W. Jorgenson, and R. Landau, 331–372. Cambridge, MA: The MIT Press.

Heston, A., and A.O. Nakamura. 2011. Reported prices and rents of housing: Reflections of costs, amenities or both?. In *Price and Productivity Measurement: Volume 1: Housing*, W.E. Diewert, B.M. Balk, D. Fixler, K.J. Fox, and A.O. Nakamura, 117–124. Victoria: Trafford Press.

Hicks, J.R. 1946. *Value and Capital*, 2nd ed. Oxford: Clarendon Press.

Hill, R.J. 2013. Hedonic price indexes for residential housing: A survey, evaluation and taxonomy. *Journal of Economic Surveys* 27: 879–914.

Hill, R.J., M. Scholz, C. Shimizu, and M. Steurer. 2018. An evaluation of the methods used by European countries to compute their official house price indices. *Economie et Statistique / Economics and Statistics Numbers* 500–502: 221–238.

Hill, R.J., M. Steurer, and S.R. Waltl. 2017. Owner occupied housing in the CPI and its impact on monetary policy during housing booms and busts. Graz Economic Paper 2018–12, Department of Public Economics, University of Graz, Graz, Austria.

Hoffmann, J., and C. Kurz. 2002. Rent indices for housing in West Germany: 1985 to 1998. Discussion Paper 01/02, Economic Research Centre of the Deutsche Bundesbank, Frankfurt.

Hotelling, H. 1925. A general mathematical theory of depreciation. *Journal of the American Statistical Association* 20: 340–353.

Hulten, C.R. 1990. The measurement of capital. In *Fifty Years of Economic Measurement*, ed. E.R. Berndt, and J.E. Triplett, 119–158. Chicago: The University of Chicago Press.

Hulten, C.R. 1996. Capital and wealth in the revised SNA. In *The New System of National Accounts*, ed. J.W. Kendrick, 149–181. New York: Kluwer Academic Publishers.

Hulten, C.R., and F.C. Wykoff. 1981a. The estimation of economic depreciation using vintage asset prices. *Journal of Econometrics* 15: 367–396.

Hulten, C.R., and F.C. Wykoff. 1981b. The measurement of economic depreciation. In *Depreciation, Inflation and the Taxation of Income from Capital*, ed. C.R. Hulten, 81–125. Washington D.C.: The Urban Institute Press.

Hulten, C.R., and F.C. Wykoff. 1996. Issues in the measurement of economic depreciation: Introductory remarks. *Economic Inquiry* 34: 10–23.

Ivancic, L., W.E. Diewert, and K.J. Fox. 2011. Scanner data, time aggregation and the construction of price indexes. *Journal of Econometrics* 161: 24–35.

Jorgenson, D.W. 1989. Capital as a factor of production. In *Technology and Capital Formation*, ed. D.W. Jorgenson, and R. Landau, 1–35. Cambridge, MA: The MIT Press.

Jorgenson, D.W. 1996. Empirical studies of depreciation. *Economic Inquiry* 34: 24–42.

Katz, A.J. 1983. Valuing the services of consumer durables. *The Review of Income and Wealth* 29: 405–427.

Koev, E., and J.M.C. Santos Silva. 2008. Hedonic methods for decomposing house price indices into land and structure components. Unpublished paper, Department of Economics: University of Essex, England, October.

Krsinich, F. 2016. The FEWS index: Fixed effects with a window splice. *Journal of Official Statistics* 32: 375–404.

Lebow, D.E., and J.B. Rudd. 2003. Measurement error in the consumer price index: Where do we stand? *Journal of Economic Literature* 41: 159–201.

Lewis, R., and A. Restieaux. 2015. Improvements to the measurement of owner occupiers' housing costs and private housing rental prices. Newport, UK: Office for National Statistics.

Malpezzi, S., L. Ozanne, and T. Thibodeau. 1987. Microeconomic estimates of housing depreciation. *Land Economics* 63: 372–385.

Marshall, A. 1898. *Principles of Economics*, 4th ed. London: The Macmillan Co.

Matheson, E. 1910. *The Depreciation of Factories and their Valuation*, 4th ed. London: E. & F.N. Spon.

McMillen, D.P. 2003. The return of centralization to Chicago: Using repeat sales to identify changes in house price distance gradients. *Regional Science and Urban Economics* 33: 287–304.

Office for National Statistics. 2010. *Consumer Price Indexes Technical Manual: 2010 Edition*. Newport, U.K.: Office for National Statistics.

Peasnell, K.V. 1981. On capital budgeting and income measurement. *Abacus* 17 (1): 52–67.

Rambaldi, A.N., R.J. McAllister, K. Collins, and C.S. Fletcher. 2010. Separating land from structure in property prices: A case study from Brisbane Australia. School of Economics, The University of Queensland, St. Lucia, Queensland 4072, Australia.

Rambaldi, A.N., and C.S. Fletcher. 2014. Hedonic imputed property price indexes: The effects of econometric modeling choices. *Review of Income and Wealth* 60 (S2): S423–S448.

Schreyer, P. 2001. *OECD Productivity Manual: A Guide to the Measurement of Industry-Level and Aggregate Productivity Growth*. Paris: OECD.

Schreyer, P. 2009. *Measuring Capital, Statistics Directorate*, National Accounts, STD/NAD(2009)1. Paris: OECD.

Schwann, G.M. 1998. A real estate price index for thin markets. *Journal of Real Estate Finance and Economics* 16 (3): 269–287.

Shimizu, C., W.E. Diewert, K. Nishimura, and T. Watanabe. 2012. *The Estimation of Owner Occupied Housing Indexes using the RPPI: The Case of Tokyo*, Meeting of the Group of Experts on Consumer Price Indices, Geneva, May 28.

Shimizu, C., K.G. Nishimura, and T. Watanabe. 2010a. Housing prices in Tokyo: A comparison of hedonic and repeat sales measures. *Journal of Economics and Statistics* 230: 792–813.

Shimizu, C., K.G. Nishimura, and T. Watanabe. 2010b. Nominal rigidity of housing rent. *Financial Review* 106 (1): 52–68.

Shimizu, C., H. Takatsuji, H. Ono, and K.G. Nishimura. 2010c. Structural and temporal changes in the housing market and hedonic housing price indices. *International Journal of Housing Markets and Analysis* 3 (4): 351–368.

Shimizu, C., and T. Watanabe. 2011. Nominal rigidity of housing rent. *Financial Review* 106 (1): 52–68.

Silver, M.S. 2018. How to measure hedonic property price indexes better. *EURONA* 1 (2018): 35–66.

Solomons, D. 1961. Economic and accounting concepts of income. *The Accounting Review* 36: 374–383.

Statistics Portugal (Instituto Nacional de Estatistica). 2009. *Owner-occupied housing: Econometric study and model to estimate land prices, final report, paper presented to the Eurostat Working Group on the Harmonization of Consumer Price Indices*, March 26–27, Eurostat, Luxembourg.

Suzuki, M., Y. Asami, and C. Shimizu. 2018. Unit-level long-run dynamics of 'sticky' housing rents. Unpublished paper, Department of Urban Engineering, The University of Tokyo. Email: suzuki@ua.t.u-tokyo.ac.jp.

Verbrugge, R. 2008. The puzzling divergence of rents and user costs, 1980–2004. *Review of Income and Wealth* 54 (4): 671–699.

Walras, L. 1954. *Elements of Pure Economics*. London: George Allen and Unwin. Translated by W. Jaffe (first published in 1874).

White, K.J. 2004. *Shazam: User's Reference Manual, Version 10*. Vancouver, Canada: Northwest Econometrics Ltd.

Chapter 7
New Estimates for the Price of Housing in the Japanese CPI

7.1 Introduction

Throughout their histories most advanced nations have experienced abrupt increases and subsequent decreases in asset prices, especially housing prices. These fluctuations have had substantial impact on the financial system, often leading to a stagnation of economic activity. The most representative examples are Japan and Sweden in the 1990s and, more recently, the global financial crisis triggered by the sub-prime problem in the United States. Reinhart and Rogoff (2008) conducted an exhaustive, long-term, comparative time series analysis of economic data from numerous countries which made it clear that the incidence of various economic phenomena is a common factor underlying banking crises. It has been noted that one of these phenomena is a significant increase in asset prices, and property prices in particular, compared to rents.[1]

This raises the following question: why do services prices not fluctuate significantly when asset prices fluctuate? If we consider housing asset prices as being determined based on the net present value of future revenue (rent) that will be produced, housing prices and housing rents should be covariant even if there is a certain lag between them. Moreover, if we assume that consumers choose housing by weighing the cost of investing in housing[2] versus rental costs, it is difficult to believe that the two would diverge significantly. However, in reality, the two do diverge

[1]Others that have been pointed out include (a) a relative rise in debt compared to income and net assets and an increase in leveraging, (b) a sustained influx of capital and (c) a lag in productivity increases compared to increases in asset values and debt.

[2]This is the so-called user cost and is calculated based on payments (including mortgage interest) and ownership-based taxes (fixed asset tax, etc.).

The base of this chapter is Shimizu, C., S. Imai and W.E. Diewert. 2015. New estimates for the price of housing in the Japanese CPI. Discussion Paper 15–02, Vancouver School of Economics, University of British Columbia. Presented at Ottawa Group Meeting 2015, Statistics Bureau of Japan, Urayasu.

W. E. Diewert et al., *Property Price Index*, Advances in Japanese Business and Economics 11, https://doi.org/10.1007/978-4-431-55942-9_7

significantly and the fluctuation of property prices in particular is a factor that has induced many economic problems.

Rent, meanwhile, occupies an important position in the goods and services market and in many countries has a weight in the CPI basket of approximately 25%.[3] The housing market plays an essential role in both the asset market and the goods and services market, and rent in particular is an important connection point linking asset prices to goods and services prices.[4]

In estimating rental costs for durable goods, statistical agencies often use the acquisition approach; i.e., they simply allocate the cost of the durable good to the period when it was purchased. It would be useful to many users if, in addition to the acquisitions approach, statistical agencies would implement a variant of either the rental equivalence approach or the user cost approach for long lived consumer durables. Users can then decide which approach best suits their purposes. Any one of the three main approaches could be chosen as the approach that would be used in the " headline" CPI.[5]

The Statistics Bureau of Japan uses the rental equivalence approach to estimate housing rents for Owner Occupied Housing (OOH). However, Diewert (2015) indicated the following disadvantages of the rental equivalence approach.

- Homeowners may not be able to provide very accurate estimates for the rental value of their dwelling unit.
- On the other hand, if the statistical agency tries to match the characteristics of an owned dwelling unit with a comparable unit that is rented in order to obtain the imputed rent for the owned unit, there may be difficulties in finding such comparable units. Furthermore, even if a comparable unit is found, the rent for that unit may not be an appropriate opportunity cost for not renting the owned unit.[6]
- The statistical agency should make an adjustment to these estimated rents over time in order to take into account the effects of depreciation, which causes the quality of the unit to slowly decline over time (unless this effect is completely offset by renovation and repair expenditures).

---

[3]Housing services represent 26.4% of the CPI for Tokyo's wards. Of this, 4.3% is private rent paid by tenants to owners while the remaining 19.4% is the imputed rent that the owner's of dwelling units pay for the services of their units. These imputed rents are the rents that owners would pay if they rented a dwelling unit of similar quality; i.e., the rental equivalence approach is used to compute imputed rents in the Japanese CPI.

[4]With regard to this point, refer to Goodhart (2001).

[5]See Diewert (2015) and Shimizu, Diewert, Nishimura and Watanabe (2012).

[6]Diewert (2007) argued that the correct opportunity cost for valuing the services of an owned dwelling unit is the *maximum* of the amount the unit could rent for in the current rental market and the user cost of the dwelling unit since this represents the financial opportunity cost of tying up ones capital in the dwelling. In most countries, the user cost of a high end home is often approximately twice as high as its rental equivalence price. For less expensive owned homes, the user cost is usually much closer to the amount it could rent for. However, the situation in Japan could be quite different since Japan has experienced widespread asset deflation which did not occur in other developed countries.

- Care must be taken to determine exactly what extra services are included in the homeowner's estimated rent; i.e., does the rent include insurance, electricity and fuel or the use of various consumer durables in addition to the structure? If so, these extra services should be stripped out of the rent, since they are covered elsewhere in the consumer price index.[7]

Recently, the Statistics Bureau of Japan started to collect housing rent data from property management companies or owners to respond to first problem listed above. However, the characteristics of the owner occupied population of dwelling units could be quite different from the characteristics of the rental population.[8] Thus in valuing the services of OOH in Japan, the current approach has some downward bias in that it does not adjust for quality declines due to depreciation (depreciation bias) and some possible bias due to the fact that the quality of rental units may be different from owned units that are thought to be comparable (quality adjustment bias).

In addition to the above possible biases in using the rental equivalence approach to the valuation of the services of OOH, there are differences between "contract rent" and "market rent". "Contract rent" refers to the rent paid by a renter who has a long term rental contract with the owner of the dwelling unit and " market rent" is the rent paid by the renter in the first period after a rental contract has been negotiated. In a "normal" economy which is experiencing moderate or low general inflation, typically market rent will be higher than contract rent. However, if there are rent controls or a temporary glut of rental units, then market rent could be lower than contract rent. In any case, it can be seen that if we value the services of an owner occupied dwelling at its current opportunity cost on the rental market, we should be using market rent rather than contract rent.[9]

It can be seen that there are many problems when we attempt to value the services of both owner occupied housing and of rented dwelling units. There have been many attempts in the literature that try to measure these possible biases. For example, Crone, Nakamura and Voith (2004) and Gordon and Goethem (2005) have pointed out the importance of addressing qualitative changes in rents and they estimated CPI bias by calculating hedonic-type quality-adjusted indexes. Crone, Nakamura and Voith (2006), focusing on changes in the estimation method of housing rents

---

[7]However, it could be argued that these extra services that might be included in the rent are mainly a weighting issue; i.e., it could be argued that the *trend* in the homeowner's estimated rent would be a reasonably accurate estimate of the trend in the rents after adjusting for the extra services included in the rent.

[8]For example, according to the 2013 Housing and Land Survey, the average floor space (size) of owner-occupied housing in Tokyo was 110.64 square meters for single-family house owner-occupied housing and 82.71 square meters for rental housing—a discrepancy of over 30 square meters. For condominiums, an even greater discrepancy exists: the floor space is 65.73 square meters for owner-occupied housing and 37.64 square meters for rental housing. Moreover, in addition to the difference in floor space between rented and owned units, the quality of the owned units tends to be higher than the rented units and these quality differences need to be taken into account.

[9]On the other hand, contract rent is the "right" rental concept to use to value the cost of rental housing for the renter and it is the correct price to use to calculate the rental income of the owner of the rental unit.

for CPIs, have analyzed the structure of these biases based on micro-data used to estimate CPI rents.

The rents used to estimate the cost of rented dwellings in the Japanese CPI is the aggregate of rents paid for rental accommodation. These rents include a combination of newly signed rental contracts and rollover contracts for existing tenants. It is appropriate to use both types of contract to measure the actual cost of rental housing (but of course, these rents should be quality adjusted for depreciation and other changes in quality). But it is not appropriate to use both types of contract to impute rents for owner occupied housing: only market rents should be used. It is known that price adjustments are basically not made for rollover contracts (i.e. renewed leases). As a result, it is to be expected that new contract rents determined freely by the market will diverge considerably from rollover contract rents.

Genesove (2003), based on a study using individual data from the American Housing Survey and survey research, has analyzed the stickiness of rents by dividing them into new contracts and rollover contracts.

In Japan, Shimizu, Nishimura and Watanabe (2010a) and Shimizu and Watanabe (2011) constructed a unique dataset using data from a housing listing magazine and a property management company to measure the extent of housing rent stickiness in the country and analyzed the micro-structure of rental adjustments.

In order to clear up remaining issues from Shimizu, Nishimura and Watanabe (2010a) and Shimizu and Watanabe (2011), this paper focuses on rent control bias or systemic bias in rental housing market and aims to construct a new dataset to re-estimate the stickiness of housing rent in Japan and the implications of this stickiness for the valuation of the services of Owner Occupied Housing (OOH). A second major objective of the present paper is to look at the effects of sampling the housing population: how much does accuracy of the housing component of the CPI decrease as the sampled population decreases?

7.2 The Macroeconomic Analysis of Housing Rent

7.2.1 Data

When attempting to conduct empirical research focusing on the housing market there are various difficulties involved in obtaining research data. This is because the organization and disclosure of information on housing lags behind other markets. Data is even more limited for the housing rental market. In both domestic and international research, analysis is conducted on a strongly hypothetical basis as is found in the studies by Shimizu, Nishimura and Watanabe (2010a) and Shimizu and Watanabe (2011).

Housing rent-related data may be broadly divided into two types. First, there are market rents, which are generated when a specific event occurs (i.e. a contract is created). These rents can be further broken down into rents based on new contracts when there is tenant turnover and rents based on new contracts for tenants who continue to reside in the same unit at the moment when the term of the previous contract ends. In general, the former are known as "new contracts" and the latter as "rollover contracts." Rents for the former are basically freely determined by the transaction market, while rents for the latter are determined based on systemic limitations such as the Act on Land and Building Leases. The other type of data is rent that continues to be paid on an ongoing basis. This rent is determined based on the new contract when a tenant arrives or the subsequent rollover contract and remains the same as long as no new event (i.e. contract) occurs. In this study, we have prepared these three types of data.

Data were provided by the company Recruit Co. Ltd. This is an insurance company that handles rental guarantees. As a result of handling insurance contracts at the time new rental contracts are drawn up, it has access to initial new rent amounts. In addition, since it provides compensation for rental defaults, it records the rental payment status each month and, by the same token, records the status of rental adjustments for rollover contracts.

The data are summarized in Table 7.1. It is limited to Tokyo's wards. We obtained data for 52,524 units covering the Tokyo ward area. In terms of the track record for rents recorded during the period covered here, there are 1,529,485 data items of which 36,832 were generated by new contracts and 41,117 were related to rollover contracts.

The average rent was ¥101,721 and the standard deviation was ¥46,210. Single-occupancy rental housing was common with an average floor space of 32 m^2. The

Table 7.1 Housing rent dataset

Sample period	January 2010–July 2014					
Frequency	Monthly					
Area	Tokyo's wards					
Type of data	Paid rent					
Coverage	New and rollover contracts					
Provided by	Recruit					
Number of units	52, 524					
Number of samples	All samples		New contracts		Rollover contracts	
	1, 529, 485		36, 832		41, 117	
	Mean	S.D.	Mean	S.D.	Mean	S.D.
Monthly rent	101, 721.2	46, 209.7	100, 423.7	45, 271.9	102, 094.6	46, 480.0
Floor space (m^2)	32.4	15.6	32.2	15.6	32.5	15.7
Price per m^2	3, 293.3	788.3	3, 271.9	756.8	3, 292.8	798.1
Age of unit (years)	13.0	9.9	12.3	10.1	13.4	9.8
Time to nearest station (min)	5.1	3.8	5.0	3.7	5.2	3.9
Time to central business district (min)	12.4	6.4	12.1	6.3	12.5	6.4

average building age was 13.0 years while the average time to the closest station was 5.1 minutes and the shortest average time by train from the closest station to a terminal station on the Yamanote Line (Tokyo, Shinagawa, Shibuya, Shinjuku, Ikebukuro, Ueno) or Otemachi was 12.4 min, meaning that rental housing was concentrated in areas that are relatively convenient in terms of transportation.

If we compare the data by separating new contracts and rollover contracts, there are no major differences in average rent, floor space, building age, time to the closest station or average time to a terminal station, which is a major (and somewhat surprising result) of our study.[10]

7.2.2 Aggregate Rent Indexes Using CPI Methodologies

Using the created housing rent database, we analyzed macro trends in Tokyo ward area housing rents to check the sample selection bias compared with official CPI rent. In order to make this comparison on a quality adjusted basis, we created a quasi-official CPI rent index using our dataset.

Our quasi-official CPI rent index created an index using the same methodology as is used by the Ministry of Internal Affairs and Communications.

We also estimated an index using the same measurement method as the private rent index published by Statistics Bureau of Japan (hereafter referred to as CPI rent). CPI rent is measured based on a housing rent survey called the Retail Price Survey Rent Survey. This surveys the rent per month and total area of housing rented from private owners in municipalities covered by the Retail Price Survey. Nationwide, 1,221 districts have been selected as rental housing survey areas from census districts in survey municipalities by means of size-proportionate sampling. All households residing in housing rented from private owners in a given rental survey area are then asked their rent and total floor space.[11]

There are 54 survey areas distributed throughout the Tokyo ward areas covered in this paper.[12] Rental survey areas are assigned to three groups and surveyed one group at a time on a rotating basis so that a given rental survey area is surveyed every

---

[10] A possible explanation for this rent invariance result is that landlords hold rents constant even though the quality of the units deteriorates over time due to depreciation. Thus given that general inflation in Japan is zero or less, landlords are actually increasing constant quality rents by holding nominal prices constant. Thus landlords that are experiencing rollover or new contracts are happy enough to just charge the previous level of rents since they are actually achieving a hidden price increase in rents. Thus we do not expect this rental invariance result to hold in other countries that are not experiencing general deflation. However, it is also possible that this invariance result is due to quality adjustment bias; i.e., the above results are based on overall average prices and do not take into account quality differences between individual units. We will look at quality adjustment in Sect. 7.3 below.

[11] This adds up to a total of around 28,000 households covered by the survey (see the 2013 Annual Report on the Retail Price Survey).

[12] Rental survey areas are distributed by survey municipality stratification.

three months.[13] In addition, the rental housing index is calculated using the total area and four categories based on the housing structure (small wooden housing, medium wooden housing, small non-wooden housing, and medium non-wooden housing) as the basic units.[14]

In order to artificially measure CPI rent using our study data, we created panel data using the 53,746 units. We then performed the following calculations.

First, using all of the created panel data, we calculated an index using the CPI rent formula. This index was created from all observable paid rent data rather than sampling the survey areas (this shall be called the Non-Sampled Rent Index).[15]

Next, after performing sampling using the same method as the Ministry of Internal Affairs and Communications (MIC), we created an index (called the MIC Method Sampled Index).[16] For the sampling, we first categorized all data by geographic neighborhood and divided them into hypothetical survey areas including roughly 30 to 60 units.[17] Secondly, based on these artificially created survey areas, we sampled 54 survey areas in the same manner as the official index. Survey areas were pre-arranged so that they included at least one unit of each of the four survey categories, and at this time four survey areas were randomly selected from the prospective survey areas. Random sampling was performed for the remaining 50 survey areas. With regard to prices used in index calculation, the sampled 54 survey districts were sorted into three groups, each of which was used once every three months.[18] Sampling was performed 200 times by means of sampling with replacement.

---

[13]The most recent survey results are used for the rents of the groups that are not surveyed in a given month. In addition, if a surveyed unit becomes vacant, the most recent survey result will be used until it is next occupied. Moreover, samples are replaced by changing the rental survey areas every five years or so.

[14]Housing with a total floor space of less than 30 m^2 is considered small and housing with a total floor space of 30 m^2 or more is considered medium. The comparative price per 3.3 m^2 is obtained by dividing the total number of rental homes by the total floor space and multiplying by 3.3. Indexes by basic unit category are calculated by dividing the comparative value by the baseline price, then the rent index is obtained by calculating weighted averages for the indexes by category.

[15]January 2010 was taken as the baseline point. For each of the four index types (small wooden housing, medium wooden housing, small non-wooden housing, and medium non-wooden housing), we divided the total rent by the total area and multiplied the result by 3.3 to obtain the comparison price per 3.3 m^2. With regard to the total area categories, we divided them by taking 30 m^2 as the reference value in the same manner as official indexes. For the housing structure, houses coded as "wooden" in the data were taken as wooden housing and all others were categorized as non-wooden housing. Indexes by category were calculated by dividing the comparative price by the baseline price. Since weights for aggregating the four category indexes have not been published, we calculated the weights based on the proportion of each category in Tokyo's ward areas in the 2009 Housing and Land Survey, in the same manner as the imputed rent for owned homes.

[16]In terms of the categories, formula and weighting, the same method as for the Tokyo ward area described above was used but not all payment information was used; instead, the calculations used only hypothetically sampled data based on the same method as the MIC.

[17]The survey area size was based on the fact that the standard census survey area is set at around 50 households. We created 982 artificial survey areas.

[18]For prices in the groups that were not surveyed in a given month, the data for the most recent applicable month were used in the same manner as the official index. Additionally, in cases where

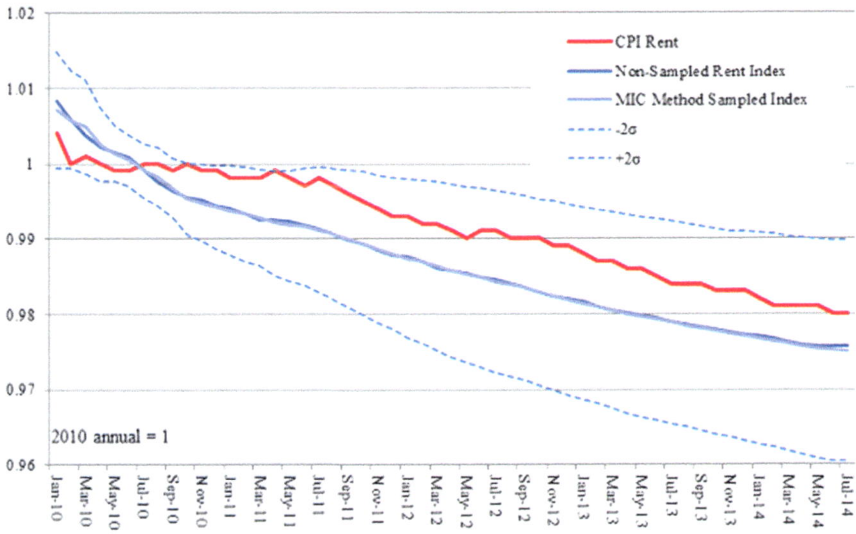

Fig. 7.1 Comparison of Tokyo ward area rent indexes

Figure 7.1 compares the Non-Sampled Rent Index using our dataset (the MIC Method Sampled Index estimated as described above) and the actual CPI rent in the Tokyo ward area. These indexes take the 2010 annual average as 1.

First, comparing the Non-Sampled Rent Index and the MIC Method Sampled Index in conjunction with the error of $\pm 2\sigma$ that occurs due to sampling, we can see that they are roughly the same. In other words, this confirms that in terms of the average value for sampling performed 200 times, the error due to sampling based on the MIC method is quite small.

Second, comparing the MIC Method Sampled Index and the actual CPI rent, we can see the same downward trend and actual CPI runs with in $\pm 2\sigma$ of MIC Method Sampled Index. This is natural because the actual CPI's sample is quite a bit smaller than the created housing rent database. Using this result, it could be assumed that the created housing rent database is not so different from the sample of the actual CPI. But the chart also shows substantial differences between the two indexes: the MIC indexes are for the most part well below the corresponding actual CPI index. To verify that this difference is real, we examine our data more detail and in particular, we look at the weighting of the different types of house in the indexes.

The weights for the four categories estimated in this study are 0.16 for small wooden housing, 0.07 for medium wooden housing, 0.38 for small non-wooden housing and 0.38 for medium non-wooden housing. These weights are estimated from the 2008 Housing and Land Survey.

---

rent was no longer paid due to a tenant departure, the most recent price was used until new payment information was recorded based on the arrival of the next tenant.

Table 7.2 Dataset by structure type

Number of samples	All samples		Small wooden housing		Medium wooden housing		Small non-wooden housing		Medium non-wooden housing	
	1,529,485 (1.000)		121,784 (0.080)		22,908 (0.015)		776,367 (0.508)		608,426 (0.398)	
Number of units	52,524(1.000)		4,106(0.078)		719(0.014)		27,045(0.515)		20,654(0.393)	
	Mean	S.D.	Mean	S.D.	Mean	S.D.	Mean	S.D.	Mean	S.D.
Monthly rent	101,721.2	46,209.7	58,487.2	11,548.7	87,521.4	25,354.3	79,801.6	17,760.7	138,879.6	50,387.7
Floor space (m^2)	32.4	15.6	18.8	4.6	39.9	9.1	22.3	3.7	47.7	13.7
Price per m^2	3,293.3	788.3	3,228.5	746.9	2,200.4	459.9	3,587.0	610.0	2,972.6	842.0
Age of unit (years)	13.0	9.9	19.1	10.9	17.7	10.0	11.6	9.2	13.4	9.9
Time to nearest station (min)	5.1	3.8	7.5	4.4	9.3	6.2	4.5	3.0	5.3	4.2
Time to city center (min)	12.4	6.4	15.5	6.8	18.0	6.0	11.5	5.9	12.7	6.6

Table 7.2 provides a summary by category of the study data. As one can see from the table, the proportions for wooden housing diverge from their weights (7.8% for small wooden housing and only 1.4% for medium wooden housing). In other words, significant weight is applied to the movement of the component prices where the calculations are based on small samples. In addition, the 2013 average for rents paid for privately owned housing in Tokyo's ward area in the Retail Prices Survey was ¥2,654 which is lower than the average in our data. Based on these facts, we may presume that distributional differences exist between the housing rent data used in this study and the samples used in the actual CPI. Thus the average quality of the housing units in the housing rent CPI may be different from the average quality of the housing units in our constructed MIC indexes.

7.2.3 Hedonic Estimation for Housing Rent

In this section, we estimate a hedonic constant quality index using new housing rent data.

Shimizu, Nishimura and Watanabe (2010a), Shimizu and Watanabe (2011) indicated that difference between new housing rent and paying rent impacts rent price indexes. They mentioned that paying rent occasionally changes during the contract period. In the opposite direction, new housing rent reflects changes in the market. As a consequence of this difference, significant difference is caused between two price indexes.

Let us begin with a hedonic price index. Suppose that we have the price and property-characteristics data of houses, pooled for all periods $t = 1, 2, \dots, T$, and that the number of data samples in period t is n_t. Then, a standard hedonic price index is produced from the following house-price estimation model:

$$\ln R_{it} = \boldsymbol{\beta}_t \boldsymbol{x}_{it} + \varepsilon_{it} \tag{7.1}$$

where R_{it} is the rent of house i in period t, $\boldsymbol{\beta}_t$ is a vector of parameters associated with residential property characteristics, $\boldsymbol{x}_{it}$ is a vector of property characteristic for house i in period t, and ε_{it} is an error term, which consists of time dummies and iid disturbance ($\varepsilon_{it} \equiv \alpha + \delta_t + v_{it}$ and $v_{it} \sim N(0, \sigma_v^2)$). The standard hedonic price index is then constructed from the time dummies.

The house characteristics coefficient vector $\boldsymbol{\beta}_t$ is usually assumed to be constant over time. However, Shimizu, Takatsuji, Ono and Nishimura (2010) and Shimizu, Nishimura and Watanabe (2010b) modified the standard hedonic model given by Eq. (7.1) so that the parameters associated with the attributes of a house are allowed to change over time. Structural changes in the Japanese housing market have two important features. First, they usually occur only gradually, triggered, with a few exceptions, by changes in regulations by the central and local governments. Such gradual changes are quite different from "regime changes" discussed by econometricians such as Bai and Perron (1998) in which structural parameters exhibit a discontinuous shift at multiple times. Second, the changes in parameters reflect structural changes at various time frequencies. Specifically, as found by Shimizu, Nishimura and Watanabe (2010b), some changes in parameters are associated with seasonal changes in housing market activity.

To allow for a gradually changing characteristics coefficient vector, we estimate the model defined by Eq. (7.1) for periods $t = 1, \ldots, \tau$, where $\tau < T$ represents the *window width*. As usual, set the first time dummy variable $\delta_1 \equiv d_1^* \equiv 1$ and denote the remaining estimated time parameters for this first regression by $d_2^*, \ldots, d_\tau^*$. These parameters are exponentiated to define the sequence of house price indexes P_t for the first τ periods; i.e., $P_t \equiv \exp[d_t^*]$ for $t = 1, 2, \ldots, \tau$. Thus the first τ price indexes, $P_1, \ldots, P_\tau$, are determined by this initial rolling window regression. Then a new τ period regression model using the data for the periods $2, 3, \ldots, \tau + 1$ can be repeated and a new set of estimated time parameters, $d_2^{2*} \equiv 1, d_3^{2*}, \ldots, d_{\tau+1}^{2*}$ can be obtained. The new *price levels* P_t^2 for periods 2 to $\tau + 1$ can be defined as $P_t^2 \equiv \exp[d_t^{2*}]$ for $t = 2, 3, \ldots, \tau + 1$. The final price index for period $\tau + 1$ is determined as $P_{\tau+1} \equiv [P_{\tau+1}^2 / P_\tau^2] P_\tau$; i.e., the price level for period τ, P_τ (obtained from the first rolling window regression), is updated by the ratio of the price indexes for period $\tau + 1$ to period τ that we obtained from the second rolling window regression, $P_{\tau+1}^2 / P_\tau^2$. Obviously, this process of adding the data of the next period to the rolling window regression while dropping the data pertaining to the oldest period in the previous regression can be continued. The focus in the Shimizu, Takatsuji, Ono and Nishimura (2010) paper was on determining how the structural parameters changed as the window of observations changed.[19]

---

[19]They called their method the *Overlapping Period Hedonic Housing Model* (OPHM).

Table 7.3 Estimation result of hedonic model of new housing rent

Estimation window	Floor space	Age of building	Time to nearest station	Commuting time to CBD	Adjusted R^2	Number of observations
2010-01–2010-12	0.0188	−0.0109	−0.0087	−0.0058	0.917	17,697
2010-02–2011-01	0.0188	−0.0109	−0.0088	−0.0058	0.916	16,707
2010-03–2011-02	0.0188	−0.0109	−0.0089	−0.0059	0.917	15,670
2010-04–2011-03	0.0188	−0.0110	−0.0090	−0.0059	0.917	14,504
2010-05–2011-04	0.0188	−0.0110	−0.0092	−0.0058	0.916	13,303
2010-06–2011-05	0.0189	−0.0111	−0.0094	−0.0058	0.915	11,684
2010-07–2011-06	0.0189	−0.0112	−0.0096	−0.0060	0.914	10,667
2010-08–2011-07	0.0190	−0.0114	−0.0097	−0.0062	0.916	9,942
2010-09–2011-08	0.0189	−0.0115	−0.0095	−0.0065	0.918	9,099
2010-10–2011-09	0.0190	−0.0114	−0.0099	−0.0065	0.919	8,346
2010-11–2011-10	0.0191	−0.0113	−0.0104	−0.0067	0.922	7,571
2010-12–2011-11	0.0191	−0.0113	−0.0105	−0.0066	0.924	6,698
2011-01–2011-12	0.0191	−0.0114	−0.0104	−0.0067	0.924	6,490
2011-02–2012-01	0.0192	−0.0114	−0.0104	−0.0067	0.927	6,446
2011-03–2012-02	0.0192	−0.0113	−0.0101	−0.0065	0.927	6,485
2011-04–2012-03	0.0192	−0.0113	−0.0102	−0.0067	0.927	6,564
2011-05–2012-04	0.0194	−0.0113	−0.0099	−0.0071	0.928	6,664
2011-06–2012-05	0.0194	−0.0112	−0.0096	−0.0075	0.929	6,782
2011-07–2012-06	0.0194	−0.0110	−0.0095	−0.0074	0.927	6,788
2011-08–2012-07	0.0193	−0.0110	−0.0096	−0.0071	0.925	6,880
2011-09–2012-08	0.0193	−0.0109	−0.0098	−0.0068	0.923	6,887
2011-10–2012-09	0.0191	−0.0109	−0.0096	−0.0071	0.922	6,913
2011-11–2012-10	0.0191	−0.0110	−0.0096	−0.0072	0.922	6,920
2011-12–2012-11	0.0192	−0.0110	−0.0094	−0.0074	0.922	6,988
2012-01–2012-12	0.0191	−0.0109	−0.0091	−0.0075	0.922	6,963
2012-02–2013-01	0.0189	−0.0109	−0.0091	−0.0072	0.918	6,968
2012-03–2013-02	0.0188	−0.0109	−0.0091	−0.0076	0.918	7,000
2012-04–2013-03	0.0188	−0.0108	−0.0093	−0.0076	0.918	7,012
2012-05–2013-04	0.0187	−0.0109	−0.0097	−0.0073	0.917	6,939
2012-06–2013-05	0.0186	−0.0109	−0.0098	−0.0071	0.916	6,785
2012-07–2013-06	0.0186	−0.0110	−0.0098	−0.0071	0.917	6,725
2012-08–2013-07	0.0186	−0.0110	−0.0098	−0.0073	0.918	6,526
2012-09–2013-08	0.0186	−0.0110	−0.0097	−0.0075	0.918	6,409
2012-10–2013-09	0.0187	−0.0110	−0.0097	−0.0074	0.918	6,260
2012-11–2013-10	0.0186	−0.0110	−0.0098	−0.0073	0.916	6,179
2012-12–2013-11	0.0186	−0.0110	−0.0099	−0.0073	0.916	6,028
2013-01–2013-12	0.0187	−0.0110	−0.0105	−0.0075	0.915	5,869
2013-02–2014-01	0.0189	−0.0109	−0.0107	−0.0078	0.918	5,718
2013-03–2014-02	0.0191	−0.0108	−0.0110	−0.0077	0.918	5,530
2013-04–2014-03	0.0190	−0.0108	−0.0109	−0.0075	0.919	5,389
2013-05–2014-04	0.0191	−0.0107	−0.0109	−0.0075	0.918	5,288
2013-06–2014-05	0.0192	−0.0106	−0.0112	−0.0077	0.918	5,273
2013-07–2014-06	0.0191	−0.0105	−0.0114	−0.0077	0.916	5,206
2013-08–2014-07	0.0192	−0.0104	−0.0113	−0.0079	0.915	5,225
Average	0.0190	−0.0110	−0.0099	−0.0070	0.9196	7,863

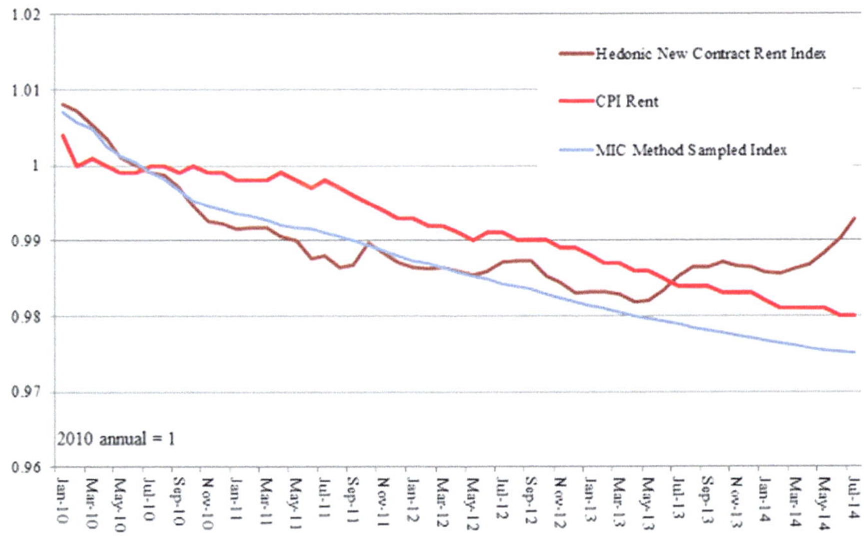

Fig. 7.2 Comparison of actual CPI and estimated indexes

In this paper, we run a rolling window regression using our information on new contract housing rents with window length $T = 12$. Table 7.3 indicates the estimation results of rolling hedonic models.

Figure 7.2 shows estimated result of our Hedonic new contract rent index and the CPI rent index and the MIC index described in Sect. 7.2.2. During 2010, the Hedonic index follows the MIC Method Sampled Index but it starts to deviate starting at November 2010. At first, it ran below the MIC Method Sampled Index but starting in the middle of 2012, it moved substantially above both the MIC and CPI indexes. This increase in rents may reflect the effect of changes in economic policy; i.e., the introduction of "Abenomics" and the attempt to end deflation.

7.3 The Micro-Analysis of Rents

7.3.1 The Frequency of Rent Adjustments

In this section we will a conduct further analysis at the micro level. We will begin by measuring the stickiness of rent. What we will measure here is the probability that rent will not change during a given year (i.e. the percentage of all units for which the rent does not change), which may be expressed as $\Pr(\Delta R_{it} = 0)$.

Rents are changed at the times when rental contracts are revised, which means either (1) there is tenant turnover or (2) the rental contract is renewed even though there is no tenant turnover. I_{it}^N is a variable that takes a value of 1 if unit turnover occurs and a new contract is agreed between the landlord and the new tenant with regard to unit i in period t, and 0 otherwise. Meanwhile, I_{it}^R takes a value of 1 if a rollover contract is agreed between the existing tenant and the landlord with regard to unit i in period t, and 0 otherwise. In addition, the rent level for unit i in period t is denoted by R_{it}, while $\Delta R_{it} \equiv R_{it} - R_{it-1}$ shows the rental adjustment amount at the time the contract is agreed. Therefore, the probability that there will be a change in rent ($\Pr(\Delta R_{it} = 0)$) can be expressed as follows:

$$\Pr(\Delta R_{it} = 0) = \left[1 - \Pr(I_{it}^N = 1) - \Pr(I_{it}^R = 1)\right] + \Pr(\Delta R_{it} = 0 \mid I_{it}^N = 1)\Pr(I_{it}^N = 1) + \Pr(\Delta R_{it} = 0 \mid I_{it}^R = 1)\Pr(I_{it}^R = 1) \tag{7.2}$$

Let us look at the terms on the right side of Eq. (7.2) one at a time. First, as seen in Table 7.1, among the total of 52,524 units, 36,832 new contracts occurred during the entire sample period. However, this does not mean that the rent was changed for all units for which new contracts were signed. This is examined in Table 7.4. The upper part of this table shows the proportion of rents that decreased, remained stable and increased among those units for which a new contract occurred within the sample period. Looking at the sample period as a whole, the rent was kept stable for 86.2% of the 36,832 new contracts. Meanwhile, the lower part of the table shows the same figures for rollover rents. Rollover contracts were renewed for 41,117 of the units during the sample period but the rent remained stable for 98.0% of these.

Taking these numbers as given, the first term on the right side of Eq. (7.2), $\left[1 - \Pr(I_{it}^N = 1) - \Pr(I_{it}^R = 1)\right]$, is 0.526, which shows that there was neither a new contract or contract renewal for 52.6% of the units. Moreover, even if a new contract did occur, there was a 0.862 probability that the rent would be kept at the same amount, which means that the second term on the right side of Eq. (7.2), $\Pr(\Delta R_{it} = 0 \mid I_{it}^N = 1)\Pr(I_{it}^N = 1)$, is 0.193. Similarly, even if a rollover contract occurred, the rent did not change for 95.8% of units, so the third term on the right side of Eq. (7.2), $\Pr(\Delta R_{it} = 0 \mid I_{it}^R = 1)\Pr(I_{it}^R = 1)$, is 0.245. Based on the above, the sum of the three terms on the right side of Eq. (7.2) is 0.964, so the proportion of units for which rent did not change in one year, ($\Pr(\Delta R_{it} = 0)$), is 96.4%.

Table 7.4 The nominal rigidity of rent

	Rent decreased	Rent unchanged	Rent increased	Total	(Rent change)
Changes accompanying new contracts	4,181 (0.114)	31,737 (0.862)	914 (0.025)	36,832 (0.224)	5,095 (0.138)
Changes accompanying rollover contracts	641 (0.016)	40,284 (0.980)	192 (0.005)	41,117 (0.250)	833 (0.020)
Total contract changes	4,822 (0.029)	72,021 (0.438)	1,106 (0.007)	164,356 (1.000)	5,928 (0.036)

How should we interpret these results showing that the rent did not change in a given year for 96.4% of units and, conversely, did change for 3.6% of units? According to Genesove (2003), who performed similar calculations for the U.S., the proportion of units for which rent did not change in a given year in the U.S. was 29%, with the rent being changed for the remaining 71%. Hoffmann and Kurz-Kim (2006), meanwhile, performed similar calculations for Germany, finding that the proportion of units for which rent did not change in a given year was 78% while it was changed for the remaining 22%. Compared to these figures, the 3.6% probability that rent will be changed in Japan is extremely low, representing a mere 1/20th of the U.S. figure and 1/6th of the German figure. It can therefore be said that rents in Japan have an extremely high degree of rigidity compared to the U.S. and Germany.

Figure 7.3a, b look at changes over time in nominal rent rigidity. Given that rollover contracts occur once every two years as a rule, they reduce the frequency of new contracts. Additionally, if we look at changes in the probability that rents will not change, gradual changes can be seen over time, but when aggregated by month, they remain stable at roughly 85%.

On the other hand, the stickiness of rollover rents (i.e. the probability that the rent will not change) hovers at around 95%. In other words, this shows that while the probability of a change in rent accompanying a new contract changes based on seasonality, there is no change in the probability of rent changing for rollover contracts, which remains uniform. To put it another way, we may consider that neither new contract rent nor rollover contract rent change depend on the contract renewal time and instead occur randomly in conjunction with contract changes.

Next, we looked at the magnitude of rental changes when a rent renewal event occurs (Fig. 7.4). Specifically, we observed the probability density for the rental comparison before and after rent revision ($\Delta R_{it} = R_t / R_{t-1} \mid I_{it}^N = 1$, $\Delta R_{it} = R_t / R_{t-1} \mid I_{it} R = 1$) excluding events in which the rent was kept at the same level. First, looking at the rent renewal range for new contracts, the scope of rent renewal was from -30% to $+10\%$. For rollover contracts, on the other hand, upward revisions were relatively few in comparison to new contracts. Even if there was a rental revision, the amount was more or less the same as before and it was most likely to be a downward adjustment. In other words, it is rare for rent to be increased for a rollover contract. If we look at the extent of decreases in rent, there was a certain likelihood of new contract rents decreasing by as much as 30%, whereas for rollover contracts, it was kept at around 20%. Thus, for rollover contracts, not only is the probability that the rent changes extremely low, but if a change does occur, the scope of the change will be small.

In addition, for both new contract rent revisions and rollover contract rent revisions, the revision probability decreases in the vicinity of 0. In other words, this shows that rent revisions are made within a certain range and it is rare for minor changes to occur. This suggests the presence of a so-called "menu cost."

Since the probability of a rent revision event occurring is extremely low, we may also consider that once such an event does occur, the range of the change will be relatively large compared to other goods and services. For example, new contract revisions occur as a result of finding new tenants via listing magazines, the Internet,

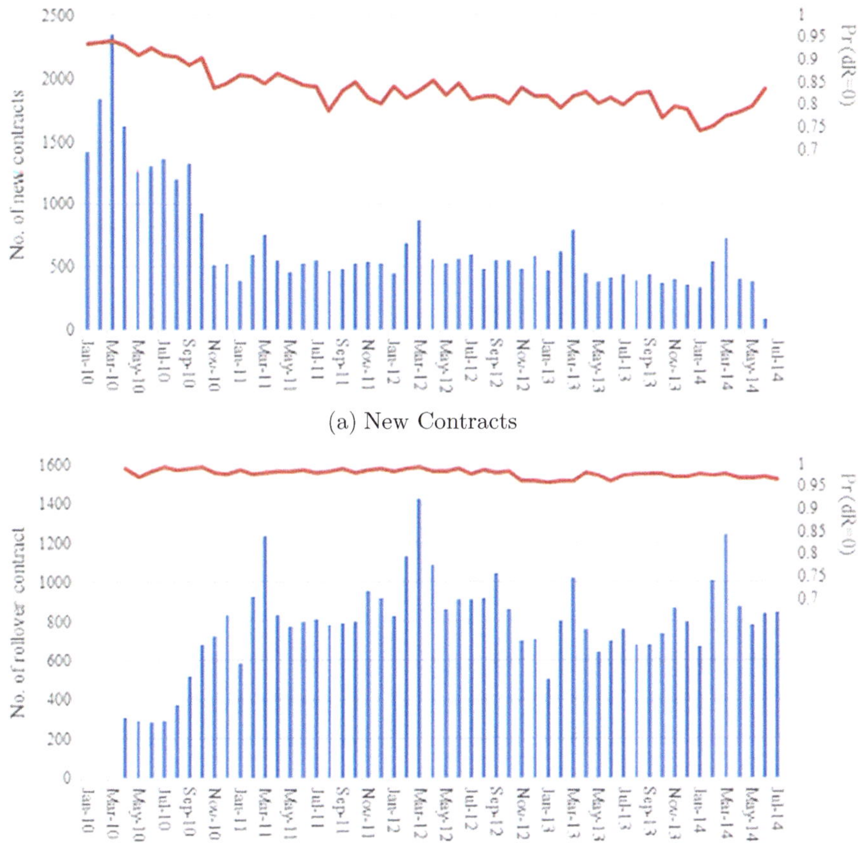

(b) Rollover Contracts

Fig. 7.3 Monthly changes in nominal rigidity of rent

etc., and if a new tenant cannot be found within a certain period of time, the search will be continued by lowering the amount of rent. In such cases, we may consider it unlikely that the price revision will be a minor one since the change must be enough to justify the time and cost involved in running advertisements and implementing the price change.

7.3.2 Time-Dependent Versus State-Dependent Adjustments

In a given month, the rent for a given unit will be revised while the rent for another unit will not be revised. What is the reason for this difference? There are two theories. The first is that there is a target rent level for different units, and when they diverge

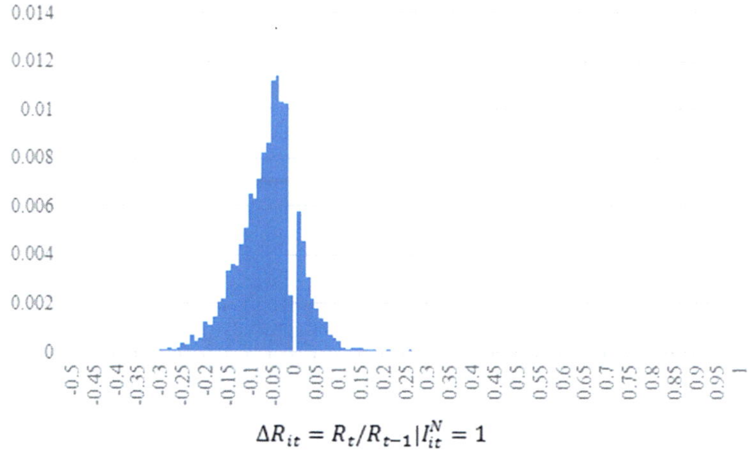

(a) New Contracts

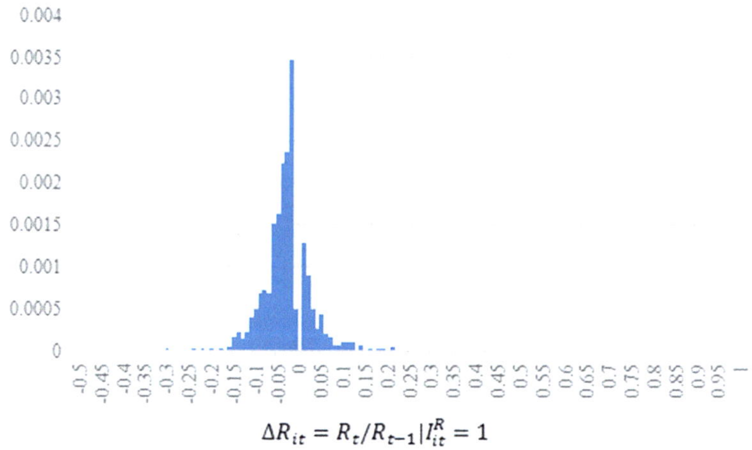

(b) Rollover Contracts

Fig. 7.4 Rent revision range density distribution

significantly from that level, the rent will be revised. According to this theory, the more the rent for a given unit diverges from the target level, the higher the probability that it will be revised. The extent to which the current rent diverges from the target rent is called the "price gap," and using this term, we can say that the probability of rent revision depends on the price gap. This theory is referred to as " state-dependent" pricing. In contrast, there is another theory which says that the probability of rent revision does not depend on the price gap at all. In other words, the probability of rent revision does not change based on how close or how far the current rent is from the target level. This is known as "non-state dependent" or "time-dependent" pricing.

Below, we will investigate whether rent revision is state-dependent or time-dependent using the method of Caballero and Engel (2007).

We will define the target rent level as R^*_{it} which we will assume is determined based on the following formula:

$$\Delta \log R^*_{it} = \Delta\xi_t + \nu_{it} \tag{7.3}$$

Here, $\Delta\xi_t$ represents aggregate shocks (shocks common to all units) and ν_{it} idiosyncratic shocks. The price gap is defined as the difference between the current rent and target rent level—i.e. $X_{it} \equiv \log R_{it} - \log R^*_{it}$. The probability that the rent will be revised based on this condition alone is expressed by the following equation:

$$\Lambda(x) \equiv \Pr(\Delta R_{it} \neq 0 \mid X_{it} = x) \tag{7.4}$$

This $\Lambda(x)$ function is called the adjustment hazard function. It was first proposed by Caballero and Engel (1993). If the probability $\Pr(\Delta R_{it} \neq 0)$ changes depending on the state variable x, it is state-dependent, and if it does not depend on x, it is time-dependent.

Using the above material, it is possible to calculate how the average rent level of all units responds to aggregate shocks.

$$\Delta \log R_{it}(\Delta\xi_t) \equiv \int \Delta \log R_{it}(\Delta\xi_t, x)h(x)dx = -\int (x - \Delta\xi_t)\Lambda(x - \Delta\xi_t)h(x)dx \tag{7.5}$$

Here, $h(x)$ is the cross-section distribution of the state variable x. Differentiating Eq. (7.5) based on aggregate shock after integrating i yields the following equation:

$$\lim_{\Delta\xi_t \to 0} \frac{\Delta \log R_t}{\Delta\xi_t} = \int \Lambda(x)h(x)dx + \int x\Lambda'(x)h(x)dx \tag{7.6}$$

The left side of this equation indicates how much the average rent for all units responds to aggregate shocks and is similar to an impulse response function. If the average rent for all units is adjusted rapidly in response to aggregate shocks, this value will be high. In this sense, the left side of Eq. (7.6) represents the elasticity of rent. According to Eq. (7.6), the elasticity of rent defined in this way is decided by two factors. The first term on the right side is the average rent adjustment probability for all units. Naturally, if the rent revision probability for all units is high, the average value will be high as well and rent will therefore be elastic. However, according to Eq. (7.6), the elasticity of rent is not just defined by this because a second term exists on the right side. In order to explain the significance of the second right-hand term, let us consider a case where $\Lambda(x)$ does not depend on x—i.e. a time-dependent case. In this case, since $\Lambda'(x)$ is 0, the second right-hand term is also 0. However, in a state-dependent case, $\Lambda'(x)$ is not 0, so the second right-hand term will not be 0 either. As shown by Caballero and Engel (2007), the second right-hand term is positive in many state-dependent models. The value of the second right-hand term

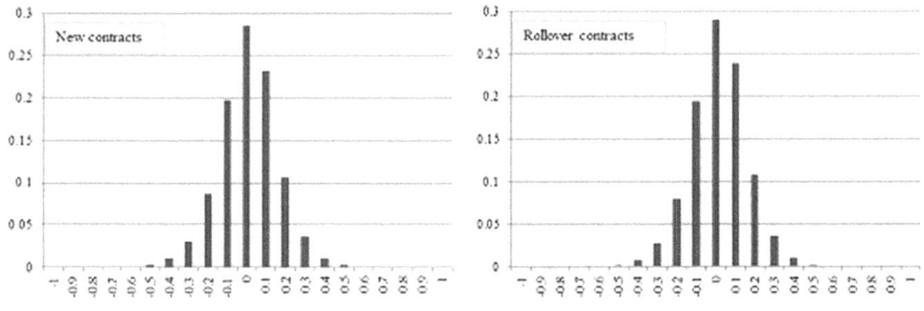

Fig. 7.5 Price gap distributions

is determined by how large $\Lambda'(x)$ is (how much it differs from 0). Caballero and Engel (2007) refer to the first right-hand term as the intensive margin and the second right-hand term as the extensive margin.

In order to apply the above analysis framework to rent, we will first define $\Lambda(x)$ for housing rent as follows:

$$\begin{aligned}\Lambda(x) =&\Pr(\Delta R_{it} \neq 0 \mid I_{it}^{N} = 1, x_{it} = x)\Pr(I_{it}^{N} = 1, x_{it} = x)\\&+ \Pr(\Delta R_{it} \neq 0 \mid I_{it}^{R} = 1, x_{it} = x)\Pr(I_{it}^{R} = 1, x_{it} = x)\end{aligned} \tag{7.7}$$

As can be understood from the right side, the rent revision probability function $\Lambda(x)$ is composed of four conditional probabilities. It is the sum of the product of the probability of a state-dependent new contract occurring ($\Pr(I_{it}^{N} = 1, x_{it} = x)$) and the probability of the rent revision based on that contract ($\Pr(\Delta R_{it} \neq 0 \mid I_{it}^{N} = 1, x_{it} = x)$) and the product of the probability of a rollover contract occurring ($\Pr(I_{it}^{R} = 1, x_{it} = x)$) and the probability of the rent changing based on that ($\Pr(\Delta R_{it} \neq 0 \mid I_{it}^{R} = 1, x_{it} = x)$).

Figure 7.5 looks at the distribution of the price gap x.[20] For both new contracts and rollover contracts, it falls within the range of roughly −0.3 to +0.4. In other words, at its highest, the rate of divergence from the appropriate rent level is around 30%. Given this distribution for x, Fig. 7.6 shows the calculated four conditional probabilities in Eq. (7.7).

First, the probability of a new contract occurring ($\Pr(I_{it}^{N} = 1, x_{it} = x)$) in the upper left of Fig. 7.6 is more or less level at around 0.025 per month (approx. 30% per year). In other words, this is not dependent on the price gap. We may consider tenant turnover as occurring when moving becomes necessary due to circumstances such as changing job, getting married, giving birth, etc., and this shows that these circumstances occur independently of the price gap. No tendency for people to move due to their current rent being higher than the appropriate level can be observed. The probability of a rollover contract occurring ($\Pr(I_{it}^{R} = 1, x_{it} = x)$) shown in the

[20] The target rent R^* was estimated based on a hedonic method in the same manner as was used by Shimizu, Nishimura and Watanabe (2010a). With regard to the choice of hedonic model, we chose the Rolling Hedonic Model proposed by Shimizu, Ono, Takatsuji and Nishimura (2010).

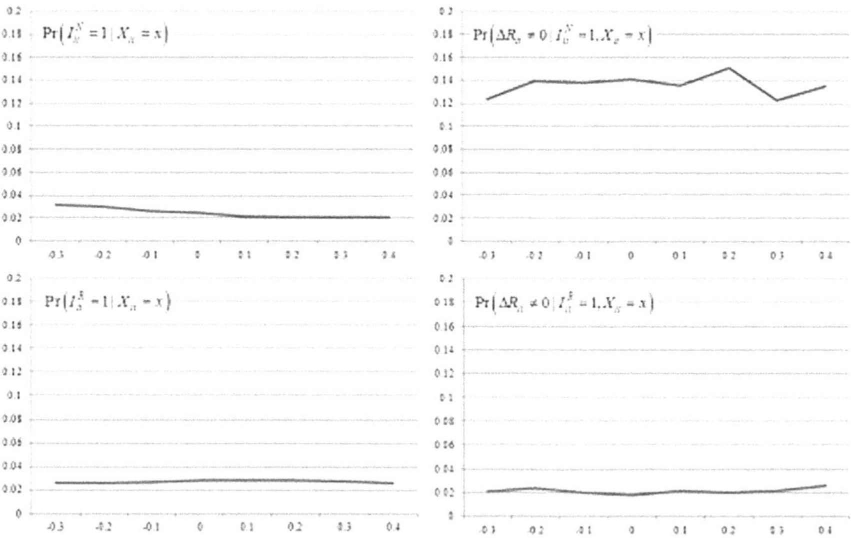

Fig. 7.6 State-dependency

lower left of Fig. 7.6 is also more or less level and not dependent on the price gap. We can see that contract renewals occur once every two years or so regardless of the price gap.

Next, if we look at the probability that rent will change based on a new contract ($\Pr(\Delta R_{it} \neq 0 \mid I_{it}^N = 1, x_{it} = x)$) in the upper right of Fig. 7.6, it is more or less flat, but when one examines it in detail, there is a slight upward slope and there is dip at 0.3. What this means is that if tenant turnover occurs in units where the current paid rent is higher than the appropriate level (market rate), the probability of the rent being changed is higher than it is in cases of tenant turnover in units where the current rent is not higher. This suggests that when searching for new tenants for units where the paid rent is higher than the market rent, it will not be possible to find one unless a lower rent is set. Finally, looking at the probability that the rent will change based on rollover contracts ($\Pr(\Delta R_{it} \neq 0 \mid I_{it}^R = 1, x_{it} = x)$) in the lower right, one can see that it is similar to new contracts: it slopes upward when the price gap exceeds the level of 0.3.

Compared to Shimizu, Nishimura and Watanabe (2010a)'s estimation results, a number of differences can be observed in these results. The reason for this may be that the distribution of price gap x varies. In Shimizu, Nishimura and Watanabe (2010a), the bubble period that occurred from the 1980s through the 1990s is included in the sample, so x changed significantly due to abrupt fluctuations in R^*. As a result, despite the strong inherent stickiness of the rental market, a tendency for paid rents to approach market rents was observed. However, Shimizu and Watanabe (2011) obtained more or less the same results in analysis using large management company

Table 7.5 Summary of estimation results

	$x \in [-0.4, -0.2)$	$x \in [-0.2, -0.0)$	$x \in [0.0, 0.2)$	$x \in [0.2, 0.4)$
$\Pr(I_{it}^N = 1 \mid X_{it} = x)$	0.035	0.029	0.023	0.021
$\Pr(I_{it}^R = 1 \mid X_{it} = x)$	0.006	0.026	0.028	0.027
$\Pr(\Delta R_{it} \neq 0 \mid I_{it}^N = 1, X_{it} = x)$	0.131	0.134	0.138	0.137
$\Pr(\Delta R_{it} \neq 0 \mid I_{it}^R = 1, X_{it} = x)$	0.015	0.022	0.020	0.021
$\Lambda(x)$	0.005	0.004	0.004	0.003
$h(x)$	0.039	0.569	0.337	0.047

data. In this sense, a certain robustness can be seen in terms of Japanese rents' rigidity and price gap dependency.

Table 7.5 summarizes the above estimation results. It shows at a glance how the four probabilities indicated on the left side are dependent on the price gap x. On the one hand, we can see that the probability $\Pr(I_{it}^N = 1, x_{it} = x)$ tends to slightly decrease somewhat as the price gap x grows bigger, whereas the probability $\Pr(I_{it}^R = 1, x_{it} = x)$ does not depend on the price gap and remains more or less fixed. Meanwhile, the probability $\Pr(\Delta R_{it} \neq 0 \mid I_{it}^N = 1, x_{it} = x)$ that the rent will be changed when there is tenant turnover becomes larger when the price gap x is positive compared to when it is negative. This suggests that when the current rent exceeds the market rate, rent will be adjusted at the time of tenant turnover. Finally, the probability $\Pr(\Delta R_{it} \neq 0 \mid I_{it}^R = 1, x_{it} = x)$ also becomes larger when the price gap x is positive compared to when it is negative.

As shown in Eq. (7.7), it is possible to calculate $\Lambda(x)$ using the four probabilities in Table 7.5. The results of the actual calculations are shown in the row for $\Lambda(x)$ in Table 7.5. $\Lambda(x)$ is more or less flat, with no relation to x. We can consider this as showing that $\Lambda(x)$ mostly does not depend on x. The level of $\Lambda(x)$ stays between 0.003 and 0.005, and this, as shown by the definition of $\Lambda(x)$ in Eq. (7.6), is an indicator representing the elasticity of rent. It signifies that in a given year, the rent will be changed for 4.1 to 5.5% of all units.

Here, a key point is how much the intensive margin and extensive margin contribute to the rent revision probability. If we actually calculate how much each contributes in line with Eq. (7.6), the formula is as follows[21]:

[21]Comparing the analysis results in Tables 7.5 to 7.3 in Shimizu, Nishimura and Watanabe (2010a), the value of $\Lambda(x)$ differs considerably. According to Table 7.3 in Shimizu, Nishimura and Watanabe (2010a), the value of $\Lambda(x)$ is around 10%, which is double the result in this paper. When we look at the source of this difference, we find that it can largely be explained by the difference in probability $\Pr(\Delta R_{it} \neq 0 \mid I_{it}^N = 1, x_{it} = x)$. In this paper, the probability that rent will be changed when there is tenant turnover is approximately 20%, but in Shimizu, Nishimura and Watanabe (2010a) it is

$$\int \Lambda(x)h(x)dx = 0.0500, \int x\Lambda'(x)h(x)dx = 0.0081, \lim_{\Delta\xi_t \to 0} \frac{\Delta \log R_t}{\Delta \xi_t} = 0.0581 \quad (7.8)$$

In other words, Caballero and Engel (2007)'s price elasticity indicator on the left side of Eq. (7.6) is 0.0621. If we separate this into two, following the example of Eq. (7.6), the intensive margin is 0.0081 and the extensive margin is 0.0082. From this we can see that the extensive margin is extremely small, accounting for only 14% of Caballero and Engel (2007)'s price elasticity indicator. We may consider it as being practically 0. The fact that the extensive margin is 0 means that rent revision is not state-dependent but time-dependent.

7.4 Re-estimation of the CPI

We have seen in the previous sections that the probability of individual rent adjustments is very low and that it depends little on price imbalances. These two facts imply that price flexibility in terms of the impulse response function is low, thus causing the CPI for rent to respond only slowly to aggregate shocks. Shimizu, Nishimura and Watanabe (2010a) simulated the estimation of the CPI depending on the change of stickiness and examined the impact. In this paper, we simplify their model: we assume that the (imputed) prices for owner-occupied housing services are very flexible and thus never deviate from the corresponding market prices. Based on this assumption, we replace the imputed rent for owner-occupied housing in the CPI by our estimate of the market rent R^*. And making a second assumption, we replace the imputed rent for OOH by our estimate of the depreciation adjusted rent R-age. A certain amount of depreciation occurs over rent properties year by year. We estimate R-age by multiplying the imputed rent of OOH by this depreciation rate as a rise of prices. The depreciation rate is estimated as -0.011[22] from Table 7.3.

Figure 7.8 shows R^*, R-age and actual CPI in 2000:1Q-2014:4Q. This treatment is perfectly consistent with the rental equivalent approach which "values the services yielded by the use of a dwelling by the corresponding market value for the same sort of dwelling for the same period of time" (Diewert and Nakamura 2009).

Figure 7.7 shows clearly that actual CPI rent continues to decrease but contrary to the Hedonic estimate, R_t^* increased 6% from 2006 to 2008. After that, it drops sharply due to the Financial Crisis but it turns up again after starting the great easing caused by "Abenomics". On the other hand, depreciation adjusted R-age lies between

around 70%. This may reflect a fundamental difference in the nature of the buildings covered by the analysis. It may also reflect the difference in the analysis periods. Specifically, Shimizu, Nishimura and Watanabe (2010a)'s sample period includes the bubble period. That was a time when major fluctuations in the market occurred rapidly, so we may consider that landlords and tenants both behaved in a way that led to rent being changed when a new contract was agreed.

[22]The average of coefficient β for "Age of Building" in Table 7.2 is -0.011. It means that the depreciation rate is minus 1.1% per year.

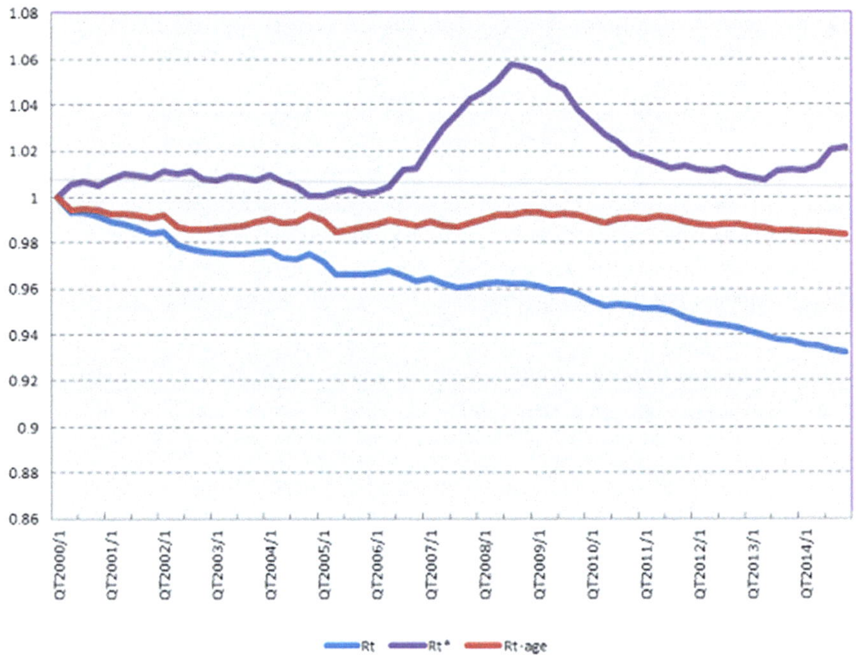

Fig. 7.7 Hedonic estimate R_t^*, R_t-age and actual CPI

R^* and the actual CPI. And it is clear that if we adjust the depreciation, the drop in hte index has practically disappeared and it stays almost flat.

Figure 7.8 shows how these changes in rents impacts the CPI. First we look at R^*. During the IT bubble in the early 2000s, it led to a 0.4% difference in the inflation rate. From 2006 to 2008 (just before the Financial Crisis), the largest difference in the inflation rate is 0.5% and the average difference is about 0.3 %.

Focusing from Jan. 2013 onward (the period that the Bank of Japan announced a new price stability target and started a monetary expansion), there is a difference starting from Q4 of 2013: a 0.2% difference repeatedly appeared during this period. This difference is an important signal because the Hedonic index R_t^* turns up while the CPI rent index continues to decrease. It implies that the difference from actual CPI seems to increase because the Hedonic index R_t^* seems to be increasingly apt to increase.

Next we turn into age adjusted CPI rent, R-age. This index exhibits a mild decline over the sample period as opposed to the actual CPI, which declined much more. This result shows clearly that the depreciation adjusted rent modifies the downward bias of actual rents as measured by the CPI. But it is also based on sticky rent prices so it hardly reflects the effect of asset price fluctuation.

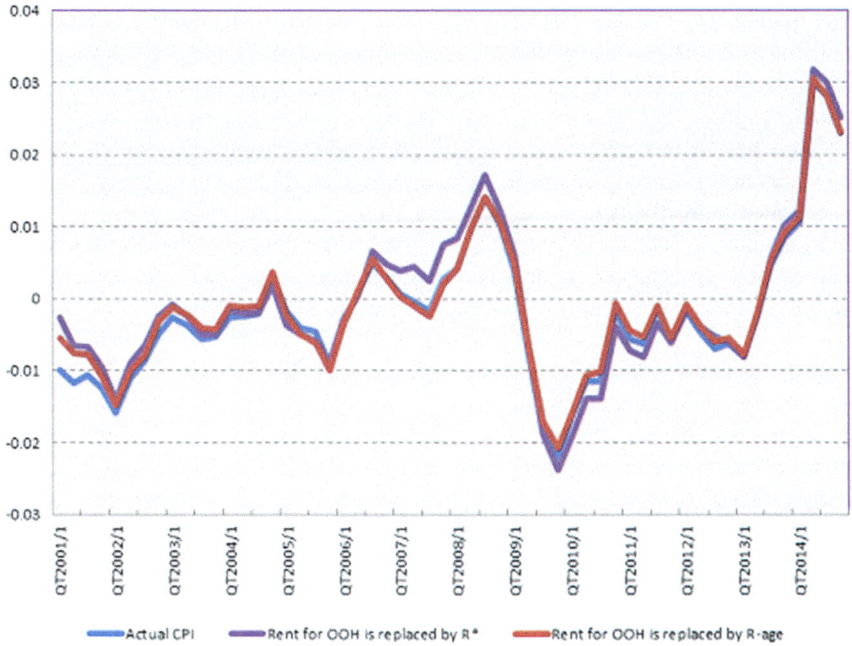

Fig. 7.8 Reestimates of CPI inflation under rent for OOH replaced by R_t^* and R-age

The above analysis show that how the CPI treats owner-occupied housing rents can make a big difference to the CPI. Hence the evaluation of the effectiveness of "Abenomics" in eliminating deflation depends to a large extent on the valuation of the services of owner-occupied housing.

7.5 Summary and Conclusion

Goods and services prices, as represented by consumer price indexes and the like, have not changed all that much in response to fluctuations in asset prices. In particular, there were no major change in goods and services prices even during the significant rise in asset prices that was one of the factors leading to the global financial crisis and subsequent decline in such prices. This lack of correlation means that business cycle management via financial policy is difficult.

Accordingly, focusing on rents, which are an important connecting point between asset market and goods and services market, we attempted to measure housing rent for Japan. Our research has two major implications for the construction of a price index for rented properties in Japan.

Our first major point is that the Japanese rent index has a downward bias due to the neglect of depreciation. In other words, the actual CPI has a strong downward bias due to the neglect of this "aging depreciation". We calculated depreciation rate for housing rent in Japan using hedonic regression techniques and it is approximately 1.1% per year.[23] In addition to this depreciation bias problem, housing rent has another problem in CPI: namely the strong rigidity of price changes.

Thus our second major result in this paper showed that, while rents based on new contracts change in an elastic manner, actual paid rents change only gradually, even when market shocks occur. In other words, average market rents, which are representative of consumer prices, have a strong tendency to change in a random manner, independently of changes in rents determined freely by the market. This rent stickiness means that consumer prices as a whole fluctuate gradually. As a result, when it comes to financial policy and the like, agile policy management targeting only goods and services price indicators is not possible.

Under this situation, the importance of developing economic statistics (residential price indexes) that are able to accurately capture fluctuations in residential property prices as an asset price has been pointed out (Diewert 2007) and the United Nations, IMF, OECD, BIS, and ILO have jointly put together international handbook on residential property price indexes.[24] Many countries in Europe are constructing these types of indexes and from March 2015, a Residential Property Price Index has been published on an experimental basis for the past 3 years in Japan.

By developing a Residential Property Price, it becomes possible to construct user cost price indexes and acquisition cost price indexes for OOH and these alternative OOH indexes can be compared with their rental equivalence counterparts. On the other hand, the fact that such an index has been developed does not mean that it is possible to respond immediately to asset bubbles or subsequent recessions. However, considering past experiences in which policy implementation delays caused significant economic confusion, it is strongly hoped that the development of asset price-related statistics will make it possible to achieve more flexible policy management.

Going forward, it will likely be necessary to clarify the relationship between asset price fluctuations and rent fluctuations. There are also still many significant questions to be addressed in the future regarding this issue.

References

Bai, J., and P. Perron. 1998. Estimating and testing linear models with multiple structural changes. *Econometrica* 66: 47–78.

Caballero, R.J., and E. Engel. 1993. Microeconomic rigidities and aggregate price dynamics. *European Economic Review* 37: 697–717.

[23]The depreciation rate is expressed as a fraction of property value, which includes the value of land. Thus the structure (net) depreciation rate is actually higher than 1.1% per year.

[24]http://epp.eurostat.ec.europa.eu/portal/page/portal/hicp/methodology/residential_property_price_\protect\penalty-\@Mindices.

Caballero, R.J., and E. Engel. 2007. Price stickiness in Ss models: New interpretations of old results. *Journal of Monetary Economics* 54: 100–121.

Calvo, G. 1983. Staggered prices in a utility-maximizing framework. *Journal of Monetary Economics* 12: 383–398.

Crone, T.M., L. Nakamura and R. Voith. 2004. *Hedonic estimates of the cost of housing services: Rental and owner-occupied units*. Price Federal Reserve of Bank of Philadelphia Working Papers, No. 04-22.

Crone, T.M., L. Nakamura and R. Voith. 2006. *The CPI for rents: A Case of understated inflation*. Price Federal Reserve of Bank of Philadelphia Working Papers, No. 06-7.

Diewert, W.E. 2007. *The paris OECD-IMF workshop on real estate price indexes: Conclusions and future directions*. Discussion Paper 07-1, University of British Columbia.

Diewert, W.E. 2015. Index number theory and measurement, economics 580: Lecture notes at University of British Columbia.

Diewert, W.E. and A.O. Nakamura. 2009. Accounting for housing in a CPI, chapter 2. 7–32 in W.E. Diewert, B.M. Balk, D. Fixler, K.J. Fox and A.O. Nakamura. 2009. Price and productivity measurement: Volume 1—Housing. Trafford Press.

Diewert, W.E., and C. Shimizu. 2013. Residential property price indexes for Tokyo. Discussion paper 13-07, Vancouver School of Economics, University of British Columbia. *Macroeconomic Dynamics*, forthcoming.

Diewert, W.E., and C. Shimizu. 2014. Alternative approaches to commercial property price indexes for Tokyo.

Diewert, W.E., K. Fox and C. Shimizu. 2014. Commercial property price indexes and the system of national accounts. Discussion paper 14-09, Vancouver School of Economics, University of British Columbia, forthcoming in the *Journal of Economic Surveys*.

Genesove, D. 2003. The nominal rigidity of apartment rents. *The Review of Economics and Statistics* 85 (4): 844–853.

Goodhart, C. 2001. What weight should be given to asset prices in measurement of inflation? *The Economic Journal* 111 (472): 335–356.

Gordon, R.J., and T. van Goethem. 2005. A century of housing shelter prices: Is there a downward bias in the CPI. NBER Working paper, No. 11776.

Hoffmann, J., and J.-R. Kurz-Kim. 2006. Consumer price adjustment under the microscope: Germany in a period of low inflation. Deutsche Bundesbank Discussion paper series 1: Economic studies, No. 16.

Reinhart, C M., and K.S. Rogoff. 2008. This time is different: A panoramic view of eight centuries of financial crises. NBER Working Paper No. W13882.

Shimizu, C., and T. Watanabe. 2011. Nominal rigidity of housing rent. *Financial Review* 106 (1): 52–68.

Shimizu, C., K.G. Nishimura, and T. Watanabe. 2010a. Residential rents and price rigidity: Micro structure and macro consequences. *Journal of the Japanese and International Economics* 24 (1): 282–299.

Shimizu, C., K.G. Nishimura, and T. Watanabe. 2010b. House prices in Tokyo: A comparison of repeat-sales and hedonic measures. *Journal of Economics and Statistics* 230 (6): 792–813.

Shimizu, C., W.E. Diewert, K.G. Nishimura and T. Watanabe. 2012. The estimation of owner occupied housing indexes using the RPPI: The case of Tokyo. RIPESS (Reitaku Institute of Political Economics and Social Studies) Working Paper,No.50. (presented at: Meeting of the Group of Experts on Consumer Price Indexes Geneva, 30 May–1 June 2012(UNITED NATIONS)).

Shimizu, C., H. Takatsuji, H. Ono, and K.G. Nishimura. 2010. Structural and temporal changes in the housing market and hedonic housing price indexes. *International Journal of Housing Markets and Analysis* 3 (4): 351–368.

Chapter 8
Imputed Rent for OOH in National Account

8.1 Introduction

Housing price fluctuations exert effects on the economy through various channels. More precisely, however, relative prices between housing and other assets prices and goods/services prices are the variable that should be observed.

Even if both assets and goods/services prices (and wages) double, the assets price hike alone may have little impact on the economy. In reality, however, housing prices posted substantial hikes and declines both in Japan and the United States while goods/services prices represented by consumer price indexes moved little (Diewert and Nakamura 2009, 2011; Shimizu and Watanabe 2010). Why? Given the substantial hikes and declines in housing prices, Shimizu et al. (2010a) look into why the substantial housing price fluctuations did not spill over to goods/services prices.

Housing rents are the most important variable for an analysis of housing price fluctuations' spillover effects on goods/services prices. Housing services account for more than a quarter of consumers' typical consumption in Japan and the United States. Therefore, if housing price hikes spill over to housing rents, consumer prices may soar. Goodhart (2001) said housing rents are a joint between assets and goods/services prices.

In order to understand why housing price fluctuations fail to spill over to consumer prices, we may have to check how housing price fluctuations spill over to housing rents. Let us look into characteristic differences between new and renewal rents.

Summarizing the Shimizu et al. (2010a)'s findings, we can conclude that while there is some mechanism for new rents to come closer to market prices, long-term relationships between house owners and tenants, as well as legal regulations, have made it difficult for renewal rents to come closer to market levels. This is one of the

---

The base of this chapter is Shimizu, C., W. E. Diewert, K. G. Nishimura and T. Watanabe. 2012. The estimation of owner occupied housing indexes using the RPPI: The case of Tokyo. RIPESS Working Paper, No. 50, Reitaku University. Presented at Meeting of the Group of Experts on Consumer Price Indexes Geneva, United Nations, Geneva, 30 May–1 June 2012.

W. E. Diewert et al., *Property Price Index*, Advances in Japanese Business and Economics 11, https://doi.org/10.1007/978-4-431-55942-9_8

reasons for the absence of any close link between the CPI rent and housing prices. The absence is also attributable to a method for measuring the CPI rent. The CPI rent includes a conventional rent and an imputed rent representing the price of housing services that a house owner receives. In Tokyo, for example, the conventional rent portion accounts for about 20% of the total rent and the imputed rent for about 80%. The imputed rent thus captures the greater part of the total rent. Conceptually, the imputed rent is a rent level that a house owner can receive when leasing the house in the rental house market today. Therefore, the imputed rent always matches the market price.

For example, Diewert and Nakamura (2009, 2011) defined the imputed rent as the services yielded by the use of a dwelling by the corresponding market value for the same sort of dwelling for the same period of time. When measuring the CPI rent, however, the Ministry of Internal Affairs and Communications collects data of real rents applied to apartment and other houses since market prices are practically difficult to survey. As noted above, such rent data include renewal rents that deviate from market prices and have little link to housing prices. Therefore, the CPI rent that substitutes renewal rents for the imputed rent has little link to housing prices.

How serious is the problem in practice? Shimizu et al. (2010a) estimated the imputed rent using market rents measured through turnover of contracted rents. Specifically, the study replaced the imputed rent out of all CPI components with the new imputed market rent index, left the other CPI components untouched and computed a New CPI. Estimation results indicate that the New CPI inflation rate exceeded the Real CPI inflation by more than 1% point during the bubble period in the second half of the 1980s. When the bubbles burst in the first half of the 1990s, the New CPI inflation was some 2% points less than the Real CPI inflation. Particularly interesting is the timing for the start of deflation. The New CPI inflation became negative in early 1993, some two years before the real CPI inflation turned negative in 1995. The estimation indicates that the replacement of imputed rent data with a more desirable indicator contributes to increasing housing prices' link to the CPI.

This kind of distortion in the estimation of imputed rent for owned-occupied housing causes major problems with respect to CPI changes.

The distortion in the estimation of imputed rent for owner-occupied housing is not just a CPI problem. The imputed rent for owner-occupied housing also represents a weight of approximately 10% in the system of national accounts (SNA). And with regard to GDP size and fluctuations, imputed rent for owner-occupied housing is the most important indicator for fiscal and monetary policies (along with the CPI), and at the same time, it is expected that the proportion accounted for by it will grow increasingly larger in future. On the other hand, it has also been pointed out that estimation of imputed rent for owner-occupied housing is the most difficult estimation subject when generating economic statistics, with various estimation methods having been proposed.

In terms of estimation methods for imputed rent for owner-occupied housing, the leading methods include the Equivalent Rent Approach, which extrapolates rent based on the surrounding rental market, and the User Cost Approach, which estimates rent using housing asset prices. However, problems have been pointed out with both of these methods. What kind of method should be used in the estimation of imputed rent for owner-occupied housing? What level of disparity arises based on the different calculation methods?

In order to answer such questions, this study will, taking Diewert and Nakamura (2009, 2011) as a starting point, estimate the imputed rent for owner-occupied housing in Tokyo using multiple previously proposed methods, with the aim of clarifying the level of difference arising due to the disparities between calculation methods.

In the 2010 national census, there were 13,161,751 people living in Tokyo (6,403,219 households), with an SNA production value of ¥71.181 trillion, of which imputed rent for owner-occupied housing accounted for ¥3.0621 trillion. The figures for both population and economic power are comparable in size to those of a small country. As well, during the latter half of the 1980s, a steep rise in real estate prices occurred, but following the collapse of the bubble in 1990, housing prices declined steadily over a long period. Given such a large-scale fluctuation in housing prices, we believe that clarifying the level of the differences that arise in imputed rent for owner-occupied housing calculated with different methods will be extremely significant when applying them to various countries in future.

8.2 The Theory of Household User Costs

8.2.1 Basic Model of User Cost Approach

Katz (2009) reviews the theoretical framework that can be used to derive both user cost and rental equivalence measures from the fundamental equation of capital theory:

> The user cost of capital' measure is based on the fundamental equation of capital theory. This equation, which applies equally to both financial and non-financial assets... states that in equilibrium, the price of an asset will equal the present discounted value of the future net income that is expected to be derived from owning it.

The user cost of capital measure provides an estimate of the market rental price based on costs of owners. It is directly derived from the assumption that, in equilibrium, the purchase price of a durable good will equal the discounted present value of its expected net benefits; i.e., it will equal the discounted present value of its expected future services less the discounted present value of its expected future operating costs. To see this, let V_v^t denote the purchase price of a v year old durable at the beginning of year t; let V_{v+1}^{t+1} denote the expected purchase price of the durable at the beginning of year $t+1$ when the durable is one year older; let u_v^t denote the expected end of period value of the period t services of this durable; let O_v^t denote the expected period t operating expenses to be paid at the end of period t for the v year old durable; and let r^t denote the expected nominal discount rate (i.e., the rate of return on the best alternative investment) in year t.

Expected variables are measured as of the beginning of year t. Assume the entire value of the durable's services in a year will be received at the year's end, and that the durable is expected to have a service life of m years. From the definition of the discounted present value, we have

$$V_v^t = \frac{u_v^t}{1+r^t} + \frac{u_{v+1}^{t+1}}{(1+r^t)(1+r^{t+1})} + \cdots + \frac{u_{m-1}^{t+m-v-1}}{\Pi_{i=t}^{t+m-v-1}(1+r^i)}$$
$$- \frac{O_v^t}{1+r^t} - \frac{O_{v+1}^{t+1}}{(1+r^t)(1+r^{t+1})} - \cdots - \frac{O_{m-1}^{t+m-v-1}}{\Pi_{i=t}^{t+m-v-1}(1+r^i)} \quad (8.1)$$

When the durable is one year older, the expected price of the durable at the beginning of year $t+1$ is:

$$V_{v+1}^{t+1} = \frac{u_{v+1}^{t+1}}{1+r^{t+1}} + \frac{u_{v+2}^{t+2}}{(1+r^{t+1})(1+r^{t+2})} + \cdots + \frac{u_{m-1}^{t+m-v-1}}{\Pi_{i=t+1}^{t+m-v-1}(1+r^i)}$$
$$- \frac{O_{v+1}^{t+1}}{1+r^{t+1}} - \cdots - \frac{O_{m-1}^{t+m-v-1}}{\Pi_{i=t+1}^{t+m-v-1}(1+r^i)} \quad (8.2)$$

Dividing both sides of (8.2) by $(1+r^t)$ and subtracting the result from Eq. (8.1) yields

$$V_v^t - \frac{1}{1+r^{t+1}} V_{v+1}^{t+1} = \frac{u_v^t}{1+r^t} - \frac{O_v^t}{1+r^t} \quad (8.3)$$

Multiplying through Eq. (8.3) by $(1+r^t)$ and combining terms, one obtains the end of period t user cost:

$$u_v^t = r^t V_v^t + O_v^t - (V_{v+1}^{t+1} - V_v^t) \quad (8.4)$$

The estimated market value of a home a year later (V_{v+1}^{t+1}) is computed in the context that the home has a remaining service life for the homeowner of m years.

8.2.2 *The Verbrugge Variant (VV) of the User Cost Approach*

The specification of the user cost implemented in Poole et al. (2005) is based on derivations presented in Verbrugge (2008), where alternative ways of handling the home value appreciation term are also investigated more fully. Here, we label the formulation of the user cost presented as Eq. (8.1) in Verbrugge (2008) as the Verbrugge variant, hereafter referred to for short as the VV user cost.

The VV user cost is derived by treating homeowners as though they costlessly sell and buy back their homes each year.[1] Stated using our notation, where V^t is

[1]This user cost variant follows naturally from application of the statement of the user cost approach given by Diewert (1974) in the opening quotation for Sect. 8.3 about how a consumer is imagined

the beginning of period value of the home ignoring, as Verbrugge does, the age of the home; r^t is a nominal interest rate; V^t is a term which collects the rates of depreciation, maintenance, and property taxes; and $E[\pi]$ is an estimate of the rate of expected house price appreciation, the VV user cost formula is:

$$\begin{aligned} u^t &= r^t V^t + \gamma_H^t V^t - E[\pi]V^t \\ &= \text{forgone interest} + \text{operating costs} - \text{expected } (t) \text{ to } (t+1) \text{ changein home value.} \end{aligned} \quad (8.5)$$

Verbrugge experiments with a number of alternative ways of measuring the final term of (8.5) for the expected change in home value from the beginning to the end of year t, but his preferred forecasting equation includes a forecast of the home price change based on 4 quarters of prior home price information. With this setup, changes in home prices have an immediate within-year impact on the user cost. When home prices are rising, the final term of (8.5) serves to offset the contribution of the first term, $r^t V^t$.

8.2.3 Diewert's OOH Opportunity Cost Approach

The time has come, we feel, to accept the evidence of Verbrugge and others that user costs and rents do not reliably move together! This verdict implies we must rethink the approach for accounting for OOH in the price statistics of nations. We argue in the rest of this paper for a shift to the new opportunity cost approach for accounting for the cost of housing.

The term opportunity cost refers to the cost of the best alternative that must be forgone in taking the option chosen. Thus, we seek to compare implications for homeowner wealth of selling at the beginning of period t with the alternatives of planning to own a home for m more years and of either renting out or occupying the home for the coming year. This comparison is assumed to be carried out at the beginning of period t based on the information available then about the market value of the home and interest rates and the forecasted average increase per year in home market value if the home is held for another m years.

Refinancing can be viewed as a way of a homeowner selling or buying back a fraction of an owned home. In contrast to selling and buying titles to properties, financing and refinancing costs for mortgages and other loans secured by liens on property titles are quite low, in the United States at least. We imagine that a homeowner mentally notes at the start of each year the market price and the forecast for the annual average growth in value for a home that the owner expects to hold for m

---

to be buying their home and then selling it back each period—(possibly to himself). We note that in Sect. 6 of his paper, Verbrugge (2008) relaxes the assumption that there are no costs of buying and selling a house and he uses this fact to try to help explain the divergence between the rental price of a home and its user cost.

more years. The homeowner is presumed to use this information as input to decisions made at the start of the year on whether to adjust their debt for the coming year, whether to sell at the start of the year or to plan on continuing to own their home for m more years, and whether to rent out or occupy the home for the coming year if they continue to own it.

Owner occupiers in period t continue to own their homes with the chosen levels of debt, and to occupy rather than renting their homes out. Thus in choosing to own and occupy, they pass up the opportunity of selling at the start of the period, and also the opportunity of renting out their home that year. At the level of an individual homeowner, the opportunity cost approach amounts to treating the cost to the owner occupant of their housing choice as the greater of the foregone benefit they would have received by selling at the start of period t or renting out the owned home and collecting the rent payments.

The owner occupied housing opportunity cost index can now be defined as follows:

For each household living in owner occupied housing (OOH), the owner occupied housing opportunity cost (OOHOC) is the maximum of what it would cost to rent an equivalent dwelling (the rental opportunity cost, ROC) and the financial opportunity costs (FOC).

The OOHOC index for a nation is defined as an expenditure share weighted sum of a rental equivalency index and a financial opportunity cost index, with the expenditure share weights depending on the estimated proportion of owner occupied homes for which FOC exceeds ROC.

8.2.3.1 The Rental Opportunity Cost Component

The rental opportunity cost component is operationally equivalent to the usual rental equivalency measure, but the justification for this component here does not rest on an appeal to the fundamental equation of capital theory and is not tied to the potential sale value for the home in the current or subsequent periods. In the present context, the ROC component is simply the rent for period t on an owned dwelling that the owner forgoes by living there that period. That is, it is the rent the owner could have collected by renting the place out rather than living there.[2]

We next turn our attention to the financial opportunity cost of the money tied up in an owned dwelling. A home, once purchased, can yield owner occupied housing services over many years. The user cost framework provides guidance on how to infer the period-by-period financial costs of OOH services using the observable home purchase data.

---

[2]Notice that, in computing the ROC component, we do not subtract the cost the owner would need to incur to live somewhere else if they rented the home out. The opportunity cost of living in an owned home, which is the maximum of the ROC and FOC components, is what the person would presumably compare with the costs of alternative housing arrangements in making their choice about where to live for period t. It does, however, make sense to think of the ROC value for an individual homeowner as a lower bound on the value they place on living in the home in light of the fact that most people, in the United States at least, seem to have a strong preference for living in owned accommodations.

We can use the user cost framework this way even in situations when the capital theory assumptions under which the user cost equals the expected rent are not satisfied.

8.2.3.2 The Financial Opportunity Cost Component

The user cost formulation we recommend for the FOC component of the opportunity cost is referred to here as the Diewert variant, or DV, user cost. For this specification, we let r^t denote the rate of return a homeowner could have received by investing funds that are tied up in the owned home. In addition, we take account of the fact that many homeowners have debt that is secured against their homes and must make regular specified payments on that debt to continue to be in a position to occupy or to rent out their homes.

Research has shown that owner occupied homes, on the whole, exhibit little physical depreciation over time given modern standards for home maintenance.[3] (This is in contrast to the situation for rental housing units that have been shown to lose significant value, on average, with increasing age.) Hence, since we are focusing on owner occupied housing here, we drop the dwelling age subscript v from this point on, as we did in introducing the Verbrugge variant (VV) user cost in Eq. (8.5).

We also take account of the fact that the vast majority of homeowners own their homes for many years. Indeed, if we take account as well of the phenomenon of serial home ownership, with owner occupiers rolling forward the equity accumulated from one owned home to the next, then the time horizon should arguably be the entire number of years a homeowner plans to continue to live in owned housing. Many people move into their own owned homes as soon as they can afford to after reaching adulthood and die still owning their own homes. The expected remaining years, m, until a homeowner expects to withdraw all the equity they have in their home is an important parameter for determining the FOC component. However, if homeowner-specific information about m is lacking, perhaps m could be set at a value no lower than the median years that homeowners report having been in their present homes.

Having stated the above choices and views, we are now ready to specify the FOC component for an individual homeowner. Here we ignore the case of homeowners who have negative home equity: a more complex and obviously important case in the present circumstances which we are considering now in separate research with Leonard Nakamura. We also abstract from transactions costs and taxes: further complications that we are also considering in our new research with Leonard Nakamura.

As of the start of period t, a homeowner with nonnegative equity could sell, paying off any debt (D^t) in the process, and could collect the (non negative) sum of $V^t - D^t$. Or the homeowner could choose to continue owning the dwelling, in which case they must make payments on any debt they have, and must pay the normal home operating

[3]Here normal maintenance for owned homes is essentially being defined to include the amount of maintenance and renovation expenditures required to just maintain the overall quality of the home at a constant level.

costs; they must do this whether they choose to live in their home or rent it out for the coming year. If they continue to own the dwelling—either living in it or renting it out—they will forego the interest they could have earned on the equity tied up in their home and will incur maintenance costs and carrying costs on any debt, but they will also enjoy any capital gains or incur any capital losses that materialize.

The financial user cost for owning the home in period t and living in it, discounted to the start of period t , is:

$$\frac{u^t}{1+r^t} \equiv [V^t - D^t] - \left[\frac{-r_D^t D^t - O^t + (\overline{V^{t+1}} - D^t)}{1+r^t}\right], \tag{8.6}$$

where $\overline{V^{t+1}}$ is the value of the home at the beginning of period t plus the expected average appreciation of the home value over the number of years before the homeowner plans to sell. Thus, the second term in square brackets is the forecasted expected value of the home as of the end of period t which is the beginning of period $t+1$ $(\overline{V^{t+1}})$ minus the period t debt service costs $(r_D^t D^t)$ and operating costs (O^t) that must be paid in order to either occupy or rent out the dwelling for period t. If we multiply expression (8.6) through by the discount factor, $1 + r^t$, we now obtain an expression for the ex ante end of period user cost:

$$u^t \equiv r_D^t D^t + r^t(V^t - D^t) + O^t - (\overline{V^{t+1}} - V^t). \tag{8.7}$$

The importance of the debt related terms in (8.6) and (8.7) can be better appreciated by considering some specific types of homeowners. Consider a type A homeowner who owns their home free and clear. For them, the end of period user cost for period t, discounted to the start of the period, is:

$$\left.\frac{u^t}{1+r^t}\right|_{\text{typeA}} \equiv [V^t] - \left[\frac{-O^t + \overline{V^{t+1}}}{1+r^t}\right] = \frac{O^t + r^t V^t - (\overline{V^{t+1}} - V^t)}{1+r^t}. \tag{8.8}$$

The user cost considered as of the end of the period is found by multiplying (8.8) through by $1 + r^t$, yielding:

$$\left.u^t\right|_{\text{typeA}} \equiv r^t V^t + O^t - (\overline{V^{t+1}} - V^t). \tag{8.9}$$

Notice that this is essentially the customary user cost expression, as derived by Katz (2009) and others. This is the same basic formulation used as well by Verbrugge; e.g., see (8.5) above.

Type B homeowners do not fully own their homes, but have positive home equity: the most prevalent case for U.S. homeowners. If the homeowner were to sell at the beginning of period t, the realized proceeds of the sale (after repaying the debt) would be $V^t - D^t$. The end of period user cost for period t for these homeowners, discounted to the start of period t, is:

$$\left.\frac{u^t}{1+r^t}\right|_{\text{typeB}} \equiv \lfloor V^t - Dt \rfloor - \left[\frac{-r_D^t D^t - O^t + (\overline{V^{t+1}} - D^t)}{1+r^t}\right]$$
$$= \frac{r_D^t D^t + O^t + r^t(V^t - D^t) - (\overline{V^{t+1}} - V^t)}{1+r^t} \tag{8.10}$$

The user cost, as of the end of the period, is found by multiplying (8.10) through by $1 + r^t$:

$$u^t\big|_{\text{typeB}} \equiv r_D^t D^t + r^t(V^t - D^t) + O^t - (\overline{V^{t+1}} - V^t). \tag{8.11}$$

Type C homeowners have zero home equity. In this case, if the homeowner sells at the start of period t, we assume simply that they get nothing from the sale. And if they continue to own and live in the home, they do so without having any equity tied up by this choice and hence are not foregoing any earnings on funds tied up in their home. The end of period user cost for period t, considered as of the start of period t, is:

$$\left.\frac{u^t}{1+r^t}\right|_{\text{typeC}} \equiv -\left[\frac{-r_D^t D^t - O^t + (\overline{V^{t+1}} - D^t)}{1+r^t}\right]. \tag{8.12}$$

The user cost considered as of the end of the period is[4]:

$$u^t\big|_{\text{typeC}} \equiv r_D^t D^r + O^t - (\overline{V^{t+1}} - V^t). \tag{8.13}$$

We next consider the extreme case in which the interest rate for borrowing equals the returns on investments (i.e., $r_D^t = r^t$). Now, (8.10) and (8.11) reduce to (8.8) and (8.9). That is, the expressions for the homeowners who have debt but still have positive equity in their homes reduce to the expressions for the user cost for the homeowners who own their dwellings free and clear. We see, therefore, that the traditional user cost expression, as derived by Katz, and the VV user cost implicitly assume that homeowners who have mortgages or other home equity loans are charged an interest rate on this debt that equals the rate of return on their financial investments.

Most well off households have mostly low cost debt whereas many poor households mostly have high cost debt. The importance of this fact can be demonstrated using the end of period user cost for a type B homeowner. For a homeowner who has positive home equity and only low cost debt with $r_D^t < r^t$, expression (8.11) can be written as:

$$\begin{aligned} u^t\big|_{\text{typeB}} &\equiv r_D^t D^t + r^t(V^t - D^t) + O^t - (\overline{V^{t+1}} - V^t) \\ &= r_D^t V^t - (r^t - r_D^t) D^t + O^t - (\overline{V^{t+1}} - V^t), \end{aligned} \tag{8.14}$$

[4]Note that in this zero equity case, it seems like the payments approach is justified at first glance. However, the payments approach neglects the expected capital gains term and during periods of high or moderate inflation, this term must be taken into account.

where the term $(r^t - r^t_D)$ is positive. Hence, for these homeowners, higher debt reduces the financial cost of OOH services. Indeed, this is a potential motivation for a Type B homeowner to increase their low cost borrowing to the greatest extent possible. The only rational constraint on doing this, from an economic perspective, is that higher debt can also bring a greater risk of home foreclosure or personal bankruptcy in the event of a downturn in the economy or personal problems such as job loss or illness.

The case of a homeowner with only high cost debt (i.e., with $r^t_D > r^t$) is different. Now (8.11) reduces to:

$$\begin{aligned} u^t\Big|_{\text{typeB}} &\equiv r^t_D D^t + r^t(V^t - D^t) + O^t - (\overline{V^{t+1}} - V^t) \\ &= r^t V^t + (r^t_D - r^t)D^t + O^t - (\overline{V^{t+1}} - V^t), \end{aligned} \tag{8.15}$$

where $(r^t_D - r^t)$ is positive. So now, higher debt means a higher financial cost of OOH services. Most subprime loans are high cost, with interest rates at least three interest rate points above Treasures of comparable maturities.

We come now to the question of how the DV user cost would behave over a housing bubble. In this portion of our analysis, we use the general (8.8) expression for the end of period user cost. Moreover, we will define $r^t_{H(m)}$ as the expected rate of home price change under the assumption a home will be held for m more years. Now, (8.7) can be rewritten as

$$\begin{aligned} u^t &\equiv r^t_D D^t + r^t(V^t - D^t) - r^t_{H(m)} V^t + O^t \\ &= (r^t_D - r^t)D^t + (r^t - r^t_{H(m)})V^t + O^t, \end{aligned} \tag{8.16}$$

where

$$r^t_{H(m)} V^t = \overline{V^{t+1}} - V^t$$

Hence the FOC for a household can be negative when, for example, the borrowing rate is less than the expected rate of return on financial assets, and the expected rate of return on financial assets is less than the expected annual rate of return on housing assets.

However, the OOHOC for a household will never be zero or negative because it is defined as the maximum of the ROC and the FOC, with the rental opportunity cost necessarily being positive.

Notice also that the FOC component will rise as home prices rise, and first and foremost, when the expected rate of return on financial investments (r^t) is greater than the expected rate of return on the housing asset $(r^t_{H(m)})$. Going into a bubble, the first term,

$$(r^t_D - r^t)D^t,$$

will be hard to forecast even in terms of sign, but we would expect the changes in this term to be small compared to the changes in the second term,

$$(r^t - r^t_{H(m)})V^t$$

During the expansion phase of a bubble, home values, and hence V^t, will grow rapidly, but the longer run return on housing assets should not change as much and hence the financial user cost of OOH, given by equation (8.16), should increase. This result underlines the importance of incorporating longer run expectations into the user cost formula. Of course, when the bubble bursts, the financial user cost will rapidly decline, although the decline will be offset somewhat by the possible decline as well in $r^t_{H(m)}$.[5]

8.3 Empirical Analysis

8.3.1 Estimation Error of Imputed Rent for OOH

Targeting the owner-occupied housing market in Tokyo, after collecting as much micro-data as possible, we estimated imputed rent for owner-occupied housing using multiple methods. First, we calculated it with the Equivalent Rent Approach currently employed in Japan.

The Equivalent Rent Approach is a method that forecasts housing rent levels in the case of leasing out owner-occupied housing, using housing rental rates formed by the housing rental market. In the case of attempting to estimate imputed rent for owner-occupied housing with such a method, it has been pointed that bias occurs due to data limitations and market structure disparities between the owner-occupied housing market and the rental housing market.

For example, according to the 2008 Housing and Land Survey, the average floor space (size) of owner-occupied housing in Tokyo was 110.71 m^2 for single-family house owner-occupied housing and 79.36 m^2 for rental housing—a discrepancy of over 30 m^2. When it comes to condominiums, an even greater discrepancy exists, at 65.84 m^2 for owner occupied housing and 36.06 m^2 for rental housing. Moreover, it is not just the area—a quality gap in structure, facilities, etc., also exists between owner-occupied housing and rental housing. As a result, when attempting to estimate imputed rent for owner-occupied housing using rental housing data, it is necessary to perform quality adjustment.

However, in estimating imputed rent for owner-occupied housing in Japan, the average rent calculated for either the country as a whole or individual prefectures is multiplied by the aggregate owner-occupied housing area. In this case, since many rental housing units are concentrated in urban areas, the average housing rent that is estimated is heavily weighted on urban data. In such a situation, there is a strong possibility of overestimating imputed rent. Meanwhile, since most rental housing units are small-scale housing of 30 m^2 or less, the quality is considerably inferior. In

[5]Locked in aspects of the financing arrangements of home buyers may also matter in this regard. We are exploring this issue now in a follow-up study.

this case, there is a strong possibility of underestimating imputed rent. As well, since it is known that housing rents and prices change significantly based on the location and building age, it is surely natural to think that major measurement errors will arise if adjustment for quality differences is not performed.

Besides these kinds of problems based on structural differences between the owner-occupied housing and rental housing markets, problems also exist in terms of the nature of the rent being surveyed. Since the rent surveyed via the Housing and Land Survey and consumer price statistics is the household's paying rent, there is a strong possibility that there is a major discrepancy with the rent determined by the current market.

The reason for this is that the lease contract period in Japan is two years, so the rent is not changed for a two-year period after the contract is concluded (in Canada it is one year, and rent is mostly not changed over the one-year period). As well, even if the lease contract is renewed, it is rare for the rent to be revised to the same level as market rent at the time of contract renewal. As a result, the rent that would likely be generated by the market at the time of the survey and the rent being paid at that time diverge significantly (see Shimizu et al. 2010a).[6]

Accordingly, we implemented two corrections for the Equivalent Rent Approach. The first correction was an adjustment to the rent data. We changed the household paying rent surveyed by the CPI and Housing and Land Survey to the market rent formed at that time. The second correction was the implementation of quality adjustment. Different rents are set depending not only on regional differences (such as proximity to city) but also on differences within the same region, such as floor space, distance to nearest station, time to city center, building age, etc. Adjustment of such quality differences was performed using the hedonic approach.

Next is the User Cost Approach, which attempts to estimate imputed rent from the asset price of owner-occupied housing. The estimation method for doing so is complicated, and it has been pointed out that there is a problem with the value becoming negative during periods of dramatic price increases. It has also been noted that this is combined with the problem of housing price volatility becoming greater than what it is perceived by market players. However, a Residential Property Price Handbook (RPPI Handbook) is published for estimating housing prices,[7] and it is anticipated that in future many countries will move forward with aligning their housing price statistics based on this handbook.[8]

---

[6]Since the Japanese Act on Land and Building Leases strongly protects renters, increasing rent is prohibited except in cases where it is allowed due to a rise in costs such as property taxes. As a result, even when housing prices rise significantly, it is difficult to change the rent during the lease contract term. As well, even when a lease contract is renewed, increases in the rent amount are not allowed to exceed the extent of cost increases.

[7]See http://epp.eurostat.ec.europa.eu/portal/page/portal/hicp/methodology/owner/occupied/housing/hpi/rppi/handbook with regard to the RPPI Handbook.

[8]In Japan, the publication of the RPPI Handbook has led to an office being set up within the Ministry of Land, Infrastructure, Transport and Tourism, and advisory board aimed at real estate price index upgrading being implemented through interaction between the Bank of Japan and Financial Services Agency (which are responsible for fiscal policy), the Cabinet Office (which is responsible for

Accordingly, in employing the User Cost Approach, we calculated the single-family housing price function and condominium price function using the hedonic approach recommended by the RPPI Handbook, and then calculated the quality-adjusted asset price. Furthermore, in the User Cost calculation, it is necessary to consider various costs. Among these, property tax has the greatest weight. The land evaluation amount for property tax varies considerably based on location. We therefore calculated a hedonic function based on published land value data that is the benchmark for property tax land evaluations, and combined it with the property tax amount for each type of dwelling unit.[9]

8.3.2 *Data*

8.3.2.1 Housing Rents, Housing Prices and Land Prices

We collect housing prices and rents from a magazine or website, published by Recruit Co., Ltd., one of the largest vendors of residential lettings information in Japan. The Recruit dataset covers the 23 special wards and Tama-area of Tokyo for the period 1986 (Rents: 1990) to 2010, including the bubble period in the late 1980s and its collapse to the 90s. It contains 251,473 listings for single family house prices, 330,247 listings for condominium prices and 1,155,078 listings for rents of single family houses and condominiums.[10] Recruit provides time-series of housing prices and rents from the week when it is first posted until the week it is removed because of successful transaction.[11] We only use the price in the final week because this can be safely regarded as sufficiently close to the contract price.[12]

SNA statistics), the Ministry of Internal Affairs and Communications Statistics Bureau (which is responsible for consumer price statistics), the Ministry of Justice (which is responsible for housing relocation statistics), and private-sector experts, and progress being made toward establishing a new housing price index. A new housing price index using the method recommended in the RPPI Handbook is scheduled to be published during fiscal 2012. The coordination of such statistics across Japan as a whole is significant not just as a benchmark for making fiscal and monetary decisions but also for creating the possibility of applying them to other statistics—the estimation of imputed rent for owner-occupied housing being a leading example.

[9]Land evaluation for property tax purposes is determined using 70% of the published land price as a base. For this study, we started by calculating the land price evaluation level using the published land price base.

[10]Shimizu et al. (2010b) report that the Recruit data cover more than 95% of the entire transactions in the 23 special wards of Tokyo. On the other hand, its coverage for suburban areas is very limited. We use only information for the units located in the special wards of Tokyo.

[11]There are two reasons for the listing of a unit being removed from the magazine: a successful deal or a withdrawal (i.e. the seller gives up looking for a buyer and thus withdraws the listing). We were allowed access information regarding which the two reasons applied for individual cases and discarded those where the seller withdrew the listing.

[12]Recruit Co., Ltd. provided us with information on contract prices for about 24% of the entire listings. Using this information, we were able to confirm that prices in the final week were almost always identical with the contract prices (i.e., they differed at a probability of less than 0.1%).

Table 8.1 List of variables

Symbol	Variable	Content	Unit
FS	Floor space	Floor space of building	m^2
GA	Ground area	Ground area of housing/building	m^2
RW	Road width	Road width in front of housing	m
A	Age of building at the time of transaction	Age of building at the time of transaction	Years
TS	Distance to the nearest station	Distance to the nearest station by walk or bus or car	m
TT	Travel time to Tokyo station	Average railway riding time in daytime to the Tokyo station	Minutes
SRC	Steel reinforced concrete dummy	Steel reinforced concrete frame structure = 1, other structure = 0	(0, 1)
RC	Reinforced concrete dummy	Reinforced concrete frame structure = 1, other structure = 0	(0, 1)
LGT	Light-gauge steel dummy	Light-gauge steel frame structure = 1, other structure = 0	(0, 1)
$Wood$	Wood frame structure dummy	Wood frame structure = 1, other structure = 0	(0, 1)
LD_k	Location (ward or municipalities) dummy	k-th administrative district = 1, other district = 0. $(k = 0, \ldots, K)$	(0, 1)
RD_l	Railway line dummy	l-th railway line = 1, other railway line = 0. $(l = 0, \ldots, L)$	(0, 1)

In addition, in order to calculate property tax amounts, we developed published land price data, which is the benchmark for property tax land evaluations. From 1990 to 2010, evaluation amount data has been published for 37,479 residential areas.

Table 8.1 shows a list of the attributes of a house. This includes ground area (GA), floor space (FS), and front road width (RW) as key attributes of a house. The age of a house is defined as the number of months between the date of the construction of the house and the transaction. We define south-facing dummy, SD, to indicate whether the house's windows are south-facing or not (note that Japanese are particularly fond of sunshine). The convenience of public transportation from each house location is represented by travel time to the central business district (CBD),[13] which is denoted by TT and time to the nearest station,[14] which is denoted by TS. We use a ward dummy, LD, to indicate differences in the quality of public services available in each

[13]Travel time to the CBD is measured as follows. The metropolitan area of Tokyo is composed of 23 wards centering on the Tokyo Station area and containing a dense railway network. Within this area, we choose seven railway/subway stations as the central stations, which include Tokyo, Shinagawa, Shibuya, Shinjuku, Ikebukuro, Ueno, and Otemachi. Then, we define travel time to the CBD by the minutes needed to commute to the nearest of the seven stations in the daytime.

[14]The time to the nearest station, TS, is defined as walking time to a nearest station if a house is located within the walking distance from a station, and the sum of walking time to a bus stop and onboard time from the bus stop to a nearest station if a house is located in a bus transportation area

district, and a railway line dummy, RD, to indicate along which railway/subway line a house is located.

Table 8.2 shows the summary statistics for the various data. The average single family house price is ¥66.23 million, while the average condominium price is ¥37.17 million. Looking at the average floor space (FS), the figures are 105 m^2 for single family houses and 57 m^2 for condominiums, which is consistent with Land and Housing Survey results. In other words, the data collected here is largely in accordance with single family housing and condominium stocks.

If one looks at rent data, the average monthly rent is ¥110,000 and the average floor space (FS) is 38 m^2. It is clear from the data collected in this study that a significant discrepancy exists between the average housing floor space produced by the owner-occupied housing market and the rental market.

The building age (A) is 15 years for single family houses, 14 years for condominiums, and 9 years for rental housing. Here, too, one can see that there is a significant discrepancy between the owner-occupied housing market and rental market.

8.3.2.2 Building Usage Data

With regard to building usage, we used the Tokyo current land and building usage survey data. This data provides information on usage status, structure, number of stories, and floor space for all buildings in Tokyo at four points in time (1991, 1996, 2001, and 2006) via an inventory survey. What's more, it is provided as a database that can be used via the Geographic Information System (GIS). With regard to housing, this study employs four types of building usage: single family houses, condominiums, housing joint industrial usage, and housing joint commercial usage.

The fact that data is provided in a form that may be used with the GIS is highly significant. It is known that there are considerable price gaps in housing prices and rent based on location in combination with building characteristics. As a result, one may expect that these location differences will cause significant bias in the estimation of imputed rent for owner-occupied housing. Accordingly, using the GIS, we obtained the "distance to nearest station" and "time to city center (Tokyo station)," which are believed to be key variables in terms of the factors determining housing prices in Tokyo.[15]

---

within walking distance from a station. We use a bus dummy, Bus, to indicate whether a house is located in a walking distance area from a station or in a bus transportation area.

[15]With regard to the distance to the nearest station, the closest station was defined as the closest station from the center of the building. Based on that, the road distance was measured using the GIS. As well, with regard to the time from the nearest station to Tokyo Station, the average day-time travel time was added, in the same way as for the rental/housing price data.

Table 8.2 Summary statistics of housing data

Single family house data: single family house price data (251,473 observations)				
	Mean	Std. Dev.	Min.	Max.
P: Price (¥10,000) of unit	6,623.83	3,619.20	1,280	29,990
FS: Floor space (m^2)	105.48	38.93	50	448
P/FS (¥10,000/m^2)	72.47	30.11	25	479
A: Age of building (years)	15.20	8.34	0	55
TS: Distance to the nearest station (m)	811.68	374.22	80	2,800
TT: Travel time to terminal station (min.)	34.48	11.12	1	144
RW: Road width	4.88	1.88	2	20
Condominium price data: condominium price data (330,247 observations)				
	Mean	Std. Dev.	Min.	Max.
P: Price (¥10,000) of unit	3,717.52	2,250.71	390	33,500
FS: Floor space (m^2)	57.83	18.29	15	110
P/FS (¥10,000/m^2)	66.22	35.73	25	315
A: Age of building (years)	14.23	8.74	0	55
TS: Distance to the nearest station (m)	682.68	366.10	80	2,480
TT: Travel time to terminal station (min.)	30.10	12.63	1	144
Land price data: land price data (37,479 observations)				
	Mean	Std. Dev.	Min.	Max.
P/FS (¥10,000/m^2)	43.11	40.90	5	1,230
GA: Land area (m^2)	191.66	128.75	40	4,069
TS: Distance to the nearest station (m)	1,142.28	1,001.50	60	9,200
TT: Travel time to terminal station (min.)	42.90	16.70	7	126
RW: Road Width	5.44	2.45	2	38
Housing rent data: housing rent data (1,155,078 observations)				
	Mean	Std. Dev.	Min.	Max.
P: rent (¥10,000/month) of unit	11.23	6.48	2	60
FS: Floor space (m^2)	38.27	20.85	10	120
P/FS (¥10,000/m^2)	0.31	0.09	0.1	2.0
A: Age of building (years)	9.74	8.11	0	55
TS: Distance to the nearest station (m)	614.87	350.25	80	7,040
TT: Travel time to terminal station (min.)	30.45	11.56	1	126

However, the data is lacking when it comes to the "Age of building (A)" for each building. Accordingly, we calculated the average building age for single family houses and condominiums by administrative district (city/ward) based on the Housing and Land Survey.[16]

[16]The Housing and Land Survey includes the number of stocks by year of construction. Accordingly, we calculated the average age of buildings by municipality based on the year of construction, and calculated the Age of Building (A) based on the time elapsed until the time of calculation.

Table 8.3 summarizes building data prepared in combination with Housing and Land Survey data.[17] First, there was little change in single family houses from 1990 (1.857 million houses) to 1995 (1.855 million houses), but the number grew considerably from 2000 (1.897 million houses) to 2005 (2.011 million houses). With regard to condominiums, there were 367,000 units in 1990, 374,000 units in 1995, and 381,000 units in 2000, which rose significantly to 417,000 units in 2005. The increase in total floor space for condominiums was especially significant.

With the Housing and Land Survey, along with the total floor space, it is possible to know the proportion of owner-occupied housing. If we focus on the percentage of owner-occupied housing, the rate was 89% for single family houses in 1990, but in 2005 it had risen to 94%. The rate rose considerably for condominiums as well, from 28% in 1990 to 39% in 2005. We believe the proportion of owner-occupied housing increased during this period because housing prices dropped substantially, along with a reduction in mortgage rates.

8.3.3 Estimation of Rental Value and Capital Value Per Housing

8.3.3.1 Hedonic Estimation Residential Rent, Condominium, Single Family House and Land

We estimated a hedonic function using housing rent data, single family house price data, condominium price data, and land price data.

In calculating the rent and housing price by dwelling unit for each year, we estimated the following hedonic function incorporating temporal changes along with structural changes in rent/price formation mechanisms.

$$\mu_{ijt} = X_{it}\beta_t + v_{it} \tag{8.17}$$

Here, μ_{ijt} is the property rent/price of type j of building i at a point in time t/m^2 while j is a characteristic vector relating to the size and building age of the property. j signifies the type of rent or price: single family house price, condominium price, or land price (published land price), along with single family house rent and condominium (apartment building) rent.

As well, it is known that the characteristic price β_t in the hedonic function changes over time (Shimizu et al. 2010b). As a result, in order to control for changes in characteristic price β_t as time passes, we estimated hedonic equations for each period t.

The estimation results are shown in Tables 8.4 and 8.5.

---

[17] We can see a differences between (a) and (e), (c) and (f). The differences come from the survey method. the Tokyo current land and building usage survey is Census, on the other hand, the Housing and Land Survey is Sample survey.

Table 8.3 Buildings survey

	Housing survey						Building survey			
	Single family house			Condominium			Single family house		Condominium	
	(a) Total[a]	(b) Owner occupied housing[a]	(b)/(a) (%)	(c) Total[a]	(d) Owner occupied housing[a]	(d)/(c) (%)	(e) Total[a]	(Units)[b]	(f) Total[a]	(Units)[c]
1990	160, 662, 570	143, 150, 350	89.10	108, 909, 068	31, 452, 939	28.88	148, 834, 033	1, 857, 722	107, 274, 134	367, 734
1995	168, 371, 522	153, 351, 080	91.08	135, 811, 068	42, 833, 050	31.54	160, 654, 688	1, 854, 315	135, 778, 868	374, 807
2000	185, 103, 543	167, 169, 249	90.31	162, 879, 280	59, 920, 560	36.79	174, 379, 864	1, 897, 345	161, 698, 203	381, 216
2005	182, 850, 330	173, 046, 939	94.64	184, 044, 399	71, 923, 616	39.08	181, 977, 956	2, 011, 068	186, 759, 564	417, 872

[a] Unit: square meter
[b] Number of condominium buildings (not unit)
[c] Number of single family houses

Table 8.4 Estimation results of Hedonic Eq. 8.1

Year	Single family house price model								Condominium price model							
	Intercept	log FS	log RW	log A	log TS	log TT	Number	Adj. R^2	Intercept	log FS	log A	log TS	log TT	RC	Number	Adj. R^2
1986	4.15	0.04	0.21	−0.05	−0.04	−0.16	2,502	0.53	4.872	−0.019	−0.152	−0.026	−0.179	−0.007	7,604	0.65
1987	4.18	0.02	0.28	−0.03	−0.02	−0.09	2,805	0.66	5.159	0.061	−0.139	0.004	−0.272	−0.034	6,312	0.71
1988	5.02	−0.06	0.26	−0.04	−0.05	−0.13	2,680	0.61	6.058	−0.072	−0.166	−0.018	−0.295	−0.025	7,368	0.72
1989	5.52	0.01	0.23	−0.01	−0.09	−0.24	2,430	0.58	6.386	−0.097	−0.176	−0.030	−0.300	−0.020	15,336	0.73
1990	6.10	−0.08	0.25	−0.02	−0.07	−0.28	2,414	0.54	6.803	−0.143	−0.159	−0.017	−0.334	−0.024	13,680	0.75
1991	6.02	−0.05	0.20	−0.03	−0.09	−0.27	2,430	0.52	6.600	−0.124	−0.195	−0.025	−0.290	−0.027	14,708	0.73
1992	5.82	−0.03	0.14	−0.05	−0.10	−0.23	2,586	0.52	6.397	−0.109	−0.207	−0.026	−0.270	−0.028	17,065	0.70
1993	5.46	−0.06	0.14	−0.04	−0.07	−0.18	2,747	0.51	5.915	−0.048	−0.210	−0.020	−0.239	−0.017	17,647	0.66
1994	5.16	−0.08	0.12	−0.03	−0.04	−0.13	3,775	0.49	5.563	−0.004	−0.224	−0.018	−0.207	−0.020	19,647	0.61
1995	5.25	−0.11	0.09	−0.04	−0.03	−0.13	4,800	0.49	5.213	0.060	−0.254	−0.021	−0.207	−0.015	19,282	0.57
1996	4.99	−0.08	0.11	−0.04	−0.03	−0.13	5,022	0.46	4.933	0.093	−0.244	−0.025	−0.196	−0.015	15,476	0.63
1997	4.67	−0.08	0.11	−0.03	−0.04	−0.04	9,706	0.46	5.018	0.080	−0.247	−0.022	−0.214	−0.016	14,037	0.63
1998	4.98	−0.13	0.09	−0.03	−0.03	−0.07	12,511	0.44	4.796	0.092	−0.228	−0.017	−0.201	−0.017	13,846	0.62
1999	4.77	−0.08	0.04	−0.04	−0.03	−0.07	11,217	0.50	4.761	0.085	−0.228	−0.020	−0.193	−0.017	13,132	0.66
2000	4.72	−0.07	0.06	−0.03	−0.03	−0.11	11,151	0.50	4.856	0.089	−0.228	−0.026	−0.218	−0.017	12,778	0.66
2001	4.71	−0.08	0.06	−0.04	−0.03	−0.10	14,212	0.59	4.918	0.063	−0.219	−0.029	−0.213	−0.019	12,879	0.66
2002	4.58	−0.03	0.03	−0.03	−0.02	−0.15	15,761	0.53	4.951	0.051	−0.201	−0.037	−0.207	−0.027	10,369	0.67
2003	4.86	−0.06	0.04	−0.02	−0.04	−0.16	18,022	0.54	5.007	0.044	−0.213	−0.037	−0.210	−0.018	9,787	0.70
2004	4.89	−0.05	0.02	−0.03	−0.04	−0.17	18,731	0.51	5.097	0.040	−0.204	−0.048	−0.219	−0.012	9,987	0.69
2005	4.63	−0.04	0.01	−0.04	−0.04	−0.12	20,732	0.55	5.050	0.023	−0.214	−0.038	−0.198	−0.013	12,223	0.72
2006	4.82	−0.04	0.01	−0.04	−0.05	−0.15	20,805	0.58	5.125	0.020	−0.218	−0.046	−0.193	−0.012	12,853	0.71
2007	5.06	−0.07	0.00	−0.03	−0.04	−0.17	19,208	0.62	4.877	0.054	−0.206	−0.041	−0.163	−0.014	13,693	0.74
2008	5.36	−0.08	0.02	−0.04	−0.07	−0.19	16,177	0.61	4.909	0.067	−0.206	−0.053	−0.158	−0.023	14,150	0.72
2009	5.70	−0.20	0.01	−0.04	−0.06	−0.17	14,429	0.63	5.042	0.072	−0.226	−0.055	−0.196	−0.031	10,920	0.72
2010	5.86	−0.22	0.03	−0.04	−0.06	−0.19	14,620	0.63	5.243	0.034	−0.219	−0.042	−0.224	−0.023	15, 468	0.72

[a] The dependent variable in each case is the log price per square meter

[b] The table indicate the coefficient of main variables which a part of hedonic estimation results per year

[c] Estimation method: robust regression

Table 8.5 Estimation results of Hedonic Eq. 8.2

Year	Published land price model								Housing rent model							
	Intercept	log GA	log RW	log A	log TS	log TT	Number	Adj. R^2	Intercept	log FS	log A	log TS	log TT	LGT	Number	Adj. R^2
1990	7.83	0.1974	0.40	–	−0.26	−0.99	1,201	0.85	2.83	−0.21	−0.05	−0.03	−0.21	−0.10	33,172	0.71
1991	7.84	0.1993	0.39	–	−0.26	−1.00	1,201	0.85	3.01	−0.22	−0.05	−0.03	−0.21	−0.10	17,622	0.69
1992	7.57	0.1839	0.38	–	−0.24	−0.95	1,202	0.85	3.00	−0.23	−0.06	−0.03	−0.20	−0.08	18,741	0.69
1993	7.14	0.1568	0.31	–	−0.21	−0.88	1,516	0.86	3.03	−0.23	−0.07	−0.03	−0.21	−0.07	22,257	0.70
1994	6.64	0.1297	0.28	–	−0.19	−0.76	1,776	0.86	3.14	−0.21	−0.10	−0.04	−0.22	−0.07	29,477	0.67
1995	6.44	0.1154	0.25	–	−0.17	−0.71	1,969	0.86	3.09	−0.24	−0.06	−0.04	−0.21	−0.04	39,609	0.67
1996	6.24	0.1059	0.22	–	−0.16	−0.66	1,969	0.86	3.05	−0.25	−0.03	−0.04	−0.20	−0.02	56,846	0.67
1997	6.15	0.0897	0.20	–	−0.16	−0.62	1,943	0.87	3.11	−0.27	−0.02	−0.04	−0.21	−0.03	62,482	0.69
1998	6.17	0.0861	0.19	–	−0.16	−0.62	1,944	0.87	3.23	−0.28	−0.03	−0.05	−0.22	−0.04	68,517	0.70
1999	6.22	0.0891	0.17	–	−0.16	−0.64	1,944	0.87	3.24	−0.29	−0.03	−0.04	−0.21	−0.04	73,701	0.71
2000	6.37	0.0931	0.16	–	−0.18	−0.68	1,949	0.87	3.22	−0.30	−0.03	−0.04	−0.21	−0.03	72,248	0.72
2001	6.56	0.0971	0.15	–	−0.19	−0.72	1,951	0.87	3.21	−0.28	−0.03	−0.05	−0.22	−0.02	90,725	0.71
2002	6.72	0.1008	0.14	–	−0.20	−0.75	1,986	0.87	3.18	−0.28	−0.03	−0.05	−0.21	−0.04	98,674	0.73
2003	6.92	0.1034	0.13	–	−0.22	−0.80	1,986	0.87	3.12	−0.28	−0.03	−0.05	−0.21	−0.04	101,845	0.74
2004	7.03	0.1082	0.13	–	−0.23	−0.83	1,984	0.86	3.07	−0.27	−0.03	−0.05	−0.20	−0.04	93,292	0.72
2005	7.15	0.1149	0.13	–	−0.23	−0.86	1,945	0.86	3.02	−0.26	−0.03	−0.05	−0.19	−0.03	82,057	0.71
2006	7.20	0.1227	0.13	–	−0.24	−0.88	1,934	0.86	3.16	−0.27	−0.03	−0.05	−0.22	−0.03	67,287	0.73
2007	7.45	0.1403	0.13	–	−0.25	−0.93	1,856	0.87	3.18	−0.27	−0.03	−0.06	−0.23	−0.02	50,159	0.75
2008	7.68	0.1513	0.14	–	−0.26	−0.96	1,809	0.87	3.16	−0.29	−0.04	−0.05	−0.20	−0.02	35,409	0.76
2009	7.60	0.1582	0.12	–	−0.26	−0.95	1,730	0.86	3.00	−0.30	−0.04	−0.05	−0.16	0.00	21,700	0.76
2010	7.58	0.1454	0.12	–	−0.27	−0.94	1, 684	0.86	2.86	−0.31	−0.05	−0.05	−0.13	−0.01	19, 258	0.78

[a]The dependent variable in each case is the log price per square meter

[b]The table indicate the coefficient of main variables which a part of hedonic estimation results per year

[c]Estimation method: robust regression

Looking at the hedonic equation estimation results, the coefficient of determination for the single family house price function fluctuates within a range of 0.5 to 0.65, with its explanatory power being lower than that of other models. For single family houses, there is a high degree of heterogeneity compared to the condominium price function, rent function, etc., and we believe it is necessary to incorporate factors such as the surrounding environment. On the other hand, the land price function using real estate appraisal prices has a strong explanatory power, at 0.85 or more across all periods. We believe this is because there is no need to consider the building's structure since it is the land price only and because much of the noise accompanying transactions is eliminated by the real estate appraisal price.

However, for the single family house price function, condominium price function, land price function, and housing rent function alike, the sign functions of the estimated values for the "Age of building (A)," "Distance to nearest station (TS)," and "Travel time to terminal station (TT)" were consistent, so it was determined that we were able to obtain reliable results.

8.3.3.2 Forecast of Rental Value, Capital Value and Rent/Price Ratio

Using the estimated hedonic function, we predicted the rent, housing price, and land price for the various dwelling units for the previously prepared building data. First, we outline the respective changes in average price for the forecast results in Table 8.6 and Fig. 8.1.[18] We calculated the price per 1 m for single family house prices and condominium prices and the rent per 1 square meter per year for single family house rents and condominium rents (in Fig. 8.1, 2000 is taken as 1). As well, we calculated the rent/price ratio for each type of dwelling unit and obtained the average value.

Single family house prices and condominium prices peaked in 1990 then reversed direction, whereas rents peaked in 1991 or 1992 before reversing direction. As well, in terms of the extent of the fluctuation, one can see that rents fluctuated less than prices.

These differences in the price changes for both types of housing can also be seen based on changes in the rent/price ratio. The rent/price ratio increased for both from 1990 through 2004. In other words, this means that the rate of decrease for housing prices was faster than the rate of decrease for housing rents.

Subsequently, prices turned to an increase with the occurrence of a mini-bubble while rents continued to decrease steadily, so the rent/price ratio turned to a decrease.

---

[18]Here, we forecast housing prices and rents using hedonic function estimate values for all periods, based on building stocks in the baseline year of 1990, and then calculated the average value. In other words, it is a weighted average based on 1990 baseline stocks.

Table 8.6 Estimation results of Hedonic indexes for housing prices and rents

Year	Single family house price (¥10,000/m²)	Condo. price (¥10,000/m²)	Single family house rent (¥10,000/m²)	Condo. rent (¥10,000/m²)	Rent/price ratio: single family house (%)	Rent/price ratio: Condo. (%)
1986	49.48	41.43	–	–	–	–
1987	90.24	73.83	–	–	–	–
1988	96.74	72.05	–	–	–	–
1989	100.03	81.86	–	–	–	–
1990	118.88	101.79	2.70	2.97	2.31%	2.96%
1991	106.19	90.96	2.94	3.28	2.82%	3.68%
1992	90.46	79.64	2.94	3.11	3.32%	3.97%
1993	80.50	71.59	2.77	3.02	3.49%	4.25%
1994	72.43	64.84	2.72	2.98	3.77%	4.62%
1995	67.19	53.41	2.68	2.95	4.02%	5.56%
1996	62.83	48.99	2.67	2.94	4.25%	6.04%
1997	60.97	47.80	2.65	2.92	4.37%	6.15%
1998	60.15	45.19	2.63	2.87	4.41%	6.37%
1999	53.84	43.17	2.62	2.83	4.88%	6.60%
2000	52.20	41.76	2.57	2.76	4.93%	6.65%
2001	48.97	40.85	2.54	2.76	5.21%	6.79%
2002	46.63	41.16	2.58	2.80	5.53%	6.85%
2003	47.81	41.17	2.54	2.74	5.34%	6.70%
2004	46.03	41.43	2.53	2.70	5.54%	6.60%
2005	46.03	42.10	2.49	2.67	5.47%	6.41%
2006	48.77	44.18	2.51	2.71	5.21%	6.22%
2007	53.09	49.60	2.57	2.68	4.93%	5.51%
2008	52.26	50.40	2.52	2.61	4.92%	5.28%
2009	51.21	47.12	2.46	2.57	4.96%	5.56%
2010	53.09	49.67	2.40	2.50	4.73%	5.13%

8.3.3.3 Estimation of Equivalent Rent

Using the estimated hedonic rent function, we calculated the equivalent rent for Tokyo's 23 wards (Table 8.6). In addition to showing the estimated equivalent rent, Table 8.7 compares it with the GDP, the imputed rent of owner-occupied housing in the GDP, and imputed rent in prefectural accounting.

First, looking at changes in the proportion of the GDP represented by the imputed rent for owner-occupied housing, the rate was 6.25% in 1990, but it has risen significantly over the years to 7.4% in 1995, 8.5% in 2000, 9.08% in 2005, and 9.92% in 2009. In Japan, not only did the proportion of owner-occupied housing rise, but we believe that the relative importance of imputed rent increased due to the accumulation of owned houses as stock that occurred with production and consumption stagnating under deflationary conditions.

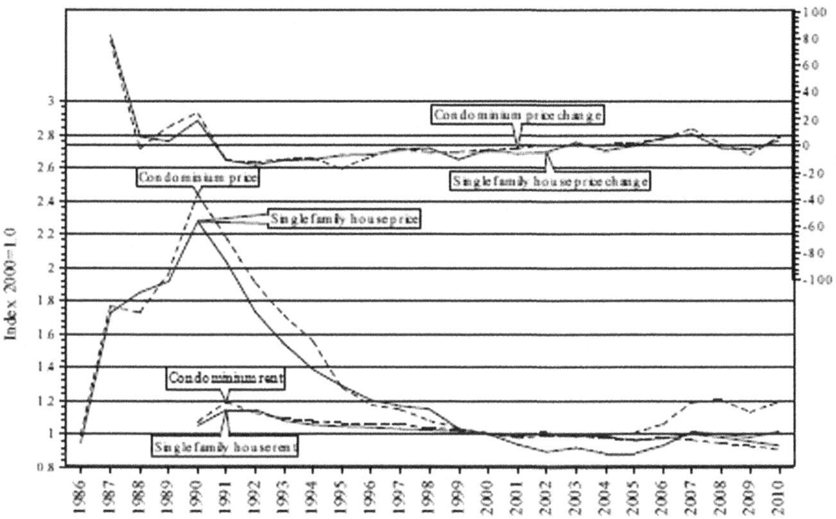

Fig. 8.1 Hedonic Price and Rents Indexes

When we compare the aggregate imputed rent for owner-occupied housing in prefectural accounting to the imputed rent for owner-occupied housing in national accounting, one can see here that a significant discrepancy exists between the two.

The imputed rent for owner-occupied housing in national accounting is calculated by multiplying rent unit prices by the total floor space of owner-occupied housing surveyed by the Housing and Land Survey.

On the other hand, in prefectural accounting, imputed rent is calculated as "owner-occupied housing" as part of the breakdown of entrepreneurial income (after receivable and payable of distributed income of corporations). This entrepreneurial income is defined as the presumed real estate income in the hypothetical case where the owner of a home operated a real estate business, and it is calculated by subtracting intermediate input such as repair costs, consumption of fixed capital, taxes such as property tax, interest payments on mortgages, and rent payments from the imputed rent for owner-occupied housing (the revenue).[19]

Here, we compared the equivalent rent estimated from the hedonic rent function estimated in this study to the SNA imputed rent for owner-occupied housing in Tokyo. The discrepancy between the two was especially significant at the bubble's peak in 1990, with an 11-fold discrepancy in 1990 and a 10.5-fold discrepancy in 1991. This discrepancy has grown smaller over the years, contracting to 1.6-fold in 2009.

[19]In national accounting as well, under the same definition, "owner-occupied housing" is calculated as part of the breakdown of "entrepreneurial income (after receivable and payable of distributed income of corporations)," with the amount being ¥22.6 trillion in 2009. Even though the definition was the same, there is a discrepancy of ¥4 trillion.

Table 8.7 Equivalent rent estimates for Tokyo's 23 wards

	National account (all Japan)					Tokyo		
Year	A. GDP[a]	B. Imputed rent (national account)[a]	B/A (%)	C. Imputed rent (prefecture account)[a,b]	C/B	C. Prefecture account[a]	D: Equivalent rent estimate[a]	D/C
1990	442,781.0	27,654.6	6.25	–	–	–	4,925.89	–
1991	469,421.8	29,595.3	6.30	–	–	–	5,381.91	–
1992	480,782.8	31,429.6	6.54	–	–	–	5,283.60	–
1993	483,711.8	33,324.3	6.89	–	–	–	5,021.95	–
1994	488,450.3	35,052.7	7.18	14, 892.63	0.42	1,217.25	4,933.06	4.05
1995	495,165.5	36,627.2	7.40	15, 686.02	0.43	1,352.16	5,268.97	3.90
1996	505,011.8	38,211.6	7.57	16, 440.75	0.43	1,442.76	5,256.77	3.64
1997	515,644.1	39,895.8	7.74	17,128.05	0.43	1,660.33	5,219.79	3.14
1998	504,905.4	41,144.5	8.15	17,743.71	0.43	1,834.53	5,155.46	2.81
1999	497,628.6	41,866.3	8.41	18,657.19	0.45	2,066.12	5,157.14	2.50
2000	502,989.9	42,772.5	8.50	19,405.15	0.45	2,174.47	5, 864.61	2.70
2001	497,719.7	43,615.6	8.76	20,229.68	0.46	2,444.69	5,831.36	2.39
2002	491,312.2	44,202.3	9.00	20,957.04	0.47	2,467.60	5,925.69	2.40
2003	490,294.0	44,754.0	9.13	21,934.66	0.49	2,769.61	5,818.97	2.10
2004	498,328.4	45,170.6	9.06	22,913.61	0.51	3,047.01	5,782.20	1.90
2005	501,734.4	45,570.9	9.08	23,686.68	0.52	3,255.94	6,001.29	1.84
2006	507,364.8	46,025.5	9.07	24,152.70	0.52	3,402.53	6,062.71	1.78
2007	515,520.4	46,358.9	8.99	24,802.42	0.54	3,529.88	6,113.83	1.73
2008	504,377.6	46,660.3	9.25	25,269.59	0.54	3,619.23	5,951.92	1.64
2009	470,936.7	46,724.1	9.92	26,411.03	0.57	3,621.54	5,815.37	1.61
2010	–	–	–	–	–	–	5,655.68	–

[a]Unit: one billion yen
[b]Sum of 47 prefectures

A more important problem here is that the imputed rent estimated with SNA increased 8.2-fold from 1990 to 2009, whereas the estimated equivalent rent has remained stable, rising 1.18-fold. How can these kinds of differences be explained?

In terms of the factors causing a more than 10-fold discrepancy at the bubble's peak, it cannot be explained simply by the difference in quality between owner-occupied housing and rented housing that has frequently been pointed out. As well, as seen in Fig. 8.1, rental housing unit prices have been on a downward trend over the years since the bubble's peak. Meanwhile, with respect to owner-occupied housing stock, condominiums increased 2.2-fold from 1990 through 2005, whereas single family houses—which have the most weight—remained stable, increasing 1.2-fold (40% increase in aggregate floor space). Given this context, it is not possible to explain the 8.2-fold increase from 1990 through 2009.

We believe the most important factor giving rise to this kind of discrepancy is that during the bubble period and subsequent collapse period, when the housing market fluctuated significantly, it was not possible to sufficiently link the "paid rent" used in calculating imputed rent to the rent determined by the market, so a significant discrepancy arose between them. This analysis is consistent with the results of Shimizu et al. (2010a). However, even though there was a discrepancy between paid rent and market rent, it cannot explain the problem of a greater than 8-fold expansion from 1990 through 2009.

8.3.4 Comparison of Imputed Rent of Owner-Occupied Housing in Tokyo

8.3.4.1 The Treatment of Cost Tied to Owner-Occupied Housing

Next, we will estimate the imputed rent for owner-occupied housing using the User Cost Approach. When attempting to estimate the imputed rent of owner-occupied housing using the User Cost Approach, whether the Basic User Cost Approach, Verbrugge Variant (VV) User Cost Approach, or Diewert's OOH Opportunity Cost Approach, it is necessary to calculate the expense of keeping a home. The expense of keeping a home is comprised of the opportunity cost when viewing the home as a financial asset, property tax arising from keeping a home, damage insurance costs, and maintenance/administration costs. Here, we take into account property tax and maintenance/administration costs.[20]

(1) Financial Opportunity Cost (FOC)

In many cases, purchasing a home involves obtaining a mortgage. In this kind of typical case, the Financial Opportunity Cost (FOC) of home ownership is calculated as $r_D^t D^t + r^t(V^t - D^t)$, as shown in Eq. 8.7. The FOC in this case is the mortgage payment interest combined with the investment gains that could have been obtained if that money had been invested. Since the mortgage amount is not considered in Eqs. 8.4 and 8.5, Eq. 8.7 is the case where the mortgage is 0. For r_D^t,[21] this study used loan interest rates from the former Government Housing Loan Corporation (now the Japan Housing Finance Agency) and the yield on 10-year Japanese government bonds for the asset investment yield.[22]

---

[20]Since damage insurance costs are extremely low, we decided not to consider them in this study.

[21]In recent years, mortgages from private financial institutions have come to be used, but prior to 2000, it was normal to use mortgages from the former Government Housing Loan Corporation. As well, even now, the interest rate set by the Japan Housing Finance Agency is the benchmark for mortgage interest. Given this, we believed that its rates were representative. The average loan interest from the Government Housing Loan Corporation was 0.0527 in 1990, which fluctuated over time to 0.0363 in 1995, 0.0278 in 2000, 0.0308 in 2005, and 0.0343 in 2010.

[22]The yield on 10-year government bonds from 1990 to 2010 peaked at 0.052 in 1990, dropping to 0.0346 in 1995, 0.0183 in 2000, 0.0140 in 2005, and 0.0117 in 2010. However, throughout the period in question, it may be considered one of the assets that offered the highest return on investment.

(2) Property Tax

It is now supposed that the owner of the housing unit must pay the property taxes T_S^0 and T_L^0 for the use of the structure and land respectively during period 0.[23] Define the period 0 structures tax rate τ_S^0 and land tax rate τ_L^0 as follows:

$$\tau_S^0 \equiv T_S^0 / P_S^0 Q_S^0 \tag{8.18}$$

$$\tau_L^0 \equiv T_L^0 / P_L^0 Q_L^0 \tag{8.19}$$

The new imputed rent for using the property during period 0, R^0, including the property tax costs, is defined as follows:

$$\begin{aligned} R^0 &\equiv V^0(1+r^0) + T_S^0 + T_L^0 - V^{1a} \\ &= [P_S^0 Q_S^0 + P_L^0 Q_L^0](1+r^0) + \tau_S^0 P_S^0 Q_S^0 + \tau_L^0 P_L^0 Q_L^0 - [P_S^0(1+i_S^0)(1-\delta_0)Q_S^0 + P_L^0(1+i_L^0)Q_L^0] \\ &= p_S^0 Q_S^0 + p_L^0 Q_L^0 \end{aligned} \tag{8.20}$$

where separate period 0 tax adjusted user costs of structures and land, p_S^0 and p_L^0, are defined as follows:

$$p_S^0 \equiv [(1+r^0) - (1+i_S^0)(1-\delta_0) + \tau_S^0]P_S^0 = [r^0 - i_S^0 + \delta_0(1+i_S^0) + \tau_S^0]P_S^0 \tag{8.21}$$

$$p_L^0 \equiv [(1+r^0) - (1+i_L^0) + \tau_L^0]P_L^0 = [r^0 - i_L^0 + \tau_S^0]P_L^0 \tag{8.22}$$

Here, the question of how P_S^0 or P_L^0 was calculated is important. We estimated P_L^0 with the hedonic function using published land prices that are the benchmark for property tax land evaluation. The estimation results are as shown in Table 8.5.

Using these hedonic function estimation results, we estimated the land evaluation amount by building unit. In addition, we obtained the building price by deducting the land evaluation amount based on the published land price from the estimated total housing price amount.

The nominal property tax rate was 1.4% of the asset amount for both buildings and land. However, the actual effective tax rate is known to be lower than that level. Accordingly, we estimated the effective tax rate for Tokyo.[24]

---

[23]If there is no breakdown of the property taxes into structures and land components, then just impute the overall tax into structures and land components based on the beginning of the period values of both components.

[24]In property tax land evaluation, various adjustments are performed, such as relief measures for small-scale residential land. As a result, tax amounts are not necessarily determined based on the land evaluation amount. Accordingly, we obtained the tax base amount for Tokyo as a whole (the total price determined as the land price for actual taxation purposes) as a proportion of the land asset amount calculated with SNA statistics. The land asset amount calculated with SNA uses published land prices for land price data and uses data adjusted for property taxes for floor space. As a result, both proportions are similar in that they are proportions of the published land price and property tax land evaluation amount.

(3) Maintenance and Renovation Expenditure

Another problem associated with home ownership is the treatment of maintenance expenditures, major repair expenditures and expenditures associated with renovations or additions.

Empirical evidence suggests that the normal decline in a structure due to the effects of aging and use can be offset by maintenance and renovation expenditures. How exactly should these expenditures be treated in the context of modeling the costs and benefits of home ownership?

A common approach in the national accounts literature is to treat major renovation and repair expenditures as capital formation and smaller routine maintenance and repair expenditures as current expenditures.

Accordingly, we calculated annual maintenance/administration costs in this study as well.

Housing maintenance/administration costs may be expected to change in accordance with home size. We therefore calculated maintenance/administration costs per square meter based on a Recruit survey of home buyers, and multiplied this cost by the size (S) of the home.[25]

The values based on this survey are for fiscal 2005 only. We therefore estimated the values for other fiscal years based on the 2005 estimate values and the rate of change for "Repairs & maintenance" in the Tokyo CPI.

8.3.5 Capital Gain

The most important element in the User Cost Approach is capital gain.

In the Basic User Cost Approach (Eq. 8.4), it is defined as $(V_{v+1}^{t+1} - V_v^t)$, which is the price change for each dwelling unit.

However, in the VV User Cost Approach and Diewert's User Cost Approach, it is defined as the expected value for a future period. The reason for this is that it is difficult to assume that in household accounting, the choice of home is made by looking at the price change for a single year and then making an investment, and because the volatility in the actual value of single-year capital gains becomes excessive.

For the present estimate, in the basic model we made the calculation with the actual value of $(V_{v+1}^{t+1} - V_v^t)$ for each dwelling unit.

On the other hand, for the calculation of VV User Cost and Diewert's User Cost, capital gain was obtained as $(\overline{V^{t+1}} - V^t)$. The anticipated growth rate ($E[\pi]$) was

[25]In Recruit's survey, housing floor space and the actual maintenance/administration costs corresponding to it were surveyed. In the 2005 survey, data was collected for 48,532 condominiums and 23,200 single family houses in Tokyo. Maintenance/administration costs for the 2005 year were ¥3,130/m^2 (annually) for condominiums and ¥920/m^2 (annually) for single family houses. Multiplying these amounts by the average floor space of 60 m^2 for condominiums and 100 m^2 for single family houses, the annual cost was ¥187,000 for condominiums and ¥92,000 for single family houses.

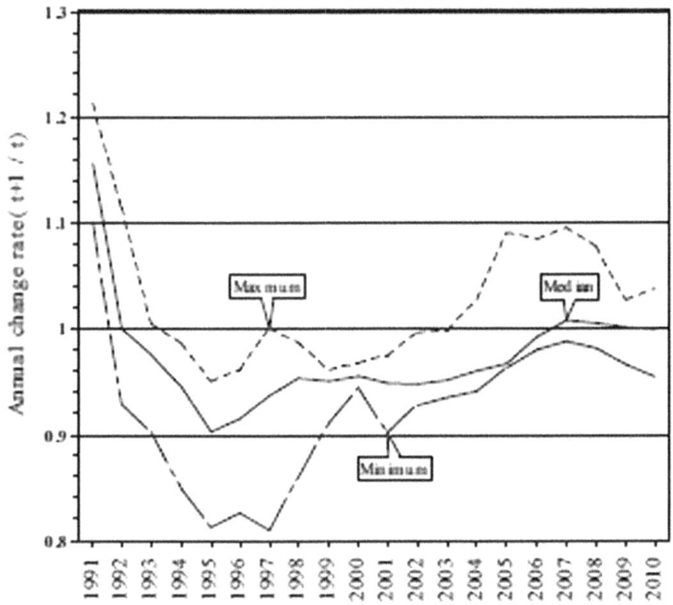

Fig. 8.2 The trend of single family house prices in municipalities

obtained as the geometric average of the rate of change over the past 5 years by municipality unit (k).[26]

We estimated the price for a future period by multiplying the anticipated growth rate obtained in the above manner by the asset price for each property unit, and obtained the capital gain with

$$(\overline{V^{t+1}} - V^t)$$

Figures 8.2 and 8.3 look at the maximum and minimum values and median value for the anticipated growth rate in municipalities (k). If we compare the average value of the change rate for the actual value (V_{v+1}^{t+1}/V_v^t) (Fig. 8.1), the volatility is considerably reduced here.

When looking at the actual value, both single family house prices and condominium prices rose by a maximum of 80% for one year during the bubble period, but when converted into anticipated growth rate, the increase is reduced to around 20%. However, even for the anticipated growth rate, during the time of dramatic price increases in the bubble period, there are municipalities demonstrating a median value of 15% and maximum value of 20% for both single family house prices and condominium prices.

[26]The city of Tokyo was divided into a total of 53 areas: 23 special wards and 30 municipalities. It has become evident that moving to a new location outside of one's administrative district happens very rarely. As well, it is known that housing price changes vary considerably by region. As a result, we deemed it appropriate to calculate anticipated growth rate by administrative district.

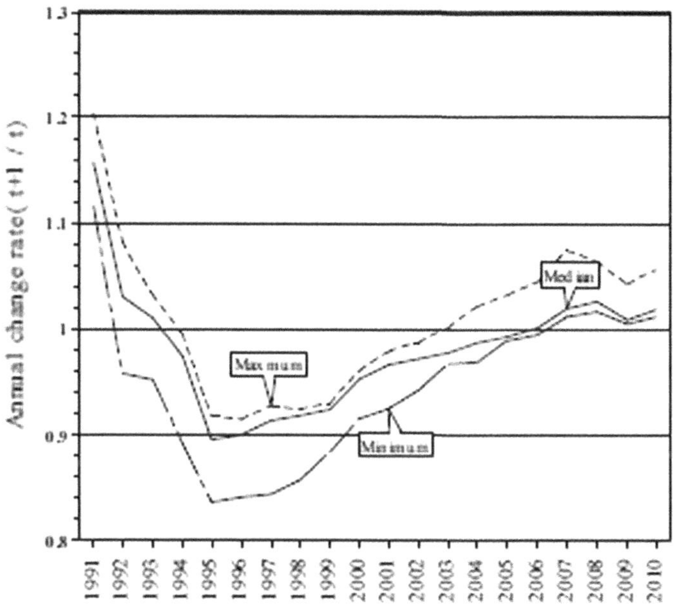

Fig. 8.3 The trend of condominium prices in municipalities

The anticipated growth rate by municipality dropped rapidly due to the bubble's collapse and became negative. It then turned upward again during the so-called mini-bubble of the mid-2000s.

8.3.6 *Comparison of Estimated User Costs*

Using the various parameters established as shown above, we obtained the Basic User Cost based on Eq. 8.4, the VV User Cost based on Eq. 8.5, and Diewert's User Cost based on Eq. 8.7. As well, we calculated Diewert's OOH Index taking the maximum value of the results obtained with Diewert's User Cost and Equivalent Rent.

Diewert's OOH Index takes the maximum value when Diewert's User Cost and Equivalent Rent are compared. Figure 8.4 looks at the changes over time in the ratio of Diewert's User Cost > Equivalent Rent for both single family house and condominium prices.

User Cost increases while the anticipated growth rate is decreasing. As a result, in 1992 and 1994 through 1995, periods when the anticipated growth rate dropped considerably, User Cost significantly surpassed Equivalent Rent. On the other hand, in the 2000s, when the rate of decrease in housing prices shrunk and then prices began to turn upward, User Cost decreased. As a result, one can see that the Diewert's User

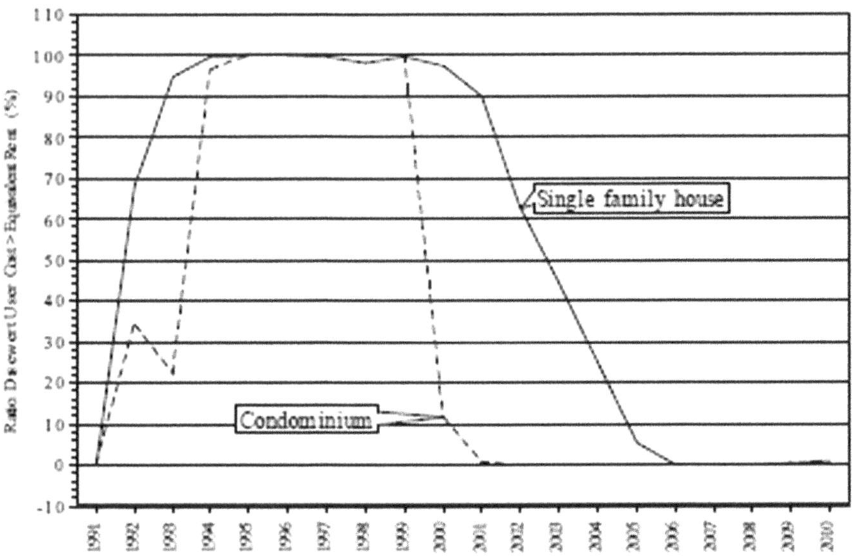

Fig. 8.4 Ratio: Diewert user cost > equivalent rent: (%)

Cost > Equivalent Rent ratio dropped rapidly, and the proportion of Diewert's OOH Index composed by Equivalent Rent grew larger.

The various User Cost estimate results are outlined in Table 8.8, while Fig. 8.5 looks at changes in them. In 1991, VV User Cost and Diewert's User Cost were negative. This was due to the residual effect of the dramatic increase in housing prices in the bubble period. On the other hand, since prices turned downward during the one-year period from 1990 to 1991, the Basic User Cost value was extremely high. It was six times higher than Equivalent Rent.

As well, in the mid-2000s, when housing prices turned upward, Basic User Cost had a negative value. And for VV User Cost as well, which uses the expected increase rate for housing prices, the value became negative in 2007, at the time of the so-called mini-bubble (Diewert's User Cost was positive).

In order to resolve this kind of problem, employing the maximum value of Equivalent Rent and User Cost in each year for each type of dwelling measurement unit with Diewert's OOH Index has been proposed. For example, in 1991, when User Cost was negative for all dwelling units, since Equivalent Rent was higher for all dwelling units, Diewert's OOH Index is the same as Equivalent Rent. From 1992 through 1995, since capital gain is negative, the weight of User Cost becomes greater. And in 1996, when User Cost exceeded Equivalent Rent for all dwelling units, Diewert's OOH Index is the same as User Cost.

Table 8.8 Estimation results of user costs

Year	(a) Equivalent	(b) Basic user	(c) VV user	(d) Diewert user	(e) Diewert			
	Rent[a]	Cost[a]	Cost[a]	Cost[a]	Index[a]	(d)−(b)[a]	(d)−(c)[a]	(e)−(a)[a]
1991	5,381.91	34,917.15	−17,249.25	−16,969.24	5,381.91	−51,886.39	280.01	0.00
1992	5,283.60	29,172.85	9 414.64	9,141.06	10,419.92	−20,031.78	−273.58	5,136.32
1993	5,021.95	22,840.21	11,742.15	11,524.01	11,589.21	−11,316.20	−218.14	6,567.26
1994	4,933.06	18,828.92	14,916.87	14,639.22	14,639.23	−4,189.69	−277.64	9,706.16
1995	5,268.97	11,404.91	18,786.03	18,624.62	18,886.70	7,219.71	−161.42	13,617.73
1996	5,256.77	8,446.97	16,425.49	16,498.50	16,498.50	8,051.53	73.01	11,241.73
1997	5,219.79	8,231.11	12,849.09	13,223.56	13,223.57	4,992.45	374.47	8,003.78
1998	5,155.46	10,184.68	9,831.25	10,367.09	10,368.52	182.41	535.84	5,213.06
1999	5,157.14	5,429.53	8,858.19	9,112.25	9,127.37	3,682.72	254.06	3,970.22
2000	5,864.61	9,214.74	7,984.24	8,189.68	8,494.76	−1,025.07	205.43	2,630.15
2001	5,831.36	3,620.13	7,063.19	7,673.58	7,729.83	4,053.45	610.39	1,898.46
2002	5,925.69	1,923.76	6,600.24	7,223.75	7,427.48	5,299.99	623.51	1,501.79
2003	5,818.97	4,383.36	5,395.85	6,012.84	6,714.04	1,629.48	617.00	895.07
2004	5,782.20	1,577.33	4,767.56	5,376.14	6,331.98	3,798.81	608.58	549.78
2005	6,001.29	−3,359.14	4,168.27	5,011.60	6,446.76	8,370.73	843.33	445.47
2006	6,062.71	−6,546.35	2,303.28	3,323.47	6,082.47	9,869.83	1,020.20	19.76
2007	6,113.83	6,050.27	−111.39	1,053.99	6,114.15	−4,996.28	1,165.38	0.32
2008	5,951.92	13,441.22	129.20	1,376.28	5,952.16	−12,064.94	1,247.07	0.24
2009	5,815.37	−1,388.15	1,594.28	2,877.89	5,817.18	4,266.04	1,283.61	1.80

[a] One billion yen

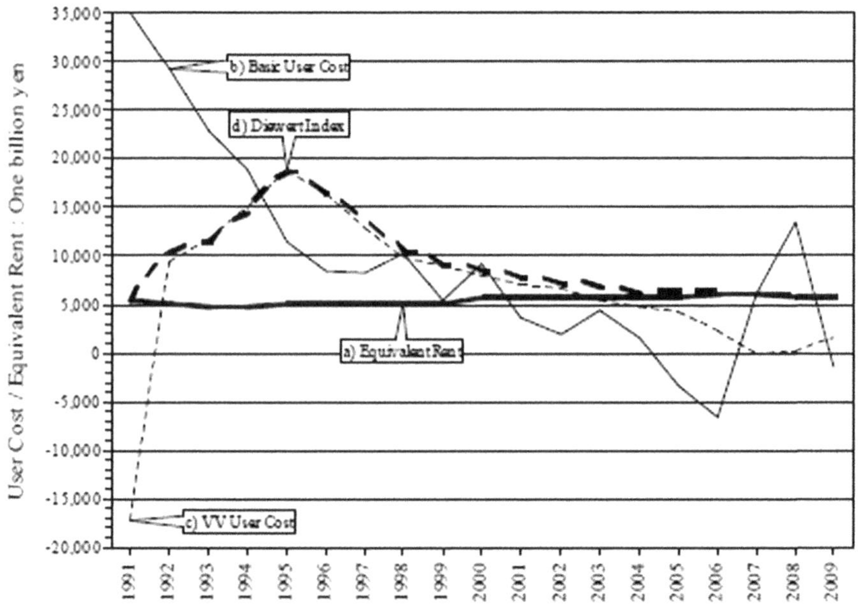

Fig. 8.5 Diewert's OOH index and user cost indexes

The discrepancy between Diewert's OOH Index and Equivalent Rent becomes greater when the Diewert's User Cost > Equivalent Rent ratio increases. It was greatest in 1995, when a 3.6-fold discrepancy occurred. One can see that it subsequently grew smaller, contracting toward the same level as Equivalent Rent.

8.4 Summary and Conclusion

Having an extremely large weight in national accounting and consumer price statistics, imputed rent for owner-occupied housing plays an important role. It has been pointed out that it is one of the most difficult estimation subjects and various estimation methods have been proposed, but there is still no standardized international approach.

Looking at the case of Tokyo, this study collected as much micro-data as possible and estimated the imputed rent of owner-occupied housing using multiple estimation methods, with the aim of quantitatively clarifying the extent of the discrepancies that arise due to differences in estimation method.

We started with estimation based on the Equivalent Rent Approach employed in Japan. In this study, for the Equivalent Rent estimation, we calculated a hedonic function using market rent data and obtained the quality-adjusted market rent for each type of dwelling unit.

Looking at the results obtained, at the bubble's peak in 1990, there was an 11-fold discrepancy between the imputed rent of owner-occupied housing calculated in prefectural accounting and the imputed rent estimated here. The divergence between the two then became smaller over the years, shrinking to a 1.6-fold difference in 2009. With regard to the causes of this discrepancy, we have assumed the following.

First, there is the gap in quality between owner-occupied housing and rental housing. In the rent estimated in prefectural accounting, quality adjustment is not performed. But a significant quality gap–such as differences in size–exists between owner-occupied and rental housing. We believe that discrepancies are caused by this quality gap. However, it is not possible to explain the 11-fold difference in scale during the bubble period with the quality gap only. It is assumed that the most significant factor giving rise to the discrepancy between the two sets of results was that during the bubble period and the subsequent collapse, when the housing market fluctuated considerably, it was not possible to sufficiently link the "paid rent" surveyed for the CPI to the market rent, so a significant discrepancy arose between them. The size of this difference was estimated by Shimizu et al. (2010a). However, even though this kind of problem is present, it is not enough to explain the 11-fold difference.

As well, the imputed rent estimated with SNA increased at least 8 times from 1990 to 2009. While the discrepancy between the two shrank over time, during this period rents were on a downward trend and the increase in owner-occupied housing stocks was stable at around 40%. This kind of change is impossible to explain, and one has to think that there is a major problem with the estimation method.

Next, we estimated imputed rent based on the User Cost Approach. Even though market rent was used in the Equivalent Rent estimation, it was easy to predict that it would be difficult to sensitively capture fluctuations during the period when housing prices changed dramatically. While estimation with the User Cost Approach has been proposed in this kind of situation, problems have been pointed out with the conventional Basic User Cost Approach: the User Cost becomes negative when there are major increases in housing prices, and it rises significantly during large-scale downward phases such as immediately after the bubble's collapse. In other words, the volatility exceeds what is expected by market players.

Accordingly, we estimated the VV User Cost proposed by Poole et al. (2005) and Diewert's User Cost and Diewert's OOH Index proposed by Diewert and Nakamura (2009, 2011).

Looking at the estimate results, a significant gap arises between the Basic User Cost and the VV User Cost and Diewert's User Cost at the start of the bubble collapse period in 1991. The bubble collapsed in 1990, and as prices dropped through 1991, the rise in the Basic User Cost was 6 times greater than that for Equivalent Rent. Meanwhile, with the VV User Cost and Diewert's User Cost, which calculated capital gain using the anticipated growth rate for housing prices by municipality over the previous 5 years, the User Cost became negative.

Even if the capital gain calculation is converted into the anticipated growth rate for the previous 5 years in order to assimilate the dramatic single-year price change, the User Cost becomes negative.

The reason for this is that the dramatic increase in housing prices during the bubble period has a residual effect on the anticipated growth rate. What's more, the Basic User Cost has a negative value during the market recovery period in the 2000s as well, and the VV User Cost also becomes negative in 2007 during the so-called mini-bubble.

This shows that even when capital gain is calculated as the anticipated growth rate, the User Cost becomes negative during large-scale price fluctuations such as the real estate bubble that occurred in 1980s' Tokyo or amid significant changes in market prices such as the "mini-bubble."

In order to resolve this kind of problem, employing the maximum value of Equivalent Rent and User Cost for each dwelling measurement unit with Diewert's OOH Index has been proposed. Looking at the difference between Diewert's OOH Index estimated in this manner and Equivalent Rent reveals that a 3.5-fold discrepancy occurred in 1995 and that there was on average an around 1.7-fold discrepancy from 1990 through 2009.

These findings show that even if Equivalent Rent approach is improved, quality adjustment is performed, and market rent is used, significant discrepancies remain between the estimation methods.

References

Diewert, W.E. 1974. Intertemporal consumer theory and the demand for durables. *Econometrica* 42: 497–516.

Diewert, W.E. and A.O. Nakamura. 2009. Accounting for Housing in a CPI, chapter 2, pp. 7-32. In W.E. Diewert, B.M. Balk, D. Fixler, K.J. Fox and A.O. Nakamura (2009),*Price and Productivity Measurement*: Volume 1—Housing. Trafford Press.

Diewert, W.E. and A. O. Nakamura. 2011. The Housing Bubble and a New Approach to Accounting for Housing in a CPI, (mimeo).

Goodhart, Charles. 2001. " What weight should be given to asset prices in measurement of inflation? *The Economic Journal*, 111(472):335-356.

Katz, A.J. 2009. Estimating dwelling services in the candidate countries: theoretical and practical considerations in developing methodologies based on a user cost of capital measure, chapter 3, pp. 33–50. In Diewert, W.E., B.M. Balk, D. Fixler, K.J. Fox and A.O. Nakamura. 2009. *Price and Productivity Measurement*: Volume 1–Housing. Trafford Press. www.vancouvervolumes.com/ and www.indexmeasures.com.

Poole, Robert, Frank Ptacek, and Randal Verbrugge. 2005. *Treatment of Owner-Occupied Housing in the CPI*. U.S. Department of Labor: Bureau of Labor Statistics.

Shimizu,C and T. Watanabe (2010), "Housing Bubble in Japan and the United States," *Public Policy Review* 6, (3):431-472.

Shimizu,C., K.G. Nishimura and T. Watanabe. 2010a. Residential rents and price rigidity: micro structure and macro consequences, *Journal of Japanese and International Economy* 24:282–299.

Shimizu, C., K.G. Nishimura, and T. Watanabe. 2010b. House prices in Tokyo—a comparison of repeat-sales and hedonic measures. *Journal of Economics and Statistics* 230 (6): 792–813.

Verbrugge, R. 2008. The puzzling divergence of rents and user costs, 1980–2004. *Review of Income and Wealth* 54 (4): 671–699.

Index

W. E. Diewert et al., *Property Price Index*, Advances in Japanese Business and Economics 11, https://doi.org/10.1007/978-4-431-55942-9

Printed by Printforce, the Netherlands